P9-CCP-095

E VIEW

AND THE DISTRICT OF COLUMBIA

TO THE GATES
OF RICHMOND

Books by Stephen W. Sears

The Century Collection of Civil War Art
Hometown U.S.A.
The Automobile in America
Landscape Turned Red: The Battle of Antietam
George B. McClellan: The Young Napoleon
The Civil War Papers of George B. McClellan
To the Gates of Richmond: The Peninsula Campaign

To the Gates of Richmond

The Peninsula Campaign

STEPHEN W. SEARS

Ticknor & Fields

NEW YORK · 1992

Copyright © 1992 by Stephen W. Sears
All rights reserved

For information about permission to reproduce selections
from this book, write to Permissions, Ticknor & Fields,
215 Park Avenue South, New York, New York 10003.

Library of Congress Cataloging-in-Publication Data
Sears, Stephen W.
To the gates of Richmond : the peninsula campaign / Stephen W. Sears.
p.   cm.
Includes bibliographical references and index.
ISBN 0-89919-790-6
1. Peninsula Campaign, 1862.   I. Title.
E473.6.S43   1992
973.7'32 — dc20   92-6923
CIP

Printed in the United States of America

BP 10 9 8 7 6 5 4 3 2 1

Front endsheet: An 1861 lithograph "Panorama of the Seat of War," drawn by John Bachmann, offers a bird's-eye perspective on the eastern theater. The two capitals, Washington and Richmond, are at right center and left center, respectively. Fort Monroe, at the tip of the Virginia Peninsula, is at lower left.
Print Collection, New York Public Library

Back endsheet: Colonel Thomas J. Cram, a topographical officer at Fort Monroe, compiled this manuscript map of southeastern Virginia early in 1862. It was on this section of Cram's map that General McClellan planned his Richmond campaign, initially to begin from Urbanna (top right center), then shifted to Fort Monroe (lower right).
Geography and Map Division, Library of Congress

For My Mother and Father

CONTENTS

....

Illustrations follow pages 84 and 276

MAPS

....

INTRODUCTION

....

"THE ENEMY are at the gates. Who will take the lead and act, act, act?" the *Richmond Dispatch* pleaded on May 16, 1862. The massive Federal army — some compared it to Napoleon's Grande Armée — was indeed very nearly at Richmond's gates that day. Soon enough Yankee soldiers could see the city's spires and hear its clock bells chime the hours. Citizens and soldiers alike believed the climax of the war was at hand.

The Peninsula campaign of 1862 — the march to the gates of Richmond — was the largest single campaign of the Civil War. More men — a quarter of a million of them — and more weapons of war were assembled on the Virginia Peninsula for this battle for the capital of the Confederacy than for any other operation of the war. Contemporaries called it, aptly enough, the grand campaign.

More than its size generated the sense of something special about the Peninsula campaign. In his journal the Comte de Paris, pretender to the French throne, recalled how anxious he was to join General McClellan's staff: "We counted upon seeing *the* campaign — because of course there was only supposed to be one campaign and that one both immediate and short." The principal army of the Federal government was to march on Richmond and fight the principal army of the Confederacy there, and if the Federals were victorious, as it was supposed they would be, the rebellion would be over.

From late March to late June of 1862 the two armies sparred and maneuvered and battled their way up the Peninsula toward the capital. At Yorktown they went to ground in a month-long siege, wielding the latest and largest weapons of war. At Williamsburg and Seven Pines there were savage battles in the woods and clearings. The armies faced each other across the Chickahominy swamps. The campaign employed the newest ways to make war — ironclad warships and 200-pounder rifled cannon and the battlefield telegraph and aerial reconnaissance.

At last the plea of the *Dispatch*'s editor was answered. Robert E. Lee, taking command of the Army of Northern Virginia, proceeded to "lead and act, act, act" with a vengeance. Lee's offensive, the Seven Days' Battles, witnessed in a week-long struggle some of the bloodiest fighting of the war, and drove the grand campaign to its climax. When the campaign was finally over, one of every four men engaged in it was dead, wounded, or missing.

The historical record of the Peninsula campaign is a uniquely rich one. Only a fraction of the men who fought there had ever fought before. These men going to war for the first time were determined to make a record of their experience, and Yankees and Rebels in remarkable numbers kept diaries and journals and wrote letters home. The Peninsula campaign was not only the largest of the war but the one most written about by those who fought it. Their eyewitness accounts — most of them used here for the first time — add a special color and texture to the story.

Corporal Sidney J. Richardson of the 21st Georgia spoke for thousands of men on both sides when he wrote home after the Seven Days, "The canons roared like perpetual thunder, the balls bombs shells whistling in the air cutting down trees killing men horses and every live thing they hit. . . . It was a horrible time, the worst time I ever saw." It was a horrible time, and it changed the course of the war.

· PART I ·

The Grand Campaign

....

I shall soon leave here on the wing for
Richmond — which you may be sure I will take.

— Major General George B. McClellan
March 16, 1862

....

· 1 ·

Seven Days to Decision

....

A T TEN O'CLOCK on the clear, cold morning of Friday, March 7, 1862, an even dozen brigadier generals assembled at army headquarters on Pennsylvania Avenue at Jackson Square in Washington. To a man they were startled to be told that forthwith they would act as a council of war. None had played the role before. Only three or four had even a vague notion of what plans the army might be considering, for General McClellan was notoriously secretive about his intentions. They had supposed they were being called to headquarters that morning to receive orders for an attack on the Confederate batteries blockading the Potomac below the capital. Instead, without preamble, they learned they would be deciding how and where and when to launch the Army of the Potomac's grand campaign to end the war.

A council of war had in fact been the furthest thing from General McClellan's mind when he scheduled the meeting the day before. The newspapers called him the Young Napoleon, and like the first Napoleon he had only contempt for generalship by committee. At age thirty-five George Brinton McClellan was at once the youngest and the senior major general in the United States army. He had commanded the Army of the Potomac for seven and a half months now, and, as general-in-chief, all the Union's armies for the last four of those months, and he appeared well cast for the part: short and broad-shouldered, with a quick eye and a jaunty confidence, he never displayed anything less than a commanding presence. He was tremendously popular with his soldiers, but in recent months his popularity with major figures in the government had plummeted almost to the vanishing point. Once he had been the toast of Washington. Now opponents in growing numbers noisily snapped at his heels.

In part this was due simply to frustration. For more than half a year the Army of the Potomac had drilled and paraded and by report been brought to the peak of military efficiency, yet in all that time McClellan had done nothing about the Confederate army camped just twenty-five miles from the capital, and nothing had stopped Confederate batteries from closing the Potomac to commercial shipping. The Rebels held the capital of the United States hostage to a partial blockade, and it was a national humiliation. In part too the outcry against McClellan was a matter of politics, for while serving a Republican administration the general made no secret of his allegiance to the Democratic opposition.

And in part it was a matter of virulent, ugly suspicion in a time when suspicion ruled the emotions of many. It was recalled that in the peacetime army George McClellan had been the protégé of Jefferson Davis, then secretary of war, now president of the Confederate States of America. It was said that in the 1850s McClellan had ties to the filibusters, the private armies that menaced Central and South America and sought the expansion of slavery. Prominent abolitionists pointed out that in taking command of the Army of the Potomac the general had said to them that he would not fight either for the Republican party or for the abolition of slavery, but only for the restoration of the old Union. "I do not believe McClellan's heart is in the right place," a newspaper editor wrote early in 1862; during the secession crisis the general had reportedly declared that "the country must be ruled by the Southern Democracy." The editor asked, "Can the ethiopian change his skin or the leopard his spots?"

As a consequence, a small army of critics — especially radical Republican critics — attacked McClellan for his inaction and his excessive caution and suspected him of worse. It was just these critics who had forced him to convert the present gathering of his generals into a council of war. He acted on the spur of the moment, impelled by a suddenly imperative need to save both his command and his grand campaign.

For General McClellan the crisis had come to a boil some three hours earlier that same morning, when he was summoned to the White House by President Lincoln. The two met alone in the president's office, and exactly what passed between them is not fully known. Only McClellan's later and self-serving recollection is on record, but it is at least certain that it was a stormy confrontation in which Mr. Lincoln carried out his vow, made a few days before, "to talk plainly" to his general. Lincoln was quoted by McClellan as raising "a very ugly matter" in regard to the proposal then current for taking the army southward against Richmond by way of Chesapeake Bay. It looked to some in the government, the president said, as if General McClellan had conceived the plan with the traitorous intention of leaving Washington unprotected and exposed to capture by the Rebels.

By McClellan's account, at the word *traitorous* he leaped to his feet and hotly demanded the president retract the charge. It was not his own view, Lincoln assured him, but he repeated that by the worst interpretation the scheme did have "an ugly look" about it. If that was the case, McClellan said, he would settle any doubts both about his plan and his loyalty at one stroke. Let the plan be judged solely on its merits by the army's general officers, he said. It so happened that most of the brigadiers commanding divisions would be meeting that very morning at his headquarters on another matter; he would appoint them a council of war with authority to decide all questions of grand strategy by majority vote. He would remove himself from their deliberations, and afterward send them with their decisions to the president for review.

This must have left Mr. Lincoln at once relieved and resigned. All through the winter he had tried with scant success to pin General McClellan down to some concrete plan and schedule of action, and now it appeared he had finally succeeded. Yet there was every chance that the plan was going to run counter to his own best judgment.[1]

At the ten o'clock meeting at headquarters Chief of Staff Randolph B. Marcy announced to the twelve surprised generals that they would be passing judgment on grand strategy. General McClellan was proposing, he said, to change the Army of the Potomac's base of operations from Washington to the lower Chesapeake — specifically to Urbanna, a little tobacco port on the Rappahannock, fifteen miles upriver from the bay. Rather than attack the Rebel batteries on the lower Potomac as planned, the army would bypass them; it would avoid the Potomac entirely and instead embark at Annapolis, directly on the Chesapeake. The movement might begin as soon as the next week. When Marcy finished this preliminary briefing, he went around to individual generals and confided to them that what was really at stake at the war council was General McClellan's future. "Gen. Marcy . . . took me aside," General Samuel P. Heintzelman recorded in his diary, "& said that there was a strong effort to have him superceded & that he would be unless we approved his plans."

General McClellan himself then joined the conference and, spreading out a large map of eastern Virginia, explained the Urbanna plan in more detail. His debate with the government over grand strategy had begun some time since, and by now his arguments were practiced. The movement to the Rappahannock by water, he pointed out, would take advantage of Federal seapower to put the army just fifty miles from Richmond. The only defenders in the landing area were reported to be a few local militia. One "long march" from Urbanna to the York River would cut off the enemy forces holding the lower Virginia Peninsula between the York and the James; then two more days' march up the Peninsula would bring the army to the gates of Richmond.

Most important strategically, the movement would turn the flank of the main Rebel army entrenched at Manassas Junction and Centreville, forcing it to give up this position threatening Washington in order to counter the threat to its own capital. The idea, one of his listeners quoted McClellan as saying, "was to leave the enemy where he was, and fight him where he was not." The Rebel army, he said, would receive no reinforcements from the rest of the Confederacy. He would have Federal forces in Tennessee cut the South's main east-west rail line to prevent help from reaching Richmond from that direction, and the force under Ambrose Burnside, recently landed on the North Carolina coast, would strike inland against Richmond's rail connections with the South Atlantic states. When the climactic battle for Richmond was fought — the battle McClellan had assured a newspaperman would be remembered as the Waterloo of the Civil War — it would be on his terms and on ground of his choosing.

The council of war had two central questions to decide, McClellan said: whether the army should change its base from Washington to the Rappahannock, as he proposed; and whether any action need be taken against the Potomac batteries. He and Marcy then left the room, and the twelve generals took up their deliberations.[2]

The council of war divided sharply on the wisdom of McClellan's plan. The three senior generals, Edwin V. Sumner, Irvin McDowell, and Samuel Heintzelman, opposed the change of base, and they were joined by John G. Barnard, the army's chief engineer. Barnard was one of the few with any previous knowledge of the commanding general's ideas. Several months earlier McClellan had sketched out for him the Urbanna scheme, and Barnard raised objection to it as impractical and even dangerous. He doubted the Federals could transport enough men to the Rappahannock by water, land them, and fortify a new base on hostile ground before the Rebels reached the scene from Manassas and assaulted the bridgehead. In any case, he said, they could hardly march from Urbanna to Richmond before the enemy arrived there by rail. Barnard and the other generals opposing the Urbanna plan urged instead a much shorter turning movement by land to the Occoquan River, hardly two days' march south of the present Washington lines, to threaten the Confederates' railroad lifeline to Manassas. As Heintzelman argued it, in that event "the enemy must come out of his entrenchments & meet us in the open field, or have his communications fall into our hands."

The eight other generals — Andrew Porter, Fitz John Porter, Louis Blenker, William B. Franklin, William F. Smith, Erasmus D. Keyes, George A. McCall, and Henry M. Naglee — were unmoved by these arguments and voted their support for the Urbanna plan. Most owed their positions to McClellan and made loyalty to the commanding general their first priority. If any among the eight gave a good reason for the army's going to Urbanna, Barnard commented, "it is more than I heard." He described the decision as cut and dried. The council reminded McDowell of a political caucus in which "the question was determined on personal grounds, not on the merits of the case," and in this General McClellan's mastery of army politics was evident. A majority also agreed with McClellan that destroying the Potomac batteries as a preliminary to the change of base was unnecessary. Before the council took its findings to the White House, the majority tried to dramatize the army's support for General McClellan by urging the votes be made unanimous. "This excited considerable feeling," Heintzelman noted dryly, and the minority indignantly rejected the idea.[3]

It was late afternoon when the twelve generals were ushered into the president's office to report on their deliberations. McDowell thought Lincoln's face fell when the eight-to-four vote to change the army's base was announced. Unknown to the generals, the president himself had proposed the Occoquan turning movement to McClellan some months earlier. (This was one reason General McClellan became so adamant about his Urbanna plan. He was not one who welcomed advice on military matters, and certainly not advice from the president.) Whatever his private thoughts, however, Lincoln expressed himself pleased that there was finally a definite plan of campaign. "Napoleon himself could not stand still any longer with such an army," he observed.

Secretary of War Edwin M. Stanton now joined the conference and began a vigorous interrogation of the generals. Stanton was a lawyer by profession and renowned for his bristling cross-examinations, and he gave the McClellan majority some uncomfortable moments. Like the president, Stanton was greatly concerned about the safety of Washington; if the Army of the Potomac sailed off down the Chesapeake, he said, it would be leaving behind, by McClellan's own admission, a very powerful Rebel army posted just twenty-five miles from the capital.

Gustavus V. Fox, the assistant secretary of the navy, was called in and asked if the navy could assist in opening the Potomac, the most direct route between Washington and the Rappahannock, should the army have to be recalled in an emergency. Fox agreed to take two big frigates off blockade duty so that they, in company with the new ironclad warship *Monitor*, then en route from New York, might silence the Potomac batteries long enough for the army to capture them. Only Sumner and McDowell argued for the army to march immediately against the batteries, before anything else was done, which moved the bellicose Stanton to complain afterward, "We saw ten Generals afraid to fight." The war council's sole unanimous vote came in approval of the president's proposal to organize the present divisions into army corps for the campaign. It was evening now, and after the last argument was exhausted Lincoln told the generals to return at ten o'clock the next morning when he would announce his decision.

At the appointed hour on Saturday, March 8, the twelve generals once again assembled at the White House. The president told them he was giving his approval to General McClellan's Urbanna plan and how greatly relieved he was to see the campaign at last going forward. "He urged us all to go in heartily for this plan," Heintzelman noted in his diary. The point of this call for unity was soon evident, for Lincoln then announced the corps commanders for the field army, chosen "according to seniority of rank." Of the four generals he named — Sumner, McDowell, Heintzelman, and Keyes — only Keyes was on record as favoring the Urbanna movement. (A fifth corps, under Nathaniel P. Banks, would remain behind as a guarding force.) "There were some blank faces, as I am confident some others expected a place," Heintzelman remarked.

Lincoln went on to list certain qualifications to his approval. No more than two corps were to sail from Annapolis until the Potomac was cleared of the enemy batteries. The capital must be left "entirely secure," with its defenders determined jointly by McClellan and the new corps commanders. Finally, there was to be no further delay: the movement must begin by March 18, ten days hence. These instructions would be incorporated in presidential war orders, he said, and with that he adjourned the council of war and sent the generals back to their commands.

General McClellan professed himself fully satisfied (he later wrote) that as a result of the war council's decisions "the Presdt dismissed from his mind the idea that I was a traitor." He was surely just as well satisfied with the council's display of support for his strategic plan, and with how nicely he had gauged the loyalty of his lieutenants. (He would later condemn the choice of corps commanders forced on him, but in fact of the president's selections only Erasmus Keyes was not duplicated on a proposed corps listing of his own, drawn up several months before.)

All in all, McClellan's gamble of calling a war council had paid off handsomely, and he could mark the date — March 8, 1862 — as the official birth of the Peninsula campaign. To be sure, circumstances would soon enough force him to alter his plan, yet its basic concept would remain intact. The Young Napoleon was going to lead his grand army to the Virginia Peninsula and to the gates of Richmond and toward his vision of an American Waterloo.[4]

....

PRESIDENT LINCOLN'S war orders officially gave life to the Peninsula campaign, but it was actually conceived some four months earlier, in November 1861, when McClellan was named general-in-chief. In its conception the plan was perfectly characteristic of George Mc-Clellan — strategically innovative, well thought out logistically, immensely ambitious in scope and aimed at nothing less than "the heart of the enemy's power in the East," yet for all that rooted in a total misconception of the enemy he faced.

At the time he was made general-in-chief, McClellan supposed General Joseph E. Johnston's Confederate army in front of Washington to be 150,000 strong, "well drilled & equipped, ably commanded & strongly intrenched." That, he claimed, was almost exactly twice the size of any force he could bring into action, making it imperative that he find some way to outmaneuver this host and fight it on better terms. (In fact — but a fact beyond McClellan's imagining — it was he who outnumbered Johnston two-to-one.) Soon he was telling the president that rather than offer battle against the Rebels near Washington, as the president urged him to do, "I have now my mind actively turned towards another plan of campaign that I do not think at all anticipated by the enemy. . . ."

McClellan selected Urbanna as his new base of operations quickly enough — on the map it looked an ideal choice — and sketched out "the shortest possible land routes" from there to the Peninsula and Richmond. The key to his plan was gaining West Point on the York, the terminus of the Richmond and York River Railroad that he anticipated using to support his drive on the Southern capital. He also anticipated his advance from the Rappahannock to the York either cutting off and capturing the Confederates holding the lower Peninsula or pressing them into retreat, thus opening the York as well as the James to the Federal navy. With that, both his flanks would be secure and he would have a well-guarded and fully adequate water and rail supply line.

Reaching Richmond ahead of Johnston's army, McClellan would have his opponent "in a vice" and might then fight the decisive battle by his own choice and on his own terms and with all the odds in his favor; only in that way might the inferior army defeat the superior one. And the battle would be decisive — a single immense contest of the magnitude of a Waterloo (but one in which the Young Napoleon, unlike the first Napoleon, would be master of the field), shattering the Confederacy at a stroke, was central to all of General McClellan's strategic thinking.

He modeled this thinking on that of the masters of the art of war he admired and had carefully studied, for no one in the army was so well read in military history as General McClellan. He could recite every detail of the campaigns of Marshal Saxe or Frederick the Great or Napoleon Bonaparte, but his own plan of campaign most closely resembled that of his onetime mentor, Winfield Scott. In 1847 General Scott had put his army ashore at Vera Cruz and marched on Mexico City, with the deliberate intent of seeking one great battle that would at once crush Mexico's principal army and capture Mexico's principal city. That General McClellan should have taken the Mexico City campaign as a model was hardly surprising, for it had been his first experience of war, as a young subaltern, and he eulogized Winfield Scott as "the General under whom I first learned the art of war."[5]

Yet for all the grandeur of his military thought, the actual planning for the Urbanna movement was sporadic and halting. McClellan overtaxed himself that winter, scattering his attention among a myriad of military matters and concentrating on none. Little was done to marshal the immense fleet of ships needed to transport the army to the lower Chesapeake, or to spell out the navy's crucial role in the campaign. The gathering of intelligence on enemy strengths and positions was unfocused. A terrain study of the Peninsula proved to be superficial and markedly inaccurate (one of its more unfortunate highlights was the assertion that the region's "good natural roads" were sandy and well drained). He made no effort to inform the president of the plan and gain his support. At the turn of the year progress ceased entirely when General McClellan fell ill with typhoid fever.

"The bottom is out of the tub," Mr. Lincoln said, and called in a council of advisers to develop some plan of action for the army. McClellan recovered his health and deflected the council with the promise that his own plan was rapidly maturing, but still no plan appeared. Only at the end of January 1862, after Lincoln impatiently ordered him to mount the Occoquan turning movement, did McClellan finally bestir himself. On February 3 he submitted a lengthy paper defending his strategy which for the first time provided some detail on the operation. Only the Urbanna plan would produce results "decisive of the war," he wrote. "I will stake my life, my reputation on the result — more than that, I will stake upon it the success of our cause." The president put his plan aside in favor of the general's.

During the month that followed progress was made in collecting shipping for the movement, but many other elements of the planning and of the army's organization remained unsettled. McClellan did his cause no good when, late in February, he attempted to clear the enemy from the upper Potomac, above Washington. He called for a crossing of the river at Harper's Ferry on a bridge of canal boats, but at the last minute these craft were discovered to be six inches too wide to pass through the Chesapeake and Ohio Canal's lift lock into the Potomac. McClellan and his divisions returned in embarrassment to Washington, and according to a White House visitor Lincoln "expressed himself angrily" on the subject. (It was perhaps just as well that McClellan did not reveal to the president the details of a second scheme, this one to employ no fewer than 118,000 men to capture three Confederate batteries on the lower Potomac.)

With the weeks passing, Lincoln once again found it necessary to intervene, this time questioning McClellan's motives — or so McClellan remembered it — in order to force his hand. On March 8 the generals' war council and the president's directives at last set the campaign in motion. At precisely that moment, with unintended but perfect timing, the enemy turned everything upside down.[6]

....

SOMETHING OVER two weeks before General McClellan's showdown meeting with the president at the White House, General Joseph E.

Johnston was summoned to a meeting of equal moment by *his* president, Jefferson Davis. The war news reaching Richmond from every quarter was grim. Two key outposts in Tennessee, Fort Henry and Fort Donelson, had been captured by the Yankees, with a very high toll of prisoners. Nashville was certain to fall as well, and everywhere in the western theater Confederate forces were in retreat. In the East, a Federal expedition had descended on the North Carolina coast, taken Roanoke Island, and was threatening to advance on Norfolk and perhaps on Richmond itself. "Dangers thicken around us . . . ," Attorney General Thomas Bragg wrote despairingly in his diary. "Our people are disheartened — 'coming events cast their shadows before,' and, do what I will, I cannot drive the horrid picture from my mind."

On February 19 Mr. Davis was discussing these various crises with his Cabinet when General Johnston arrived from Manassas. The general joined the conference, and the discussion turned to the eastern army. In his character and his careful caution Joe Johnston bore a strikingly resemblance to George McClellan, and indeed the two had been close friends in the old army. A gray, erect, soldierly man of fifty-five, Johnston (like McClellan) was much beloved by his men while suffering an uneasy and touchy association with his president. He had made a distinguished record in the Mexican War, where he was wounded five times — Colonel Johnston's only failing, said Winfield Scott, was his "unfortunate knack of getting himself shot in nearly every engagement" — and he had gained further renown for his role in the Confederate victory at Bull Run in 1861. Just now, however, General Johnston's overriding concern, like Attorney General Bragg's, was the shadows cast by coming events.

President Davis told the gathering he was certain that with the coming of spring McClellan's army would take the offensive. The Confederate stance must be defensive. In its present position near Washington Johnston's army was overextended and outmanned — by the latest count he had but 42,200 effective troops — and must withdraw to better defensive ground and to better protect Richmond. "Gen'l J. admitted the propriety of falling back to the line of the Rappahannock," Bragg recorded in his diary, but warned that it would be an uncommonly difficult maneuver to make. Virginia's roads were too deep in winter mud to move even the light field artillery, much less the heavy battery pieces. Johnston also doubted the ability of the single-track Orange and Alexandria Railroad to carry off much of the army's supplies and equipment. In any event, he had not investigated any new position — an admission, Davis later wrote, that came as "a great shock to my confidence in him." General Johnston was told to give further thought to the matter and return the next day.

On February 20 president, general, and Cabinet met again and for weary hours debated ways to withdraw the heavy guns so important to Richmond's defenses. Johnston repeated that the task would be next to impossible until the roads dried, and even then he doubted the enemy would hold off long enough for him to conduct an orderly evacuation.

After the conference adjourned and he returned to his hotel, Johnston encountered one of his colonels in the lobby. Was the rumor making the rounds true, the colonel wanted to know — was the Cabinet really discussing the evacuation of Manassas? If this breach of security was not alarming enough, the next day Johnston was further alarmed when on the train returning to Manassas an acquaintance asked him the same question. This was all the worse, he thought, from the fact that his friend was too deaf to have overheard the tale accidentally; it was told him deliberately. With government leaders so careless of security, Johnston wondered what chance he had to carry off the evacuation of Manassas without disaster.[7]

Praying that none of the rumors had reached the ears of Yankee spies, General Johnston set about preparing for the withdrawal. He faced a problem unique in the history of the Confederacy. For what would prove to be the one and only time in four years of war, the army's much-maligned commissary department had outdone itself, stockpiling at Manassas some 3,240,000 pounds of subsistence stores, nearly a two months' supply. There was as well an immense accumulation of soldiers' baggage; every man in the army, Johnston concluded, had brought a trunk with him to war. To make matters worse, fifteen miles behind his lines was a government-operated meat-curing plant, the largest in the South, currently stocked with more than 2 million pounds of bacon and salted meat. The Orange and Alexandria, which had delivered all this tonnage to the front, was now able to make only scant headway carrying it away, and day by day through late February and into March Joe Johnston grew more apprehensive and morose.

In the midst of these trials came word that the Federals were attempting a crossing of the Potomac at Harper's Ferry, threatening his left flank. "We may indeed have to start before we are ready," he warned one of his officers, but to his great relief nothing more came of that threat. Then on March 5 the detachment guarding his other flank reported "unusual activity" among the Yankee troops in lower Maryland. This immediately aroused Johnston's worst fears. Perhaps word of his evacuation had leaked out after all; perhaps the Federals were attempting just what he had warned President Davis they might try — a surprise crossing of the Potomac from lower Maryland to turn his right flank and strike him in midflight.

What in fact his scouts had seen was nothing more than preparations for McClellan's soon-to-be-abandoned scheme to seize the Potomac batteries, but Johnston was determined not to award his opponent the first move. Orders went out for the army to fall back behind the Rappahannock without a moment's delay. Whatever could not be carried away was to be destroyed.

All through the weekend of March 8 and 9 the Confederates slipped quietly out of their lines and set off southward. A number of the heavy guns in the batteries on the Potomac had to be abandoned. At Manassas the troops were marched to the supply depots and told to help themselves. Rushing from one pile to the next, they loaded up with everything they could carry. A few lucky ones discovered stocks of whiskey and filled their tin cups and canteens. In one company of South Carolinians the men took turns hefting a ten-gallon keg of whiskey all the way to the Rappahannock. More often the roadsides were littered with supplies of every description that had grown too heavy to carry.

The cavalry rear guard put the depots and the meat-curing plant to the torch, and behind the plodding columns the horizon blazed with fire. Cavalryman William Blackford never forgot the peculiar mix of yellow and blue flames that curled up from the huge piles of meat and the overwhelming smell of frying bacon that followed them for twenty miles. "Manassas was burnt up and . . . it was the greatest destructing I ever saw in my life," a Georgian wrote his parents, and he complained that his regiment lost everything in the retreat "but a few frying pans, water buckets and bread pans." Another man recorded in his diary that the farther they marched the more their spirits fell, and he concluded, "I do not think that I ever saw as many men in an ill humor." Joe Johnston, however, could take satisfaction on one count — there was no pursuit. The Federals seemed unaware of his going.[8]

....

BY SHEER happenstance and without notice to General Johnston, the Confederate navy had chosen this particular weekend to strike out at the Federals and rivet their attention. On Sunday morning, March 9, as Johnston's men were abandoning their entrenchments, stunning news reached the White House from Union-held Fort Monroe, at the tip of the Virginia Peninsula. The day before, General John E. Wool's dispatch announced, the huge Rebel ironclad ram *Merrimack* had emerged from Norfolk and attacked the Federal blockading squadron in Hampton Roads. The monster destroyed the *Cumberland* and the *Congress* and drove the *Minnesota* and the *St. Lawrence* aground and to seemingly certain doom. Another telegram, from a newspaperman on the scene, described how the cannon shot fired at the *Merrimack* "had no effect on her but glanced off like pebble stones." No war news had so shocked President Lincoln and his advisers since the army's defeat at Bull Run the previous summer.

The news threw Secretary of War Stanton into a frenzy, leading one of Lincoln's secretaries to compare him to a caged lion. Stanton rushed to the windows of the president's office as if expecting to see the dreaded ironclad steaming up the Potomac to hurl shells at the White House, then rushed back to the conference table to demand that something be done. What was to prevent the *Merrimack* from destroying the rest of the blockading squadron this very day and then going on to lay waste to Washington and New York and Boston, he asked. All the Federal footholds in coastal Virginia and the Carolinas were endangered, and the Army of the Potomac's advance by way of Urbanna and the Peninsula would have to be abandoned.

General McClellan, while not sharing in Stanton's panic, did share his apprehensions. He hurried off orders to protect the army's transports assembled at Annapolis and instructed General Wool at Fort Monroe on defenses to meet the enemy. "The performances of the Merrimac place a new aspect upon everything," he told Wool, "& may very probably change my whole plan of campaign, just on the eve of execution."

Secretary of the Navy Gideon Welles was the chief target of Stanton's blustering. Welles responded calmly that the *Merrimack* could not be in all those places at the same time, and in any case she would probably not reach any of them. He was sure that by now the Union's own ironclad, the *Monitor*, had reached Hampton Roads and he had confidence in her fighting prowess. In fact, he said, if only the *Monitor*'s builders had finished their work on schedule there would be no crisis this day. Spies had been tracking the *Merrimack*'s progress for months, and it was intended that the *Monitor* should long since have attacked the Norfolk navy yard and destroyed the Rebel ironclad in her dry dock. Then it was the army that had dragged its feet on proposals to attack Norfolk. Now, he told the impatient Stanton, there was nothing to do but await further word from Hampton Roads. One of the naval officers at the meeting wrote afterward that he and his colleagues waited that day "with no despair of the Republic, though all of us were thoughtful enough." Secretary Stanton had considerably less faith in the new Union ironclad, and he turned to preparations for blocking the Potomac's channel to prevent the Rebel monster from reaching Washington.[9]

The reports from Hampton Roads began a Sunday crowded with momentous events. Army headquarters was suddenly barraged by telegrams. From the upper Potomac came word that the Confederates were gone from their outpost at Leesburg. Dispatches from the lower Potomac told of the enemy battery positions on the river blown up and abandoned. An escaped slave came into the Union lines west of the capital with a report that over the past two days the Rebels were seen leaving their entrenchments at Manassas and Centreville and falling back. Columns of smoke from the burning supply depots marked the western sky.

General McClellan hurried across the river to learn the truth of the matter for himself. That evening he telegraphed Washington that the enemy was indeed gone, and he promised that the next day he would "move forward to push the retreat of the rebels as far as possible." To climax his day, a message from Gustavus Fox, the assistant navy secretary, was forwarded to him from Fort Monroe. Fox had watched from the fort that day as the *Monitor* steamed out into Hampton Roads to challenge the *Merrimack* and battled her to a draw. Neither vessel appeared seriously damaged, Fox added. In a subsequent dispatch, he described the Confederate ironclad as "an ugly customer" but assured the general that the *Monitor* was her equal. McClellan's plan for his campaign against Richmond by way of the Peninsula might yet be salvaged.[10]

....

THE NEXT MORNING, amid great fanfare, the Army of the Potomac marched out of Washington bound for the Confederate works at Manassas and Centreville. By the time the Yankees reached the scene, however, the last of the Rebels had been gone twenty-four hours, and

McClellan's promise to press the retreating foe was gone as well. He recast the expedition as simply a practice march. There was nothing to be seen but smoldering fires and acres of destruction and fortifications guarded by cannon that on closer inspection turned out to be logs painted black. Newspaper reporters found these "Quaker guns" the most newsworthy feature of the expedition. "The fortifications are a damnable humbug and McClellan has been completely fooled," the *New York Tribune*'s Bayard Taylor concluded, and his judgment was widely echoed. In fact, McClellan's intelligence chief Allan Pinkerton had reported on this wooden ordnance six weeks earlier, but since the general had no plans to assault the enemy entrenchments he cared nothing for how they were defended. Nevertheless, the Quaker guns, like the undersized canal lock at Harper's Ferry, came as one more public embarrassment to a general who had not blushed at being compared to the great Bonaparte.

On March 11 the president called his Cabinet into session, with General McClellan as the main topic of discussion. Most of McClellan's remaining friends in the administration were already disillusioned by his lack of accomplishments, and the news that the Rebel army had slipped out of range so easily was the last straw. The contrast between the good news from other war fronts and "all quiet on the Potomac" was particularly marked. Attorney General Edward Bates noted in his diary that he was not alone in believing the general "has no plans but is fumbling and plunging in confusion and darkness." He characterized McClellan's Manassas march as a fool's errand, with a fool's reward. Mr. Lincoln was not so discouraged as that, but he did conclude that his general must no longer overtax himself by acting as general-in-chief of all the Union armies now that he was on campaign. By presidential war order General McClellan, "having personally taken the field," was relieved of command of all but the Army of the Potomac.

The president deputized William Dennison, the former governor of Ohio and McClellan's confidant during his earlier wartime command in the Ohio Valley, to see the general and explain the order and to assure him that his command of the Potomac army was paramount. Chief of Staff Marcy telegraphed McClellan to return immediately to Washington "as Mr. Dennison desires to see you before you see any one else. . . . All this is very important." The summons only aroused McClellan's suspicions; it must signal a plot by his enemies. "I think the less I see of Washington the better," he replied, and remained in the field. "I regret that the rascals are after me again," he wrote his wife that night. ". . . If I can get out of this scrape you will never catch me in the power of such a set again — the idea of persecuting a man behind his back."

As a result, McClellan learned of his relief as general-in-chief the next morning from Washington's *National Intelligencer*. He nursed this as an insult until Dennison reached his headquarters later in the day and explained the change, and told him that he retained the president's confidence and would command the Army of the Potomac "wherever it may go." Thus mollified, McClellan called together his new corps commanders to decide where the Army of the Potomac should go.[11]

When he first contemplated the changed state of affairs from his field headquarters at Fairfax Court House, McClellan had determined not to let the enemy's retreat deflect him from his cherished Urbanna plan. As soon as he arranged for the occupation of the old Confederate positions, he telegraphed Secretary Stanton, he intended "at once throwing all the forces I can concentrate upon the line agreed upon last week."

Soon afterward, however, McClellan was struck by sobering second thoughts. What he had always argued as the singular advantage of the Urbanna route — the chance to steal a march on his opponent and beat him to Richmond — was all but gone with Johnston back behind the Rappahannock and within easy railroad distance of his capital. Furthermore, there was now the danger that the *Merrimack* might break out of Hampton Roads and devastate the landing force on the Rappahannock, stranding the army on enemy ground. Finally, General McClellan (like General Johnston) suspected he had been victimized by a security leak. Word of the council of war's decision to change the army's base of operations must somehow have reached the Confederates and caused them to withdraw, and McClellan (like Johnston) acted on his misapprehension. If the Rebels knew enough about his plans to pull back out of harm's way, he reasoned, they must also know about Urbanna and would spring an ambush there before his beachhead could be securely established. He must instead take a surer and safer base.

So far as McClellan was concerned, there was but one choice in the matter once he gave up Urbanna. He would instead open his grand campaign against Richmond from a point seventy-five miles southeast of the Confederate capital but already in Union hands — Fort Monroe, at the tip of the Peninsula.

Fort Monroe had always been a fall-back position in his planning. "Should circumstances render it not advisable to land at Urbanna . . . ," he wrote in his February 3 strategy paper, "— the worst coming to the worst — we can take Fort Monroe as a base, & operate with complete security, altho' with less celerity & brilliancy of results, up the Peninsula." He was now willing to settle for less celerity and brilliancy because the alternative — an overland advance against the Rebel army on the Rappahannock — was to him unthinkable. Fort Monroe on the Peninsula and Fredericksburg on the Rappahannock might offer certain similarities as starting points, and the natural obstacles to overcome on the two routes might be similar, but McClellan had long and vehemently argued against the overland route and to take it now would be to admit that he had been wrong and President Lincoln right, and that was something George McClellan would never allow himself to admit.[12]

Late on the afternoon of March 12, in the shabby parlor of an abandoned house at Fairfax Court House, General McClellan convened his second council of war in less than a week. Like the earlier war council, he called it for much-needed reinforcement against enemies who might revoke his design. Present this time were three of the new corps commanders, McDowell, Sumner, and Heintzelman — the fourth, Keyes, only arrived some hours later — and John Barnard, the army's chief engineer. As he had done in Washington, McClellan presented his intended plan of operations and then left his lieutenants to deliberate among themselves. Although originally these four had argued against the Urbanna route, they now agreed without dissent that in the changed circumstances the army should advance by way of the Chesapeake and take Fort Monroe as its new base.

They were gravely concerned about the *Merrimack*, however. As Barnard put it, the possibility of another sortie by the Rebel ironclad "paralyzes the movement of this army by whatever route is adopted." (Although the Confederates had rechristened their ironclad at her commissioning the *Virginia*, all Northerners, and a good many Southerners as well, continued to call her by her original name, and the new name was not widely used in these weeks.) McClellan telegraphed anyone he thought might have an informed opinion on the matter: General Wool at Fort Monroe, navy ordnance expert Henry A. Wise, Assistant Navy Secretary Gustavus Fox. "Can I rely on the Monitor to keep the Merrimac in check so that I can take Fort Monroe as a base of operations," he asked Fox. The war council adjourned until the next morning to await the replies.

The replies were encouraging. Wool and Wise were confident the *Monitor* could again checkmate the *Merrimack*. Fox thought so too, although he warned "this is hope, not certainty." He added that in his view "the Merrimac does not intend to pass by Fort Monroe. I am also of opinion that we shall take her if she does so pass. I think the above is sure enough to make any movement upon." With this assurance, the council of war voted its unanimous consent to the new plan. Complying with the president's March 8 war order, the corps commanders further specified that when the army departed for the Chesapeake, Washington would be left fully garrisoned and additionally guarded by a 25,000-man covering force.[13]

Once he declared the Manassas expedition's purpose to be unwarlike, McClellan had sent for his wife to join him in the field, and she and the general now hosted a picnic lunch for the corps commanders to celebrate the occasion. Afterward General McDowell was dispatched to Washington to explain the new plan to the government. Through his favorite lieutenant, Fitz John Porter, McClellan confidently announced to the *New York World*, his strongest ally in the press, that despite the best efforts of enemies in high places his campaign would go ahead as planned. In a follow-up note, McClellan told the *World*'s reporter, "I believe that we are now on the eve of the success for which we have been so long preparing. . . ."

That evening Mr. Lincoln telegraphed his approval of the new plan. After stipulating that Manassas as well as Washington must be left "secure," he said the Army of the Potomac might take as its new base Fort Monroe "or anywhere between here and there" in order to move "at once in pursuit of the enemy by some route."

So it was that on March 13, 1862, the last of seven eventful days, General McClellan finally gained victory in his battle to retain his command and to lead his grand campaign against Richmond. In due course, in a nice touch of symmetry, victory and defeat in that grand campaign would also be determined in seven days.[14]

Stride of a Giant

···

G ENERAL MCCLELLAN always spoke of the Army of the Potomac
as "my army" — it belonged to him, he once said, "as much as
any army ever belonged to the man that created it" — and he made
a particular point of communicating directly with his soldiers. For that
purpose the headquarters baggage train included a portable printing
press with which to mass-produce general orders and addresses to the
troops. Within twenty-four hours of the decision to open the Peninsula
campaign, the Yankee camps were flooded with copies of the latest
exhortation from the general commanding.

"I have held you back that you might give the death-blow to the
rebellion that has distracted our once happy country," McClellan explained. Through training, arms, and discipline the Army of the Potomac was now a real army. "The moment for action has arrived, and I
know that I can trust in you to save our country. . . . I will bring you
now face to face with the rebels . . . where I know you wish to be, —
on the decisive battlefield." He promised to watch over them "as a
parent over his children; and you know that your General loves you
from the depths of his heart. It shall be my care, as it has ever been, to
gain success with the least possible loss. . . ." In the coming campaign
he would demand of them "great, heroic exertions, rapid and long
marches, desperate combats, privations, perhaps," but he was confident of victory in a righteous cause.

For his closing McClellan adapted a favorite passage he had copied
from Napoleon's address to the Army of Italy: "We will share all these
together; and when this sad war is over we will all return to our homes,
and feel that we can ask no higher honor than the proud consciousness
that we belonged to the ARMY OF THE POTOMAC." The *New York
Herald* called it "a thrilling and patriotic address." The *St. Louis Republican* thought the general had out-Napoleoned even Napoleon: "There

is nothing finer in the published literature of war," it announced. The army redoubled its cheers for the Young Napoleon.[1]

His civilian critics were only inspired to redouble their attacks. Members of the Joint Committee on the Conduct of the War, appointed by Congress to investigate the way the administration and the army were managing the war, visited the abandoned Confederate fortifications at Manassas and Centreville and came back enraged. They saw the Quaker guns and were told the Rebels had spirited away men and equipment for weeks before McClellan discovered what was happening, and they declared the general a failure and demanded his replacement.

These were radical Republicans, described by one observer as "ruthless sleuth-hounds" when it came to rooting out Democrats in uniform (like General McClellan) who did not appear to share their dedication to making the hardest kind of war against the Southern traitors. They took particular offense at the phrase *this sad war* in McClellan's address to his troops; to them any war against the slave power was a glorious war. On March 17 a vote to censure the general and recommend his dismissal failed only narrowly to pass the Senate. Secretary of War Stanton cast about for a replacement — and for some way to persuade the president to make the change. "The fire in the rear is a terrific one," Democratic senator Benjamin Stark told McClellan's most prominent home-front supporter, Samuel L. M. Barlow, although he believed that Lincoln remained firmly committed to the general's campaign. In the end, Stark warned, only victory on the battlefield would silence the anti-McClellan party.

McClellan was very much aware of this fire directed at him from the rear, and it impelled him to get his army and himself into the field and out of range as quickly as he could. With the Potomac now clear of the enemy's batteries he shifted his port of embarkation from Annapolis to Alexandria, a half-dozen miles downstream from the capital, and ordered the troops to be assembled there for passage to the Peninsula. He wrote his friend Barlow on March 16 that history would mark the Rebels' retreat from their stronghold so close to Washington "as the brightest passage of my life." He would ignore all his enemies on the home front and instead stake everything on his army and its "magnificent spirits," and on Mr. Lincoln, who had promised him he would command that army wherever it might go: "*The President is all right —* he is my strongest friend." The next day the lead contingent of the Army of the Potomac set sail for Fort Monroe, with the general himself directing its embarkation. "I shall soon leave here on the wing for Richmond — which you may be sure I will take," he assured Barlow.[2]

Nothing comparable to the movement of the Army of the Potomac to the Virginia Peninsula had ever before been seen in America. Nothing comparable to it would ever be seen again during the four years of civil war. Some troops and equipment were loaded at Annapolis and at Washington, but by far the largest share of the army set off from Alexandria. Vessels of every imaginable kind arrived by the hundreds at the wharves of the historic little brick town that had marked the head of deep-water navigation on the Potomac since colonial days. John Tucker, assistant secretary of war, was in charge of collecting the shipping for the movement, and Tucker had chartered every available steamer on the eastern seaboard. There were Philadelphia ferryboats and Long Island Sound side-wheelers and big Hudson River excursion boats and crack transatlantic packets — 113 of them in all, at a charter cost of more than $24,300 a day. An additional 276 schooners and barges and canal boats, fitted out to transport artillery, animals, and war materiel of every sort, were carried to Fort Monroe under tow.

The troops were happy to be free of their winter quarters and on the move, and many of them viewed the expedition as a lark. Sergeant Elisha Hunt Rhodes of the 2nd Rhode Island noted in his diary that the Hudson River steamer *John Brooks* carrying his regiment was "gaily decorated with flags, and it looks more like a pleasure excursion than an army looking for the enemy." As they passed Mount Vernon the Rhode Islanders' band struck up "Washington's March" in honor of the Father of His Country, and continued its concert as they steamed on downriver. Major George Monteith of General Fitz John Porter's staff counted twenty-five steamers and schooners and tugs lined up at Alexandria to ferry his division. The men marched up the gangplanks in steady procession, and steam derricks hoisted aboard wagons and guns and supplies and even artillery horses in slings. As the loaded vessels pulled away from the wharves, with the men cheering and ships' whistles shrieking, Monteith thought the sight "exceeds anything in grandeur I ever beheld."

On occasion the high spirits got out of hand. The men of the 37th New York, the Irish Rifles, smuggled aboard a barrel of whiskey and before long most of them were drunk and brawling with the 2nd Michigan sharing the transport with them. Order was not restored until the colonel of the Michigan regiment, a tough regular named Orlando Poe, personally "ended the performance" by knocking three of the

Irishmen down a hatchway and kicking two more after them. It is recorded that after that their voyage passed quietly enough.

Daily through the last weeks of March and into early April the parade of ships on the Potomac and Chesapeake Bay continued without pause. River and bay were never empty of heavily laden southbound traffic or northbound steamers and tugs riding light with their tows as they returned for more men and cargoes. All the while navy gunboats prowled the Virginia shoreline on the lookout for Rebel raiding parties that might hope to get off a cannon shot or two at the crowded transports. The only mishap was a tow of nine barges driven ashore in a storm; with the exception of eight mules drowned, their cargoes were saved.

In less than three weeks, John Tucker reported, his 389 vessels delivered to Fort Monroe 121,500 men, 14,592 animals, 1,224 wagons and ambulances, 44 artillery batteries, "and the enormous quantity of equipage, &c. required for an army of such magnitude." Once the kinks were worked out of the system, the Army of the Potomac set off for the Peninsula at the rate of one division starting each day. With pardonable pride, Tucker declared that "for economy and celerity of movement, this expedition is without parallel on record." A British military observer traveling with the army was so impressed with the operation that he called it "the stride of a giant."[3]

....

IT COULD TRULY be said of Major General John Bankhead Magruder that his reputation preceded him. A tall, mustachioed, resplendently uniformed Virginian with a theatrical manner, Magruder had been known to everyone in the prewar army as "Prince John," and Prince John stories were legion. At a post on the Canadian border, for example, Lieutenant Magruder once invited the officers of several famous British regiments stationed nearby to a dinner elaborately staged in the regimental mess with fine china and glassware and silver he had begged, borrowed, and rented. One of his awed guests inquired what salary an American lieutenant commanded that he might lay on such a gala. "Damned if I know," the insouciant Magruder replied. On another occasion, assigned to duty in Washington, he attended a fancy-dress ball as the King of Prussia, authentically costumed down to the last velvet cuff and silver collar button. In 1857, stationed at Fort Adams on the Rhode Island coast, Lieutenant Colonel Magruder was acknowledged to be the centerpiece of the social season in fashionable

Newport. No one could match Prince John at stretching limited resources into plausible illusions.

Magruder found full play for his talent in the straitened Confederacy. He was assigned the command of the Army of the Peninsula, and through the winter and into the spring of 1862 he struggled to create a respectable defense for this eastern gateway to Richmond. He found himself short of every sort of war materiel, and particularly short of manpower. On March 24, with reports reaching him of growing numbers of Union vessels arriving off Fort Monroe, Magruder telegraphed Richmond, "The enemy are evidently concentrating their forces against this line." He added that he could muster hardly 10,000 troops to oppose an advance up the Peninsula.[4]

The enemy's intentions were a good deal less clear to Magruder's superiors in Richmond, President Davis, Secretary of War George W. Randolph, and Mr. Davis's new military adviser, General Robert E. Lee. Thus far the fortunes of war had not been kind to General Lee. His attempt to reverse the Federal gains won by McClellan in 1861 in western Virginia ended in failure. He was then assigned the thankless task of organizing defenses for the South Atlantic coast. In mid-March President Davis brought him to Richmond and named him, in effect, chief of staff of the Confederacy's armies. With Davis taking a very active view of his function as commander-in-chief of the nation's forces, Lee would only be as effective a strategist as he determined to be. In the event he proved to be highly effective. At the moment, however, he had no way of knowing just where the Federals might be headed.

When he contemplated the military chessboard he had inherited, Lee found the Confederacy's pieces on the defensive and widely scattered. Southeast of Richmond, in addition to Magruder's Army of the Peninsula, was Benjamin Huger's contingent guarding Norfolk. To the south, Theophilus Holmes stood vigil against General Burnside's Union foothold in the North Carolina sounds. Joe Johnston's main army was posted to the north, behind the line of the Rappahannock and Rapidan rivers. Along Virginia's western frontier were three small outposts of observation. Farthest north, in the Shenandoah, was the modestly sized Army of the Valley under Thomas J. Jackson, the Stonewall Jackson of Bull Run fame.

The Federals pouring ashore at Fort Monroe might be planning to move against either Richmond or Norfolk, or they might simply be using the fort as a staging ground to reinforce Burnside in North

Carolina. Or they might be making only a feint on the Peninsula while advancing in force from the Rappahannock against Joe Johnston. Lee could promise Magruder only minimal reinforcements until the enemy revealed his hand.

Behind Prince John Magruder's love of display and his voluble excesses — the general, one of his lieutenants wrote, "is fond of dress and parade and of company . . . can talk twenty four hours incessantly" — was an experienced artillery officer of shrewd intelligence. A dozen or so miles from Fort Monroe Magruder had drawn what he called his advanced line across the Peninsula, made up of infantry outposts and artillery redoubts. Adequately manning this line, however, required at least twice the force he had and it could be easily turned, and all in all it was more sham than substance. Its primary value was to keep the Yankee garrison at Fort Monroe at arm's length and prevent it from observing the main defensive line Magruder was constructing a few miles farther up the Peninsula. This line ran from Mulberry Island on the James across the tapering waist of the Peninsula to Yorktown on the York, and included, across the York's narrow channel, the fortified outpost of Gloucester Point on the north bank of the river.

The strongest parts of this Yorktown line were its flanks. Heavy guns in battery at Yorktown and Gloucester Point were sited to block any passage of the York, hardly a thousand yards wide at this point. Batteries on Mulberry Island, supported by the ironclad *Merrimack*, guarded the James River flank. Between these outer works Magruder had constructed an array of redoubts and rifle pits and fortifications behind the Warwick River, a boggy, sluggish stream originating a mile or so from Yorktown and meandering across the Peninsula to empty through tidal marshes into the James at Mulberry Island. There were two gristmill dams, at Lee's Mill and Wynn's Mill, on the Warwick, and Magruder had considerably enlarged the millponds by building three more dams on the stream, turning the Warwick into a watery military obstacle for most of its length.

From end to end this line was strong in artillery firepower — it mounted eighty-five pieces of heavy artillery and fifty-five field guns — but exceedingly thin in manpower. It required 6,000 men to garrison the fixed positions on the two rivers, leaving Magruder with just 7,600 troops to man the line of defenses fourteen miles long between them. This number included 3,600 reinforcements Lee scraped up for him late in March. Beyond that, Prince John would have to depend on his particular skills as an illusionist.

General Magruder, like General McClellan, was handy with pen as well as sword, and he composed an address of his own to his troops. Magruder's was a stirring call to repel invasion by "the ruthless tyrants who have . . . vowed our conquest or our destruction." He reminded his little army that it guarded the hallowed ground where General Washington had met Cornwallis and his invading redcoats eighty-one years before. "The long war of the Revolution culminated at length in victorious triumph on these very plains of Yorktown," he proclaimed. "These frowning battlements on the heights of York are turned in this second war of liberty against the enemies of our country." Southerners liked to call this war the second American Revolution, and Prince John Magruder liked to imagine winning the second Battle of Yorktown.[5]

....

FORT MONROE was the largest coastal fortress in America, an enormous hexagonal masonry work a third of a mile across that had been completed fifteen years before the war on Old Point Comfort, the finger of land marking the tip of the Virginia Peninsula. Monroe's great guns commanded the channel from Chesapeake Bay into Hampton Roads, the spacious roadstead into which flows the James, Elizabeth, and Nansemond rivers, and they commanded as well the passage between Hampton Roads and the mouth of the York. The fort had been too strongly defended for the Rebels to capture at the outbreak of the war, and now it was a secure sally port from which the Federals might advance on the Rebels' capital. Few postings in the old army had been more favored than Fort Monroe, for Old Point Comfort with its Hygeia Hotel was one of the antebellum South's most celebrated watering places. Among the officers once stationed there who now wore Confederate gray were Robert E. Lee, Joseph E. Johnston, and John B. Magruder.

Never had the fort witnessed such a display of military might. By late March Hampton Roads, already the main base for the North Atlantic Blockading Squadron, was so crowded with the ships transporting McClellan's army that Edmund Ruffin, the well-known Virginia secessionist, described his view from Norfolk as simply a forest of masts. "It was impossible to count the vessels, though aided by a glass," he noted in his diary, and he was persuaded that the entire Northern army must be arriving "& the 'march to Richmond' will be again attempted, up the peninsula." The sheer numbers also impressed a Yankee diarist. "The bay is covered with vessels," wrote the 2nd Michigan's Lieutenant Charles B. Haydon, and when he reached

100 he stopped counting. Among them were a visiting British man-of-war and the French *Gassendi*, "for whose benefit our band played the Marseilles Hymn as we passed."

Other sights in the roadstead were reminders of the recent battle there: the topgallant masts of the sunken *Cumberland*, slanting up out of the water with flags still flying, and at anchor the little *Monitor*, which one soldier described for his wife as "the oddest looking thing in the shape of a boat I have ever looked upon." Several of the newly arrived Federals observed that the much-quoted description in a Southern newspaper of the *Monitor* looking like a Yankee cheesebox on a raft was right on the mark.

Ashore the scene was equally crowded. As they landed, the Federal troops were marched to hastily laid-out camps on the outskirts of the fort and at nearby Newport News and Hampton. Historic Hampton, whose settlement dated back to 1610, was already a casualty of war. The previous fall General Magruder, acting on a newspaper rumor that the Yankees were planning to turn Hampton into a settlement for runaway slaves, had burned the village to the ground rather than see it suffer such desecration. Now nothing remained but a grim forest of blackened chimneys, like an illustration of some ancient ruin, a monument to the particular passions unleashed by this civil war. The armies left their marks in smaller ways as well. A homesick Massachusetts boy found the Virginia landscape pleasing to the eye but rapidly changing. "When we first came here," he wrote his parents, "the woods were full of whippoor-wills, they made me think of home, but they have been all scared away now." Day by day the ground around Fort Monroe grew into a great armed camp.[6]

During these opening weeks of the operation General McClellan remained behind at Alexandria, working out the logistics for his offensive and pondering his strategy. The enemy kept putting crimps in his grand campaign. He had been forced to abandon the Urbanna scheme after Joe Johnston pulled back behind the Rappahannock. Then the *Merrimack* restricted his options even further. He had always counted on using the James as well as the York as an artery to supply his army and as a springboard for possible flanking operations against the Confederate capital. Now the *Merrimack* had taken the James right out of his calculations. The navy promised him it would protect Fort Monroe as the army's new base, but it would not promise to challenge the Rebel ironclad for control of the James. McClellan would have to narrow his focus to an advance by land up the Peninsula and to gaining control of the York.

The suddenness of his decision to shift from Urbanna to Fort Monroe set off a hurried scramble at headquarters to calculate what opposition might be met in any advance from the fort. Until now the intelligence about the lower Peninsula had not had a high priority, and Allan Pinkerton, the Chicago private detective who directed intelligence-gathering for the general, found only three reports on the area in his files. Late in 1861 Timothy Webster, the most skilled of Pinkerton's spies, had stopped at Gloucester Point and Yorktown on his way into Richmond and counted the batteries there and learned from a talkative Rebel lieutenant of Magruder's advanced line facing Fort Monroe. A few weeks later a free black who had worked as a steward on a steamer plying the York River before escaping north furnished additional details about the Yorktown and Gloucester Point positions. The third report was by a deserter from Magruder's command who provided recent firsthand information on the advanced line between Yorktown and Fort Monroe, where his regiment had been posted.

All this intelligence was highly detailed and had every evidence of being reliable. None of it, however, contained a single word about any defensive line across the Peninsula along the course of the Warwick River, for none of the informants had happened on a description of it. Indeed, military maps made of the region gave little notice at all to the Warwick. General McClellan raised no questions about this intelligence and seemed satisfied that it told him all he needed to know about what he might encounter. Alexander S. Webb, a Federal artillery officer and the Peninsula campaign's first historian, would describe himself as dumbfounded by the extent of McClellan's ignorance of the enemy's position.[7]

For an up-to-date estimate of Magruder's numbers, McClellan turned to John E. Wool, in command at Fort Monroe. John Wool was the old soldier of the Civil War — seventy-eight years old, white-haired and ramrod-straight and sharp-tongued, beginning the fiftieth year of a service record that stretched back to the War of 1812. He had been a major general by brevet since the war with Mexico and had persuaded himself that he outranked the upstart McClellan, a major general only since 1861, albeit by a regular commission rather than by brevet. This would create occasional awkwardness in the coming weeks but no real difficulty; McClellan's problems with John Wool would come instead from the old soldier's efforts to inject reality into the way the enemy was viewed.

At first there was no dispute on that score. On March 12 Wool had telegraphed headquarters that he believed Magruder "has from 15,000 to 18,000 men, extending from James River to Yorktown." (This report stemmed from a bit of espionage trickery. Wool had one of his men desert to the enemy and enlist in a Confederate regiment, then return "with precise information of the rebel works between York and James Rivers." The double-deserter's information on the Rebel works was as misleading as Pinkerton's, however, for he had been posted only in Magruder's advanced line.) Fitz John Porter, when he arrived at Fort Monroe, seconded this figure after a reconnaissance that tapped the enemy's advanced line. "From all I learn . . . ," Porter telegraphed McClellan on March 30, "no greater force this side than 15,000 men." This was the number McClellan told Secretary Stanton he expected to face when he advanced on Yorktown.

This estimate was notable on two counts. First, it was remarkable for its accuracy, overstating Magruder's defenders by just 1,400 men; and second, it proved to be the only time during the entire Peninsula campaign that Federal intelligence came anywhere close to an accurate count of the opposing army. After this singular moment of reality, the Army of the Potomac would always confront a phantom Rebel army that existed only in the mind of the general commanding.[8]

At the moment, however, from what detective Pinkerton and General Wool told him, and from these first estimates of Magruder's strength, General McClellan concluded that he would encounter no great obstacle in reaching the same objective he had set for himself in a landing at Urbanna — West Point, the terminus of the Richmond and York River Railroad which was to support his final march on Richmond. He planned to make that march with 130,000 men, and ordered locomotives and cars to be readied for shipment to the Peninsula to operate on the captured railroad. To be sure, instead of a single "long march" from Urbanna it would now be necessary to force a passage of thirty-five miles up the York to reach West Point. This might lack the "celerity & brilliancy" of the original plan, but it appeared perfectly feasible, for it looked as if General Magruder was repeating General Cornwallis's error of walling himself up inside Yorktown.

Some considerable force might be needed to lever the Confederates out of their fortifications there and open the river, and McClellan would bring along heavy siege guns for that purpose and ask the navy for help, but the operation looked simple enough. An amphibious column landing below Yorktown would turn the advanced line of enemy defenses facing Fort Monroe. A second column marching straight up the Peninsula would then turn Yorktown itself and cut off the garrison from Richmond. To complete the encirclement, in due course he would land General McDowell's First Corps on the north bank of the York, overrun the Gloucester Point batteries, and go on to "turn in that manner all the defences of the Peninsula." Of course the enemy might flee on his approach, but if not, a second siege of Yorktown would surely end as successfully as the first, and no doubt more quickly.[9]

He set his staff to working out the details with the navy. McClellan's naval counterpart was Flag Officer Louis M. Goldsborough, commanding the North Atlantic Blockading Squadron from his flagship *Minnesota* in Hampton Roads. Goldsborough was a bulky, imposing man of fifty-seven who, remarkably, had been in service for fifty of those years, having gone to sea as a midshipman at the tender age of seven. A hot argument would later arise about the navy's part in the campaign, but the situation was certainly made clear enough at the beginning. Goldsborough told all those who conferred with him that he would be glad to put his gunboats at the disposal of the army to support any landings it might want to make on either side of the York, and perhaps once Gloucester Point fell a gunboat or two might be able to run past Yorktown and help take its defenses in reverse. But beyond everything else he wanted it understood that his first and primary duty was to check the *Merrimack*.

Nothing in living memory had so shaken the navy's high command as the *Merrimack*'s foray into Hampton Roads. The ease with which she destroyed two of the wooden navy's finest warships had been frightening. Admittedly the *Monitor* had demonstrated she was the equal of her ironclad adversary, but even that fact haunted Goldsborough and his captains. What if in her next sortie the *Merrimack* simply ignored the *Monitor* and went in pursuit of every wooden vessel in sight, including the Potomac army's transports and supply ships? On that day if the *Monitor* could do no more harm to the *Merrimack* than she had on March 9, the navy would be driven from Hampton Roads and McClellan's campaign would be over before it was fairly begun.

Goldsborough's solution to this nightmarish prospect was to plot the *Merrimack*'s destruction not by gunfire but by ramming, and he assigned all his largest and heaviest warships to that tactic. Old Commodore Vanderbilt had even turned over his fast side-wheeler *Vanderbilt* to the navy, and she stood by with steam up as part of Goldsborough's ramming squadron. With these rams added to the *Monitor*, the flag

officer wrote his wife, he was "spoiling for a fight with the Merrimac. . . . I expect to sink her in ten minutes."

Giving this priority to the *Merrimack* left the navy with but seven
gunboats — all of them of wood and none of them armored — to
support the operations of the Army of the Potomac. These craft were
perfectly adequate to furnish escort and fire support for any landings
the army cared to undertake, but they were not up to challenging shore
batteries, especially the batteries of heavy guns known to be at Yorktown and Gloucester Point. Indeed, their guns would not even elevate
sufficiently to reach the batteries sited on Yorktown's bluffs. General
McClellan would later complain bitterly of Goldsborough's timidity,
but on the eve of his campaign he knew very well what to expect. He
must have heavy weapons of his own and the engineers to serve them,
McClellan wrote the chief of the Corps of Engineers on March 28:
"The first operation will be the capture of Yorktown & Gloucester, this
may involve a siege (at least I go prepared for one) in case the Navy is
not able to afford the means of destroying the rebel batteries at these
points."[10]

The general's final task before leaving Alexandria to take command
on the Peninsula was to arrange for the defense of Washington. In his
original scheme this had seemed simple enough. To make up the
forces specified by the council of war at Fairfax Court House, he
intended to call in most of General Nathaniel Banks's corps from the
Shenandoah Valley to furnish the "covering force" for the capital's
garrison. Toward the end of March, however, two events conspired to
upset his calculations. From the Valley on March 23 came word that
Confederates under Stonewall Jackson had attacked one of Banks's
divisions at the village of Kernstown. Jackson was driven off, but the
fact that he had dared to make the attack at all gave pause; Banks's
corps would have to remain in the Valley until the troublesome Jackson
was disposed of.

Then, on March 31, President Lincoln announced he was transfer-
ring Louis Blenker's division from the Army of the Potomac to the
newly formed Mountain Department commanded by John Charles
Frémont. Lincoln admitted to McClellan that he acted from political
motives; General Frémont was a hero to radical Republicans everywhere, and they were heavily pressuring the president to find him a
command. It was supposed that in due course Blenker's transfer would
profit the Army of the Potomac: thus reinforced, Frémont might advance into east Tennessee and cut the Confederacy's only direct east-

west rail link, long a favorite project of McClellan's, to help isolate Richmond in the coming campaign. (In the event, Frémont's generalship failed to match his partisanship, and he never came close to his objective.) McClellan appeared to accept Blenker's detachment with good grace — "I cheerfully acquiesce in your decision without any mental reservation," he told Lincoln — but in fact, whether from that cause or some other, he abruptly adopted an ill-conceived, even cavalier course toward the defense of Washington.[11]

This attitude was rooted in his conviction that the best way to defend Washington was to attack Richmond. The Rebels, McClellan insisted, would call in every available soldier to defend their capital; therefore he must have every available soldier to attack it. In any case, General Banks's corps posted in the Shenandoah Valley was just as much a part of Washington's defenses as the city's garrison. If by some chance Joe Johnston should turn back and launch a new campaign against Washington, he would have to pause to rebuild his railroad supply line destroyed during the withdrawal from Manassas, giving Banks plenty of time to come to the rescue.

But that possibility struck McClellan as highly unlikely. "It seems clear that we have no reason to fear any return of the rebels in that quarter," he assured Banks. He quite dismissed the possibility that an enemy raiding force, moving fast and traveling light, might attempt a coup de main by seizing and sacking Washington simply for political gain and to impress world opinion. Such a raid would not be militarily sound and hardly anything his old friend Joe Johnston would consider. (It would have deeply shocked McClellan to hear his old friend propose, hardly a month later, to "take the offensive, collect all the troops we have in the East and cross the Potomac with them. . . .")

Secure behind his convictions, McClellan was unable to comprehend the deep concern Lincoln and Stanton felt for the capital's safety. The president had clearly stipulated, in approving the general's plan, that no change of base be made "without leaving in, and about Washington, such a force as . . . shall leave said City entirely secure." In approving the decisions of the Fairfax Court House war council he was equally direct: "Leave Washington secure." Yet McClellan, when he worked up the final details for the capital's defense, made no effort to meet Lincoln and Stanton to discuss and explain his ideas. Instead, on April 1, he hurriedly dashed off a paper outlining his dispositions and dispatched it to the War Department, and even before the courier reached Washington he set sail for Fort Monroe in the headquarters ship *Commodore*. That afternoon, as the *Commodore* steamed down the Potomac, he wrote his wife to boast how he had gotten under way with all due speed: "I feared that if I remained at Alexandria I would be annoyed very much & perhaps be sent for from Washn. Officially speaking, I feel very glad to get away from that sink of iniquity."[12]

At first glance, McClellan's paper appeared to assign more troops to the capital's defense than even Secretary Stanton could wish. Two days earlier, Stanton had obtained a general accounting of manpower from McClellan that listed under the heading "to be left around Washington" 50,000 men — the city's garrison troops, plus Banks's corps. Now the general wrote that he was leaving nearly 55,500 from his army, which, when added to the 18,000 in the Washington garrison, totaled no fewer than 73,500 men to defend the city. When Stanton took a closer look at McClellan's calculations, however, he discovered that nearly half this imposing total was in the Shenandoah Valley, a very different matter from being stationed "in, and about Washington," as the president had directed. Stanton put staff officers to analyzing the general's paper down to the last comma.

The staff reported serious problems both with McClellan's troop placements and with his arithmetic. Of the men he had listed, fully one-quarter of them — 18,600 — simply did not exist. They were overcounted on returns, or counted twice, or were not with the army at all. Blenker's division was counted with the troops in the Valley, but shortly it would have to join Frémont's Mountain Department. Instead of the 50,000 men Stanton had been told would be "left around Washington" — instead of the 40,000 the army's corps commanders had specified as the minimum number needed to guard the capital — General McClellan had assigned just 26,761 troops to this task. What was worse, the majority of these were raw recruits, poorly equipped and totally without training. The verdict was unanimous, Stanton wrote, that General McClellan had disregarded the president's orders: "They agreed in opinion that the capital *was not safe*." It was reported that when Mr. Lincoln was told these facts, "he was justly indignant."[13]

....

IN THE MEANTIME, late on the afternoon of April 2, the *Commodore* anchored off Fort Monroe, and General McClellan immediately boarded the *Minnesota* to confer with Flag Officer Goldsborough. The navy's scheme for coping with the *Merrimack* was again explained to him. The part the gunboats might play in the envelopment of Yorktown and Gloucester Point was examined in detail. "The whole subject was fully discussed by Genl McClellan & myself . . . ," Goldsborough reported to the Navy Department. "McClellan was perfectly satisfied . . . & freely & frankly expressed himself so." Returning to the *Commodore*, McClellan met with his generals until the small hours of the morning, drawing up plans for the march on Yorktown. "The grass will not grow under my feet," he assured his wife Ellen. Everything appeared to be going according to plan, and he was optimistic. "The great battle will be (I think) near Richmond as I have always hoped & thought," he told her. "I see my way very clearly. . . ."

"Forward to Yorktown!!" the 15th Massachusetts's Sergeant Jonathan Stowe wrote exuberantly in his diary on April 4. True to his word that no grass would grow under his feet, General McClellan put his army on the march just thirty-six hours after he arrived at Fort Monroe. He had with him, when he set out early that morning, just half the force he expected eventually to command in the great battle for Richmond, yet even so it was the largest Civil War army yet assembled for the field.

Advancing on the right, on the direct road to Yorktown, were two divisions and a cavalry regiment under Samuel Heintzelman. On the left, making up the column intended to outflank Yorktown by way of the Lee's Mill Road, were two divisions and cavalry under Erasmus Keyes. Following along behind with McClellan was the reserve — a fifth infantry division, a brigade of regulars, the reserve artillery, and the sizable headquarters guard. In all there were 66,700 men marked for duty, of which some 55,000 could be put on the firing line, along with nineteen batteries of field artillery and the artillery reserve. The day was pleasant and the marching easy. The green of spring had touched the countryside and orchards glowed pink and white with blossoms. The few Rebels sighted faded back before the advance. During the noontime halt Sergeant Stowe's brigade lined both sides of the road to cheer General McClellan and his staff as they cantered past. The sergeant thought the general looked too young to be commanding an army.[14]

By day's end they were more than halfway to their objective, and it was clear that the Rebels were making no attempt to defend their advanced line. Positions McClellan had expected he would have to turn with an amphibious landing fell without a fight. This seemed to confirm his latest intelligence. A few days earlier Confederate deserters from Yorktown had reported that beyond his troops in garrison General Magruder could put no more than 8,000 men into the field against the invaders. McClellan's spirits soared. That evening he wrote Ellen, "Everything has worked well today — I have gained some strong positions without fighting & shall try some more maneuvering tomorrow." The next day, he told her, he would invest Yorktown itself "& may have a fight." His only concern was that Magruder might escape, and he ordered Heintzelman not to unduly alarm the enemy at Yorktown: "I wish to cut off their retreat with Keyes' column before pressing them on our right."

Word flashed to Richmond that the Yankee army was on the march. McClellan was tipping his hand at last, and General Lee acted quickly. He telegraphed Joe Johnston, "Enemy advancing in force from Old Point," and ordered him to send troops to the Peninsula without delay. That movement was going to take time, however, and Magruder must somehow delay McClellan's advance. Magruder did not rate his chances as very good. Recent deserters from his army had "probably warned the enemy of our strength & movements," he said. "I have made my arrangements to fight with my small force, but without the slightest hope of success."[15]

Day Two of the operation — Saturday, April 5 — proved to be a day of great disillusionment for General McClellan. First came the unhappy discovery that those advance reports of the region's "good natural roads" — roads with a sandy surface that drained well — were as far wrong as it was possible to be. During the morning's march there was a downpour of rain lasting several hours, and the whole Yankee army promptly sank in mud. A man in the 38th New York writing home described it as "our weary march through rain of the worst I ever saw & mud (without any stretching) up to our knees. . . ."

Major Charles S. Wainwright, a Yankee artillerist, would take it upon himself to study the Peninsula's roads simply as a curious phenomenon of nature. He discovered that the topsoil tended to be a foot or so of mostly light, sandy loam that rested on a bed of shell marl, which in turn lay on a subsoil of heavy clay. The roads were not crowned, and water sank straight through the topsoil to be trapped in the marl, converting it "into the consistency of soft mortar." Whenever anything broke through the surface crust, Wainwright observed, "there is nothing to stop its sinking until it reaches the hard clay." This was a lesson both armies learned to their pain, and the Yankees who advanced on Yorktown learned it first. Another Union officer rendered a verdict both simple and heartfelt: "Such depth of mud & such frightful roads I never saw."

General McClellan's second great shock of the day was the discovery that enemy forces were in position where they were not supposed to be. Certainly it came as no surprise that Heintzelman's column on the right ran into opposition as it approached Yorktown. The colonel of the lead regiment sent back a message that their movement "brought upon the parapets a large number of men & a battery out of the woods & into action." From their fortifications Confederate gunners and riflemen opened a sharp fire on any Yankee who came within range. The opposition here was expected, but the report from General Keyes, in command of the column on the left on the Lee's Mill Road, was quite unexpected.

A man in the 7th Maine, which was heading Keyes's march, wrote that as they emerged from a patch of woods "we saw across the open space a long line of rebel earthworks with a stream in front, the rebel flag was flying and we could see the secesh officers riding along their lines inside the works." Keyes notified headquarters that his advance was halted by enemy works "which offer a severe resistence." He said that a column of Rebel troops 2,000 or 3,000 strong was clearly visible moving off through the woods toward the James River, sealing the enemy's line against any attempt of his to outflank it. To attack would simply waste lives. Keyes thought he had at least impressed the Rebels with his own numbers: "Wherever the enemy has shown himself I have shown a force to confront him. . . ."[16]

What in fact these Yankees were viewing, for the most part, were the Prince John Magruder players, strutting and fretting their hour upon the stage. Their performance was exhausting but good theater all the same. "This morning we were called out by the 'Long roll' and have been traveling most of the day, seeming with no other view than to show ourselves to the enemy at as many different points of the line as possible," a tired Alabamian noted in his diary. As Lieutenant Robert Miller of the 14th Louisiana explained it, "The way Magruder fooled them was to divide each body of his troops into two parts and keep them travelling all the time for twenty four hours, till reinforcements came." Before the charade was over, Miller's regiment had marched from Yorktown to the James and back six times.

Captain James H. McMath of the 11th Alabama described a variation on the theme. When the Yankees first came in sight, McMath wrote, his regiment was ordered out of its entrenchments and sent at the double-quick through the enemy's fire "untill we got out of sight just around the point of a hill. We were halted there some 1/2 hour, when we were counter-marched over to the place we started from." Sound effects from behind stretches of concealing woods heightened the illusion: frequent drum and bugle calls, much shouting of marching orders, periodic outbursts of firing all along the line. Prince John had never been in better form. "It was a wonderful thing," the diarist Mary Chesnut recalled, "how he played his ten thousand before McClellan like fireflies and utterly deluded him. . . ."[17]

Magruder's illusion did not depend entirely on stage-managing his little army. Equally important was the impression made on McClellan of finding fortifications stretching all the way across the Peninsula. General McClellan had a highly systematic cast of mind; he liked events to proceed according to careful plan, and suddenly his best-laid plan for taking Yorktown was falling to pieces. Everything he had counted on in his planning was going wrong.

His intelligence information was wrong, and so was his notion that the Peninsula's roads "are passable at all seasons of the year." His maps that showed the Warwick River as insignificant and of no military importance were wrong. And from all reports, his estimate of 15,000 Confederate defenders at Yorktown was as wrong as all the rest of it. Logic had persuaded him that with a total of only 15,000 men Magruder would never try to hold a line from river to river — it was against every military precept to attempt so extended a defense with hardly a thousand troops to the mile — and he had supposed his opponent would simply make Yorktown a citadel and hold out there for as long as he could. Now a new plan was necessary, and he adopted one with uncharacteristic speed.

"Our neighbors are in a very strong position . . . ," McClellan explained to Flag Officer Goldsborough. "I cannot turn Yorktown without a *battle*, in which I must use heavy artillery & go through the preliminary operations of a siege." He sent orders to Fort Monroe to bring forward the siege train and to repair the roads and establish forward depots for the heavy paraphernalia of a siege.

Offsetting his disappointment, however, was an inner sense of confidence, for if there was one military art General McClellan knew better than any other, it was siege warfare. His first experience of war as a young lieutenant had been at the siege of Vera Cruz in the Mexican War. During a mission to observe the Crimean War in 1855 he had made a long and careful study of the siege of Sevastopol. No officer in either army knew more about conducting a siege than George McClellan.[18]

At his field headquarters that evening, as he worked out the details of the siege and planned reconnaissances to mark out the best approaches to the Rebel works, General McClellan received the final shock in this day of shocks. A telegram from Washington announced that McDowell's First Corps was detached from his command. The president, it was subsequently explained, considered the forces McClellan had left for the defense of Washington "insufficient to insure its safety." The one infantry corps not yet sent to the Peninsula was McDowell's, and he was ordered to remain behind to guard the capital.

The news drove McClellan to a towering rage. In his nightly letter to his wife he called the president's action "the most infamous thing that history has recorded." He telegraphed Lincoln that in his "deliberate judgment" the loss of the First Corps imperiled his entire campaign. Now more certain than ever of playing the underdog's role in the fighting to come, he erased from his mind the least thought of an immediate assault on the "formidable" enemy line in front of him. Prince John's bluff was safe. "I am now of the opinion," McClellan concluded, "that I shall have to fight all of the available force of the Rebels not far from here." The British observer who termed the Army of the Potomac's first step of the campaign "the stride of a giant" would describe the second step as "that of a dwarf."[19]

· 3 ·

Siege

....

WHEN HE came to write his official report on the Peninsula campaign a year later, General McClellan was still incensed. He
labeled the withholding of McDowell's First Corps a "fatal error,"
making it impossible for him to execute the "rapid and brilliant operations" he had so carefully planned. "I know of no instance in military
history where a general in the field has received such a discouraging
blow," he wrote. What was worse — and he made this charge from the
first — it was all part of a deliberate plot, conceived by "a set of
heartless villains" in Washington, to sacrifice him and his army on the
altar of abolitionism.

As McClellan viewed it, the real reason for holding back the First
Corps was to make sure he would not have force enough to capture
Richmond and end the rebellion before the abolitionists could enlarge
the conflict from civil war to revolution, from the reuniting of the
sections to the forcible abolition of slavery in defiance of the Constitution. As he told his friend Samuel Barlow, it was all a conspiracy
originating in "the stupidity & wickedness" of his enemies in the
government.

There was no substance whatever to McClellan's conspiracy theory,
but there was also no doubt of his fervent belief in it. Unable to
recognize failings in himself, he needed to invent failings in others to
excuse whatever went wrong with his grand campaign. His list of
conspirators was a long one, headed by Secretary of War Stanton and
seconded by radical Republicans of every stripe, and it included General McDowell, whom he suspected of plotting to replace him as
commander of the Army of the Potomac. President Lincoln was on the
list as well, but more as Stanton's tool than as instigator. Throughout
the campaign McClellan would rarely find a good word to say for the
president — and would never grasp the reality that it was Lincoln,

rather than Stanton, who made the decisions affecting him and his army. Although he had glimpsed the truth earlier when he remarked to Barlow that the president "is my strongest friend," he would not return that friendship. This matter of the defense of Washington was just the first of many instances when General McClellan's refusal to trust the president or to take him into his confidence would cost him dearly.

Nor was there any substance to McClellan's claim that holding back McDowell to guard Washington dislocated all his plans for getting the Peninsula campaign off to a fast start. He had already brought the campaign to a dead stop, before learning of the First Corps's detachment, by electing to lay siege to Magruder's line across the Peninsula. The First Corps was not even a high priority in his planning — by his scheduling it was to be two weeks or more before its divisions began to reach Fort Monroe. In any event, his original idea of using McDowell to outflank all the enemy positions on the Peninsula was gone beyond recall the moment he decided that the main army could not turn Yorktown.

Should he land the First Corps on the north bank of the York and send it past Gloucester Point while the rest of the army was immobilized in its siege lines before Yorktown, he would be committing what was for him a cardinal military sin: dividing his army in the face of what he now had no doubt was a superior foe. It would invite his opponent to leave a holding force in his own siege lines, cross the York with the rest of his army, and fall on McDowell like an avalanche. General McClellan's declarations to the contrary, the president's decision to hold back McDowell did not dictate the decision to besiege Yorktown. It did not affect the way the siege was conducted, or even how long it lasted. The sole author of the siege of Yorktown was George Brinton McClellan.[1]

Sunday, April 6, dawned clear and pleasant, and at first light the balloon *Intrepid*, piloted by "Professor" Thaddeus S. C. Lowe, the New Hampshire Yankee who headed McClellan's aeronaut corps, rose majestically from behind the trees to spy out the Yorktown defenses. On the ground dozens of other Yankees crept forward with telescopes and field glasses on the same mission. Prince John Magruder, continuing his game of bluff, provided them with a good deal to see, but little that was distinct. His artillerists and sharpshooters continued to fire at the slightest movement, and the Yankee observers had to keep their distance.

Some of McClellan's generals were eager that morning to see what was really behind the fierce front Magruder displayed. Charles S. Hamilton, leading a division in Heintzelman's Third Corps, said he could not see much in the way of any actual defenses in the gap between Yorktown's ramparts and the headwaters of the Warwick River. Heintzelman and Hamilton went to headquarters to seek permission for a reconnaissance in force to probe the spot. They got nowhere with the idea. McClellan's favorite lieutenant, Fitz John Porter, and his chief engineer, John Barnard, both strongly seconded the general's decision to do nothing more than dig in where they were. As Barnard wrote in appraising the siege, "The project of an assault was mere hare-brained folly. . . ." Just then, however, an actual reconnaissance in force was being launched against another part of Magruder's line, and it very nearly succeeded.

Leading the left wing of the Federal advance was the Fourth Corps division of General William F. Smith, who since his West Point days had been known as "Baldy" for his thinning hair. Baldy Smith was an aggressive, contentious sort, with little faith in the resolve of his corps commander, Erasmus Keyes, and that morning he acted on his own in ordering two regiments to investigate the Warwick River line to see if there were any holes in it. Smith assured the leader of the expedition, Brigadier Winfield Scott Hancock, that if a hole was found he would send him strong reinforcements to exploit it.

After seeing off his reconnaissance, Smith rode to Keyes's headquarters to let his superior know "in a conversational way" what he had done. As they talked, a messenger arrived from McClellan's headquarters. Keyes read the dispatch and without a word handed it to Smith. No action was to be initiated against the enemy, it read, until the engineers had thoroughly studied the Rebel line and determined the best approach. Smith, "very much chagrined," rushed back to the front to recall Hancock. Hancock said that he had already discovered the weak spot they were looking for, and that it could be taken easily. No matter now, Smith told him: it was out of their hands. Baldy Smith always believed that had McClellan's order arrived an hour or two later, he would have broken the enemy's line and ended the siege of Yorktown the day it began.[2]

Ironically, this aborted assault furnished General McClellan with the evidence he needed to prove he had done the right thing in putting Yorktown under siege. Hancock came back with four prisoners from the 14th Alabama who were so talkative that it is likely they were members of Prince John's acting company. Under questioning by one of Pinkerton's detectives, the Alabamians revealed that the Rebel line on the Warwick was manned by 40,000 men, which would grow "in a few days" to 100,000. Joe Johnston himself was expected that day, along with 8,000 reinforcements.

McClellan took the baited hook. On April 7 he telegraphed Washington, "All the prisoners state that Gen. J. E. Johnston arrived in Yorktown yesterday with strong reinforcements. It seems clear that I shall have the whole force of the enemy on my hands, probably not less than 100,000 men & possibly more"; as a result of the government's deductions from his command "my force is possibly less than that of the enemy. . . ." To take the offensive now would be fatal: "Were I in possession of their entrenchments and assailed by double my numbers I should have no fears as to the result." Simply to continue the siege he must have more men and more heavy guns.

President Lincoln urged him to break the enemy's line in front of him immediately. "They will probably use *time*, as advantageously as you can," he warned, and sought to reason with his general. Yorktown would only become another Manassas: "You will do me the justice to remember I always insisted, that going down the Bay in search of a field, instead of fighting at or near Manassas, was only shifting, and not surmounting, a difficulty — that we would find the same enemy, and the same, or equal, intrenchments, at either place." The country could not fail to note "that the present hesitation to move upon an intrenched enemy, is but the story of Manassas repeated. I beg to assure you that I have never written you, or spoken to you, in greater kindness of feeling than now. . . . *But you must act.*" McClellan ignored the overture. He wrote his wife that the president had urged him to make an attack, and added, "I was much tempted to reply that he had better come & do it himself."[3]

....

PRINCE JOHN MAGRUDER continued to direct his charade bravely enough, but he was not confident that it would hold together much longer. On the evening of April 6 he telegraphed General Lee in Richmond that enemy observers, in the air and on the ground, had been active along every part of his line throughout the day. "They discovered a weak point," he reported, and while he would make every effort to shore up the spot he worried that "numbers must prevail." Reinforcements were reaching him very slowly "and will probably be too late." The previous evening a brigade had arrived from General Huger's command at Norfolk, but that day had brought him just two regiments from across the James and no troops from Johnston's army.

Prince John was not one to display his concerns outwardly, however. In full regalia, with staff and escort, he rode his lines from one end to the other, radiating confidence, encouraging his troops, looking every inch the part of commanding general — or more accurately in his circumstances, every inch the part of leading actor.

Richmond was almost sixty miles from the scene of conflict at Yorktown, but already there was a palpable sense of crisis in the Confederate capital. Martial law was imposed on the city, the sale of liquor prohibited, and all military furloughs canceled. Additional state militia were called to the colors to supplement the half-dozen militia units already serving with Magruder on the Peninsula. The women of Richmond, responding to an appeal from the authorities, stitched together 30,000 sandbags for Yorktown's defenders in thirty hours. The Confederate Congress sitting in the Virginia State Capitol debated a revolutionary bill to conscript men into the army, and Richmond's city council appropriated funds to bolster the city's defenses. According to one Southern newspaper, the issue building at Yorktown was "tremendous, . . . for the stake is enormous, being nothing less than the fate of Virginia." The editor went so far as to compare the army McClellan was assembling to march on Richmond to the Grande Armée Napoleon had assembled to march on Moscow fifty years before.[4]

The capital's mood brightened considerably when Joe Johnston's army began to arrive from the Rapidan. A steady parade of Johnston's troops started through the city on April 6, the very day Magruder remarked on how slowly help was reaching him. While there was no official announcement of the fact, it was obvious to all that the army was on the march to meet McClellan on the Peninsula, and spirits soared.

"Richmond is one living, moving mass of soldiers & to day the streets show nothing but a continuous stream on their way to York-town — infantry, cavalry & artillery," a Mississippi soldier wrote home. Citizens filled the windows overlooking Main Street and lined the sidewalks to cheer column after column as they made their way to the depot of the York River Railroad or to the wharves at Rocketts for passage down the James. Women welcomed them with food and drink and bouquets of flowers. The men responded with the Rebel yell, and regimental bands swung into "The Bonnie Blue Flag" and "Maryland, My Maryland" and "Dixie." Flamboyant Robert Toombs, one of the founders of the Confederacy and now a brigadier in Johnston's army, was especially noticeable. Looking revolutionary in a flaring black slouch hat and tossing red scarf, he personally led each regiment of his brigade in turn past the cheering throng in front of the Spottswood Hotel, making sure all Richmond knew that Toombs's brigade was on its way to war.

The first two brigades reached Yorktown on April 7, and a third the next day. On the tenth another brigade arrived, and on the eleventh, three more. By that date, General Magruder's force stood at 34,400, two and a half times his strength just a week earlier when the Federals began their march on Yorktown, and he finally began to breathe easier. Prince John expressed himself utterly surprised that his opponent had "permitted day after day to elapse without an assault," but he was properly grateful nonetheless. Joe Johnston was equally surprised. After inspecting the Warwick line and hearing what Magruder had to say about those first days of the siege, he told General Lee, "No one but McClellan could have hesitated to attack."[5]

On April 11, taking a leaf from General Magruder's book on bluff, the *Merrimack* appeared suddenly out of the morning haze and steamed slowly and menacingly toward the Federal squadron in Hampton Roads. "The cry was raised, 'There comes the Merrimack!!' " a Northern diarist wrote. ". . . Such a scatteration of vessels as ensued was quite a sight: the roads were full of transports of all sorts, steam and sail, and those which lay farthest up got underway in a hurry." The *Monitor* and her consorts cleared for battle, seeking to draw the monster deeper into the roadstead to give the ramming vessels the sea room they needed to make their runs at the enemy. By contrast, the *Merrimack*'s commander, Flag Officer Josiah Tattnall, was determined to lure the *Monitor* into the narrow waters of the upper bay, engage her there, and capture her. He knew of the Yankee rams and was heard to say that he was not going out into enemy waters "to get punched. The battle must be fought up there."

It was Tattnall's idea for sailors from his escorting gunboats to close with the Yankee ironclad, board her, jam the turret with wedges, blind her by throwing a wet sailcloth over the pilot house, and smoke out her crew by tossing lighted, turpentine-soaked cotton waste down the ventilators. Tattnall expected to lose half his gunboats in the attempt;

Flag Officer Goldsborough expected to lose half his ramming squadron if it engaged. Hour after hour the contestants feinted and challenged and exchanged random shots at long range, but neither commander would forgo his tactical plan, and at last the *Merrimack* steamed back to her lair in Norfolk. The stand-off would be repeated several times in the coming weeks. By threat alone the *Merrimack* succeeded in guarding Norfolk and sealing off the James and in neutralizing every major fighting ship in the Federal squadron.[6]

General Johnston first reached Richmond from the Rapidan on April 12, to be greeted by President Davis with new orders. Magruder's Army of the Peninsula and Huger's command at Norfolk were thereby folded into Johnston's command, which was officially styled in these orders the Army of Northern Virginia. This ought to have made him, in history's eyes, the famous first commander of this most famous of Confederate armies, but Joe Johnston would never be a general blessed by fame, and his name — in contrast to Robert E. Lee's — would never be automatically coupled with that great army. Johnston himself preferred to continue calling his command the Army of the Potomac, as if in deliberate defiance of the Federal army of the same name. Some who communicated with Johnston in these weeks used the one name for his army and some the other; Jefferson Davis even addressed him as commander of the Army of Richmond. Despite these eccentricities, most people found it most convenient to call the army now defending Yorktown the Army of Northern Virginia.

Joseph E. Johnston was by nature a fault-finder, seldom satisfied with his circumstances, always first calculating risks before profits. A story was told of him on a grouse-hunting outing before the war. Johnston was known to be a crack shot, but on the hunt he could not seem to find the perfect moment — the birds flew too high or too low, the dogs were not properly positioned, the odds for a sure shot were never quite right. His companions blazed away and ended the day with a full bag; Johnston was blanked. "He was too fussy, too hard to please, too cautious. . . ."

Much the same could be said of him when he inspected General Magruder's Yorktown line. Magruder was certainly to be commended for his efforts, Johnston said, but everything was wrong with his position — the line was incomplete and badly drawn; it was purely defensive, with no avenues for an offensive; the artillery was inadequate; the Federals, with their naval and arms superiority, would surely turn one or both flanks. On the morning of April 14 Johnston was back in

Richmond and delivering his gloomy report to President Davis. He wanted to abandon Yorktown immediately and pull right back to Richmond, the better to contend against the enemy host.[7]

Davis called together a council of advisers to take up this momentous question. He had General Lee and Secretary of War Randolph join them, while Johnston brought in his two senior generals, Gustavus W. Smith and James Longstreet. In the president's office in the Confederate White House, from eleven that morning until one o'clock the next morning, with only a break for the dinner hour, the six of them debated the proper strategy for meeting the invaders.

Collectively they possessed a remarkable range of personal knowledge of the general opposing them. Lee had commanded young Lieutenant McClellan in the Corps of Engineers during the Mexican War, and Longstreet too had made his acquaintance in the old army. Joe Johnston had been McClellan's close friend in the decade before the war, and G. W. Smith his closest friend. As a junior officer McClellan was the protégé of then secretary of war Jefferson Davis. Mr. Davis, Longstreet recalled, took special note of the "high attainments and capacity" of General McClellan.

Repeating his arguments for abandoning the Yorktown line, Johnston urged that all the forces from his command and from Magruder's on the Peninsula and Huger's at Norfolk, reinforced by garrison troops from the Carolinas and Georgia, be massed at Richmond for a showdown battle against the invading army. Alternatively, he proposed leaving Magruder to hold Yorktown for as long as he could while the rest of the army marched north to menace Washington and (as Longstreet phrased it) "call McClellan to his own capital." Longstreet predicted that McClellan, being a careful-minded military engineer, would not be prepared to assault Magruder before May 1. Smith added his support for Johnston's plan and strongly pressed for an invasion of the North that would not stop at Washington but go on to Baltimore, Philadelphia, and New York.

Randolph and Lee took an opposite tack. Randolph pointed out that giving up Yorktown would also mean giving up Norfolk and its important navy yard, where there were ironclads and gunboats under construction and where the *Merrimack* was based. Lee added his voice to the argument for continuing to hold the lower Peninsula, primarily for the time it would gain them: time to complete the difficult transformation of the Confederacy's one-year volunteer army into a "for the war" army; time to begin enlarging that army through the conscription law then being acted on by the Congress; and time to forestall the call-up of reinforcements from other areas. Immediately stripping the Carolinas and Georgia of troops, he warned, would very likely lead to the loss of Charleston and Savannah. In any case, Lee said, the lower Peninsula was well suited defensively for fighting the Yankees.

The debate continued hour after hour until all the arguments — and all the participants — were exhausted, and then Mr. Davis announced his decision. Johnston was to shift the rest of his army — the troops of Smith and Longstreet — to Yorktown and make a stand there for as long as it was practical to do so. Whatever General McClellan gained on the Peninsula he would have to fight for. Joe Johnston accepted the decision without protest. He later wrote that he knew Yorktown could be held only so long before the government would come around to his plan to fall back on Richmond; that, he said, "reconciled me somewhat to the necessity of obeying the President's order."[8]

....

THE TWO ARMIES went to ground, and the siege of Yorktown settled into a sometimes deadly but more often dull routine. Reinforcements would raise the number of men involved to 169,000, with the Federals enjoying a final superiority of almost exactly two to one. On the Confederate side Magruder's redoubts and trenches — including some first dug by Cornwallis's redcoats in 1781 — were extended and deepened and weak points strengthened, using slave labor impressed from the Peninsula's plantations. Starting their fortifications and trench lines from scratch, the Federal troops had much the heavier labor, which was multiplied by McClellan's decision to emplace 111 of the largest siege pieces in the Union arsenal in order to blast his way through Yorktown's defenses.

He had a choice, McClellan explained: an approach "blocked by an obstacle impassable under fire" — the Warwick River — "& another that is passable but completely swept by artillery. I think we will have to choose the latter, & reduce their artillery to silence." He sent to his wife for his books on the siege of Sevastopol in the Crimea, which he had studied intensively. In planning the siege of Yorktown, he told her, "I *do* believe that I am avoiding the faults of the Allies at Sebastopol & quietly preparing the way for a great success."[9]

Day after day at one point or another in the disputed ground in this hugely scarred landscape there were exchanges between pickets or sharpshooters or artillerymen. "There is scarcely a minute in the day when you cannot hear either the report of a field-piece and the explosion of a shell, or the crack of a rifle," Lieutenant Colonel Selden Connor of the 7th Maine wrote. In a letter home Lieutenant Robert Miller of the 14th Louisiana described one of these outbursts of firing. The Yankee shells, he wrote, "get to us some seconds before the report . . . so that the first thing we know of them is a shrill whistle unlike any thing you or I ever heard before, then the sharp bell-like crack of the bomb — the whistle of the little balls like bumble-bees — then the report . . . but it all comes so nearly at the same time that it takes a very *fine ear* to distinguish which is first." Lieutenant Miller counted 300 shells fired at his sector in one twenty-four-hour period; miraculously the only casualties were three men wounded.

"I believe if there is anybody in the world that fulfills the Apostle's injunction, 'beareth all things,' and 'endureth all things,' it is the soldier." Thus the 2nd Vermont's Wilbur Fisk opened his weekly letter to his hometown paper on April 24. At its best, life in the trenches meant endless boredom. "This is the dullest place I ever saw, nothing to arouse one from the oppressive monotony but an occasional false alarm . . . ," the 19th Mississippi's Oscar Stuart wrote bitterly after three weeks in the lines. "I am afraid we will stay in this abominable swamp for a long time without a fight." Another Mississippian, Augustus Garrison, said that after a while the boys began to wish for a nice safe flesh wound, one that would get them home and "that they might show the girls." His friend Pink Perkins got his flesh wound, Garrison noted, being nicked in the hip by a piece of shell, "which was very painful but which he could not show to any of the fair ones."

Life in the trenches was at its worst during the periods of miserable weather that marked these April weeks. Soldiers sent their letters home datelined "Camp Muddy" and "Camp Misery." A Georgian in Toombs's brigade, which had marched so gaily through Richmond a few days before, recorded in his diary one particular pitch-black night when his brigade had to crouch for twelve hours in a waterlogged trench knee-deep in mud and water while a cold rain poured down on them without letup. In the middle of the night there was an alarm and much firing, and at daylight they discovered two of their men badly wounded and one dead, all three, it was decided, shot accidentally by their comrades. "It was a night that will long be remembered not only by me, but all that were in that disagreeable hole," he wrote.

As often as not the killing was random and without purpose. Another diarist, Lieutenant Charles Haydon of the 2nd Michigan, was off duty one day and well behind the lines when he noticed a soldier walking idly by himself across an empty field. With no warning a shell burst over the man's head, killing him instantly. It was the only Confederate shell fired within a mile of that spot during the entire day. "Some men seem born to be shot," Haydon decided.[10]

By far the most dangerous siege duty was the advanced picket line, which called for keeping a close watch on the enemy while at the same time avoiding becoming a sharpshooter's target. Captain William F. Bartlett of the 20th Massachusetts, in command of a company assigned to picket duty every third day, expressed a universal complaint when he called it "very unpleasant duty. No glory in being shot by a picket behind a tree. It is regular Indian fighting." Four days after writing this, Bartlett had his knee shattered by a sharpshooter's bullet and had to have the leg amputated.

Early in the siege it was the Union sharpshooters who had the decided edge in this deadly contest, and any Rebel showing himself was liable to catch a bullet. Among the units in the Army of the Potomac was a regiment of sharpshooters recruited by Colonel Hiram Berdan that contained expert marksmen armed with special rifles, among them finely crafted target pieces equipped with telescopic sights. "Our Sharp Shooters play the mischief with them when they come out in daylight," one of Berdan's men told his wife.

A rough balance was restored with the arrival at Yorktown of John Bell Hood's Texas brigade from Johnston's army. Hood's men had a sizable number of British-made Enfield rifles and knew how to use them. When the Yankee sharpshooters grew too bold, the Texans would slip into the forward picket line for what they liked to call a little squirrel shooting. Soon their fire would drive the Federals out of the trees and other hiding places they favored and back into their fortifications, where sharpshooting continued but on more even terms. The marksmen on both sides at Yorktown considerably exaggerated their prowess, especially to credulous newspaper correspondents, yet there was no doubt that because of them the prudent learned to keep their heads down. The story quickly got around, for example, of the Confederate soldier who woke up one morning in his cramped trench and unthinkingly stood up to stretch and was instantly shot through the heart.[11]

In spite of the sharpshooters' threat the siege had its lighter moments. One day a Louisiana soldier searched out his colonel in the

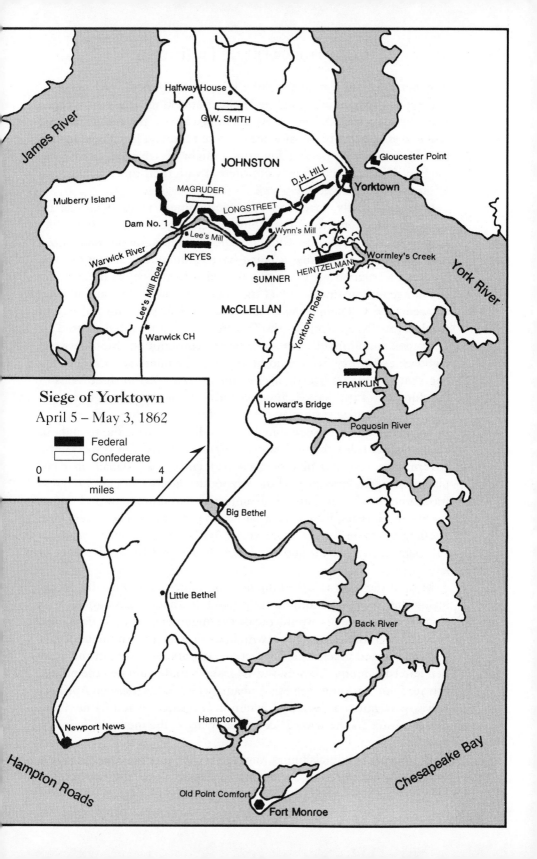

Siege of Yorktown
April 5 – May 3, 1862

■	Federal
□	Confederate

0 ——————— 4
miles

James River

Halfway House
G.W. SMITH

JOHNSON

Gloucester Point

Mulberry Island

MAGRUDER
LONGSTREET
D.H. HILL
Yorktown

Dam No. 1
Lee's Mill
Wynn's Mill
KEYES
Warwick River
SUMNER
HEINTZELMAN
Wormley's Creek

Lee's Mill Road
York River

McCLELLAN

Warwick CH

Yorktown Road

FRANKLIN

Howard's Bridge

Poquosin River

Big Bethel

Little Bethel

Back River

Newport News

Hampton

Hampton Roads

Chesapeake Bay

Old Point Comfort
Fort Monroe

trenches to report "an awful thing has just happened!" What was it, the colonel demanded: were the Yankees attacking? It was worse than that, the man said. A Yankee shell had just struck the colonel's camp tent and smashed a barrel of whiskey stored there. The colonel rushed to his tent in the hope that something might be salvaged, but he was too late. His men had already crowded in with their tin cups to rescue whatever had survived the wreck.

One particularly novel form of entertainment in the Confederate ranks was electioneering. For months Richmond had been struggling with what General Lee termed "the fermentation of reorganization" — keeping its army in being beyond the one year that the volunteers had signed up for in the first rush to the colors in 1861. To encourage re-enlistments it had tried bounties and furloughs and even allowed men to change their branch of service, but with indifferent results. Finally on April 16 the Congress, acting on a bill drafted by Lee, took the ultimate step and decreed conscription. Men between eighteen and thirty-five would be subject to military service, and the one-year volunteers had their enlistments extended to three years or the duration of the war. Regiments had forty days in which to reorganize under the new system and to hold elections for their officers.

For those who had seen enough of soldiering, even the thought of changing the rules this way was a betrayal. "I have no respect for a government that is guilty of such bad faith," an Alabamian complained. Private Jesse Reid of the 4th South Carolina thought Congress was taking the law into its hands unjustly; if volunteers were kept on for two more years, he asked, what was to prevent the lawmakers from keeping them on for ten more years? With conscription, he warned, "all patriotism is dead, and the Confederacy will be dead sooner or later."

Most of the men accepted the new law more philosophically, recognizing that there was nothing they could do about it anyway. At least electing their officers would break the monotony of their days, and they followed the campaigning with interest. Certain candidates found one time-tested electioneering tactic that worked as well in the army as it had back home. "Passed the Whiskey round & opened the polls," Private John Tucker of the 5th Alabama wrote in his diary on April 27. It was very much a "Big day" when his brigade elected its field and company officers, he wrote, "& a great many of the men got gloriously *tight*."[12]

Resourceful Federals found ways to vary the monotony of their days as well. It did not take them long to discover that the tidal creeks emptying into the York below Yorktown contained the most succulent oysters they had ever tasted, and that the gray squirrels infesting the thick woods made a delicious stew (wearing the enemy's colors, it was said, made them fair game). The hogs that roamed the woods were also declared contraband of war and subject to capture, although the headquarters prohibition on firing guns behind the lines forced a resort to the bayonet; it was admitted that considerable effort was required for the enjoyment of roast pork. Pennsylvanian Oliver W. Norton felt obliged to justify such foraging by explaining that whatever they found in Virginia "is nothing else than a *secesh*, and when Uncle Sam can't furnish food, I see nothing wrong in acquiring it of our enemies." A Virginia woman who lost most of her pigs and chickens to the light-fingered Yankee cavalrymen encamped on her farm near Yorktown had taunting advice for her guests. Want to get into Yorktown did they? "General Magruder's thar, an' he kin drink more whiskey nor enny general you'uns got, but he won't be thar when you git thar. . . ."

Informal truces, usually arranged when no officers were around, also served to break the siege routine. These sometimes produced odd coincidences. The men of the 2nd Rhode Island discovered that the Rebel pickets opposite them had haversacks and canteens stenciled "2nd R.I." that they had picked up when fighting the Rhode Islanders at Bull Run nine months earlier. (One of the Rhode Islanders got a big laugh from the Rebels when, called on for the name of his regiment, he shouted back, "150th Rhode Island!") The men of the 2nd Michigan found that the Georgians posted in their sector were from the same regiment they had faced the previous fall at Munson's Hill near Washington. They talked this over at a parlay between the lines and agreed that as old acquaintances they would refrain from firing at each other when on picket duty.

In places where the lines were close together there was a good deal of bantering back and forth. "As they have only a large swamp between them," a man in the 61st Pennsylvania wrote his family, "they can talk as well as if in a room together, they throwing up Bull Run to our boys & we Fort Donaldson & other places." At the James River end of the Warwick line, where tidal marshes 300 or 400 yards wide made the prospect of any attack highly unlikely, informal truces might stretch on for as long as the stints of duty lasted. When one side or the other was due to be relieved, the pickets shouted across to watch out and everybody keep their heads down, for they could not be responsible for what the new men might do. [13]

Federal general Philip Kearny was struck by the ironies of the situation. "Is it not odd to think," he wrote his wife, "that Magruder, one of my best friends, is one of the chief men here. This is surely a most unnatural war." At one of the nearby farms, Kearny went on, he had the disconcerting experience of talking to an elderly slave of at least ninety who distinctly remembered, as a child, hearing cannon fire once before at Yorktown — during the first siege in 1781. Union engineers examined old maps made by Cornwallis's army for clues to the Confederates' Yorktown defenses.

Whenever the weather was good Professor Lowe's war balloons — by April 10 he had the *Constitution* as well as the *Intrepid* at the front — soared high in the air over Yorktown like great yellow soap bubbles, searching out information about the enemy positions. Generals frequently went up with the professor, to cast a professional eye on what the Rebels might be doing. Confederate artillerists did their best to shoot down the intruders, and while they scored no hits they did force Lowe to keep his distance and thus limited what he could see. For all the drama of these ascensions, balloon reconnaissance brought very little real enlightenment to General McClellan; certainly they furnished him nothing that brought any reality to the way he was counting the Army of Northern Virginia.

Indeed, the *Intrepid* very nearly deprived him of his favorite general. On April 11, in Professor Lowe's absence, Fitz John Porter went up alone, and the balloon broke free of its moorings and began drifting straight toward the enemy lines. Fortunately for Porter, a last-minute wind shift carried him back to Union territory, and he managed to reach the gas valve and bring himself to the ground. General McClellan termed the episode "a terrible scare," and Professor Lowe admitted that it was some time before he could persuade any other generals to go up with him.

Determined not to be outdone in aeronautics, the Confederates countered with a balloon of their own. Lowe was scornful: it was nothing but a hot air balloon — he called it a fire balloon — and could only stay aloft a half hour or so before the air in the envelope cooled and lost its aerial buoyancy. Lacking a portable hydrogen generator of the sort Lowe had developed, the Rebels had to stoke a hot fire of pine knots soaked with turpentine to get their aeronaut, Captain John Bryan, off the ground. Captain Bryan had the same visibility problems as the Yankee aeronauts, complicated by the fact that his balloon had but a single mooring rope whose strands tended to unwind and spin him around dizzily like a top. On his third ascension he duplicated

General Porter's experience. His balloon broke loose, drifted over the Federal lines, then was finally blown back to safety by a Confederate breeze. "This was indeed luck of the greatest kind," Captain Bryan observed, and never went up again.

Easily as unusual as the war balloons were the coffee-mill guns, a Yankee invention getting a tryout in General Keyes's Fourth Corps. This crank-operated prototype machine gun fired cartridges rapidly from a hopper mounted atop the barrel; President Lincoln, an enthusiast for new weapons, coined its name. Its promoters called it "an Army in six feet square." Rhode Islander Charles E. Perkins, for one, was impressed. "And we have got 4 other guns that shute a ball a little larger than our muskets do and thay can shute it a hundred times a minit," he wrote home. "Thay are drawed by one horse and are very handy and I should think that thay might do a grate work." A newspaper correspondent was sure this example of Yankee ingenuity "must have astonished the other side." No Confederates recorded any reaction to the novel weapon, however. In any event, as well sheltered as the Rebels were from the Federal artillery it is doubtful that the coffee-mill guns claimed any victims during the siege.[14]

On April 16 General McClellan took his first aggressive action against the enemy since arriving in front of Yorktown. He ordered Baldy Smith to stop the Rebels from strengthening their defenses behind the Warwick River at a place called Dam No. 1 — the "weak spot," as it happened, that General Hancock had wanted to seize ten days earlier. There was no truly pressing need for the operation — it was not the spot McClellan had selected to pulverize with his siege guns to force a breakthrough — and he hedged his orders with cautions. There was to be no general engagement; his last words to Smith were to "confine the operation to forcing the enemy to discontinue work." Smith dutifully advanced his divisional artillery close to the dam, along with the Vermont brigade — five regiments from his native state, including the 3rd Vermont that he had led at Bull Run back in 1861 — for infantry support. For most of the day the Yankee gunners and skirmishers blazed away at long range at the enemy across the millpond.

The Confederates prudently took shelter from this barrage ("Break ranks and take care of yourselves, boys," one of their officers shouted, "for they shoot like they know we are here") and nothing could be seen of them, and presently an adventurous Yankee lieutenant waded across the waist-deep pond and came back to report he thought the enemy's works could be taken. Four companies from General Smith's old regiment, the 3rd Vermont, holding their rifles and cartridge boxes high, splashed across the pond on a reconnaissance. As the Rebel pickets scattered, the Vermonters rushed into the rifle pits on the far bank and opened a steady fire into the woods beyond. Having gained this much, no one in the Federal high command seemed to know what to do next.

Baldy Smith was victimized by an unruly horse, which twice threw him and left him stunned and incapable of "seeing the advantage I had obtained." General McClellan, who had come to observe the operation, offered no advice and then left, having concluded that "the object I proposed had been fully accomplished. . . ." After clinging to their foothold for forty minutes, the Vermonters were counterattacked by a brigade of Georgians and Louisianians and sent flying back across the pond, losing men at every step. "As we waded back," one of them wrote, ". . . the water fairly boiled around us for bullets." Of the 192 who began the ill-fated reconnaissance, 83 were killed, wounded, or captured. The Vermont brigade's commander, William T. H. Brooks, belatedly sent in reinforcements, but their assault was shot to pieces before it fairly began. Recalling McClellan's injunction not to bring on a general engagement, Brooks finally ordered everyone back. The day's Federal casualties came to 165.

The operation left a sour taste. "This Battle took place at Dam No. 1 in Warwick creek," a Federal diarist wrote, "and was a Dam failure." It was rumored that General Smith had not been thrown by his horse but was in fact drunk and had fallen off. In Washington a Vermont congressman introduced a resolution calling for the dismissal of any officer "known to be habitually intoxicated by spirituous liquors while in service," and left no doubt who it was aimed at. Smith's defenders, and Smith himself, hotly denied the charge and eventually a congressional investigating committee found it groundless. It was clear enough that the operation had been bungled, but less clear where the fault lay. All he could see, General Brooks remarked ruefully, was that his brigade had gotten itself involved "in something we did not exactly finish."[15]

....

"THE ROADS have been infamous," General McClellan wrote Winfield Scott, his predecessor as general-in-chief; "— we are working energetically upon them — are landing our siege guns, and leaving nothing undone." His sense of accomplishment was understandable. The complex arrangements for commencing siege warfare were proceeding on schedule. Two weeks into the siege, he already had 100,000 troops under him. He had persuaded the president to let him have the First Corps division commanded by a favored lieutenant, William B. Franklin, and he was promised the second of McDowell's three divisions, under George A. McCall, as soon as "the safety of the city will permit."

Prospects for naval cooperation were improving. A new ironclad warship, the *Galena*, was slated for his use, to break through between Yorktown and Gloucester Point and cut the enemy's communications on the York. Critics were muffled by the release to the press of "official" estimates of Confederate strength that ranged up to 100,000 men and 500 guns. "The task before Genl McClellan, reduction of fortified entrenchments, is that for which he is held specially qualified and the result is not doubted," one correspondent wrote.

A suddenly docile Secretary Stanton even volunteered to put General Franklin in command of the Fourth Corps, in place of the ineffectual Erasmus Keyes, an offer McClellan was quick to accept. Although nothing finally came of this idea, it at least suggested a thaw in his chilly relationship with the contentious secretary of war. There was a strong gleam of optimism in the letter McClellan wrote his wife on April 19. "I know exactly what I am about," he told her, "& am confident that with God's blessing I shall utterly defeat them."

He grew increasingly confident the next day as a result of new intelligence about the enemy's high command. He had heard, he told President Lincoln, that Joe Johnston was now under the command of Robert E. Lee, and that greatly encouraged him. "I prefer Lee to Johnston," he explained. To his mind, General Lee was "*too* cautious & weak under grave responsibility . . . wanting in moral firmness when pressed by heavy responsibility & is likely to be timid & irresolute in action." (He added the opinion, a few days later, that "Lee will never venture upon a bold movement on a large scale.") McClellan did not elaborate on how he had arrived at this singular appraisal; mercifully for him, it was never made public during his lifetime.[16]

The Yankees pursued their siege operations with great energy and according to the latest principles of military science. However much he overestimated Confederate numbers, General McClellan never doubted his own superiority in artillery, especially heavy artillery. His confidence in ultimate victory rested on his guns. His siege train contained no fewer than seventy heavy rifled pieces, including two enormous 200-pounder Parrotts, each weighing more than 8 tons, and a dozen 100-pounders, all of which greatly outgunned any cannon the Rebels had at Yorktown. The balance of McClellan's heavy rifled pieces were 20-pounder and 30-pounder Parrotts and 4.5-inch Rodman siege rifles. For vertical fire he had forty-one mortars, ranging in bore size from 8 inches up to massive 13-inch seacoast mortars that when mounted on their iron beds weighed almost 10 tons and fired shells weighing 220 pounds. Once they were finally all emplaced and opened fire simultaneously, as McClellan intended, these siege guns would rain 7,000 pounds of metal on Yorktown's defenders at each blow. Such firepower dwarfed even that of the Sevastopol siege.

Fifteen batteries for these heavy guns were dug and fortified. "It seems the fight has to be won partially through the implements of peace, the shovel, axe & pick," a New Hampshire soldier observed. To reach the battery sites new roads had to be cut through the forest and bridges built and old roads made passable by corduroying them with logs. The best at this road-making proved to be the 1st Minnesota regiment, whose skilled woodsmen could clear a mile of road and corduroy a quarter of it in a day. According to a Minnesota diarist, the Rebel gunners heard them felling the trees and fired at the sound. The heaviest pieces in the siege train had to be carried forward in canal boats on the York and then up Wormley's Creek to the front. To mount one of the great seacoast mortars in battery, the side of the canal boat was cut down, tracks were laid to the bank, and the piece was raised by a hoisting gin and dragged ashore on rollers and finally hauled to its platform suspended under a high-wheeled sling cart. Simply to stock the battery magazines required 600 wagonloads of powder and shot and shell.

Much of the digging for batteries and trenches and redoubts was done at night and under fire. "Night work in the trenches is a sight to be remembered," a man in an engineer battalion wrote in his journal, "to see a thousand strung along like a train of busy ants in the night, shoveling away, with now and then a shell bursting near. It is strange . . . to have a piece of shell come so near you, you can feel the wind. . . ." Although Fitz John Porter was put in direct command of the siege operations, General McClellan, a military engineer by training, visited the batteries constantly, directing construction, planning for the final assault, encouraging the troops. "Gen. McClellan & staff have just rode along the line," a Pennsylvanian recorded in his diary on April 16. "Took a view of the rebel fortifications, gave some orders to the Gen. & passed on. While riding along he stopped and lit his cigar from one of the private's pipes." Such homely touches by the general sent morale soaring.[17]

....

THE IMPORT of all this immense effort was not lost on Joe Johnston. As the siege dragged on and the Yankees continued to fire only their field artillery in the periodic exchanges, it became obvious that Mc-Clellan was holding back his big siege guns until all were emplaced and ready to open simultaneously. General D. H. Hill, now in command of the Confederate left at Yorktown and Gloucester Point, observed that with his control of the water McClellan could "multiply his artillery indefinitely, and as his is so superior to ours, the result of such a fight cannot be doubtful." One of his lieutenants, Gabriel J. Rains, predicted that when the enemy opened fire it would be with 300 shells a minute. One day Hill was discussing their prospects with Johnston. Johnston asked him how long he could hold Yorktown once the Federal siege batteries opened. "About two days," Hill said. "I had supposed, about two hours," Johnston replied.

Scouts and spies reported evidence of the rapidly multiplying Federal batteries and sightings of numerous transports entering the York, suggesting preparations for a drive up the river. It was reported too that the Yankees now had one or two more "iron-cased" war vessels in addition to the *Monitor*. To the trained military eye, a certain sign of impending attack was the appearance of parallels, the advanced trench lines from which the final assault would be launched once the siege guns had battered down Yorktown's defenses.

On April 27 General Johnston warned Richmond that the enemy's parallels were well along and he would be compelled to fall back to avoid being trapped in his lines. On April 29 he made it official: "The fight for Yorktown, as I said in Richmond, must be one of artillery, in which we cannot win. The result is certain; the time only doubtful. . . . I shall therefore move as soon as can be done conveniently. . . ." Once Yorktown and the line of the Warwick were abandoned, Norfolk could not be held for long; it too must prepare for evacuation.[18]

Johnston sent an appeal for the *Merrimack* to come to his aid by attacking the Federal shipping in the York and upsetting McClellan's best-laid plans. (He also repeated his earlier call for a strike on Washington so as to distract his opponent further.) This idea of a sortie by the *Merrimack* had already caught General Lee's imagination, and he several times urged the navy to send the big ironclad by night past Fort Monroe and the cordon of Federal warships to get in among McClellan's transports in the manner of a fox in a henhouse. "After effecting this object," he explained, "she could again return to Hampton Roads under cover of night." For Robert E. Lee, a weapon in war was only as good as the use made of it.

Flag Officer Tattnall complained that too much was expected of the *Merrimack*. Her fight in March in Hampton Roads, in which her first captain, Franklin Buchanan, was wounded, had raised expectations too high, Tattnall said; "I shall never find in Hampton Roads the opportunity my gallant friend found." The truth of the matter was that the *Merrimack* was altogether a dubious proposition — unseaworthy except in a flat calm and ponderous to maneuver, inadequately armored, powered by engines that constantly broke down. In truth too the adventurous spirit that had marked Josiah Tattnall in long-ago battles against the Royal Navy and the Barbary pirates had cooled. Now, at age sixty-five, his first impulse was to catalogue all the possible risks in any plan, and certainly here was a plan freighted with risks.

Tattnall was appalled at the thought of navigating the *Merrimack* by night across Hampton Roads and up the York. To attempt such a sortie by day would mean running the gauntlet of Fort Monroe's guns and those of the *Monitor*, the forty-seven-gun frigate *Minnesota*, and assorted other Federal warships, not to mention the threat of being "punched" by the Yankee rams. Even if he somehow reached the York safely, McClellan's transports would probably find shelter from his guns in shoal water and in the tidal creeks. Flag Officer Tattnall could see only hazard in the operation. General Johnston would have to manage without any aid from the *Merrimack*.

Evacuating an army of twenty-six brigades of infantry and cavalry and thirty-six batteries of field artillery — 56,600 men all told — and their equipment, and carrying out the evacuation secretly in the face of the enemy, was a truly challenging task. It was also a complicated task, and Johnston had to endure delays caused by every imaginable complication. "I am continually finding something in the way never mentioned to me before," he complained. He finally set the withdrawal for the night of May 3 and made it a "without fail" order. Anyone and anything not ready to move by that night would be left behind. And unlike the earlier Manassas evacuation, this time the entire Federal army was only a few hundred yards distant.[19]

Perfect security proved impossible, and hints of the movement leaked out. Northern newspaper correspondent Uriah H. Painter, for example, interviewed an escaped slave from Yorktown who had seen the Rebel wagon trains pulling out behind the lines. When Painter reported this to Chief of Staff Randolph Marcy, however, he was told it could not be so; headquarters had "positive intelligence" the enemy was going to put up a desperate fight at Yorktown.

That was indeed the message in most of the intelligence reaching General McClellan. On May 2 another contraband reported the Confederates were 75,000 strong and intended to hold out until 75,000 more men reached them. On May 3 detective Pinkerton announced the enemy's strength to be between 100,000 and 120,000, and since that was merely a "medium estimate" it was very likely "under rather than over the mark of the real strength of rebel forces at Yorktown." McClellan was thus confirmed in another of his intuitive leaps of logic. Just as he had been sure in early April that Magruder would never attempt to hold a line all the way across the Peninsula with a mere 15,000 men, he now concluded that with eight times that number the enemy would certainly stay and make a showdown fight of it. "I can not realize an evacuation possible," he told Baldy Smith.

He pressed ahead with his plan for the grand assault. The heavy batteries would simultaneously open fire at dawn on Monday, May 5, the thirty-first day of the siege. Once the enemy shore batteries were silenced, gunboats and the new ironclad *Galena* would run past to take Yorktown's defenses in reverse. General Franklin's reinforcing division from Washington, held on shipboard for ten days while McClellan debated what to do with it, was brought ashore to add weight to the attack. After a day or two of unremitting bombardment — or only a few hours, some predicted — it was supposed that every gun and fortification between Yorktown and the headwaters of the Warwick would be demolished. Heintzelman's Third Corps would then storm the position. "I see the way clear to success & hope to make it brilliant, although with but little loss of life," McClellan told President Lincoln.[20]

After nightfall on May 3, a Saturday, the Confederates opened a tremendous bombardment with their heavy guns. The shells were not directed at any one spot but seemed rather to be aimed at random, driving the Yankees to ground everywhere. Their burning fuzes traced brilliant red arcs across the dark sky. The surgeon of a New York regiment called it "a magnificent pyrotechnic display." At last the guns fell silent, and for the first time in a month it was utterly still. At first light General Heintzelman went up in the balloon *Intrepid* with Professor Lowe. "We could not see a gun on the rebel works or a man," the general would write in his diary. "Their tents were standing & all quiet as the grave." He shouted down that the Rebel army was gone.

The Yankees on picket duty rushed forward and clambered into the empty redoubts, and the color bearer of the 20th Massachusetts laid claim to being the first to plant the Stars and Stripes over Yorktown. "The soldiers gave tremendous cheers," wrote the 20th's Lieutenant Henry Ropes, "and it was altogether a glorious occasion." Another Massachusetts soldier, wandering through one of the abandoned Rebel camps, was struck by the message scrawled in charcoal across one of the tent walls: "He that fights and runs away, will live to fight another day. May 3."[21]

· PART II ·

Enemy at the Gates

....

*The enemy has now ditched himself up to
the very gates of Richmond.*

— MAJOR GENERAL D. H. HILL
JUNE 10, 1862

....

A Fighting Retreat

....

G ENERAL MCCLELLAN'S regular morning telegram to Washington on May 4, 1862, was dramatically brief: "Yorktown is in our
possession." It was as if he was too surprised to say more. In a later
dispatch he announced, "Our success is brilliant," and he was in
pursuit and would "push the enemy to the wall." Northern papers
proclaimed the news with bulletins, and some put out extra editions.
REBELS RAN AWAY LAST NIGHT — THE "LAST DITCH" FILLED,
read the headline in the *New York Tribune*'s extra. "The beginning of
the end is visible," wrote the editor of the *Journal of Commerce*. In
Albany, New York's capital, the authorities fired 100 guns and rang
church bells in celebration.

Others had second thoughts. This was the second time, a government official remarked to a friend, that General McClellan "has let the
rat escape, after having it fairly in a hold; I agree with you, he is no
great rat-dog." Reflecting on the news from Yorktown, William Cullen
Bryant, editor of the *New York Evening Post*, detected a note of the
ridiculous. He recalled the numerous reports from McClellan's headquarters "of the immense numbers of men which the rebels had
congregated on the peninsula, of the impregnable nature of their
defences, of the necessity of our slow and careful approach" — reports
that had aroused "the universal expectation of some grand result when
everything should have been prepared" — and was reminded of a
metaphor used by the Roman poet Horace. The enemy's "rapid retreat
from the place," Bryant told his readers, "is the mouse brought forth
by the laboring mountain."

There was no denying the disappointment in the Federal camp.
"Our army would all much rather that they had stood a fight," a New
Jersey officer, Robert McAllister, told his family, "as we could have
taken them all prisoners and ended the war." In the opinion of General

Joseph Hooker, "The retreat of the rebels I fear will play the devil with McClellan." The Comte de Paris, the French nobleman serving on the headquarters staff, noted in his journal the particular disappointment among the artillery and engineering officers, who "have counted down the hours that separated them from the bombardment which promised them no end of pleasure." After the prodigious effort that had gone into erecting fortifications and digging parallels and emplacing siege guns — only one of the fifteen siege batteries had gone into action, firing 141 rounds — once again, by a margin of just twenty-four hours, Joe Johnston had evaded giving battle on his opponent's terms.

To be sure, Johnston had to leave behind at Yorktown and Gloucester Point seventy-seven pieces of artillery too heavy to carry away, yet nearly all were antiquated smoothbore ship's guns of comparatively little military value which had been seized from the navy yard at Norfolk in 1861. Casualties for the two sides at Yorktown totaled fewer than 500, most of them occurring in the affair at Dam No. 1 on April 16. The siege ended on its thirtieth day, and that gain of a month's time marked the Confederates' profit for the operation. What the Federals' profit might be was not yet clear.[1]

Capturing almost as much attention as the evacuation itself was the discovery that the retreating Confederates had planted torpedoes — land mines in the parlance of later wars — in all manner of places in and around the fortifications. These "infernal machines" were devised by General Gabriel J. Rains, whose brigade had manned the main Yorktown redoubt and who was convinced of "the vast advantages to our country to be gained from this invention." Rains had experimented with such devices as far back as 1840, during the army's war with the Seminoles in Florida. His torpedoes were artillery shells buried in roads and pathways and rigged with pressure-sensitive percussion fuzes or hidden tripwires. Rains's idea was simply to slow up the pursuing Federal columns, but some of his men became carried away with their assignment to hide the torpedoes and put them inside houses and around wells and in flour barrels, which struck the Yankees (and some Southerners as well) as a highly uncivilized kind of warfare. General McClellan adjudged the enemy "guilty of the most murderous & barbarous conduct" and made Confederate prisoners disarm the devices.

Yankee Richard Derby's experience with a torpedo was typical. Lieutenant Derby wandered into the Yorktown fortifications to look at a big cannon that had burst during the siege just as a fellow soldier "on the same errand trod on a torpedo, and the shell exploded, throwing him ten feet into the air, tearing off one leg, and burning him black as a negro!" No one kept an accurate count of the casualties caused by the torpedoes and rumor greatly magnified their toll, but General McClellan was probably close to the truth when he listed four or five men killed and a dozen or so injured. Torpedoes that were discovered were marked by stakes tied with little strips of fluttering cloth, and sentries were posted to steer the marching columns clear of them. The ethics of the matter became the subject of debate in the Confederate high command, and eventually General Rains would be transferred to the James River defenses, where his particular talents could be applied to the more acceptable activity of blowing up Yankee warships.[2]

McClellan was taken quite unawares by Johnston's withdrawal. When the Comte de Paris awakened him at six o'clock that morning to report Yorktown evacuated, he refused to credit the news and went back to sleep. "The American mind is slow to grasp an idea to which it is not accustomed beforehand," the Frenchman observed in his journal. McClellan's subsequent pledge to Washington to "push the enemy to the wall" required him to improvise. He had made no plans for the occasion, and had no organized *corps des chasseurs* with standing orders to pursue.

He called out the available cavalry under George Stoneman, along with four batteries of horse artillery, to head the pursuit, backed by one infantry division each from the Third and Fourth corps. Most of the Yankees had anticipated nothing more arduous that day than the usual Sunday morning inspection, and it took them a good deal of time to get organized to march. The last of the enemy had been gone twelve hours before the first Federal infantry took up the chase.

The sudden opening of the York finally gave General McClellan the chance to pursue his cherished strategy of a turning movement by way of the river. Half the troops would follow on the heels of the enemy while the other half steamed upriver to the vicinity of West Point to try to cut off all or some part of the Rebel army.

Had the Rebels evacuated Yorktown twenty-four hours earlier, he would have had at hand the ideal spearhead for this flanking movement: General Franklin's 11,300-man division, riding at anchor aboard its transports at the mouth of the York. On May 3, however, driven by his delusion of vast enemy numbers, McClellan had abandoned his original plan to put Franklin ashore on the north bank of the river to attack Gloucester Point and instead had him disembark his division to support Heintzelman's proposed attack on Yorktown. Now, after hardly a day ashore, Franklin's men were ordered to re-embark. The army, they complained, always found a way to do everything the hard way. Getting the troops aboard their transports again was slow enough work, but loading the artillery back aboard seemed to take forever. Franklin termed it "a tedious and exasperatingly slow process." General McClellan was determined to supervise the start of this flanking operation personally, but even so it would take him two days to get the flotilla under way.

The Yorktown evacuation gave Joe Johnston the opportunity to pursue his own cherished strategy, which was to retreat rapidly to the immediate vicinity of Richmond. Johnston was alert to the danger of being cut off by a Yankee force advancing up the York, and he had no thought of making a stand until that particular danger was past. Once in front of Richmond, he reasoned, he need no longer worry about being outmaneuvered by an opponent taking advantage of his command of the waters around the lower Peninsula. The prospect "that the Federal army might pass us by water" (as Johnston phrased it) acted as a powerful stimulus to putting as much distance as possible between the Army of Northern Virginia and Yorktown.[3]

....

GENERAL JOHNSTON took his army back along two roads, one from Yorktown that angled westward and then turned northwest up the center of the Peninsula, and one that crossed the Warwick at Lee's Mill and then ran parallel to the Yorktown Road and a mile or so from the James River. The two roads came together eleven miles beyond Yorktown and two miles short of Williamsburg, Virginia's old colonial capital. For his retreat Johnston had his forces organized in four commands, under James Longstreet, D. H. Hill, G. W. Smith, and David R. Jones, who was replacing the ailing Prince John Magruder. Jeb Stuart's cavalry formed the rear guard.

The marching was tedious and frequently slowed by boggy stretches in the roads, and it progressed at hardly one mile an hour. "And so it went on all night," Major Porter Alexander remembered, "— march or wade two minutes and halt ten or longer." At one point an artillery piece became so deeply mired in the mud that a troop of Stuart's cavalry was called on to assist the gunners. Among the cavalrymen was a monocled Englishman come to witness the war in the colonies, and as he observed the struggle to free the gun he noticed Yankee cavalry coming into sight on the road behind them. Turning to his captain, he asked why they were bothering with "that damned thing." "We can't afford to leave it," he was told. "Pardon me again," said the Englishman, "if I ask how much it is worth." The captain said he supposed the gun was worth about a thousand dollars. The Englishman glanced again at the approaching enemy, who were now close enough to loose a few shots at the party. "Well then, Captain, let's move on," he said briskly. "I'll give you my check for it at once."

They did manage to move on, with the gun in tow, and the army as a whole had a sufficient head start over the pursuers that by afternoon on May 4 all four commands were at or beyond Williamsburg. Private John Tucker of the 5th Alabama recorded in his diary that as they marched through the town "all the eligible places in the buildings were crowded with men women & children all of whom wore a countenance of Sadness & deep regret." He felt sorry for them beyond measure. "They knew we were on the retreat and . . . burning with a feeling of humiliation at the prospect of their quiet firesides soon being visited by a set of 'yankee Mauraders' & made desolate."

Only Stoneman's cavalry managed to close with Stuart's rear guard, and late in the afternoon there was sharp skirmishing between the opposing troopers. As the sound of this musketry echoed through Williamsburg, a woman rushed up to a passing column of Mississippians and pleaded with them to turn back and repel the Yankee invaders. They must defend this cradle of liberty just as their forefathers had defended it against the redcoats, she cried. "If your captain won't lead you, I will be your captain!" Just then, from the head of the column, the order came back to about-face and double-quick. The radiant Joan of Arc, as one of the Mississippians described her, inspired by the seeming success of her appeal, was preparing to lead the men into battle until one of them cautioned her, "Oh no, sis, don't go — you might tear your dress!"

Once his sorties began to draw fire from Confederate infantry, General Stoneman prudently withdrew until his own infantry could come up. In the process he lost forty-four of his men and one of his guns. A South Carolinian described his repulse with phonetic economy: "The bauls whisld and bums busted over us but God was with us and we pushed on them and they gave back." The stand-off between pursued and pursuer seemed likely to continue. Then that evening it began to rain, and it continued to rain for thirty straight hours.[4]

Monday, May 5, dawned gray and bleak in a cold, hard downpour, and it was soon apparent to General Johnston that his supply trains and artillery would be a long time moving any distance on the single muddy road leading out of Williamsburg toward Richmond. He would have to buy time for them to escape. The commands of Jones and Smith and D. H. Hill were set in motion; Longstreet's division would act as a rear guard to block pursuit. It was Longstreet's good fortune that at Williamsburg he had a good place to make a defensive fight.

The Peninsula here is only seven miles wide, and the area Longstreet had to defend was further narrowed by the courses of two streams, Queen's Creek and College Creek. The area between them was barely three miles wide. Indeed, in General Magruder's original plan for defending the Peninsula Williamsburg was designated his fallback position should he not obtain enough men to hold the Warwick River line or if the Yankees broke through there. To that end, during the winter he had constructed a large earthen redoubt — which he pridefully named Fort Magruder — which commanded the junction of the Yorktown and Lee's Mill roads in front of Williamsburg, and thirteen small redoubts and redans to cover the rest of the shallow V of open ground that ran west to College Creek and east-southeast to Queen's Creek. To enlarge the defenders' field of fire and hamper an attacking force, a wide belt of timber was felled to form a tangled slashing — in military terminology, an abatis — along the face of the woodland fronting this line. Major Wainwright, the Union artillerist, was not alone in calling it a very ugly place to have to attack.[5]

The two Federal infantry divisions ordered to pursue on May 4 — Joe Hooker's and Baldy Smith's — had labored slowly through the bad stretches of road cut up by the guns and wagons of the retreating Confederates and only caught up with Stoneman after dark. Hooker on the Lee's Mill Road and Smith on the Yorktown Road were not within mutual supporting distance, however. Rather than coming together at a narrow angle, the two roads turned sharply toward each other and met at a virtual 90-degree angle, and with the junction under the Rebels' guns Hooker and Smith at their closest were still a good mile apart and separated by swampy, impenetrable woods. They might as well have been on different battlefields, as would soon become evident.

The Federal command at Williamsburg that day was top-heavy with general officers. Electing to remain behind at Yorktown to launch his flanking expedition, General McClellan had placed the pursuing half of his army under Edwin V. Sumner, who by seniority was his second-in-command. Sumner had none of his own Second Corps troops with him; McClellan was holding them all for the York River operation. With Sumner, and under his orders, were the army's two other corps commanders, Erasmus Keyes and Samuel Heintzelman. Keyes's Fourth Corps was represented at the front that morning only by Baldy Smith's division, with Keyes's other two divisions somewhere off to the rear in the mud. Heintzelman's Third Corps command consisted solely of Hooker's division; his second division, under Phil Kearny, was some miles to the rear, and his third division was at Yorktown under McClellan's orders. Thus the Army of the Potomac opened the Battle of Williamsburg with three corps commanders in command of two divisions, totaling just 18,500 men. Three other divisions might or might not reach the battlefield in time to take part in the fighting.

Brigadier General Edwin Vose Sumner was sixty-five years old and had been in the army longer than many of his fellow generals (including General McClellan) had been alive. He had led the 1st Dragoons in countless frontier battles with Indians and had performed gallantly in the Mexican War, and he was called "Bull" for his great booming voice, loud enough to be heard over the thunder of a cavalry charge, and for his bravery under fire. No one in the Union army was more admired as a leader of men in the heat of battle; no one had risen in rank further beyond his capacity. McClellan was diplomatic in describing Sumner as "in many respects . . . a model soldier, but unfortunately nature had limited his capacity to a very narrow extent." The Comte de Paris was less kind but expressed the more common opinion when he wrote in his journal that the Bull Sumner he saw at Williamsburg, "the grand old man, wizened, white-bearded, has an air of stupidity that perfectly expresses his mental state." From first to last that day General Sumner would be unable to grasp the battle unfolding in front of him.[6]

Joe Hooker was hard-living and intensely ambitious, and he had little patience with the caution that seemed to mark everything about the Army of the Potomac. He was ordered to pursue a retreating foe, he said, and "deemed it my duty to engage him without regard to numbers and almost without regard to position" so as to hold him until the rest of the army came up.

At seven o'clock that morning Hooker and his artillery chief, Major Wainwright, went on foot up the road to the edge of the forest to reconnoiter and to locate a position for the divisional artillery. The only open space they could find was the road itself and an old cornfield on their right that faced the junction of the Lee's Mill and Yorktown roads and beyond that Fort Magruder. Hooker believed his lead brigade already skirmishing in and behind the slashing of felled trees could protect the guns, and Wainwright ordered up the six pieces of Battery H, 1st United States Artillery. As the regulars splashed forward in the mud and rain and unlimbered, the Confederate gunners in Fort Magruder and the adjoining redoubts opened on them. The Battle of Williamsburg was joined. The first General Sumner knew of it was the sound of the guns off to his left beyond the thick forest.

Battery H had been under fire before, at Fort Sumter in the war's first hours, but that experience had been bloodless. This was more its true baptism of fire, and very different. Even as the battery was taking position men and horses were shot down, and suddenly the gun crews were seized by an unreasoning panic and dived for cover. It was a miserable beginning to his first battle, Major Wainwright thought. "Never in my life was I so mortified, never so excited, never so mad." He raged at the cowering gunners and whacked them with the flat of his saber and even drove some of them back to the guns at sword's point. But nothing could keep them there. Reflecting on it later, Wainwright decided "it was a very hot place for men . . . and they were a wretched lot of men." In desperation he spurred back to his reserve, a New York battery that had been his first command, and pleaded with the gunners to save him from disgrace. "I have no doubt all heard me, for I was very much excited, and don't know now what I said," he later wrote in his journal. He was rewarded by a rush of volunteers, and in minutes the guns of Battery H were manned and pouring shot and shell into Fort Magruder. The enemy's fire slackened.

As the rest of his infantry arrived at the front, Hooker pushed most of it into the woods and the abatis west of the Lee's Mill Road, and Major Wainwright ordered up reinforcements until he had ten guns posted in the road and in the old cornfield to the east. Although greatly increasing their volume of fire, the Federals did not attempt to storm Fort Magruder or its supporting redoubts. Hooker was waiting for a joint advance by the Fourth Corps troops on his right. There was no movement there, however. As the stand-off lengthened, General Longstreet and his lieutenants seized the initiative.

When the pitch of battle that day grew loud enough to draw Joe Johnston back to the scene, he observed matters for a time at Longstreet's side and then left everything in his hands. James Longstreet was big and rough-hewn and radiated self-assured competence the way other men radiated charm or high fervor. He commanded without hesitations or false moves. Earlier, while the army was still at Manassas, his aide Thomas J. Goree wrote of "Old Pete" that he "seems to manage a division of eight or ten thousand men with as much ease as he would a company of fifty men." In notable contrast to his opposite number, Bull Sumner, Longstreet would manage the fighting at Williamsburg without a misstep.

Beginning the day with just two of his brigades in the Fort Magruder line, Longstreet soon brought three more brigades into action and a fourth into close reserve. He put his senior brigadier, Richard H. Anderson, in immediate command of his offensive. Anderson sent Cadmus Wilcox's brigade — 9th and 10th Alabama and 19th Mississippi — advancing through a sheltered ravine and into the thick woods off to the west. The lead Mississippians loped through the trees in loose skirmishing formation, looking for Yankees under Wilcox's order "to advance until forced to halt & find out what is in front." Soon enough they found Yankees in front. More troops came up and before midday the fighting was general along this entire western flank, 10,350 Confederates matched against 9,000 Federals. The Rebels had the initiative and the advantage of position, and Hooker was in growing danger of having his flank turned.[7]

As the fighting quickened, Hooker called for reinforcements to "take post by the side of mine to whip the enemy." General Sumner refused to part with any of the forces with him, however; Hooker would have to rely instead on the other Third Corps division, under Phil Kearny, coming up from the rear. At his headquarters well back on the Yorktown Road, Sumner was blind to the battlefield. At any event, just then he was distracted by another development requiring his decision. Earlier that morning, a contraband had come in to report that off to the right, on the opposite side of the field from Hooker, there was a woods road that crossed a branch of Queen's Creek called Cub Creek on a dam and went on to outflank the Confederate defenses. The Rebels had a redoubt covering the dam, he said, but there was no one in it. An engineer officer sent out to confirm the Negro's story came back to say the man was being entirely truthful — the eastern flank of the enemy's line was unguarded.

Baldy Smith urged Sumner to let him take his division in that direction "and do some good work." Too dangerous, Sumner replied:

here was the center of the Federal position, and here he expected the enemy to attack him. Smith complained to the Prince de Joinville, another of the French noblemen traveling with the army, that there was simply no reasoning with old Sumner. Finally Sumner unbent enough to let Smith send a single brigade to the right, but his approval was hedged about with cautions. Smith chose his best brigadier, Winfield Scott Hancock, and quietly reinforced Hancock's command to five regiments and two batteries.

As Hancock's column set off on a circuitous two-mile march through the woods toward the dam on the right, on the left the sounds of battle intensified and drew closer. Unable to budge Sumner into giving him reinforcements, a disgusted General Heintzelman rode off to support Hooker with at least his own presence. General Keyes could think of nothing better to do than to ride back toward Yorktown to see what had happened to his other two Fourth Corps divisions. Bull Sumner resolutely faced ahead, ready to repel any assault.[8]

The rain had slackened but continued to fall steadily in a misty curtain. On Hooker's front the battle smoke hung in the windless air like broad streaks of white fog among the trees, making it hard to tell friend from foe and indeed making it hard to see anything at all. Battle flags became targets simply because they alone were visible; the men of the 7th Virginia counted twenty-three holes in their flag at day's end. Private Francis P. Fleming of the 2nd Florida complained that his regiment fired volley after volley at a range of twenty or thirty paces into what they took to be a Yankee battle line in the timber slashing and had no idea whether they hit anyone or not. Lieutenant David Steele of the 2nd New Hampshire stumbled blindly into a knot of Wilcox's men in the slashing, yelled, "Surrender, you damned cusses or I'll blow you to hell!" and despite the fact that he had nothing but his sword to back up his threat the surprised Rebels threw down their rifles. In the slashing and the woods men on both sides made use of tree trunks as shelter against the hail of bullets. When a Yankee urged a comrade to find a tree to get behind, the reply came back, "Confound it, there ain't enough for the officers!"

Hooker's battle line west of the Lee's Mill Road, its outer flank overlapped by Anderson's reinforcements, was bent sharply back and pushed steadily toward the road. Four New York City regiments of the Excelsior Brigade — 70th, 72nd, 73rd, and 74th New York — were hit the hardest, with the 70th losing very nearly half its men and the brigade as a whole taking 772 casualties, almost a third of them marked down as missing. "Alas the field is literally covered with our dead," one of the Excelsiors wrote. Ammunition ran short, and men scrambled among the cartridge boxes of the dead and wounded.[9]

With a triumphant yell the Rebels broke through to the road. Major Wainwright's guns at the front had to be abandoned, the gunners escaping into the woods to the east. They told everyone they encountered that it was another Bull Run. The 19th Mississippi's Lieutenant Columbus Jones leaped atop the barrel of one of the captured pieces and waved the regimental flag to signal the gunners in Fort Magruder to hold their fire. The Confederates carried off four of the guns and an ammunition limber; the other six were so deeply bogged in the mud they could not be dragged out. "We took their ammunition and shot it back at them," a Confederate gunner in Fort Magruder said with satisfaction.

A half mile to the rear Major Wainwright positioned his remaining battery right across the road where there was a little clearing, ordered canister loaded, and when the charging Rebels were 150 yards away opened fire and blew away the head of the column. The survivors took cover from the guns in the woods. Joe Hooker spurred his big white horse in among his retreating men to rally them. At the discharge of one of Wainwright's guns the horse reared and threw him into a ditch, but he came up muddy and blowing and continued to shout at the fugitives. "Don't fall back — the rebels are whipped!" he told them. "Reinforcements will be here in a few minutes." A cavalry detail from the 3rd Pennsylvania took more direct action, opening fire on the fugitives to hold them.

Corps commander Heintzelman joined the desperate struggle to close the broken ranks. He hit on the novel idea of rallying them with music. Finding several regimental bands standing by bewildered as the battle closed in, Heintzelman ordered them to take up their instruments. "Play! Play! It's all you're good for," he shouted. "Play, damn it! Play some marching tune! Play 'Yankee Doodle,' or any doodle you can think of, only play something!" Before long, over the roar of the guns, came the incongruous sound of "Yankee Doodle" and then "Three Cheers for the Red, White, and Blue." One of Hooker's men thought the music worth a thousand men. "It saved the battle," he wrote.[10]

What in fact saved the battle for the Federals was the arrival at that moment of Kearny's division. Phil Kearny was the general most experienced in war on the field, and the most colorful as well. An inher-

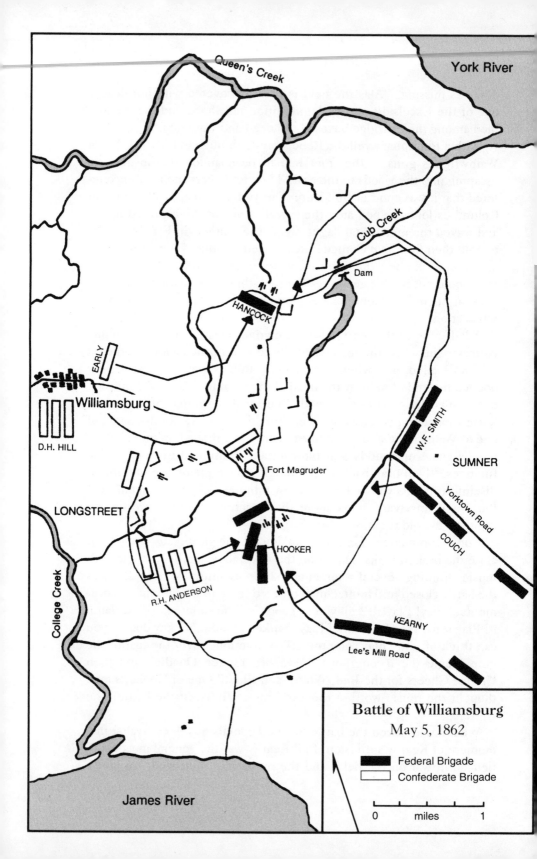

York River

Queen's Creek

Cub Creek

Dam

HANCOCK

EARLY

Williamsburg

D.H. HILL

W.F. SMITH

SUMNER

Fort Magruder

Yorktown Road

COUCH

LONGSTREET

HOOKER

R.H. ANDERSON

KEARNY

College Creek

Lee's Mill Road

James River

Battle of Williamsburg
May 5, 1862

■ Federal Brigade
□ Confederate Brigade

0   miles   1

itance allowed him to indulge himself as a soldier of fortune, and he had traveled to France to learn the advanced arts of war at the cavalry school at Saumur. In a cavalry charge at Churubusco in Mexico in 1847 he had lost his left arm, but he proved no less of a warrior for it. In Italy in 1859 he fought with Napoleon III's Imperial Guard at Solferino and Magenta and won the Legion of Honor. Winfield Scott once called him "the bravest man I ever saw, and a perfect soldier."

On this day at Williamsburg Kearny drove his men through the quagmires of mud toward the sound of the guns, pushing past or through other troops less driven. Coming up behind Hooker's lines, he encountered a battered company from the New Jersey brigade he had earlier commanded. Where were their officers, he demanded. They had none. "Well, I am a one-armed Jersey son-of-a-gun, follow me!" Kearny cried. "Three cheers!" One of Hooker's men saw the reinforcements coming up at the double-quick and "at their head was General Kearny flourishing a sword in his only arm. Never was our eyes more gladdened than at this sight."

Kearny had only been a division commander a few days and most of his men had never seen him, but now he made sure they knew who was in command. To reconnoiter the field he rode right out in front with the skirmishers to draw the enemy's fire and locate their positions. Two staff aides with him were killed, but he was unharmed and rode back to his troops and pointed out where they should fire. As each unit came up he coolly directed it into position. "Men, I want you to drive those blackguards to hell at once," he told the 2nd Michigan, and Lieutenant Haydon reported that the general "was answered with a yell which reached the enemies line above the roar of battle." Haydon also recorded his amazement at seeing his corps commander, Samuel Heintzelman, standing by the roadside haranguing the men as they passed. "He swung his hat, hurrahed for Michigan most lustily & swore as hard as ever saying, 'Give them hell God damn them, give the steel, dont wait to shoot,' " Haydon wrote in his diary. "He was more enthusiastic than I ever supposed he could be."

The Rebels were pushed off the Lee's Mill Road and back into the woods and the abatis to the west, but they held on there stubbornly, and in the late hours of the afternoon there was a series of sharp and bloody firefights in the gloomy, dripping thickets. Williamsburg was the first battle for the large majority of the men who fought there, and like many others Joseph B. Laughton, a color bearer in the 38th New York in Kearny's division, had wondered how he would react under fire for the first time. "To tell the truth John," he wrote his brother a few days later, "when I first came on the field at a double quick tramping over the dead of the whole day & hearing the cries of the wounded & dying . . . & surrounded on all sides by the enemy I came near fainting but . . . as soon as our line came to the 'charge' & I saw the enemy retreat back it filled me with new courage & I thought no more of fear. . . ." What inspired Corporal Laughton and thousands like him on both sides who were seeing battle for the first time was inspiring leadership. "General, I can make men follow me to hell," Kearny confided to Heintzelman that afternoon, and so it seemed.[11]

At 3:00 P.M., as Kearny led his men into the fight, at the opposite end of the battlefield General Hancock was posting himself squarely athwart the Confederates' left flank. Hancock had led his column through the woods and across the Cub Creek dam without event, and advanced past the empty redoubt there and ahead to a second empty redoubt, taking a position just over a mile from Fort Magruder. He arranged his batteries and his 3,400 men on a low rise overlooking a field of early wheat and sent back to Baldy Smith for reinforcements so that he might exploit his good fortune and turn the enemy out of Fort Magruder.

Smith responded by sending him a brigade, only to have General Sumner recall it. In the grip of one of his frequent alarms, Sumner husbanded his forces and ordered Hancock back to the redoubt overlooking Cub Creek; whatever he may have originally expected of Hancock's expedition, his idea now was simply to guard his own flank. The disbelieving Hancock sent one of his staff to argue the matter directly with Sumner, and meanwhile opened fire at long range with his artillery.

Earlier in the day, as the fighting intensified, Longstreet had taken the precaution of calling on D. H. Hill, the rearmost command in the order of march, to furnish him a reserve force in case of trouble. Hill sent the brigade of Jubal A. Early, which marched back to Williamsburg and stacked arms on the green of the College of William and Mary and awaited orders under whatever cover could be found from the rain. The wait was not a long one. The two Confederate redoubts on the far left were unguarded that day because they went unnoticed in the rain and mist that was making everything difficult to see. General Magruder's old Army of the Peninsula had built the Williamsburg defenses and knew all about them, but it was at the head of the retreating column that day and somehow a full description of the defensive line never filtered back down to the rear guard. The shells from Hancock's guns came as a surprise and raised a considerable alarm. Early's brigade was called up from the college green and marched toward the left, and Hill ordered back the rest of his division to take up a supporting position behind it.

Jubal Early was a caustic, harsh-spoken West Pointer who years before had given up the army for the law and who displayed on his return to the military the aggressiveness of the prosecuting attorney he had been in civilian life. His first action on reaching the battlefield was to go to D. H. Hill and propose to outflank and capture those Yankee guns that could be heard firing from behind a concealing strip of woodland. Hill concurred and took the plan to Longstreet and Joe Johnston. They too approved, so long as Hill went along with Early and they proceeded with appropriate caution against an enemy whose exact position and strength were not yet known. Like Jubal Early, however, Daniel Harvey Hill was not one to look carefully before he leaped. "Genl Hill made us a slight address," one of Early's men recounted, "telling us not to fire a shot but give them the cold steel." It was nearing five o'clock and growing darker in the rain and mist when Early's brigade marched to the left and then turned into the woodland opposite the point where the sound of the Yankee guns seemed to be coming from.[12]

Early's four regiments entered the woods side by side in line of battle, 24th Virginia on the left, then the 38th Virginia, 23rd North Carolina, and 5th North Carolina. Early led the two left-hand regiments, Hill the two on the right. The strip of woodland was half a mile deep and swampy and thickly tangled by undergrowth and very dark, and the alignment of the regiments was soon lost and never regained. The 24th Virginia, which Early had led as its colonel at Bull Run back in 1861, emerged first from the woods to face an unexpected sight. Rather than encountering the rear or the flank of the Federal battery as planned, the guns were a quarter of a mile farther to the left. The Confederates had badly miscalculated their direction and come out into the open well in front of their target.

Without waiting for the rest of the brigade, shouting "Follow me!" Early rashly wheeled the Virginians to the left and straight toward the guns. At just this moment, a disgusted General Hancock was starting his command back in obedience to Bull Sumner's repeated order to withdraw to Cub Creek. The Confederate attack came as a reprieve. His skirmishers and gunners were heading for the rear as Early's charge began, and the Virginians, seeing this and remembering their last encounter with Yankees on a battlefield, began shouting "Bull Run! Bull Run!" as they pushed across the soggy wheatfield. The cry died in their throats as it became clear that the Yankees were not running away but instead taking up a strong position. The volume of their fire made it equally clear that they were there in strength. Casualties mounted rapidly among the Virginians and included General Early himself, shot through the shoulder by a rifle bullet. Losing blood and in severe shock, he had to go to the rear.

As the 24th Virginia was making its charge, a second Confederate regiment, the 5th North Carolina, emerged from the woods, and D. H. Hill had his first, shocked look at the battlefield. Posted as the right-hand regiment in the line of attack, the Carolinians were 800 to 900 yards from the Federal guns off to their left; to make matters worse, there was a huge gap between them and Early's Virginians. The two intervening regiments, the 38th Virginia and the 23rd North Carolina, were nowhere to be seen. They were still deep in the woods, tangled in the thickets and marshes.

With Early under heavy fire and clearly in need of help, Hill could not wait for the laggards. "If you attack," he said, "attack quickly." The 5th North Carolina made a left wheel and started through the wheatfield. It seemed to Major Peter Sinclair that they were advancing through "the valley of death — our line as perfect and unbroken as if on parade, at each step our gallant boys would fall. . . ." He was certain he had "never read of anything that surpassed it in bravery."

It was doomed bravery, however. Hancock had his forces marshaled in line along the crest of the rise: 3,400 rifles and eight artillery pieces to oppose the assault by the two regiments, not quite 1,200 men, mounted without any artillery support at all. As the strength of the Federal line became increasingly evident, General Hill realized to his horror that the situation was about to become, as one of his officers put it, "fatally destructive." He ordered the assault broken off.

The attacking spearheads had reached as far as a rail fence a hundred yards in front of the Federal line when Hill's order reached them. They were starting to fall back when Hancock ordered a counterattack. The newspapers later had him make the cool announcement, "Charge, gentlemen, charge," but as Major Thomas W. Hyde of the 7th Maine recalled, no one who knew Winfield Scott Hancock would ever believe that. "He was more emphatic than that," Hyde wrote; "the air was blue all around him." Another Maine soldier,

Selden Connor, wrote that he and his fellow Yankees charged over the crest "with a terrible yell . . . and poured in a volley following it up with a steady fire. . . . The enemy, who doubtless thought we sprung from the earth, halted with terror and amazement, their dead were dropping like tenpins, one after another. . . ."

Harper's Weekly artist Alfred R. Waud, making a quick sketch of the scene, wrote on his drawing, "Line of infantry all broken and running . . . enemy dead and wounded covering the field." The 24th Virginia had the shortest distance to cover to reach the woods and escaped without many additional casualties, but the 5th North Carolina, which had slanted well out into the wheatfield so as to come in on the right of the Virginians, had a murderous gauntlet to run to reach safety. "The slaughter of the 5th N.C. regiment was one of the most awful things I ever saw," D. H. Hill would say. It lost 302 dead, wounded, and captured, a casualty rate of 68 percent. Early's brigade as a whole lost 508 men in the disastrous assault. Hancock's loss was an even 100.[13]

At about the time Hancock was repulsing the attack of Early's brigade, there was an outburst of cheering at General Sumner's headquarters back on the Yorktown Road. The commanding general had reached the battlefield. An admiring Comte de Paris marveled at the impression created by General McClellan's arrival. "As they recognize him the troops welcome him with heart-felt cries," he wrote in his journal. McClellan would tell his wife that the moment he came on the field "the men cheered like fiends & I saw at once that I could save the day." In truth the day no longer needed saving and soon enough the firing died out of its own accord without the general seeing any of it, but he was not to be deterred from claiming his triumph.

Francis W. Palfrey fought in the 20th Massachusetts on the Peninsula and was an early historian of the campaign, and he concluded that the commanding general's belated arrival at Williamsburg signaled a pattern of behavior. "Curiously enough," Palfrey wrote, "there was almost always something for McClellan to do more important than to fight his own battles."

In this instance the general had considered the loading of Franklin's division aboard its transports at Yorktown — a task General Franklin himself was eminently qualified to handle — more important than investigating the unmistakable sound of pitched battle heard clearly throughout the day. As early as 9:00 A.M. McClellan was reporting "heavy firing" from Williamsburg in telegrams to Washington and to his wife. He was not easily persuaded to hurry toward the sound of the guns, however. Baldy Smith remembered sending messages "all day long . . . to General McClellan begging him to come to the front," and Smith was not alone in making this appeal, but McClellan only acknowledged learning "that everything was not progressing favorably" at about one o'clock in the afternoon. Even then he cannot have set out for Williamsburg "without delay" on his big, fast bay, Dan Webster — and then required four hours to ride eleven miles, even in the rain and mud. (A staff aide reported making the same journey that afternoon in an hour and a half.) Clearly the Young Napoleon did not relish the prospect of commanding in battle, and on this day — and on other days to come — he would demonstrate his reluctance to do so.[14]

....

TUESDAY, MAY 6, dawned clear and pleasant, and the scene of two days earlier was repeated: Yankee pickets edging forward at first light discovered the Rebel lines deserted. Longstreet and D. H. Hill had quietly slipped away through Williamsburg and taken the road to Richmond. General McClellan boasted of another "brilliant victory" gained by his outmanned army. "My entire force," he announced to Secretary Stanton, "is undoubtedly considerably inferior to that of the Rebels. . . ." (Seeing this dispatch, General Wool at Fort Monroe expressed his "surprise" that an enemy in such numbers should ever have abandoned Yorktown in the first place.)

If any victory was to be awarded at Williamsburg, however, the Confederates had by far the better claim. Joe Johnston's rear guard had beaten back the Federal pursuit, as he intended, and the Army of Northern Virginia was able to continue its retreat unmolested. Confederate casualties in the fighting, including the cavalry skirmishing on May 4, came to 1,682. Federal casualties, at 2,283, were considerably greater, and Federal management of the fighting considerably worse. The Union's high command at Williamsburg, Baldy Smith summed up with blunt candor, was "a beastly exhibition of stupidity and ignorance."

Some 13,750 Confederates in the divisions of Longstreet and D. H. Hill saw action at Williamsburg, with another 8,750 at hand in reserve, most of those to counter the threat of Hancock's flanking operation — a threat that never materialized. At every stage of the fighting the Federals had more men at the front, but only at day's end did they gain anything by it. During most of the day-long battle against Joe Hooker west of the Lee's Mill Road, the five brigades under Richard Anderson enjoyed a better than 1,300-man advantage over Hooker's unsupported division. Only late in the afternoon, after the arrival of Kearny's troops and then a brigade of Keyes's Fourth Corps, did the Federals finally gain a manpower advantage there. Meanwhile, in the center on the Yorktown Road, two of Baldy Smith's brigades — 6,100 men — idled away the hours virtually without event, having just twelve men wounded by stray shots. Off to the rear, six other Yankee brigades never reached the field at all or were too late to have any effect on the fighting. Indeed, Silas Casey's division was discovered at midday halted a mile or so from the fighting with arms stacked and the men boiling coffee over smoky little fires in the rain. Hooker's angry complaint that while his division was nearly bled to death (he lost 1,575 men, almost 70 percent of the day's Union casualties) there were 30,000 Yankee soldiers standing idle within supporting distance was an exaggeration, but not a very great one. The actual figure was 25,000.[15]

For the Federals the one note worth cheering was the repulse of Early's brigade by General Hancock, which McClellan quickly seized upon to support his claim of brilliant victory at Williamsburg. He described the incident as "a real charge with the bayonet," and that bit of inflation and his comment that "Hancock was superb" were released to the press. Thereafter Hancock was "Hancock the Superb," and his bayonet charge became for Northerners the single memorable feature of the Battle of Williamsburg.

Joe Hooker and Phil Kearny were infuriated by this "puffing and blowing." They bombarded influential acquaintances with tirades against the general commanding and contrived to get their own reports into print, and eventually McClellan issued a revised account that mentioned others besides Hancock, but the two generals never forgave him for the slight. "The blazoning about the bayonet charge of Hancock is all stuff," Hooker told one senator, and to another he confessed he was unsure whether McClellan's lapse "arises from his ignorance of soldiership . . . or whether it results from a consciousness of his own negligence. . . ."

The newspapers' expansive coverage of Hancock's part in the battle was balanced by highly negative accounts of Sumner's role. "Genl. Sumner seems troubled by the newspaper attacks," one of his subordinates wrote. "Some of them are virulent," he added, so that the tough old warrior "often profanes the name of God." Behind the false front of victory he erected for public consumption, General McClellan was himself coldly furious at the way Williamsburg had been managed. He claimed it as his first battle as head of the Army of the Potomac, and told his wife he was appalled by "the utter stupidity & worthlessness of the Corps Comdrs. . . . Heaven alone can help a General with such commanders under him." He was particularly unsparing of old Sumner, who had "proved that he was even a greater fool than I had supposed & had come within an ace of having us defeated." The one silver lining he detected in the otherwise dismal picture was the army's morale. Perhaps it was just as well that he arrived on the field the way he had, McClellan said, "for the officers & men feel that I saved the day. . . ."

For the men in the ranks Williamsburg had been marked by the hardest kind of fighting they could imagine. Veterans of Bull Run insisted that that fight did not compare in intensity with this one. Far fewer had run; most stayed and fought, and died where they stood. Men wandering over the silent, sunny battlefield that Tuesday had an irresistible urge to inspect the dead. They lay in all postures, Lieutenant Haydon recorded in his diary, "but most of them on their backs, their heads thrown back, mouth slightly open, elbows on the ground by the sides, with the hands up, folded . . . or frequently one of them placed over the wound. . . . One I saw on his hands & knees with his head shot off. Two men were found lying opposite each other with each his bayonet through the other's body." Burial details interred the dead in rough graves and the wounded were collected in field hospitals. Virtually every building in Williamsburg flew a yellow hospital flag. Four hundred Confederates, too badly wounded to move, were left behind to be cared for by the Federals.[16]

....

AMONG THE ARMY of the Potomac's general officers William B. Franklin was considered one of the most accomplished. He had graduated first in his class from the Military Academy in 1843 and had directed major engineering projects in the prewar army, and he was highly skilled in all the arts of military administration. He was careful and cautious and George McClellan's friend of twenty years' standing, making him in General McClellan's eyes the perfect subordinate. Franklin had trained and equipped his division for an amphibious landing, and when he set off on his flanking movement up the York early on May 6, the day after the fight at Williamsburg, every factor

Century Collection

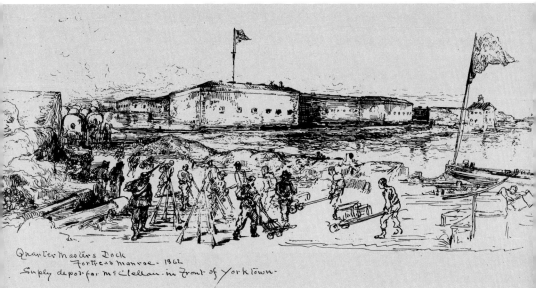

Fort Monroe, at the tip of the Virginia Peninsula, as seen from a supply dock. Newspaper artist Theodore R. Davis based this view on his 1862 sketch.

Musée de la Marine, Paris

The Army of the Potomac disembarks from steamers at Fort Monroe. A watercolor by Prince de Joinville, the French nobleman serving on McClellan's staff.

National Archives

Library of Congress

Left: General McClellan with members of his military family prior to the campaign. General George Morell is at left of the tree stump; behind it is aide Albert Colburn. At right are Prince de Joinville (black hat) and his nephew, the Comte de Paris.

Lower left: John R. Chapin of *Harper's Weekly* made this drawing of Yankee troops coming ashore at Hampton.

Right: General John B. Magruder — "Prince John" — resplendent in his full-dress Confederate uniform.

Below: The Confederates' Water Battery of 32-pounders at Yorktown commanded the York's channel. George N. Barnard photographed it after the evacuation.

Louisiana State University Library

Library of Congress

Cooper-Hewitt Museum

Winslow Homer covered the early part of the campaign for *Harper's Weekly*. In this sketch, the 6th Pennsylvania cavalry prepares to embark at Alexandria.

Cooper-Hewitt Museum

In this Homer drawing, the 61st New York, of Sumner's Second Corps, makes a bivouac at Ship Point, a position behind the Federal lines at Yorktown.

M. and M. Karolik Collection, Museum of Fine Arts, Boston

Willis A. Gorman's brigade of the Second Corps begins a reconnaissance in force at Yorktown; beyond the woods, as Homer notes, is a Rebel battery.

Cooper-Hewitt Museum

Homer's sketch captures the motion of ramrods on the firing line. The scene is Lee's Mill on April 16, the largest infantry clash of the Yorktown siege.

Library of Congress

Battery No. 1, mounting big Parrott rifled cannon, was the only Union battery to open fire during the Yorktown siege. Drawing by combat artist Alfred R. Waud.

Library of Congress

Battery No. 4 mounted the heaviest weapons — 13-inch seacoast mortars — of any of the fifteen heavy batteries at Yorktown. Photograph by James F. Gibson.

National Archives

After the siege, the Federals turned Yorktown into an enormous artillery depot, pictured here by a Brady photographer, for the next phase of the campaign.

Library of Congress

Alfred Waud sketched George Stoneman's cavalry, along with a battery of horse artillery, in pursuit of the Confederates after the evacuation of Yorktown.

National Archives

Brigadier General Philip Kearny, in a photograph by John W. Kuhl.

Library of Congress

Harper's Weekly's combat artist Waud did this dramatic pen and wash drawing of Phil Kearny, on horseback, leading his troops to the rescue of Joe Hooker's embattled Yankee division during the Battle of Williamsburg on May 5.

Library of Congress

Waud also sketched Winfield Scott Hancock repulsing an assault by Jubal Early's Virginians at Williamsburg. At the right is an abandoned Rebel redoubt.

Captain James Hope of the 2nd Vermont painted this panorama of the great Federal encampment at Cumberland Landing on the Pamunkey. At center is General McClellan leading his staff.

M. and M. Karolik Collection, Museum of Fine Arts, Boston

Another Federal soldier, Lieutenant John Donaghy of the 103rd Pennsylvania, did this pencil sketch of his regiment marching through New Kent Court House.

William B. Franklin, Sixth Corps commander, and his generals and staff pose for James F. Gibson's camera. Seated from left: Joseph J. Bartlett, Henry W. Slocum, Franklin, William F. Barry (chief of artillery for the Army of the Potomac), John Newton.

M. and M. Karolik Collection, Museum of Fine Arts, Boston

Library of Congress

U.S. Naval Historical Center

Flag Officer Louis M. Goldsborough commanded the Federal naval forces during the Peninsula campaign.

The Battle of Drewry's Bluff on May 15 is pictured below by an unidentified amateur artist, probably a crewman aboard one of the Yankee vessels. His ship renderings are intended to picture (from left) the *Aroostook*, *Monitor*, *Galena*, *Port Royal*, and *Naugatuck*.

U.S. Naval Historical Center

National Archives

James Gibson took this view of the Richmond and York River Railroad's Pamunkey bridge at White House being reconstructed. A locomotive awaits on a barge.

Library of Congress

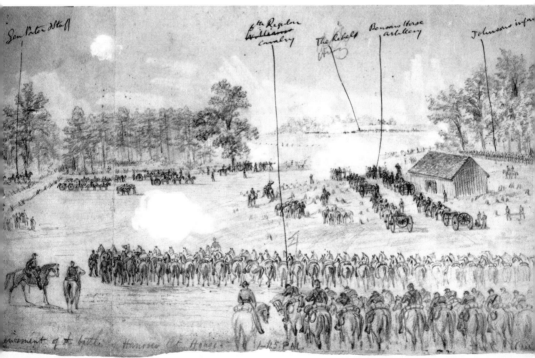

Waud sketched Fitz John Porter's artillery in action at Hanover Court House on May 27. The 6th Cavalry is in the foreground, General Porter at left rear.

National Archives

Cook Collection, Valentine Museum

Joseph E. Johnston   James Longstreet

Library of Congress

National Archives

Samuel P. Heintzelman   Silas Casey

Library of Congress

A Federal officer poses in one of Thaddeus Lowe's war balloons for photographer James Gibson. The achievements of Lowe's aerial corps were inflated by Lowe.

Century Collection

In Waud's watercolor, Sumner's reinforcements make their perilous way across the Grapevine Bridge over the flooding Chickahominy during the Seven Pines battle.

Library of Congress

Arthur Lumley sketched Yankee wounded from Seven Pines put aboard railroad cars bound for White House Landing. In the foreground is a horse-borne litter.

Library of Congress

In Alfred Waud's drawing, the dead are buried and the dead horses burned on the Seven Pines battlefield. Casey's Federal division was routed in this area.

seemed to be in his favor — but one. The missing ingredient — as was so often the case with McClellan's Army of the Potomac — was timing. General Franklin was starting his expedition forty-eight hours too late.

West Point, the terminus of the Richmond and York River Railroad, occupied the narrow tongue of land between the Pamunkey and Mattapony rivers where they join to form the York. Opposite West Point, on the south bank of the York was the open ground of Eltham plantation, where Franklin was to put his division ashore. To negotiate the shallows off Eltham's Landing the lead infantry came ashore in light pontoon boats, under the guard of five gunboats. A 400-foot-long floating wharf was then assembled from pontoons, canal boats, and planking, and by working through the night by torchlight Franklin was able to land all his artillery and supplies and the rest of his infantry. Had it been the morning of May 5, he might then have set out for Barhamsville, five miles away on the main road and eighteen miles beyond Williamsburg, to block the Rebels' escape route.

But it was the morning of May 7, and Franklin chose caution as the better part of valor. He set up picket lines in the woodland fringing the plantation and gave thought simply to holding his landing ground until the three other divisions still at Yorktown joined him. "We were told to act on the defensive and contest every tree and every inch of ground," said a man in the 96th Pennsylvania. Franklin's caution was well advised. Joe Johnston's entire army was then at or near Barhamsville, and there was no longer any real opportunity for Franklin to get across its path.

It was not Johnston's intention to bring on a new fight with this Yankee force but only to hold it at bay until the army and its trains were safely past. His instruction to John Bell Hood's Texas brigade that morning was "to feel the enemy gently and fall back." General Hood was a giant of a man, blond-bearded and looking like a Viking warrior of yore, and he genuinely liked to fight. His brigade — 1st, 4th, and 5th Texas, plus the 18th Georgia, which the Texans had adopted as the "3rd Texas" — appeared perfectly willing to follow Hood wherever he might lead. With Hood as support went half a dozen other regiments from Chase Whiting's division.[17]

Although the fighting on May 7 ranks as a heavy skirmish rather than a full-fledged battle, it was marked by the same aggressive Southern tactics that characterized Williamsburg. The penchant of officers for leading from up front at Williamsburg had cost the Confederacy one brigade commander (Jubal Early) wounded, and three regimental commanders killed and three others wounded. At Eltham's Landing Hood's notion of personally leading his men to feel the enemy very nearly cost him his life.

To avoid the chance of accidents from friendly fire in the thick woods, Hood had his men advancing with guns unloaded when abruptly they stumbled on a squad of Yankee pickets in a clearing. Hardly fifteen paces away, Hood wrote, "a corporal of the enemy drew down his musket upon me as I stood in front of my line." Fortunately for him, Private John Deal of the 4th Texas had disobeyed orders and loaded his rifle, and Deal shot down the Yankee corporal before he could fire.

The Texans pushed on through the woods, driving the pickets ahead of them until they collided with a solid line of Federal infantry in brigade strength. The firing became general and there was great confusion. A Maine soldier familiar with the wilderness forests of his native state remarked on the difficulty of keeping anything straight when "proceeding through one of the closest growths of pine trees and underbrush I ever saw." After charges and countercharges, fearing their flanks were being turned, several of the Federal regiments broke for the rear. North Carolinian Bartlett Malone, serving in a regiment in support of Hood, summed up this turn of events in his diary: "And from that time untell 12 oclock we was a scurmishing and a running from one place to another hunting the scamps." After falling back more than a mile to the open ground above the landing, the Yankee line was reinforced and held there. Seeing no further opportunity for gain and having more than carried out General Johnston's instructions, Hood broke off the action. His casualties came to 48 men. The Federals lost 186. "I congratulate myself that we have maintained our position," Franklin told McClellan.

In the wake of the Eltham's Landing fight the Army of Northern Virginia continued its retreat toward Richmond, not in the least troubled by McClellan's attempt to outflank it. The manner in which this came about, however, was not as Johnston had expected. "General Hood, have you given an illustration of the Texas idea of feeling an enemy gently and falling back?" he asked. "What would your Texans have done, sir, if I had ordered them to charge and drive back the enemy?"

Hood considered the question soberly before answering. "I suppose, General," he said, "they would have driven them into the river, and tried to swim out and capture the gunboats."[18]

· 5 ·

March to the Chickahominy

....

I T IS DISTRESSING to see how many persons are leaving Richmond,
apprehending that it is in danger," Judith White McGuire noted in
her diary for May 3. Four days later she recorded the exodus continuing, with wagonloads of furniture and family belongings rumbling
through the streets even in the small hours of the morning. Refugees
filled the railroad depots and hurried aboard westbound packets on the
James River Canal. At the same time, other refugees from the Peninsula crowded into the city from the east, fleeing the advancing Yankees. President Davis sent Mrs. Davis and the children to safety in
North Carolina. The Confederate Congress had already adjourned,
and its members rushed off to their homes with what the newspapers
considered unseemly haste. Secretary George Randolph ordered the
War Department's archives to be boxed for shipment in case of emergency. Secretary Christopher Memminger had the Treasury's gold
reserves readied for evacuation. The Richmond press might describe
the engagements at Williamsburg and Eltham's Landing as Confederate victories, but it was evident that the victories did not signal an end
to the retreat of Joe Johnston's army. McClellan's grand army came on
relentlessly, growing in menace each day.

These developments were only the latest in a month-long rush of
bad news washing over Richmonders. Simultaneously with the report
that McClellan was laying siege to Yorktown had come word from
western Tennessee that Albert Sidney Johnston's army had failed to
turn back the Yankees on the Tennessee River at a country church
called Shiloh, and that General Johnston himself was dead on the field.
At the same time, the Mississippi River fortress of Island No. 10 was
lost to the enemy. Fort Pulaski at Savannah and Fort Macon in North
Carolina were next to fall. But worst of all was the news that on April
25 New Orleans, the largest city in the South, had been captured by

the Federals. When she came to write her memoir of life in wartime Richmond, Sallie Putnam would title this chapter in the story "Accumulating Disasters."

On May 7 Joe Johnston told General Lee that the presence of the Yankee gunboats on the York made it impossible for him to attack the enemy's landing ground at Eltham's. "The sight of the iron-clad boats makes me apprehensive for Richmond, too," he wrote, "so I move on. . . ." Yet knowing he must move on did not make the going any easier, and abruptly General Johnston's temper boiled over. Mounting his charger Sam Patch and without a word to anyone, he set off at a gallop right through his marching army. His staff tried desperately to keep up. When an ambulance blocked his way, Johnston cursed the terrified driver and threatened to shoot him. It was the only occasion his aide Porter Alexander ever saw him in such a fury. "I will remember that ride as long as I live," Alexander wrote. Finally reaching the day's stopping place, the general reined in both his horse and his temper and was his usual calm self again. The episode suggested, however, that the Fabian strategy of retreat was wearing Joe Johnston's toleration very thin.[1]

The retreat after Williamsburg was an experience not soon forgotten by Johnston's troops. "Proceed on march *hungry as wolves*," North Carolinian Henry C. Wall began his diary entry for May 7, and his complaint was echoed by virtually every diarist and letter-writer in the army. The Confederate commissary, inefficient enough to begin with, was thrown into a shambles by the condition of the roads. "We had very little to eat, our commissary wagons being stuck in the mud and many being compelled to throw out rations in order to get along," Private Henry R. Berkeley of the Hanover Artillery explained. When the Georgians of Cobb's Legion ran out of provisions, ten men from each company were ordered out into the countryside "to buy and, if not to be bought, to press and give receipt." Other foragers showed less concern for such niceties. "We were for days together without a morsel of food, excepting occasionally a meal of parched corn," Mississippian Ruffin Thomson wrote, and he watched men descend on farmers' gardens and smokehouses like clouds of locusts. "Whenever a cow or hog were found it was shot down & soon dispatched." Alabamian John Tucker reported his company "so hungary that they ate corn, collard stalks, Turnips, Beets or any thing they could get hands on." Getting only half enough to eat at least made them mad enough to fight, another man remarked, and there was a certain grim satisfaction in knowing that when the Yankees reached this part of the Peninsula there would be nothing left for them to steal.[2]

At Barhamsville Johnston divided his army to continue the march back toward Richmond. Longstreet's and D. H. Hill's divisions followed a road paralleling the Chickahominy River to a crossing of that stream called Long Bridge. Farther to the north, paralleling the Pamunkey River, G. W. Smith's and David Jones's divisions took the old Williamsburg Stage Road as far as the junction known as Baltimore Cross Roads. The Federals offered no pursuit, and the movement was completed by May 9. The commissary, now able to make use of the York River Railroad, began issuing rations once again.

The stragglers and the skulkers did not stop there, however. They always brought up the rear of any army on attack but led the way in retreat. During the week after Williamsburg the Richmond observer Thomas C. DeLeon watched them trickle into the capital, "muddy — dispirited — exhausted; and throwing themselves on cellar doors and sidewalks, slept heavily, regardless of curious starers. . . . Never had the Southern Army appeared half so demoralized. . . ." From his camp at Baltimore Cross Roads, Georgian Joel Barnett wrote his wife, "Some say there must have been 10,000 of these sick men who could not march but could beat anybody to Richmond!" General Johnston called on the provost marshal to round up this division of stragglers for return to the army.

He had the army now less than twenty miles from Richmond, but at last it was out of reach of the Yankee gunboats on the York and the Pamunkey. On May 12 President Davis and General Lee rode out from the capital to confer with Johnston at his headquarters. Johnston could provide them little satisfaction. The enemy was still in superior force and still held the initiative, he said; he could do no more than await the next movement and look for an opening for a counterstroke. The president had no better suggestion. General Johnston's policy seemed to be, Davis later wrote, to "improve his position as far as practicable, and wait for the enemy to leave his gun-boats, so that an opportunity might be offered to meet him on land."[3]

....

ON THE EVENING of May 6 the Treasury Department's revenue cutter *Miami* tied up at Fort Monroe with a distinguished passenger list: President Abraham Lincoln, Secretary of War Edwin M. Stanton, and Secretary of the Treasury Salmon P. Chase. Spurred by the news of the fall of Yorktown, the president and his Cabinet officers were determined to see if vigorous personal intervention might speed the war along. General McClellan explained that he was too busy at the front just then to see them, so they turned to the local commanders, General Wool and Flag Officer Goldsborough. As he studied the map, it appeared to Mr. Lincoln that Norfolk was now quite isolated and ripe for capture, and that it was time to challenge the Confederates for control of the James River. With General McClellan apparently indifferent to the matter and taking no action, the president, commander-in-chief of the nation's armed forces, took matters into his own hands.

The Confederate authorities had no illusions about holding out for very long in Norfolk once Johnston announced his intention of giving up the Yorktown line, and General Benjamin Huger had begun the intricate task of quietly evacuating men and guns and munitions and as many of the vessels and as much of the machinery from the nearby navy yard as possible. The *Merrimack* continued to serve as his shield. "Of course everything is in confusion . . . ," one of Huger's men wrote home on May 6; "the cars are full of troops, provisions, and ammunition every day." For more than a week Huger's bluff held and the Federals made no move against him. Then on May 8 a Norfolk tugboat captain, a Northerner by birth, deserted to the Yankees and reported all the details of the evacuation. Lincoln had already ordered Flag Officer Goldsborough to dispatch a gunboat squadron up the James; now he pressed General Wool to move rapidly against Norfolk.

The navy took the batteries defending Norfolk under fire, and the president and Secretaries Chase and Stanton boarded small craft and set out across Hampton Roads on a personal reconnaissance to find a suitable landing place. Lincoln went ashore himself to inspect one likely spot. On May 10 Wool's troops landed on an outlying beach and began their march on the town. A squabble soon developed among the officers over who was supposed to do what, but "General" Chase, who took as much interest in military affairs as in money matters, untangled things, and in due course the warlike Treasury secretary and the elderly General Wool, in joint command, had the column headed right toward Norfolk. Mr. Lincoln was meanwhile hurrying reinforcements to them. A soldier aboard one of the transports watched in amusement as the commander-in-chief went into action: "Abe was rushing about, hollering to someone on the wharf — dressed in a black suit with a very seedy crepe on his hat, and hanging over the railing, he looked like some hoosier just starting for home from California, with store clothes and a biled shirt on."

The Yankees encountered hardly even token resistance, for General Huger had by now evacuated nearly all his troops and their equipment. A partially completed ironclad and two unfinished gunboats had been towed up the James to Richmond and what remained in the navy yard was set on fire. As Norfolk's mayor with ornate ceremony surrendered the keys to the city to the invaders, Huger's rear guard boarded the last train out of town. The victors ran up the Stars and Stripes and appointed a military governor and then returned to Fort Monroe. The report of their bloodless conquest delighted everyone, particularly Secretary Stanton. "He fairly hugged General Wool," Chase wrote. ". . . So ended a brilliant week's campaign of the President. . . ."[4]

The most lasting effect of the president's campaign was to hasten the *Merrimack* to her fate. In the event he lost his base at Norfolk, Flag Officer Tattnall had intended taking the big ironclad far up the James to a new base at Harrison's Landing, some thirty-five miles from Richmond, where he might obtain the coal and other supplies he needed and once again block off the river to the Federals. To negotiate the shallows and sandbars in the river he would have to lighten ship substantially, reducing her draft from twenty-two and a half feet to eighteen feet. The river pilots assured him that such a reduction would be enough to make good his escape.

The sudden haste of General Huger's evacuation gave Tattnall only a few hours to carry out his plan, however, and no choice at all on its timing, and on the night of May 10 his crew worked frantically to remove the ship's ballast and everything else that could be spared and still allow her to fight. After five hours' labor they had her raised three feet when the river pilots came again to Tattnall and said the prevailing wind was wrong — high tide at daylight would not be high enough to carry the *Merrimack*, even with an eighteen-foot draft, over the first bar in the river.

Tattnall already mistrusted the pilots and would later accuse them of "palpable deception" and cowardice, yet his real dilemma in these dark early morning hours stemmed from his overwhelming premonition of disaster. Cautious by instinct, he knew entirely too much of the *Merrimack*'s frailties — her wretched engines that had already failed him twice; her vulnerability to damage when lightened, which exposed her thinnest armor; her poor prospect of survival should the Yankees press an attack relentlessly — and entirely too little of the advantage given him by the *Merrimack*'s fearsome reputation among his enemies. Flag Officer Goldsborough confessed he passed that night sleepless in his anxiety at the prospect of a fight at dawn against the dreaded Rebel ironclad. Tattnall could not bring himself to finish the lightening and then force the frightened pilots, at gunpoint if need be, to guide him upriver toward Richmond, challenging hell and high tide to save his ship. That would risk his crew as well as his ship, and he found the risk too great. He ran the *Merrimack* aground near the mouth of the Elizabeth River, took off the crew, and set her afire. Early Sunday morning, May 11, just before dawn, the flames reached the magazine and the *Merrimack* blew to pieces with a thunderclap.

Yankee ships were soon on the scene, confirming the death of the ironclad and collecting trophies for the president and others from the huge circle of floating debris. At last the James was open to the Federal navy, perhaps as far as Richmond itself. "The hasty evacuation of the defences below and the destruction of the Virginia hastens the coming of the enemy's gun-boats," Jefferson Davis wrote his wife on May 13. "I know not what to expect when so many failures are to be remembered, yet will try to make a successful resistance. . . ." Diarist Judith White McGuire called the news "a dreadful shock to the community. We can only hope it was wisely done." Weeks later, as the Peninsula campaign ran its course, Richmonders would speculate on the direction events might have taken had the *Merrimack* been posted during these weeks as a mighty floating battery in the James at Harrison's Landing.[5]

On May 14 the Virginia General Assembly, meeting in Richmond, called for the capital to be defended "to the last extremity," and assured President Davis that any destruction or loss of property this might entail "will be cheerfully submitted to." In a Cabinet discussion that day General Lee announced, with a vehemence that startled his colleagues, "Richmond must not be given up; it shall not be given up!" The *Dispatch* echoed his thought: "To lose Richmond is to lose Virginia, and to lose Virginia is to lose the key to the Southern Confederacy." The next day the governor, John Letcher, led a mass meeting in front of City Hall to enroll citizens' committees for defense. Richmond's mayor, Joseph Mayo, told the crowd that if he was ever asked to surrender his city to the Yankees, as the mayor of Norfolk had done, they would have to get another mayor. "So help me God, I'll never do it," he cried. In spite of his three score and ten years, he would take up a musket and man the barricades. His audience responded with three rousing cheers. In counterpoint to the day's excitement, the dull booming of cannon could be heard off to the south, coming from somewhere down the James. The enemy was nearing the gates.[6]

This particular enemy was a squadron of Union warships — ironclads *Monitor*, *Galena*, and *Naugatuck*, and wooden gunboats *Aroostook* and *Port Royal* — under Commander John Rodgers. "Let loose from all fear & constraint by the destruction of the Virginia," the diarist Edmund Ruffin wrote bitterly, the squadron had been steaming slowly up the James, methodically pounding Confederate shore batteries, clearing the way for a naval coup de main — bombarding Richmond into surrender. Now just one obstacle remained, but it promised to be the greatest challenge to the navy since the *Merrimack*. At 6:30 A.M. on May 15 Rodgers's squadron came in sight of the battery on Drewry's Bluff.

The bluff, on the south or right bank, overlooks a sharp bend in the river seven miles downstream from Richmond. The spot, on property owned by Augustus H. Drewry, had always been considered both the city's last line of defense on the James and its strongest one. A redoubt built atop the bluff that winter and mounting three heavy cannon had recently been reinforced by five naval guns removed from the Rebels' James River gunboat squadron. From their position 110 feet above the water these guns — four rifles and four smoothbores — commanded a straight, mile-long stretch of the river below the bend. As important defensively as the battery was the obstruction of the river below the bluff by pilings and sunken cribs of stone and other debris, supplemented by the hulks of several vessels scuttled in the channel. The James here was too narrow for the Union warships to maneuver, and the obstructions prevented them from forcing their way past the battery. Commander Rodgers would have to challenge Drewry's Bluff head-on and overwhelm it by gunfire. It would be the first real test for his flagship *Galena*, he said, "and I resolved to give the matter a fair trial."

Leading the army cannoneers on the bluff was Augustus Drewry himself, defending his own property as captain of the Southside Heavy Artillery. Equally appropriate, the gunners manning the navy pieces included crewmen from the *Merrimack*, preparing to duel once more with the *Monitor*. Sharpshooters were posted along the riverbanks, and the gunboat *Patrick Henry* took position behind the river obstructions to add her 8-inch smoothbore to the defenses. The majority of the defenders being navy men, Commander Ebenezer Ferrand, a veteran of service in the old navy, held the command at Drewry's Bluff. At 7:45 A.M. Rodgers boldly steered the *Galena* to within 600 yards of the bluff and anchored broadside to the channel to bring his guns to bear.

Before he could even complete the maneuver, Ferrand sent his first two shots straight into the ironclad's port bow.

The *Galena* was something of a makeshift, a conventional wooden gunboat with layered armor made of iron bars and plates bolted to the sides. She looked to a Union nurse "like a great fish with iron scales." Flag Officer Goldsborough was appalled when he first saw the *Galena*, calling her "a most miserable contrivance" and refusing to send her into action until shields of boilerplate were installed inside the bulwarks to prevent the armor-securing nuts from flying off from the concussion of a hit and decimating the gun crews. Even with that improvement, Goldsborough said, "She is a sad affair."

In three and a half hours of battle that day the *Galena* was hit forty-four times and damaged severely. Her armor was repeatedly penetrated or knocked loose; her timbers and frames were splintered and broken. Shells exploded in the below-decks spaces and a solid shot went completely through one bulwark and embedded itself in the other. She began to take on water and was briefly set afire. Rodgers finally had to slip his cables and fall back out of range. He counted fourteen dead or mortally wounded and ten injured.

While the *Monitor* suffered no damage and the Confederate gunners soon stopped wasting shot and shell on her, she proved wholly ineffective when it was found that her guns would not elevate sufficiently to reach the battery on the bluff. The *Naugatuck* went out of action midway in the fight when her 100-pounder Parrott rifle burst. The two unarmored gunboats had to remain at extreme range and contributed little to the attack; to add injury to insult, the *Port Royal*'s captain was wounded by a sharpshooter. When Rodgers turned his squadron back downriver, the Drewry's Bluff gunners saw them off with three cheers. The losses on the bluff were seven killed and eight wounded. As the *Monitor* steamed away, a Rebel sharpshooter on the bank called out to her pilot, "Tell the captain that is not the way to Richmond!"[7]

....

"THE FOLLY of sending this army down the Peninsula," Joe Johnston told one of his staff, "is only equalled by our good fortune in getting away from there." His new position between Long Bridge and Baltimore Cross Roads, facing east, seemed proof against his left flank being turned by the enemy advancing up the York. He had hardly settled into this new line when he learned of the *Merrimack*'s destruction and of the Yankee warships on the James, and he took alarm for his other flank. With both rivers under Union control, General Mc-Clellan might now advance along either one or along both.

It was Johnston's best guess that his opponent would shift his line of advance over to the James, simply because the James led straight into Richmond, and he acted quickly. On May 15 the order went out to fall back across the Chickahominy River so as to bring the army's right closer to the James. Wearily his men took up the march once more. "Out of provisions & make a draw of rations — 1 cracker & a slice of meat to each man, to march 11 miles," Henry C. Wall of the 23rd North Carolina wrote in his diary. "Take up march in the evening in a slight shower of rain, march back a mile or so to the main Richmond road, have a laborious march of 11 miles thro' mud, swamp, & water. . . ." It was two o'clock in the morning when they finally bivouacked in a pine thicket. Two more marches brought them nearly to the outskirts of Richmond. Sergeant Wall confessed that in the two weeks since he left Yorktown "I have gone thro' an extent of suffering as regards hunger, hardship & exhaustion, that I might once have considered surpassing my powers of endurance. . . ."

When word came of the repulse of the Federal squadron at Drewry's Bluff, Johnston took that spot as his right-flank outpost. The Army of Northern Virginia still faced eastward, but now it was behind the Chickahominy and directly in front of Richmond; at their closest the lines were just three miles from the city. This was where Joe Johnston had always wanted to take his stand, to be sure, but in taking it he drastically reduced his military options. He could retreat no farther without giving up Richmond.

His second reason for the hurried withdrawal was to put the Chickahominy in front of him rather than behind him. It was not considered good military form for a general to give battle with a river at his back, where it might impede his retreat if beaten, and in any event Johnston much preferred seeing the Chickahominy a barrier to his opponent rather than a potential problem to himself. Indeed, the Chickahominy was not the sort of river that any general would relish having anywhere near him.

Taking its rise some ten miles northwest of Richmond, the Chickahominy makes its way in a generally east-by-southeast direction around and in front of the city — coming as close as three and a half miles at one point — before stretching away down the center of the Peninsula to empty into the James thirty-six straight-line miles away. One of McClellan's men described it feelingly as "a narrow, sluggish stream flowing through swamp land . . . covered with a rank, dense, tangled growth of trees, reeds, grasses and water plants. Vines climb and mosses festoon the trees; . . . its stagnant water is poisonous; moccasins and malaria abound; flies and mosquitoes swarm. . . ." In dry weather the Chickahominy did not seem unduly imposing to the military eye, but in the rainy season its bottomlands quickly flooded and what had been a river became a broad lake as much as a mile across. "It was hard to say at the best of times where its banks were," wrote Francis Palfrey of the 20th Massachusetts, "and . . . no man could say to-day where its banks would be tomorrow." The Federals would soon enough come to call it the cursed Chickahominy, and worse.[8]

General Johnston had always coupled his argument for making the fight for Richmond right at Richmond itself with a demand for substantial reinforcements. Concentration of force was his invariable strategic design. "My general idea," he explained, "is to gather here all the troops who do not keep away from McClellan greatly superior forces." He was certain his army would be the underdog in any battle for the capital; the only question was how much of an underdog.

Johnston's view of the army opposed to his was a great deal more clear-headed than General McClellan's. He had originally calculated McClellan's numbers by the simple expedient of having scouts along the Virginia shore of the Potomac count the Federal transports passing on their way to Fort Monroe and estimate the troop-carrying capacity of each. By late April, when he decided he must evacuate Yorktown, he believed he was outnumbered five to two. (This overstated the Federals' manpower advantage by 20 percent; at the same time, McClellan was overstating the Confederate numbers by 112 percent.) President Davis and General Lee promised him a sizable increase in numbers: Huger's force from Norfolk and three brigades from the Carolinas, plus two contingents then posted to the north to watch the Yankees on the Rappahannock and guard important railroads. When they all finally reached him, Johnston would have better than 75,000 men at his command. With the exception of Stonewall Jackson's forces in the Shenandoah Valley, this would represent virtually every armed Confederate soldier in northern and eastern Virginia.[9]

So far as Robert E. Lee was concerned, one of the major dividends earned by holding the Yankees at Yorktown through the month of April was the time it gave him to assemble further combinations to confound the enemy. During the siege Confederate intelligence reported that

the Federal army corps under General McDowell was not with Mc-
Clellan on the Peninsula but was instead some fifty miles due north of
Richmond, on the Rappahannock opposite Fredericksburg. Other
Federal forces, in addition to the Washington garrison, were identified
as two divisions with General Banks in the Shenandoah Valley, and the
troops of General Frémont's Mountain Department in the Allegheny
range west of the Valley.

As Lee viewed the strategic situation, the most immediate and most
dangerous threat posed by this combination of enemy forces was an
advance southward from Fredericksburg by McDowell's corps to join
McClellan before Richmond. Possibly Banks might join this advance,
or at least reinforce it. Should this happen, the odds against Joe Johnston would lengthen alarmingly and the chances of holding Richmond
would diminish accordingly. Lee's sole weapon to prevent this from
happening was Stonewall Jackson's little Army of the Valley.

Since his repulse at Kernstown on March 23, Jackson had been
withdrawing slowly up the Valley so as to keep good position against
the advancing Banks while at the same time staying out of harm's way.
Under his command and within his reach were three separate columns:
his own, composed of 8,000 infantry, another 8,000 men under Richard
S. Ewell, and 3,000 under Edward Johnson. It now became General
Lee's thought to turn Jackson back to the offense. If he could seize the
initiative in the Shenandoah, Lee wrote him on April 21, "it will prove
a great relief to the pressure on Fredericksburg." On April 25 Lee
made note of the wide dispersal of the enemy forces and suggested
that by "a rapid combination of our troops" Jackson might deal a blow
to the Yankees' strategic plans. He granted him wide latitude as to
target, and added a significant proviso: "The blow wherever struck,
must, to be successful, be sudden and heavy."

Jackson welcomed the change. "Now, it appears to me, is the
golden opportunity," he said, and proposed to strike first at Frémont's
advance guard under Robert Milroy posted on the western edge of the
upper Valley. Lee's endorsement was prompt. It appeared to him, he
telegraphed, that the Federals were preparing to reinforce McDowell
for a push southward from Fredericksburg. "If you can strike at Milroy
do it quickly. . . ."[10]

....

LARGE QUESTIONS of strategy were crowding in on General Mc-
Clellan as well. His high hopes for Franklin's flanking movement by

way of the York had turned to ashes when Franklin was rudely pushed back into the landing ground at Eltham's. Only on May 10, when the vanguard of the main army advanced beyond Williamsburg and linked up with Franklin, did McClellan breathe easy once more. "The dangerous moment has passed," he telegraphed Secretary Stanton. He told his wife, "We are now again united and Joe has lost his best chance of catching us in detail." His own best chance of catching his old friend in detail was gone as well, although he was silent on that point.

McClellan had gained West Point and the terminus of the Richmond and York River Railroad, the first objective of his original plan back in March for basing his campaign at Urbanna, but gaining it had required a long and costly detour by way of Fort Monroe, Yorktown, and Williamsburg. The climax of his grand campaign also seemed bound to proceed differently from the way he had planned it. Joe Johnston's army was squarely blocking his path to Richmond, and his dream of fighting an American Waterloo on his own terms and on ground of his own choosing now seemed unlikely to occur in just that way.

By every indication, from every source, he announced to President Lincoln on May 14, it would be "the fixed purpose" of the Rebels to defend their capital to the last ditch, "offering us battle with all the troops they can collect from East, West, and South. . . ." In numbers this was certain to be a host: "I must attack in position, probably entrenched, a much larger force, perhaps double my numbers." He said it would be insane to count on anything less than a desperate resistance by the enemy before Richmond, and he begged to be reinforced "without delay by all the disposable troops of the Government. I ask for every man the War Department can send me." While the general was entirely earnest in his plea, his measurement of the task he faced was entirely illusionary.

To be sure, this was hardly a new state of affairs. George McClellan's conviction that he was forever outnumbered was the one constant of his military character. Ten months earlier, soon after taking command of the Army of the Potomac, he began issuing estimates of the Confederate army confronting him that showed him capable (as one disbelieving observer put it) of "realizing hallucinations." Having started off the Rebel army at 100,000 men — almost three times its actual strength at the time — he could never retreat from that figure; by logical progression it would only increase in size. Detective Pinkerton subsequently attempted to document the great Rebel army his chief had invented, but poor Pinkerton was unable to match the general's imaginings and grew less and less scientific and more and more desperate in his estimating methods. By the time he reached the Peninsula, Pinkerton was reduced simply to guessing, giving headquarters "medium estimates" and "general estimates," sometimes without any supporting evidence at all. Like his chief, he too was realizing hallucinations.[11]

The estimates of Johnston's strength that McClellan endorsed and passed on to Washington during May came from Pinkerton's interrogation of Virginia civilians at Yorktown and Williamsburg who had served in the state militia and who seemed perfectly happy to tell the Yankees all they knew, or said they knew. None of these Sunday soldiers had the slightest claim to being authoritative. Their estimates for the Army of Northern Virginia ranged up to 150,000 men, and all agreed that the Rebels had 400 to 500 pieces of artillery. In this fashion General McClellan reached the conclusion that he was facing "perhaps double my numbers."

Against these daunting odds, he told the president, "I cannot bring into actual battle against the enemy more than eighty thousand men at the utmost. . . ." McClellan's recital of the weakness of his own army was nothing new either, and it left Mr. Lincoln bemused. It struck him as a "curious mystery," he said, that so many of the troops sent to the Peninsula by the War Department were taking no part in the fighting. It indeed seemed a mystery. According to the latest return, there should have been 102,236 fighting men armed and present for duty with the Army of the Potomac on the Peninsula, yet here was the general saying that one out of five of those men would not fire a shot in the next battle.

One explanation for the mystery was slack organization. There were any number of able-bodied soldiers in this army who were customarily detailed to duty as orderlies and servants and guards and a score of other noncombatant jobs; the equivalent of two regiments did nothing more than serve as escort for the general commanding. Another explanation lay in General McClellan's exceedingly conservative method of troop-counting. His 80,000 figure referred only to enlisted men, and only to those with rifles in their hands assigned to the firing line on the day of battle. He never troubled to explain to his superiors how this differed from "present for duty" on the returns; more important, he never applied the same strict accounting to his opponent's army. By this manipulation of the numbers he made the odds against him — which were entirely imaginary to begin with — seem even longer.

While the president did not directly challenge McClellan on these odds, there can be little doubt that he viewed them with skepticism; certainly they were a topic discussed with a skeptical Cabinet. After Secretary of the Treasury Chase returned from his expedition to the Peninsula with the president, he wrote to a friend that he was convinced "McClellan has a force which, properly handled, is vastly superior to any that can be brought against him." In his diary Secretary of the Navy Welles would remark, on the subject of numbers, "the talk of McClellan, which none of us have believed." (McClellan's generals were similarly skeptical. Corps commander Heintzelman, told the enemy had 130,000 men, believed the figure inflated and much swollen by conscripts likely to be unreliable in battle. Many of his fellow generals agreed, Heintzelman said, that the general commanding "was in the habit of overestimating the Rebel forces.") Yet despite whatever he may have thought of his general's view of the enemy, Lincoln did not waver in his support for the campaign. Indeed, he decided to furnish General McClellan with even more reinforcements then he had called for.[12]

Late in April, as Stonewall Jackson withdrew up the Shenandoah ahead of him, General Banks announced to Washington that his task was done. Jackson would surely be called in momentarily by the Confederate authorities to help defend Richmond, he said. "There is nothing more to be done by us in the valley." This news was exceedingly welcome to the president, who with the aid of Secretary Stanton had been acting as his own general-in-chief since he removed McClellan from the post in March. It appeared that the capital was safe from an attack or a raid, and General McDowell's First Corps might now be released to join McClellan as originally intended.

Following the dispatch of Franklin's division to the Peninsula in mid-April, McDowell's corps was brought back up to strength by the addition of a newly organized division. Had the First Corps thus reconstituted and 30,000 strong been promptly marched south from Fredericksburg, it might have joined hands with McClellan's army on the Pamunkey as early as mid-May. McDowell anticipated its taking him no more than four days of easy marching. The greatly outnumbered Confederate force keeping watch on Fredericksburg would have been helpless even to delay the link-up. In such an event, armed with thirteen divisions and more than 130,000 men — just as he had planned it all back in March — General McClellan might have continued his grand campaign with confidence restored.

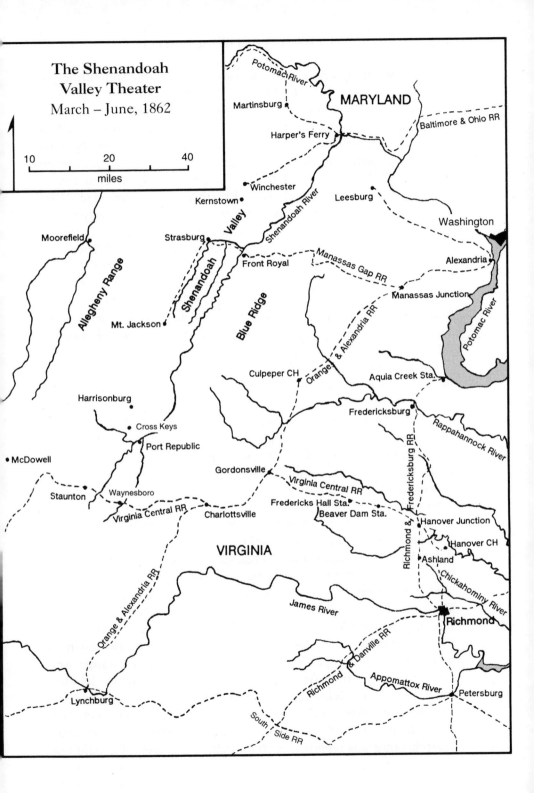

The Shenandoah Valley Theater
March – June, 1862

10   20   40
miles

Potomac River

MARYLAND

Martinsburg

Harper's Ferry

Baltimore & Ohio RR

Winchester

Kernstown

Leesburg

Washington

Moorefield

Strasburg

Front Royal

Manassas Gap RR

Alexandria

Manassas Junction

Mt. Jackson

Potomac River

Culpeper CH

Aquia Creek Sta.

Harrisonburg

Fredericksburg

Rappahannock River

Cross Keys

Port Republic

McDowell

Gordonsville

Virginia Central RR

Fredericks Hall Sta.

Staunton

Waynesboro

Virginia Central RR

Charlottsville

Beaver Dam Sta.

Hanover Junction

Hanover CH

Ashland

VIRGINIA

James River

Chickahominy River

Richmond

Orange & Alexandria RR

Lynchburg

Richmond & Danville RR

Appomattox River

Petersburg

South Side RR

Mr. Lincoln, however, was determined to go a large step further for his general. He would make McDowell's corps a full-fledged army for the march to the Peninsula. On May 1 James Shields's division was detached from Banks's corps in the Valley and ordered to join Mc-Dowell at Fredericksburg. This would raise the count of the First Corps to 41,000. The president's one stipulation was that McDowell advance overland so as not to leave Washington uncovered and to enable him to return quickly should the capital be threatened. (Lincoln pointed out that it had recently taken two weeks to carry Franklin's single division to the Peninsula by water; McDowell could march his entire army corps overland in considerably less than half that time.) On the face of it, it seemed a plan of considerable foresight. Jackson was credited with 20,000 men; thus when Jackson joined the Army of Northern Virginia at Richmond, McDowell's countermove would bring twice that number to the Army of the Potomac in front of Richmond. All that was required now was for Stonewall Jackson to follow the script the Federals had drawn up for him.[13]

Once assured that matters were nicely under control in the Shenandoah, Washington ordered General Banks to fall back from his advanced position there and take a posting at the town of Strasburg, where he might simply act as a guard for the lower end of the Valley. At the same time he made this withdrawal, Banks was to release Shields's division to begin its march to join McDowell's First Corps. From one cause or another, however, neither Banks nor Shields seemed able to get himself or his men properly organized for these movements. Twelve days would pass before Shields even started his march, and then it would take him eleven more days to reach Fredericksburg. No sense of urgency marked the operation. In the meantime, it developed that General Banks had been somewhat hasty to assume that there was nothing more to be done in the Valley.

On May 8 came word of a sudden stir in John Charles Frémont's Mountain Department. A few days earlier Stonewall Jackson had abruptly disappeared from the Federals' sight; now he just as abruptly reappeared, in front of General Milroy at the town of McDowell in the far reaches of the upper Valley. (First reports of the encounter were garbled, and for a time Washington believed Confederate Joe Johnston and Federal Irvin McDowell were involved. Finally it was straightened out: the Confederate officer in question was Edward Johnson, Jackson's lieutenant, and McDowell was a place rather than a general.) Sharp fighting was reported at McDowell, and General Frémont telegraphed that Milroy and the advance guard were rapidly falling back into the mountains to evade the enemy's pursuit. Finally, with an almost audible sigh of relief, Frémont reported Jackson "now in full retreat" from his front.

Just what this might portend was not yet clear, but after Shields and his men took their leave on May 12, General Banks began to cast nervous glances over his shoulder as he fell back down the Valley. He now had only a single division with him, and his closest support, Frémont's command, was not actually anywhere nearby, and somewhere in that silent Valley to the south might well be Stonewall Jackson and 20,000 soldiers.

The Federal high command in Washington did not blink and went ahead with its plans for McDowell's movement to the Peninsula. On May 17 McDowell received his instructions to march for the Pamunkey as soon as Shields's division reached him. General McClellan was notified to expect the First Corps to appear on his right flank in due course. [14]

....

IN COMMON with just about everyone else in the Army of Northern Virginia, General D. H. Hill anticipated a battle for Richmond "on the grandest scale and of the most desperate character in the war." He told his wife that the Confederacy's best defense might turn out to be the offense. "I do not feel sure that McClellan will venture to attack at all. His movements have been characterized by great prudence, not to say great timidity."

In the three weeks following Williamsburg and Eltham's Landing General McClellan did indeed move with glacial deliberation. He spent the time organizing his supply line, reorganizing his army, and trying to refine his strategy. "Tomorrow I will get up supplies — reorganize — arrange details & get ready for the great fight . . . ," he explained to his wife at one point. "Secesh is gathering all he can in front of me — so much the better — I will finish the matter by one desperate blow. I have implicit confidence in my men & they in me! What more can I ask. . . ."

After its link-up with Franklin at West Point, the Army of the Potomac pushed slowly up the winding Pamunkey, taking successive supply bases at Eltham's Landing, Cumberland Landing, and finally at White House Landing, the point at which the York River Railroad from West Point crossed the Pamunkey to run eastward twenty-three miles straight into Richmond. McClellan designated White House as his base of operations for the final advance on the Confederate capital.

White House was the plantation of William H. F. "Rooney" Lee, General Lee's son, and a hundred years or so earlier it had been the site of George Washington's courtship of the widow Martha Custis. General Lee's wife was a Custis and had been staying at White House until just a few days before the Yankees came. Their advance guard found a note from her pinned to the front door: "Northern soldiers who profess to reverence Washington, forbear to desecrate the home of his first married life, — the property of his wife, now owned by her descendants. — A Grand-daughter of Mrs. Washington." General McClellan obligingly posted a guard on the house and prohibited its use by the army.

Before the army came, a nurse with the U.S. Sanitary Commission wrote, White House "must have been a very pretty place — a green lawn sloping to the river with trees, locusts, I think, and on the north of the house along the shore a line of tall cedars, under which are the tents of our soldiers. Forward from this fringe of trees is an immense plain trampled dead by the feet of McClellan's army."

Overnight the landing became an enormous depot. A newspaper correspondent found the Pamunkey "marked for leagues by sails, smoke-stacks, and masts. The landings and wharves were besieged by flat-boats and sloops. . . ." The shallows between riverbank and deep water were bridged by floating docks constructed of planked-over barges and canal boats. Acres of boxes and barrels and crates holding rations and ammunition and supplies and equipment of every sort covered the landing. There were wagon parks and artillery parks and great piles of baled forage. Vessels freighted with locomotives, boxcars, and flatcars soon arrived from Baltimore, and in a matter of days as much of the railroad as the Yankees controlled was in operation. Except for burning a few bridges, the retreating Confederates had left the line intact, much to the disgust of Jefferson Davis. "The York River Railroad which not being useful to our Army nor paid for by our treasury was of course not destroyed," he observed bitterly. This failure went into Mr. Davis's book as one more black mark against Joe Johnston.[15]

In the months and years ahead, General McClellan would roundly condemn President Lincoln's insistence on dispatching McDowell's First Corps to the Peninsula by the overland route. Just as the president's decision in April to hold back McDowell was "a fatal error," this decision in May "incurred great risk . . . and frustrated the plan of campaign." It tied his hands, he said; he was forced to base his campaign on the York and Pamunkey and approach Richmond from the north and east across the Chickahominy because of the need to position his army to extend a welcoming hand to McDowell marching south from Fredericksburg. Had the First Corps instead been ordered to him by water, as he wanted, he would have been free to approach Richmond by way of the James River and so avoid all the problems that in time would plague his operations. He might even have crossed the James and made his approach to Richmond from the south, by way of Petersburg — as General Grant did successfully in 1864–65 — and thereby shortened the war by two years.

This construction of unerring logic was entirely an afterthought, however. General McClellan's decision in May 1862 to base his campaign at White House Landing and to march on Richmond by way of the York River Railroad was entirely his own doing, made without compulsion from Washington and without reference to the First Corps and how it might reach him. It was only hindsight that furnished him with second thoughts and a scapegoat on which to lay the blame.

The James River route, to be sure, had always been one of the options in McClellan's planning. In his February 3 paper for the forthcoming campaign he had listed as one possibility to "cross the James & throw ourselves in rear of Richmond, thus forcing the enemy to come out & attack us. . . ." On May 10, when it appeared that Norfolk would be taken and with it the *Merrimack*, he told Secretary Stanton that in that event "I can change my line to the James River & dispense with the Railroad." This assumed, however, that the Federals would gain control of the entire James, right to Richmond, a presumption quickly put to rest by the navy's repulse at Drewry's Bluff.

"Without the Army the Navy can make no real headway towards Richmond," Flag Officer Goldsborough explained. "This is as clear as the sun at noonday to my mind." The flag officer went to White House on May 19 to consult with the general on what might be done about Drewry's Bluff. McClellan could not promise any troops for an attack on the fort there for some time to come. Goldsborough said that even after the fort was taken it would require considerable time to clear all the obstructions from the river to allow passage. There seemed no chance any time soon of coming closer to Richmond than seven miles by way of the James.

So far as General McClellan was concerned, that stark fact made the James useless to him as an avenue of advance. To win the battle for

Richmond he must have his siege train right at the front with him. It was the equalizer, the one way to counter his great disadvantage in numbers. His strategy was now to lay siege to Richmond, just as he had laid siege to Yorktown. With sufficient labor the smaller pieces in the siege train could be moved to the front by road, but not so the larger pieces, the huge 10-inch and 13-inch mortars and the 100-pounder and 200-pounder Parrott rifles. At Yorktown he had been able to float these great guns to their battery sites by way of Wormley's Creek. In operating below Drewry's Bluff on the James, however, there was no corresponding waterway to bring them within besieging range of the enemy lines.

Possession of the York River Railroad, on the other hand, enabled McClellan to carry his heavy ordnance right to the gates of Richmond. The order went out to have the big guns at Yorktown placed aboard barges and canal boats for passage up the York and Pamunkey to the railroad. Not once in these weeks — neither before he knew the First Corps was to come overland, nor after its subsequent recall — did he propose to change his base to the James. The possibility was not even seriously discussed. As for crossing the James and moving on Petersburg, through which passed all but one of the rail lines serving Richmond, he was silent on that possibility as well. This would have required of General McClellan a stroke so bold, with an army so outnumbered, that the idea of it simply did not then cross his mind. His thoughts were focused instead on a siege. If the enemy stood and fought, he wrote his wife on May 22, "he must do so in the very outskirts of Richmond, which must in that event suffer terribly, & perhaps be destroyed." He prayed that in the aftermath of a victorious siege he would not have to witness outrage and pillage in the Rebel capital.

However that might be, General McClellan did not doubt that what lay ahead would rank as "one of the great historic battles of the world." God had called him to lead in this battle to save the Union, and "I pray for God's blessing on our arms. . . . I can almost think myself a chosen instrument to carry out his schemes." He would strive to do his best, but with the awareness of "the uncertainty of all human events — I know that God may even now deem best to crush all the high hopes of the nation & this army. . . ." With all human events thus ordered by the Creator, he could hardly be blamed for their outcome.[16]

As if to demonstrate his commitment, McClellan substantially reorganized his army for the final struggle. In his anger at the conduct of affairs at Williamsburg, he demanded of Washington "full & complete authority" to alter the corps organization and to relieve incompetent corps commanders. From the moment the corps system was forced on him back in March, he later wrote, "many of my difficulties & delays grew out of the fact that I could not trust any of the Corps Comdrs." His solution to this problem did not include any dramatic dismissals from high command, however. Instead, he diluted the authority of the present corps commanders — Sumner, Heintzelman, and Keyes — by restricting them to the control of only two divisions each. He then organized new two-division corps for his two favorite generals: the Fifth Corps, under Fitz John Porter, and the Sixth, under William B. Franklin. The reorganization went into effect on May 18, just as the army began to close in on the line of the Chickahominy.[17]

....

THE MEN OF these two armies were now in their second month of campaigning, and in that time many of them had experienced their first taste of combat, and collectively they were developing a rough code of soldiering. It dealt with what they believed was fair (and not fair) in making war. The unofficial truces during the Yorktown siege were carefully honored by both sides, for example, but great indignation was expressed at the Rebels' "inhuman" use of torpedoes there. At Williamsburg men in both armies complained of being cruelly ambushed after opponents signaled surrender, and both sides condemned the practice. After the fight at Eltham's Landing a Federal soldier was found on the field with his throat cut, which was widely reported as an atrocity. Hood's Texans had a different view of the matter. As they told it, the Yankee had been wounded and his position overrun, and therefore they considered him out of the action. But he had pulled out a pistol and opened fire at the Texans who had advanced past him, hitting several, and for that unsoldierly act he was dispatched with a bowie knife. In a later skirmish the same sort of harsh justice was meted out to a Confederate picket who surrendered to the Irish Brigade and then opened fire on his captors. The man was summarily hanged from the nearest tree. The general rule in such cases, one man said, was quite simple: "No quarter will be given."

The Federals, being deep in enemy territory, faced the additional problem of dealing with enemy civilians. General McClellan issued strict orders regarding the respect due Southern civilians and their property. As Fitz John Porter explained it to a Northern newspaper editor, "This army moves as a disciplined body — not an armed mob — compelled to respect private rights and to win the respect of the people we will mingle with. . . ." Yet the men in the ranks were not sure it was quite as simple as General Porter would have it. A New York cavalryman, for example, fairly bristled at being ordered "to guard the property, women, and children of the rebels, because their husbands and fathers have left to fight against us. . . . Oh Lord, how long. How long shall we sacrifice our lives to save those of our enemies?"

Here again a rough code of conduct began to emerge. Those civilians who stayed on their property and in their homes when the Yankee army came were generally not molested much beyond the loss of a stray chicken or two or perhaps a raid on their kitchen garden when army rations were late. If owners abandoned their property and fled to the Confederate lines, however, the men took it as a sign of their hopelessly secessionist spirit, in which case their property did not deserve respect. It was under such an unofficial edict that the Governor John Page mansion in Williamsburg was wantonly vandalized of its many colonial-era treasures and manuscripts for no better reason than the presumed disloyalty of its absentee owner.

Pennsylvanian Luther C. Furst remarked in his diary on how few civilians were to be seen as they advanced. "Nearly everybody has left, leaving house & home with niggers, horses & furniture. . . . The cattle, hogs & colts are running at large & our men confiscate all they want. . . ." Slaves not carried off by their masters flocked to the Union lines. "The niggers all want to be free," Furst reported, "& ask me if they had to go to work or not." With those civilians who remained informal truces became common. Lieutenant Haydon of the 2nd Michigan found a "very amiable Secession lady" who sold him a rooster for a dollar and for a quarter more consented to cook it for him. She admitted, Hayden wrote, that "Lincolnite Yankees" were not as bad as she had first supposed.[18]

The topic of most consuming interest to these Yankee soldiers, however, was how incredibly difficult it was to get from one place to another on this Virginia Peninsula. "Our marches since the battle have been very monotonous," one of Phil Kearny's men wrote on May 17, "only varied by changes from heat and dust to rain and mud, and vice-versa." After two or three days of hot sun the roads would dry and turn to thick powdery dust; after an hour's rain they turned back to bottomless mud. A Massachusetts man explained to his family that the mud here was nothing at all like the mud back home. "It is a light yellow and as sticky as wax," he wrote, and it was deep beyond all belief. General McClellan reported on May 16 that one division's supply train had required thirty-six hours to move exactly five miles.

Tales were told of Peninsula mud which lost nothing in the telling and retelling — the time, for example, that an army mule (not, admittedly, a very large army mule) sank so far into a mudhole that finally only its ears were visible — but often enough truth matched exaggeration. The day following Williamsburg Major Wainwright returned to his batteries that had been overrun during the fighting and found a pair of wheel horses still harnessed to the traces of a limber. Both were dead. One had been killed in the battle and it sank down into the mud, dragging its mate down with it to suffocation. Men groped for words to describe these conditions. One old regular who thought he had seen it all in his travels was reduced to a simple admission in a letter to his wife. The roads of the Virginia Peninsula, he wrote, "have been very bad in fact I never saw a 'bad road' until I came here. . . ."

Major Thomas Hyde of the 7th Maine took note one day of a weathered signpost at a crossroads pointing west and reading RICH-MOND 21 MILES. Beneath it, pointing north, was a brand-new sign, put up by a homesick Yankee, reading GORHAM, MAINE 647 MILES. In the two weeks after Williamsburg, the Yankee soldiers marched on average a total of only forty to fifty miles, but all too often they were wearying, exasperating miles.

Lieutenant Haydon described the routine in his diary for May 19: "It seems some times of late as if the whole object was to see how much trouble and vexation can be given us. We usually pull up at daylight, march a mile, lie on our arms in rain or hot sun till dark, then go 4 or 5 miles at double quick & halt for supper when it is too late to find either wood or water." Was the illogic of this General McClellan's fault, he wondered, "or that of some one under him or is it really unavoidable?" To ward off the effects of exposure the men were given a quarter-pint of whiskey a day. The whiskey ration was issued at the end of the day's march, and was found to be the most effective deterrent to straggling yet found.[19]

On May 20 Silas Casey's division of Keyes's Fourth Corps, advancing along the Williamsburg Stage Road, reached the Chickahominy at Bottom's Bridge, a dozen miles due east of Richmond. The retreating Confederates had burned the bridge, and also the railroad bridge three-quarters of a mile upstream, but they made no attempt to contest the crossing, and Casey's men easily forded the stream. The next day General McClellan crossed at Bottom's Bridge and made a personal reconnaissance. He expressed himself puzzled. Unless the enemy "has some deep laid scheme that I do not fathom," he told Ellen, "he is giving up a great advantage in not opposing me on the line of the Chickahominy. . . ."

Accepting what he was given, he pushed additional troops from Keyes's corps across the river and ahead six miles to the crossroads of Seven Pines, where he anchored his left flank. On May 24 the lead elements of Baldy Smith's division chased the Rebels out of Mechanicsville, on the Chickahominy five miles north-northeast of Richmond, and established the army's right flank at that point. From these advanced positions the spires of Richmond were clearly visible and church bells and clock bells clearly heard.

May 24 was also the day that disturbing news reached General McClellan from Washington. It had been arranged that McDowell's First Corps, reinforced at last by James Shields's division, would set out for the Peninsula on the twenty-sixth; by the end of the month McDowell was expected to be united with the Army of the Potomac. Now, however, the president telegraphed, "In consequence of Gen. Banks' critical position I have been compelled to suspend Gen. McDowell's movement to join you." Although it was not clear just where he had come from, it seemed that Stonewall Jackson had surprised and routed a part of Banks's force at a place called Front Royal and was now hot on the trail of Banks's main body in the lower Valley. The president said that he was attempting to bring Frémont's troops and at least a part of McDowell's to the rescue.

During the next twenty-four hours the situation in the Valley worsened rapidly. Word came that General Banks had attempted a stand at Winchester but was beaten badly and was now in flight down the Valley toward the Potomac, with Jackson close on his heels. "The enemy is moving North in sufficient force to drive Banks before him . . . ," Lincoln told McClellan. "I think the movement is a general and concerted one. . . . I think the time is near when you must either attack Richmond or give up the job and come to the defence of Washington. Let me hear from you instantly."[20]

Battle at the Seven Pines

··

G ENERAL MCCLELLAN was in his headquarters tent writing a
Sunday afternoon letter to his wife when President Lincoln's
telegram was handed to him. He reacted with predictable fury at this
second recall of McDowell's corps. It was one more sickening proof of
the "hypocrisy, knavery & folly" of those in Washington, he raged.
"Heaven save a country governed by such counsels!" In his reply to
the president he announced coldly, "Telegram received. Independently of it the time is very near when I shall attack Richmond. The
object of enemy's movement is probably to prevent reinforcements
being sent to me." Stonewall Jackson's game was clear to him and he
would not be fooled by it. Should the army actually be ordered back to
the defense of Washington because of it, he told Ellen, "you can
imagine the course I had determined to pursue. . . ." He had discussed such matters with her before, and the implication was clear that
if it came to that he would resign his command.

In due course the president too came to see the purpose behind
Jackson's offensive, especially after Banks was able to get his battered
force to safety across the Potomac and the alarm in Washington began
to subside. Yet the question of what to do next about the situation in
the Shenandoah Valley found Lincoln and McClellan in fundamental
disagreement.

McClellan clung to his argument that the best defense for Washington (and for the Valley) was his army's moving against Richmond with
every available soldier. The Rebels would soon enough be obliged to
recall Jackson to help defend their capital and his threat would evapo-
rate. The president, on the other hand, saw in Jackson's foray north all
the way to the Potomac an opportunity for a counterstroke. If Mc-
Dowell and Frémont moved swiftly, he said, they had the opportunity
to trap and crush Jackson before he could escape from the Valley,

which event ought substantially to ease General McClellan's burden on the Peninsula. Mr. Lincoln liked to remind his general that every Rebel soldier not at Richmond was one less soldier he had to fight, and the president preferred throwing McDowell against Jackson in the Valley immediately rather than see the two meet at Richmond at some future time. Further to the argument, he felt that McDowell and Frémont would give battle in short order; he was less confident that General McClellan, on his record and regardless of how many men he had, would fight anytime soon. In issuing his orders Lincoln told McDowell that everything depended "upon the celerity and vigor of your movement." To Frémont he telegraphed, "Put the utmost speed into it. Do not lose a minute."[1]

Resignedly shrugging his shoulders, McClellan returned to his dogged preparations for putting Richmond under siege. He was quick to file a self-fulfilling prophecy with Washington. "I feel forced to take every possible precaution against disaster," he telegraphed on May 26, "& to secure my flanks against the probably superior force in front of me." Having gained a foothold across the Chickahominy with his left wing, he needed to bridge the Chickahominy securely to ensure communication between that wing and the rest of the army still north of the river.

George McClellan's particular forte was engineering — during and after the Mexican War he had officered the army's first engineering unit, the Company of Engineer Soldiers — and no one in the Army of the Potomac saw more arduous duty than his engineers. The engineering brigade consisted of two volunteer regiments, the 15th and 50th New York, and a battalion of regulars, some 1,500 men in all. On the Chickahominy their first priority was rebuilding Bottom's Bridge, where the Williamsburg Stage Road crossed the stream, and the nearby Richmond and York River Railroad bridge.

As Lieutenant William Folwell of the 50th New York explained it, the railroad bridge was altogether more than a quarter of a mile long, but "the Rebels, fortunately for us, burnt only some 80 ft. of the bridge over the channel. . . . What fools the Rebs were not to do their work better. . . ." The engineers soon put a nearby sawmill in operation and replaced the burned-out section of the trestle and laid new rails brought up from White House, and on May 27 the first supply train steamed across the Chickahominy to Savage's Station three miles beyond. Just a week after reaching the river the Yankees had this crucial link in their supply line in working order.

The rank and file in Sumner's Second Corps were also put to work at bridge building. Sumner's corps, north of the Chickahominy, was less than three straight-line miles from the advance of Keyes's neighboring corps south of the river at Seven Pines, but when measured by the road that looped back across Bottom's Bridge the distance was more than twelve miles, which made General McClellan decidedly nervous. Sumner set the lumberjacks of the 1st Minnesota and 5th New Hampshire to heading the construction of a pair of bridges upstream from Bottom's Bridge and in a direct line with Seven Pines.

Details of axmen were sent out into the bottomlands to fell trees by the hundreds and float them to the bridge sites. There log piers were assembled and sunk into the mud and connected by long stringers to which a corduroyed log causeway was fastened. His entire regiment was assigned to this fatigue duty, wrote diarist Matthew Marrin of the 1st Minnesota. "About 3 companys had to work in the water waist deep all day. . . . The whiskee ration taken on going to bed kept us all rite I guess — at least I kept warm." The main channel here was only some forty feet wide, but the bridges had to be more than a quarter of a mile long to traverse the lesser channels and the spongy bottomlands on both sides. Sumner's two bridges were completed by May 29. The upper one, soon to become the better known of the two, was christened the Grapevine Bridge, after an old bridge formerly on the site that took its name from the river's twisting channels. The task was completed none too soon, for Heintzelman's Third Corps now joined Keyes's Fourth, putting fully a third of the army south of the river.[2]

McClellan's next step, as he explained it to Heintzelman, would be to edge the Third and Fourth corps upstream along the southern bank of the Chickahominy so as to uncover more crossing sites and allow more bridge building. That in turn would enable him to shift the bulk of his army across the river and by advancing along the axis of the railroad, to carry his siege guns directly to the gates of Richmond. Before continuing this movement with his left, however, he felt obliged to deal with a threat to his right.

It was reported to him that a certain Dr. Pollock, a civilian, had been heard to say that the Confederates were advancing a force of 17,000 men to Hanover Court House, fourteen miles north of Richmond and on the right rear of the Army of the Potomac. Unaccountably the Federals always paid heed to such talk by Virginia civilians, and General McClellan grew apprehensive. Although a cavalry reconnaissance reduced the threatening number to perhaps 6,000, he moved quickly to clear his flank of this menace. He assigned the task to his favorite general, Fitz John Porter, and at first light on May 27, in a driving rainstorm, Porter set his troops on the road to Hanover Court House.

At that moment, the furthest thing from Confederate general Lawrence O'Bryan Branch's mind was an assault on McClellan's flank. Branch was on duty guarding the Virginia Central Railroad, Richmond's main link with the Shenandoah Valley, and was unsuspectingly posted near Peake's Crossing on the railroad four miles southwest of Hanover Court House. He had a reinforced brigade of six North Carolina regiments and one Georgia regiment, some 4,000 men in all. General Branch's background was congressional politics rather than the military, and his only previous command experience was the failed defense of New Bern, on the North Carolina coast, back in March. On that day he had been outnumbered by almost three to one; on this day he would face exactly the same odds.

The road to Hanover Court House, a man in the 22nd Massachusetts complained, "was eighteen miles in length, and about one foot in depth." Although the rain ended in midmorning the mud remained, and when an enemy outpost was encountered at noon at a crossroads south of the court house, the tired Yankees felt they had already put in a full day's soldiering. Infantrymen of the 25th New York were with the cavalry in the advance, and they took heavy skirmishing losses before the rest of Porter's command could make headway in the mud to relieve them. There was an hour or so of brisk fighting in a woodlot and around the house and barn of a Dr. Kinney at the crossroads, and then the outmanned Rebels beat a hasty retreat. Most of them were driven off to the north, up the road to Hanover Court House, and Porter set off in pursuit with the bulk of his troops. He left behind a slim force of three regiments, including the battered 25th New York, to hold the crossroads.[3]

Porter misjudged the case by expecting to find the main Confederate force at Hanover Court House, and so marched past and then away from Branch at Peake's Crossing. For his part, Branch misjudged the Yankees' numbers and gave battle when his wiser course was retreat. "We was defeated through General Branchs bad management," one of his men would write bitterly. "He was told by a Citizen that the enemys force was small & he believed it. . . ." Branch threw his main body, five regiments strong, against the Yankee rear guard at the crossroads.

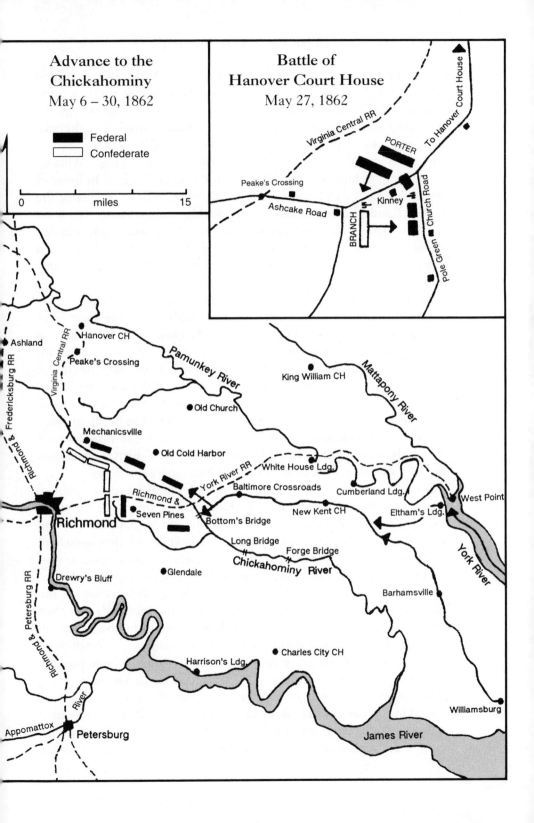

Advance to the Chickahominy
May 6 – 30, 1862

Federal
Confederate

0   miles   15

Battle of Hanover Court House
May 27, 1862

Virginia Central RR

To Hanover Court House

PORTER

Peake's Crossing

Ashcake Road

BRANCH

Kinney

Church Road

Pole Green

Ashland

Hanover CH

Virginia Central RR

Peake's Crossing

Pamunkey River

King William CH

Mattapony River

Richmond & Fredericksburg RR

Old Church

Mechanicsville

Old Cold Harbor

York River RR

White House Ldg.

Baltimore Crossroads

Cumberland Ldg.

West Point

Richmond &

Seven Pines

Bottom's Bridge

New Kent CH

Eltham's Ldg.

Richmond

Long Bridge

Forge Bridge

Chickahominy River

York River

Drewry's Bluff

Glendale

Barhamsville

Richmond & Petersburg RR

River

Harrison's Ldg.

Charles City CH

Appomattox

Petersburg

Williamsburg

James River

The Federals here — 2nd Maine, 44th New York, what remained of the 25th New York, and a two-gun section of artillery — were immediately in trouble, and staff officers went pelting off up the Hanover Court House Road to recall General Porter. The Rebels, wrote the colonel of the 2nd Maine, "appeared boldly in front, advancing in perfect order, . . . the Stars and Bars defiantly flying." What he saw coming at him was the 18th North Carolina. William Bellamy of the 18th recorded in his journal that they were "ordered to charge the Yankee Battery after marching to the double quick at charge Bayonets for about 300 yards." As they stormed out of the woods and across a wheatfield they were greeted by repeated blasts of musketry. "In consequence of our men being mowed down like grass," Bellamy continued, "we fell back to our original stand. . . ."

Maine men and Carolinians settled into a vicious, prolonged struggle for a hedgerow fence between two fields, ramming their rifles through the hedgerow to fire on each other. Their weapons became so hot from firing that the men cooled them with water from their canteens. The Federals had started their march with sixty rounds of ammunition, but this was their second fight of the day and they began to run short. As their fire slackened the Rebels drove the gunners away from their pieces and then the center of the Yankee line began to break in what the brigade commander, John H. Martindale, admitted was "a disorderly movement." The 44th New York lost a quarter of its men and later would count exactly forty-four holes in its battle flag.

Just in time the rest of Porter's command, rapidly reversing course, reached the field. "The woods all round were swarmed with rebels," Lieutenant Colonel Patrick A. Guiney of the 9th Massachusetts wrote his wife. ". . . We met the rebels on the verge of the wood and whipped them out of it in no time — such quick work I never saw — the rebels made a stand in the open field. . . . Again we pressed upon the enemy — captured one of their flags — and drove them in the most indescribable disorder." As Yankees by the hundreds and then the thousands poured onto the field, Branch had to fall back with all possible speed. Finally darkness ended the fighting. "We whipped them and have driven them from the ground, killing a large number and taking a great many prisoners," Porter reported to McClellan.[4]

Porter acknowledged large losses in some of his regiments, and indeed in the Battle of Hanover Court House the killed and wounded of the two sides were about the same. The Yankees had 285 men hit on May 27, with more than three-quarters of that total in the Maine and New York regiments that fought so desperately at the crossroads. The count of Confederate dead and wounded was incomplete, but it probably came to between 270 and 300. (In that count was one particularly melancholy statistic — three of the four Robinett brothers of Company G, 37th North Carolina, were found dead on the field.)

The real measure of Federal victory was in the number of prisoners. Porter lost 70 men captured, while Branch lost 731. Many of these, demoralized by the hurried retreat, were scooped up as stragglers after the battle by Porter's cavalry. The cavalrymen went on to burn all the railroad bridges in the vicinity and even to capture a trainload of Confederate stores, including a boxcar full of tobacco. After their return to camp Porter's men amused themselves by rolling the largest cigars any of them had ever seen.

For General McClellan, Hanover Court House was yet another "glorious victory over superior numbers." Porter's expedition, McClellan explained to Washington, "has entirely relieved my right flank which was seriously threatened," and he ranked it as "one of the handsomest things of the war. . . ." Behind his overblown rhetoric was a rather different balance of results. Set against the railroad cutting and the thousand casualties inflicted on Branch was a full week's delay in securing the Federal foothold across the Chickahominy. For however long his reserve was depleted by the absence of Porter's corps, McClellan had refused to chance putting more than the Third and Fourth corps over the river; in sending out Porter, he said, "I run some risk here, but I cannot help it." The actual risk he ran would soon prove entirely different, and far greater than he imagined.[5]

....

JOE JOHNSTON intently watched the Federals position themselves astride the Chickahominy. This division of their forces was the opening he had been waiting for, and he let them come on unopposed. His first impulse was to attack the column that had crossed to the south bank and advanced up the Williamsburg Road to the area of Seven Pines. The ground there appeared good for fighting and all the approaches from Richmond toward Seven Pines were in his hands. Then on May 27, the day that Porter fought Branch at Hanover Court House, word reached Johnston that the Yankee army corps under McDowell was marching south from Fredericksburg. "We must get ready for this," he told his second-in-command, G. W. Smith. To prevent McDowell from linking up with McClellan's right wing at Mechanicsville, they must cross the river and attack that wing, and they must do it quickly.

Johnston called his generals to headquarters at the Stubbs house the evening of May 28 to plan the operation. Smith, who was to command the assault, said the Federals were well posted at Mechanicsville and predicted that dislodging them would be "a bloody business." With no doubt a sigh of relief, Johnston was able to report fresh news. Jeb Stuart's cavalry had seen McDowell turn back to Fredericksburg, and it was thought he was bound for the Shenandoah to fight Stonewall Jackson. (McDowell had actually been ordered to the Valley by President Lincoln four days earlier; the Yankees seen south of Fredericksburg were simply making a diversion to screen the movement.) Johnston now determined to return to the better target south of the Chickahominy.

He shifted the army so as to strike the enemy's left wing instead of the right, and ordered the Federal position at Seven Pines reconnoitered. On May 30 D. H. Hill, commanding the division opposite Seven Pines, reported that two days of reconnaissances had convinced him that he was facing General Keyes's entire corps. Hill did not indicate whether he knew Heintzelman's corps was also across the Chickahominy, but that knowledge would not have altered Johnston's decision in any case. He intended to mass enough force to overwhelm two Federal corps if it came to that. He set the attack for the next day, Saturday, May 31. For the first time in the war, the Army of Northern Virginia would be taking the offensive.[6]

Johnston's plan appeared simple and straightforward. Intending to throw two-thirds of his army — including twenty-two of its twenty-nine infantry brigades — into battle south of the river, he decided to approach the enemy there along three roughly parallel roads so as to strike him head-on and on both flanks simultaneously. The center column would use the Williamsburg Stage Road, which ran in an almost straight line eastward from Richmond seven miles to Seven Pines. (The name Seven Pines was a literal one, however, taken from the seven large pine trees standing at the crossroads there.)

For the column on the left, the Nine Mile Road ran from the capital northeast to Old Tavern, then turned southeast to cross the York River Railroad at Fair Oaks Station (another site named for a handsome grove of trees) and intersected the Williamsburg Road at Seven Pines. It was named for its distance — nine miles — from Richmond to Seven Pines. To the south, branching off the Williamsburg Road some two miles out of Richmond, was the Charles City Road. It diverged gradually from the Williamsburg Road until, due south of Seven Pines, it was two and a half miles from that point; the column on the Charles City Road would have to follow a rough forest track through White Oak Swamp to reach the Yankees at Seven Pines.

As the Rebel troops were now arranged, the main attack would be made by the right wing of the army, under James Longstreet, and Johnston put Longstreet in tactical command of the opening of the operation. When battle was joined Johnston intended to take the overall command himself. To make up the three columns of attack, Longstreet had his own division and those of D. H. Hill and Benjamin Huger. He would be supported, and reinforced, by troops drawn from the left wing, under G. W. Smith, and from the reserve, under Prince John Magruder. The remaining third of the army would hold the line of the Chickahominy against the Federals north of the river.

Johnston based the composition of this three-column attack on the current positioning of the troops. Already D. H. Hill had three brigades out on the Williamsburg Stage Road; with these, plus his fourth brigade brought over from outpost duty on the Charles City Road, Hill would spearhead the attack on the Federal center. Benjamin Huger and his three brigades from Norfolk were to march out the Charles City Road, relieve Hill's brigade posted there, and then join the battle from the southern flank. Longstreet had three of his six brigades already on the Nine Mile Road to the north; his other three, in camp in the Richmond suburbs, were to join him for the advance along the Nine Mile Road to form the left wing of the assault.

G. W. Smith's division, led that day by Chase Whiting, would come up behind Longstreet in close support, and four of Magruder's brigades from the reserve might join the battle on that flank if called upon. D. H. Hill was to open the fight about 8:00 A.M., the moment his fourth brigade joined him. The sound of his guns would signal the two flanking columns into action.[7]

By massing fifteen brigades on the Nine Mile Road, and by posting himself there as well, General Johnston clearly anticipated the heaviest weight of his attack driving through Fair Oaks Station toward Seven Pines, splitting off the Federal left wing from the rest of McClellan's army and crushing it. Including the brigades from Magruder's reserve, there were to be as many as 51,600 Confederates in action on May 31, and Johnston was confident his assault would achieve a decisive edge in manpower. In fact the Federal troops marked present for duty that day in the Third and Fourth corps south of the river totaled just under 33,000. In return for achieving his advantage in numbers, Johnston ran the risk of a counterattack on Richmond through his thinned lines by McClellan's other three army corps still north of the Chickahominy.

The apparent simplicity of Johnston's plan was deceptive, for it involved one of the most difficult tests of military command in that day: coordinating several separate columns advancing to battle at the same time but out of sight of one another. Joe Johnston was not a general noted for his attention to detail, and Seven Pines would demonstrate how careless he could be. From the outset he quite failed to make himself understood or obeyed. Longstreet was to command the troops of two other generals — Huger and Smith — who outranked him, a situation that Johnston never bothered to clarify in his orders. Furthermore, his orders to Huger and Smith were poorly drawn and incomplete; those to Huger did not even state Johnston's intention to fight a battle on May 31, leaving Huger in bewilderment. For Longstreet, his chief subordinate in the operation, Johnston wrote nothing at all. He gave him instead verbal orders during a long private meeting at the Stubbs house on the afternoon of May 30. There is no record of their conversation; all that can be said of it for certain is that it produced a monumental misunderstanding of how the battle was to be fought.

As General Johnston put the final touches on his battle plan that evening, the two armies were battered by a thunderstorm of such violence that men called it quite simply the worst they had ever seen. Rain fell in torrents and lightning flashed almost continuously, and the thunder was described as hell's artillery. A bolt of lightning hit the tent of the 44th New York's quartermaster, killing him instantly and stunning twenty other men. Near Richmond one encampment came to be remembered as Camp Lightning after four men of the 4th Alabama were killed by a single strike. In his journal Major Wainwright described the storm as "another of those rains in which the very sluice gates of heaven seem to be opened, and the water drops in masses for hours."

Joe Johnston viewed the storm as a godsend. Now the Chickahominy would surely rise in flood and make it difficult — perhaps even impossible — for McClellan to reinforce his advance across the river during the battle. The flooding might also act as insurance against any Yankee attempt to counterattack toward Richmond over the upper Chickahominy crossings. G. W. Smith described Johnston as "elated" at his prospects.[8]

At first light on Saturday, May 31, the storm was over but the day dawned gray and overcast. At his headquarters along the Nine Mile Road, which he expected to be the main theater of action, General Johnston was joined by second-in-command Smith. Soon a message arrived from General Whiting, whose division was to support Longstreet's on the Nine Mile Road. Whiting complained that his way was blocked by Longstreet's troops crossing in front of him. Johnston was not unduly alarmed and assured Whiting that Longstreet was to precede him on that road in any case, but an aide, Captain Robert Beckham, was ordered to find Longstreet to straighten out the delay.

In due course Captain Beckham sent back to say that he had ridden all the way out the Nine Mile Road to the advanced Confederate outpost there and found no trace of Longstreet or his men. That did alarm Johnston. It was nine o'clock now and the battle should have opened an hour before this, but no firing could be heard and his principal subordinate had vanished, along with his entire division. Johnston dispatched a second aide, Lieutenant James B. Washington, to find out what was going on. That was the last Johnston saw of him: Lieutenant Washington rode so far out the Nine Mile Road in his search that he was captured by the Yankees. Finally, at 10:00 A.M., Captain Beckham sent word that he had discovered Longstreet and his troops — on the Williamsburg Road some two miles out of Richmond.

Joe Johnston would never admit publicly that his plan for the Battle of Seven Pines miscarried right from the start, and later he even persuaded G. W. Smith to alter his official report so as to say nothing of Longstreet's misadventures. At the moment, however, he considered the mixup serious enough that he nearly canceled the whole operation. For his part, Longstreet never acknowledged any failing of his own. Perhaps, Johnston confessed to Smith, the misunderstanding was all his fault, yet it is hard to believe that his instructions of the day before were so vague that Longstreet confused something so simple as which road he was to use. More probably, Longstreet believed his command of the army's right wing allowed him the independence to change the plan, and that by shifting his division over to the Williamsburg Road he would not have to come under Johnston's eye — and Johnston's direct supervision — once the fighting began. It would not be the last time in the war that Old Pete revealed a relish for independent command.[9]

However that may be, the consequences of his changing the plan were made even more serious by two further mischances that morning.

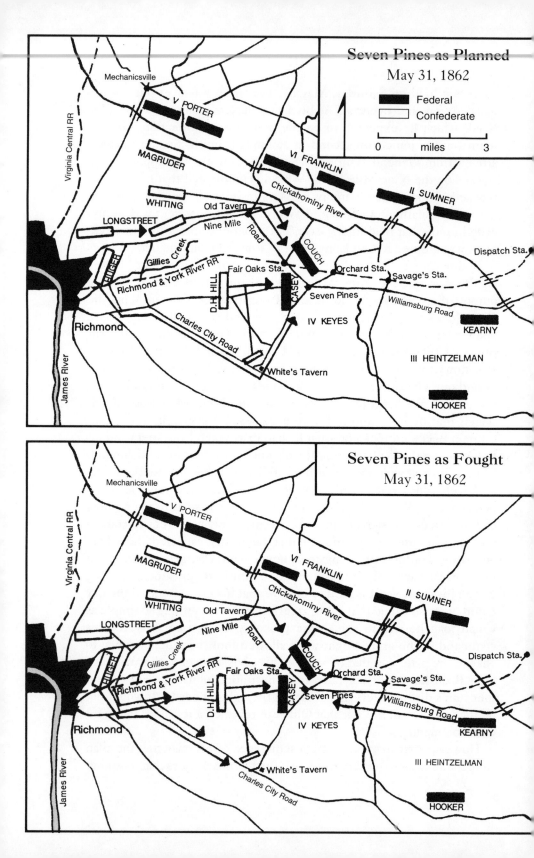

Seven Pines as Planned
May 31, 1862

Federal
Confederate

0   miles   3

Mechanicsville

V PORTER

Virginia Central RR

MAGRUDER

VI FRANKLIN

Chickahominy River

II SUMNER

WHITING

Old Tavern

Nine Mile Road

LONGSTREET

COUCH

Dispatch Sta.

HUGER

Gillies Creek

Richmond & York River RR

Fair Oaks Sta.

Orchard Sta.

Savage's Sta.

D.H. HILL

CASEY

Seven Pines

Williamsburg Road

Richmond

Charles City Road

IV KEYES

KEARNY

James River

White's Tavern

III HEINTZELMAN

HOOKER

Seven Pines as Fought
May 31, 1862

Mechanicsville

V PORTER

Virginia Central RR

MAGRUDER

VI FRANKLIN

Chickahominy River

II SUMNER

WHITING

Old Tavern

Nine Mile Road

LONGSTREET

COUCH

Dispatch Sta.

HUGER

Gillies Creek

Richmond & York River RR

Fair Oaks Sta.

Orchard Sta.

Savage's Sta.

D.H. HILL

CASEY

Seven Pines

Williamsburg Road

Richmond

IV KEYES

KEARNY

James River

White's Tavern

Charles City Road

III HEINTZELMAN

HOOKER

The first of these was Longstreet's choice of a march route for his division. Of the two lateral roads connecting the Nine Mile and Williamsburg roads he might have used to bring him in behind D. H. Hill, one was far enough to the east that it entered the Williamsburg Road beyond the point where the Charles City Road branched off, leaving the way clear for Huger's column. Instead, Longstreet chose the lateral road nearest to Richmond, which put both his and Huger's division on the same few miles of road.

The second mischance was General Huger's rising late on this day of battle. Benjamin Huger came from an old and distinguished South Carolina Huguenot family that pronounced its name in the French manner (*U*-zhay), and in his own manner he was proudly aristocratic. He had been well known in the old army as an ordnance expert, and six months into the war he was named a major general. Huger would be blamed for much that went wrong on May 31, but in truth his only real failing was sleeping late. D. H. Hill recorded that an aide he sent to Huger's camp at daylight found the general and all his officers still in bed.

Huger's three brigades had camped for the night along the Richmond lateral road close by Gillies Creek, which they would have to cross to reach the Williamsburg and then the Charles City roads. His orders were to start out "as early in the morning as possible," but by the time he finally woke and got his men down to Gillies Creek, Longstreet's division had already reached there from the Nine Mile Road and was crossing slowly on an improvised bridge over the creek in flood from the previous night's storm. Huger's orders did not tell him the battle would only open after he relieved D. H. Hill's brigade out on the Charles City Road so that it might join Hill for the attack on the Federal center — Huger in fact only learned there was to be a battle when he talked to Longstreet that morning — and in any event Longstreet claimed (falsely) that he was the senior general of the two and refused to relinquish the right-of-way at the crossing.

The scene took on the look of comic opera. Hour after hour the fuming Huger waited while Longstreet's column inched its way across the creek, and then, once on the Williamsburg Road, Longstreet politely had his men step aside so that Huger's following troops might pass them. It was now 10:00 A.M., and rather than striking at the Yankees over three roads in three parallel columns, the three divisions under Longstreet were now all crowded onto a single road — and were a good four hours behind schedule. All the while General Johnston, watch in hand, was trying to find out what had happened to his battle.

At his outpost on the Williamsburg Road, D. H. Hill was as per-plexed as General Johnston. Harvey Hill was short-tempered and blunt-spoken and easily irritated and he had been primed for battle since sunrise, and as the hours passed and there was no sign of his brigade from the Charles City Road, his impatience boiled over. At 11:00 A.M. he sent to Robert Rodes, commander of the missing bri-gade, to bring his troops across to the Williamsburg Road without waiting any longer for Huger to relieve him. Rodes's men floundered along the muddy forest track and through waist-deep White Oak Swamp as fast as they could, but even before they had all arrived and taken position Hill ordered the signal guns fired and sent his lines forward. It was one o'clock in the afternoon, five hours after the battle's scheduled starting time.[10]

....

THE ARMY of the Potomac's position astride the Chickahominy that day was shaped like a giant fishhook. At the top of the twelve-mile-long shank, at Mechanicsville, was Porter's Fifth Corps. To Porter's left, stretching down the length of the shank and paralleling the river on the north bank, were Franklin's Sixth Corps and then Sumner's Second. The curve of the fishhook crossed the Chickahominy at Bot-tom's Bridge and passed through Heintzelman's two Third Corps divisions on the south bank: Phil Kearny's division guarding Bottom's Bridge and the railroad, and Joe Hooker's on the southern flank facing White Oak Swamp.

Keyes's Fourth Corps formed the barb of the hook. Silas Casey's division was the point, three-quarters of a mile up the Williamsburg Road beyond Seven Pines; behind it Darius Couch's division covered Seven Pines and the Nine Mile Road as far as Fair Oaks Station on the railroad. McClellan had put Heintzelman in overall command of this wing south of the river, with authority over Keyes's corps as well as his own. The general commanding, still basking in Porter's glorious vic-tory at Hanover Court House, believed himself firmly in control of the strategic initiative. The Richmond newspapers were urging Johnston to attack him, McClellan said, but he doubted such an attack was imminent: "I think he is too able for that."

"This country is three-quarters woods, low and swampy — in a word, a most miserable, forelorn looking place," a Union officer wrote. Casey's division had been advanced beyond Seven Pines by the need to hold one of the area's few large clearings, a mile long and half a mile wide, on the Williamsburg Road. A belt of timber along the western face of this clearing was felled to form a tangled abatis, and 500 yards behind this barrier, astride the road, was a line of rifle pits and a rough earthen redoubt for artillery. A thousand yards farther to the rear, at the Seven Pines crossroads, there was another clearing and a second line of rifle pits, also fronted by an abatis, and almost a mile and a half farther back was a third line. McClellan's engineers had laid out these lines only a short while before and they were far from complete when the attack came. Casey's division was equally unready.

Silas Casey was an old regular of thirty-six years' experience who had written an infantry tactics manual and whose role in the war so far had been drillmaster to the Army of the Potomac. His own division was only lately organized and contained the rawest of recruits, and its training, health, and morale were poor. Just four days earlier headquarters had felt obliged to send over an inspector "to examine the extraordinary state of things" in the division. This made Casey's corps commander, Erasmus Keyes, very nervous. On May 30 Keyes warned headquarters that the enemy had again probed sharply at Casey's undermanned line, and he added, "I shall be glad when I learn Gen. Sumner has crossed so as to strengthen my right."

Keyes and Casey, in the aftermath of Seven Pines, would insist that the Confederate attack did not catch them unawares. The capture in midmorning of Lieutenant Washington of Johnston's staff, they said, was only one of the clues that put them on the alert, and it is true enough that they then took certain precautions. Yet their precautions were more suited to defending against a renewal of D. H. Hill's probing reconnaissances of the past two days than to meeting a full-blooded assault, and by no means were all the Yankee troops under arms. No word of warning was sent to the commander of the sector, General Heintzelman. One of Casey's front-line generals, Innis N. Palmer, would admit he was so surprised by the first rush of firing that he had to bolt for safety from his tent, leaving behind his midday meal and all his personal belongings, including a letter just received from his wife. The Confederates' plan may have fallen into confusion and delay, but the operation itself was not compromised.[11]

To the Rebels' good fortune, the Yankees did not have any aerial reconnaissance in operation that morning. Professor Lowe had two balloons stationed north of the Chickahominy on May 31, with a good view of the Richmond suburbs, but because of high winds aloft neither

got into the air before two o'clock in the afternoon, well after the
fighting had started. Even then the countryside south of the river was
too heavily wooded for Lowe to see anything of the battlefield maneuvers, and Federal commanders on the ground gained nothing of value
from the Balloon Corps that day.[12]

Three solid shot that whistled over Casey's camp and landed at the
Seven Pines crossroads signaled the Confederate advance. Harvey Hill
had arranged his brigades in four columns, with Samuel Garland's
brigade leading on the left of the Williamsburg Road, supported by
George B. Anderson, and Rodes's brigade on the right of the road,
backed by Gabriel Rains. Their numbers came to just over 9,000. On
Hill's order the men had fastened bits of white cloth to their caps so
they could distinguish friend from foe.

Rodes had not quite gotten his late-arriving men into line when the
impatient Hill ordered the advance, so at first Garland carried the
assault alone. Samuel Garland was new to command, having replaced
Jubal Early, wounded at Williamsburg. In line of battle with a battalion
of Mississippians in the lead in skirmish formation, Garland's troops
pushed forward through the thick woods. There was no preliminary
artillery bombardment. Thomas Learn of the 85th New York, posted
in Casey's picket line, saw a squad of men in butternut appear suddenly and trot silently past the thicket where he was concealed. Without delay, Private Learn remembered, "I left the place and took a
course to get away. . . ."

He and the other Yankee pickets fell back, yelling the alarm. The
103rd Pennsylvania, ordered forward earlier as a precaution, had just
taken position behind the picket line when the woods in front erupted
in a sheet of flame. These Pennsylvania boys were among the rawest
in Casey's division and they had never been under fire before, and
they panicked. Hardly pausing to return fire they broke for the rear,
clambering over the abatis, and ran for safety. Garland pushed after
them to the edge of the cleared ground and struck Casey's main
defenses.

Directly in front of Garland's men, 200 yards beyond the abatis, was
a battery of 3-inch rifled guns supported by four regiments of infantry,
with a second battery on the flank farther to the rear. They were also
within range of the guns in the redoubt just south of the road, and with
Rodes on the right not yet caught up with the advance, all this Yankee
fire focused on them. "The balls were falling around us as thick as hale
all the time," Leonidas Torrence of the 23rd North Carolina wrote

home. "It did not look like there was any chance for a man to go through them without being hit." A bullet snipped his coat and shirt sleeve, and a cannon shot narrowly missed his head and struck the trunk of a large pine tree, which "did not appear to check the Ball at all." Losses mounted rapidly on both sides. The 23rd North Carolina would suffer 169 casualties this day, including its colonel, lieutenant colonel, and major all wounded, the last mortally. "It was a verry distressing place," Private Torrence concluded. Garland's supporting brigade under George B. Anderson now joined them and Rodes too came up on the right, and the battle widened.[13]

The advance of Anderson's fresh brigade overlapped the Federals north of the Williamsburg Road and endangered Captain Joseph Spratt's rifled battery, which was posted farthest to the front. To allow the battery to withdraw, General Casey ordered a counterattack by its supporting infantry. Their charge, he said, "would have honored veteran troops," but the Confederate fire was hitting them now in flank as well in as in front, and they were repulsed and had to retreat along with the battery. Captain Spratt lost one of his guns in the confusion. James Carr of the 56th New York believed that had they remained five minutes longer everyone in his regiment would have been shot or captured. He was halfway across the field when he heard a wounded comrade calling after him, and he ran back and dragged the man to safety. Like North Carolina's Leonidas Torrence, James Carr remembered the bullets in this part of the field flying thick as hail. "I came out safe with a hole in my cap . . . ," he wrote. "This is what I call pretty close work. . . ."

General Hill had sent two batteries forward along the Williamsburg Road to support his offensive, but the first to reach the field was heavily outgunned by the Federal artillery and forced to retire. When Virginian Thomas H. Carter's King William Artillery reached the scene, however, enough of the Yankee guns had been driven back by the infantry attack that he could challenge on more equal terms. Carter first aimed his fire at a column of infantry seen coming up from the rear — these were some of Couch's men called to the front — and drove it off into the woods. Then he turned his five guns on the Yankee redoubt. In the ensuing duel Captain Carter saw his brother manning one of the guns shot through the chest, and he sent him to the rear without hope of seeing him alive again.

The redoubt and the nearby rifle pits now became the focus of the Confederate assault. At the head of Rodes's brigade was the 6th Alabama under Colonel John B. Gordon, and Gordon would remember the enemy fire on this day being as murderous as any he experienced in the war. One of those facing the Alabamians was Corporal William E. Dunn of the 85th New York, who wrote home that when the Rebels charged his line "they were mown down like grass before the sythe. . . . No men could stand before such a fire." Dunn's was a deadly accurate simile. Colonel Gordon listed every one of his field officers killed; he alone survived after his horse was killed under him. The 6th Alabama took 632 men into the fight that afternoon and 259 survived unhurt, a casualty rate of 59 percent. (At the same time as Captain Carter, Colonel Gordon saw his own brother off to the rear with an apparently mortal wound. Both brothers would somehow survive their severe injuries.)

Bryan Grimes's 4th North Carolina was another of the Confederate regiments taking heavy losses from the fire of the Yankee redoubt. One of his officers went up to Major Grimes, who was sitting his horse in the din, tugged at his pants leg to get his attention and pleaded, "Major, we can't stand this. Let us charge the works." That seemed to Grimes a sensible solution. "All right. Charge them! Charge them!" he yelled, and led the assault himself. A cannon shot from the redoubt took off his horse's head and in falling the stricken animal pinned Grimes to the ground, but he continued to wave his sword and to urge on his men. Finally he was pulled free, and picking up the regiment's fallen battle flag he led the rest of the charge on foot. Stephen R. Mallory, the Confederacy's secretary of the navy, was watching the charge and became so caught up in the excitement that he joined in the Rebel yell, "as exhilirated as if I had just swallowed a bottle of champaigne."

These various storming parties, combined with a flanking attack by Gabriel Rains's brigade, at last became too much for the Yankee defenders, and they broke for the rear. Casey's artillery chief, Colonel Guilford Bailey, was shot through the head as he tried to spike the guns in the redoubt, and all six of the pieces were captured intact. It was three o'clock now and Casey's first line of defense was entirely gone. The Rebels pressed on toward the second line, at Seven Pines.[14]

. . . .

AS THE STRUGGLE on the Williamsburg Road grew rapidly in intensity, the high commands of both armies reacted in a kind of slow motion. There was uncertainty about the fighting and how serious it was, and there were difficulties with communications.

At 1:30 P.M. General Heintzelman, learning nothing from the front to explain the sounds of musketry he was hearing, had sent two of his staff forward to investigate. His headquarters, at Savage's Station on the railroad, was connected by telegraph to Army of the Potomac headquarters across the river at New Bridge, and within a few minutes he received a query about the firing from General McClellan. The commanding general had been suffering for several days from the effects of malaria and was resting as quietly as possible in his tent, with no wish to face a battle. While waiting for Heintzelman's reply, he ordered General Sumner to be ready to advance the Second Corps across the river if his help should be needed.

Bull Sumner was still smarting from criticism of his handling of the Williamsburg battle, and he was determined there be no further question about his willingness to fight. Rather than simply alerting his troops and issuing ammunition, he marched them right up to the two bridges on his front and kept them standing in ranks, ready to cross the moment orders came from headquarters. Old Sumner was reacting to the sound of battle the way a veteran fire horse reacted to the smell of smoke.

Keyes was very slow to get word of the attack back to his superior, and as late as 2:30 P.M. army headquarters had a telegram from Heintzelman saying, "No report has been received from Genl Keyes yet, therefore I presume there is nothing serious." But the rising sound of battle was leading Heintzelman to suspect otherwise, and he alerted Phil Kearny of the Third Corps to send reinforcements forward. A few minutes later his two aides returned to report that Keyes's front line, Casey's division, "was being driven in." Heintzelman forwarded this report to McClellan and then set off for the front himself. At last, at three o'clock, as the fighting was entering its third hour, Bull Sumner received McClellan's telegraphed order to march to the battlefield.

On the Confederate side, mischance continued to plague Joe Johnston and his plan. It seemed that everyone for miles around learned of the battle raging at Seven Pines before General Johnston did. People in Richmond to the west heard the musketry. McClellan and Sumner across the Chickahominy heard it, and so did Heintzelman to the east. But Johnston heard nothing. Toward noon he had moved out the Nine Mile Road to Old Tavern, and by a freakish combination of atmospheric conditions having to do with layers of air of different densities — the clouds were low and leaden gray with moisture and it had grown warm and muggy — an "acoustic shadow" fanned out that afternoon in a narrow cone north-northwest from Seven Pines and fell across Johnston's field headquarters hardly two and a half miles away. It so muffled the sounds of the struggle that Johnston believed nothing more than a sporadic artillery duel was taking place. Until someone arrived from the front to tell him, the general commanding the Army of Northern Virginia did not know that his battle had commenced — and the battle would be three hours old before he was told.

Meanwhile James Longstreet was managing the independent command he had arranged with surprising indecisiveness. Following the hours-long entanglement with Huger's division, he had split his own division in half, keeping three brigades on the Williamsburg Road and sending the other three out the Charles City Road. Of the three on the Williamsburg Road, only one went into action to support D. H. Hill, and Longstreet himself look no direct part in the battle there. "Hill is on the ground and knows his business," he said. On the Charles City Road, the scene once again took on the look of comic opera.

Longstreet had directed Huger to march out the Charles City Road to a point opposite Seven Pines and wait there for further orders. Those orders never came, and none of Huger's 7,000 men fired a shot on May 31. At the same time, on the same road, Longstreet's three brigades were marching and countermarching as the general tried to decide what to do with them. Captain James McMath of the 11th Alabama, whose regiment had been shifted back and forth like this at Yorktown during Prince John Magruder's charade, wondered if they were somehow trying to fool the Yankees again.

The 11th Alabama would be one of just two regiments (out of ten) in this force to see action at Seven Pines before nightfall. Captain McMath carefully recorded all the day's marching in his diary, including the final march: "We went again towards the battlefield at quick time over the worst road I ever saw . . . & when we arrived on the field our men were much exhausted. . . ." Of the 29,500 men in the three divisions under his command that day, Longstreet managed to get just 12,500 into the Seven Pines battle. [15]

As for Silas Casey's division, its failed defense of the first line of entrenchments finished it as an effective force. The rookies of the 103rd Pennsylvania had run at the first fire and heavy straggling drained other regiments, but perhaps two-thirds of the 6,200 men on duty in the division that day stood and fought, at least for a time. Now they had had enough, and great numbers of them did not stop at the second line of defense at Seven Pines but hurried on toward the rear. General Heintzelman and other officers eventually managed to rally some of them, but Heintzelman warned headquarters that the division could no longer be relied on. A column of Third Corps reinforcements found the road so crowded with stragglers from the front that the men had to fix bayonets to force their way though. Part of the 3rd Michigan was deployed as a provost guard and in an hour collected a thousand fugitives, most of them Casey's men. It was said that another thousand escaped across the Chickahominy.

The battle at Seven Pines was now carried on by Darius Couch's division and by two of Phil Kearny's brigades from the Third Corps. A major problem for the Federals in this fighting was disjointed command. From the outset regiments from different brigades were intermixed in meeting the crisis, and there was confusion over who should be obeyed. In the absence of their own brigade commanders regiments tended to advance or retreat according to the best judgment of their colonels. At one point General Casey called on the 10th Massachusetts of Couch's division to come to his aid, but its colonel refused to advance without orders from his own general. Later General Keyes happened by and the Massachusetts colonel agreed to accept the corps commander's order to advance.

Early in the fighting General Couch led a counterattack personally, was repulsed and cut off, and with Rebels after him "at a full run" had to beat a retreat to Fair Oaks Station a mile away. For the rest of the day Couch's division fought at Seven Pines without its general. Corps commanders Keyes and Heintzelman were leading from up front by necessity, and both generals had their horses hit and narrowly escaped injury themselves. (D. H. Hill also exposed himself to the enemy's fire this day, but he did so deliberately. "I saw that our men were wavering," he explained, "and I wanted to give them confidence.")[16]

In this struggle for the second line of Federal defenses, Robert Rodes's brigade south of the Williamsburg Road was pitted against a brigade of Couch's and a reinforcing brigade from Phil Kearny's division, and the result was a bloody stalemate in which neither side could gain advantage. In addition to his three Alabama regiments and one from Mississippi, Rodes had a regiment of Virginians originally trained as artillerymen whose particular skills now became very useful. Rodes posted the Virginians in the captured redoubt, where they turned Casey's guns around and fired them at the Yankees. Captain Carter brought his battery forward to add to the Confederate artillery display. There was a fierce struggle for the tangled abatis between the battle lines, with Brigadier Charles D. Jameson telling the 63rd Pennsylvania,

"Go in there and don't come out until you have driven every Rebel out of that brush!" Any depressions in the ground were filled with water from the storm, and wounded men had to be propped up by their comrades so they would not drown.

Even the men in combat for the first time saw how costly straight-ahead frontal assaults against enemy battle lines were likely to be, and any sort of flanking approach found favor with the attackers. One of Couch's men, Lieutenant George E. Hager of the 10th Massachusetts, recorded with graphic simplicity what it was like to face a flanking attack: "So we filed into an open space in the slashing, our left resting in the woods. We had not been there long when they came upon our flank & fired a raking fire across our line. The men had no chance & were obliged to run. Here Capt. Parsons was wounded & many others. It was a terrible fire." General Longstreet would remark that day, rather more indelicately, on the same phenomenon. Any flanking fire, he said, "was exceedingly annoying, particularly with fresh troops, who were always as sensitive about the flanks as a virgin."[17]

Joe Johnston had designed his battle to gain victory by flanking attacks on both the left and the right, but now D. H. Hill was wondering how it could all have gone so wrong. Only his division, in the center, was doing any fighting. There was no sign of a flanking column coming up from the Charles City Road to the south. There was no sound of battle from the Nine Mile Road to the north. Even Gabriel Rains of his own division seemed overcome by caution and would not repeat his flank movement that had helped turn Casey's Yankees out of their first line. "Had my boys been supported," Hill would tell his wife, the enemy "would have been driven like chaff before the wind."

Hill determined on a new flanking movement of his own to maintain his offensive. He sent Colonel Micah Jenkins, who had just reached him with reinforcements from Longstreet, to the extreme left "to scour along the railroad and the Nine-mile road, and thus get in rear of the enemy. . . ." At 3:00 P.M., leading the Palmetto Sharpshooters and the 6th South Carolina, and picking up the 27th Georgia from Hill's division on the way, Jenkins set off on his adventure. Captain Thomas Goree of Longstreet's staff would write, with pardonable pride, that in the next few hours Jenkins's command "*immortalized* itself."

Swinging northward almost as far as Fair Oaks Station on the railroad and then turning southward across the Nine Mile Road to strike the Williamsburg Road well behind the Federal second line at Seven Pines, Colonel Jenkins (as Goree calculated it) "fought 5 separate & distinct lines of the enemy, whipping each one. . . . He passed over several abattis of felled timber, 2 lines of breastworks, captured . . . 250 prisoners & several stands of colors."

What made Jenkins's three regiments seem so imposing — a fourth, the 5th South Carolina, came up to reinforce him near the end of his march — was that each Yankee force they encountered was of a size they could successfully attack — and attack was their unfailing tactic. Much of their movement was concealed by the thick woods, and the first enemy met, the 23rd and 61st Pennsylvania regiments of Couch's division, was caught by surprise and wrecked in just twenty minutes. The 23rd Pennsylvania lost 129 men and the 61st Pennsylvania 263 (out of 574), including its colonel and most of his field officers. A party of the Palmetto Sharpshooters, 47 men strong, surprised a Yankee picket post and came away with 139 prisoners.

Colonel Jenkins, a twenty-six-year-old graduate of The Citadel in South Carolina who was demonstrating a pure instinct for fighting, continued to drive his men forward and to catch one Federal unit and then another unprepared. Sometimes the fighting lines were seventy-five yards apart, sometimes only thirty or forty yards. Jenkins kept attacking and the Yankees kept falling back in disorganization before him.

It was toward dusk when Jenkins reached the Williamsburg Road. The moment this force of Rebels was reported behind them, the shocked Yankee defenders of the Seven Pines line scattered for safety as best they could — it seemed that an enemy to the rear was worse even than an enemy on the flank. A considerable number of Couch's men and Kearny's had to march off southward toward White Oak Swamp to avoid being trapped, and a Pennsylvania battery lost one of its guns in the retreat. It was the eighth gun lost by the Yankees that day.

A new Federal line, the third of the day, was finally established on the Williamsburg Road a mile and a half in rear of Seven Pines. "Thus at 7:40 P.M. we closed our busy day," Jenkins wrote in his report of the action, "the last seen of the enemy being his broken and disordered squads of from 5 to 20, visible for one-half mile over an extensive wheat field." Jenkins had taken only 1,900 men into the fight and had lost 700 of them, but he had changed the face of the battle.[18]

....

IN RICHMOND the mutter of gunfire grew steadily louder as the afternoon advanced. Rooftops and church belfrys were crowded with spectators listening to the guns and watching the clouds of battle smoke rise slowly against the leaden sky to the east. Stragglers and walking wounded from the battlefield were pressed for news. On Main Street and Broad Street and in Capitol Square rumor was the common coin. "I again went among the excited crowds in the streets & in the halls of the hotels, & also we went to the War Office, to gather the latest rumors of the battle," Edmund Ruffin wrote in his journal that night. "They were too many, & too variant, to be noted," and he added, "There was much carnage on both sides."

Hardly more was known of the battle at Joe Johnston's field headquarters in a farmhouse overlooking the Nine Mile Road. The atmosphere there was quiet but thick with tension. General Lee had ridden out from Richmond to offer what assistance he could, but Johnston was grimly determined to fight his own battle and volunteered little of his plans. Lee ventured the opinion that on his ride he had heard sounds of battle off to the south, but Johnston insisted it was merely some artillery firing. There had been no word at all from Longstreet since he was located at midmorning on the Williamsburg Road.

In midafternoon, with rising impatience, Johnston sent off yet another aide to find out what was happening. Finally, at four o'clock, news of the battle came to him in a rush, as both his aide and a courier from Longstreet arrived at the same time. The aide reported a heavy engagement at Seven Pines, with the Confederates getting the better of it. Longstreet added confirmation. In several hours of severe fighting the Federals had been defeated, he said, but he complained of heavy losses and the lack of any supporting attack by way of the Nine Mile Road. Even now, late as it was, he would welcome help for his exposed left flank, and to emphasize the point he added his tart remark about the troops being as sensitive about the flanks as a virgin. Armed at last with authentic intelligence, General Johnston hurried into action.

G. W. Smith's division, under Chase Whiting, originally intended to back up Longstreet's offensive along the Nine Mile Road, was waiting nearby in reserve at Old Tavern, and Johnston ordered it forward as a substitute left-wing attack. To make sure that nothing further went wrong, he would ride with Whiting himself.

Just after Johnston headed off southward from his headquarters, Jefferson Davis rode up from the other direction. Johnston's staff whispered that the general was no doubt happy to have avoided meeting the president, with whom relations had been decidedly cool. Mr. Davis told General Lee that all the way out from Richmond he had been hearing the sound of musketry. What did it mean? Lee explained what little he knew of events, and then he and the president joined Whiting's troops crowding toward the battlefield. "It is scarcely necessary to add," Davis later wrote bitterly, "that neither of us had been advised of a design to attack the enemy that day."

As Whiting's lead brigade, under Evander M. Law, neared Fair Oaks Station, it was unexpectedly hit by a barrage of shells from a battery of long-range guns posted a thousand yards off to the left and rear. Whiting brought the column to a halt and deployed Law's brigade to contend with this threat, but Johnston rebuked him for his caution. The Yankees could not be in any real force this far from Seven Pines, he said, and certainly none could have crossed the flooded Chickahominy. Then Law's men advanced against the battery, and a solid line of Federal infantry rose up and poured a killing fire into them. They fell back into the woods in confusion, pursued by shells from the battery. Clearly the Yankees were here in some force, and clearly Whiting had a fight on his hands.

This opening fire in the contest for Fair Oaks Station came from a pickup force of Federals to the strength of a brigade that just then was feeling very lonely and threatened. The 65th New York and 31st Pennsylvania, with Captain James Brady's Pennsylvania battery of Parrott rifles, had started the day here as the right-flank outpost of Couch's division, standing guard at the station. The 7th Massachusetts and the 62nd New York had arrived more recently, as a consequence of a failed counterattack early in the fighting at Seven Pines. Along with General Couch they had been forced to seek safety at the station, and now Couch was hoping to buy time enough for reinforcements to arrive which he had been promised were on the way. Providentially the head of the relief column now came into sight half a mile away, and, Couch wrote, "I felt that God was with us and victory ours."[19]

This relieving column was from John Sedgwick's division of the Second Corps, and simply getting that far had been an adventure. It was 3:00 P.M. when General Sumner had received McClellan's order to march to the battlefield. Sedgwick's division was already lined up ready to cross the river on the Grapevine Bridge; Israel Richardson's division was at Sumner's Lower Bridge, a mile and a half downstream. The Chickahominy, thick with reddish mud, was booming past in full flood. The bridge causeways were under water and the main spans were twisting and wrenching loose and about to break up and float away in the torrent, and an engineer rushed up to the corps commander at the Grapevine Bridge and warned him, "General Sumner, you cannot cross this bridge!"

Bull Sumner had been in the army forty-three years and had seen it all, and no upstart engineer officer was coming between him and his duty. "Can't cross this bridge!" he roared. "I can, sir; I will, sir!" But the bridge was breaking up before their eyes, the engineer said; it would be impossible to make it to the other side. "Impossible!" Sumner roared, "Sir, I tell you I *can* cross. I am ordered!" That closed the debate, and Sedgwick's men started across.

Their crossing was slow and perilous. "To get through our artillery seemed impossible," observed Captain William Sedgwick, the general's brother. "Men went in up to their waists; horses floundered and fell down." The Lower Bridge soon collapsed and was swept away, and Richardson's division had to shift over to the Grapevine crossing. Somehow that structure held together, kept in place on its piers by the weight of the marching columns. Just one of Sumner's batteries, Lieutenant Edmund Kirby's Battery I, 1st United States Artillery, made it across, and then one of Kirby's six guns bogged down hopelessly in a swamp on the other side. But the infantry slogged on steadily through the flood and the mud. One Yankee soldier called it "the most damnable bog I ever went through, clear up to our knees in solid mud."

It was three miles from the Grapevine Bridge's northern approach to Couch's position at Fair Oaks, and the first of Sedgwick's men did not reach there much before 5:30, but that proved soon enough. A man in the 15th Massachusetts in Sedgwick's lead brigade summed it up nicely in a letter home: "After a hard march through swamps and mud we arrived on the ground just in time to save the day, and a second Bull Run. . . ."

The Bull Run analogy had particular meaning for Lieutenant Kirby's Battery I, for in that battle of the year before the regulars had lost all their guns and twenty-seven of their gunners, and they had some paying back to do. Kirby went into battery on a low rise in front of a peach orchard and opened fire on the Rebels with what one observer called "astonishing rapidity." The chaplain of the 1st Minnesota remembered that at Fair Oaks the guns of Battery I "sounded like the incessant pounding in some great steam-boiler shop. . . ." In this fight the Yankee artillery — Kirby's five Napoleons and Brady's four Parrotts — would prove a decisive factor, for in yet another of the mischances confounding the Confederates this day, Chase Whiting failed to advance any of his own batteries to the front and had to fight entirely without artillery support.

The Yankee guns took a murderous toll, especially when firing canister. When Captain Brady ran short of canister, he had his gunners fire shell and case-shot without fuzes, so that like canister they burst leaving the muzzles with the lethal effect of giant shotguns. At each discharge the recoil drove the pieces deep into the mud, and the artillerymen had to call on infantry volunteers to help drag them free. Lieutenant Kirby recorded that his five guns fired 343 rounds at the enemy on May 31, "a tremendous fire . . . which they were unable to stand." So far as he and the men of Battery I were concerned, Bull Run was avenged.[20]

Whiting put three more brigades into the widening struggle at Fair Oaks, throwing them one after another against a Federal position growing steadily stronger as more of Sedgwick's men came up from the river crossing. By nightfall Couch and Sedgwick between them had 10,700 men in action, a substantial edge over the 8,700 Whiting brought to the fight.

The ground for 800 yards in front of the Federals was mostly open and slightly rolling and the Rebels attacked straight ahead in line-of-battle formation, with little attempt at flanking maneuvers. Like Colonel Gordon earlier at Seven Pines, Whiting's men would never forget the fire they faced that day. Thomas Herndon of the 14th Tennessee remembered how they "fought and scratched our way to within twenty to forty yards of the enemy's line, when they gave us the deadliest volley we received all during the war." Ben Coleman of the same regiment told his parents how a piece of shell hit him and "it knocked me down as flat as if I had been struck with an axe," and he said that all that saved him was his haversack "which was filled with hard crackers."

A Confederate staff officer, Major Joseph Brent, watched Wade Hampton's brigade — Georgians, North Carolinians, and Hampton's own South Carolina Legion — make its attack. Hampton led them in careful alignment from the Nine Mile Road over a low rise and through a patch of woods and across fields and through a swampy pond full of fallen tree trunks "sleek as eels," as one man put it. Major Brent heard the gunfire rise to a crescendo, and then he saw the men running back across the fields and through the trees in increasing numbers. "The victorious enemy did not show himself," he wrote, "but a constant stream of rifle and artillery fire made the retreat a rapid one."

The scene was repeated with the brigades of Robert Hatton and James J. Pettigrew, with the same result. One of Sedgwick's men later came upon a neat rank of Rebel dead, killed by a single volley, "their heels on the very spot where they stood and fought." All three brigade commanders were hit — Hampton wounded, Pettigrew wounded and captured, Hatton killed. The Federals' line was unbroken, and in the growing darkness they began spontaneous counterattacks.

The 20th Massachusetts's Captain Oliver Wendell Holmes, the future Supreme Court justice, tracked the progress of the fighting by the lines of bright flame as the men fired on command, "splendid and awful to behold." Another 20th Massachusetts man, Lieutenant Henry Ropes, had a similar impression. "The noise was terrific . . . ," he wrote, "the whole scene dark with smoke and lit up by the streams of fire from our battery and from our infantry in line on each side." Finally the firing died out as it became too dark to see anything. The fruitless series of assaults cost Whiting 1,270 men. The Federal loss was but 468.[21]

Few battles ever go entirely as their generals plan them, but seldom does a battle stray so far from plan as Seven Pines on May 31, 1862. General Johnston intended twenty-two of his infantry brigades to assault the Federals south of the Chickahominy that day. Instead, just nine brigades and part of a tenth did all the fighting; better than 30,000 men who were supposed to join the battle did not fire a shot. He intended a coordinated three-pronged offensive against the front and flanks of the enemy. Instead, two separate and distinct battles were fought, entirely without coordination. He intended to cut off and overwhelm the left wing of the Army of the Potomac before it could be reinforced. Instead, the battle only opened long after it was supposed to close, and the Federals, while driven back two and a half miles, were not overwhelmed and were substantially reinforced from across the river. For the Confederates the cost of this bungled, tangled day of fighting added up to 5,002 men, with the most notable single casualty occurring just at dusk on the Nine Mile Road.

Joe Johnston had elected to observe Whiting's battle from a knoll 200 yards north of Fair Oaks Station and well within range of the Yankee guns. One of the young staff officers with him instinctively ducked whenever a bullet sang past, but Johnston, a veteran of hostile fire in the old army and five times wounded by it, laughed and told him, "Colonel, there is no use of dodging; when you hear them they have passed." A moment later the general was struck in the right shoulder by a bullet, and a moment after that a shell exploded directly in front of him and a large fragment slammed into his chest with force enough to knock him off his horse.

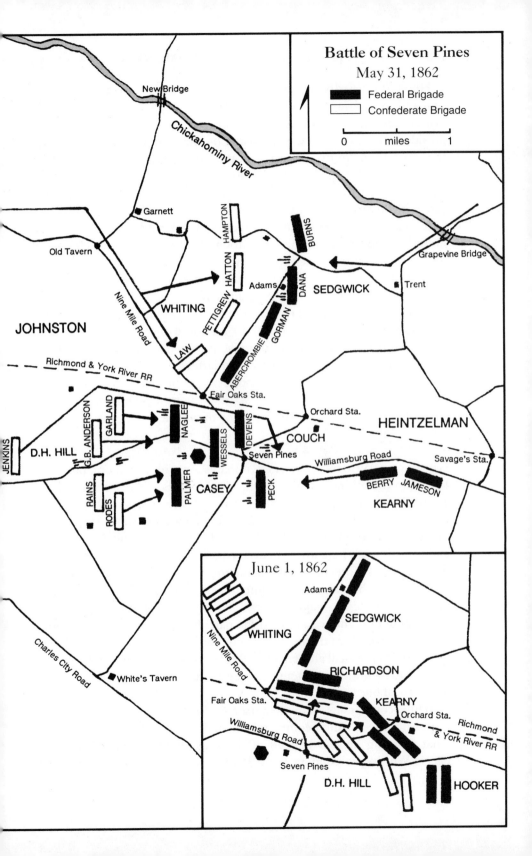

Battle of Seven Pines
May 31, 1862

■ Federal Brigade
□ Confederate Brigade

0   miles   1

New Bridge

Chickahominy River

Grapevine Bridge

Garnett

HAMPTON

BURNS

Old Tavern

PETTIGREW HATTON

Adams

DANA

SEDGWICK

Trent

WHITING

Nine Mile Road

LAW

GORMAN

JOHNSTON

ABERCROMBIE

Richmond & York River RR

Fair Oaks Sta.

Orchard Sta.

HEINTZELMAN

GARLAND

NAGLEE

DEVENS

COUCH

G.B. ANDERSON

JENKINS

D.H. HILL

WESSELS

Seven Pines

Williamsburg Road

Savage's Sta.

RAINS

PALMER

CASEY

PECK

BERRY

JAMESON

RODES

KEARNY

June 1, 1862

Adams

SEDGWICK

WHITING

Nine Mile Road

RICHARDSON

Charles City Road

White's Tavern

Fair Oaks Sta.

KEARNY

Orchard Sta.

Richmond & York River RR

Williamsburg Road

Seven Pines

D.H. HILL

HOOKER

His staff hurriedly carried him up the Nine Mile Road to a sheltered spot and sought out stretcher bearers. Johnston regained consciousness just as President Davis arrived to commiserate with him. No doubt the president was as shocked as Johnston by the turn of events. This was the second time in two months that the Confederacy had witnessed an army commander struck down in the midst of a battle, and Davis could only hope that this time the wound was not mortal, as had been the case with Albert Sidney Johnston at Shiloh back in April.

Johnston discovered that his brace of pistols and his sword, which his father had carried in the Revolution, were not with him. He asked if someone would go back for them, expressing particular concern for the sword. "I would not lose it for ten thousand dollars," he said. One of his couriers, Drury L. Armistead, raced back to the scene of the wounding, now under increasing enemy fire, and managed to retrieve both the pistols and the sword. In gratitude the general presented young Armistead with one of the pistols. Stretcher bearers then bore him, in great pain, back to his headquarters, and later that night he was carried to Richmond. His wounds were not fatal, but they were serious enough that he required six months to recover. Joe Johnston would never again serve with the Army of Northern Virginia.[22]

....

Gustavus Woodson Smith remains one of the more puzzling figures in the military history of the Confederacy. A West Pointer with a capable but limited record in the war with Mexico, Smith had given up the army in 1854 for a career in civil engineering, becoming Commissioner of Streets in New York City. He was a Kentuckian by birth and like his state he chose a neutral course early in the war, and it was five months before he declared for the Confederacy. He arrived in Richmond with qualifications more imagined than real and was immediately appointed a major general, perhaps because in his bluff and self-confident manner he looked the part. From the first his health was suspect, however, and Porter Alexander of Johnston's staff termed him "a martyr to physical ailments which greatly reduced his energy. . . ." In fact G. W. Smith's ailments derived more from his mental state than his physical one.

While courageous enough personally, simply the thought of the responsibilities of high command seemed to unnerve General Smith. That morning he had begged off leading his own division, leaving Chase Whiting to conduct the fighting and acting instead only as an adviser. Then at 8:30 that night, as senior officer on the field, he found himself abruptly in command of the Army of Northern Virginia.

President Davis wanted to know his plans. Smith's is the only account of their meeting, at which General Lee was also present, but it is evident that he did not make a good impression on the president. He tried to explain what he knew of Johnston's battle plan and how that plan had gone awry, and said he "could not determine, understandingly, what was best to be done" until he learned Longstreet's situation. Could Mr. Davis tell him anything of what had taken place that day at Seven Pines?

Smith's plea for information was certainly understandable, yet his labored explanation did not inspire confidence. Perhaps, he said, he could hold his ground and resume the battle; perhaps he would have to fall back; he was not sure which was the better course. His hesitant, indecisive speech belied his usual self-confident manner. "Mr. Davis did not seem pleased with what I said," he admitted. President Davis and General Lee rode back to Richmond over the dark roads. Smith would have to see the present battle through, Davis decided, but no more than that. The army must have a new commander.[23]

General McClellan had meanwhile risen from his sickbed at army headquarters at New Bridge and ridden five miles closer to the battle, to Second Corps headquarters north of the river. Exhausted from the effects of his malaria, he lay on a cot there and attempted to follow events by telegraph. In his journal the Comte de Paris recorded how painful it was to watch the general trying to marshal his remaining energy to chart a course and issue orders. McClellan's primary concern that night was bridging the Chickahominy so as to link his divided army. He roused himself to ride in the darkness to Dispatch Station on the railroad to meet Heintzelman for a first-hand account of the fighting, then returned to the Second Corps camp. Everyone on the headquarters staff, the young Frenchman wrote, "thought the battle lost and badly lost."

The men of the two armies passed the night as best they could. The black woods seemed lit by bright fireflies as stretcher bearers with lanterns searched out the wounded. Lieutenant Henry Abbott of the 20th Massachusetts noted approvingly that wounded prisoners were treated kindly by his men, although to his eye the Rebels were an unsoldierly lot. "They were horrible looking devils," he wrote, "lank, long haired, clad in a nasty brick colored stuff that a beggar in the North would be ashamed to wear. . . ." The dead were left where they fell. The 5th New Hampshire, which reached Fair Oaks Station after the fighting there ended, took position along the railroad in the darkness and was told to sleep on its arms. "Some dark forms lay around which might have been the dead," Thomas Livermore remembered, "but I chose to lie down and not search." Reconnoitering the area, the 5th New Hampshire's commander, Edward E. Cross, came upon a tent off to the side and called out for the name of the regiment. It was headquarters for a Texas regiment, came back the answer, and Colonel Cross quietly moved on. Before the night was over, the colonel would make a prisoner of a Rebel courier who rode up to him in the darkness to ask for directions.

The lines were not so close together on the Williamsburg Road, and the Rebels there made the best of their capture of the camps of Casey's division. D. H. Hill took General Casey's tent for his lodging that night. A Louisianian in Longstreet's division described his good fortune in a letter home: "I had the pleasure of drinking General Caseys coffee, eating his ham, drinking his claret and sleeping in one of his regimental tents. . . ." Several barrels of liberated whiskey were quickly disposed of. Private John Tucker of the 5th Alabama recorded in his diary the same sort of booty, and added, "Most of the Boys exchanged their Guns for better ones." General Hill would report to Richmond that 6,700 Federal small arms were collected in the area of Seven Pines. Federal casualties on that part of the field had totaled 3,358, suggesting that fully half the captures were from stragglers who had thrown down their rifles in their flight.[24]

In the small hours of the morning — it was now Sunday, June 1 — General Smith decided to carry on the battle. He told Longstreet to pick up the advance where it had left off on the Williamsburg Road, but this time to turn to the north, toward the railroad, rather than continuing eastward. Whiting's division on the Nine Mile Road would join the fighting once Longstreet's attack "was fully developed." The action was to open as soon as it was light.

The Federals positioned themselves during the night to meet just the sort of offensive Smith was planning. Sedgwick's division held its lines facing west toward the Nine Mile Road. The other Second Corps division under Israel Richardson, which had reached Fair Oaks too late on May 31 to join the contest, was posted along the railroad tracks facing south. Troops from Kearny's and Hooker's Third Corps divisions formed a link with Richardson and blocked the Williamsburg Road at what on the day before had been the Yankees' last line of defense. At first light old Sumner rode the lines and told his men to be ready. "If they come out here, give 'em the bayonet!" he said in a voice loud enough for a whole brigade to hear. "Give 'em the bayonet, they can't stand that."

The Confederates' second-day offensive began on schedule but soon bogged down. This time Longstreet put in troops he had held out of the battle the day before — four of his own brigades and two of Huger's — but they could make little headway, especially in the thick woods between the Williamsburg Road and the railroad. It was exceedingly difficult for men on either side to see what they were shooting at, and at one point two Virginia regiments opened fire on each other. Colonel Cross sent the 5th New Hampshire into action with the cry, "Charge them like hell, boys! Show 'em you *are* damned Yankees!" and Thomas Livermore dutifully fired into the smoky woods where he supposed the enemy to be, but he had no real idea whether he hit anyone.

Yet there was no doubt that the enemy was there. Stray bullets showered leaves and twigs down on the Yankees and better-aimed bullets found their marks. In a neighboring regiment, the 61st New York, Colonel Francis Barlow reported that "a most violent firing began on both sides. . . . In about three minutes men were dying and groaning and running about with faces shot and arms shot, and it was an awful sight." One of every ten men in the 61st New York would die in this morning's fight. The brigade commander, O. O. Howard, was among the wounded. (General Howard's right arm had to be amputated, and the next day Phil Kearny, who had lost his left arm in the Mexican War, consoled him. "General, I am sorry for you, but you must not mind it; the ladies will not think the less of you!" Howard laughed and observed that at least the two of them could now buy their gloves together. "Sure enough!" Kearny said with a grin, and the two generals shook hands on it with the hands left to them.)[25]

Benjamin Huger's troops had so far in the war seen only comfortable garrison duty in Norfolk, with no field experience at all, and now in their first time under fire they gave way in confusion. D. H. Hill was again in tactical command — "You have here taken the bull by the horns and must fight him out," Longstreet told Hill that morning and rode away — and he was ungentle with the fugitives. After the first of Huger's brigades "was stampeded about sunrise," as Hill put it, he ordered the second one in its place, and soon it too came streaming back. As the men cowered in a ditch the general railed at them and called them cowards. William Mahone, the brigade commander, protested Hill's language and told him it was he who had ordered the troops back, at which Hill turned his considerable wrath on Mahone. "Little Billy" Mahone, thin as a fence rail but large of temper, "fairly foamed" at this rebuke and for a time debated challenging Hill to a duel. Hill meanwhile pushed another brigade into the gap in his line and concluded that this battle was going nowhere and would have to be broken off.

Farther to the east, on the Williamsburg Road, Joe Hooker pushed against the Rebels facing him. In this fighting Alfred Bellard of the 5th New Jersey, like so many other men this day, complained that it was almost impossible to spot the enemy troops in the woods. He concluded it was their gray and butternut uniforms that made them hard to see, "while we wore the blue and marching were in plain sight."

Private Bellard's brigade commander, Colonel Samuel H. Starr, faced a problem of a different sort. Starr rode an Indian pony acquired during his frontier service before the war, and he had found it an ideal mount but for one thing — whenever it came under fire it turned its tail to the enemy. The pony did not run or balk or otherwise cause any difficulty and Colonel Starr was quite attached to it, so he tolerated this idiosyncrasy and skewed himself around in the saddle until he, if not his horse, was facing the enemy properly. General Hooker was equally tolerant, reporting that on June 1 Colonel Starr's "energy and courage were conspicuous."[26]

Over on the Nine Mile Road General Smith listened to the battle and tried to decide if it signaled the full-blooded offensive by Longstreet that he had promised to support. The action there was certainly intense enough for one Federal observer, who wrote, "It never fell to my lot to hear such musketry-fire as I heard then." But Smith's nerve failed him and he could not bring himself to act, and finally the firing died away as the last of D. H. Hill's attacks was repulsed. Whiting's division remained idle, suffering just thirteen wounded that day.

The fighting on June 1 ended about 11:30 A.M., the losses of the two sides were about the same — 1,132 Confederate, 1,203 Union — and when it was over nothing had changed. Sumner and Heintzelman had held their ground against the attackers and were content with that and launched no counteroffensive. The new commander of the Army of Northern Virginia had expended even less personal effort to secure victory at Seven Pines than had his predecessor.

As the sound of the gunfire began to fade away it was replaced by the sound of Yankee soldiers cheering. General McClellan had arrived on the battlefield. "Minnesota 1st give him six cheers and two tigers," Private Isaac Taylor wrote in his diary. Private Bellard of the 5th New Jersey reported that his regiment too welcomed the general with loud cheers. McClellan doffed his cap in acknowledgment and said, "Boys, we've licked them, right, left, and center, and we're going into Richmond," and Bellard added, "This sounded well and put the boys in good humor."

After inspecting some of the troops and consulting briefly with his lieutenants, McClellan returned to headquarters in a state of near collapse. His command role in the battle had been as slight as Joe Johnston's or G. W. Smith's, but he told his wife that what he saw that day at the front disturbed him deeply. "I am tired of the sickening sight of the battlefield, with its mangled corpses & poor suffering wounded!" he wrote. "Victory has no charms for me when purchased at such cost."

It was two o'clock on the afternoon of June 1 when General Lee rode up to the house of a man named Hughes, on the Nine Mile Road, which G. W. Smith had taken as his headquarters. Jefferson Davis was there before him and had told Smith of his decision, so there was little to be said on the subject. Without ceremony Smith turned over command of the Army of Northern Virginia to Robert E. Lee.[27]

Lee Takes Command

....

BEGINNING ON THAT SABBATH, hour after hour, by daylight and through the night, the roads leading into Richmond were crowded with vehicles bringing in the wounded and the dead of Seven Pines. Major Heros Von Borcke, the Prussian serving on Jeb Stuart's cavalry staff, was struck by the contrast of sounds — the moans and cries from the parade of ambulances bound for the city, and passing in the opposite direction the shouts and curses of teamsters driving their supply wagons to the front. Other casualties came to Richmond aboard the cars of the York River Railroad. On the battlefield Georgian Thomas Ware watched as "wounded & dying, any quantity," were loaded on the cars. "It was a sad sight," Ware confided to his diary, "some with their legs & arms shot off, . . . dangerously wounded."

Richmond's streets were soon jammed with ambulances and the sidewalks with walking wounded, and their numbers quickly overwhelmed the city's medical facilities. Richmonders had experienced problems enough caring for the 1,500 wounded from Bull Run back in 1861; now suddenly there were more than three times that number — Confederate losses at Seven Pines came to 6,134: 980 killed, 4,749 wounded, 405 missing — and the authorities simply ran out of space.

After the military hospitals were full and then the private hospitals, the wounded had to be put in public buildings and private homes. When official organization broke down under the strain, the women of Richmond stepped in. "Their wants were supplied in a few hours by the citizens, who cooked and sent refreshments, beds, pillows and blankets, water, soap, and all that could for the time relieve the helpless sufferers," Sallie Putnam wrote. ". . . Our summer's work had begun."

The dead were brought to Richmond too, by the wagonload, the bodies stacked like cordwood, their stiffened, rigid feet exposed to view. After several days of this, wrote Alexander Hunter of the 17th Virginia, "the passer-by, grown rapidly familiar with such fearful sights, glances hastily and passes on." Anxious civilians crowded into Capitol Square searching for news of those who had been in the battle, or gathered before the public bulletin boards as the casualty lists were posted. In these spring weeks, even as McClellan's grand army came ever closer, the war had seemed somehow unreal and out of sight; now Seven Pines made it all very real and starkly visible. "No city in the world was sadder than Richmond in those days," Private Hunter recalled.[1]

However makeshift their accommodations, the Confederate wounded were better off than most of the Yankee wounded from Seven Pines. Charles S. Tripler, the Potomac army's medical director described by General McClellan as "an old & faithful officer," was at heart a spinner of bureaucratic red tape, and he was quite unprepared to handle the casualties of a major battle like Seven Pines. The Federals lost some 1,100 fewer men than the Confederates — 790 dead, 3,594 wounded, 647 missing, a total of 5,031 — but even that number overwhelmed Dr. Tripler's facilities.

Tripler's ambulance corps was rudimentary. His field hospitals were largely filled with the sick, whom he was trying to keep with the army rather than sending them away to recuperate in the North, and consequently there was nowhere to put the wounded when they were finally collected from the battlefield. George W. Barr, a regimental surgeon with the 64th New York, wrote his wife angrily, "Even *Hell* cannot be more hateful than the murderous effects of war as we are seeing them now; . . . the horrors we behold are sickening enough to drive humanity to madness. . . ."

For the Union wounded, the counterparts of the ministering women of Richmond were the female nurses of the U.S. Sanitary Commission. The commission, a civilian agency dedicated to the welfare of the troops, had joined the Peninsula campaign by the expedient of staffing a fleet of hospital ships. Dr. Tripler disapproved of such civilian involvement in army affairs — he derided Sanitation Commission volunteers as "sensation preachers, village doctors, and strong-minded women" — but those vessels of the hospital fleet that happened to be at White House Landing proved the salvation of the Seven Pines wounded.

Just as the Confederates used the western section of the York River Railroad to bring their wounded to Richmond, the Federals utilized the eastern section to transport casualties to White House. They came several hundred at a time, packed tightly in the cars, many with no initial treatment of their wounds, and all of them hungry and exhausted from their ordeal. "They arrived, dead and alive together, in the same close boxcar, many with awful wounds festering and alive with maggots," reported Frederick Law Olmsted, manager of the Sanitary Commission's hospital-ship fleet. "The stench was such as to produce vomiting with some of our strong men, habituated to the duty of attending the sick & wounded of the army." With the field hospitals already filled with sick, the casualties were carried aboard the steamers. Some had to be left lying by the tracks in the rain for long periods until room could be found for them.

Nurses and surgeons labored to feed and wash the men and care for their wounds, but hardly did they gain headway with the task before a new trainload of wounded arrived at the landing. Nurse Katharine Wormeley described it as a "long nightmare." After four days of it, hardly pausing to eat or sleep, she reflected on the experience in a letter to her family. "I do not suffer under the sights," she wrote, "but oh! the sounds, the screams of men. It is when I think of it afterwards that it is so dreadful. . . ."[2]

In the meantime the task of cleaning up at Seven Pines went on. He could hardly find words to describe the battlefield, one of D. H. Hill's men told his wife. "I would to God it could be the last & our country saved. The dying and the dead, the rebel & and the federal side by side. The groans of the wounded, & the lifeless corpse of the foe prostrate on the field, half covered with water." He shrank at the prospect that he too might find such a last resting place.

General Lee had ordered the troops back to their original lines, and the Federals moved up in their place. They buried their dead and any the enemy had left, and burned the dead horses, but they did the job of interment imperfectly and for weeks afterward the field stank of putrefaction and was uninhabitable. Rain washed away the earth over the makeshift graves, a man in the 2nd New Hampshire explained, "and here and there a leg or hand or head could be seen protruding in all its ghastliness. . . ."

The Confederates had carried off everything of any use from Casey's camps, and the Federals found little that was worth scavenging. Their largest prize was a double-decker omnibus from the Exchange Hotel in Richmond which the Rebels had used as an ambulance before it bogged down in the mud. Some of Joe Hooker's New Yorkers dug it out and paraded it through the camps, with one of them on the rear platform crying out, "Broadway, ride up here!" It was about the only cheerful thing anyone found to do after the battle.[3]

The Federals had done their best fighting around Fair Oaks Station and so took Fair Oaks as their name for the battle. The Confederates, for the same reason, called it Seven Pines. The most compelling reason for history to remember it as the Battle of Seven Pines is that it was around the Seven Pines crossroads that most of the fighting took place and most of the casualties occurred. Yet except for the examples of fighting prowess displayed by the men in the ranks, there was little that either side could point to with pride about this battle, regardless of what name they gave it.

General McClellan, as was his custom, proclaimed a glorious victory. He put his portable printing press to work and on June 2 issued an address on the subject to the troops. He told them he had now fulfilled the first part of his promise made to them at the beginning of the campaign: "You are now face to face with the rebels, who are at bay in front of their Capital. The final and decisive battle is at hand." Every trial of combat had proved them superior to the enemy, he said, and now they faced the final trial. "Let us meet and crush him here in the very centre of the rebellion." Then he offered a new pledge. "Soldiers! I will be with you in this battle, and share its dangers with you. . . . Let us strike the blow which is to restore peace and union to this distracted land." The address was well received. Lieutenant William Folwell of the engineers thought it "quite Napoleonic in its style and sings finely. It will no doubt have a very inspiring effect."

In truth the Young Napoleon could count himself exceedingly fortunate that the Third and Fourth corps he had posted in isolation south of the Chickahominy had not been destroyed. He was equally fortunate that Bull Sumner had had one of his good days on May 31 and had marched without a moment's delay to the sound of the guns through every obstacle. (It was fortunate too, the staff whispered among themselves, that old Sumner had found the right target straight in front of him or otherwise he would never have discovered it.) Beyond ordering Sumner's advance, McClellan played no active role in the battle, due in large measure to his malarial attack.

For a time on June 1, however, he did give thought to an immediate counterattack toward Richmond by the right wing of his army. By the account of the Comte de Paris, the two corps commanders on that wing, Fitz John Porter and William Franklin, "judged the passage impracticable" and discouraged the idea. The young Frenchman watched the general read their dispatch and then crumple it in his fist, "but he limited himself to this gesture of impatience." McClellan's critics would contend that by failing to override his lieutenants he thereby missed a golden opportunity to win his grand campaign.

Yet such a counterstroke would have required of General McClellan a fundamental change in the way he viewed his situation on the Peninsula. Convinced beyond all doubt that he had been attacked at Seven Pines by an army much larger than his own — Keyes, Heintzelman, and Sumner, he told Washington, had "engaged greatly superior numbers" — he was well satisfied simply to have fought off this host and lost no more than 5,000 men in the process. "I have to be very cautious now," he said in reporting his situation to President Lincoln on June 4. ". . . I mention these facts now merely to show you that the Army of the Potomac has had serious work & that no child's play is before it."[4]

In Richmond much was made of the rout of Casey's division on May 31, and on that count the Battle of Seven Pines was declared a Southern victory. At the same time, there was disappointment at the lack of any other accomplishments to justify the loss of better than 6,100 men, for the fact remained that on June 2 the two armies were exactly where they had been on May 30. One of Micah Jenkins's men, surveying the thinned ranks, remarked that if this battle was being called a victory, "I never want to be in a battle that is not a victory."

Few then understood that Joe Johnston's perfectly sound battle plan had gone completely astray; in any event, with the general himself among the gallant wounded, it would hardly be proper to charge him with misdirecting the battle. General Longstreet, who had in fact misdirected every aspect of the battle that he touched, was able to avoid censure by blaming everything on Benjamin Huger. Huger protested this injustice but could not make himself heard, for the government would not grant him a court of inquiry. Thus first by rumor and then by official report, Huger was accused of standing idle with his division on the Charles City Road while the rest of the army fought on unsupported. "Just to think that Huger's slowness has spoiled everything!" was one of the comments heard in Richmond in the days after Seven Pines.

President Davis took the true measure of the failure but did not lose heart. "Unaccountable delays in bringing some of our troops into action prevented us from gaining a decisive victory on Saturday," he told his wife. "The opportunity being lost we must try to find another."[5]

....

FINDING ANOTHER opportunity to get at McClellan's grand army precisely described General Lee's thoughts. Unlike Joe Johnston, Lee was not content to wait for McClellan to make some incautious move and open himself to attack. He would create opportunity himself. "It would be necessary to strike a blow," he said.

Nothing in Robert E. Lee's military character was more fixed than his determination to seize the initiative; to his mind, gaining the initiative strategically and tactically was the essential first step to gaining the victory. In hardly more than three weeks that June he took firm hold of the army, shaped it to his needs, and laid careful plans for capturing the initiative from his opponent. During Johnston's tenure as army commander there had been indecision even about what to call the army. That indecision, and much else, changed when Lee took command. It was now and forever the Army of Northern Virginia, and Lee made it his instrument for turning the war in favor of the Confederacy.

One of his first acts as commanding general was to call together his lieutenants so they might acquaint themselves with him and he with them. The gathering was held on June 3 at the Chimneys, a house on the Nine Mile Road near the late battlefield. Lee revealed nothing of any plans he might be considering but instead invited his generals to give their opinions of the state of the army and its position. This was a departure from the secretive Johnston, and they spoke freely. Several, concerned with the reach of McClellan's heavy guns, wanted to pull back farther toward Richmond. Chase Whiting was grimly pessimistic about even the attempt to hold the city against the enemy's superior force. At that Lee broke his silence to suggest a stop to such talk. "If you go to ciphering," he said, "we are whipped beforehand." That at least indicated he intended to make a fight for Richmond, and the majority of his generals left the conference reassured.[6]

Lee had in fact begun to shape the cornerstone of his evolving strategy from his first day of command. On June 1 a telegram had arrived in Richmond from Alexander R. Boteler, member of the Confederate Congress and staff officer to Stonewall Jackson. "I left Maj. Genl. Jackson at Winchester yesterday," Boteler reported. "The enemy is threatening his flanks & front." He described the numerous

Federal forces gathering in the Shenandoah from all directions and added, "Jackson wants reinforcements immediately if possible." Just then Lee could spare no troops from Richmond, but he ordered whatever garrison troops were in the upper Valley to march to Jackson without delay. Soon Boteler himself reached the capital, and he and President Davis conferred with Lee on the larger question of the future employment of the Army of the Valley.

There could no longer be any doubt about General McClellan's purpose. Lee came out of the army engineers, and he read the mind of his engineer opponent. "McClellan will make this a battle of posts," he predicted. "He will take position from position, under cover of his heavy guns, & we cannot get at him without storming his works, which with our new troops is extremely hazardous." They had witnessed the result of such an "experiment" at Seven Pines. He noted too McClellan's dependence on the York River Railroad to move up his big guns, which tied his supply line to White House on the Pamunkey. By Lee's estimate, 100,000 men would be required to resist a regular siege of Richmond, "which perhaps would only prolong not save it."

Alexander Boteler had brought with him a proposal by Jackson to raise the Army of the Valley to 40,000 men so that he might cross the Potomac and invade Maryland and Pennsylvania. Lee acknowledged that such a move would change the character of the war, and considered it feasible if the South Atlantic states — Georgia and the Carolinas — would give up all their garrison troops for the attempt. Having thus endorsed Jackson's idea, he quietly abandoned it. While Lee did not reveal the reason for his change of mind, he seems to have feared that an invasion of the North by Jackson would trigger the recall of McClellan's army to counter it, which was not what he wanted to see happen. His ambition was far greater than simply to thwart a siege of Richmond. General Lee intended to destroy McClellan's army, and he felt the best place to do that was right where it was — at the gates of Richmond.

All this talk of Jackson's future was carried on in the quiet confidence that that general would evade the trap the Federals were laying for him. By Boteler's report, when he left Winchester on May 31 Jackson had just started to retreat southward, up the Valley. Ahead of him on his right flank was General Frémont with a substantial force. Ahead of him on his left flank was General Shields's division, newly returned to the Valley from Fredericksburg. Behind him was General

Banks, earlier chased out of the Valley by Jackson but now reinforced and returning to the fight.

By all appearances the Army of the Valley was at risk of being trapped between these converging columns. Yet Jackson had expressed no alarm at this prospect beyond calling for reinforcements, and Lee took him at his word. Alexander Lawton's Georgia brigade, then en route to Richmond from Savannah, was diverted to Jackson to fill his depleted ranks. Jackson's plan, Lee told Secretary of War Randolph, was to march against Shields and crush him, "and as he is a good soldier I expect him to do it."

Lee's confidence was rewarded. "The hero of the war," as the newspapers were calling him, slipped between Frémont and Shields, and the Federal pincers closed on empty air. Now the Shenandoah became the setting for what navy men called a stern chase, and the pursuing Yankees could not overhaul their quarry. On June 8 at Cross Keys and on June 9 at Port Republic, Jackson, "through God's blessing," turned on both enemy columns and sent them tumbling back down the Valley. Now the Army of the Valley was free to take up whatever course General Lee might choose for it.[7]

Learning of these victories, Lee determined to play a double game against the enemy. He would further reinforce Jackson — two brigades this time, taken from the army at Richmond — to enable him if need be again to "hit the Yankees in the Valley, so as to keep them quiet," but in any case to make him strong enough to quit the Valley entirely and deliver a major blow against McClellan in front of Richmond. At the same time, Lee would conceal his purpose behind a smokescreen of deception, and he designed his deception with some care.

His scheme made a virtue of necessity by not attempting to disguise the hard-to-disguise fact that reinforcements were going to Jackson. General Lawton's Georgia brigade, 3,600 strong, went west by rail from Petersburg to Lynchburg and from there northward toward the Valley. The two brigades from the main army, 4,500 men under Chase Whiting, were marched in broad daylight through Richmond to the depot for the trip to Lynchburg, "the object of which was not concealed," as one of Lee's staff put it. All this was done, Lee said, "knowing that the news would reach the enemy, and induce the belief that Jackson was to be pushed north." He expected the news to get out by means of Yankee spies, which he believed were everywhere. (In fact this was one channel that carried none of these reports. All of detective Pinkerton's spies in Richmond had been captured and his best agent, Timothy Webster, hanged.) So that the deception would not become too obvious, Lee urged Richmond's newspapers to avoid comment on the troop movements.

It is likely too that deserters and refugees were employed to spread the deception. A deserter from the 8th Georgia, for example, told the Federals a good deal more about Whiting's force than he could have known about a division not his own. A Frenchman claiming to be a refugee from Richmond displayed remarkably detailed knowledge of Confederate rail movements. Seeing these reports, Mr. Lincoln raised the question with McClellan "whether the Frenchman & your deserters have not all been sent to deceive." McClellan harbored no such doubts. "If ten or fifteen thousand men have left Richmond to reinforce Jackson," he told the president on June 18, "it illustrates their strength and confidence." That was precisely what General Lee wanted his opponent to think.[8]

Lee moved with equal dispatch to develop a plan of attack. He explained its general outlines to President Davis on June 5: "I am preparing a line that I can hold with part of our forces in front, while with the rest I will endeavor to make a diversion to bring McClellan out." Unlike Joe Johnston, Lee was at pains to explain and discuss his every step with Mr. Davis, and he was rewarded with the president's unstinting support. In promptly approving command appointments that Lee had requested, Davis told him, "I give you the material to be used at your discretion."

Jefferson Davis was himself a man of no small military accomplishment — West Point graduate, Mexican War command, chairman of the Senate's military affairs committee, secretary of war — and he took his constitutional role as commander-in-chief seriously, and he expected his generals to acknowledge that fact. Johnston would never do so and suffered for it, and Johnston was one of the first to recognize the change in the once chilly atmosphere of the high command. "The shot that struck me down is the very best that has been fired for the Southern cause yet," he told a visitor to his bedside soon after Lee's appointment. "For I possess in no degree the confidence of our government, and now they have in my place one who does possess it. . . ."

On Lee's orders Confederate engineers laid out new defenses facing the Yankees east of Richmond, and the troops were put to work with pick and shovel. At first there was grumbling in the ranks that digging trenches and throwing up earthworks was work for slaves, not white men, and they took to calling their new general the "King of Spades." The previous year, when Lee was struggling with the intractable problems of the campaign in western Virginia, a newspaperman christened him the "Great Entrencher" and complained of his "dilly-dally, dirt digging, scientific warfare," and now all that was brought up again. Lee was bemused by the complaints. Manual labor was one of the soldierly virtues, he remarked to Mr. Davis, and so it had always been: a "happy combination" of labor, valor, fortitude, and boldness "carried the Roman soldiers into all countries. . . ." Then he gave the matter no further thought. In due course his critics (and his soldiers) would come to see that instead of going to ground with his army he was only making Richmond more easily defended, thus freeing him for a campaign of maneuver.[9]

In addition to formulating a plan of action and fitting Jackson into that plan, Lee set about reorganizing and strengthening the army for the coming battle. He faced an immediate problem concerning G. W. Smith. On June 2, the day after giving up command of the army, Smith suffered what later generations would describe as a nervous breakdown. The doctors prescribed complete rest. "All business and all exciting questions must be kept from him for awhile" was the verdict. Having observed Smith's performance at Seven Pines and found it wanting, Lee now quietly but firmly determined that Smith must not return to field command.

Joe Johnston's partitioning of the army into two wings and a reserve was abandoned, and with it Smith's role as wing commander. Then Lee dissolved Smith's division command as well. Two of his brigades, under Chase Whiting, were sent to Stonewall Jackson. One was broken up and its regiments dispersed to other commands, and the remaining two were put into an enlarged division under A. P. Hill. On June 21, when Smith inquired about these changes and about re-forming his division as soon as his health was restored, Lee put him off. Saying nothing of his battle plans, he urged the general to leave Richmond for a complete rest. All this was done, Smith would later complain, "in a semi-pius, semi-official" manner, but in a fashion that left him no recourse. Smith would return to duty some two months later, but he never again held a field command with the Army of Northern Virginia. Assigned behind-the-lines duties, he eventually resigned his commission when passed over for promotion. G. W. Smith had failed Robert E. Lee's test for command in battle, and from that verdict there was no appeal.[10]

The break-up of Smith's division triggered other changes. Before Seven Pines A. P. Hill had led a single brigade; by June 12, at age thirty-six, he was the youngest major general in the army and commanded its largest division, which he christened the Light Division. Prince John Magruder's old command was reworked into three divisions from two. No fewer than thirty regiments from Johnston's army found themselves in different commands in Lee's army. Old organizations were disbanded and new ones formed, producing a net gain of ten new infantry regiments to be inserted into existing brigades. The artillery, which had been poorly used at Seven Pines, was extensively reorganized, and nine new batteries were added. Most significantly, entire new commands came into the army.

In addition to Lawton's Georgia brigade, sent on to Jackson, a fresh brigade under Roswell Ripley arrived from Charleston and was attached to D. H. Hill's division. Robert Ransom's North Carolina brigade was assigned to Benjamin Huger's division. Also from North Carolina came Theophilus Holmes with three new brigades. When all these troops were finally in place, and when Jackson should arrive with his forces from the Valley, Lee would command 92,400 men.

General McClellan's prediction that the Rebels would call up every available soldier to defend their capital was proving precisely true, if in nothing like the numbers McClellan imagined. Robert E. Lee would never again command an army as large as this, nor ever again come as close to parity with the enemy, nor would the Confederacy ever again assemble so many men in one place. In expectation of the climactic battle for Richmond, each side was assembling its equivalent of a grand army.[11]

....

THE YOUNG NAPOLEON was also welcoming reinforcements. Much to his relief, the government replaced thorny old John Wool at Fort Monroe with John Dix, and placed the Fort Monroe garrison under McClellan's direct control. He was quick to call up nine of Dix's regiments to fill the gaps left by the Seven Pines fighting. These troops, plus a regiment from Washington and two batteries from Baltimore, brought 10,300 replacements into his ranks. He also persuaded Washington to release to him another element of the First Corps, and George McCall's division — a dozen regiments of the Pennsylvania Reserves — began arriving at White House on June 10. These reinforcements, which nearly matched the number of new men Lee brought up from Georgia and the Carolinas, raised the present-for-duty count in his field army to 105,900. In addition to the 9,300 men still at Fort Monroe, McClellan was told that the 7,000 men under Ambrose Burnside then on the North Carolina coast were also his to command.[12]

To be sure, General McClellan was hardly satisfied that Washington was giving him all the reinforcements that it might. He cast an eye on the western theater, where General Beauregard's Confederate army had given up the rail center of Corinth and retreated deeper into Mississippi, and deduced that Beauregard and a substantial part of his army must now be hurrying to the defense of Richmond. To meet this threat he wanted the Federal western army of Henry Halleck to furnish substantial reinforcements to the Army of the Potomac. He had not yet positively confirmed Beauregard's arrival, he told Secretary Stanton, "but it is possible & ought to be their policy." It ought to be Washington's policy to put the battle for Richmond ahead of everything else. "It would seem that Halleck has now no large organized force in front of him, while we have."

Halleck lost little time in pointing out that his own intelligence sources were certain beyond any doubt that neither Beauregard nor any of his troops had left Mississippi for Richmond. Indeed, he said, should he be required to send any of his troops east, Beauregard would most certainly turn back and fall on him. From that McClellan gloomily concluded (as he told his wife) that he would have to win his campaign entirely on his own, "notwithstanding all they do & leave undone in Washington to prevent it." In striking contrast to his opposite number in Richmond, General McClellan was convinced that he had not a single friend in the high councils of his own government. He was certain that Secretary of War Stanton wished to see him defeated, and that the president had turned against him as well. "Honest A has again fallen into the hands of my enemies," he told Ellen, "& is no longer a cordial friend of mine!"[13]

Far from abandoning his general, Mr. Lincoln remained intent on reinforcing him. When he told Stanton, "Richmond is the principal point for active operation," he was echoing McClellan. When on June 8 he instructed Stanton to have the rest of General McDowell's First Corps "move upon Richmond," he was affirming McClellan's fondest hope. Yet in the end this third order to McDowell to join the Army of the Potomac met the same fate as the first two.

Earlier only Franklin's division was sent from the First Corps. This time only McCall's division reached the Peninsula. It developed that

Shields's travel-worn and battle-worn division was, as Lincoln put it, "so terribly out of shape, out at elbows, and out at toes," that it could not make the journey. Then McDowell's remaining two divisions, under Rufus King and James Ricketts, became victims of the deception laid out by General Lee.

Lincoln saw clearly enough what Jackson was doing in these weeks in the Valley — his game, the president said, was to magnify his numbers and movements "and thus by constant alarms keep three or four times as many of our troops away from Richmond as his own force amounts to" — and he had tried very hard to break up this game, but his fumbling generals in the Valley had failed him. Now they had become entirely befuddled and could not begin to tell him where Jackson had gone or what his numbers were or what he intended to do. If only they knew the truth of the matter, Lincoln told McClellan on June 20, "we could send you some more force, but as the case stands, we do not think we safely can." King and Ricketts stayed where they were, guarding an empty landscape. The true measure of Jackson's Valley campaign became not the battles won or the enemies outwitted, but the final disabling of these Yankee divisions. As Lieutenant Folwell of the 50th New York engineers put it in a letter home, camp rumor had Jackson "coming down upon our rear. If so, where is McDowell?"[14]

However discouraged he became with the actions of his government, General McClellan's spirits invariably rose when he contemplated his own actions. Day by day he pursued his campaign plan confidently and methodically. The Grapevine Bridge was repaired, and upstream from it his engineers constructed eight additional bridges to ensure that there would be no repetition of the near breakdown in communications of the Seven Pines battle. (A weary bridge builder remarked that when the war was over the local people would be able to cross the Chickahominy just about anywhere they pleased.) Miles of existing roads were corduroyed, and new ones cut through the woods. McClellan also tried to ensure that his lines would be better guarded in another attack. From White Oak Swamp on the south to the bluffs overlooking the Chickahominy bottomlands on the north, a three-mile-long line of fortifications sprang up facing Richmond. Barricades of felled trees marked the line, and anchoring it were six extensive earthen redoubts mounting forty guns.

As the engineers' work progressed, Sumner's Second Corps and Franklin's Sixth dug in south of the river, joining the Third and Fourth corps of Heintzelman and Keyes. McClellan himself crossed the river, shifting his headquarters to the Trent house on the Grapevine Bridge Road. "We are now encamped behind the works which have been thrown up along the whole line of our front," Colonel Francis Barlow of the Second Corps wrote home on June 18. "One would think we were acting on the defensive instead of the offensive."

In fact, McClellan was pursuing what his West Point instructors had called an "active defense" — a tactic for advancing against an opponent from behind one's own fortifications while providing protection, McClellan said, "against the consequences of unforeseen disaster." It was as well the tactic by which he believed he could gain final victory over the enemy host. As a close student of military history, General McClellan was well aware of instances when, by the display of one advantage or another, the smaller army had defeated the larger. In this instance, his carefully defensive offensive, when combined with his great siege train, ought to offset the Rebel advantage in numbers and make his campaign a success.

He spelled out his battle plan for his wife. On a map he had sent her he told her to find Old Tavern, on the high, open ground along the Nine Mile Road a mile and a half south of the Chickahominy. "It is in that vicinity that the next battle will be fought," he explained. "If we gain that the game is up for Secesh — I will then have them in the hollow of my hand." He expected the battle to be primarily one of artillery. First he would bring some 200 guns to bear "& sweep everything before us." Once he gained Old Tavern, "I will push them in upon Richmond & behind their works — then I will bring up my heavy guns — shell the city & carry it by assault. I speak very confidently. . . ."[15]

Like Lee, McClellan reorganized his command for the battle to come. He rearranged the batteries in the Second, Third, and Fourth corps to provide each corps commander with a reserve and to make their artillery tactics more flexible. He determined to replace Silas Casey, whose division had been badly beaten at Seven Pines. While Casey's personal bravery was not in question, he said, "he does not command the confidence of his soldiers." He gave the division to John J. Peck and placed Casey in command of the "important depot" at White House Landing.

He handled his displeasure with Erasmus Keyes, whom he would describe as "very prissy & entirely unfit to command a corps," in a different way. When he arranged his forces in the shift south of the

Chickahominy, he posted Keyes as far from the scene of any probable fighting as possible. His solution to potential problems with Bull Sumner was to keep a close check on the old man while taking particular care for his own safety. Should he be disabled, he confided to Ellen, Sumner as senior general would assume command of the army: "I must be careful. . . . Sumner would ruin things in about two days." By contrast, he displayed perfect confidence in Fitz John Porter by assigning him the key role of guarding both the army's right flank north of the river and its supply line. The attachment of McCall's fresh division to Porter's Fifth Corps made it the largest corps in the army.[16]

....

WITH EVENTS seeming to point to a classic siege of the Confederacy's capital, visitors hurried to the Peninsula for a personal view of the war. As was the custom of the day, the European powers had dispatched teams of military observers to take note of this newest of wars, and their little enclaves soon dotted the Federal camps. The most recent arrival, McClellan noted, was "a large dose of Spaniards": General Juan Prim y Prats and his retinue. General Prim was reported to be greatly impressed with the feats of engineering he saw. From Washington came senators and congressmen and Cabinet officers and other notables, who dined at the headquarters mess and were taken on tours of the front. "Crossed the Chickahominy swamps," reported Pennsylvania congressman James H. Campbell, ". . . ran to the front — to the first parallel — within four miles of Richmond, the spires of which could be seen from that point." General McClellan took time to brief his visitors and to send them back to Washington with pleas for more men and more guns and more of everything.

In a like fashion he cultivated the press. Newspapermen on the Peninsula worked under the tightest of restrictions, with Chief of Staff Marcy acting not only as their chief source of information but as their chief censor as well. As a consequence, what appeared in Northern newspapers was what General McClellan wanted known about the enemy he was confronting and the trials he was facing.

"We inquire if it is fair, right or politic to underestimate the strength of the enemy simply to discredit the prudent preparations of Gen. McClellan," the *St. Louis Republican* editorialized. The *New York Tribune* demanded that if any available force "can be used to rectify the fearful mistake of weakening McClellan, in God's name let it be so used, and used on the instant!" Henry J. Raymond, editor of the

New York Times, insisted that if General McClellan should fail to take Richmond, "the responsibility must rest with those who compelled him to fight, and withheld the means which he deemed important to an assured success." The general commanding was making certain that if it should ever come to a matter of blame, he would be blameless.[17]

In these crowded weeks McClellan even found time to explore the prospects of peace. He was in communication with Richmond on the exchange of prisoners, and when he assigned Thomas M. Key of his staff to a flag-of-truce meeting on that subject with General Howell Cobb, a founding father of the Confederacy, he told Key to expand the talks to include a discussion of what might be done to end the war. The fact that only the civil authorities could properly discuss such matters did not trouble General McClellan. He had Key explain to Cobb that the North's sole object in the war was maintaining the Constitution and upholding the nation's laws. Cobb rejected the proffered olive branch, and when he learned of the meeting Secretary Stanton reminded his general that flags of truce were to discuss military questions only. Continuing his efforts to impose policy, McClellan offered to send Mr. Lincoln his thoughts on "the present state of military affairs throughout the whole country."[18]

Another flag-of-truce meeting resolved the problem of Mrs. General Lee, as she was known to both armies. After leaving White House in May ahead of the invaders, Mrs. Lee had taken up residence at Marlbourne, the Pamunkey River plantation of Edmund Ruffin. Before long the Yankee army occupied that property as well, and guards were posted around the house. The general's wife, whose manner was imperious, took outspoken offense at this and the matter became an embarrassment to General McClellan and his sense of gallantry. Arrangements were made to pass her through the lines. On June 10, in a plantation carriage flying a makeshift white flag from its whip stand, Mrs. General Lee was brought to McClellan, who greeted her with due ceremony and sent her on her way with an escort of well-turned-out cavalry from the headquarters guard. She was driven across Meadow Bridge between the two armies and into the Confederate lines, where she was welcomed by her husband and cheered by his troops.[19]

General McClellan's carefully engineered advance and his design for taking Richmond by siege rested, as it had since Yorktown, on the premise that he was confronting an army vastly larger than his own.

"The rascals are very strong & outnumber me very considerably," he assured Ellen. Detective Pinkerton reported on June 15, "It is variously estimated that the Rebel army at Richmond and vicinity numbers from 150,000 to 200,000 men." Pinkerton afterward settled on a "general estimate" of 180,000, but cautioned that this was very probably an undercount.

McClellan did not question this conjuring; if anything, it fell short of his own. Dismissing General Halleck's reports, he continued to credit the arrival in Richmond of Beauregard and a good part of his western army. At the same time, relying on the protection of his entrenchments and the great guns of his siege train, he predicted that in due course Richmond must fall. "After tomorrow we shall fight the rebel army as soon as Providence will permit," he promised the president on June 18. "We shall await only a favorable condition of the earth and sky & the completion of some necessary preliminaries."

These delusions about the enemy invariably blinded McClellan to opportunity. When he told Mr. Lincoln his offensive awaited only the cooperation of earth and sky, he was in the midst of the longest period of good weather of the entire campaign. Between June 11 and June 23 it rained twice, briefly and lightly. Lee had but two men to his three, and only on June 16 did Lee send for Jackson and the Army of the Valley; only on the eighteenth did Jackson begin the long journey. Thus far in the campaign McClellan had not seized the slightest advantage from the fact that while Jackson's two divisions in the Valley might be holding up reinforcements for the Potomac army, at the same time those two divisions were absent from the army defending Richmond. Nor did he act now.

Incapable of seeing or even imagining the truth of the case, General McClellan continued to delay, to worry the "necessary preliminaries." He wanted more heavy guns for his front lines. He wanted final touches on his entrenchments. He wanted Burnside's troops from North Carolina. He wanted supplies stockpiled on the James so that in due course he might capture Drewry's Bluff and open the river for the navy's gunboats to bombard Richmond "in the final attack." He wanted the navy to make good on a plan to blow up the railroad bridge between Richmond and Petersburg and thus delay the arrival of Beauregard's phantom battalions.

"We are making slow progress here — but I dare not rush this Army on which I feel the fate of the nation depends," McClellan wrote his friend Samuel Barlow on June 23. "I will succeed, but for the sake of the cause must make a sure thing of it." Day by day he delayed and his opportunity slipped away and then was gone, and when finally he did fight the Battle of Richmond, it was against the full strength of the Army of Northern Virginia.[20]

. . . .

WHEN GEORGE McCALL's Pennsylvania Reserves arrived at White House Landing that June, their first impression of the war on the Peninsula was not quickly forgotten. Piled on a wharf were scores of rough pine coffins awaiting shipment to the North, and several of the shedlike buildings lining the shore bore such signs as UNDERTAKERS & EMBALMERS OF THE DEAD. PARTICULAR ATTENTION PAID TO DECEASED SOLDIERS. For those who cared to investigate the matter, prices were $25 for privates and $50 for officers, with business reported brisk for the fever-killed as well as the battle-killed. "The scene as we disembarked at the landing," Captain Robert Taggart recalled, "was neither cheerful nor encouraging."

As spring turned toward summer the health of the two armies grew poorer every day. The Army of the Potomac's return for June 20 listed 11,000 men sick enough to be declared unfit for duty, almost one-tenth of those with the army. Among the Confederates the count was proportionally about the same. The Federals' death count from disease on the Peninsula in June came to 705; when deaths among the severest cases sent north were added, the toll was greater than the army's fatalities at Seven Pines.

Private A. W. Stillwell of the 5th Wisconsin summed up the soldier's life as "digging, entrenching, mortifying, and dying in the Chicka-hominy swamps." Private Josiah Patterson of the 14th Georgia pursued the same thought in more detail. "The weather has been unusually cold and wet," Patterson wrote home on June 13. "We have had no shelter save what we could lug on our shoulder, no bedding except what we transported in the same manner. Our rest has been short and frequently disturbed, our meals scant, irregular and badly cooked. . . . When standing we were in a bog of mud; when lying down to refresh ourselves in sleep we were in a pool of water." He added, not surprisingly, "My health has been very bad. . . ."

The worst scourges were dysentery and chronic diarrhea, and what everyone called simply the Chickahominy fever, which might be ma-laria or typhoid or typhus or some other of the numerous fevers of the time and place. The constant diet of salt pork and salt beef and hardtack produced outbreaks of scurvy. Rank was no guarantee of good health. General McClellan was felled by malaria and attacks of acute neuralgia. Nine other Union generals were seriously ill of disease at one time or another during the campaign, and one of them, William H. Keim, died of the Chickahominy fever. In the Confederate army, in addition to the collapse of G. W. Smith, five generals were incapacitated at least for a time by illness.

This is not to suggest that the rest of the men, those marked present for duty on the returns, were in fact entirely healthy. It was generally agreed among the troops that they would have to be desperately ill before they would report to a military hospital. Mississippian Edward Burruss vowed, "Unless they take me there when I am insensible or too weak to resist I will never get in one. They are the most loathsome holes that I ever visited. . . ." Jesse Reid of the 4th South Carolina reported on June 7 that in just one day five men of his company were carried off to the hospital, and a sixth had died there two days before. The worst of it, he said, was that the dead man's only brother had been killed in the Seven Pines fight. A man in the newly arrived Pennsylvania Reserves, Jacob Heffelfinger, noted in his diary that from their camp next to a field hospital they saw three or four patients carried out every day "in plain view" for burial. "The grave is dug, four men carry the corpse from its couch in a blanket, and thus it is buried without coffin, and without ceremony."[21]

Medical knowledge of the causes of the diseases afflicting the armies was limited, but few doubted that bad water and the pestilential atmosphere, called "miasma," of the Chickahominy swamps and bottomlands had a great deal to do with their illnesses — and there was very little they could do about it. The very name of the Chickahominy became infamous, a regimental historian remembered: "The mention of that name causes a shudder to run through the survivors of the Army of the Potomac, and brings sad memories to thousands. . . ." Back in May, in reply to criticism of his inactivity, Joe Johnston insisted, "I *am* fighting, sir, every day! Is it nothing that I compel the enemy to inhabit the swamps, like frogs, and lessen their strength every hour, without firing a shot?"

A surgeon complained that the army's engineers gave no thought to hygiene when they laid out their lines. "As there is no spring near, we shall have to drink surface water," he wrote in his journal. "Of course, we shall get sick, but protest is unavailing." Where no wells or natural springs were to be found, the usual method of obtaining water was to dig a hole two or three feet deep, insert in it an empty commissary barrel or hardtack box with the bottom cut out, and wait for subsurface water to well up and fill it. Using the wells of the local inhabitants was no guarantee of good water. The 2nd Michigan's Lieutenant Haydon noted without comment in his diary on June 14, "A dead rebel soldier was today fished out of the well where we got what was supposed to be the best water."

The urge to supplement the army diet was universal. Those with money indulged in pies and cakes from the sutlers. Others hoped to vary their menus with packages from home. Lieutenant Giles Ward of the 92nd New York wrote his mother that a bottle or two of sherry for his bilious stomach and soft bread and fresh biscuits and crullers "would be luxuries which you cannot tell the worth of." Selden Connor of the 7th Maine was desperate for anything green: "For a bunch of lettuce I believe I would part with my shoulder straps." Georgian Frank Coker gratefully informed his wife, "Most of the cordial, the honey, the butter and eggs were safe, only eight or ten of the eggs broken." Off-duty men on both sides foraged the spring strawberry crop and anything else fresh they could find. One man explained that there was a farm near his camp where slaves milked the cows, "and sometimes the soldiers milk them after dark so they get milked enough."[22]

The opposing lines east of Richmond and south of the Chickahominy were a mile or so apart and much of the area between them was heavily wooded, and daily there were picket-line clashes somewhere in this disputed ground. A turn on the picket line was dreaded, for sharpshooters were alert for the slightest movement. Officers on picket duty removed their marks of command so as not to become particular targets. The 2nd Delaware was stationed along the York River Railroad where the ground was open, and James Miller recalled that whenever they had to cross the railroad "we had to go it on the run and would always draw a shot or more, and many a poor fellow got winged as he crossed." John Fite of the 7th Tennessee described sharpshooting duty. He was behind a log one day "watching for Yankees," he recalled, when he sighted someone "slipping down along through the bushes." He watched the man, and when he reached a small clearing "I pulled away at him. . . . He was the only man I killed during the war, that I knew I had killed. . . ."

Private Edgar Allan Jackson of the 1st North Carolina described a scouting expedition on June 15 in which his colonel determined "to find out the whereabouts of the Yankees." He ordered them to push through White Oak Swamp until they found the enemy, but what Private Jackson and his company found instead was water waist-deep and undergrowth so thick that they lost all sense of direction and were in as much danger of being shot by their own men as by the enemy. Abruptly they stumbled on a Federal picket post, "and in a minute bullets were flying around our heads altogether too unpleasant. . . ." In the confusion two men were lost, "either prisoners or killed, we do not know which," and eventually they found their way back to their lines. It was fortunate, Jackson thought, that the Yankees were not better shots.[23]

Like the Yorktown siege, however, not every meeting between the two sides was a violent one. "We used to have good times picketing in front of Richmond," James R. Strong of the 5th Wisconsin admitted. In the lines opposite the Wisconsin boys was Robert Toombs's Georgia brigade, and one morning a Georgian was seen to step out from behind a tree and wave a copy of the *Richmond Examiner*. "We returned the salute by raising the New York Herald," Strong wrote, and shortly there was a parley between the lines in which the newspapers were exchanged and an agreement made not to open fire unless one side should advance on the other. Afterward that section of the line was peaceful, Strong recalled, and the Rebels would "come out in an open field without arms and pick cherries in plain sight of our boys. . . ."

Robert Taggart of the 9th Pennsylvania recorded in his diary another such between-the-lines meeting, on one of the Chickahominy bridges, in which the opposing pickets "enjoyed themselves talking over the war news . . . and exchanged an old Meadville paper for yesterday's Richmond Examiner." More than newspapers were traded at these parleys. A Vermont man gave a pint of coffee beans for two pounds of tobacco, and for the coffee-less Rebel and the tobacco-less Yankee it was a happy arrangement. On June 23 Baldy Smith notified headquarters that the captain of one of his picket posts had been invited to a ball in Richmond that night in celebration of Stonewall Jackson's recent victories, at which the hosts "promised to be civil to him & bring him back in the morning." The records do not reveal whether this particular example of chivalry was carried out.[24]

There was considerable speculation in the ranks about the course of the campaign. Captain Robert Haile of the 55th Virginia did not approve of all the entrenching undertaken by the two armies. "I go for their meeting each other in open ground — fight it out and be done with it," he observed. At the present rate he could see the digging continuing all summer. South Carolinian Jesse Reid agreed. "I don't see the sense of piling up earth to keep us apart," he told his wife. "If we don't get at each other sometime, when will the war end? My plan would be to quit ditching and go to fighting." On the other hand, Sergeant Charles Perkins of the 2nd Rhode Island remembered the battle at Bull Run the previous summer, and he thought General McClellan had exactly the right idea. "I like to go slowe and sure," he wrote home on June 23, "for I know what it is to go in a hurrey and come back in a hurrey, for I remember I went to bulls run once and come back agane and I dont want to see aney more such cind of work." General McClellan might have improved the orthography, but he would not have changed the thought.[25]

....

As JUNIOR OFFICER on the staff of the Fifth Corps, Lieutenant Stephen M. Weld had the duty of "improving" the headquarters mess, and on the afternoon of June 13, with wagon and driver, he was visiting farms in the backcountry behind the army for eggs and butter and chickens and anything else the inhabitants would sell him. From a byway off the main road he caught sight of a considerable cloud of dust ahead. Directing the wagon into the woods, he crept forward to the cover of a stone wall. "To my horror," as he put it, he saw an immense column of Rebel cavalry filling the road as far as the eye could see. Soon afterward, "I saw a battle going on, tents burning, and pretty lively times." When things quieted down he made his way back safely with his load of provender. Lieutenant Weld was one of the first to glimpse a legend in the making — Jeb Stuart's "Ride Around Mc-Clellan."

James Ewell Brown Stuart, the twenty-nine-year-old Virginian commanding Lee's cavalry brigade, was already a legend of sorts for the way he dressed for war. With his gold-braided jacket and yellow sash and cavalry cape, his gauntlets and jackboots and plumed hat, he was a figure from the age of cavaliers. Yet for all that, Stuart had demonstrated a particular talent for the most mundane and most essential role cavalry played in this war — reconnaissance and intelligence gathering. No intelligence source surpassed his eye for seeing and evaluating a military landscape or an enemy's strengths and dispositions. "I know no one more competent than he to estimate the occurrences before him at their true value," Joe Johnston had said of him, and that trust was shared by General Lee.

Stuart anticipated his chief's determination to take the offensive.

As early as June 4 he proposed that Lee "move down with a crushing force" against McClellan's left flank at White Oak Swamp. The Confederate army, he insisted, was better suited to attack than to defend: "Let us fight at advantage, before we are forced to fight at disadvantage." Not content to rest on this proposal, over the next few days he and his chief scout, John Singleton Mosby, explored McClellan's other flank, north of the Chickahominy. As it happened, that was where Lee's thoughts were focused as well; it was there he intended to attack with Jackson's force from the Valley.

On June 10 Lee called Stuart to headquarters and instructed him to assemble an armed reconnaissance to examine the ground beyond and behind the Federals' right flank, where the Fifth Corps was posted. Stuart was to pay particular attention to the ridgeline between the Chickahominy and Totopotomoy Creek, a tributary of the Pamunkey, over which Jackson would have to march to launch his attack. He was to find out if the Yankees were shifting farther to their right into this area and how they guarded their supply line to the Pamunkey. "To gain intelligence for the guidance of future operations," Lee said, Stuart must exploit secrecy and surprise.

Stuart had already gathered some of this intelligence through his own efforts and those of his scout Mosby, and the idea of the expedition came as no surprise. When he gave Stuart the results of his scouting, Mosby recalled, "I remarked that as the cavalry was idle, he could find on the Pamunkey something for them to do." Stuart described for Lee his "favorite scheme." Instead of simply examining the Yankees' flank and returning as they came, why not continue on, making a complete circuit of McClellan's army and returning to Richmond by way of the James River shoreline? The very unexpectedness of the move would ensure its safety, he said, and better disguise the expedition's purpose.

Lee's response to this is not known, except that he did not forbid it. His orders issued the next day told Stuart he must exercise all due vigilance and caution, but did not dictate his every move. There can be little doubt that unless the enemy interfered, Jeb Stuart fully intended the expedition to follow his "favorite scheme."[26]

At two o'clock on the morning of June 12 Stuart awakened his staff with the announcement, "Gentlemen, in ten minutes every man must be in his saddle." By daybreak the long cavalry column was well out of Richmond on the turnpike leading north, and troopers in the ranks wondered if they were bound for duty with Jackson in the Valley. For the expedition Stuart had selected the 1st and 9th Virginia cavalry and part of the 4th Virginia, two squadrons of the Jeff Davis Mississippi Legion, and a two-gun section of horse artillery. In all there were 1,200 horsemen. Among his colonels were the 9th Virginia's Rooney Lee, the general's son, and the 1st Virginia's Fitz Lee, the general's nephew. Among the scouts were men from the various localities Stuart intended to traverse. Camp was made the first night some three miles beyond Ashland, after a march of twenty-two miles.

The next day, June 13 — Friday the thirteenth — the column took an easterly heading through Hanover Court House and then southeast on the road to Old Church, and there was no more talk of joining Stonewall Jackson. They were greeted warmly by the citizens along the road, who had not seen Confederate uniforms since General Branch was routed out of Hanover Court House in May. The few Federal outposts they encountered were easily scattered or overrun and captured. All were cavalry pickets; clearly the Yankees had not extended their lines this far north. Totopotomoy Creek might have posed a barrier, but to Stuart's relief the bridge was intact and undefended.

A mile or so beyond the creek they encountered a Yankee picket post that refused to give way without a fight. There was a sharp clash of horsemen. As if in a tournament, the respective commanders faced off in individual combat, Captain William Latané of the 9th Virginia against Captain William Royall of the 5th United States. Latané wounded his foe with a saber thrust, but Royall was better armed and killed the Virginian with two pistol shots. The rest of the clash went the Confederates' way. At Old Church they captured and burned the camp of the 5th U.S. Cavalry. This was the "lively times" witnessed by Lieutenant Weld.

When they reached Old Church, shortly after 3:00 P.M., Stuart described it as the turning point of the expedition. He now had the essentials of what Lee wanted to know and might return the way he had come. Or he might continue on south and east nine miles to cross the York River Railroad and, eleven miles beyond that, to cross the Chickahominy at Forge Bridge. From there the course would be westward back to Richmond along the James. He did not hesitate in his decision; the lack of serious opposition no doubt confirmed him in his determination to ride all the way around McClellan's army. He called his lieutenants together and told them the plan. As they digested the startling news, John Esten Cooke of his staff remarked, "I think the quicker we move now the better." Stuart agreed: "Right. Tell the column to move on at a trot."[27]

The Confederates were already an hour beyond Old Church when the first reports of their presence behind the army reached Fifth Corps headquarters. Philip St. George Cooke's reserve cavalry was called to action. That Friday the thirteenth was General Cooke's fifty-third birthday and it promised to be a decidedly unlucky occasion. The Union cavalry, lacking the unified tactical command that Stuart enjoyed, was scattered all through the army, and Cooke could muster hardly 500 horsemen for the challenge. The challenge itself must have disconcerted him, for Jeb Stuart was General Cooke's son-in-law. And if these were not handicaps enough, Cooke was victimized by a wildly imaginative report of the enemy's strength. Lieutenant Richard Byrnes of the 5th Cavalry, one of the first on picket duty to encounter the Rebels, insisted that in addition to the cavalry he had seen "five or six regiments of infantry."

Lieutenant Byrnes's delusion all but paralyzed General Cooke. When he finally picked up the Confederates' trail at Old Church that evening, he insisted on making his pursuit at the pace of the infantry brigade with him. The infantry commander, Gouverneur Warren, argued that there was no actual evidence of any infantry with the enemy column, and urged Cooke to push ahead with his cavalry alone. Cooke would have none of it: he was not going to throw cavalry unsupported against infantry. A disgusted Warren described the whole operation as "a weary tramp, and an unsuccessful one foolishly managed."[28]

Stuart meanwhile had struck the York River Railroad at Tunstall's Station, less than five miles from the great Federal supply base at White House Landing. His lead scout sought to decoy the picket post at the station by claiming he was from the 8th Illinois cavalry, but his ruse failed when the head of the column came up behind him. The Yankees wheeled away, one of them shouting back that he could go to hell with his 8th Illinois cavalry. As the Rebels were securing the station, a shrill whistle announced the arrival of a train from the Chickahominy. Hurriedly Stuart's men tried to barricade the tracks, but there was not enough time. The train's engineer cracked on steam and roared through the station, knocking the obstructions aside. A trooper galloped up alongside the locomotive and shot the engineer, but the fireman took the controls and the train made it safely to White House.

The temptation to go after it and raid the White House base was

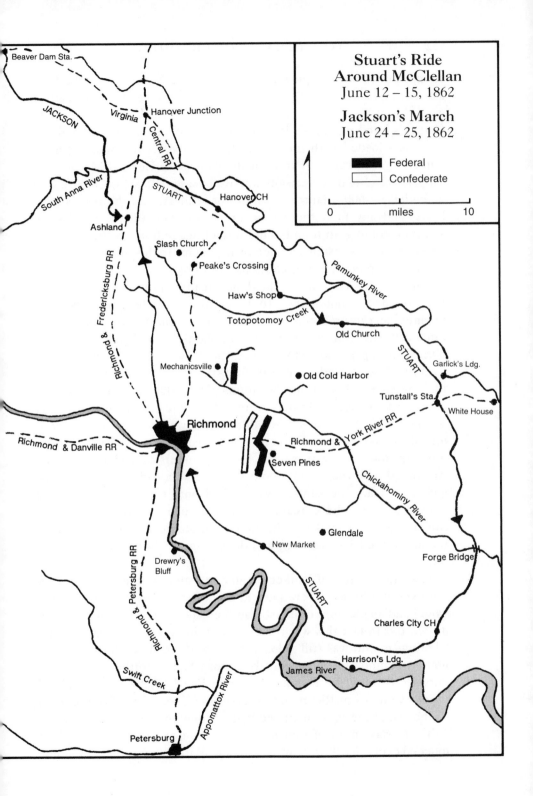

**Stuart's Ride
Around McClellan**
June 12 – 15, 1862

Jackson's March
June 24 – 25, 1862

Federal
Confederate

0   miles   10

Beaver Dam Sta.

JACKSON

Virginia

Hanover Junction

Central RR

South Anna River

STUART

Hanover CH

Ashland

Slash Church

Richmond & Fredericksburg RR

Peake's Crossing

Pamunkey River

Haw's Shop

Totopotomoy Creek

Old Church

STUART

Garlick's Ldg.

Mechanicsville

Old Cold Harbor

Tunstall's Sta.

White House

Richmond

Richmond & York River RR

Richmond & Danville RR

Seven Pines

Chickahominy River

Glendale

New Market

Drewry's Bluff

Richmond & Petersburg RR

STUART

Forge Bridge

Charles City CH

Harrison's Ldg.

Swift Creek

Appomattox River

James River

Petersburg

strong, but Stuart recognized that by now the Yankees must be fully alerted, night was coming on, and time was running short. Instead he gave the order to march for the Chickahominy. A party he sent to Garlick's Landing, on the Pamunkey above White House, burned two schooners loaded with forage and fired a seventy-five-wagon supply train, and that was the extent of the damage to General McClellan's supply line. Stuart's decision was well reasoned. White House was defended by 600 infantry, a battery of artillery, and the navy's gunboats, and any fight there was sure to be hard on the cavalry. In addition, coming up from behind was a brigade from the Fifth Corps, which reached Tunstall's Station by midnight. In this instance General Stuart's discretion was the better part of valor.

The cavalry column plodded on steadily through a long night brightly lit by moonlight. To keep the pace the prisoners were mounted on captured mules. At daybreak on June 14, the expedition's third day, the Chickahominy was in sight. Forge Bridge had been burned during Joe Johnston's retreat in May, but it was thought the river could be crossed at a nearby ford. But the Chickahominy was still running high and fast from the storms of late May and early June, and only the strongest swimmers were able to breast the current. After several hours' effort only a few dozen men were across. Stuart determined to stake everything on rebuilding Forge Bridge. A nearby barn was torn down and a pair of its longest timbers extended across the streambed with the aid of an old skiff the men had found. With just inches to spare the timbers were lifted onto the abutments of the burned bridge. The crossing was quickly planked over with siding from the barn. By 1:00 P.M. the entire column, including the two guns, was across the Chickahominy and the emergency bridge was put to the torch.

Just then a party of Yankee cavalry appeared on the north bank of the river and loosed a few shots at Stuart's rear guard. The incident would add an element of hairsbreadth escape to accounts of the expedition, but in fact this was merely a scouting party. General Cooke's laboring column was still a dozen miles to the rear. With the Chickahominy behind him and unfordable, Stuart had no further worry about pursuit. Turning the command over to Fitz Lee, he rode on ahead thirty-five miles to Richmond to report to General Lee. Late on June 15 the rest of the column arrived in the capital to a hero's welcome.[29]

There was an air of romantic adventure to Stuart's exploit which touched every Southerner who read of it. With the exception of Stonewall Jackson's recent victories, the war news for the past months had not been good, and this acted as a tonic for the nation's spirit. Newspapers printed column after column of fulsome praise. "The more we think of Stuart's late feat the more wonderful it seems," wrote the correspondent for the *Charleston Mercury*. "It is a question of whether the annals of warfare furnish so daring a deed." One of Stuart's officers remarked in wonder that all the papers "were filled with accounts of the expedition, none accurate, and most of them marvelous."

There was particular poignancy in the fate of Captain Latané, Stuart's sole loss of the expedition. Latané's body was brought to a nearby plantation, where the mistress of the house and her sister-in-law arranged for burial in the family plot and performed the services themselves. The poet John R. Thompson composed a threnody titled "The Burial of Latané" which appeared the next month in the *Southern Literary Messenger*. The historical painter William D. Washington committed the funeral scene to canvas, and prints of his work hung in Southern parlors for a generation. Captain Latané became a martyr to the cause and Jeb Stuart's Ride Around McClellan became one of the lasting legends of the Confederacy.[30]

Stuart's raid, a man in the Fifth Corps wrote home, "was a day of great excitement, you may be sure. The whole army was under arms supposing that an attack was to be made upon us from all sides. . . ." After the alarm passed away, he decided "there must have been an awful leak in our lines somewhere." A day or two afterward an enterprising young Richmond newsboy made his way into the Federal lines with an armful of *Examiners* and sold every copy to Yankee soldiers eager to find out what had happened. Stuart's raid did not greatly disturb General McClellan. "The stampede of last night has passed away," he assured Washington on June 14. Neither the railroad nor the supply base at White House had been damaged, he noted, and he blamed the whole episode on a lack of proper vigilance by his cavalry.

McClellan's order of June 18 to send several vessels loaded with rations and forage around to the James River might suggest that Stuart's exploit alerted him to the need to change his base to the James. His actual purpose in dispatching the supplies, however, was to support an impending attack on Drewry's Bluff so as to open the James to the navy's gunboats. McClellan remarked after the war that Stuart's ride "was a very minor consideration" in his planning. His major consideration was that his army needed 600 tons of food and forage and other supplies every day, and he needed to move his siege guns to the front, and only the York River Railroad met both those needs. Rather than planning to change his base, he ordered the heavy mortars and Parrott guns of the siege train put aboard barges at Yorktown ready for delivery to the railhead at White House. As patiently and doggedly as ever, he continued his plans to lay siege to Richmond.[31]

....

GENERAL LEE now knew what he needed to know to formulate a final plan for his offensive. The Federal right flank, anchored close by the north bank of the Chickahominy near Mechanicsville, did not extend far enough north to block the roads he wanted to use to bring Stonewall Jackson to the scene. Furthermore, the York River Railroad running back to the Pamunkey was the Federals' primary supply line and was vulnerable; if he succeeded in turning McClellan's flank he would cut McClellan's communications at the same time. On June 16, the day after Stuart made his report, Lee sent orders to Jackson. "The sooner you unite with this army the better," he told him.

"To be efficacious the movement must be secret," Lee said in his dispatch, and Jackson surely nodded in agreement as he read it. Old Jack's passion for secrecy was legendary; his staff insisted he even kept secrets from himself. In the small hours of the morning on June 18 he set his army in motion toward the Virginia Central Railroad at the head of the Valley.

Jackson told no one where they were bound, and left cavalry behind to screen the movement from the enemy. When Chase Whiting arrived with the two brigades of reinforcements from Richmond and reported to Jackson for orders, he was greeted politely enough but told only to return twenty miles to the railroad where he had left his troops and orders would be sent him there. Jackson's lieutenants were used to this sort of thing, but Whiting was outraged. Back at his camp, he burst out that he had no idea what Jackson was doing. "I believe he hasn't any more sense than my horse." The staff could only tell him that that was Old Jack's way.

The Virginia Central, the most direct rail route (130 miles) between Richmond and the Shenandoah Valley, had been put in a bad way by Fitz John Porter's bridge-burning expedition near Hanover Court House in late May. The destruction of the railroad's South Anna River bridge caught its regular passenger cars on the Richmond side of the break; on the western section toward the Valley there was only a miscellany of freight cars, work-train flatcars, and caboose cars. When

Jackson's men were ordered aboard these makeshift accommodations, trainman Carter Anderson recalled, "the soldiers, and officers especially, complained heavily and curses thick and fast fell on us. . . ."

They operated the trains in "riding and tiring" fashion, Anderson explained. A train full of infantry would be delivered to a certain point and unloaded, and the empty train then backed up to the rear of the column where "we reloaded the tired ones" and carried them to the head of the column. "It was amusing to see the men so unaccustomed to riding," an officer said. "They looked uneasy."

Their destination was the subject of intense speculation. "There is a thousand-and-one rumors about matters and things," one of Jackson's officers remarked. Before they reached the Gordonsville junction everyone thought they were heading for an attack on Washington. After they turned east at Gordonsville, their target was thought to be the Yankee force at Fredericksburg. Few guessed Richmond was the goal. What was the sense of sending reinforcements from Richmond, they asked, if they were going right back there? Jackson kept his own counsel. At one point he boarded the cars and bade his staff farewell, "shaking hands all round and saying good-bye as earnestly as if he was off for Europe. . . ." At one o'clock on the morning of June 23, at the Fredericks Hall Station on the railroad, he mounted his horse and with three aides simply disappeared.[32]

Fourteen hours later, at three o'clock that Monday afternoon, Jackson reappeared, riding up to Lee's headquarters at High Meadows, the home of the widow Dabb on the Nine Mile Road. He was told he was expected; would he wait a few moments until General Lee was free? Jackson, worn and dust-covered, went outside and leaned tiredly on the fence in front of the house. In a few minutes D. H. Hill rode up the lane to headquarters and was startled to recognize Jackson, who so far as anyone knew was far away fighting Yankees in the Shenandoah Valley.

Jackson and Harvey Hill were brothers-in-law, husbands of the sisters Morrison, and in a letter to his wife the next day Hill described the gathering of generals he had been summoned to attend. "Two of these," he explained, "were sons-in-law of Rev. R. H. Morrison, one of whom had ridden on horseback without resting 48 miles and expected to ride 38 miles back without sleeping." He added that great efforts were made to keep that fact secret, but "how long the secret can be kept is doubtful."

Soon they were joined by two other major generals, James Longstreet and A. P. Hill, and Lee welcomed the four of them into his office and shut the door. This June 23 meeting at the Dabb house would be described as a council of war, but Lee, unlike McClellan back in March, did not submit his plan of campaign to the vote of his generals. They were here to learn the plan and discuss its details and how to carry it out, but he did not invite their approval or disapproval.

Lee began by explaining the arrangements he had made for reinforcing Jackson and bringing him to Richmond. He had determined, he said, to assume the offensive rather than see Richmond besieged. The objective was the army corps — General Porter's Fifth Corps — forming the Federals' right flank north of the Chickahominy near Mechanicsville and guarding their supply line. From a starting point due north of Mechanicsville, Jackson would march down behind Porter's position to take it in flank and rear. A. P. Hill would cross the Chickahominy upstream from the enemy and move forward along the north bank, uncovering the Mechanicsville Bridge for D. H. Hill and Longstreet to use to join the movement.

As Lee phrased it in written orders the next day, together in a great turning movement the four commands "will sweep down the Chickahominy, and endeavor to drive the enemy from his positions. . . . They will then press forward towards the York River Railroad, closing upon the enemy's rear and forcing him down the Chickahominy." The whole idea, as he had explained it earlier to President Davis, was to force McClellan out of his fortifications by threatening his communications. The commands of Generals Magruder, Huger, and Holmes would remain on the defensive guarding the capital.

Lee then excused himself for a time, leaving the four generals to agree on the details of the plan and its timing. They agreed that Jackson, with the longest way to come to reach the battlefield, should appoint the starting hour for the operation. Accounts differ on how this was decided. Harvey Hill remembered that Jackson set the date three days hence, at daylight on June 26. Longstreet remembered it differently: the date Jackson first set was June 25, but Longstreet warned him that he was certain to encounter difficulties in marching to that schedule and he should allow himself more time, and Jackson then agreed to the twenty-sixth. By General Lee's account, it was he who "insisted" to Jackson that he give himself those additional twenty-four hours to reach the field. However it happened, the starting hour for the offensive was finally established as 3:00 A.M., Thursday, June 26.

Many more details must have been examined, for the meeting lasted four hours altogether, with Lee returning to participate in most of it, but the records are silent on what else they discussed and exactly what each man understood of his role. Lee said he would issue written orders the next day, and at dusk he adjourned the war council and sent the four generals back to their commands. Stonewall Jackson rode off northward into the dark, rainy night, disappearing as mysteriously as he had appeared.[33]

· PART III ·

The Seven Days

....

There is something mysterious connected with the
movements. Our troops are continually retreating —
enemy turning our right flank. Some suppose it
to be a link in McClellan's strategy.

— PRIVATE A. W. STILLWELL
JUNE 27, 1862

....

"Stonewall Is Behind Them!"

A T D A Y B R E A K the next morning, June 24, along the Virginia Central tracks half a dozen miles north of the Fifth Corps lines, a
young man stepped out of the woods in front of a troop of Federal
cavalrymen on outpost duty and asked to be taken to their headquarters. There he eagerly told his story to Colonel John F. Farnsworth of
the 8th Illinois cavalry. He gave his name as Charles Rean and his age
as seventeen, and explained that despite his civilian clothes he was a
Union soldier. A month before, he and most of his Maryland regiment
had been captured by Stonewall Jackson in the Shenandoah Valley.
Later he escaped and wandered all across northern Virginia, and now
he wanted to see General McClellan to tell him all he knew, which he
said was a great deal, about Jackson's army and where it was at that
moment.

Colonel Farnsworth was suspicious, and sent the young man under
guard to Fifth Corps headquarters with the suggestion that General
Porter question him personally. Any number of rumors were circulating
about Jackson's whereabouts and Fitz John Porter had heard them all,
and he gave Rean's story a careful hearing. "The boy was bright,
quick, intelligent and evidently confident in his show of honesty,"
Porter recalled, but he did not believe he was who he said he was, and
he sent him on to army headquarters at the Trent house, "asking that
he be forced to tell the truth." There Allan Pinkerton took over the
interrogation.

As Rean told it, Jackson's Army of the Valley was not in the Valley at
all but as of June 21 was only some fifty miles away, at Fredericks Hall
on the Virginia Central. Rean claimed to have seen units making up
Jackson's division and Ewell's division; he described both Whiting's
division and a Georgia brigade recently sent to Jackson as reinforcements. He gave Jackson's strength as fifteen brigades. Nor was that

all. He reported that he heard "officers and also privates say, 'Wish to God it was the 28th,' " and at Fredericks Hall a lieutenant told him the plan was for the army from Richmond to "attack in front on that day and for Jackson to co-operate simultaneously in the rear."

Pinkerton had him searched and found concealed in his drawers a scrap of paper bearing the name of a local man Pinkerton described as "an active rebel." With that the pressure was stepped up — no doubt by the threat to hang him summarily as a spy — and finally young Rean broke down and confessed. He admitted he was actually a Texan who had deserted from Jackson's army three days earlier. Pinkerton thought him a special kind of deserter, one who "has been sent within our lines for the purposes of conveying to us the precise information which he has thus conveyed." The confession got Rean his audience with General McClellan.

Detective Pinkerton had more reason than he knew to suspect Charles Rean of deception. He was another of those Confederate deserters who knew too much. A Texan in the Texas brigade in Whiting's command could have known details about the reinforcements sent from Richmond, but hardly as much as he claimed to know about Jackson's Valley army. Certainly no "officers and also privates" under the secretive Jackson had any knowledge of a proposed attack on the Yankees' right flank on June 28. To mislead the Yankees into thinking that, however, and to make them think Jackson had fifteen brigades instead of his actual nine, might be all to the good.

That night a worried McClellan telegraphed Secretary Stanton in Washington that according to a "very peculiar case of desertion," Jackson, Whiting, and Ewell with fifteen brigades "were moving to Frederickshall & that it was intended to attack my rear on the 28th." He asked for all the information then available "as to the position and movements of Jackson. . . ." Stanton replied that every report reaching Washington put Jackson in a different place. The warning by the deserter might well be a blind, he said, yet perhaps it should "not safely be disregarded."

Charles Rean probably was a blind, one of several deceptions intended by Jackson to plant doubts about his movements, but if so the plot went awry. His story proved ill-timed and too convincing. Had Jackson actually struck the next day, the twenty-fifth, as he originally intended, the Yankees would have had time enough to worry but not to prepare. Rean's "confession" seemed to erase any doubts McClellan had about the story and decided him to act on it. (Pinkerton was sufficiently convinced to want the young man "liberated and well paid" and turned into a double agent.) The next day parties were ordered out to the north to reconnoiter and to obstruct the roads Jackson would have to use to reach Porter's flank and rear. Porter prepared his lines for attack. So it happened that the Federals were neither misled by the story nor surprised by Jackson's arrival on the field.[1]

In spite of his concern about Jackson, McClellan determined to go ahead with his own plan. He had finally completed his lengthy preparations to open the campaign — the final campaign — against Richmond. His first step would be short and decisive, he told his wife, "& if I succeed will gain a couple of miles towards Richmond." He was no longer predicting a single, great, war-winning battle, an American Waterloo. "It now looks to me as if the operations would resolve themselves into a series of partial attacks, rather than a general battle." He set June 25 as the date for the first of these partial attacks. Unknowingly, he was setting the date for the first of the Seven Days' Battles.

McClellan's larger goal remained the seizure of Old Tavern, the high ground on the Nine Mile Road a mile and a half in advance of the Federal lines and the same distance south of the Chickahominy. From there he would be able to breach the enemy's main defenses with his siege guns. To properly mount the attack on Old Tavern he wanted to strike it from the flank as well as the front, and thus his initial step would be to seize the woodland to the south, in the area of the Williamsburg Stage Road and the York River Railroad. Known locally as Oak Grove, for a particular stand of tall oaks, this was the ground from which D. H. Hill had launched the Confederates' attack on Seven Pines on May 31, and it had been hotly disputed by the opposing pickets ever since. An advance here by Heintzelman would put his Third Corps and Sumner's Second in position to take Old Tavern in flank at the same time that Franklin's Sixth Corps advanced from the front. As McClellan scheduled it, that event would take place in a day or two, on the twenty-sixth or twenty-seventh. "If we gain that," he said of Old Tavern, "the game is up for Secesh. . . ."[2]

....

THE JUMPING-OFF place for the Oak Grove operation was to be General Casey's old redoubt a thousand yards west of Seven Pines, now enlarged and strengthened and numbered Redoubt No. 3 in the long line of Federal fortifications. The advance would be due west, straight toward Richmond, along the axis of the Williamsburg Road. At this point both the Federal and Confederate lines fronted on open ground, but midway between them was a thick strip of dense forest some 1,200 yards wide. Bisecting this woodland was a swampy little creek, the headwaters of White Oak Swamp, which by tacit agreement had become the dividing line between the opposing pickets. The Third Corps divisions of Joe Hooker and Phil Kearny were to carry the main weight of the assault, as they had at Williamsburg, with a brigade each from the Second and Fourth corps serving as a reserve in case of need.

The stretch of Confederate line facing them was held by the three brigades of Benjamin Huger, the Charlestonian pilloried for his alleged inactivity at Seven Pines. Huger's men did not appreciate their notoriety and were in no mood to back down from any fight that might come their way. On the night before the battle Private Thomas B. Leaver of the 2nd New Hampshire, Hooker's division, wrote home to Concord that his regiment was under marching orders. "I hope the day of decision will soon come. . . . I believe the Rebels will skedaddle as they did at Yorktown and Corinth. Keep up good courage, dear Mother, *'the end is near at hand.'* "

At 8:30 A.M. on Day One — Wednesday, June 25 — Joe Hooker sent the brigades of Daniel Sickles and Cuvier Grover in line of battle through the woods toward Richmond. A Yankee soldier described the day as a "perfection of weather." The New Yorkers of Sickles's Excelsior Brigade made up the right wing, straddling the Williamsburg Road, while Grover's Massachusetts, Pennsylvania, and Rhode Island men were on the left. Extending the line farther to the left, or south, was a single brigade from Kearny's division, under John C. Robinson.

Sickles advanced behind a conventionally light force of skirmishers, but Grover put out two full regiments, the 1st and 11th Massachusetts, as a skirmish line and had quick success pushing back the enemy pickets. Robinson's brigade kept pace with him on the left. Sickles's New Yorkers, however, were slowed getting through their own abatis of felled timber and the swampy streamed in the woods, and then they encountered a stubborn Rebel picket line, and gradually the entire right wing of the advance fell behind.

Grover's brigade out ahead reached a considerable clearing in the woods where they found a little one-room schoolhouse and beyond that the fields and farmstead of a man named French. They also encountered a series of sudden, sharp counterattacks by Ambrose

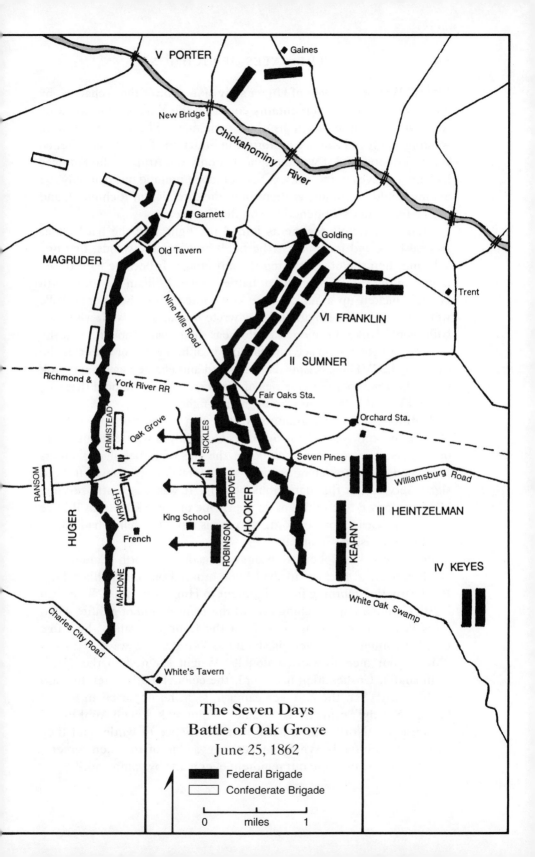

V PORTER

Gaines

New Bridge

Chickahominy River

Garnett

Golding

Old Tavern

MAGRUDER

Nine Mile Road

VI FRANKLIN

II SUMNER

Trent

Richmond &

York River RR

Fair Oaks Sta.

Orchard Sta.

ARMISTEAD

Oak Grove

SICKLES

Seven Pines

Williamsburg Road

RANSOM

WRIGHT

GROVER

HOOKER

ROBINSON

III HEINTZELMAN

HUGER

King School

French

KEARNY

IV KEYES

MAHONE

White Oak Swamp

Charles City Road

White's Tavern

The Seven Days
Battle of Oak Grove
June 25, 1862

■ Federal Brigade
□ Confederate Brigade

0   miles   1

"Rans" Wright's brigade of Huger's division. One of these charges, by a Georgia regiment, momentarily confused the Yankees into thinking they were being attacked by their own men. The Georgians were wearing gaudy red Zouave uniforms, in imitation of the famous French colonial troops, and it was thought that only the Army of the Potomac had any Zouaves in its ranks. Then someone pointed out that only the enemy would be coming at them from the direction of Richmond, and the Federals quickly opened fire on the Zouaves.[3]

More of Wright's regiments joined the fight, and the battle lines swayed back and forth across the fields and into the woods, first one side and then the other gaining the advantage. It became hard to see targets in the spreading cloud of battle smoke. William Gay of the 4th Georgia picked up a Yankee rifle and turned it on the enemy. "We were very close to each other," Gay wrote his parents, "and, when the balls would strike our men, I could hear them plain enough. And the next instant you would see him fall and hear him groan or holler, as the case may be." The 1st Louisiana charged and charged again and took the highest number of casualties of any regiment on the field that day, losing 135 of the 355 men who began the fight.

Additional Federal regiments were drawn to the front as well, including the 2nd New Hampshire. Its Company B was sent out ahead of the first line to try to put down the fire of Rebel sharpshooters concealed in the French house and, as General Grover phrased it, "did signal service" in this dangerous posting. It was also costly service, and Company B lost a third of its men. One of those killed was Private Thomas B. Leaver of Concord, who in his last letter home had hoped the day of decision was at hand.

Providentially, Robert Ransom's brigade of North Carolinians, newly arrived in Richmond, had been ordered out the Williamsburg Road early that morning for assignment to Huger's division. The 25th North Carolina was marching toward the rising sound of gunfire when Rans Wright came riding back from the front at a gallop, his huge beard streaming back over his shoulders like the bow wave of a ship. "Move your men forward, colonel!" Wright shouted to the 25th's commander. Unsheathing his sword, the colonel led his men forward at the run. When the Yankees came in sight he deployed in line of battle. "Steady!" came his command. "Front rank, kneel! Aim! Fire!" This was the North Carolinians' first experience of battle, and they delivered a perfectly synchronized volley. One of the men remembered it as "the only fire our regiment ever made by command."

The Yankees they faced were the New Yorkers of Sickles's Excelsior Brigade, on the scene of action at last, and the North Carolina rookies had the good fortune to get their first fire in against another regiment of rookies, the 71st New York. The rest of the Excelsiors had experienced their baptism of fire at Williamsburg, but the 71st did not reach that field in time to go into action and then was only lightly engaged at Seven Pines, and now it had the misfortune to be surprised by this explosion of fire coming from an unexpected quarter. Someone in the regiment — Sickles never learned who — shouted out that they were flanked and must retreat, and a good part of the 71st panicked and ran for the rear in what Sickles described as "disgraceful confusion." Eventually their flight was halted, but not before some men rushed all the way back through the woods to their original line. This was particularly mortifying to Sickles, for one of the witnesses to the flight was his division commander, Joe Hooker.

Hooker relayed reports back to corps commander Heintzelman of the opposition Sickles was encountering and estimated that he was outnumbered, and Heintzelman ordered reinforcements forward and dutifully relayed the reports to General McClellan at army headquarters. McClellan was attempting the novel tactic of managing a battle from three miles away at the Trent house by telegraph, and without any understanding of what was actually happening on the firing line he took sudden alarm. Heintzelman's dispatches, he later wrote, "led me to believe Hooker was hard pressed and I then directed him to fall back quietly to his entrenchments. . . ." At 10:30 A.M., just two hours after the Oak Grove operation began, the Federal commanders at the front were baffled by an order to break off the action and withdraw. Hooker termed it a "misapprehension of my true condition. . . ." General McClellan sent word that he would come to the front himself to take command. An uneasy lull settled across the field.[4]

It was one o'clock before General McClellan rode up to Redoubt No. 3, escorted by staff and the headquarters cavalry guard. He conferred with his generals and then ordered the advance renewed. The Federals pushed ahead over ground they had already won once that day. This was the kind of advance that was hardest to bear, Sergeant Edgar Newcomb of the 19th Massachusetts wrote home that night. "It is not the marching nor the firing that wears men, but the suspense of the slow advance and frequent halt . . . till finally when at once the storm of bullets whirs over and on each side, and men begin to fall, and orders come thick and fast, the sweat oozes from every pore. It is not fear but uncertainty, that makes men live days in every moment."

The strain was magnified for anyone going into combat for the first time. Lieutenant Colonel Samuel H. Walkup of the 48th North Carolina of Ransom's brigade gave a candid account of his regiment's baptism of fire that day. The first thing they encountered as they neared the battlefield was a stream of wounded coming back, and Walkup noted that "some of our Regt. suddenly took sick and fell back to the rear." They endured shelling from the enemy and errant shells from their own artillery that wounded two men. Ordered into action at French's farm, the North Carolina rookies advanced at the double-quick, "fought under a most galling and murderous fire for 10 minutes," saw men fall on every side, and then retreated. Colonel Walkup was trying to rally survivors sheltering behind a woodpile when General Ransom rode up and told him to shoot any man who refused to answer the colors. The flag bearer had lost his nerve but another man volunteered to carry the colors and he and Walkup led a hundred men back into the fight and regained the ground they had lost. It cost the regiment 88 men for the day, Walkup wrote, including "the best and most gallant boys. . . ."

The experience of the 20th Indiana of Robinson's brigade, on the same part of the field, was strikingly similar. Here too were rookies under fire for the first time, and as they advanced through the woods, Private Joshua Lewis wrote, "once and awhile we got sight of a Johnnie as he dodged from tree to tree." They were ordered to charge. "We so far had never made a charge, so some had blanched cheeks. . . ." In their attack a gap opened between them and their neighboring regiment, exposing them to a deadly flanking fire, and they stampeded. "So it was then, every man for himself. . . . So I ran as fast as I could, some ran for camp, but . . . stopped as soon as they were out of immediate danger." Like Colonel Walkup's North Carolinians, the Indiana boys were successfully rallied and returned to the front, but they lost 125 men that day, second only to the 1st Louisiana.[5]

Like General McClellan, General Lee came to the front that afternoon to see for himself the turn of events. He was concerned about Ransom's inexperienced brigade, but concluded that in their first battle the men performed better than their officers. He was especially concerned that this might be a spoiling attack, that McClellan had discovered his own plan to attack the next day across the river. Lee decided to take the risk. He told General Huger that he would have to hold the line here the next day "at all hazards." He told President Davis, "I have determined to make no change in the plan."

Charge and countercharge continued into the dusk. Lieutenant Haydon, whose 2nd Michigan was held in reserve, followed the action by sound. "The clear ringing Union cheers & the sharp wild yells of the rebels were every few minutes heard with great distinctness," he wrote in his diary. Back at Redoubt No. 3 General McClellan had the unique experience of coming under enemy fire, as a Confederate solid shot ranged high over the infantry and buried itself in the parapet, scattering staff and onlookers.

Finally the Oak Grove fighting died out in the darkness. McClellan professed himself satisfied that Heintzelman had gained the required ground. "It will be a very important advantage gained," he told Washington. The bill for advancing his picket line some 600 yards was costly, however: 68 dead, 503 wounded, and 55 missing, a total of 626. The Confederates' loss was about a third less: 66 killed, 362 wounded, and 13 missing, a total of 441. For a fight over advanced picket lines to generate more than a thousand casualties suggested just how intense any fighting between these two armies was likely to be.

The night was miserable for the men in the ranks at Oak Grove. There were frequent alarms and bursts of firing along the new picket lines, and more than once friends fired on friends. Colonel Alexander Hays of the 63rd Pennsylvania reported that in one such exchange "every picket and regiment opened fire upon the 63rd. . . . Even our own pickets became bewildered and faced about to fire upon us." He thought he was fortunate to escape with two dead and two wounded. Diarist Elisha Hunt Rhodes of the 2nd Rhode Island remarked that the rifle pits they were ordered to dig immediately filled with water. "We struck across a trench where the dead of Fair Oaks were buried, and the result was simply horrible." A fellow diarist on picket duty that night made the heartfelt entry, "At daylight, we fell back to the rifle-pits & I never wish to pass another night such as that."[6]

....

SHORTLY BEFORE 5:30 on the afternoon of the twenty-fifth, while he was watching Heintzelman's advance with satisfaction from Redoubt No. 3, General McClellan was handed a dispatch from Fitz John Porter. Porter reported that a contraband had just come into his lines from Richmond with important intelligence. The man claimed to have seen "a large portion" of Beauregard's western army arrive in the capital the day before "and heard the cheering welcome to them." He also heard that there were now 200,000 Confederate troops at hand, "and that Jackson is to attack in the rear." Officers there "expected to fight today or tomorrow and fight all around. . . .'' McClellan immediately called for his horse and rode hard for the Trent house.

The contraband's fantastic story was just the latest of numerous fantastic stories reaching Army of the Potomac headquarters in these days. Rumors of Beauregard's impending arrival from Mississippi had been circulating for weeks. (What the contraband saw in Richmond on June 24, if he saw anything, was the arrival of Robert Ransom's brigade from Petersburg.) Rumor had Jackson threatening the Potomac army well before young Rean put him within striking distance; another contraband had described ''an almighty lot of the enemy'' somewhere north of Hanover Court House. Detective Pinkerton's June ''general estimates'' of the enemy's strength had ranged as high as 200,000 and beyond; the next day he would set the figure at 180,000 but warn that this was ''probably short of the real strength of their army. . . .''

It was the consistency and the pattern of all these stories that gave weight to the contraband's story and turned fantasy to reality in General McClellan's mind. All the pieces now fitted together and fulfilled all his self-fulfilling prophecies, and he lost all composure. As soon as he reached his headquarters he sent a despairing telegram to Secretary Stanton in Washington.

''I shall have to contend against vastly superior odds,'' he announced. The Rebels would attack him 200,000 strong, ''including Jackson & Beauregard.'' He had repeatedly warned Washington this would happen if he were not reinforced; if the consequence should be disaster, ''the responsibility cannot be thrown on my shoulders — it must rest where it belongs.'' He anticipated calamitous defeat and martyrdom. ''I will do all that a General can do with the splendid Army I have the honor to command & if it is destroyed by overwhelming numbers can at least die with it & share its fate.'' He then set to work frantically to try to save his splendid army. His first thought was not of seeking victory in the coming battle but of salvaging what he could from defeat.

He sent new orders to Ambrose Burnside on the North Carolina coast to march inland with his division and cut the railroad over which the rest of Beauregard's phantom army would come to Richmond. ''I wish you to understand that every minute in this crisis is of great importance,'' he said. He pursued a second scheme to block Beauregard's arrival, which had the navy pushing up the Appomattox River to destroy a bridge on the railroad from Petersburg to Richmond.

McClellan then alerted the four corps commanders south of the

Chickahominy to prepare to fight for their entrenchments, for with 200,000 men Lee would surely attack at every point. "I wish to fight behind the lines if attacked in force," he told them. He prepared a line of retreat, ordering his quartermaster to have a "good supply of assorted ammunition afloat on James River" in addition to the provisions and forage already stockpiled there for the Drewry's Bluff operation. He hurried across the river to Porter's headquarters to prepare for Jackson. He was certain now that the battle would begin the next day, June 26. "If I had another good Division I could laugh at Jackson," he told Washington. He told his staff he "greatly doubted" his ability to hold position against an army so much stronger than his own.[7]

....

GENERAL MCCLELLAN got at best two or three hours of sleep that night, but his nemesis, Stonewall Jackson, got even less. Jackson was encountering severe difficulty bringing his army to the field on time. His inflexible, highly individualistic style of command which had produced ruthlessly decisive results on the battlefields of the Shenandoah Valley was proving a failure on this march. An army that had gained fame as "Jackson's foot cavalry," marching great distances at great speeds, was advancing now by fits and starts.

Back on June 22, when as was his custom he called for a day's halt for most of the army in observance of the Sabbath, Old Jack had men scattered along more than twenty-five miles of the Virginia Central at roughly the midpoint in their journey from the Valley. When he rode off early the next morning to attend Lee's council of war in Richmond, he left Major Robert L. Dabney, his chief of staff, in charge of moving the troops along. The Reverend Dabney, who held his post more for the spiritual guidance he provided the general than for his military prowess, lacked the skill and authority to direct the complex road-and-rail movement. Then he fell ill and was unable to direct anything at all. To compound the problem, Jackson had taken with him to Richmond the best administrator on the staff, his strong-willed quartermaster, John Harmon. Since no one else, not even Jackson's second-in-command, General Richard Ewell, was permitted to know where the army was going or when it was supposed to get there, not a great deal was accomplished that Monday.

The rearmost division, Jackson's own now under the command of Charles S. Winder, marched sixteen "very hot and dusty" miles but was still twenty miles behind the rest of the army at nightfall. Chase

Whiting's division marched only ten miles; "travel easy, stop frequently," was how a soldier-diarist described its day. Ewell's division experienced an adventurous rail journey at the hands of Virginia Central trainmen who during the Sunday layover had generously sampled a locally distilled apple brandy; somehow the trains stayed on the tracks and there were no collisions, but they gained just twenty miles. That night there was a driving rainstorm, described as "a perfect flood." When Jackson returned from Richmond at midmorning on June 24, he found the vanguard of his drenched army at Beaver Dam Station, only ten miles in advance of where he had left it, with the rearmost elements a good twenty miles back. He now had two days to assemble his forces at the appointed place and at the appointed hour for the offensive.

Even though the Virginia Central was still open some distance to the east, Jackson determined to quit the railroad at Beaver Dam Station and march southward from there by road, to avoid detection by the enemy. Lee's orders directed him to the village of Ashland and then southeast along the Ashcake Road five miles to a location known as Slash Church, due north of Mechanicsville. He was to reach that point by evening on June 25. "At 3 o'clock Thursday morning, 26th instant, Genl Jackson will advance," Lee wrote in his general orders, opening the offensive that along with the commands of A. P. Hill, D. H. Hill, and Longstreet was to turn the Yankees out of their lines. The distance from Beaver Dam Station to Slash Church was twenty-four miles by road, seemingly not an unreasonable march over two days for the foot cavalry, yet Jackson would fail to reach his objective.

The first day went well enough. On June 24 the rearmost division, Winder's, was carried to Beaver Dam Station in the cars and then marched five miles down the road toward Ashland. The rest of the army closed to within five miles of Ashland. The roads were muddy and the creeks high and the marching was hard; still, by nightfall the lead division was within ten miles of Slash Church and the trailing division within nineteen miles. That evening there was a rain shower that produced a spectacular rainbow, and optimists took it as a good omen for the future.

On June 25, the day of Heintzelman's contest with Huger at Oak Grove and one day before Lee's offensive was to open, Stonewall Jackson gave priority to closing up his column. His old division, under Charles Winder, still trailed well to the rear, but Old Jack was not with it to apply any driving urgency to its march that day. He had never before directed so large an army as this, and commands that were beyond his personal reach tended to move at their own pace. His staff was described by his medical director, Dr. Hunter McGuire, as "inexperienced and awkward." The Reverend Dabney complained that it was an hour after sunrise before the movement started: "The brigade commanders would not or could not get rations cooked, their own breakfasts, and their men under orders earlier, probably because their supply trains were rarely in place, by reason of the indolence and carelessness of julep-drinking officers." Diarist John Melhorn of Winder's division was only slightly more generous toward the high command. "Left camp at sunrise," he wrote that day, "without breakfast my rations having given out except one biscuit. . . ." Winder's division would make only fourteen miles on June 25, bringing it only as far as Ashland.

As a consequence, those units of the Valley army in the advance did little more than mark time that day. The 2nd Mississippi's Sergeant A. L. P. Vairin, in the vanguard, recorded in his diary, "June 25 Wednesday. Clear. 6 AM marched 3 miles & rested til 12 AM then marched 1 mi. to Ashland and filed off toward Richmond 1½ mi. & rested. . . . Camped for the night, drew 2 days rations of crackers. . . ." Another man reported reaching Ashland "by a circuitous route. . . ." Late that night Jackson sent off a courier to Lee to say that he had been held up by mud and high water and was only as far as Ashland. That was five miles short of his objective, Slash Church. He said he would move up the next day's starting time to 2:30 A.M.[8]

．．．．．．．．．．．．．．．．．．．．．

EVERY MAN in the Richmond army recognized that a battle was coming from the orders passed down the chain of command that evening: two days' rations to be issued and cooked and put in haversacks. They had now been on campaign long enough to know that that signaled a fight the next day. Thomas Ware of the 15th Georgia complained that he and his mess mates were up until 1:00 A.M. baking a dozen biscuits each and frying their bacon. Between their cooking chores and their general nervousness, Ware wrote, "most of the boys were up all night." Whether they had been able to sleep or not, the troops were up and moving toward their positions by 3:00 A.M. To one of his lieutenants James Longstreet announced, "In thirty-six hours it will all be over." It was Thursday, June 26, Day Two of the Seven Days.

At Ashland to the north, Jackson's Army of the Valley had also been up late cooking rations. Reveille found James Dinwiddie of the Charlottesville Artillery "up at peep of dawn, in high spirits, expecting to meet the enemy by noon. . . ." Despite Jackson's promise to Lee to be on the march by 2:30 A.M., however, it was nearly 5:00 A.M. before the columns started. Jackson's usual iron grip seemed relaxed, and small, nagging things held them up, such as finding water for their canteens. Already Old Jack was beginning the day five miles in arrears; to that handicap was now added two and a half hours' delay getting the march started. To turn Porter's Federals out of their line behind Beaver Dam Creek, just east of Mechanicsville, would require of his three divisions a march, on the two roads assigned them, of between seventeen and nineteen miles. Even at the pace of their famous Valley marches, that was not going to leave them much time that day for either maneuvering or fighting.

General Lee's orders for the day were designed more for maneuver than for fighting. Ideally, Jackson's turning movement would force the Federals out of their lines without a fight; at worst, any fighting should only be against the enemy's rear guard as it retreated. Lee was emphatic in not wanting to attack the Yankees in their entrenchments with infantry. That "experiment," as he told Mr. Davis, had failed at Seven Pines and he was not going to repeat it. Furthermore, there was a definite respect for the Beaver Dam Creek position in the Confederate high command, for Joe Johnston's engineers had intended it as an anchor for their own line had they taken a stand north of the Chickahominy in May. When Johnston elected instead to fall back behind the river, Porter Alexander remarked, "the enemy took the beautiful Beaver Dam position for his own right."9

Coordinating the movements of several columns out of sight of one another — the problem that plagued Joe Johnston at Seven Pines — promised to be Lee's greatest challenge on June 26. The most difficult linkage was sure to be between Jackson and A. P. Hill; Hill was to spearhead the threat to Porter's front while Jackson threatened Porter's flank and rear. The link-up depended on one of Hill's brigadiers — Lawrence O'Bryan Branch, Porter's opponent at Hanover Court House back in May — who was sent with his brigade upstream to an unguarded Chickahominy crossing called Half Sink. Jackson was to communicate the progress of his march to Branch, who would then cross the Chickahominy and take the road leading downriver eight miles to Mechanicsville.

Within a mile of Mechanicsville, Branch would uncover the Meadow Bridge crossing and drive off any Federal guard there, allowing the rest of Powell Hill's division to cross and join him. In due course the Light Division's advance would uncover the Mechanicsville Bridge crossing for the divisions of D. H. Hill and Longstreet. After that, the four commands would sweep southeastward down the north bank of the Chickahominy in a steplike echelon formation, with Jackson on the left in the lead. It was a complicated plan, but one beautiful in concept.

Like Joe Johnston at Seven Pines, Lee lacked detailed intelligence on the numbers in the Federal force he would face, but like Johnston he determined to make his turning movement strong enough to overwhelm whatever it might encounter. Against Porter's Fifth Corps — which in fact numbered 28,100 — he massed 55,800 men in the combined forces of Jackson, A. P. Hill, D. H. Hill, Longstreet, and a part of Jeb Stuart's cavalry brigade. To achieve this margin, Lee was risking a counterstroke directly on Richmond by the four corps of McClellan's army — 76,000 men — posted south of the Chickahominy. The Yankees there were less than six miles from Capitol Square.

Such a counterstroke greatly worried President Davis, for Lee would be marching most of the army well away from the city's defenses. "The stake is too high to permit the pulse to keep its even beat . . . ," Davis told his wife in describing the plan. (Joe Johnston also worried. He was still disabled by his Seven Pines wounds, and when he learned of Lee's turning movement he had a special train readied to take him south to safety should McClellan storm the city.) Left to defend Richmond would be only the 28,900 men in the commands of Magruder and Huger. Holding the James River flank, and serving as a general reserve, was another 7,300, under Theophilus Holmes.

Lee had surely thought of Austerlitz, where in 1805 an ill-conceived turning movement by the Allies opened the way for Napoleon's most brilliant victory. However, he did not believe the Young Napoleon a bold enough general to seize that sort of opportunity (the word Lee used for his opponent was *timid*); McClellan would only think of defense, not offense. Indeed, Robert E. Lee's entire scheme for capturing the initiative was based squarely on that reading of his opponent.[10]

As Lee had originally scheduled it — Jackson beginning his march on June 26 from Slash Church at 3:00 A.M. — the Army of the Valley should arrive in position to turn the Federal flank between eight and nine o'clock that morning. Before eight o'clock the Richmond army was in position. Harvey Hill and Longstreet had their men concealed in the woods alongside the Mechanicsville Turnpike running northeast out of Richmond toward Mechanicsville Bridge. Powell Hill was a mile and three-quarters farther up the Chickahominy, waiting to cross at Meadow Bridge with five brigades. His sixth brigade, under Lawrence Branch, was farther upriver at Half Sink. The lines in front of Richmond were fully manned. "We are looking for them every moment," one of Prince John Magruder's men wrote home that morning. "Batteries, breast-works, entrenchments, and redoubts are as thick here as fences at home." Everyone waited on Jackson's signal.

It was about this time that Lee learned from Jackson's courier that the signal would be later than expected. Lee could calculate that starting out from Ashland rather than from Slash Church would delay Jackson by two to three hours. He left the Dabb house and rode out the Mechanicsville Turnpike to an observation post on a bluff overlooking the Chickahominy crossing, and waited. He was not unduly worried. There should still be at least half a day in which to carry out his scheme.

The Yankees too were waiting. The general commanding had gone to bed at dawn, having been up all night conferring with Fitz John Porter about the defenses north of the river and afterward riding the lines south of the river to coordinate those defenses as well. Porter had manned the Beaver Dam Creek position with George McCall's recently arrived division of Pennsylvania Reserves. His advanced outposts of observation at Meadow Bridge and Mechanicsville were under orders to fall back to the main line if attacked; Porter was going to offer battle only from behind Beaver Dam Creek.

His two other Fifth Corps divisions were held farther back in reserve. Porter's line faced west; his worry was Jackson on his open flank to the north. He had cavalry patrolling the roads north and west, with details of axmen felling trees across every narrow defile. While Porter anticipated an attack, he gained no advance notice that morning on the direction of the enemy's approach. Repeating his Seven Pines failure, Professor Lowe did not have an observation balloon in the air that morning, and contributed no useful sightings all that day.

In the Sixth Corps, south of the Chickahominy, there was a sense of routine and quiet confidence on June 26. "McClellan has ordered that there must be no more skirmishing and picket firing," the 1st New Jersey's Lieutenant Colonel Robert McAllister confided to his wife.

"He evidently intends to invest the city, starve them out, complete the surrender, and save life. If so, we may not have to do much fighting. . . ."[11]

....

I T W A S 9:00 A.M. before Stonewall Jackson's Valley army reached Slash Church on the Ashcake Road, where his march that day was to have begun. He was now running six hours behind Lee's schedule. He dutifully sent a courier with his position to General Branch. At 10:00 A.M. he notified Branch that he had advanced two more miles and turned off to the south on the road toward Mechanicsville. That proved to be the sum total of his communications with anyone in Lee's army that day. Jackson had in fact turned southward toward the enemy on two roughly parallel roads, Ewell's division on the direct road to Mechanicsville, and Jackson, with Winder's division and Whiting's, on the Pole Green Church Road farther to the east.

Their pace was far from typical of the Valley campaign. Captain Melhorn of Winder's division noted in his diary, "We advance very slowly . . . we turn toward Richmond & find where the Enemy has been . . . & tried to blockade the road." Later the column was held up nearly an hour at a stream crossing where Yankee cavalry burned the bridge and obstructed the road. One of Dick Ewell's staff remembered the march as "strange & dreary," with dense woods on every side and "no extended views," and apparently Jackson felt the same sense of uneasiness. He proceeded cautiously, halting and deploying skirmishers to drive off each cavalry picket they encountered, bringing up a battery to shell the woods when he suspected ambush.

That day there was little about him of the great captain marching resolutely to battle. When the column passed the birthplace of Henry Clay, he was moved to discuss the high qualities of that statesman. When General Evander Law sought him out to deliver a report, he found Jackson leaning carelessly against a roadside fence with Chase Whiting. "They were both perfectly silent, not a word passing between them," Law wrote, "and, so far as I could judge from their attitudes, had been so from the time I came in sight." Law made his report, Jackson asked a question or two, "and again relapsed into silence, which was unbroken by a word until I left them."

Stonewall Jackson's puzzling behavior on June 26 suggests that he did not really understand what Lee expected him to accomplish that day. He seemed unaware that time was the critical factor in the plan.

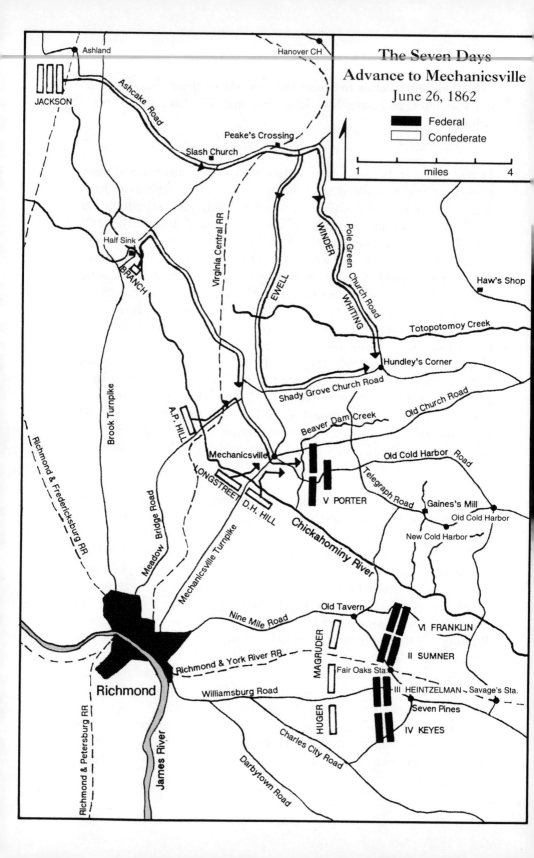

The Seven Days
Advance to Mechanicsville
June 26, 1862

Federal
Confederate

1   miles   4

Ashland
Hanover CH
JACKSON
Ashcake Road
Peake's Crossing
Slash Church
Virginia Central RR
Half Sink
BRANCH
EWELL
WINDER
Pole Green Church Road
WHITING
Haw's Shop
Totopotomoy Creek
Hundley's Corner
Shady Grove Church Road
Old Church Road
Brook Turnpike
A.P. HILL
Beaver Dam Creek
Mechanicsville
Old Cold Harbor Road
LONGSTREET
D.H. HILL
Telegraph Road
Gaines's Mill
V PORTER
Old Cold Harbor
Meadow Bridge Road
Chickahominy River
New Cold Harbor
Richmond & Fredericksburg RR
Mechanicsville Turnpike
Old Tavern
VI FRANKLIN
Nine Mile Road
II SUMNER
MAGRUDER
Richmond & York River RR
Fair Oaks Sta.
III HEINTZELMAN
Savage's Sta.
Richmond
Williamsburg Road
Seven Pines
HUGER
IV KEYES
Richmond & Petersburg RR
James River
Charles City Road
Darbytown Road

Possibly he did not realize that the entire plan hinged on his movements; Lee's orders, except for a starting time, had included no time-
table. Furthermore, not knowing the ground troubled Jackson. He
seemed uncomfortable with the guide Lee sent him and with what Jeb
Stuart, furnishing him flank protection, told him of the countryside.
Certainly he had no clear notion of where or when he might meet the
enemy in force; he seemed to expect a major confrontation around
every bend in the road.

It was five o'clock in the afternoon when Jackson's column reached
Hundley's Corner, where the Pole Green Church Road intersected the
Shady Grove Church Road. Supposedly here A. P. Hill's division
would take position on his right and D. H. Hill's division would come
up in support. Ewell rejoined Jackson at Hundley's Corner as arranged, but there was no one else there and no word of anyone, either.
There was only the sound of heavy musketry and artillery fire off to
the southwest, in the direction of Mechanicsville.

By the account of the Reverend Dabney, Stonewall Jackson was
perplexed and disturbed by this turn of events. He might be late by
half a day and more in reaching this point, but now he was isolated well
behind enemy lines without orders and without anyone to tell him
what was going on. So far as he knew, he had carried out his part of the
plan, but something about the plan must have gone wrong.

Conflicting orders and a poor map contributed to Jackson's dilemma. At the council of war on June 23, it was agreed that Jackson
would "endeavor to come into the Mechanicsville Turnpike in rear of
Mechanicsville" — the turnpike at that point, east of the village, also
being called the Old Church Road. Yet in Lee's plan of battle issued
the next day, Jackson was directed only to "the road leading to Pole
Green Church." Although not reflected on his map, that particular
road ended at Hundley's Corner and left him, in effect, one road
short — at Hundley's Corner he was two and a half miles north of the
Old Church Road and that much short of turning the Federals' flank.
He seemed not to realize that fact. As for the battle going on, whatever
and wherever it might be, Jackson apparently reasoned that it would
be late before he could reach the scene and to move there blindly
would be dangerous in any event. He elected to put his army in
bivouac for the night and await the new day to set matters straight.[12]

Some hours earlier Fitz John Porter's cavalry pickets had reported
on all three Confederate columns then on the march — Jackson's,
Ewell's, and Branch's — but the reports were fragmentary and failed

to identify the columns and estimate their numbers. As late as 3:00 P.M. General Porter was complaining to headquarters, "I cannot judge where the enemy will strike, so conflicting are the reports." On this second day of the Seven Days General McClellan would entirely misread the whereabouts of Jackson's Valley army. Throughout the subsequent attack at Beaver Dam Creek he would be convinced that Jackson was the attacker, and so failed to react to Jackson's threat to Porter's flank. Ironically, the whole premise of Lee's plan went unrecognized by his opponent.[13]

....

ALONG THE Chickahominy events moved in slow motion. The sun climbed and the day warmed and then turned hot, and on both sides of the river men waited and tensions rose. At noon General McClellan telegraphed Washington that it was unnaturally quiet on all fronts, and he added, "I would prefer more noise." In the Richmond lines Prince John Magruder took a hurried noontime meal and paced impatiently, and finally sent his aide Major Joseph Brent out the Mechanicsville Turnpike to try to discover what was going on. Brent found the woods along both sides of the turnpike crowded with troops as far as he could see. In a grove near the river was a knot of civilians that included President Davis, Secretary of War Randolph, and Secretary of the Navy Mallory. "I have never in my life seen more gloomy faces," Brent recalled. Everyone wore "an expression of weary waiting and anxiety."

In a second group was the army's high command. Outwardly General Lee, dressed in full uniform, appeared as calm and self-possessed as usual, but then Brent saw that unnoticed the general's cravat had slipped around under his collar and "his eyes were restless with the look of a man with fever." It was nearly four o'clock now and Lee had been waiting in suspense for eight hours for his offensive to begin, and still there was no word from Jackson. General Branch, the intended link with Jackson, had failed to forward even Jackson's two morning dispatches, and then there were no more dispatches. Branch, on Jackson's first signal, had crossed the river at Half Sink and started his march toward Mechanicsville, but he made slow progress and was still some distance from his objective.

Suddenly there was a scattering of rifle fire from across the river and through their glasses the generals could see men in blue coming tumbling out of an orchard, followed closely by a line of skirmishers in gray. "Those are Hill's men," General Lee said quietly. Turning to Longstreet, he said, "General, you may now cross over." The plan was at last in operation, and the battle joined.

The plan was not at all operating as Lee assumed, however. Without notice, A. P. Hill had taken matters into his own hands. Powell Hill was ambitious and high-tempered and anxious to pass his first test of high command. For the occasion he wore a shirt of red calico, soon to be celebrated as his "battle shirt." As the hours passed Hill had heard nothing from Branch either, and at three o'clock he decided he must act. As he put it in his report, he determined to cross Meadow Bridge without reference to either Branch or Jackson — or Lee — "rather than hazard the failure of the whole plan. . . ." He felt sure that by the time he was in position to confront the Yankees, Jackson would be on their flank. He sent the Light Division across Meadow Bridge on the run, scattering the Yankee pickets there, and formed up for the march on Mechanicsville.[14]

Mechanicsville was a modest crossroads village on the turnpike not quite a mile north of the river, consisting of half a dozen shops and stables and two blacksmiths (this "superiority in mechanic arts," a Yankee soldier decided, explained the village's inflated name) and an equal number of houses. In a grove of oaks nearby was a beer garden where in better times Richmonders enjoyed bucolic outings. In occupying the place in May the Federals had shelled the Confederates out, damaging most of the buildings and frightening the residents into leaving for Richmond.

A regiment of Federal infantry and a battery were posted at Mechanicsville and, farther west at Meadow Bridge, six companies of the 13th Pennsylvania, the Bucktails. The Bucktails took their nickname from the tails of bucks they pinned to their hats to proclaim their marksmanship. As ordered, they fell back when Powell Hill's men approached, but not before getting in a volley or two. "We took a rest from the fence and trees and fired," Private Cordello Collins wrote home. "Oh! you ought to have seen them jump up and fall. . . ." Someone missed an order, however, and an entire company of Bucktails, seventy-five men, was trapped and surrounded and forced to surrender. The rest of the Yankees did not linger at Mechanicsville but ran for their lines behind Beaver Dam Creek.[15]

Flowing southward past Mechanicsville and within easy artillery range to the east, Beaver Dam Creek traversed a valley some 200 yards wide before emptying into the Chickahominy. The bottomland along much of the stream was swampy, and half a mile from the creek mouth was the gristmill and millrace of a man named Ellerson. Bluffs rose irregularly sixty feet on both sides of the valley. It was approached from Mechanicsville by two roads, the Old Church Road and the Old Cold Harbor Road, which crossed Beaver Dam Creek on bridges that the retreating Federal pickets destroyed.

George McCall had his division of Pennsylvania Reserves, 9,500 strong, posted on the high ground east of the creek, dug in securely in a mile and a half of rifle pits and field fortifications. The Reserves had been recruited by Pennsylvania's Governor Andrew G. Curtin during the first flush of patriotism back in 1861, and when Washington found itself unable to arm or equip so many new men Governor Curtin performed the task at state expense. The Reserves were in the Federal service now, to be sure, but they still displayed a spirit and a sense of being special from the early days. They had not seen combat before, but were well trained and their morale was good and they had promise of being formidable fighters.

McCall put the brigades of John F. Reynolds and Truman Seymour in the main line and George G. Meade's brigade in close support. The line was braced, in position or in reserve, by thirty-two guns in six batteries, and the woodland in front cleared for fields of fire. Timber was felled on the west bank of the creek to form an abatis. It was a position, said the Confederate engineer and artilleryman Porter Alexander, "absolutely impregnable to a front attack."

Nevertheless, it would be attacked, for General Lee believed he had no alternative. A. P. Hill had advanced four of his brigades beyond Mechanicsville as a threatening demonstration while waiting for Jackson's turning movement to take effect. There was no sign of Jackson, however, and Hill's men were being severely pounded by the Yankee guns. Hill's artillery responded, and Willie Pegram's Purcell Battery rushed up to within 800 yards of the Yankee line. Pegram's recklessness pinned the battery in a deadly crossfire and it was shot to pieces. "A solid shot bowled past me, killed one of our men, tore a leg and arm from another, and threw three horses into a bloody, struggling heap," gunner Francis Dawson wrote of these moments. Four of Pegram's six guns were disabled, and 47 of his 75 men killed or wounded. It was stark evidence of how poorly the Confederates were still managing artillery tactics.

Lee crossed the bridge into Mechanicsville to confer with Powell Hill and only then discovered that Hill knew nothing more of Jackson than anyone else and instead had acted entirely on his own. Lee faced a Hobson's choice; as he later put it, he "was obliged to do *something.*" If he did nothing, halting the operation where it was for the day, the initiative would pass to his opponent. Recognizing Lee's turning movement for what it was, McClellan might strike directly for Richmond through the thinned defenses before the city. Or he might elect to take the offensive north of the river, bringing troops across to hold off Lee with one hand while with the other falling on Jackson's now isolated Valley army. The hunter would become the hunted. In order for Lee to retain the initiative the Young Napoleon must be distracted and his attention captured. To do that Powell Hill's demonstration must become an attack.

At that moment the Young Napoleon was debating just the sort of counterstrokes Lee feared. At 4:30 P.M. at his headquarters at the Trent house south of the Chickahominy, listening to the rising sound of gunfire from Mechanicsville, General McClellan composed a telegram to his wife. He had somewhat recovered from his despairing mood of the evening before. The battle was joined, he told her, but she must not worry, for the Rebels were "making a great mistake. . . . I give you my word that I believe we will surely win & that the enemy is falling into a trap. I shall allow the enemy to cut off our communications in order to ensure success." He had his corps commanders south of the river on alert "to be ready to move in any direction called for," and asked them what reinforcements they could spare for Porter if called upon. Entrapping his foe and storming Richmond were very much in McClellan's thoughts, and when he consulted with them, Generals William Franklin and Baldy Smith encouraged him in that direction.

Yet for all that, these designs of General McClellan's were only tentative, to be dictated by the course of events. Rather than seizing the moment he would march to his opponent's pace, waiting always for a clearer picture before acting. Nothing said or done that day lessened his conviction of the "great odds" arrayed against him.[16]

Powell Hill made his first attempt against the Federal right, the northern flank that Jackson was to have turned, advancing along the Old Church Road with the brigades of Joseph R. Anderson, James J. Archer, and Charles W. Field. Manning this section of the defenses was John Reynolds's brigade, well positioned and supported by eighteen guns and abundant reserves. The Rebels came on, one of the Federals wrote, "from the woods, out of the swamps, down the roads, along the entire front, with shriek and yell. . . ." There was some cover for them at first in the woods and thickets along the western bluffs, but coming down the slope toward the creek there was no cover at all. Secure behind works of logs and earth the Pennsylvanians had little trouble repulsing this initial assault, and every subsequent assault.

A Rebel color bearer in Archer's brigade remembered how difficult it was just to get through the abatis to reach the creek bank. He had to wind the flag tightly around the staff before he could crawl through the tangle. Afterward he counted ten bullet holes in the flag and an eleventh in the staff. Beaver Dam Creek was more swamp than stream here, and only the 35th Georgia, on the extreme left of the battle line, could find a way across to the Yankees' side. They could go no farther, however, as Captain Mark Kerns's battery of Napoleons opened on them with double rounds of canister. When it was dark the Georgians would fall back from their hard-won beachhead.

The infantrymen of the 5th Pennsylvania fired so fast that they soon exhausted all their ammunition, and a regiment from George Morell's Fifth Corps division had to move in to spell them. McCall inserted Meade's regiments and others of Morell's into the line wherever they were needed. Powell Hill went himself to the front to cheer his men on, and from that perspective could see that his prospects were hopeless. The Yankee position here, he admitted, "was too strong to be carried by direct attack," and he ended the effort. The Light Division lost 553 men in these fruitless assaults on the Federal right. The Federals opposite them lost less than a third of that number.[17]

....

GENERAL LEE had positioned himself on a rise of open ground outside Mechanicsville for a view of the fighting. Shells from long-range Federal guns were bursting in the immediate area when he noticed that President Davis and his entourage had arrived on the scene and were standing nearby. He rode up to Davis, bowed from the saddle, and inquired politely, "Mr. President, am I in command here?" Davis acknowledged that he was. "Then I forbid you to stand here under the enemy's guns. Any exposure of a life like yours is wrong. And this is useless exposure. You must go back." According to James Chesnut of the presidential party, who recorded this exchange, Mr. Davis agreed to Lee's request, but only went far enough away to be out of the general's sight — but not out of the enemy's range — and from there continued to watch the fighting.

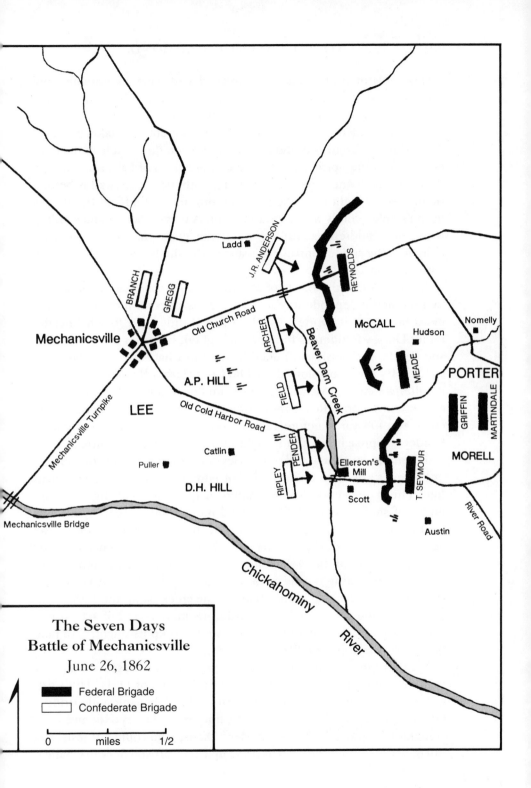

Ladd

J.R. ANDERSON

REYNOLDS

BRANCH

GREGG

Old Church Road

ARCHER

McCALL

Hudson

Nomelly

Mechanicsville

Beaver Dam Creek

MEADE

PORTER

A.P. HILL

FIELD

GRIFFIN

MARTINDALE

LEE

Old Cold Harbor Road

Mechanicsville Turnpike

Catlin

RIPLEY

PENDER

Ellerson's Mill

T. SEYMOUR

MORELL

Puller

D.H. HILL

Scott

Mechanicsville Bridge

Austin

River Road

Chickahominy

River

**The Seven Days
Battle of Mechanicsville**
June 26, 1862

Federal Brigade
Confederate Brigade

0   miles   1/2

The hills of Richmond were crowded with citizens watching and listening. The earlier troop movements had alerted them to expect a battle, and that morning's *Dispatch* seemed a confirmation: "It is generally expected that operations of great moment will take place today." Rumors circulated everywhere, but when the rumble of the guns began off to the north across the river and clouds of battle smoke rose over the trees, one rumor dominated all others: "Stonewall is behind them!" As twilight deepened, the gunfire intensified and the flashes lit the smoke clouds with pulsating light. A newspaperman on a hilltop wrote of "children gambolling upon the grass and crying out with delight as the sudden, fitful explosion of the shells strewed the horizon with meteors. . . ."[18]

In the twilight the Battle of Mechanicsville took on a life of its own that seemed independent of logic. Like a whirlpool, it drew more and more men into its vortex. A. P. Hill had ordered a fourth brigade, under Dorsey Pender, to form on the right of his other three brigades, and Pender recklessly embroiled himself in what was soon a hopeless attack. His advance followed the Old Cold Harbor Road from Mechanicsville, which approached Beaver Dam Creek a half mile or so south of the Old Church Road, then turned to the right and paralleled the creek for 400 yards before turning again to cross at Ellerson's mill. Pender's approach led him straight into the crossfire of fourteen guns and then the musketry of Truman Seymour's Pennsylvania brigade.

"I never saw such a storm of shot and shells before," Lieutenant John Hinsdale, Pender's aide, noted in his diary that night. "Fragments of shells literally hailed around me. I thought that my life was worth very little. . . . The noise was deafening." In a rifle pit on the opposite bank, with the Federal guns firing right over his head, diarist Robert Taggart of the 9th Pennsylvania had the same impression. "The artillery firing was heavy beyond description," he wrote. Under this fire, and entangled in the abatis by the creek bank, the 38th North Carolina would lose well over a third of its men — 152 of 420 — in a matter of minutes. One of its officers summed up its plight: "To take the works was impossible."

Yet there seemed no choice but to go to Pender's rescue. The only reinforcement immediately available was the first of D. H. Hill's brigades, Roswell Ripley's, which had crossed at Mechanicsville Bridge. Orders sending Ripley to the front came from Harvey Hill and from General Lee and even from President Davis, who could not resist the call of battle. Ripley's men had come up from garrison duty in Charleston and this was their first fight. They followed the same route as Pender's men, and faced the same murderous fire. Looking back on the battle in later years, Harvey Hill would write ruefully, "We were lavish of blood in those days, and it was thought to be a great thing to charge a battery of artillery or an earth-work lined with infantry."

Seventeen-year-old Edgar Allan Jackson of the 1st North Carolina, Ripley's brigade, would write home describing his first battle. "As we approached nearer the bullets flew by us in torrents," he wrote. The officers dismounted and led them on foot, then had them lie down to shelter from the fire. Then the order to charge: "Col. Stokes soon orders us to rise up and charge and at it we go with a yell; we proceed half way down the hill, halt and exchange shot for shot with the yankees, who had the very best of covering." They were stopped there short of the creek and stranded, unable to go forward or back, "firing by the light of the enemys guns." Only after it became fully dark could they withdraw.

That charge cost the 1st North Carolina 142 casualties, including its colonel and major dead, its lieutenant colonel wounded, and six company captains dead or wounded. The toll in the 44th Georgia fighting alongside came to 335, by far the heaviest loss of the day and a casualty rate of 65 percent. Between them, Pender and Ripley lost 851 men. "I have passed through a fiery ordeal of grape, canister shells, round-shot and musket balls," Private Jackson summed up, "and was permitted by the All Wise Being to pass through unscathed. . . ."

Late in the day General McClellan crossed the Chickahominy to Porter's headquarters and watched the last of the fighting from there. He was exultant. "We have again whipped secesh badly . . . ," he telegraphed his wife. "Stonewall Jackson is the victim this time." He told Secretary Stanton, "Victory of today complete & against great odds. I almost begin to think we are invincible." To Chief of Staff Marcy back at headquarters south of the river he boasted, "We have completely gained the day — not lost a single foot of ground. McCall has done splendidly as well as Morell. Tell our men on your side they are put to their trumps & that with such men disaster is impossible." When these tidings were announced to the troops, great bursts of cheering traveled along the lines, and regimental bands struck up impromptu concerts of national airs. On the battlefield there was no cheering and no music. "Nothing could be heard in the black darkness of that night save the ghastly moans of the wounded and dying," one of Dorsey Pender's men remembered.[19]

General Lee met that night with his division commanders at the house of a Dr. Lumpkin in Mechanicsville. (In a twist of irony, Dr. Lumpkin was the "active rebel" whose name was found on the planted deserter Charles Rean two days before, leading the Federals to anticipate Lee's offensive.) Lee's plan of battle had gone as far off track as Joe Johnston's at Seven Pines. Even yet there was no word of Stonewall Jackson's whereabouts; Lee knew only that Jackson, for whatever reason, had failed to carry out his part of the plan.

All the day's other failures stemmed from that. Instead of 55,800 men bearing down on the enemy's flank, only five brigades, hardly 11,000 men, had gotten into action. Their loss was 1,475 and they failed even to dent Porter's defenses. (The Federals engaged more men at Mechanicsville, 14,000, and lost but 361 of them.) The plan designed with such care had utterly fallen apart.

Lee said nothing of it at the time, but his staff, Porter Alexander recalled, recognized that he was "deeply, bitterly disappointed" by Jackson's performance. Lee himself would admit after the war that he was "disappointed" at not finding Jackson that day. The cause of most of what went wrong at Mechanicsville on June 26, however, was simply a breakdown in communications among virtually everyone involved.

Jackson surely misunderstood his role as explained at the council of war in Richmond, and Lee's subsequent written orders were not drawn precisely enough to clarify matters. Too many questions about the time and place and route of Jackson's march, and its objectives, went unanswered. However late he was on June 26, Jackson did not even then actually turn the Beaver Dam Creek position, nor did he make his presence known so as to alarm the Yankees into retreating; it is likely he did not know where their position was. After his two morning messages to Branch he made no further effort to communicate with Lee's army.

For his part, Lee counted too much on Branch as the link with Jackson, and when the delay lengthened he sent no one of his own to discover its cause and set it right. Branch was seriously derelict in not communicating with A. P. Hill and through him with Lee. Powell Hill set events in motion without communicating with anyone at all, although his (and Ripley's) subsequent assaults on the Beaver Dam position were made on Lee's orders and under his eye.

Mechanicsville was General Lee's first battle in command of the Army of Northern Virginia, and the course of the day demonstrated that neither he nor his lieutenants were masters of so complicated a battle plan. Like all generals in this war, Lee was having to learn his trade while practicing it. Nothing in his experience and training had sufficiently prepared him to manage so large an army in so complex an operation.

The same can be said of his lieutenants, even of Stonewall Jackson. Much debate would be generated as to why Jackson was "not himself" in these days on the Peninsula. It was suggested that his exertions of the previous weeks in the Valley and since had exhausted him both physically and mentally, and it is true enough that during the Seven Days his health troubled him. "During the past week," he would tell his wife, "I have not been well, have suffered from fever and debility. . . ."

However that may be, it is closer to the truth to suggest that Jackson simply found making war in the Shenandoah Valley and on the Peninsula as different as day and night. In the Valley he had studied every foot of ground beforehand and prepared carefully every movement, and had benefited immensely from the fumbling and incompetence of his opponents. On the Peninsula he lacked these advantages and the assurance they provided him, and like Lee he had now to learn in the hard school of experience.

Yet however grim the failures of the day, General Lee had succeeded in one vitally important respect: he had captured the initiative. Equally important, he had indelibly impressed that fact on the mind of his opponent. Just five hours after the fighting at Mechanicsville ended, General McClellan determined he must retreat from Richmond. In losing his first battle, Robert E. Lee had dressed the stage for winning the campaign.[20]

Gaines's Mill

··

G ENERAL MCCLELLAN stayed late that night at Fitz John Porter's headquarters north of the Chickahominy, "discussing the situation and arranging for the future," as Porter phrased it. Porter argued for remaining where he was; with suitable reinforcement he believed the Fifth Corps could beat off a renewed Confederate assault the next day. McClellan's earlier euphoria was leaking away, and he was unsure and undecided. Perhaps any continued fighting north of the river should be made from another position. The two did agree that it was now too late that night to bring the Fifth Corps back across the Chickahominy so as to concentrate the Army of the Potomac for operations on the Richmond side of the river.

At 1:00 A.M. on June 27 McClellan left to return to his own headquarters, saying he would give the matter further thought before rendering a decision. As they parted he told Porter, "Now, Fitz, you understand my views and the absolute necessity of holding the ground, until arrangements over the river can be completed." Porter took this, he recalled, as indicating McClellan would decide to have him resist Lee's attacks north of the river "even to my destruction" in order that the general commanding might storm into Richmond with the rest of the army.

If that was actually the trend of McClellan's thoughts, he soon had second thoughts. Rather than attack Richmond he would give up his campaign and retreat; and his retreat would not be back down the Peninsula the way he had come but due south to the nearest haven, the James River.

What decided him on this radically different course was the sobering discovery that Stonewall Jackson had not after all been the "victim" of Porter's triumphant defense of Beaver Dam Creek. Instead Jackson was reported to be somewhere off to Porter's right and rear, unbloodied and menacing. Still imagining overwhelming force wherever he

looked, McClellan vowed to save his army by retreating to the protection of the navy's gunboats on the James. To be sure, he would not call
it a retreat but rather a change of base — in the presence of a powerful
enemy, he said, "one of the most difficult undertakings in war" — yet
in truth he was quitting his grand campaign, surrendering the initiative, and giving up all hope of laying siege to Richmond from the line
of the Chickahominy. Confiding his decision to his staff but not to his
generals, he issued a barrage of orders. The Comte de Paris noted in
his journal that the decision to retreat reflected "a firmness of decision"
the general had seldom displayed during the campaign.

Porter was ordered to pull back to a defensible position directly
covering the Chickahominy bridges, his unstated mission to prevent
Jackson from crossing the river until the heavy guns and the supply
and baggage trains could be started for the James. Engineers were
dispatched to White Oak Swamp to survey crossings there. The headquarters staff was to break camp and be ready to move at a moment's
notice. The quartermaster at White House was to rush all the supplies
possible to the front by rail and wagon, and if the Rebels approached
to evacuate the base, burn whatever could not be gotten away by water.
General Franklin was alerted to send a division to support Porter.
(McClellan already had answers from the other corps commanders on
reinforcements for Porter: Sumner was willing to give up half his corps
for that purpose and Heintzelman a third of his; cautious Keyes did
not want to part with a single man.) That morning, Friday, June 27,
General McClellan signaled Washington that he was now ready to
"take advantage of the first mistake made by the enemy." General
Lee had judged his opponent with uncanny precision.[1]

Fitz John Porter, thirty-nine and handsome and assured, looked
every inch the fighting general. McClellan rated Porter his favorite
lieutenant by a wide margin. In April he had placed him in overall
charge of the Yorktown siege, and in May he entrusted him with the
Hanover Court House expedition, and currently posting him with the
Fifth Corps north of the Chickahominy was critically important to the
campaign against Richmond. In his skill as a military administrator and
in his confident handling of high command Porter mirrored McClellan.
Indeed, he mirrored McClellan in most respects — except that he,
Porter, would fight if it was required of him — including a careful
caution. On this third of the Seven Days Fitz John Porter would
passively allow events to shape his course in precisely the same way his
chief did.

It was not until three o'clock that morning that General McCall

received the order to withdraw his division from the Beaver Dam
Creek position. He had to move fast. While the Fifth Corps's heavy
guns and baggage had been started back earlier, there were still numerous supply and ammunition wagons and ambulances to move, half
a dozen batteries, and the three brigades of infantry. Rear guards
supported by artillery screened the movement and held the creek
crossings until after sunrise, and there was heavy firing as the Confederates pushed against the guards as soon as it was light enough to see.
The Yankees burned or abandoned a good deal of camp gear but all
the men and guns made good the four-mile withdrawal to the new
line — all but the 13th Pennsylvania, the Bucktails. For the second
day in a row someone in the regiment missed an order, and this time
the better part of two companies were scooped up by the Rebels.
Failure to get the word had now cost the hapless Bucktails 171 men in
prisoners.

General Lee arrived in Mechanicsville at dawn during this firing
determined to accomplish everything on June 27 that was left undone
on June 26. All his forces were now in position to turn the Federals'
flank and force McClellan out of his entrenchments and to the defense
of his supply line. Lee intended to maintain the pressure, keeping his
opposite number off balance and not allowing him the leisure to
become aware of the logic of a counterstroke. Otherwise, he later
admitted, "disaster was to be apprehended." He had A. P. Hill push
ahead across Beaver Dam Creek when it became clear that the Yankees
were falling back. Magruder and Huger in the Richmond lines were on
notice to hold their entrenchments "at the point of the bayonet if
necessary," which meant that they must hold to the last man if attacked.

The 2nd North Carolina made a wide flanking march through the
woods to the north and came in on the newly evacuated Beaver Dam
works from the rear. "Three cheers announced our victory," Private
William Calder wrote, and added that in the Yankee camps "we found
all manner of things." Powell Hill's men advancing straight across the
ground of the previous day's battle had nothing to cheer about as they
encountered the bodies of comrades killed in the fighting. "They were
lying very thick on both sides of the road," a Georgian wrote. "They
were lying in every position you could think. . . ." Some had been
wading knee-deep through the muddy bottomland when they were
hit, and now in death were standing rooted in the mud like grotesque
wilted flowers. The historian of Maxcy Gregg's South Carolina brigade

announced piously that "our ardor prevented us from pillaging" in the abandoned Federal camps, but others were less restrained and thoroughly looted all the knapsacks and commissary stores they found. Columns formed up on all the roads leading eastward from Beaver Dam Creek for the pursuit of the retreating enemy.[2]

....

DURING THE late afternoon and evening of June 26, while the Mechanicsville battle was fought, John G. Barnard, chief engineer of the Army of the Potomac, had searched for a new position for Porter's Fifth Corps in case of need. On McClellan's orders Barnard was to mark out a line north of the Chickahominy that would guard the bridges tying Porter to the rest of the army; however the Mechanicsville fighting turned out, Porter ought to have a better line of retreat than the one he had from Beaver Dam Creek.

Within the space of a mile and a quarter, opposite army headquarters at the Trent house south of the river, four military bridges crossed the Chickahominy: Sumner's Grapevine Bridge, and Alexander's, Woodbury's, and Duane's bridges, named for the engineers who built them. On high ground beyond the river Barnard laid out a defensive position to cover the four bridges, and late that night reported his work to McClellan and Porter. When the early morning order came to fall back, Porter went with Barnard to reconnoiter the new ground. It was a formidable position.

The heart of the Fifth Corps's new posting was a largely open, oval-shaped plateau, varying in height from forty to eighty feet, some two miles wide and a mile deep, its long outer side facing north. There were several residences on the plateau — the Watt house and the McGehee house and the Adams house — and the highest elevation was known locally as Turkey Hill, yet the day's fighting here would take its name from a site fully a mile away, the gristmill of Dr. William G. Gaines.

The Battle of Gaines's Mill was so called because of Dr. Gaines's prominence. He was the area's largest landowner and his plantation the most imposing, and he was further renowned for his ardent support of the rebellion. Federal troops had been camped on the doctor's land for more than a month now, and over his protests they had buried a number of fever-killed men there, and he defiantly announced that the moment the Yankees were driven away (which he predicted would be very soon) he would dig up the bodies and feed them to his hogs.

Sergeant Jonas D. Richardson of the Fifth Corps remarked that "it is rather tough to be compelled to protect such a man's property."

Rising at the northeast corner of the plateau and curving around its northern and western sides before emptying into the Chickahominy was a sluggish little stream called Boatswain's Swamp. (In this part of tidewater Virginia, slow-flowing, marshy streams were often known with refreshing candor as swamps; another example was nearby White Oak Swamp.) Its banks and bottomlands were heavily overgrown with trees and underbrush. Except toward its mouth, where it was steep-sided and particularly boggy, Boatswain's Swamp did not present quite the military obstacle that Beaver Dam Creek had been on the twenty-sixth, but still it was difficult enough.

To the north and west beyond the plateau the ground was largely open and under cultivation and sloped down toward Boatswain's Swamp. On the Federals' side of the swamp it rose more steeply. The area was sufficiently framed in thick woods that Confederate artillery and wagons could only approach over five roads: two from the west through Dr. Gaines's plantation and mill; two from New Cold Harbor to the north, one of them leading to the Watt house and the other to the McGehee house; and a road from Old Cold Harbor, off to the northeast, which joined the one from New Cold Harbor at McGehee's before continuing southward to cross the Chickahominy at Grapevine Bridge. Porter Alexander, who termed the Beaver Dam Creek position "absolutely impregnable" to frontal assault, wrote that at Gaines's Mill the Army of Northern Virginia "had no margin to spare over the size of its task."

Fitz John Porter arranged his Fifth Corps on the plateau that morning facing west and north in the shape of an archer's bow a mile and three-quarters long, with George Morell's division of three brigades covering the left or western flank, and George Sykes's division — two brigades of regulars and one of volunteers — on the right, looking north. They were posted in a first line in and behind Boatswain's Swamp and in a second line halfway up the hillside. McCall's division, which had fought the day before at Mechanicsville, was in reserve in a third line on the crest of the plateau. Porter did not regard himself as strong enough to extend the line back to the Chickahominy on the right, trusting instead to the broken, boggy ground there, called El-der's Swamp, to discourage a flanking movement. He did not call on McClellan for reinforcement to strengthen the line. As posted, he could count 27,160 men of all arms in the Gaines's Mill position.

Seventeen Federal batteries, totaling ninety-six guns, were ranged in line or in reserve across the plateau, and in Franklin's Sixth Corps south of the river three batteries of long-range guns were positioned to fire on any assault against Porter's left. The infantry hurriedly fashioned rough fieldworks of logs and fence rails and felled trees and even of knapsacks. Porter called for axes to fell more trees, but when they arrived they were not helved and could not be put to use very rapidly. Unlike the Beaver Dam Creek position, these defenses were prepared in hours rather than days, but they were imposing nonetheless.

Amidst Porter's preparations for battle were small matters of routine: a mail call bringing the men of the Fifth Corps letters from home, and newsdealers hawking the daily New York and Philadelphia papers. The regulars of the 12th U.S. Infantry could all be seen smoking cigars, confiscated from a sutler's stock before it was put to the torch during the morning's withdrawal. A captain in another regiment of regulars, looking back from the hilltop to the open ground fringed with woods over which he had come, and over which the enemy would have to come to attack, remembered thinking, "We felt we could mow them down as they moved out."

General McClellan's first major decision on June 27 was flavored with the indecision that would characterize everything he did that day. It had been arranged for Franklin to send one of his Sixth Corps divisions, under Henry W. Slocum, to Porter's support, but when Slocum started across the river that morning he was suddenly recalled by the general commanding; McClellan feared that Franklin would thin his lines facing Richmond, and so invite attack, before Porter actually needed help. Porter for his part believed his task was simply to hold off the attackers — which he estimated in McClellanesque fashion at 80,000 — long enough for the rest of the army to march on Richmond. Porter would call for Slocum in due course, but only to brace his lines. That with an early and more powerful reinforcement he might aggressively seek a victory north of the Chickahominy apparently did not occur to him, and he did not propose it. Certainly that thought did not enter into McClellan's calculations. He continued thinking only in terms of how much he might salvage from defeat.[3]

What especially alarmed General McClellan was the notice of impending attacks all along his lines south of the river. This brought to a halt all his immediate plans for changing his base. Beginning before 9:00 A.M. and flowing into army headquarters in a steady stream came warnings from observers from one end of the Richmond front to the other. Baldy Smith, posted closest to the Chickahominy, reported six to eight enemy regiments — two full brigades — moving from his front toward Sumner's Second Corps on his left. "Enemy threaten an attack on my right near Smith," Sumner announced. Joe Hooker sighted another large force, 3,000 to 4,000 men, moving toward Sumner's other flank; then General Franklin reported several regiments shifting away from Sumner's front and back toward Baldy Smith's.

Bugle and drum calls were clearly audible from behind the Confederate lines, indicating units being alerted for action. All this was accompanied by a series of sharp skirmish-line clashes and bursts of artillery firing. "The enemy would make a rush & then skedaddle," a man in Sumner's corps noted in his diary. Professor Lowe went aloft in his balloon and at 9:20 A.M. warned, "By appearances I should judge that the enemy might make an attack on our left at any moment." Not long afterward Chief of Staff Marcy assured one of his officers that they had managed to beat off "all his attacks on us on this side. . . ." In the view of another staff man, "The enemy appears to be intending to sweep down the Chickahominy on both sides."

What captured Professor Lowe's attention as much as anything else that morning was the sight of a rival balloon, brightly colored and floating serenely above the lines in front of Richmond. For the occasion of General Lee's offensive the Confederacy had once again improvised an aerial corps. The balloon this time was a multicolored affair of silk, the work of Captain Langdon Cheves of South Carolina. Captain Cheves had collected virtually every yard of dress silk in Charleston and Savannah (not, as a later tale would have it, all the silk dresses from the ladies of those cities), stitched together an envelope and filled it with illuminating gas from the Richmond gas works, and dispatched it to the front roped to a boxcar on the York River Railroad. The aeronaut was Porter Alexander, who gained a view of the fighting and that afternoon discovered the movement of Slocum's division across the Chickahominy. Far more important, however, was the impression the Confederate balloon gave of overseeing preparations for an assault on the Yankee lines.

What the Federals south of the Chickahominy were seeing on June 27 was another grand illusion staged by Prince John Magruder and his troupe of players. Magruder revived the deceptions he had practiced in those first days back at Yorktown, and once again he found a credulous audience. He shifted troops here and there and back and forth, making sure they were seen and heard by Yankee observers on the ground and in the air. One of his more imaginative ploys was unmasked by Samuel K. Zook, the enterprising colonel of the 57th New York in Sumner's corps, who personally scouted far out in front and caught a glimpse behind the enemy lines. What he saw, according to one of his officers, was "a whole lot of niggers parading, beating drums, and making a great noise. . . ." Colonel Zook's indignant report was over-looked in the flood of messages reaching headquarters, however, and Magruder's illusion held.

General McClellan did not test these reports against reality because by now reality was the captive of his delusions. He did not doubt for a moment that he was under attack that day on both sides of the river — under attack "by greatly superior numbers," he said — because that was just what he expected; had the roles been reversed it is what he would have ordered in Lee's place and with Lee's vast numbers. Several weeks later, when his conduct of the campaign was challenged by Secretary of War Stanton, McClellan was outraged even to be questioned on the subject. "Stanton's statement that I outnumbered the rebels is simply false — they had more than two to one against me," he told his friend Samuel Barlow. "I could *not* have gone into Richmond with my left." Prince John Magruder could not have asked for a better audience for his play-acting. As a consequence, General McClellan spent Day Three of the Seven Days in an agony of indecision.[4]

....

INDECISION was not one of General Lee's problems that day. Lee knew precisely what he wanted to do. His problems rose from the fact that now, for the first time, he misjudged his opponent. While he correctly judged General McClellan to be defensive-minded, it did not occur to him that General McClellan would give up so easily: that after a single battle — which the Federals won — he would decide to abandon his campaign, cut his losses, and run for safety. Lee followed the more logical reasoning that on June 27 McClellan was making a major effort to defend his White House supply line. "The principal part of the Federal Army was now on the north side of the Chickahominy" was how Lee put it in his official report of the day's events.

One of Lee's first actions that morning was to establish communication with Stonewall Jackson, and he sent his aide Walter Taylor to guide Jackson by the shortest route to join the rest of the army. Had this order reached Jackson the night before, he might have started south from Hundley's Corner early enough to strike McCall's Pennsylvania Reserves as they fell back from Beaver Dam Creek. As it was, McCall had too early a start and Jackson too long a march — three and a half miles — and the Federals made good their escape.

D. H. Hill's division pushed eastward from Mechanicsville on the left along the Old Church Road. A. P. Hill's division was on the Old Cold Harbor Road in the center and Longstreet on the right followed the River Road along the bluffs overlooking the Chickahominy. It was close to 10:00 A.M. when Maxcy Gregg's skirmishers, at the head of Powell Hill's division, came under artillery fire near Walnut Grove Church and two men fell wounded. They drew little comfort from the fact that it turned out to be Confederate fire. Stonewall Jackson had arrived at last. General Gregg called for a cease-fire, as he put it, "to avoid the risk of further mischief." The day was hot and hazy and still, and, as the sun rose toward its zenith, gave promise of becoming hotter.

In the shaded churchyard at the Walnut Grove crossroads Jackson and A. P. Hill had a brief discussion about their respective commands. It was understood that their positions relative to each other would remain as originally planned, with Hill continuing to advance on Jackson's right. Just then the general commanding rode up. After an exchange of greetings Hill saluted and turned his division off to the right down the Telegraph Road toward Dr. Gaines's mill and New Cold Harbor. Lee and Jackson dismounted and walked together through the churchyard, too distant for any on their staffs to hear what was said. Lee seated himself on a cedar stump and Jackson stood before him, the Virginia Military Institute cadet cap he wore in his hand, and they continued their quiet conversation.

Most of their two staffs knew one or the other of the generals only by reputation, and they watched the scene with rapt attention: Lee, strikingly distinguished-looking, turned out in full uniform, termed in the Reverend Dabney's first impression simply "a gentleman," his mount the handsome gray, Traveller; and Jackson, his uniform dusty, seeming awkward in his great jackboots, looking somehow as dingy as his dingy cadet cap, his horse a gaunt and raw-boned sorrel that one amused Southerner likened to Don Quixote's steed, Rosinante. The Defender of Richmond and the Hero of the Valley, it was agreed, appeared as unalike as it was possible to be.[5]

From their subsequent movements it is clear enough what they discussed in the Walnut Grove churchyard. Lee concluded from his map that the Federals must have fallen back from Beaver Dam Creek to the next good defensive position, Powhite Creek, which flowed southward into the Chickahominy and on which Dr. Gaines's house and mill were located. Against this second north-south line he determined to repeat his first tactic: a turning movement by Jackson, supported by D. H. Hill, to flank the enemy out from behind the creek. Jackson would march northeast on the Old Cold Harbor Road around the headwaters of Powhite Creek to Old Cold Harbor, where he would be joined by D. H. Hill, already well along on a wider turning movement over the Old Church Road farther to the north. At Old Cold Harbor Jackson and Harvey Hill, with better than half the army — fourteen of its twenty-six brigades — would threaten the Yankees' path to the York River Railroad, forcing them to fall back from Powhite Creek or lose their communications. A. P. Hill and Longstreet would harry them along from in front, driving them onto Jackson's guns.

It was 11:00 A.M. when the two generals parted, Jackson setting off along the Old Cold Harbor Road and Lee taking the right-hand fork from the Walnut Grove crossroads in the wake of Powell Hill's division. After a mile Lee turned off on a track toward the Chickahominy and Selwyn, the home of William Hogan. Taking Selwyn as his field headquarters, he called together A. P. Hill and Longstreet to coordinate the movement against Powhite Creek. Already the morning's advance had greatly relieved Lee's mind, for it secured a new river crossing at New Bridge. This put him in direct touch with Magruder south of the river, replacing the roundabout route via Mechanicsville Bridge. In the haste of their retreat the Federals had only damaged the New Bridge span, and also a smaller military bridge upstream, and Confederate engineers promised to have them repaired by afternoon. It was thus with a feeling of optimism that Lee ordered A. P. Hill to take the lead against the Powhite Creek line.[6]

The first engagement of the Battle of Gaines's Mill, however, would take place some three miles away and entirely unknown to General Lee. D. H. Hill's troops had made a rapid flanking march that morning, crossing Jackson's track from Hundley's Corner ahead of that general and then three miles beyond swinging south off the Old Church Road to reach Old Cold Harbor still well ahead of Jackson, whom they were supposed to support. They were even swift enough to surprise a fleeing Union sutler and thoroughly rifle his wagon; it was, an appreciative Rebel soldier wrote, "heavily laden with good things." Hill marched on through Old Cold Harbor without waiting for Jackson.

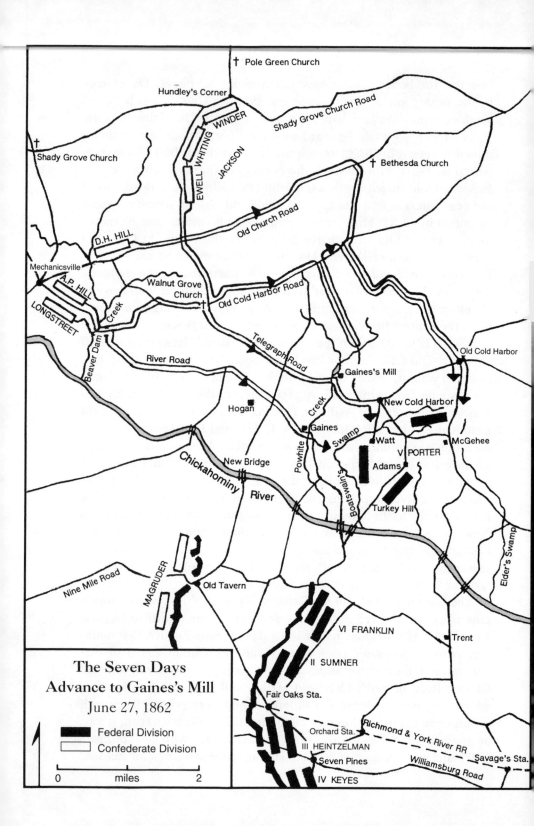

† Pole Green Church

Hundley's Corner

WINDER

EWELL WHITING JACKSON

Shady Grove Church Road

† Shady Grove Church

† Bethesda Church

D.H. HILL

Old Church Road

Mechanicsville

A.P. HILL

Walnut Grove Church

LONGSTREET

Beaver Dam Creek

Old Cold Harbor Road

River Road

Telegraph Road

Old Cold Harbor

Gaines's Mill

New Cold Harbor

Hogan

Gaines

Powhite

Creek

Boatswain's Swamp

Watt

V PORTER

McGehee

Chickahominy

New Bridge

River

Adams

Turkey Hill

MAGRUDER

Nine Mile Road

Old Tavern

VI FRANKLIN

Elder's Swamp

II SUMNER

Trent

Fair Oaks Sta.

Richmond & York River RR

Orchard Sta.

III HEINTZELMAN

Seven Pines

Savage's Sta.

Williamsburg Road

IV KEYES

The Seven Days
Advance to Gaines's Mill
June 27, 1862

███ Federal Division
☐ Confederate Division

0   miles   2

The name of the place, a crossroads hamlet with but one principal structure, Burnett's tavern, puzzled the men of both armies. It was well away from any body of water, they said, and at least at this time of the year was certainly not cold or even cool. The local people had various explanations for the name; one Union soldier was told that an Indian had once frozen to death there. In fact the name dated from the early days of settlement and was English in origin, referring to an inn or tavern furnishing unheated shelter for travelers. New Cold Harbor, a mile and a half to the west and presumably settled more recently, also had a country tavern catering to travelers.

General Hill pushed two brigades ahead on the road leading toward the Chickahominy from Old Cold Harbor, and their skirmishers soon ran into sharp infantry fire from behind some sort of watercourse and from high ground beyond. The Jeff Davis Battery from Alabama, led by Captain J. W. Bondurant, was hurried to the front to put down this fire, but like Willie Pegram and his battery at Beaver Dam Creek the previous day, Bondurant was outgunned and roughly handled. From the crest of the hill a pair of six-gun rifled batteries manned by U.S. regulars, under Captains Stephen Weed and John Tidball, pounded the Alabama battery so severely that it had to be withdrawn, losing 3 gunners dead and 14 wounded and 28 horses killed or disabled.

Harvey Hill concluded that he had run into far more substantial opposition than was supposed to be here, and furthermore he seemed to be facing its front rather than its flank. He thought it best now to wait for Jackson. The very position of the enemy was a mystery. The stream behind which the Yankee infantry sheltered was not shown on Hill's map at all; on it the whole area was blank except for the cryptic label "Turkey Hill." Poor maps would mystify more than one Confederate general this day.

From the Federals' perspective this opening skirmish went well enough, being mostly artillery fire that did no particular harm to the infantry. These were George Sykes's regulars, and one of their few losses in these moments was the commander of the 4th U.S. Infantry, Major Delozier Davidson. Under the opening fire of the Confederate battery Major Davidson lost his nerve and ran for the rear and, as one report put it, "has not been seen or heard of since." The next day the unfortunate major would be captured as a straggler by Jeb Stuart's cavalry.

This clash took place between noon and 1:00 P.M., but back at Selwyn General Lee learned nothing of it, or of the Yankees' new position. Normally the sound of artillery at that distance was easily heard, but on this hot and sultry day there would be acoustic shadows, like that at Seven Pines, scattered all across the field. Little of the Gaines's Mill fighting would be heard at McClellan's headquarters at the Trent house just across the river, for example, and from high ground in the Richmond lines Confederate Secretary of War Randolph would see the fighting across the river with perfect clarity but hear no sound of it.[7]

....

GREGG'S South Carolina brigade had been held in reserve during the Mechanicsville fighting, and so on this day Powell Hill had Gregg in the van for the pursuit along the Telegraph Road. Maxcy Gregg was a polished and cultured forty-seven-year-old lawyer from Columbia who carried the sword his father had carried in the Revolution; for him and for his South Carolinians this would be their first experience of combat. It was noon when they reached Powhite Creek at Dr. Gaines's mill. Lee had warned Gregg to expect a battle here, but instead he met only desultory fire from across the creek. Seizing the opportunity, Gregg had engineers quickly rebuild the road bridge at the mill, and on that and a nearby milldam the South Carolinians rushed across. To Gregg's surprise — and to General Lee's — the Yankees on the scene hurried away.

These were men from the 9th Massachusetts, and they had orders not to stay long at this outpost. Going back across an open field, one of the Yankees was hit and went down, only to get up and start running for his life. He was now the only target in sight, and an entire company opened on him, excited by the chase. "Cries of 'Kill him!' 'Shoot him!' 'Down with the fellow!' and others of rougher cast resounded from every side," one of the South Carolinians wrote. Bullets kicked up spurts of dust all around him, yet try as they might they could not bring down their elusive quarry. Eventually they would come on him, spent and collapsed from loss of blood, and with frank admiration send him to the rear for treatment. Entering New Cold Harbor on the Telegraph Road, Gregg's men turned south there and ran ahead at the double-quick down a slope to a belt of trees marking the base of a long hill.

Abruptly they were met with a withering fire that stopped their charge at the trees and drove them back in confusion. From the high ground beyond, Yankee artillery joined in with shell and solid shot.

Gregg rallied his broken ranks and regained his advanced line, and reported back to Powell Hill that he had brought the enemy to bay. Hill was soon up to see matters for himself, and there Lee joined him. It became clear, as they studied the scene through their glasses, that the Federals had taken their stand not behind Powhite Creek as expected but in a position considerably more imposing. They were facing north as well as west, and they were there in great force. Presumably a local guide identified the obstacle Gregg had struck as Boatswain's Swamp, so that General Lee might mark it on the empty space on his map.

Lee concluded that his opponent was making a showdown fight of it, apparently with the largest part of his army, and he accepted the challenge. Maxcy Gregg was told to hold on where he was until the rest of the Light Division joined him for a renewed offensive. Longstreet was ordered up in support behind A. P. Hill and to his right. On the far left, as arranged earlier in the Walnut Grove churchyard, Jackson and D. H. Hill should soon add their considerable weight to the contest, forcing the Federals to shift eastward to meet them or be cut off from their base. All told, Lee mustered 54,300 men in six divisions north of the Chickahominy that afternoon.

The largest of these divisions, with 12,200 men, was Powell Hill's, and beginning about 1:00 P.M. Hill's other five brigades began deploying for action alongside Gregg's brigade. Gregg was posted on the left, just east of the track running from New Cold Harbor to the McGehee house on the plateau, and to his right the brigades of Branch, Pender, Joseph R. Anderson, Field, and Archer formed up, making a continuous, convex battle line more than three-quarters of a mile long. Initially Hill had just two of his batteries in support, although later two others joined the fight; once again, the Confederates were failing to mass their guns to concentrate their fire, and both their gunners and their infantry would suffer as a result. While the woods along the Telegraph Road offered some cover during this deployment, most of A. P. Hill's men would have at least a quarter mile of open ground to cross before they reached Boatswain's Swamp.

From his headquarters on the hilltop at the Watt house, Fitz John Porter was carefully observing the enemy build-up. George Sykes, one of his division commanders, would describe the midday pause as "only the lull that precedes the storm." Already Porter had noted the skirmishing and probing against his right and center; off to his left, to the west along the Chickahominy, rising dust clouds along the River Road indicated a further gathering of the Rebel host. He decided he must strengthen his defenses, and at 2:00 P.M. signaled army headquarters, "If you can send Slocum over please do so."

General McClellan, repeating his experiment of two days before at Oak Grove, was attempting to direct the battle by telegraph from his Trent house headquarters south of the river. Unlike that earlier battle, however, he would not go to the front this day to direct any action personally. He expected action on every front; anticipating attacks at every point of his lines, he dared not leave headquarters and his communications. He would judge none of the fighting — and on Prince John Magruder's front, none of the pseudofighting — for himself, trusting entirely to his lieutenants for his impressions. He relayed Porter's request to Sixth Corps headquarters, and Henry W. Slocum's division was ordered to cross the Chickahominy at Alexander's Bridge.[8]

It was 2:30 P.M. when A. P. Hill signaled the advance. Gregg's men had the most forest cover approaching Boatswain's Swamp and had forced a lodgement there. They were at the center of the Federal line, where the divisions of Sykes and Morell joined, and they soon got into so savage a fight there that one Southerner remembered it as the heaviest fire of the war. A Federal officer said simply, "Hell itself seemed to break loose on our division."

The 1st South Carolina Rifles charged with bayonets fixed toward a Massachusetts battery that had raked them since they first reached the field. Moving to meet the assault was the battery's support, the 5th New York, called the "Red Legs" for their baggy red Zouave pants. Answering the Rifles' Rebel yell, the Red Legs shouted out a cheer of their own: "Zou-zou-zou!" The range closed until it was point-blank, and there were swirls of hand-to-hand fighting. Finally, with the aid of a regiment of Sykes's regulars, the Zouaves drove the South Carolinians back to their starting point.

The 1st Rifles would count 309 casualties that day, the greatest loss in any Confederate regiment on the field and 57 percent of their numbers. The rest of Gregg's brigade fared little better. Sergeant Barry Benson of the 1st South Carolina volunteers remembered his regiment being ordered to lie down to try to shelter from the incessant fire. "Men were killed and wounded amongst us everywhere in rapid succession," he wrote. "As I lay, a man on my right (I could have touched him) . . . suddenly vomited up blood, turned over and died. The wounded were steadily rising and running to the rear." Benson himself was nicked by a bullet and at last the order came to fall back. He recalled the sound of the musketry as a continuous roar, like some great waterfall. The air was smoky and scorching hot. Gregg's brigade was fought to exhaustion. It would suffer 815 casualties on June 27, the largest toll in any brigade in Lee's army.[9]

George Morell's division contained a thousand fewer men than A. P. Hill's, but with a part of Sykes's division also engaged, the defending Federals had a small advantage in numbers over the attackers. The Yankees had a considerable advantage in artillery. There were three batteries posted on the lower slopes of the plateau to meet Hill's attack, and higher up on the crest were several more. The Confederate gunners made little impression on this array. Captain William Crenshaw's Virginia battery, for example, retired with two of its Napoleons disabled with broken axles and the other two too hot from continuous firing to be safely fired again. When Captain D. G. McIntosh's Pee Dee Artillery of South Carolina came on the field, battle smoke so obscured the hill that McIntosh could not tell friend from foe and ceased firing after three rounds. So many Federal guns crowded the crest that they endangered the infantry they were firing over. Several Union regiments in the first line would report casualties from misaimed canister or from poorly fuzed shells that exploded prematurely.

Lawrence Branch's brigade, which like Gregg's had been held out of the Mechanicsville fighting, was also badly battered during this assault and lost 401 men. Branch's 7th North Carolina had particular misfortune with color bearers. The regular color bearer, Corporal Henry Fight, was badly wounded almost the moment the charge began. Corporal James Harris took up the flag and was wounded soon after. Colonel Reuben Campbell then carried the colors out ahead of the line and told the men to hold their fire and follow him at charge bayonets. He was within twenty paces of the Yankee line when he was killed. Lieutenant Duncan Haywood was the next flag bearer, and the next to be killed. Finally a Corporal Peavey bore the flag safely away on the retreat. The staff was splintered and the banner was found to have thirty-two holes in it.

Hiram Berdan's regiment of U.S. Sharpshooters contributed to this toll. Posted as skirmishers they dropped back from tree to tree, sharpshooter Brigham Buswell recalled, "loading as we ran, in Indian style according to our usual custom. . . . We dropped their colors several times while falling back through the forest. . . ." Another of Berdan's men reported firing as fast as he could fit cartridges into his Sharps breech-loader, and at forty yards' range it was hardly necessary to aim: "We couldn't help hitting them. . . ."

None of A. P. Hill's brigades, except Maxcy Gregg's, was able to gain even a toehold beyond Boatswain's Swamp. Archer's brigade, like Branch's, reached to within twenty paces of the Federal line — close enough to lose two battle flags — before being driven back. Two of Dorsey Pender's regiments actually broke Morell's line, but only for a moment. Joseph R. Anderson's brigade made three unavailing charges. The brigade of Charles Field became so entangled in the swampy undergrowth that the second line unseeingly poured deadly volleys into the backs of the men in the first rank. The colonel of the 47th Virginia had to order his men to fall flat to avoid the fire coming at them from both front and back. A Virginian wrote his wife, "Our Generals was not hiding from the balls but facing the music, all the time commanding Forward which was promptly obeyed, but thousands of our men fell in the action. . . ."

Far over on the Federal left, Private Oliver Norton and the men of the 83rd Pennsylvania had an experience not unlike that of the 47th Virginia, except that they were a good deal safer. The Pennsylvanians' brigade commander, Daniel Butterfield, had posted them right down in the bottomland of Boatswain's Swamp, next to the streambed. Behind them, atop the bank of the ravine, was the 12th New York, and beyond them atop the far bank but out of their sight was James Archer's Rebel brigade. Throughout this assault Norton and his comrades trained their rifles on the far bank but saw no one to shoot at, and all the while Federal and Confederate fire crisscrossed over their heads. Their only danger was from falling tree limbs clipped off by the intense gunfire.

Powell Hill's men maintained their attack for nearly two hours, but in the end they were no closer to the enemy than when they started. "These brave men had done all that any soldiers could do," Hill said. He would lose 2,154 men on June 27, nearly all of them in this fruitless series of attacks. Two days of such attacks had cost him nearly a quarter of the Light Division, and he must have wondered at the ill fate dogging his steps. For the second day in a row his division carried the brunt of the battle virtually unsupported. And for the second day in a row the same question was running through the minds of the Confederate high command: Where was Jackson?[10]

....

AT THE HEIGHT of A. P. Hill's assault, Captain William Biddle of McClellan's staff arrived at Fitz John Porter's to get an appraisal of the situation. Biddle found Porter calmly sitting his horse behind a strip of woods overlooking his left flank. A tide of wounded men streamed past, and bullets and shells were dropping all around. Biddle asked the general if he had any message for headquarters. "You can see for yourself, Captain," Porter said. "We're holding them, but it's getting hotter and hotter." Just then the head of Slocum's division came up from the river crossing, and Porter hurried off to place his reinforcements. Slocum's arrival raised his total count of men to 36,400. Porter did not send Captain Biddle back to McClellan with a demand for additional forces with which to mount a counteroffensive. "The design of battle," a Fifth Corps brigadier observed, "seemed to contemplate that we should simply hold our position."

Porter's telegram reporting A. P. Hill's repulse momentarily brightened General McClellan. "If the enemy are retiring and you are a chasseur, pitch in," he telegraphed Porter. In the same mood, he told William Franklin, on the south bank of the river, "If you see a chance to go over the Duane bridge and take the enemy in flank please do it." He was taken aback by Franklin's reply. He had seen Rebels near the northern end of Duane's Bridge, Franklin explained somewhat apologetically, and fearing they would cross over and attack him, he had had the bridge destroyed. Soon after, General Sumner reported to headquarters an enemy force in the Richmond lines drawn up in line of battle threatening him; soon after that, it appeared that an assault on Baldy Smith was imminent.

McClellan's optimism evaporated, and he became resigned to events taking their course. Captain Biddle never forgot the scene around the Trent house when he returned: all the headquarters tents down and packed away, wagons loaded, horses saddled, only the telegraph office still operating, and in the shade of a tall walnut tree General McClellan sitting silently by himself on a stump and the staff standing around in little groups, everyone "waiting the result of Porter's fight."[11]

Stonewall Jackson was meanwhile experiencing yet another bad march. At Walnut Grove Church he had obtained a guide, to whom he apparently said only that he wanted to go to Old Cold Harbor. Something less than two miles into the march the guide dutifully turned the column off on a woods road that forked to the right, a road that led past Gaines's Mill and near New Cold Harbor intersected the Telegraph Road running eastward to Old Cold Harbor. This was more direct and shorter than the more northerly Old Cold Harbor Road they had been following.

A mile and a quarter down the woods road, as they neared Dr. Gaines's millpond, the rising sound of battle could be heard ahead. "Where is that firing?" Old Jack demanded of the guide. The man replied that he supposed it came from around Gaines's Mill. "Does this road lead there?" Jackson wanted to know. That it did, the guide said, and then on to Old Cold Harbor. But he did not want to go to Gaines's Mill, Jackson said with some heat, only to Old Cold Harbor "leaving that place to the right," by which he meant approaching it from a northerly direction in a flanking movement. The guide replied with equal heat that had he been told that in the first place, "I could have directed you aright." Back at the turning they should have taken the left fork, not the right one.

There was nothing for it but to reverse the column and retrace their steps to the Old Cold Harbor Road. Jackson seemed strangely resigned to the prospect. When the Reverend Dabney expressed his concern at the inevitable delay in reaching the field of battle — this misdirection would cost the Valley army at least an hour and a half of marching and countermarching — Jackson replied that they must trust to "the providence of our God . . . that no mischief shall result."

As it happened, the fortunes of the Confederacy would have benefited greatly had God's providence directed Old Jack to continue the way the guide was leading him. In the course of events that day, Dick Ewell's division at the head of Jackson's column would go into battle hardly a mile and a quarter from the point where it turned back — but only some three hours later and after a roundabout march of six miles. Jackson, however, determined to hew to Lee's order to outflank the Yankees by way of the Old Cold Harbor Road so as to intercept their retreat.[12]

A. P. Hill's brigades were still making their thrusts against the Boatswain's Swamp line when Ewell and his division reached Old Cold Harbor. Jackson himself was farther back in the column, and Lee's aide Walter Taylor, sent out after any of Jackson's troops he could find, came on Ewell first and told him to bring his men to the battleground as quickly as possible. Much had changed since the meeting in the Walnut Grove churchyard; battle was joined, and General Lee's concern now was that the Federals would counterattack Powell Hill's fading Light Division.

At the same time, Lee told Longstreet on the right to make at least a diversion in Hill's favor. It was 3:30 P.M. or a little after when Lee greeted Dick Ewell on the Telegraph Road near New Cold Harbor and gave him directions for putting his three brigades into the fight. He also told the first staff man he found there, Ewell's aide Campbell Brown, to locate the rest of Stonewall Jackson's forces and bring them to the field without delay.

Richard Stoddard Ewell was forty-five and bald and had pop eyes and a bushy beard and a squeaky voice, hardly the image of the professional soldier he was. His men called him "Old Bald Head" and were devoted to him. He had fought well under Jackson in the Shenandoah Valley but confessed his perplexity at that general's ways. His directions from Lee were straightforward enough — to attack as soon as he could where the brigades of Gregg and Branch, of Powell Hill's division, had gone in and been repulsed, so as to maintain the momentum of the offensive. His target would be the center of the Federal position.

Without waiting for the rest of his division to deploy, Ewell sent in his lead brigade, the famous (and notorious) Louisiana Tigers. The Louisianians were under the command that day of their senior colonel, Isaac Seymour, in place of the ill Richard Taylor, and under Seymour's inexperienced hand they soon became confused in the woods and boggy thickets of Boatswain's Swamp. In only fifteen minutes, the 9th Louisiana's Henry Handerson wrote, four of his company were killed and four severely wounded, all within ten paces of him, and he himself took a bullet through his hat. "We fired only at the smoke of their guns," he wrote. Colonel Seymour fell dead in the storm of fire, and the leaderless Tigers milled about in confusion.

Major Roberdeau Wheat, the celebrated soldier of fortune who ruled the most unruly of all the Tigers, the 1st Louisiana Special Battalion, pushed out in front to direct the charge and died instantly with a bullet through his brain. Just before the assault, Wheat had shared a drink from the flask of staff man Moxley Sorrel. "Moxley," he said, "something tells old Bob that this is the last drink he'll ever take in this world and he'll take it with you." Wheat's death demoralized the Tigers. "They have killed the old Major, and I am going home," one of his men cried. "I wouldn't fight for Jesus Christ now!" The Louisiana Tigers fell back from Boatswain's Swamp and out of the battle.

Ewell's next brigade, Isaac Trimble's, began its charge in piecemeal fashion with just two of its regiments, the 15th Alabama and 21st Georgia. The Georgians' colonel had drunk himself to sleep under a tree, and Major Thomas Hooper led them into battle, only to fall badly wounded. (Major Campbell Brown would report another of the division's officers drunk that afternoon, this one a staff man always considered sober as a judge, who galloped about the field wildly and issued incoherent orders until he was shot off his horse and killed.) Going forward the men of the 21st Georgia met some of the Louisiana Tigers coming out. "Boys," one of them called out, "you are mighty good but that's hell in there." The Georgians soon found reason to agree. Corporal Sidney J. Richardson wrote his parents afterward that he still had no idea how he escaped alive, "for there was five wounded and two killed in the crowd I was in, all I can see it was the will of the lord to spair my life a little longer." The 21st Georgia did not back away from this murderous fire, but it could not advance beyond the swamp, either.

The 15th Alabama went in alongside the Georgians and had the same experience. Between them these two regiments of Trimble's would lose one man of every five on June 27. As the Alabamians reeled back under the enemy's fire, they were rallied by a horseman riding up and down behind the firing line, commending them on their shooting and urging them to stand fast. They took him for an officer and obeyed his exhortations, but in fact he was a high private from Company F, Frank Champion, who had come upon a riderless horse and took it upon himself to lead his comrades to victory. General Ewell went himself right to the front to gauge the action, and had his horse killed under him. He continued to command on foot, pausing only long enough to shake a spent Yankee bullet out of his boot.[13]

The Yankee battle line behind Boatswain's Swamp stood fast against these repeated attacks, but each one took a toll. The men of the 9th Massachusetts in the center had been issued sixty rounds that morning, but by this time few had any left. "We took the ammunition from the boxes of the dead and wounded and fired that also," a diarist in the 9th wrote, and after that resource was exhausted they were relieved and marched to the rear to resupply. Since their midday skirmish at Dr. Gaines's gristmill, the Boston Irishmen of the 9th had fought off assaults by Branch, Pender, and now Trimble, and their battle was not done yet; for the day they would count 231 casualties. The nearby Red Legs of the 5th New York Zouaves finally went back as well to refill their cartridge boxes, having lost a third of their number in a succession of charges and countercharges. A row of red-clad bodies, like a high tide line, marked their most advanced position.

In the still air the plateau was thickly wreathed in low-hanging

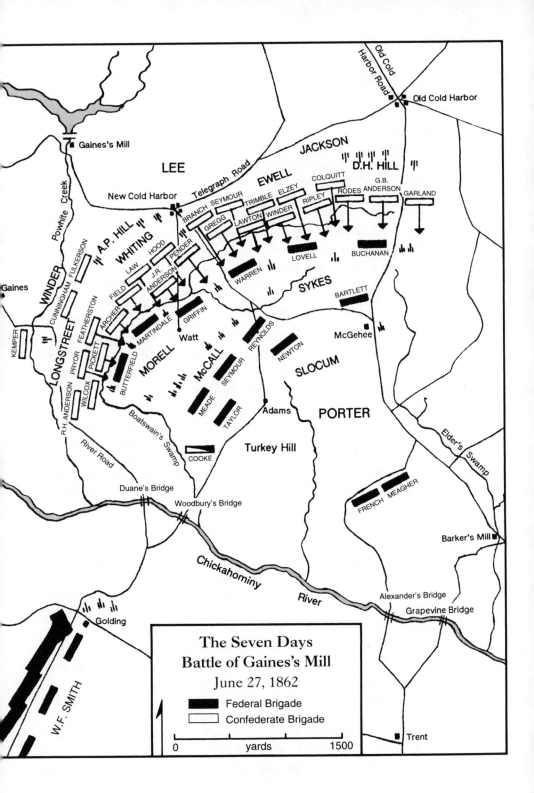

The Seven Days
Battle of Gaines's Mill

June 27, 1862

■ Federal Brigade
□ Confederate Brigade

0   yards   1500

smoke from the musketry, so that from a distance only the treetops were visible. Above the Federal artillery positions were slow-rising columns of white smoke, providing the only guide for the firing of the Rebel batteries. A Northern officer was struck by the sight of trees tossing as if in a storm on this windless day, and then realized that it was a manmade storm of shot and shell and musketry.

Fitz John Porter pushed troops from the reserve into gaps in his battered line. The 13th Pennsylvania, the Bucktails, went forward into what Private Cordello Collins called "a hard fight; we slaughtered them big, and they killed a great many of us; the ground was spotted with dead rebels." Another of George McCall's Pennsylvania regiments, the 9th, sent to the front to relieve the 9th Massachusetts, advanced at charge bayonets. "We chased them across a field into some woods," Corporal Adam Bright told his homefolks, "but then they got reinforcements and we had to fall back. Three times we reformed our lines and charged them but could not get them out of the woods."

Slocum's Sixth Corps troops were also coming into action now, inserted like McCall's regiments into the lines at whatever point the need seemed greatest. Just as George W. Taylor's New Jersey brigade reached the field, a youthful-looking captain galloped up to General Taylor and burst out at him in rapid French, gesturing and pointing to the front. The bewildered Taylor turned to his aide, Lieutenant E. B. Grubb, and asked, "Who the devil is this, and what is he talking about?" Grubb recognized him as the Comte de Paris, of General McClellan's staff; the count spoke English well enough, he said, but apparently overcome by the excitement of the moment he had reverted to his native tongue in urging Taylor to give him a regiment to plug a gap in the line. Was he sure about this, the general said, eyeing the young captain still spewing French at him. Lieutenant Grubb assured him that he was indeed the Comte de Paris. "Very well then," Taylor said grudgingly, "give him the Fourth Regiment and go see where he puts it. . . ."

At Mrs. Price's house on high ground within the Confederate lines south of the river scores of officers and dignitaries from Richmond, including President Davis, gathered to watch the battle a mile or so distant. Their view was of the Confederate right, where Longstreet was preparing to send in George Pickett's brigade of Virginians to divert the Yankees' attention from A. P. Hill and Ewell.

Major Joseph Brent of Magruder's staff remarked on the panoramic view from Mrs. Price's. He watched as Pickett's brigade, nearly 2,200 strong, deployed in a double line under its Confederate and regimental flags, field officers and file closers taking position, skirmishers melting back to clear the fields of fire. "A moment's pause," Brent wrote, "and then the long line streamed forward, descending the slopes leading into the wide bottoms of the stream, and as they entered and disappeared into the woods and thickets their ranks were fringed with the curling white smoke of musketry fire." An acoustic shadow muffled the sounds of battle, giving an eerie tone to the scene.

As Brent watched, Federal artillery on the hilltop joined the contest and battle smoke increasingly obscured the picture. Before long a trickle of men was seen to come out of the smoky woods and hurry toward the rear, and then numbers of stretcher bearers with their burdens. "In a little while, after the first stragglers appeared, their numbers increased, and then after an interval, large bodies of men without any order came out, not running, but evidently under the control of their officers, and after this it was evident that our whole line was repulsed and retreating." General Longstreet watched as well, and recognized that his diversion had failed. The only way to push the Yankees off their hill, Old Pete decided, was by a full-fledged assault by his entire division, perhaps by the entire army.[14]

....

SHORTLY AFTER four o'clock that afternoon, after repulsing the assaults by A. P. Hill's division, Fitz John Porter had telegraphed headquarters that everything was "most satisfactory. . . . Our men have behaved nobly and driven back the enemy many times, cheering them as they retired. . . ." But as the Rebels continued their attacks — these were Ewell's troops and Longstreet's — Porter's optimism turned to anxiety. "I am pressed hard, very hard," he telegraphed an hour later. "About every Regiment I have has been in action." Unless he was reinforced, "I am afraid I shall be driven from my position."

Awash in his own anxieties, General McClellan had given no thought to anticipating Porter's need. Even now, with Porter's telegram in his hand, he did not immediately act. Instead of ordering reinforcements across the river he merely asked his lieutenants if they had any men to spare. Franklin replied, "I do not think it prudent to send more troops from here." Sumner said to do so would be "hazardous." The general worried these replies for a time and then decided to brace Porter with a bold promise. "Hold your own," he telegraphed. ". . . You must beat them if I move the whole Army to do it & transfer all on this side."

General McClellan's actual move was considerably less bold. Sumner was told to send Porter two brigades — one-tenth of the Federal army "on this side." Furthermore, as Sumner's brigades were posted some distance south of the Chickahominy, it would be nearly three hours before they could reach the battlefield. Brigadier Andrew Humphreys of the staff thought McClellan would at least go himself to the battlefield. "We waited for him expecting every moment to mount," Humphreys confided to his wife. The general commanding, however, had now done everything he would do in regard to the Battle of Gaines's Mill.[15]

When he first reached Old Cold Harbor that afternoon, Stonewall Jackson had dutifully arranged D. H. Hill's division so as to entrap the Federals as they were driven eastward by A. P. Hill and Longstreet. By now, however, with the fresh instructions from General Lee delivered by Campbell Brown, Jackson finally had some grasp of the true situation and of the position of the Federal army, and he was taking decisive steps to bring his own forces into the battle. But for Old Jack the day's mischances were not yet over.

Two divisions of the Valley army, Whiting's and Winder's, were just then stretched out in a miles-long column on the Old Cold Harbor Road to the north. Jackson's chief of staff, the Reverend Dabney, was the logical one to guide these troops to the battlefield, but because he was solicitous of Dabney's still frail health, Jackson had turned instead to the only other staff man present, quartermaster John Harmon. He gave Harmon rapid-fire verbal instructions for the two divisions to fill in the battle line between Harvey Hill and Dick Ewell by advancing in a somewhat complicated "echelon movement beginning from the left," with the left-hand regiment of each brigade guiding on the right-hand regiment of the brigade to its left and keeping at all times within supporting distance; "if this fails at any point" (so Dabney remembered Jackson saying), the commanders should form line of battle and move toward the heaviest sound of firing "to attack the enemy immediately wherever found."

Major Harmon was perhaps the best quartermaster in the Confederate army, but of battlefield tactics he knew very little, and when he tried to relay these instructions to the generals involved he became hopelessly confused. What was worse, he had got it in his head that Jackson wanted these generals to begin their advance only on his further orders. As a consequence, Chase Whiting and Charles Winder, as puzzled as ever by their chief's strange ways, obediently stayed right where they were on the Old Cold Harbor Road.

An hour passed, and Ewell and Longstreet became hotly engaged and there was a rising fire all along the front, and still there was no sign of the rest of the Valley army. Perplexed by the delay, Jackson distractedly rode back and forth behind the battle line. The Reverend Dabney, suspecting what had happened, slipped away and galloped off to find the missing troops. When he came to Chase Whiting and asked if Harmon had delivered the general's instructions, Whiting grumbled that indeed he had: "That man Harmon has been here with a farrago of which I could understand nothing." Dabney delivered the correct instructions and rode along to the next division. He explained to Charles Winder that he was acting entirely on his own initiative in ordering him forward, but he was sure that was Jackson's intention. "Yes, you are right," Winder said, "and I shall do so at once." One after another, Whiting's and Winder's six brigades began moving toward the front.

Some of these brigades had two miles and more to march, and they encountered further confusion about where they were supposed to go in when they reached the battlefield, but overriding everything else was a sense of urgency. The daylight was beginning to fade and there would probably be time for only one concerted attack before it became too dark to see. Sensing this, Lee and Jackson both gravitated toward the center of the battlefield. General Lee, his aide Charles Venable recorded, "galloped across the field in the rear of the line of battle under a sharp artillery fire."

Lee and Jackson met on the Telegraph Road. "Ah, General, I am very glad to see you," Lee said. "I had hoped to be with you before." If Jackson noticed the subtle rebuke he gave no sign, only nodding. "That fire is very heavy," Lee continued. "Do you think your men can stand it?" "They can stand almost anything," Jackson said. "They can stand that!" After a brief discussion of troop dispositions, Jackson returned to the left of the line to put the Valley army into action.[16]

The fire of battle was on Stonewall now. His face was flushed, a staff man noticed, and his blue eyes blazed "with a species of glare." As was his custom on a day of battle, he began sucking on a lemon. He barked out his orders and spurred his mount from place to place, seeming to be in "a sort of concentrated rage." He sent off couriers to his principal lieutenants with a curt directive: "Tell them this affair must hang in suspense no longer; sweep the field with the bayonet!"

No doubt impatience contributed to Jackson's concentrated rage, for placing the troops in attacking positions in this wooded ground was a painfully slow business. Even then the Valley army was scattered widely. Two of Charles Winder's brigades ended up as a reserve behind Longstreet's division on the extreme right and almost a mile from the rest of Winder's troops; in the process brigade commander Samuel V. Fulkerson was mortally wounded by a stray shot. Chase Whiting had drifted well to the right in his approach to the field, and by marching his two brigades to the sound of the heaviest firing he would go into action under Longstreet's direction.

It was nearing 7:00 P.M. now, and the sun low on the western horizon was glowing a dull red through the haze of battle smoke, giving the scene a hellish cast. From a distance all that could be seen was the incessant gun flashes in the smoke. Something over an hour and a half remained before the twilight would fade into darkness.

General Lee was making this final, supreme effort to win the day, as Porter Alexander noted, with no margin to spare. Virtually everyone on both sides at Gaines's Mill on June 27 would report facing "superior enemy forces" or "overwhelming odds" or some other such description, yet in fact this climactic phase of the battle would pit closely equal forces one against the other.

On the Confederate side, A. P. Hill's six brigades and the Louisiana Tigers of Ewell's division were too battered from the earlier fighting to join the final advance, and two of Winder's brigades and one of Longstreet's remained in reserve. This left the Army of Northern Virginia sixteen brigades, 32,100 men, to put into the battle. Their line, in the shape of a great arc, faced due east on the right and due south on the left and stretched two and a quarter miles from end to end.

Fitz John Porter's force, after accounting for the addition of Slocum's division and the losses earlier in the day, was at some 34,000 men slightly larger. Many of these, however, especially in the divisions of Morell and Sykes, were badly strained from being under fire for hours. Additional Confederate batteries had finally come on the field, especially on D. H. Hill's front on the left, but the Yankees still maintained their strong advantage in artillery. (John Pelham of Stuart's horse artillery would receive wide notice for gallantly fighting his single gun, primarily because he was one of the few Southern artillerists that day whose fire was effective.)

Offsetting the Federals' artillery advantage was a potential confusion of command. In haphazard fashion Porter had inserted individual regiments of McCall's and Slocum's divisions into gaps in the line or to bolster weak points, with the result that McCall and Slocum and their lieutenants found their troops scattered far beyond their reach. This posed no real problem so long as the defenders held their positions. In any crisis, however, there was likely to be command confusion of the same sort that had hampered Heintzelman and Keyes during the fighting at Seven Pines.

The climax of the battle that evening was hardly a picture-book charge, with the entire Confederate line advancing in unison and seamless alignment. It was instead a matter of fits and starts, of rushes and repulses. On D. H. Hill's front on the left his five brigades immediately became entangled in Boatswain's Swamp and lost all alignment. Regiments came out of the trees intermixed and piled up one behind another, unable to return the enemy's fire. While they were being untangled, Harvey Hill and his lieutenants contemplated the daunting prospect ahead. The slope rising to the crest of the hill in front of them was 400 yards long and entirely open, planted in corn in early growth. Before ordering a general advance, Hill determined to storm a battery in front of the McGehee house that had them in an accurate enfilading fire.[17]

He sent five regiments to take the guns in front and flank, but only one of them, the 20th North Carolina, a new regiment under fire for the first time, managed to reach the battery. The Carolinians seized the guns, a section of the U.S. 3rd Artillery, and even turned one of them against the Yankee line but promptly lost them to a counterattack by one of Slocum's Sixth Corps's regiments.

This was the 16th New York, one of the most easily recognized outfits on the field. The colonel's wife back in Albany, thinking to shade the boys from Virginia's summer sun, had sent along a large stock of white straw hats, one for every man in the regiment. At first they had liked their distinctive headgear, but now suddenly they were not so sure. Private Cyrus Stone noticed that most of the 16th's casualties were struck in the head or upper part of the body, "but the most of the enemy firing was too high, they must have aimed at our hats. . . ." He did his own firing down on one knee, "and I think it saved me from being shot." His regiment's loss came to 40 percent, but the 20th North Carolina would take 272 casualties, the second largest Confederate regimental loss — after the 1st South Carolina Rifles of Gregg's brigade — that day.

As the Carolinians and the New Yorkers struggled for the battery, the rest of D. H. Hill's division pushed toward the crest of the hill. Bryan Grimes, personally leading his 4th North Carolina from out front as he had at Seven Pines, once again had his horse killed under him. This time he was able to appropriate a remount from the Federals before the day was over. One of Grimes's men remembered how "the roaring of musketry, the thundering of cannon, the shouting of men &c &c but served to heighten the scene." Private Stone of the 16th New York had a similar recollection, and he added, "The air at this time was too full of lead for standing room."

The first line of Yankee defenders here were hard-bitten regulars from Sykes's division, and they only gave up ground stubbornly and deliberately. The McGehee house was a substantial brick structure, and it and its several outbuildings and the family orchard became a bloody battlefield. Sergeant Thomas Evans of the 12th U.S. Infantry remembered his company rising up and firing in unison, then pulling back a few yards and repeating the process; the order was "Step now, men, if you ever stepped." In the McGehee orchard, Evans wrote, "Every post, bush, and tree now covers a man who is blazing away as fast as he can." Ahead of him all he could see was a gray sea of men. "Column after column melts away like smoke but is quickly re-formed and again rushes on." The 12th Infantry and its neighboring regulars, the 14th, would between them lose 452 men in this struggle, most of them in the fight around the McGehee house.[18]

Immediately to the west, at the center of the Federal position, Alexander Lawton's Georgia brigade, the trailing command in Jackson's column, was finally getting into the fight. Lawton found Dick Ewell, still on foot, stamping about the woods urging on his troops, and got some direction as to the enemy's position. When he saw Lawton's big brigade — its 3,600 men made it one of the largest in the Army of Northern Virginia — Ewell waved his sword and pointed it toward the hill ahead and cried out, "Hurrah for Georgia!" Lawton's was one of the army's better traveled brigades, having recently come up from Georgia and then been sent on to Jackson in the Shenandoah. Certainly it was one of the better armed, being largely equipped with English-made Enfields, the best rifle in the Confederacy's arsenal.

This was the Georgians' first battle, and their enthusiasm matched their innocence. Private I. G. Bradwell of the 31st Georgia always believed their officers did not sufficiently appreciate their mettle. They passed through a line of Gregg's South Carolinians recuperating from their earlier repulse, who called out, "Come on, boys, walk right over us." Then they came under the fire of a Yankee battery and began taking casualties. The 31st was the only regiment in Lawton's brigade still carrying the old smoothbore muskets, and they were out of range for returning the fire. With that, Bradwell wrote, they "dashed forward, without orders, with a hideous yell." Their officers did their best to restrain them, fearing they would get too far ahead of the rest of the brigade and be cut off. On they went anyway, until the colonel got the color company stopped by threatening to run the men through with his sword, and then the rest of the regiment halted as well. Private Bradwell was certain they could have continued on and taken the battery and saved a good many of the 170 casualties they suffered that day.

Corporal Richard Robins of the 11th U.S. Infantry was on this same part of the field and described the charge of Lawton's Georgians. "The enemy which had halted," he wrote, "now uttered that fiendish yell and rushed toward us. I seemed fascinated by the sight and waited to pick out a color bearer, fired twice more and looking around, found the regiment had marched off." Robins hastened back to better cover with the rest of the regulars. "Looking back I saw the rebels pouring over the crest. . . ."

On the crest of the hill Lawton's brigade, "disunited by the smoke, dust, and confusion of the battle-field" (as Lawton reported it), paused to regroup for the final push. Here the Stonewall Brigade of Winder's division pushed into line between Lawton and D. H. Hill, and Arnold Elzey's brigade and Isaac Trimble's of Ewell's division added their weight to the attack. The 1st Maryland of Ewell's division was standing by just then without orders when Lieutenant McHenry Howard of General Winder's staff happened by and asked them accusingly, "Are you going to remain here like cowards while the Stonewall Brigade is charging past?" Presently the regiment joined the charge, but Lieutenant Howard narrowly escaped being shot at by one of the Marylanders resenting his accusation.[19]

Far over on the Confederate right, at the same time, James Longstreet was putting in an attack of his own with methodical force. Longstreet's front was the most difficult that any Confederate general faced that day. It was closest to the Chickahominy and therefore under harassing fire from the Federal guns south of the river. From his starting point, behind a low ridge west of the Federals, he faced a quarter mile of entirely open ground, part of it planted in wheat, sloping down to Boatswain's Swamp and the first line of Yankee fieldworks. On the hillside behind the swamp were two additional tiers of defenders. "I was, in fact," Longstreet remarked in his report, "in the position from which the enemy wished us to attack him." He now had no choice but to oblige the enemy.

In his diary Corporal Edmund Patterson of the 9th Alabama recorded the opening of Longstreet's assault. "Up to the crest of the hill we went at a double quick," he wrote, "but when we came into view on the top of the ridge we met such a perfect storm of lead right in our faces that the whole brigade literally *staggered* backward several paces as though pushed by a tornado." To stay where they were would be annihilation; to fall back would be unthinkable. "Just for one moment we faltered, then the cry of Major Sorrel, 'Forward Alabamians — forward!' and . . . we swept forward with wild cheers. . . ." Lieutenant Robert Miller of the 14th Louisiana, going in on the Alabamians' left, sensed the bullets coming at them so thickly in these moments, he told his homefolks, "that I felt a desire to see how many I could catch with my open hand stretched out." During the charge one of the Louisiana companies lost 29 of its 45 men.

Farther yet to the left, Chase Whiting had also been contemplating the well-posted Yankee defenders. Whiting, going astray in approaching the field through the woods, had been directed first by General Lee and then by Longstreet, and he now made up what amounted to the left wing of Longstreet's assault. The news that Jackson's men were here at last sent a cheer through Longstreet's ranks.

Whiting's two-brigade division was the smallest in the army, but no division had any tougher fighters: Evander Law's brigade of Mississippians, Alabamians, and Carolinians, and John Bell Hood's Texas brigade, containing the only three Texas regiments in Lee's army as well as the 18th Georgia and Wade Hampton's South Carolina legion. Lee searched out Hood and explained the enemy's position. "This must be done. Can you break this line?" he asked. "I will try," Hood promised.[20]

Gaines's Mill was a battle fought entirely without subtlety; the tightly contained Federal position appeared to offer no opportunity for maneuver. The result was a straight-ahead slugging match in which the defenders held all the advantages of position. It had already been amply demonstrated how difficult it was even to approach their position. Chase Whiting had a different idea. He wanted Law's and Hood's brigades to advance without pausing to fire, to cover the open ground down to Boatswain's Swamp as swiftly as they could without losing order, then to storm right over the Yankee line. Whiting rode through the ranks calling out, "There will be no order for retreat! Boys, you can take it!"

Hood split his command, making the charge on both flanks of Law's brigade. For the occasion he took personal command of his old outfit, the 4th Texas. Hood had once boasted he could "double-quick the 4th Texas to the gates of hell and never break the line." On this day, leading from in front on foot, he proceeded to prove it.

"Steady! Steady!" he shouted as the first Yankee fire reached out for them. "I don't want you to run." No one was to return fire until he gave the order. Law's men kept pace alongside. There was no firing and no sound in the ranks. The count of dead and wounded mounted rapidly; between them, Law and Hood would lose 1,018 men on June 27, nearly one man in every four, and easily two-thirds of that number fell during the charge. It was much the same in Longstreet's five brigades on the right — some 2,000 casualties for the day, one in four, a large share of them falling in these few minutes.

Now they were within 100 yards of the swamp, and the order went out to double-quick and to fix bayonets on the run. "Forward! Forward!" Hood shouted. "Charge right down on them. . . ." They hit the swamp and at point-blank range from the first line of Federals raised the Rebel yell. At the same time, off to the right, a half-mile-wide line of Longstreet's men were crashing into the swamp, jumping the creek, scrambling up the bank. Their screams, one of Old Pete's men said, "sounded like forty thousand wild cats."

The Federals here were from George Morell's division — the brigades of Charles Griffin, John Martindale, and Daniel Butterfield — with bracing from McCall's and Slocum's divisions. Their numbers were at least equal to those of the attackers, but with even the best infantryman able to get off only three shots a minute they simply could not fire fast enough to break this swift advance. As the yelling horde in gray and butternut bore down on them, those in the first line panicked and turned and fled. So great was their rush to the rear that they blocked the fire of the second line and then carried those defenders along with them. The Comte de Paris, watching Griffin's brigade, described it as "debris . . . completely broken." A tide of blue washed back toward the crest. The Confederates were stopping to fire now. "One volley was poured into their backs," a Texan said, "and it seemed as if every ball found a victim, so great was the slaughter." The enemy looked twenty ranks deep, one of Longstreet's men said, "and we could not miss them. . . ."

It would be argued for years who had the honor of being the first to break the Federal line at Gaines's Mill. In the annals of the Confederacy it became a legendary feat, deserving of recognition. There were many claims for Hood's brigade of Chase Whiting's division. D. H. Hill and his men said it was in fact they who first broke the Yankee line, over on the left at the McGehee house. Others said that one or another of Longstreet's brigades was first, on the right. In later years Hood would admit to Cadmus Wilcox of Longstreet's command that Wilcox's Alabamians might have reached a certain line of Federal guns first, "but you could not hold them" and his Texans had to retake them.

In fact the Federal collapse in those twilight minutes was complete enough on every hand to suggest that the breaks right, center, and left were all but simultaneous. A single break in the line anywhere ought to have drawn a sharp counterattack, but nowhere was there any sustained counterattack. Everywhere the defenders were too busy on their own fronts; everywhere the Confederates were successful, or about to be successful.[21]

....

GEORGIA cavalryman N. J. Brooks had a posting that gave him a panoramic view of this drama, and he tried to get his impressions down on paper for those back home. "I tell you of a truth, a battlefield is awful when you see thousands of angry warriors rushing upon each other, yelling like so many hell hounds from the infernal regions . . . ," he wrote, "and when you see hundreds of bombs bursting and men falling, horses running away, killing themselves and riders, cannons firing, clouds of dust rising, . . . ambulances and men running hither and thither getting the wounded away, many wounded getting themselves and other wounded away as bloody as butchered hogs." Brooks decided that if only the people at home, North and South, could once see such a scene, "there would be a ten-fold greater clamor for peace among them than there ever was for war."

What moments before was a vast panorama now became a disjointed series of miniature battles in the woods and fields of the plateau, some as small as man against man. Major John Cheves Haskell, attaching himself to Whiting's division in the charge, had picked up a fallen Confederate flag and carried it with him right over the Federal field-works, where his horse was killed under him. A captain of the 25th New York of Morell's division rushed at him and tried to wrest the flag away, crying out, "You damned little rebel, surrender!" Haskell hacked at him with his sword and the captain retaliated with two wounding pistol shots. He then turned to join the retreat, but Haskell dashed after him and struck him a mortal blow. He stopped to assure the dying Yankee that his family would be notified. Minutes later Major Haskell was himself out of the battle, hit by a shell that mangled his right arm.

In the charge of the 4th Texas the sole field officer to survive unhurt was General Hood himself. Half the regiment, 253 men, would be killed or wounded. One of these wounded, Val Giles, never forgot the act of a Good Samaritan whom he credited with saving his life. Giles was down with a severe wound and squarely in the line of fire of a Yankee battery when a passing Rebel grabbed him by the collar "and unceremoniously snaked me along for a few yards and landed me behind a big apple tree. He handled me without gloves and hurt me fearfully, and in return for that act of humanity I cursed him. He made no reply, but hurried on. . . ."

There were incidents at the other extreme. Generals Lee and A. P. Hill were riding behind the advance when they came on a Confederate captain who had deserted his command to take shelter behind a tree. The high-tempered Hill leaped cursing from his horse, snatched away the man's sword, and attempted to break it over his knee. "The sword was of as bad metal as the man" (as Lee's aide Charles Venable put it) and merely bent. Hill hurled it as far as he could and resumed his ride toward the battle.

Down in the bottomland on the Federal left, Private Oliver Norton and the 83rd Pennsylvania of Butterfield's brigade were finally in action. They repulsed several assaults on their position behind the streambed, but suddenly they were taken under fire from the rear. The Rebels had broken through on their right and the rest of Butterfield's brigade had retreated, but the word did not reach the 83rd Pennsylvania or its neighboring regiment, the 16th Michigan. Their attackers were South Carolinians from Longstreet's division. Eventually the two Yankee regiments fought their way out of the closing trap, but in doing so the 16th Michigan lost 220 men and its regimental colors. The 83rd Pennsylvania lost 196 men, a third of its numbers. "God only knows why or how I came out alive," Private Norton wrote. Three times rifles were shot to pieces in his hands, and three times he was hit, fortunately all flesh wounds. All were healing nicely, he assured his family.[22]

For the Federals there was now no recourse but to retreat, in the best order possible. As the light faded the battlefield contracted rapidly toward the Chickahominy crossings. Those regiments still under firm control — especially the regulars — went back without panic, halting to fire on command, then going back again. Others calmly walked off the field without stopping, saying they had had enough fighting for one day. Still others, particularly those who had been in the front line or who had lost their officers, fell into more disorder.

O. T. Hanks of the 1st Texas remembered how "crossing a large rolling field we had nothing to do but shoot them as they went panic-stricken. . . ." Charles Page of the *New York Tribune*, who had crossed to Porter's headquarters to report the battle, watched as the first wave of panic surged toward him: "They ran back, broken, disordered, routed." These were mostly the stragglers and the skulkers who marked the rear of every army in every battle, and Page was reminded of the scene at Bull Run the summer before. He was astonished by the sight of a madly galloping horse "carrying a man's leg in the stirrup — the left leg, booted and spurred. It was splendid horse, gayly caparisoned."

After the breakthrough the Confederates' most obvious target became the Federal artillery. As the range closed the Yankee gunners went to firing deadly canister, but when their infantry supports began leaving the field they in turn came under equally deadly short-range rifle fire. A Mississippian in Law's brigade reported that he and a comrade paused and took deliberate aim and "shot down some of the finest horses in McClellan's army, which was to prevent the guns from being taken off." Brigadier Charles Griffin, a veteran artilleryman in the old army and now commanding infantry in Morell's division, rushed to the defense of the divisional batteries, pleading with passing Yankee infantry, "Men, this battery must not be taken. I will not abandon my guns. I cannot cover your retreat; you must cover mine."

Despite Griffin's efforts, only one of the front-line batteries in Morell's sector got all its guns safely away, and even then lost three of its caissons. Battery E, Massachusetts Light Artillery, lost all four of its guns, and Battery C, 1st Rhode Island Light, lost three of its six. Near the McGehee house the guns of the 3rd U.S. Artillery, which earlier were taken by the 20th North Carolina and retaken by the 16th New York, were now captured a third time, by the 5th Virginia of the Stonewall Brigade. All told, the batteries making up the first line of artillery defense on the plateau lost ten guns to the Confederate assault.[23]

As they continued pursuing the Yankee defenders toward the river the Confederates encountered a second line of Federal guns in reserve near Porter's headquarters at the Watt house. Most were McCall's batteries, with others from Slocum's division and the army's artillery reserve. As the Rebels advanced on this gun line there occurred the most unexpected happening in this long day of happenings — a Napoleonic-style cavalry charge.

General McClellan had posted Philip St. George Cooke's reserve cavalry north of the Chickahominy, under Fitz John Porter's direction, and for this battle Porter had placed the troopers down in the bottomlands on the far left flank, behind Boatswain's Swamp. His orders to Cooke (so Porter later claimed) were simply to guard that flank and, in effect, to stay out of the way: "He was told that he would have nothing to do on the hill." When General Cooke saw the fortunes of the day turning against the Federals and the reserve artillery opening fire, he pushed his command up the hill ("without orders, of course," he said) to the support of the threatened batteries.

Cooke's orders at that point would become a matter of no small dispute. He claimed he told Captain Charles J. Whiting, commanding five companies of the 5th U.S. Cavalry, to charge only when "the support or safety of the batteries required it." As one of Whiting's men heard it, however, Cooke ordered something quite different: when he saw the enemy on the crest of the hill, he was to "charge at once, without any further orders, to enable the artillery to bring off their guns." In the event, that was exactly what Captain Whiting proceeded to do.

With sabers drawn, the 250 men of the 5th Cavalry charged in two lines toward the advancing Confederate infantry some 275 yards away. These were Chase Whiting's men and some of Longstreet's, and their first warning was the ground trembling "like an earthquake and . . . a noise like the rumbling of distant thunder." Quickly they closed ranks to meet the charge, wrote Corporal Edmund Patterson of the 9th Alabama, "not such a line as would have stood an infantry charge, but plenty strong to resist cavalry." They opened a deadly fire. In moments they shot down almost a quarter of the attacking troopers, including six of their seven field officers. Under the weight of this fire most of the survivors sheered off before reaching the Rebel line, but at least two galloped close enough to be bayoneted. There were apparently no Confederate casualties. "We gave them a well directed and murderous fire . . . ," Corporal Patterson summed up, "and taught them a lesson that when infantry are fighting they should keep out of the way."

Riderless and wounded horses and scores of mounts running wild beyond their riders' control plunged back through the line of guns, upsetting efforts to limber up and go to the rear. At the same time, the cavalry did give pause to the Confederate advance, and under cover of the charge others of the guns were gotten away. Nine of the pieces would finally be taken, raising the total of Federal guns captured to nineteen. (In the rush of the evacuation that night, three additional pieces would be lost, tipped into the river at the crossings.)

In General Cooke and the 5th Cavalry Fitz John Porter found an excuse for the events of the day. By his reckoning, before the charge of the cavalry, "victory, so far as possession of the field was concerned, had already settled upon our banners. . . ." Then the foolhardy charge: "To this alone is to be attributed our failure to hold the battle-field and to bring off all our guns and wounded." By the time he came to make this accusation in his report of the battle, however, General Porter was intent on concealing his own failings on June 27, and the facts of the case were very different. The Battle of Gaines's Mill had already been well lost and the retreat well started by the time the 5th Cavalry made its charge. Moreover, probably as many guns were saved under cover of the charge as were lost in the confusion that followed it. The singular consequence of the rash attack was its toll of 55 Yankee troopers.[24]

The 5th Texas and the Hampton Legion were bringing up the rear of Hood's brigade when abruptly from their rear came a blast of fire. They about-faced and fired a volley in return, and that was enough for their opponents. The Yankees waved handkerchiefs and their hats in token of surrender, and threw down their rifles. Their officers ceremoniously offered their swords to Lieutenant Colonel J. C. Upton of the 5th Texas. Upton was not one for military protocol — rather than carrying a sword himself he went to battle wielding a long-handled frying pan — and he accepted all these swords with considerable reluctance. Just then he noticed one of his men involved in a commotion in the Federal ranks. "You, John Ferris!" he shouted. "What in hell and damnation are you trying to do now?" Ferris replied that he was trying to keep a number of their prisoners from escaping. "Let them go, you infernal fool," Upton said. "We'd a damned sight rather fight 'em than feed 'em."

The Confederates found themselves encumbered by two entire Yankee regiments. The 4th New Jersey of Slocum's division and the 11th Pennsylvania of McCall's were victims of the confusion in command that followed the Federal collapse. Once the line was broken Slocum and McCall and their brigadiers found it all but impossible to direct their scattered units. These two regiments were lost in the confusion and trapped and surrounded, with little choice but surrender. Between them their losses would come to 1,269 on June 27, of which 949 were made prisoners of war. The Jerseymen and Pennsylvanians did not appreciate being described in the newspapers as the first regiments in McClellan's grand army to reach Richmond.

One of those who witnessed the fate of the 4th New Jersey but managed to escape capture himself was Lieutenant E. B. Grubb, who earlier had seen the Comte de Paris direct the 4th to the battle line. Lieutenant Grubb hastened to find his brigade commander, George W. Taylor. "Where is the Fourth?" General Taylor asked him. "Gone to Richmond, sir," Grubb replied. Taylor turned on him with a rebuke for such levity at a time like this. "They are captured, every man of them," poor Grubb explained. "My God, My God," said the general. General Taylor would earn the unhappy distinction of suffering the largest loss — 1,072 men — of any brigade in the Potomac army that day.[25]

As the Confederates were mustering forces for their all-out final attack on Porter, General McClellan had been distracted by an attack on Baldy Smith's front south of the river. The thrust was made on the James Garnett farm not far from Old Tavern, and of all the threatening Rebel movements from the Richmond lines that day it seemed to have the most substance. It was in fact the only one of Prince John Magruder's illusions with any substance to it at all, and it was made quite by mistake.

Ordered at dusk "to feel the enemy," Georgian Robert A. Toombs instead embroiled his command in a sharp and sustained fight with Winfield Scott Hancock's brigade. Hancock repulsed the misguided attack easily enough, inflicting 271 casualties on the attackers. The Toombs incident was not entirely without profit, however, for it sharply etched on General McClellan's mind the idea that he was under fierce and simultaneous attack on both sides of the Chickahominy. He was being assaulted "by greatly superior numbers in all directions," he announced to Washington that evening. "On this side we still hold our own, though a very heavy fire is still kept up."[26]

It was growing dark now, and in the diminishing visibility the Confederates' advance began to slow, out of fear of hitting their own men. No one could really tell where he was, and direction was easily lost in the dimness and the slowly drifting clouds of battle smoke. Suddenly from the retreating Federal columns ahead came the incongruous sound of cheering. Reinforcements had finally arrived.

The brigades of Thomas F. Meagher and William H. French, from Sumner's Second Corps, pushed their way across the Chickahominy bridges and up to the plateau. "I was obliged to charge bayonets by the heads of regiments to force a passage through the flying masses," General French reported. General Meagher, who led his Irish Brigade with the courage found in a bottle, galloped about drunkenly trying to rally everyone he saw. One of French's men watched Meagher ride into a group of walking wounded and single one man out: "He struck him over the head with his sword, knocking him down, then galloped on. . . ."

Behind this shield of reinforcements Porter's defeated command fell back to the river crossings in the darkness. Gradually the firing slackened and then died away. "And instead of the rattle of guns," wrote Sergeant Barry Benson of the 1st South Carolina, "I now heard on all sides groans, and cries from the wounded: Water! Water! Water! We gave from our canteens till they were empty. And from dark till late in the night men were calling for their regiments. . . . All over the field of battle it was First South Carolina! Eleventh Mississippi! Fourth Alabama! — and so on, men seeking for their commands. . . ."[27]

The Flight

··

W HEN THERE WAS time to make a count, Gaines's Mill proved
to be the largest and costliest battle of the Seven Days, and the
largest and costliest of the entire Peninsula campaign. Including reinforcements, the two armies between them put 96,100 men on this
field. For concentrated fury, only Shiloh among the war's earlier battles
even approached it; few later battles would exceed it.

Fitz John Porter's command lost 894 killed, 3,114 wounded, and
2,829 captured, a total of 6,837. Lee suffered 1,156 more casualties:
1,483 killed, 6,402 wounded, and 108 missing, a total of 7,993. For the
Federals the number of captured was very high, and there were as well
the twenty-two pieces of artillery lost. For the Rebels the role of
attacker on June 27 proved very costly, their toll of dead and wounded
being nearly twice that of the defenders. For the day, and including
Toombs's fight south of the Chickahominy at dusk, the two armies lost
altogether 15,223 men in less than nine hours of fighting. There would
be veterans of four years' fighting in both armies who insisted that the
volume of fire at Gaines's Mill was unmatched in all their wartime
experience.

Gaines's Mill was beyond any doubt a major defeat for General
McClellan, yet in common with the fight at Seven Pines he was
exceedingly fortunate that it was not a great deal worse — that he did
not lose one-third of his army on June 27 rather than the 6.5 percent he
did lose. Fitz John Porter, committed like his chief to the delusion that
he was hugely outnumbered, fought the battle not to win but only in
the hope of not losing, and only darkness and the last-minute arrival of
the two Second Corps brigades saved his command from being driven
against the Chickahominy and shot to pieces as it tried to escape across
the narrow bridges. But for Stonewall Jackson's mishaps — his misdirected march and his poor staff work — the full-blooded assault Lee

mounted at 7:00 P.M. would have opened three or four hours earlier and left Porter in the gravest jeopardy and without any last-minute reinforcements. Porter Alexander put the case concisely: "Had Jackson attacked when he first arrived, or during A. P. Hill's attack, we would have had an easy victory — comparatively, & would have captured most of Porter's command."[1]

While the numbers were not yet known to McClellan, he did not doubt the dimensions of the defeat. As he put it to General Heintzelman that evening, "On the other side of the Chickahominy the day is lost." In the hour before midnight he called together his generals to announce to them his decision to retreat to the James. The clearing at army headquarters was lit by a blazing fire of pine logs, next to which, in a bower of fir-tree branches, the high command gathered about the general commanding. Sentries patrolled the outskirts of the clearing, and the leaping flames cast dramatic lights and shadows on the surrounding trees. A newspaper correspondent watching the scene thought it a fitting subject for some great historical painter: the Young Napoleon and his ranking generals pondering the army's fate, perhaps the country's fate as well.

All the corps commanders were present except Erasmus Keyes, who had already been ordered to begin the retreat across White Oak Swamp. McClellan had also previously announced his decision to retreat to Flag Officer Goldsborough in making a request for the navy's gunboats on the James to protect the army. To the present gathering, however, he offered the fiction that he had not yet decided to retreat — that in fact he was debating gambling everything on one dramatic cast of the dice and fighting to a final decision across the Chickahominy. Of course, he said, defeat in such a battle would mean the loss to the country of its principal army; of course this led his lieutenants to urge him not to risk such a calamity but instead to take the alternate course and preserve the army to fight another day. Feigning reluctance — Heintzelman reported the general commanding insisted he was still inclined to risk all on one great battle — McClellan agreed to do what he had privately decided to do some time since: the Army of the Potomac would abandon its campaign and seek a new base on the James River.[2]

No matter how and when General McClellan arrived at this decision, it was clearly a wrenching experience for him. After he sent the generals back to their commands he remained alone by the fire, by its light composing a long telegram to Secretary of War Stanton in Washington. At this midnight hour he was physically and emotionally exhausted, and the composure he had affected through the long day abruptly crumbled. His demoralization, which had begun two days before with the report that Stonewall Jackson was approaching, was now complete. In an outburst composed equally of venom and self-pity, he charged the government with treason.

"I have lost this battle because my force was too small," he insisted. "I again repeat that I am not responsible for this. . . ." He claimed he had brought his last reserves into action: a few thousand more men "would have changed this battle from a defeat to a victory." He said nothing of the 64,000 men who sat by idly south of the Chickahominy while Porter's lines were driven in. "I feel too earnestly tonight," he told Stanton, " — I have seen too many dead & wounded comrades to feel otherwise than that the Govt has not sustained this Army." He said nothing of the fact that he had not been within two miles of the battlefield and its dead and wounded that day. He concluded his dispatch with an indictment: "If I save this Army now I tell you plainly that I owe no thanks to you or any other persons in Washington — you have done your best to sacrifice this Army."

Neither Secretary Stanton nor President Lincoln ever reacted to McClellan's charge of treason, which fact McClellan laid to their guilty consciences. What he did not know was that neither man even saw the charge. Colonel Edward S. Sanford, head of the War Department's telegraph office, was so shocked by McClellan's accusation that he simply deleted the closing sentence and had the dispatch recopied before showing it to Stanton. The result was to fix General McClellan's delusions even more firmly in his mind.

The president's response was forbearing. "Save your Army at all events," he telegraphed McClellan. He would send what reinforcements he could. "Of course they can not reach you to-day, to-morrow, or next day. . . . If you have had a drawn battle, or a repulse, it is the price we pay for the enemy not being in Washington. We protected Washington and the enemy concentrated on you. . . ." General McClellan was spared replying to that interpretation when Rebel cavalry reached his telegraph line and cut it.

Writing to his fiancée that day, Lincoln's secretary John Nicolay reported Washington "almost wild with rumors and suspense." The loss of the telegraph meant no news at all from the Peninsula, official or unofficial. A crowd gathered at Willard's Hotel to sift the latest rumors, which ranged from the capture of Richmond to the capture of the Army of the Potomac. "Of course the suspense is terrible," Nicolay wrote.

In Richmond the news of Gaines's Mill created a mood of optimism. In his diary for June 28 Edmund Ruffin wrote, "From so many different informants, I trust that at least half of this good tiding may be true — & that will be enough to ensure to us a signal victory." John Graeme of the *Richmond Whig*, when asked if there was now any way for McClellan to reach his gunboats, was heard to reply, "None under heaven that he could see except with his balloon." A Georgia soldier in Huger's command shared the mood. "One thing is certain," he told his wife; "we have now got them scattered and squandered, and all we have got to do is *push the thing to an end*. . . . "[3]

....

THROUGH THE NIGHT most of the Federals north of the river made their way to and across the Chickahominy bridges. Theirs was a dismal night. "Sleep on the sand without any blanket," John M. Bancroft of the 4th Michigan wrote in his journal. "Woke up about 1 o'clock and crossed the river. One of those awful marches — night marches where we move 150 or 100 ft. to rest ten minutes or one-half hour." Few of the men had tents or even blankets, and many had lost their knapsacks as well. Like Sergeant Bancroft, once they were safely across the river and the column halted, they turned into the nearest field or woods and threw themselves down exhausted, without food or shelter. Sykes's regulars were the last to cross, at daybreak, burning the bridges behind them.

The badly wounded had to be left behind, and they and a good many stragglers were collected by the Rebels. Stonewall Jackson, reconnoitering out front, personally captured a group of fifteen or twenty Yankee stragglers, who proclaimed themselves honored to be taken by the famous Rebel chieftain. But the biggest catch was a brigadier general, John F. Reynolds, commander of a brigade in McCall's Pennsylvania division. Exhausted after two days of continuous duty, Reynolds had thought to catch some sleep in a supposedly secure place and was overlooked in the retreat, and the next morning was awakened by some of D. H. Hill's men. Taken to Hill's headquarters in the McGehee house, Reynolds admitted to being mortified by the circumstances of his capture. The two had served together in the old army, and Hill assured Reynolds that everyone knew him to be a good soldier and would think none the less of him. "Reynolds," he said, "do not feel so bad about your capture, it is the fate of wars."

Among thousands of weapons the Confederates gleaned from the battlefield were several of the coffee-mill guns favored by Governor Curtin for his Pennsylvania regiments. Private Norton of the 83rd Pennsylvania saw one of these machine gun–like contrivances in action and described it as making "a noise like the dogs of war let loose." They were proving unreliable in battle, however, especially the cartridge-feed mechanism. This may have been the problem with those captured, for there is no record of their further use by the Confederates.

To the victors belonged the spoils, and to hungry, threadbare Rebels there seemed no end of good things to be found on the field. "Knapsacks were captured by thousands and rifled," wrote Barry Benson of the 1st South Carolina, "while the whole Confed. army refitted itself with blankets, rubber clothes, tentflies, haversacks, and canteens." Union beef, hardtack, and coffee were consumed in great quantities. In almost every respect the Yankee goods were found to be superior to Confederate issue, and the former were promptly substituted for the latter. W. A. Kenyon on Hampton's Legion wrote home to South Carolina that day on stationery colorfully decorated with the state seal of New Jersey and the engraved figure of a Union soldier which he had found in a Jerseyman's knapsack. "We have been living high," Kenyon assured the people at home. He was no doubt but one of countless Confederate soldiers writing to the homefolks on liberated Yankee stationery.

Among the relics found on the battlefield were numerous steel breastplates that Yankee inventors had sold to safety-conscious soldiers. What they all had in common was considerable weight, and in the haste of the retreat most had been simply discarded by their owners. Some, however, were found still strapped in place on the dead. Porter Alexander later examined one such case. He counted the dents of six musket balls and what he took to be a piece of canister, all of which had failed to penetrate the plate. But a single shell fragment had sliced a hole an inch by two inches and killed the wearer. The Rebels observed that a breastplate faced the wrong way on a retreat and served only to slow up the wearer. Yankee soldiers apparently agreed, and the use of body armor fell off considerably thereafter.[4]

The main activity on the battlefield that night and the next day, June 28, was caring for the wounded and disposing of the dead. "I never had a clear conception of the horrors of war untill that night and the morning," Texan A. N. Erskine wrote home. ". . . Friends and foes all together. . . . Oh the awful scene witnessed on the battle field. May I never see any more such in life. . . ." Burial parties were everywhere at work. Dr. Gaines, who earlier had so vehemently resented the burial of a few Federal soldiers on his land, now witnessed far more interments on his property than he could have ever imagined. They were buried in mass graves, Lieutenant John W. Hinsdale noted, "without ceremony or decency even." Virginian William G. Morris, assigned to one of the burial details, confided to his wife that of the Federal dead "a great many they throughed in the River & creeks when convenient." Many others they simply left unburied.

Dr. James L. Boulware, a surgeon with the 6th South Carolina, remarked in his journal that "now came the busiest time for the surgeons. Ambulance after ambulance came up with its load until a two acre lot was filled completely." Every house and outbuilding on the north bank of the Chickahominy from Mechanicsville to Old Cold Harbor held its quota of casualties, from both armies, and when the buildings were filled the yards around them became checkerboards of wounded, with narrow aisles left for the doctors and stretcher bearers. A Georgia cavalryman took notice of two men, apparently with mortal wounds, who were set aside to die while the doctors worked on those they might save. The two were in an attitude of prayer, one silent, the other intoning over and over, "Oh, my Jesus, sweet Jesus, come, take me home!" The cavalryman could only give them water and then turn away.

As they had after Seven Pines, the women of Richmond came forward to care for those wounded once again pouring into the city. Confederate gunner Henry Berkeley was at the Virginia Central depot, newly converted into a dressing station where casualties were brought for preliminary treatment. "The ladies of Richmond, may God ever bless them . . . ," he wrote in his diary, "moved like ministering angels among these sufferers. . . ."

The Yankee wounded from Gaines's Mill who had been carried back across the Chickahominy were in worse straits, for with the White House base abandoned they could not be transported to Northern hospitals for advanced care. Instead they were crowded into a huge field hospital at Savage's Station on the York River Railroad, where surgeons labored around the clock to treat them. A New Jersey man having his wound dressed there matter-of-factly noted in his diary, "Four tables amputating all day."[5]

SATURDAY, JUNE 28, would be remembered as the eye of the hurricane that was the Seven Days. For three days, with increasing fury, the storm had torn at the two armies. Three more days of such fury were yet to come. On Day Four, however, as if the eye at the center of the storm was passing over, it was quiet, almost serene. There was fighting, to be sure, but with a total of only 235 casualties it was hardly noticeable compared with what had passed and what was to come. June 28 was instead a day of intense calculation on the part of the two commanders.

Although he had succeeded in seizing the strategic initiative, General Lee found himself in the peculiar position of having to wait for General McClellan to make the first move. The Federals' retreat back across the Chickahominy effectively broke contact between the two armies. Federal guns controlling the river crossing sites from the south bank made direct pursuit impossible. The two lines still faced one another closely in front of Richmond, yet there was no real way for the Confederates to discover what was happening behind those formidable entrenchments if the Yankees chose to keep their movements secret. Even the smallest of rear guards might hold there against a reconnaissance by Magruder or Huger, and a planned balloon ascension that day by Porter Alexander was frustrated by high winds. Lee calculated that McClellan would make one of three movements on June 28, and he did what he could to gain the necessary intelligence, yet the entire day would pass before he felt certain of his opponent's decision.

The first possibility was that McClellan would remain on the Chickahominy and fight for his railroad supply line to White House — as Lee believed McClellan had done the previous day at Gaines's Mill — thereby hoping still to put Richmond under siege. His second choice would be instead of fighting to fall back down the Peninsula, recrossing the Chickahominy farther downstream and regaining his link with the York River — in effect withdrawing along the way he had come and from there perhaps starting his campaign over again. The third possibility would be to give up the Chickahominy line entirely and retreat southward to a safe haven under the guns of the Federal navy on the James. (General Lee apparently concluded that since his opponent had not rushed straight for Richmond on the twenty-sixth or twenty-seventh, he was not going to attempt it now.)

The only way to discover whether McClellan was making for the James, however, was to discover that he was not adopting either of the two other alternatives. To find this out, Lee sent Dick Ewell's division and Jeb Stuart's cavalry downstream to try to seize both White House and the railroad and to observe the lower Chickahominy crossings. With the rest of his main striking force he would remain on the north bank of the river, so as to be in a commanding position against either of the first two movements. He could only then wait for answers as the hours ticked away.

The network of roads south of the Chickahominy and east of Richmond did not favor the Federals in their retreat. Most travel in the region was east and west, and there were comparatively few north-south roads. Consequently, to reach the James from their lines in front of Richmond they had first to fall back southeasterly some six miles, then at the crossings of White Oak Swamp turn south. For most of the Yankee troops the march over these roads would be no more than fifteen miles, yet better than three days would be required for the army to cover that distance.

This slow pace was due in part to the limited number of roads and bridges, and in part to the sheer size of the Army of the Potomac: over 99,000 men, 281 pieces of field artillery and 26 heavy guns of the siege train, something over 3,800 wagons and ambulances, and 2,500 head of beef on the hoof. But the primary reason for the deliberateness of the movement proved to be General McClellan's obsessive caution in disengaging his forces from what he took to be overwhelming numbers of Confederates on every hand. Withdrawal from in front of a superior foe, he would explain, is "always regarded as the most hazardous of military expedients." As a consequence of his misguided caution — the Young Napoleon was in fact fleeing from an army four-fifths the size of his own — Lee was granted the opportunity to catch McClellan on the march and destroy him.[6]

By dawn on June 28 Yankee engineers were in White Oak Swamp to construct crossings. Before this the swamp had served to anchor the left flank of the Federal line before Richmond, and the bridges there had been cut down; now they had to be reconstructed to permit the army to make good its escape. Lieutenant William Folwell's 50th New York engineer regiment was assigned to rebuild White Oak Bridge. "What the Bridge was for," Folwell wrote his wife, "we did not know but some of us had our guess. At 20 min. to 5 our bridge was begun, 20 min. to 7 the word done was passed, and the head of Gen. Peck's (Casey's old) Division filed on to the bridge. So the stream began to flow and so poured in steady tide. . . ."

A mile and a half upstream, at Brackett's Ford, engineers built a second bridge. By noon that day the head of Keyes's Fourth Corps was across the swamp, and the supply trains began crossing. During the afternoon Porter's battered Fifth Corps began moving through the corridor. The word that it was a retreat swept through the ranks. In his diary that day a Rhode Island artillerist wrote, "A deep gloom is prevailing over the whole army." Lieutenant Haydon of Phil Kearny's division, who expected to be in the rear guard and who believed "our situation is one of uncommon danger," used his diary entry for June 28 to settle accounts and make his testament to the members of his family "if I fall."

Understanding so little of the point or purpose of the movement was unsettling to the men and heightened their fears. In a marching column of McCall's Pennsylvanians a sudden noise of approaching horses raised the alarm that Rebel cavalry was attacking, sending the men tumbling into the woods on either side and emptying the road in a matter of moments. A few moments more brought the cause of the panic into view — a sutler's wagon proceeding along peacefully enough at a trot. Sheepishly, shaking their heads, the men resumed their places in the column.[7]

In his defense of his change of base, General McClellan would claim much for the efficiency of the march to the James. The movement, he told President Lincoln afterward, was without a parallel "in the annals of war." It was in truth managed with much inefficiency. The route was so poorly reconnoitered that for much of the time the entire army was unnecessarily crowded onto a single road, the Quaker Road; a second nearby woods road was only discovered by accident, then went unused until it was finally rediscovered, again quite by accident. Two roads farther to the east were never found at all. Baldy Smith would remember the march as "without much except accident to direct it." Giving priority to a slow-moving, mile-long herd of beef cattle also contributed to the lagging pace. Having started with a twenty-four-hour lead, the Federals soon enough squandered that advantage and were forced to fight for their lives.

Over the previous three days the sun had baked the roads hard and dry, and as that Saturday wore on the Confederates began seeing slow-rising clouds of dust south of the Chickahominy. The Yankee army was moving. The dust clouds suggested a movement to the east, which was little help to General Lee in deciphering the Federals' intentions; a shift eastward fitted any of McClellan's alternatives. In midafternoon, however, a courier from Jeb Stuart arrived with more certain news. Stuart and Dick Ewell had reached the York River Railroad at

Dispatch Station and reported it undefended. After tearing up track and cutting the telegraph line, the Rebels pushed on to the nearby Chickahominy crossings, and at their approach the enemy fired both the railroad bridge and the Willamsburg Stage Road crossing at Bottom's Bridge. This was conclusive — beyond any doubt General McClellan was abandoning his railroad supply line.

In due course Stuart reached White House and found it evacuated and great piles of stores and forage ablaze. A Federal straggler had fired the plantation house that Mrs. General Lee earlier persuaded McClellan to safeguard, and soon nothing remained standing of the building but its chimneys. Stuart's troopers would manage to rescue sufficient sutlers' stock from the wreck to enjoy a memorable feast that included iced lemonade, pickled oysters, canned ham, French rolls, and cake, concluding with fresh-ground coffee and fine Havana cigars. A trooper in the Jeff Davis Mississippi Legion described the scene at White House as "an awfull destruction," but added that the entire brigade dined well and "filled their haversacks with good things. . . ." Jeb Stuart and the cavalry experienced few of war's hardships on the Peninsula.[8]

High-tempered Bob Toombs, a Georgian with a long career in politics, was outspoken in his contempt for professional soldiers — he described his superior as "that old ass Magruder" — and on June 28, as on the day before, his overaggressiveness entangled him in an unhappy clash with the Yankees. It again took place at the James Garnett farm, three-quarters of a mile from Old Tavern and the same distance from the Chickahominy. David R. Jones, commanding a division under Magruder, suspected that the Federals might be pulling back that morning, and he initiated a reconnaissance in force to test his theory. Taking it upon himself to order his fellow brigade commander, George T. Anderson, to advance along with him, Toombs converted Jones's reconnaissance into an attack. Before higher command could countermand the move, two Georgia regiments were badly cut up. The repulse, as on the twenty-seventh, was delivered by Baldy Smith's command.

Ironically Toombs's brigade escaped with minimal casualties, but "Tige" Anderson's 7th and 8th Georgia lost between them 156 men. The Georgians managed to drive into the outer Yankee works, but the farther they advanced the more fire they drew. They faced at least one of the coffee-mill guns, in the lines of the 49th Pennsylvania. "It seemed impossible for a man to escape," a private in the 7th Georgia wrote his wife. "The bullets fell just like hail." When the order finally came to withdraw it was little better. "We could not form under such a fire, so every man had to look out for himself." The outcome left him embittered: "I hope our generals are now satisfied that the 7th and 8th regiments cannot whip the whole Yankee nation. . . ." Over two days political general Toombs's ill-starred adventuring had cost the Confederacy 438 men, against a Federal loss of 189.[9]

On another front, however, there was reason for Richmonders to rejoice that day. From Petersburg, twenty miles to the south, came a dispatch announcing that the Yankees "have suddenly and unexpectedly left the Appomattox." Over the past several days the Rebels had watched apprehensively as a Union flotilla came up the James and turned into the Appomattox River, obviously intent on a mission of some sort. Abruptly, giving up whatever was intended, the flotilla steamed away.

The whole affair had a comic-opera flavor to it that was entirely appropriate to its origins. A few days before, General McClellan had called on the navy to mount an expedition to destroy the Swift Creek Bridge on the railroad between Richmond and Petersburg, over which he supposed Beauregard's thousands were pouring in from the West to reinforce Richmond. Dutifully the navy assembled a flotilla that included the *Monitor*, the *Galena*, and an odd sort of submarine propelled by oars called the *Alligator* to run up the Appomattox to Swift Creek. The water proved too shallow for the *Alligator* to submerge, however, and she was sent back in disgrace. The other vessels were also hampered by the shallows and obstructions in the Appomattox and harassed by Rebel sharpshooters and artillerists, and finally the commander gave up in disgust, having to set fire to one vessel that was hard aground as he left. Richmond's southern flank was once again secure.[10]

McClellan had shifted army headquarters two miles southeast to Savage's Station on the railroad, and the order went out that after dark the three corps still holding the lines in front of Richmond must start pulling back down the railroad to a new position well behind the old Seven Pines battlefield and in front of Savage's. They would compose a rear guard of half the army to cover the White Oak Swamp crossings. McClellan also called on Ambrose Burnside to abandon all operations on the North Carolina coast and instead bring his division as reinforcement for the Potomac army on the Peninsula. Finally, the general commanding issued a circular to all commands ordering that everything "not indispensable to the safety or maintenance of the troops must be abandoned and destroyed." This sacrifice, he said, is "for the short season only, it is hoped. . . . "

Lieutenant Colonel Barton Alexander of the engineers went to McClellan and urged him to rescind the order. It would demoralize both officers and men, he said, telling them in no uncertain terms "that they were a defeated army, running for their lives." Alexander testified that he was successful in getting the recision, yet even so a good many units had already gotten the circular and carried out its provisions. No fires were permitted for fear of tipping off the enemy, so the destruction was carried out with knives, bayonets, axes, and anything else that came to hand. Tents and clothing were slashed to ribbons, officers' baggage destroyed, and camp equipage of every kind wrecked. Then the troops were marched to the commissary stores and told to help themselves to all they could carry. As had been the case with the Rebel troops at Manassas back in March, it was evident to everyone that what they could not eat on the spot or carry away was going to be destroyed.

At 2:00 A.M. Sunday morning, in a rain shower, McClellan's short-lived field headquarters at Savage's Station was broken up and the headquarters train marched five and a half miles east and then south, crossing White Oak Bridge and setting up again on the south edge of the swamp. The general commanding snatched an hour or two of sleep, but no more than that, so intent was he on supervising the smallest detail of the saving of his army. By contrast, the previous evening General Lee, certain now that the James River was his opponent's objective, issued orders for pursuit in the morning and by 11:00 P.M. was asleep in *his* latest field headquarters, at Dr. Gaines's house. Robert E. Lee's principles of command included the determination to be well rested and fully alert for the battle, so that he might properly exercise the command.[11]

. . . .

THE ROAD NETWORK the Federals found awkward to use in their retreat to the James was, on the other hand, nicely suited to their Confederate pursuers. Fanning out east and south from Richmond were four main roads that might be used to intercept McClellan's march. Interception was General Lee's objective — not simply to lift the siege of Richmond, which he had now accomplished, but to bring the Army of the Potomac to battle away from its entrenchments and crush it. Lee believed that taking the North's principal army in front of Richmond would mean independence for the Confederacy. General McClellan believed precisely the same thing.

Lee assigned the direct and immediate pursuit to Prince John Magruder, who was to push ahead with his command due east along the Williamsburg Road and the York River Railroad against the Federal rear guard, his purpose to force the Yankees to turn and fight. Benjamin Huger, guarding Richmond on Magruder's right, would take the next road to the right, the Charles City Road, to intercept the enemy's line of march south of White Oak Swamp at the hamlet of Glendale, on the Quaker Road.

The divisions of Longstreet and A. P. Hill had the longest march. From the Gaines's Mill battlefield they were to turn back to the New Bridge crossing of the Chickahominy, follow that to the Nine Mile Road and from there to a north-south lateral road behind Magruder and Huger, then turn back to the southeast on the next road beyond Huger, the Darbytown Road. This would bring them to the Long Bridge Road that led to Glendale. The last of the roads fanning out from Richmond, the River Road, the southernmost of the four, reached the James at an eminence known as Malvern Hill. It was assigned to the division of Theophilus Holmes.

Stonewall Jackson, with D. H. Hill still attached to his command, had orders to join the pursuit by the shortest route, due south. Rebuilding the Grapevine Bridge and crossing the Chickahominy there, he would take position to close with the Yankee rear guard in the area of Savage's Station, to Magruder's left. In thus attempting to bring the enemy to bay, Lee's plan was much like Joe Johnston's three-pronged plan for opening the Seven Pines battle. This time it would be Prince John Magruder in the center, with Huger on the right and Jackson on the left.

Meanwhile, Dick Ewell's division and Jeb Stuart's cavalry were to remain north of the Chickahominy, at Bottom's Bridge and to the east, to make sure McClellan was not shamming a move to the James while escaping across the Chickahominy downstream and retreating down the Peninsula. This struck General Lee as unlikely, however. "His only course seemed to me was to make for James River . . . ," he told President Davis that day; "the whole army has been put in motion upon this supposition."

Lee's plan for the pursuit of the Army of the Potomac on June 29 was as aggressive as his earlier plan for attacking Porter's Fifth Corps north of the Chickahominy. It involved the same kinds of movements. To catch the enemy at the difficult White Oak Swamp crossings would require coordinating the marches of three separate, widely dispersed columns — those of Magruder, Huger, and Jackson — so that they would fall simultaneously on an enemy whose actual position was not yet precisely known. The movements of the divisions of Longstreet and A. P. Hill, and of Holmes, were less critical to the events of June 29, for they had the longest marches and Lee anticipated their crucial roles in the pursuit being played the next day, June 30. As it was on the days of Mechanicsville and Gaines's Mill, much would depend this Sunday on Stonewall Jackson's arriving at the right place in good season.

Considering that the Grapevine Bridge had yet to be rebuilt while New Bridge was already back in service, Lee might have arranged his maneuvers differently on June 29. He might have put Jackson's command, as well as Longstreet's and A. P. Hill's, across the Chickahominy at New Bridge. He had to question, however, whether New Bridge (and the small infantry bridge nearby the engineers had repaired) had the capacity to cross that many troops within a reasonable period of time. Furthermore, the New Bridge route would increase Jackson's march from two miles to eleven miles, and leave him poorly positioned to strike the enemy's rear guard. The experienced engineer in General Lee concluded that rebuilding the Grapevine Bridge would be the least of problems that day. It turned out to be the largest of problems.[12]

During the night Longstreet had dispatched two of his engineer officers to scout across the Chickahominy, and at first light on Sunday morning they sent back word that the Federal entrenchments were empty. Here finally was direct testimony to the Yankees' retreat. Soon afterward a report to the same effect arrived from General Magruder, along with the dramatic announcement that he was preparing to advance to battle. Magruder's grandiloquence brought from Lee the caution that he take care during his assault not to injure Longstreet's engineers, who now occupied the works. Lee then crossed the river himself at New Bridge and sent word to Prince John to meet him to confer; the general commanding wanted no misunderstanding of his intentions that day.

The two generals met on the Nine Mile Road and as they rode together toward Fair Oaks Station Lee outlined his plan and the disposition of his forces. Magruder was in a nervous, agitated state and did not grasp everything Lee said; he thought, for example, that Huger's division would be close by on the Williamsburg Road instead of several miles farther to the right on the Charles City Road. Prince John had been up all the previous night and furthermore was suffering from acute indigestion, and his surgeon had treated him with a mixture that included morphine, which was acting on him as an irritant. What Lee did manage to impress on him was that he had primary responsibility for the pursuit of the Federals that day. What Lee did not realize was that Magruder was not in condition for such responsibility. At Fair Oaks Station they parted, and Lee rode on to consult with Benjamin Huger. Magruder was left to face the test alone.[13]

It was soon evident on this clear and very hot Sunday just where General Magruder would find the enemy. Roiling black clouds of smoke rose high over Orchard Station and Savage's Station on the railroad as the Yankees began destroying everything they could not carry away. Witnesses groped for words to describe the immensity of the destruction. Chaplain J. J. Marks of the 63rd Pennsylvania watched as troops and teamsters hurled articles of every description into the spreading flames and termed the scene "altogether unearthly and demoniac." One particularly huge stack of blazing hardtack boxes and provision barrels attracted everyone's attention. A farmer in the ranks compared it in size to several large barns pushed together. A Philadelphian thought it the size of a city block of two-story houses; a Bostonian considered it as large as Faneuil Hall. They all agreed it made a spectacular bonfire.

Whiskey from stove-in barrels intensified the fires and flowed in flaming rivers in every direction, and men burned themselves trying to salvage a canteen-full. Rifles were destroyed by smashing the stocks against trees and throwing the barrels into the fires. Medicines were poured into springs and down wells. Beef and pork and coffee and vinegar were thrown into lakes of molasses. "The flames roared and snapped, and its vicinity was exceedingly hot," Lieutenant Thomas Livermore wrote, "and we had a sort of savage joy in seeing the destruction which would keep our rations from the enemy."

One of the last trains to come up from White House and not yet unloaded was set afire on a siding at Savage's Station, and soon the flames and smoke were punctuated by the rapid-fire explosions of artillery shells which produced a rain of flaming debris. Yankee ingenuity was applied to a second train loaded with ammunition. The cars were set afire and the locomotive, with a full head of steam and the

throttle tied down, was sent rushing down the tracks toward the Chickahominy with its lethal cargo. On the other side of the river Campbell
Brown, General Ewell's aide, saw the train coming, the boxcars flashing and exploding like a bizarre fireworks display, and told his men to
run for it when it looked as if the train would jump the stream. Instead
it plunged off the broken bridge and into the river in a cataclysmic
explosion that shook the ground and broke windows three-quarters of
a mile away. An enormous mushroom-shaped cloud of smoke surged
upward, whitish gray on top and dark gray underneath, reaching more
than a thousand feet. Major Brown would remember it as "one of the
grandest sights I ever looked at."[14]

As the wagon trains started south and east and the reserve artillery
and the columns of infantry joined the stream, it became obvious to
those in the Savage's Station field hospital that they were going to be
left behind in the retreat. To be sure, there was no official announcement from headquarters, but they saw many of the surgeons being
called back to their regiments and the army's ambulances going with
them — going empty so as to be available for the next battle.

Before long Chaplain Marks saw a "long, scattered line of the
patients staggering away, some carrying their guns, and supporting a
companion on an arm. . . . They retired one by one across the fields,
and were lost in the forest. . . ." Corporal John S. Judd, wounded in
the arm at Gaines's Mill, spoke for hundreds when he wrote in his
diary that day, "Ordered to leave in morning or be taken prisoner. . . . Walked 8 miles." Judd and his comrades were the lucky
ones. Some 3,000 men in the field hospital, too ill or too badly
wounded to move, would be made prisoners by the Rebels. Leaving
them to their fate, Major Thomas Hyde of the 7th Maine wrote home,
made his blood boil: "Their cries are yet ringing in my ears."

Like the slow current of a sluggish river, the wagon trains and
artillery batteries made their way southward. "The halting of a single
wagon for any purpose checked the entire movement," wrote William
Le Duc, quartermaster of the Second Corps. "There was no such
thing as passing unless a new road was cut around the obstruction."
Whenever a wagon or a caisson or a team broke down, it was pushed
off to the side so that the march might continue. At such times, wrote
Sergeant Thomas Evans of the U.S. 12th Infantry, "a convocation of
teamsters assembles, and we have as much blasphemy — horrid, out-
landish, and newly-invented oaths — as can be heard anywhere this
side of hell." Even so, the head of any column leaving Savage's Station

reached White Oak Swamp five miles distant before the rear of the column had even started. Hour after hour, without pause, the labored movement continued.

As yet it was a movement untroubled by the enemy. General Keyes had pushed ahead a mixed picket of infantry and cavalry to hold the Quaker Road, beyond the swamp, and at 9:00 A.M. a reconnoitering force of Confederate cavalry collided with this picket, with unhappy consequences. The Rebels, led by the 1st North Carolina cavalry, incautiously rode right into an ambush. "With the help of two guns with us we about ruined this Cavalry Regiment . . . ," Elisha Hunt Rhodes of the 2nd Rhode Island reported in his diary. "As we were concealed in the woods the enemy rode right up to us and did not hit even one of our men." The cost to the Rebels was 62 troopers, 48 of them taken prisoners; the Federals lost just 6 men, all from the 3rd Pennsylvania cavalry. The clash demonstrated to General Lee that the Yankees were well on their way to the James, and that it would take more than cavalry to block their escape.[15]

....

IN SHIFTING army headquarters from Savage's Station to the far side of White Oak Swamp, General McClellan was once again leaving any fighting that might take place that day to his lieutenants. He left orders for the rear guard's retreat but appointed no one to command it in his absence. This was no doubt deliberate; Bull Sumner, the senior general, was the last general McClellan wanted in command of anything. As he told his wife, Sumner in charge "would be utter destruction to the army. . . ."

Consequently, the three corps commanders in the rear guard — Sumner, Franklin, and Heintzelman — acted according to their own best lights. The first to go his own way was Sumner, who opposed even the idea of a retreat. Early on June 29 he took his Second Corps back from the fortifications as ordered, but only as far as Allen's farm on the railroad near Orchard Station, two miles short of Savage's Station where the rest of the rear guard was headed. At 9:00 A.M. Magruder's advance found him there, and Sumner promptly made a sharp fight of it in Mr. Allen's peach orchard.

Tige Anderson's Georgia brigade bore the brunt of this fight, as it had the day before at the Garnett farm, but this time it had better fortune. For nearly two hours two Georgia regiments fought it out with two Pennsylvania regiments, and when it was over the Georgians had lost 28 men and the Pennsylvanians 119. Then, wrote a Second Corps diarist, "the enemy skeddadled one way & we went the opposite."

There was one additional Confederate casualty that morning: Brigadier General Richard Griffith, commanding a brigade of Mississippians well to the rear in reserve, who was mortally wounded by a stray Federal shell. Major Brent of Magruder's staff described the Federal artillery fire as entirely harmless but for that one shell, and wondered at the fate that had singled out the general for death.

The rest of the Federal rear guard was meanwhile falling into what Baldy Smith described as "a muddle." It presented nothing like a continuous front to the enemy. Sumner in the center was well out ahead of Heintzelman on the left. Baldy Smith on the right discovered his division had no protection on either flank. Franklin discovered that his other Sixth Corps division, under Henry Slocum, had without notice been ordered away to White Oak Swamp by General McClellan. Confederates were reported across the river and as close as the Trent house, McClellan's old headquarters. When Franklin sent a dispatch to Sumner pointing all this out and suggesting they take up a more unified position, old Sumner sent back to say he was in battle and would not turn his back to the foe.

Franklin and Smith and Heintzelman met together and (Smith recalled) "it was agreed to try and inveigle General Sumner back. . . ." Franklin made it a personal effort, going to Sumner at Allen's farm and explaining that Baldy Smith was in grave danger of being cut off unless the Second Corps fell back to support him. A plea to help a fellow general was always enough for Bull Sumner, and by midafternoon the entire Federal rear guard was reassembled at Savage's Station.[16]

In a muddle himself, General Magruder was persuaded by the clash at Allen's farm that rather than retreating the Yankees were preparing to attack him. This was in fact a common enough concern with Prince John. At Yorktown in early April and in the Richmond lines a few days before, the conviction that he was on the verge of being overwhelmed had inspired him to heights of bluff and deception so as to forestall the enemy. He hurried Major Brent to General Lee to plead for reinforcements. He instructed Brent to say that he had "found the enemy in numbers far exceeding him . . . ," and in addition to Jackson's command already promised him he wanted help from Benjamin Huger.

Lee received the message in disbelief; surely an army in retreat would not want to bring on battle deliberately. Nevertheless, he agreed to have Huger send two brigades around to the Williamsburg Road to support Magruder, but if they were not engaged by two o'clock that afternoon they would be ordered back; Huger had "important duty" that must not be unduly delayed. This did little to calm the agitated Magruder. He had since learned from Jackson that his bridge building was going slowly and would not be completed for another two hours. Prince John therefore determined to wait for Huger's men to come up on his right and Jackson's on his left before resuming the movement. That prospect ought to have reassured him. If all these troops did indeed come together as promised, it would throw 46,600 men — well over half the army — against the Federal rear guard. And that would surely be enough to contend with the counterattack Prince John feared.

General Heintzelman was the next of the Yankee generals to go his own way. Sam Heintzelman was a grizzled veteran of thirty-six years' service who viewed events with calm calculation. He observed that in front of Savage's Station and extending from the Williamsburg Road to and across the railroad was a clearing half a mile wide, and that Sumner's two divisions and Baldy Smith's one — 26,600 men — were more than adequate to hold this ground against whatever force Sumner had fended off earlier at Allen's farm. He saw no space and no need for his Third Corps troops there. In any event, he regarded Sumner as an alarmist; in his diary in these weeks Heintzelman often remarked how the old soldier called out the troops to meet attacks that invariably proved to be the mildest of threats or no threats at all. Having discovered an open road south from the station and with McClellan's retreat orders in mind, Heintzelman proceeded to march the Third Corps toward the White Oak Swamp crossings. He neglected to tell anyone of his departure, however, and in the concealing woods south of the Williamsburg Road no one saw him go.

Meanwhile, Prince John's agitation had if anything increased. Two o'clock came and with it General Huger, who noted the quiet that prevailed on Magruder's front and said he was honoring the order to reclaim his two brigades and resume his march down the Charles City Road. On the heels of that came a fresh message from Stonewall Jackson, in which that general announced he would be unable to cooperate with Magruder after all, "as he has other important duty to perform."

This left Prince John to contemplate Lee's order to pursue and attack the enemy, but now with none but his own troops to do so. That morning the prospect had been for a battle along the railroad perhaps as large as Gaines's Mill, involving more than 90,000 men. Now, after the various defections on both sides, it promised only to pit Magruder's 14,000 against Sumner's 26,600. He sensed these odds. It was close to five o'clock in the afternoon when Magruder, with understandable caution, made contact with the Yankees at Savage's Station.[17]

Neither then nor later did the secretive Jackson reveal the "important duty" that prevented him from intercepting the Federals' retreat that day. In fact, that duty was the consequence of a poorly drawn order sent out that morning by General Lee's chief of staff, Colonel Robert H. Chilton. In the event McClellan might yet try to escape to the east the way he had come, crossing the Chickahominy downstream, Lee wanted Jeb Stuart to picket those crossing points, "advising Gen'l Jackson, who will resist their passage untill reinforced." At 3:05 P.M. Jackson received Chilton's dispatch, forwarded to him by Stuart. Writing on it "Genl. Ewell will remain near Dispatch Station & myself near my present position. T.J.J.," he sent it back with Stuart's courier. His important duty, then, was to stay where he was north of the river, ready to defend the Chickahominy crossings and prevent the enemy from escaping down the Peninsula.

Since later that day General Lee assured Magruder that "General Jackson has been ordered . . . to push the pursuit vigorously" — any other view of that order, he said later, was a "mistake" — Lee had obviously intended in the earlier dispatch for Jackson to continue as originally planned, crossing the river and advancing on the enemy. Then, if Stuart should signal him, he could move downriver on the south bank to resist a Yankee crossing. It was, in short, a contingency plan. Colonel Chilton's dispatch failed to make this distinction clear, however, and since by three o'clock Jackson's forces had not yet crossed the river (although Old Jack himself did cross and with a scouting party reconnoiter as far as the Trent house, thereby alarming the Federals), Jackson saw it as his duty to hold the Valley army right where it was.

As it happened, this mixup in orders made no real difference in Jackson's progress that Sunday. Once again, he was plagued by unexpected delay in moving his command. Porter Alexander would blame this on Jackson's rigid observance of the Sabbath, and initially at least Jackson's fervid Sunday morning devotions may have distracted him from personally pressing his bridge building. However that may be, about midday he made the discovery that he was going to need more than one bridge to put his entire force across the Chickahominy in good season.

The Grapevine Bridge put up by Bull Sumner's troops back in May was a narrow, ramshackle, amateurish affair that was rarely used by the Yankees after Lieutenant Colonel Barton Alexander of the engineers completed the far superior military bridge 400 yards upstream that bore his name. On the testimony of Confederate general Wade Hampton, Sumner's Grapevine Bridge was repaired by noon on June 29, but it was soon evident that it would take far too many hours to cross all five divisions then under Jackson's command by this tortuous route. Jackson had put the Reverend Dabney in charge of rebuilding Alexander's Bridge (which Jackson and Dabney, among others, insisted on calling Grapevine Bridge, after the prewar crossing site of that name nearby). Engineering was not one of Dabney's skills, however, and he had no idea how to direct the detail of soldiers assigned to the task; he remembered it only as a "shilly-shally" operation.

Finally recognizing the futility of Dabney's efforts, Jackson replaced him with an experienced engineer, Captain C. R. Mason, who directed an equally experienced squad of slave laborers. Progress on Alexander's Bridge became more rapid. Shortly before receiving Chilton's dispatch from Stuart, Jackson reported the bridge "will from appearances be completed in less than 2 hours. . . ." It was night when it was finished, but even so it was considered an accomplishment. Note was made of a sign the Yankees had nailed to a tree announcing that Lieutenant Colonel Alexander, U.S. Engineers, had constructed this bridge in five days. In due course both bridges were used to cross Jackson's command.[18]

....

PRINCE JOHN MAGRUDER announced his arrival before Savage's Station with a characteristic flourish. Advancing slowly from Richmond over the York River Railroad at the pace of the infantry was a locomotive pushing ahead of it history's first armored railroad battery. Early in June, when he decided his opponent would try to carry his siege guns to Richmond by way of the railroad, General Lee sought to blockade the route with a siege weapon on his own. Since mounting a heavy gun capable of traverse on a railroad flatcar was not unlike mounting a pivot gun on a warship, he turned to the navy. The result, ready for use on the eve of the Seven Days, was a big 32-pounder Brooke naval rifle, shielded by a sloping casemate of railroad iron and nicknamed the

"Land Merrimack." It easily outranged any gun the Yankees had on the field that day, and, as a Rebel soldier told his wife, "during our progress . . . would be turned loose on the enemy to their great dismay."

General Franklin was making a personal reconnaissance out in front of Savage's Station with one of Sumner's division commanders, John Sedgwick, when they sighted what they took to be a column of Heintzelman's troops coming out of the woods ahead. Then Sedgwick took a closer look and exclaimed, "Why, those men are rebels!" "We then turned back in as dignified a manner as the circumstances would permit," Franklin wrote, and thus the high command at Savage's Station learned that Heintzelman's Third Corps was nowhere to be found. When he was told this Sumner was particularly outraged, and seeing Heintzelman the next day he refused to speak to him. For old Sumner, one general leaving another's flank uncovered was not easily forgiven. The Federal batteries opened fire and skirmishers went forward to locate the Rebels.[19]

The Confederate force spotted so fortuitously by Franklin and Sedgwick was the South Carolina brigade of Joseph B. Kershaw, of Lafayette McLaws's division leading Magruder's march. Kershaw established his battle line in the woods along the western edge of the cleared ground in front of the station and opened a fierce firefight with one of Sedgwick's brigades, led by William W. Burns, posted out in advance in the middle of the field.

Before long McLaws's other brigade, under Paul J. Semmes, came up on Kershaw's right, extending the Confederate battle line to and across the Williamsburg Road. As he advanced, Colonel Alfred Cumming of the 10th Georgia in Semmes's brigade could see a Federal skirmish line moving toward him on the far side of a strip of trees separating two fields. "Forward double quick! March!" Colonel Cumming shouted, then decided that the situation required something stronger. "Run, men, run! Get into that wood before the enemy does." The Georgians gained the woods but it was a close-run race, so close that the two lines opened fire just thirty paces apart. "I was surprised that all were not killed on both sides," one of the Georgians remembered.

General Burns's Philadelphia Brigade was now stretched dangerously thin in order to match this widening enemy front. The larger force was in danger of being outflanked by the smaller one. Burns sent back "in haste" for help. As it was of most engagements in which Bull

Sumner played a leading role, the Federal management of the Battle of Savage's Station was erratic.

In response to his call, two of Burns's own regiments were sent forward, and then the 1st Minnesota from another brigade in Sedgwick's division, and finally one regiment each from two different brigades in Israel Richardson's division. Sumner's way was to send in the first regiment that came under his eye. The Irishmen of the 88th New York rushed up to Burns's position primed for a charge by old Sumner himself, who waved his hat and shouted out the order in his booming voice. Burns got them aimed in the right direction, down the Williamsburg Road, which was being swept by the fire of a Virginia battery. "They went in with a hurrah," Burns said, "and the enemy's battery fell back."

The arrival of the Federal reinforcements put the two sides in rough equality, two brigades apiece, and the fighting in front of Savage's Station settled down to a bloody stalemate as the daylight faded. "Water was awful scarce," wrote a diarist in the 1st Minnesota. "I had to drink slough water as the weather was fairly scorching hot." With measured, thundering regularity, the railroad battery dropped its heavy shells into the woods and fields on the Yankee front. Before its aim was corrected, several reached as far as the field hospital. With each firing the locomotive engineer released his brakes, and the train rolled backward to absorb the recoil of the big gun. In the dusk, wrote the historian of Kershaw's brigade, only "the long line of fire flashing from the enemy's guns revealed their position."

Of his twenty-six Second Corps regiments General Sumner engaged but ten at Savage's Station, and General Magruder was equally cautious. Of his six brigades he engaged only Kershaw's and Semmes's and half of Griffith's Mississippi brigade, now commanded by William Barksdale. It was clear enough to Prince John that to attempt anything more would be essentially pointless. Lee's purpose of forcing the Federal rear guard to fight had been achieved, and Magruder could see enough of the Union forces in front of him to know that he was substantially outnumbered. He was satisfied just to maintain the fight and the position.[20]

Barksdale's Mississippians and part of Semmes's brigade were in the thick woods south of the Williamsburg Road where simply locating the enemy was difficult enough. The 5th Louisiana came on a body of troops in the woods some forty yards away but could not tell who they were. Private John Maddox was sent out ahead to find out. "Who are you?" he called out. "Friends," was the reply. That was not assurance enough for Private Maddox, and he asked, "What regiment?" The reply came back, "Third Vermont," and with that the battle was joined.

The 53rd Georgia was one of the new regiments inserted into Lee's ranks just before the Seven Days, and Savage's Station was its first fight. During the day-long advance the 53rd seemed always to be crossing muddy swamps or briary thickets. "You may know that it was tough working," John Wood wrote home, "charging through such a place, with a knap sack, and it crammed chug full, and also my gun and other equipments." Finally the 53rd went into action, but to its dismay, its first experience of war proved to be against friend rather than foe. It delivered a volley into the ranks of the 10th Georgia, which made a hasty march by the flank to escape. Then the rookies of the 53rd exchanged fire with a Mississippi regiment on the right. "The only damage we done, I believe, was that of killing our Major's horse," Private Wood reported. That at least seemed to settle them down, and afterward, Wood said, "I fired as coolly as if I had been shooting a squirrel."

Before the battle began Baldy Smith had started his division on the road to White Oak Swamp but was soon recalled by Sumner. It was Smith's Vermont brigade, under command of William T. H. Brooks, that made the fight in the dark woods to hold the flank south of the Williamsburg Road. The Vermonters charged into the woods only to be met by a withering fire, and suffered by far the most casualties of any brigade on the field that day. The 5th Vermont was hit particularly hard, losing nearly half its men — 209 of 428, with one company having 25 of its 59 men killed — and the brigade as a whole taking 439 casualties.

Much of this loss was inflicted by Rebel soldiers equipped with old smoothbore muskets firing "buck and ball" — a cartridge containing a ball and three buckshot — which proved deadly at the short ranges of so much of the fighting here. At times it was hand-to-hand. General McLaws made note in his report that a Federal soldier attempted to wrench the flag away from the 10th Georgia's color bearer "but was immediately knocked down and killed."[21]

When darkness ended the Battle of Savage's Station about 9:00 P.M. the two sides were holding the same ground they had held at 5:00 P.M. Federal casualties were considerably greater, 919 against 444 for the Rebels. Including the morning's clash on the Allen farm, Magruder

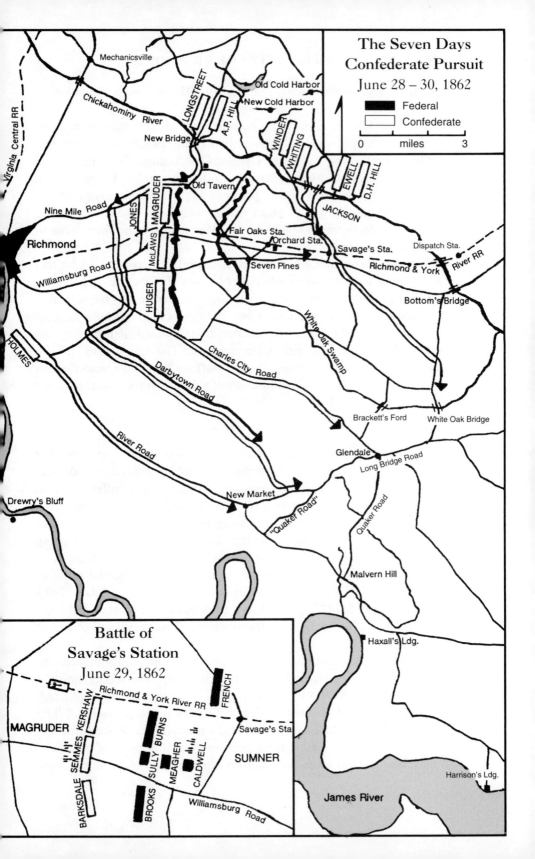

The Seven Days
Confederate Pursuit
June 28 – 30, 1862

■ Federal
□ Confederate

0   miles   3

Mechanicsville

Old Cold Harbor
New Cold Harbor

Chickahominy River

LONGSTREET
A.P. HILL
WINDER
WHITING
EWELL
D.H. HILL

New Bridge

Virginia Central RR

Nine Mile Road

Old Tavern

JONES
McLAWS MAGRUDER

JACKSON

Fair Oaks Sta.
Orchard Sta.

Savage's Sta.

Dispatch Sta.

Richmond

Williamsburg Road

Seven Pines

Richmond & York River RR

Bottom's Bridge

HUGER

White Oak Swamp

Charles City Road

HOLMES

Darbytown Road

Brackett's Ford   White Oak Bridge

River Road

Glendale
Long Bridge Road

New Market

"Quaker Road"

Quaker Road

Drewry's Bluff

Malvern Hill

Haxall's Ldg.

Battle of
Savage's Station
June 29, 1862

Richmond & York River RR

FRENCH

MAGRUDER

KERSHAW

SEMMES
BARKSDALE

SULLY BURNS
MEAGHER CALDWELL

Savage's Sta.

SUMNER

BROOKS

Williamsburg Road

Harrison's Ldg.

James River

inflicted a loss on the enemy that day of 1,038, against his own loss of just 473.

Even so, Day Five proved a considerable disappointment to General Lee. The pursuit had showed hardly any profit; the enemy had not been brought to bay against White Oak Swamp. To Magruder he sent an uncharacteristically sharply worded dispatch. "I regret much that you have made so little progress today in the pursuit of the enemy," he told him. "In order to reap the fruits of our victory the pursuit should be most vigorous. . . . We must lose no more time or he will escape us entirely."

There was considerable injustice in his rebuke. If Prince John had been wrong to announce earlier that he was about to be attacked by the Yankees, he had been right to point out that he was considerably outnumbered — by better than two to one, in fact. Without Jackson on the scene there was little chance that June 29 of inflicting any serious damage on the Federal rear guard. The true failings of the day's pursuit were to be found in poor staff work at Lee's headquarters and in Stonewall Jackson's failure to put a driving force into the matter of bridge building.[22]

....

PHIL KEARNY sardonically informed his men they were "the rear guard of all God's creation." On the Charles City Road late in the day Benjamin Huger halted his pursuing column three miles short of Glendale, his objective, when he encountered Kearny's Yankees on his left in White Oak Swamp. Fearing he would be outflanked, cautious Huger quit his march for the day. Kearny, also fearing being outflanked, pulled back and took another crossing of the swamp.

The retreat went on. "I did not expect this would be the result of our campaign," Elisha Hunt Rhodes wrote in his diary that day, "but I suppose it is all right." "Have drawn back most of our forces and hope for the best," a Massachusetts diarist wrote. "Perhaps all will come out in *strategy*. . . ."

During the day and into the night Federal columns were halted for hours in miles-long traffic jams. Men fell asleep where they stood or sat. "Officers nodded and swung this way and that in their saddles," wrote a regimental surgeon. "The stillness of death prevailed." The *New York Tribune*'s Charles Page thought it must have looked like this when Napoleon retreated from Moscow — "this herd of men and mules, wagons and wounded, men on horse, men on foot, men by the roadside, men perched on wagons, men searching for water, men famished for food, men lame and bleeding, men with ghostly eyes, looking out between bloody bandages. . . ."

By day the heat and dust were suffocating. Night compounded the confusion. Quartermaster Le Duc of the Second Corps found a stalled supply train piled up behind a single wagon blocked by some obstruction or other and its driver fast asleep. Le Duc kindled a roadside fire to locate and clear the obstruction and drove the mules ahead with his sword's point. Keep moving, forget proper march order, he kept repeating; they must get to the James or be taken.

General Keyes, interrogating a local farmer "under fine of death," learned of an old unused woods road east of the Quaker Road and used it to carry his Fourth Corps trains to the river. The Fifth Corps, by contrast, lost its way entirely in the darkness and took a heading straight for Richmond. It was General Meade, able to navigate by the stars, who realized they had turned in the wrong direction and got the column stopped before it stumbled into the enemy lines. "March and wait and march and wait and then countermarch," was how a Fifth Corps soldier summed up the night. "May you never experience how tired we were." It would be remembered as the "blind march."

No one knew when Rebels might be encountered in the blackness, and the columns moved in enforced silence. "Nothing was heard but the steady tramp, tramp of the men, and the creaking of the wheels of the artillery and the ammunition train," wrote the historian of the 10th Massachusetts. ". . . Hour after hour this march was kept up in the narrow, forest-lined road leading to the river. Streams were forded by the light of pitch-pine torches held on either bank." In the cavalry escort troopers were seen to give up their saddles to wounded and sick from the Savage's Station field hospital. A sudden thunderstorm drenched everyone, but at least the way was revealed by the flashes of lightning. "No one who participated in the march that Sunday night," the regimental historian wrote, "will ever forget it."[23]

The last scheduled to take up the retreat on June 29 was the rear guard that had fought at Savage's Station, and once again Bull Sumner balked. General McClellan's orders were shown to him, but Sumner's blood was up and he said the general commanding did not know how circumstances had changed since he issued those orders. He had stopped the enemy that day and could do it again, Sumner told General Franklin. "I never leave a victorious field. Why! if I had twenty thousand more men, I would crush this rebellion."

Franklin could do nothing with him, and finally he sent an aide to find McClellan and report the old soldier's intransigence. Back to Savage's Station came McClellan's inspector general, Colonel Delos Sacket, with written orders for Sumner to take up the retreat. Sacket had his own orders as well: "If he fails to comply with the order you will place him in close arrest and give the necessary orders to Genl Richardson & Sedgwick and tell them that the orders must be complied with at once." Sumner's new orders were read to him, and that was enough. With a sigh he turned to his staff. "Gentlemen," he said, "you hear the orders; we have nothing to do but obey." The Second Corps promptly took up the march for White Oak Swamp.

Captain George W. Hazzard's battery of the 4th U.S. Artillery had seen hot action during all the fighting that day, and immediately afterward the captain and his gun crews bedded down for the night. When the corps pulled out no one thought to look for Hazzard's battery. At first light the artillerymen were awakened by reveille sounding from an unexpected direction, where no Yankee troops were supposed to be. Clearly they were the only Yankees on the field. Hazzard had the guns and caissons limbered up as silently as possible. Just as silently, they slipped off the field at a walk. As soon as the road entered the forest the pace was advanced to a trot. "We bowled along in fine style," reported one of the relieved officers. Soon they began encountering numerous stragglers, to whom they announced that there was no one behind them but Rebels. That advanced the stragglers' pace.

As the sun came up Hazzard's battery reached White Oak Bridge, which the trailing brigade of Richardson's division was just then preparing to fire. The moment the guns had clattered across and as many of the stragglers as were in sight, the bridge was set ablaze. The Army of the Potomac was safely across White Oak Swamp.[24]

Library of Congress

These pictures show the Federal lines facing Richmond erected in June. The view above, by George N. Barnard, is Redoubt No. 3, on the Seven Pines battleground; McClellan would witness the Oak Grove fighting from here. The battery below, by James F. Gibson, guarded Redoubt No. 5, near Fair Oaks Station.

Library of Congress

National Archives

General Sumner (center), commander of the Second Corps, and his staff prepare to bivouac in front of St. Peter's Episcopal Church, near White House Landing.

Library of Congress

Above: White Oak Swamp, photographed by James Gibson. Below: the corduroyed approach to Grapevine Bridge over the Chickahominy, built by the men of the 5th New Hampshire and the 64th New York, photographed by David B. Woodbury.

Library of Congress

Library of Congress

The Federal line north of the Chickahominy was anchored at Mechanicsville, shown in a misdated Alfred Waud drawing being occupied by Yankee troops on May 24.

Print Collection, New York Public Library

Leslie's artist William Waud (Alfred's brother) sketched Generals McClellan and Franklin and Prince de Joinville personally reconnoitering in Mechanicsville.

Schoff Collection, Clemens Library, University of Michigan

Where is Jackson? ... Here I am!

David H. Strother, a Union staff officer serving in the Shenandoah Valley, had been an artist for *Harper's Weekly* under the name Porte Crayon. He did these satirical drawings for his own amusement. Above, a lurking Stonewall Jackson answers "Here I am!" to the query of bewildered Federals. Below, President Lincoln tries to prod some life into the slow-moving Peninsula campaign.

Schoff Collection, Clemens Library, University of Michigan

TO RICHMOND

The "Little Napoleon" receives another pointed reminder. 1862

M. and M. Karolik Collection, Museum of Fine Arts, Boston

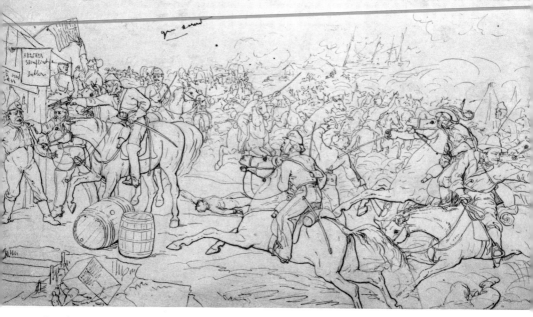

Southerner Adalbert Volck did this imagined view of the capture of McClellan's supply base at White House Landing by Jeb Stuart's cavalry during the Seven Days. This is an original drawing for Volck's series, *Confederate War Etchings*.

Print Collection, New York Public Library

In William Waud's drawing, a Federal battery near Mechanicsville shells Rebel positions across the valley of the Chickahominy. The view is southeast, toward Richmond. The bridge visible at center is on the Mechanicsville Turnpike.

Cook Collection, Valentine Museum

Ambrose Powell Hill

Museum of the Confederacy

Robert E. Lee

Library of Congress

The village of Mechanicsville, the Federals' right flank, was the initial target of Lee's Seven Days offensive. James Reekie took this photograph at war's end.

Library of Congress

Anne S. K. Brown Military Collection, Brown University

Fitz John Porter

Library of Congress

Alfred Waud's drawing pictures one of the numerous Confederate frontal attacks hurled against Fitz John Porter's battle lines at Gaines's Mill on June 27.

In Prince de Joinville's lithograph of Gaines's Mill, the view is northwest, with the Chickahominy at left. Porter (center) gives orders to the Comte de Paris.

Library of Congress

The measure of Lee's victory at Gaines's Mill is represented in Waud's drawing of an abandoned Federal battery overrun by exuberant Confederate troops.

Library of Congress

James Gibson photographed sick and wounded at the Savage's Station field hospital on June 28. Within 24 hours most of them were abandoned to the enemy in the retreat. Men of the 16th New York wear white straw hats issued by the regiment.

Library of Congress

Against a backdrop of burning stores the Sixth Corps of the rear guard joins the retreat June 29. Waud shows the 16th New York in its distinctive straw hats.

Library of Congress

Arthur Lumley sketched the scene at Savage's Station on June 29. An ammunition train is blown up at the station as Rebels push against the rear guard's skirmish line. A shell strikes near General Sumner and staff in the foreground.

Library of Congress

In Waud's drawing, a second Federal ammunition train is sent hurtling to its spectacular destruction at the burned-out rail bridge over the Chickahominy.

Library of Congress

At Glendale on June 30, drawn by Alfred Waud, Emory Upton's and Josiah Porter's batteries of Slocum's division duel with Huger's guns on the Charles City Road.

Library of Congress

In Waud's wash drawing, a Federal battery of Franklin's rear guard at White Oak Bridge is taken under fire by Stonewall Jackson's guns across White Oak Swamp.

Library of Congress

Waud did this sketch of the central action at the Battle of Glendale. These are Phil Kearny's men on the firing line in the thick woods near the crossroads.

Library of Congress

Cook Collection,
Valentine Museum

Benjamin Huger   Stonewall Jackson

Library of Congress

Anne S. K. Brown Military Collection, Brown University

Henry J. Hunt

McClellan lounges on the *Galena* during the Malvern Hill fight; an 1864 cartoon.

Cook Collection, Valentine Museum

Library of Congress

Daniel Harvey Hill

Theophilus H. Holmes

M. and M. Karolik Collection, Museum of Fine Arts, Boston

An unknown artist sketched the gunboats *Galena* (left) and *Mahaska* shelling the Rebels beyond Malvern Hill on July 1. Hunt's reserve artillery is at center.

Library of Congress

In Alfred Waud's drawing of the Malvern Hill battle, a Federal gun fires over Fitz John Porter's infantry lines at advancing Confederates in the distance.

Print Collection, New York Public Library

With McClellan's army at Harrison's Landing, a Lowe war balloon reconnoiters the banks of the James from the tender *Custis*, drawn by Arthur Lumley of *Leslie's*.

Library of Congress

When the Army of the Potomac evacuated the Peninsula, it left behind at Harrison's Landing, as sketched by Alfred Waud, straw sentinels and wooden "Quaker guns."

· 11 ·

Opportunity at Glendale

....

A T FIRST LIGHT AT 3:30 A.M. of Day Six — Monday, June 30 —
Stonewall Jackson rode up unannounced to General Magruder's
headquarters on the Williamsburg Road. During the night Jackson had
word from General Lee that must have clarified his orders about
holding the line of the Chickahominy, for he now informed Magruder
that the Valley army was crossing the river and would be up shortly.
Prince John was greatly relieved. He had continued to worry about an
enemy counterattack and had stayed up all night preparing for one.
Now he felt it safe to catch an hour's sleep — "the first in forty-eight,"
he said. With sunrise came General Lee himself, with Magruder's
orders for the day. Lee explained that Jackson would take over the
direct pursuit of the enemy's rear guard, and that Magruder was to
march his command back and around to the Darbytown Road to act as
a reserve for the day's operations by Longstreet and A. P. Hill.

Afterward, farther out on the Williamsburg Road, where the dead
of the Savage's Station battlefield were being collected, Lee met with
Jackson. As with their meeting three days earlier in the Walnut Grove
churchyard, no record was made of what passed between them. No
one on their staffs was close enough to hear them, and neither man
later related the conversation. Lieutenant Robert Stiles, an artillerist
in the Richmond Howitzers, was watching closely, however, and by his
account Jackson "began talking in a jerky, impetuous way" and marking out a triangle of lines in the dirt with the toe of his right boot,
seemingly proposing or describing some plan with great earnestness.
As if to emphasize his point, Jackson stamped his boot on the diagram
and Stiles heard him exclaim, "We've got him!" With that the two
generals mounted and went their separate ways.

It is clear enough that on this early morning of June 30 Lee assigned
Jackson the pursuit of the Yankee force Magruder had engaged the day

before, but it is less clear, from subsequent events, what he expected of Jackson when he caught up with that force — whether he was to bring it to battle, or simply to halt its retreat and hold it there, away from any fighting elsewhere that day.

What was known of the enemy must have been mentioned. From the many prisoners taken at Gaines's Mill it was known that the Federals had been at least four divisions strong there. From prisoners taken the day before, Magruder learned that he had faced at least three divisions at Savage's Station — divisions different from those met on June 27. Furthermore, the enterprising Porter Alexander, affixing Captain Cheves's silk balloon of many colors to a steamer and taking it down the James River to Drewry's Bluff, discovered enemy camps and campfires on the James itself, at Malvern Hill.

Most probably, then, Lee only described to Jackson his general plan for battle that day and left it to Jackson to determine how best to participate in that battle. That was Lee's usual way. The triangulation Lieutenant Stiles saw Jackson mark out in the dirt suggests forming a trap around McClellan's army. In the event, Lee would make no criticism of Jackson's actions on June 30, and Jackson would admit no failings. Some days later, overhearing his staff speculating on what might have been done differently that day, Old Jack said pointedly, "If General Lee had wanted me he could have sent for me."[1]

With Jackson and his command positioned to operate against the rear of McClellan's army, Lee turned next to marshaling forces to take the enemy in flank from the west. At the farthest extreme, moving toward the head of the Federal columns by way of the River Road, was the division of Theophilus Holmes, 7,200 men of all arms and six batteries of artillery. These were new troops, and Lee originally intended them simply to act as a reserve on his right flank and perhaps to interrupt and damage the Federal supply trains if opportunity arose. At ten o'clock that morning General Holmes reported himself at New Market, on the River Road three and a half miles west of Malvern Hill.

The main focus of Confederate operations on June 30 was easily seen: Glendale, the little crossroads community of scattered farms and houses and the shop of blacksmith Riddell two and a quarter miles south and west of White Oak Bridge. All the roads led to or toward Glendale. The Long Bridge Road ran on a long slant southwesterly from the Chickahominy through Glendale and on to an intersection with the River Road at New Market. The road from White Oak Bridge entered the Long Bridge Road barely a mile east of Glendale. The Charles City Road, starting from the outskirts of Richmond, ran southeasterly directly to Glendale. The Darbytown Road paralleling it entered the Long Bridge Road less than three miles west of Glendale. The Quaker Road ran due south from Glendale to Malvern Hill and the James River.

The Federal columns, whichever White Oak Swamp crossing they used, all had to funnel through Glendale. From there, except for a few of Keyes's men and later some of Baldy Smith's who discovered the nearby woods road, the entire Army of the Potomac followed the Quaker Road toward the James. Glendale was therefore a place the Yankees had to defend at any cost if their army was to escape. The Prince de Joinville of General McClellan's staff carefully studied the map and pointed this out to the general, who, it was said, grasped his point at once.

It was Lee's intention to throw the largest part of his army, six divisions, 44,800 men, directly against Glendale to cut McClellan's army in two. At the same time, Jackson with his four divisions, 25,300 men, would confront McClellan's rear guard, thought now to be guarding the White Oak Swamp crossings against any pursuit. Lee could not know just how many of the enemy would be encountered at Glendale and behind the swamp, so in common with his earlier operations north of the Chickahominy he determined to mass sufficient force to overwhelm whatever might be encountered. In this case, that meant every man at his command but Holmes's division and Jeb Stuart's cavalry.

Lee had in fact so outmaneuvered his opponent that McClellan, with an army superior in numbers but widely scattered, faced a battle on June 30 at Glendale and White Oak Swamp outnumbered 71,000 to 61,500. As Lee planned it, Benjamin Huger's division — with 12,000 men and thus far in the Seven Days lightly engaged, now the largest in the army — would open the battle at Glendale by reason of having the shortest march, just three miles along the Charles City Road, to reach the enemy. Jackson at the same time would confront the Yankee rear guard. The divisions of Longstreet and Powell Hill, with Longstreet in command, had marched the longest distance the day before from across the river and still had seven miles to go to reach Glendale over the Darbytown and Long Bridge roads. In addition to Longstreet's and Hill's 19,200 men, acting as a reserve, would be Magruder's three divisions with 13,600 men. General Lee took a central position, with Longstreet and Hill, and waited expectantly for Huger's guns to signal the start of the battle.

Looking back on this day years later, Porter Alexander observed that there were only a handful of times during the four years of war when "we were within reach of military successes so great that we might have hoped to end the war with our independence. . . . This chance of June 30th '62 impresses me as the best of all."[2]

....

IT MIGHT BE supposed that at this moment, a few miles to the east, General McClellan was also waiting expectantly for the battle to commence. It was as obvious to him as to Lee that here was the decisive hour in the retreat to the James. The Federal supply trains and cattle herd were still making their labored way south from White Oak Swamp. Of the Army of the Potomac's fighting men, only Keyes's Fourth Corps and two divisions of Porter's Fifth Corps had so far reached the river. Two-thirds of the army still guarded White Oak Swamp and the Glendale crossroads, and those men, by McClellan's hallucinatory arithmetic, might be facing as many as three times their number. He personally reconnoitered their entire position, from White Oak Bridge to the Quaker Road below Glendale. By any reckoning, here was the moment for the Young Napoleon to fulfill the pledge he had made to his army after Seven Pines: "I ask of you now one last crowning effort. . . . Soldiers! I will be with you in this battle, and share its dangers with you."

General McClellan, however, would not be sharing any dangers in this battle. Instead he was five miles away, at Haxall's Landing on the James behind Malvern Hill, without telegraphic communications and too distant to command the army. Among general and staff, the Comte de Paris reported, each one expressed great pleasure "upon seeing with his own eyes the goal of our efforts, the end of our retreat." (A newspaper correspondent compared it to what the Greek Xenophon must have felt upon reaching the sea after *his* epic retreat.) At four o'clock that afternoon, distancing himself even further from the responsibilities of command, General McClellan boarded the gunboat *Galena*, and forty-five minutes later, with McClellan aboard, the *Galena* steamed off upriver to shell an enemy column sighted on the River Road west of Malvern Hill. That evening the general would dine at Commander John Rodgers's table aboard the *Galena* where, the Comte de Paris noted appreciatively, the linen was white and there was "a good dinner with some good wine."

When he was later asked about General McClellan's riding off to the James on the eve of the Battle of Glendale, his friend William Franklin suggested that the general must have believed his forces "safe against any attack" at Glendale, while he had real concern for the safety of the Malvern Hill position and felt he had to consult personally with the navy on the best place finally to put the army. "I am not sure that these views were correct," Franklin added, "but I think they actuated him." Assuming these concerns about the James River position were real, however, both Fitz John Porter and John Barnard, the army's chief engineer, were already at Malvern Hill and entirely capable of arranging matters there. The general commanding's peculiar conduct on June 30 has another explanation.

The truth of the matter is that George McClellan had lost the courage to command. With each day of the Seven Days his demoralization had increased, and each day his courage to command decreased accordingly. By Day Six the demoralization was complete; exercising command in battle was now quite beyond him, and to avoid it he deliberately fled the battlefield. He was drained in both mind and body. Brigadier Andrew A. Humphreys of his staff saw him the next morning aboard the *Galena* and, Humphreys wrote his wife, "never did I see a man more cut down than Genl. McClellan was. . . . He was unable to do anything or say anything."[3]

When he rode off toward the James at noon on June 30, General McClellan, as he had done the day before at Savage's Station, failed to appoint anyone to command in his stead. Once again, his motive was to keep Bull Sumner from that post. Once again, the three corps commanders, as Heintzelman put it, "fought their troops entirely according to their own ideas." McClellan also left the forces there in a considerable tangle, which made directing them even more difficult.

Behind White Oak Bridge was William Franklin with one of his two Sixth Corps divisions, under Baldy Smith, and four of Smith's batteries. With him as well and falling informally under Franklin's command was the Second Corps division of Israel Richardson, and Richardson's two batteries. Franklin also had one additional brigade that he had collared as it passed by after performing guard duty at Bottom's Bridge — Henry M. Naglee's brigade from the Fourth Corps. Somewhat later, after an appeal to Sumner, Franklin was reinforced for a time by two more brigades, these from the Second Corps. This reinforcement raised Franklin's maximum strength that day to 25,200 men and six batteries of artillery. It was a rear guard only slightly smaller than what had confronted Magruder the day before at Savage's Station. Posted as it was behind White Oak Swamp, it was in a far better position defensively.

Farther to the west, on the right of the Charles City Road a mile beyond Glendale, was Henry W. Slocum with Franklin's other Sixth

Corps division. Slocum had three batteries of his own and two others loaned him by the Third Corps. His task was to hold the Charles City Road and also the road leading to the White Oak Swamp crossing at Brackett's Ford. Because of his separation from Franklin, Slocum for all practical purposes had an independent command.

The balance of the Federal forces at Glendale were posted west of the crossroads and the Quaker Road, facing west, extending in an irregular line nearly two miles long. Each corps commander, and sometimes each division commander, had placed his men as he saw fit, and consequently it was far from being a seamless line of battle. Some units were advanced, some drawn back, and there were numerous gaps. It was a rare Federal general that day who knew the identity of the units on his flanks.

Heintzelman had both his Third Corps divisions at hand, but somehow in all the confusion and shifting about they had become widely separated. Phil Kearny was on the right of the line, connecting loosely with Slocum along the Charles City Road. Joe Hooker's division was on the extreme left, well down the Quaker Road. Corps commander Heintzelman was faced with directing two divisions that were, at the closest, three-quarters of a mile apart.

Straddling the Long Bridge Road and squarely between Kearny and Hooker, yet not securely connected with either, was George A. McCall's division from the Fifth Corps. McCall's Pennsylvanians had been in the hottest fighting at Mechanicsville and Gaines's Mill and had lost one-fifth of their numbers, and by all rights should not have been asked to make this fight, yet they found themselves at the very center of the battle line. (The rest of the Fifth Corps had already left for the James. The Fourth Corps, with just 51 casualties so far in the Seven Days, had left even earlier. General McCall had not moved fast enough.) McCall, like Slocum, was commanding independently.

So was Bull Sumner. He had just one of his Second Corps divisions under his eye, John Sedgwick's, and had posted it behind and to the left of McCall. When Franklin called on him for help that afternoon and he sent two of Sedgwick's brigades, corps commander Sumner was left in command of a single brigade. After that detachment the Glendale line, running from Slocum on the right to Hooker on the left, totaled 36,300 men and thirteen batteries of artillery. Lee's intended concentration at Glendale would thus pit five Rebels against every four Yankees.[4]

No announcement had come down from the high command, but it was plain to those in the Federal ranks that they would be expected to hold this position for however long it took for the trains to pass. In any case, the infantry could march no farther toward the James until the road was clear. Corporal Asa Smith of Joe Hooker's division watched the unbroken line of wagons passing down the Quaker Road behind him. "If anything broke about wagon or harness," Smith wrote, "the mules were detached from the wagon and it was pulled out of the line and burned, together with its contents. This procession was passing nearly all day." Not infrequently fights broke out for places in the line, an angry quartermaster reported, "degenerating sometimes into personal contests . . . and very often in the breaking of wagons and the killing or maiming of public animals."

The fighting men kindled their little fires for coffee to wash down their hardtack, if they had even that. Long lines formed at every spring and well to fill canteens. Afterward they waited and rested in whatever shade they could find. The heat was oppressive; many remembered it as the hottest day yet. "Each man seemed to think that he could not live 15 minutes from the burning sun that was shining & not a sign of any wind," Matthew Marrin noted in his diary. Yet army routine would be served. It was the last day of the month and the 9th Pennsylvania was mustered for payday. Before the day was over 137 men of the 9th would be dead, wounded, or prisoners with their pay in their pockets.[5]

....

IN SPITE OF its early start that morning, Stonewall Jackson's Army of the Valley made poor time in its pursuit of the Federal rear guard. There was a great deal of booty to collect. Georgian Frank Coker assured his wife that at Savage's Station "you could find anything you wanted from a siege gun to a cigar." Colonel Bryan Grimes of D. H. Hill's division found even a large pile of metallic coffins. John Casler of the Stonewall Brigade found great mounds of burned coffee beans, but "some was scorched just enough to be good, and we went for it. . . ." For all their effort, the Yankees had carried out the destruction imperfectly, and great quantities of equipment, stores, and ammunition were salvaged. "For weeks afterward," the Reverend Dabney recalled, "the agents of the army were busy gathering in the spoils; while a multitude of the country people found in them partial indemnity for the ruin of their farms." The Rebels also succeeded in gathering up a thousand Federal stragglers who had not been quick enough to escape across the swamp.

Jackson took a moment to inspect the large Federal field hospital at Savage's Station. It looked like a city of tents, and he marveled at "the extent and convenience of its accommodations." Corporal Patrick Taylor of the 1st Minnesota, wounded in the fighting the day before at the station, assured the general that all the wounded, of both armies, were treated alike there. That was how it should be, Jackson agreed, and asked, "How many men had you engaged here yesterday?" He did not know, Corporal Taylor replied. "I don't suppose you would tell if you did know," Jackson remarked. "No, sir, I should not," Taylor said, "but I don't know." Old Jack rode on with his column.[6]

Major General Benjamin Huger was at heart a headquarters bureaucrat, devoid of imagination and enterprise and even of energy. In the old army he had been a staff man, specializing in ordnance, and field command in the Confederate army was testing him beyond his depth. While he had been unjustly blamed for his role in the Seven Pines failure, the experience seemed only to have increased his caution. On June 29 he had advanced his brigades, one of his generals wrote, "cautiously feeling for the fleeing foe." His march out the Charles City Road that Sunday covered but five miles and ended prematurely at the Brightwell farm, three miles short of Glendale, allowing the Yankees to escape across White Oak Swamp without hindrance.

Like Prince John Magruder, Huger expected every moment to be attacked by the Yankees. Lee might have explained to him that an army under General McClellan that was retreating with all speed was highly unlikely to launch attacks, but of all his lieutenants Huger was the only one Lee did not see personally on June 30. As it happened, Huger's excessive caution would take him right out of the battle.

Early Monday morning, still concerned the enemy would come through White Oak Swamp on his left and attack him, Huger sent one of his four brigades, under Rans Wright, to the rear and around to the north side of the swamp. Wright was there all day, and the only troops he encountered were Stonewall Jackson's. Huger's other three brigades pushed ahead cautiously along the Charles City Road. At the next swamp crossing a second brigade was sent to the left on another careful reconnaissance. It was led by "Little Billy" Mahone, whose quarrel with Harvey Hill at Seven Pines had nearly resulted in a duel. Mahone found no one in the swamp but a civilian, who told him that the Yankees had indeed been there, but the night before they had crossed the swamp to the Charles City Road and now were no doubt somewhere ahead. With that Huger was persuaded to push on, only to discover that the road ahead was blocked by felled trees. It had taken him all morning to advance just over a mile, and General Slocum had made good use of the time to send out teams of axmen to block his path.

This unexpected development perplexed General Huger. He might have sent a company or two of skirmishers loping ahead through the woods to put a stop to the tree cutting, but that did not occur to him. The Yankee woodsmen, undisturbed, continued blockading the road well into the afternoon, stopping only when they reached a clearing and ran out of trees. The felled trees were not overly large and Huger might have put squads of men to lifting them aside to make way for his men and guns, but he did not do that either. Instead, on the advice of Little Billy Mahone, who had been a construction engineer in civilian life, it was decided to cut a new road through the woods alongside the blocked road.

In this battle of woodsmen, marked by the whacking of axes and the crash of falling trees, the Confederates proved to be a good deal less skilled than the Yankees, and it was late afternoon before they came even within artillery range of Slocum's Federals. Huger had a substantial edge in infantry, but he elected to attempt no trial of strength. He elected to attempt no attack at all. He settled instead on an artillery duel — for his part, he said, he "only kept up a moderate fire" — in which he was worsted. Slocum put five batteries against the two Huger sent forward. The casualty list in Huger's entire division on June 30 would come to just 78 men, all due to artillery fire. Of Huger's performance at Glendale one of his Seven Pines critics now wrote, "As usual, that commander was behind time. . . ." On this occasion there was no disputing the point.[7]

While Huger inched forward along the Charles City Road, Jackson's Valley army was covering the five miles from Savage's Station to White Oak Bridge. In the van was Jackson's chief of artillery, Stapleton Crutchfield, who found an observation post from which to survey the prospect ahead. The road slanted down to the bridge from the northwest, then on the other side ran straight ahead and disappeared to the south over a low rise. White Oak Bridge itself was burned and its timbers tumbled into the shallow stream, and the marshy bottomland barred a crossing by wagons and artillery nearby.

Several Federal batteries supported by infantry could be seen across the stream and distant 300 yards on the left (east) of the road, but on the right dense woodland covered the slope and shielded any defenders there from Crutchfield's view. His artillerist's eye soon found a good position for his own guns. To his right was a low, open ridge paralleling the swamp, allowing a clear line of fire diagonally over the bridge toward the Yankee guns. He set to work cutting a pathway through the woods to reach the rear of the ridgeline. Except for a scattering of sharpshooters' fire from the swamp the enemy was silent and waiting.

Jackson himself arrived on the scene about noon and approved Crutchfield's dispositions. The ridgeline was some 600 yards long, and seven batteries, containing thirty-one guns, were quietly driven up behind it with pieces shotted and gunners ready. Shortly before 2:00 P.M., with a rush, the batteries deployed on the ridge and unlimbered and abruptly opened a thunderclap of fire against the Federal lines.

Lieutenant Thomas Livermore of the 5th New Hampshire, dozing like many others in the midday heat, was jolted awake "by the thunders of artillery, the shriek of shells, and the horrid humming of their fragments. Hell seemed to have opened upon us." Everything near him was sudden movement. Infantrymen fell into ranks and gunners rushed to their pieces. Terrified teamsters drove their wagons wildly into the woods. Teams of mules being watered in the swamp ran hellbent up and over the slope, wrecking bivouacs and trampling men. "Stragglers and non-combatants of all kinds fled in all directions from the fire," Lieutenant Livermore wrote. Horses went down screaming and he saw a shot strike into the 2nd Delaware, "which threw a man's head perhaps twenty feet into the air, and the bleeding trunk fell over toward us."

Baldy Smith had his headquarters on the grounds of the Britton house behind the artillery line, and was refreshing himself with a cool bath in Mr. Britton's bathhouse when the shells began raining down. General Smith would recall dressing "in what I judged was dignified haste" and calling for his horse. General Franklin sent back a call to Glendale for reinforcements. The Federal gunners answered with a few rounds before their batteries were riddled and they pulled back to safer ground. A disabled gun and its limber were left on the field. The infantry lay flat, a man in the 57th New York wrote, "eyes fixed on the rising ground in front, where most of the shells struck and then came ricocheting down the slope amongst us. We could do nothing but try and dodge them. . . ."[8]

Jackson called for Colonel Thomas Munford and his 2nd Virginia cavalry to cross near the wrecked bridge and seize the abandoned gun and reconnoiter the enemy position. He and D. H. Hill, commanding the lead division, would cross with them. Munford said he doubted their horses could make it through the swamp. "Yes, Colonel, but you haven't tried it," Old Jack said. "Try it, Colonel!" In they went, Munford recalled, "belly deep to the horses in mud and mire," and finally struggled up the far bank.

Going forward, however, the expedition soon came under a heavy fire from artillery and massed infantry that had been concealed from their earlier view by the woods. One shell, Munford noted, came "uncomfortably near" Jackson and Hill, and with that the party concluded it had seen enough and retired. The two generals were able to recross the swamp near the bridge, but Munford's cavalry made too large a target at the constricted crossing and so rode off downstream a quarter mile and discovered a crossing Munford described as a cowpath. There were no Federals there, and he sent back to Jackson to say that infantry crossing here would be on the enemy's flank. There was no response from the general. "Why, I never understood," Munford later wrote.

Equally enterprising was Wade Hampton, who had recovered from his Seven Pines wound and was now commanding a brigade in Charles Winder's division. Off to the east of White Oak Bridge, but not as far as Colonel Munford's crossing point, General Hampton discovered a second usable passage across the swamp. Crossing there and cautiously scouting ahead, he found himself well to the rear of the line of Yankee infantry holding the eastern flank at the bridge. He withdrew unobserved and reported his finding to Jackson. Could the crossing be bridged, Jackson asked him. Hampton said it could easily be bridged, but only to carry infantry; cutting a road through the woods for the artillery would make too much noise and alert the enemy. Jackson told him to build a bridge for the infantry.

Hampton collected a detail of fifty men, cut sufficient trees for a crossing, carried them to the site, and soon assembled a rough but workable footbridge. Returning, he found Jackson seated on a log, his dingy cadet cap pulled low over his eyes, displaying no animation. Hampton reported his bridge finished and volunteered his brigade for the movement, and waited for orders. "He sat in silence for some time," Hampton recalled, "then rose and walked off in silence." On that awkward note Hampton returned to his troops.[9]

Jackson's personal reconnoiter across the swamp left him in no doubt that he was facing a substantial force at White Oak Bridge — a local resident identified it for him as General Franklin's corps — and one capable of "obstinately disputing" any crossing he might attempt. Whether or not he recognized Franklin's force for what it was —

virtually identical in size to his own — he certainly recognized the strength of Franklin's position. An infantry attack could not be forced through the swamp barrier here in any numbers or with any speed, and artillery could not cross at all. Two attempts to rebuild the bridge collapsed under the heat of the enemy's fire. Jackson was checkmated.

Yet there were the two other passages across the swamp discovered by Munford and Hampton. These crossings, to be sure, were only usable by infantry, and were not by themselves likely to produce a decisive victory. Even so, at small risk they were certain to produce another important result — a flanking movement so threatening to Franklin that he would not dare send reinforcements to the contest at Glendale. If the Federal rear guard at White Oak Bridge was too large and too well posted for Jackson to challenge in pitched battle, at least he could hold it away from the larger battle. The two foes at the swamp would then checkmate each other. As it happened, the two brigades sent to Franklin by Sumner were returned in time to play an important role at Glendale, and two of Richardson's brigades also entered that fight. These 11,700 Yankee reinforcements were the literal measure of Stonewall Jackson's failure on June 30.

There would be critics (among them Longstreet) who found failure in Jackson's not moving by the flank to Longstreet's support at Glendale once his direct way was blocked at White Oak Bridge. "Jackson should have done more for me than he did," Old Pete said. Here, as at Mechanicsville, the failure was one of communication. Jackson did not send to Lee to report he was stymied at the bridge. Lee did not send to Jackson to find out his situation and to change his mission.

Changing Jackson's mission would have meant a long march to the west to search out an unobstructed upstream crossing of White Oak Swamp and to cut through Huger's division, and would have required an early decision by Lee if Jackson were to arrive before nightfall. For Jackson to initiate this on his own would have meant exercising more discretion in his orders than even Lee permitted. It was on this point that Jackson said, "If General Lee had wanted me he could have sent for me."

Whatever the merits of the various alternatives to stalemate at the bridge, Jackson attempted none of them and instead went to sleep under a tree. "It looked to me as if on our side we were waiting for Jackson to wake up," McHenry Howard of General Winder's staff wrote of that afternoon. The hours passed in a desultory artillery exchange, much of it between batteries out of sight of each other and firing by sound. Porter Alexander, an artillerist himself, dismissed it as an "absurd farce of war." The total casualties in Jackson's command on June 30 were three men killed and a dozen wounded, all of them artillerymen. (Among the Federal dead in the exchange was Captain George Hazzard, who earlier in the day had led his battery safely away from capture at Savage's Station.)

What happened to Stonewall Jackson that Monday afternoon is obvious enough — with stiking suddenness he reached the end of his physical endurance. That morning he had been himself; the next morning he would be himself again. But even awake in these afternoon hours he was as benumbed and unresponsive to everyone he encountered as he was to Wade Hampton. He made no effort to communicate with his fellow generals. When Rans Wright of Huger's command searched him out to report the ground north of White Oak Swamp clear of the enemy, and to ask for orders, Jackson had none and advised Wright to return to Huger south of the swamp. A staff man sent by Longstreet learned nothing of Jackson's intentions, for Jackson had no intentions. That evening he fell asleep at the mess table, the Reverend Dabney reported, "with his supper between his teeth." He only roused himself sufficiently to announce, "Now, gentlemen, let us at once to bed, and rise with the dawn, and see if to-morrow we cannot *do something!*"[10]

....

BEFORE NOON that day the divisions of James Longstreet and A. P. Hill entered the Long Bridge Road from the Darbytown Road and turned eastward toward Glendale. General Lee and his staff were with the head of the column, and soon President Davis and his entourage joined as well. Why was he here in so dangerous a position, the president asked Lee. "I am trying to find out something about the movement and plans of these people," Lee replied. He added that this was certainly not the proper place for the commander-in-chief. "Oh, I am here on the same mission that you are," Davis said, and the two began discussing what they knew about the situation.

Within a mile or so of Glendale the advance encountered Yankee pickets. If it was not clear before, it was clear now that McClellan was not using the Long Bridge Road for his retreat, and that his trains had to be on the Quaker Road, heading south toward the James. Porter Alexander soon arrived to verify this. He said that from the balloon at Drewry's Bluff the night before and again at dawn that morning he had seen signs of the enemy on the James in the area of Malvern Hill.

The troops took their ease in the shade of the woods along the road, waiting for Huger's guns on the left to signal the start of the action. Huger had reported his road obstructed but after that nothing further was heard from him. Prince John Magruder reported his command several miles to the rear and coming forward. As it happened, the opening guns of the Battle of Glendale were Jackson's, beginning his barrage at White Oak Bridge at 2:00 P.M. Thinking they were Huger's, Longstreet had a battery fire in acknowledgment. In reply from beyond the trees ahead came a hail of Federal shells.

At that particular moment a large part of the high command of the Confederate States — President Davis, army commander Lee, Generals Longstreet and A. P. Hill, all their staffs — were gathered in a rough clearing among the pines behind the front line. Firing blindly but with uncanny accuracy, a Yankee battery began dropping shells into the clearing. Horses were killed and staff men wounded. A. P. Hill galloped up to Davis and Lee and announced without preamble that this was no place for them. "As commander of this part of the field, I order you both to the rear!" Dutifully president and general rode farther to the rear, but shells continued to fall in their vicinity. Hill rode after them and exclaimed, "Did I not tell you to go away from here?" A single Yankee shell, he said, could in an instant deprive the Confederacy of its president and the Army of Northern Virginia of its commander. With that Davis and Lee finally rode beyond the range of the enemy guns.[11]

It became apparent that the gunfire heard from the left was a false alarm. Its intensity soon fell off and it seemed too distant for Huger's column, nor was there any subsequent sound of musketry to signal an attack going forward. Longstreet's guns continued their long-range exchange with the Yankees and there was some firing on the skirmish lines, but Lee determined to hold up his attack here until Huger and Jackson were engaged as planned.

Three o'clock came and still there was no change. Then a courier arrived for Lee from Colonel Thomas Rosser, 5th Virginia cavalry, scouting on the army's right flank. Rosser reported sighting Federal columns "moving hurriedly and confusedly" over Malvern Hill in the direction of the James. General Lee knew little enough of what was happening in front, and even less of Huger and Jackson on the left, but on the right it appeared that the enemy was getting away. He would see for himself. Leaving Longstreet in command on the Long Bridge Road, he rode off to find General Holmes.

Theophilus Hunter Holmes, thirty-two years in the old army, was fifty-seven and old before his time. He was a stiff-backed regular and quite deaf, and like Benjamin Huger he was beyond his depth in a field command. Earlier, at New Market, he had been informed by Colonel Rosser of the cavalry and by his own officers that the Yankees were at Malvern Hill, and when Lee encountered him that afternoon on the River Road Holmes was sending forward six rifled guns to shell them. Lee, just back from personally reconnoitering the position, told him to bring up his whole division. While Holmes was calling up his infantry, Lee returned to the Glendale front. Reaching there at four o'clock or a little after, he made a fateful decision.

By his own observation he saw that the head of McClellan's army had already reached the James at Malvern Hill, or was reaching there. He saw that the tail of McClellan's army was still at Glendale and White Oak Swamp. He determined to attack both head and tail simultaneously. For that he ordered Magruder's divisions, in reserve at Glendale, to march to Holmes's support for the attack on Malvern Hill. The logic of his decision was sound enough, yet unknown to Lee his logic was already undermined by reality.

Reinforcing Holmes with Magruder would raise the force on the River Road to better than 20,000 men, a number large enough for an attack. What Lee did not realize, however, was that when he ordered Magruder away from the Glendale front he was grievously weakening his chances of victory there. He assumed that even without Magruder he was still left with seven divisions for the battle. In fact he was left with just two divisions. It never entered his calculations that on June 30 not a single infantryman in either Huger's command or Jackson's would fire a shot.

General Holmes proceeded with his plan to bombard the Federals on Malvern Hill. Six 3-inch rifled pieces were brought forward to within half a mile of the steep western face of the heights, known locally as Malvern Cliffs. The rest of Holmes's division moved into the woods behind the guns in support. What the Confederate observers had seen on and around Malvern Hill that day were mostly wagon trains. What they did not know was that Fitz John Porter had the better part of two divisions of the Fifth Corps posted there facing the River Road or within easy supporting distance. More important, the better part of the artillery reserve of the Army of the Potomac was there. Seven batteries — thirty-six guns, most of them 3-inch Ordnance rifles and 20-pounder Parrott rifles — were deployed atop Malvern Cliffs to overlook the River Road to the west. So confident was he of the position that at his headquarters at the Malvern house, a hundred yards behind this gun line, General Porter slept right through the subsequent engagement.[12]

The cloud of dust raised by the marchers announced Holmes's approach, and his guns had hardly unlimbered when the Yankees opened fire. By the account of a man in the 50th North Carolina, "in a few minutes there was a perfect shower of shells of tremendous proportion and hideous sound. . . ." The "shower" of shells came from the rifled guns of the artillery reserve on Malvern Cliffs; those of "tremendous proportion" were from the gunboats *Aroostook* and *Galena* (which had General McClellan on board as an interested spectator) in the James, whose 9-inch and 11-inch Dahlgrens and 100-pounder Parrott rifles sent their great shells plunging into the woods along the River Road.

Lieutenant Colonel Samuel Walkup, whose 48th North Carolina had first experienced combat five days earlier at Oak Grove, wrote in his diary that this Federal gunnery "frightened the boys terribly." Shell fragments and tree trunks and broken branches rained down everywhere, and the noise was overwhelming. A battalion of Virginia cavalry, two months in the service, panicked and galloped off to the rear, knocking over men and guns on the way. That spread the panic to the infantry, and the many new levies among them (as one of them wrote) "ran back like a flock of sheep with a pack of dogs after them." A battery in reserve tried to turn back and became tangled in the woods. The drivers cut the traces and rode off on their mounts, leaving behind two guns and three caissons.

The gunners manning the six rifles in front stayed at their posts and tried to maintain the contest, but they were so outgunned and so battered by the shelling that they soon had to retire. Two of their caissons were blown up. In the midst of the chaos, old General Holmes stepped out of the house he had taken as his field headquarters, cupped a hand behind his ear, and observed, "I thought I heard firing."

Eventually Holmes managed to collect his scattered forces some distance to the rear. He had lost but 3 dead and 50 wounded, but his repulse was complete nonetheless. He was virtually speechless with anger. When Magruder's aide Major Brent rode up to inquire if Holmes could suggest where Magruder's troops might be placed and where the enemy might be found and other such matters, Holmes's replies were brief and blunt. "I left him in wonder," Brent recalled, "after having extracted from him four No's as the sum total of my results."

General Magruder was meanwhile having troubles of his own. There was confusion in his orders and among those delivering them, and his own agitation of the day before had if anything increased. Attempted shortcuts in the march only extended it. Officers unfamiliar with the ground to begin with were further confused by the mysterious name Darby, which all their guides used but which they could not find on their maps.

It seemed that at some time past, back in England, in an inheritance dispute, the family Enroughty had grudgingly agreed to call itself Darby but perversely retained the old spelling. The maps showed numerous Enroughtys living in this part of the Peninsula, but every one of them answered only to Darby — thus the Darbytown Road — all of which thoroughly befuddled Prince John. He would arrive too late to be of use to Holmes, and was then recalled to support Longstreet again, and was too late there as well. When the day was over, Magruder's command had marched twenty miles and more to no result at all, and like Huger's men and Jackson's, had not fired a shot.[13]

....

THE AFTERNOON was fast slipping away and there were only four hours of daylight remaining, and General Lee determined he could wait no longer for Huger and Jackson. He ordered Longstreet to attack at Glendale. Old Pete had already posted the troops and the movement began promptly.

The Confederates' advance would be guided by the Long Bridge Road, running here in a northeasterly direction through heavy woods to the Glendale crossroads. Longstreet's initial line of assault, nearly half a mile wide, consisted of 4,700 men in the three brigades of James L. Kemper, Micah Jenkins (commanding Richard Anderson's brigade this day while Anderson commanded the division), and Cadmus Wilcox. The remaining three brigades of the division were in close support, and Lawrence Branch's brigade of A. P. Hill's division acted as support for the right flank. Longstreet held the rest of Hill's division in reserve — to be employed, it was hoped, in the pursuit of the broken Yankee forces. It was 5:00 P.M. when the two armies came to grips.

Posted squarely in front of this advance was George McCall's division of Pennsylvania Reserves, facing their third battle in five days. McCall's line ran in a shallow concave curve west of the Glendale crossroads, George Meade's brigade straddling the Long Bridge Road on the right, Truman Seymour's on the left. John Reynolds's brigade, led since Reynolds's capture by Colonel Seneca G. Simmons, was in reserve. Of McCall's 7,500 infantry, some 5,000 were in the front line. Out in front of the infantry was an artillery line — five batteries, with twenty-six guns.

Off to the north, between the Long Bridge and Charles City roads and separated from McCall's line, was Phil Kearny's division of the Third Corps. Off to the south, down the Quaker Road, also separated from McCall, was Joe Hooker's division of the Third Corps. To the rear, between McCall and Hooker, was a single brigade from John Sedgwick's Second Corps division, just now the sole unit under Bull Sumner's direction. There was not even a semblance of unified command over these variegated forces. McCall's men on the firing line were tense and waiting; everyone knew, as one of the officers put it, that "the whole woods were full of rebels."

Much of the Battle of Glendale would be fought back and forth across a farm of some 200 acres owned by R. H. Nelson. Mr. Nelson's house, on the Quaker Road not far from the Willis Methodist Church, was taken by General Sumner for his headquarters. The farm had belonged in years past to the Frayser family and was still called by many local people Frayser's farm. The open ground opposite the Nelson house and west of the Quaker Road, 800 yards wide and 1,000 yards deep, was defended by Truman Seymour's brigade and, out front, by three batteries of artillery. All four sides of the clearing were wooded, with the heaviest woods to the west, where the Confederates were advancing. General McCall would call it "a beautiful battle ground, but too large for my force to find cover or protection on both flanks."[14]

James Kemper's Virginians had not yet been in any of the Seven Days fighting, and at the command "Forward!" they started ahead without thought to order or discipline, rushing headlong through the woods and underbrush and clearings, hallooing the Rebel yell. Kemper admired their spirit but despaired of keeping them under command. In ragged order or no order at all they burst out of the woods into the open ground in front of two batteries of the German Light Artillery.

Recruited in New York City from among first- and second-generation Germans, commanded by Captains John Knieriem and Otto Diederichs, these gunners were not themselves very well disciplined. Furthermore, they had been posted too far out in front of their infantry supports, inviting every Rebel on the field to take aim at them. Their first shells were more damaging to their own pickets falling back than to the enemy. Then, in the face of the yelling Virginians rushing at them, they broke for the rear. Captain Knieriem managed to take back with him two of his four guns. Captain Diederichs kept up a fire longer, using canister, but soon enough all his men had disappeared into the woods, leaving behind all four of their guns. "Drivers, cannoneers & all . . . ignominiously left the field," a fellow artilleryman would write contemptuously.

The 10th and 12th Pennsylvania regiments, anchoring General Seymour's left flank, had made a strongpoint out of the log farmhouse of a man named Whitlock, piling up fence rails in the yard as a rough breastwork. The Virginians stormed right over the position, driving the Pennsylvanians before them. The fugitives, along with some of the German artillerymen and assorted other Yankees knocked loose by Kemper's attack, turned off to the south and into Joe Hooker's lines. Officers and men "broke through my lines, from one end of them to the other," Hooker reported angrily, "and actually fired on and killed some of my men as they passed. Conduct more disgraceful was never witnessed on a field of battle." McCall would later feud bitterly with Hooker over the accusation, but just then the Pennsylvania Reserves' left flank was broken in.[15]

The rush of Kemper's brigade had taken it out ahead of the rest of Longstreet's assault. At the center of the attacking line the South Carolina brigade led by Micah Jenkins now engaged the rest of Truman Seymour's command. Colonel Jenkins, who had commanded a bold flanking march at Seven Pines, had no opportunity for maneuver on this day. His South Carolinians went in head-on, straight for Captain James H. Cooper's Battery B, 1st Pennsylvania Light Artillery. Cooper's gunners were made of sterner stuff than those in the German batteries, and their infantry support was more effective, and the fight for the guns was prolonged and bitter and at times hand to hand.

Regiments from Colonel Simmons's brigade in McCall's reserve came forward to support Cooper. Charge and countercharge crisscrossed the field. "If there was one Ball Whistled past my devoted head that day there was thousands," Michael Miller of the 1st Pennsylvania told his wife. "It appeared to me they flew in every Square inch of air around me except the little Space I stood in." Miller's regiment would suffer 133 casualties, and the fight for Cooper's battery would take the life of his brigade commander, Colonel Simmons.

With a desperate effort Jenkins's South Carolinians finally overran

Cooper's six 10-pounder Parrott rifles. Captain Cooper and his gunners fell back into the woods where they encountered the 9th Pennsylvania coming up in support. "The Capt. seemed down-spirited," Robert Taggart of the 9th wrote of Cooper. "Our Reg. rallied, charged, & retook the guns, much to his joy." In the smoky confusion around the battery Captain Taggart "got in with a lot of Rebels. Thought I was rallying my own men. Managed to get away. . . ."

Micah Jenkins refused to admit defeat. He later told Captain Goree of Longstreet's staff that as he rode up and down his line during the fight, his men would look at him as if to say they could go no farther, then he would wave his hand, "and they would again dash forward." This time they had the help of two Alabama regiments of Wilcox's brigade on their left. The enemy's fire seemed almost to scorch their faces, wrote Edmund Patterson of the 9th Alabama. "Those of us left standing poured a volley at a distance of not more than ten paces into the faces of the gunners. They fell across their guns and under the wheels, whole teams of horses plunging about in their mad agony, trampling under foot the wounded." Cooper's battery was taken again.

The effort cost Corporal Patterson's 9th Alabama 130 casualties. It cost Colonel Jenkins, from first to last, 532 casualties, the highest number in any Confederate brigade on June 30. The Palmetto Sharpshooters, his old regiment, lost 254 of its 375 men, a casualty rate of 69 percent. Jenkins's own survival, Goree wrote, "was almost miraculous." His horse was hit twice, his saddle blanket and a coat tied behind his saddle riddled with shell and bullet holes, his bridle reins cut in two, his sword hit three times, and he himself wounded three times by shell fragments. Major Porter Alexander saw one of Jenkins's color bearers come out of the fight shot through the lungs. Did the major think there was any chance for him, the man asked. Alexander replied that he had known men to survive such a wound. He certainly hoped so, the man said; he was willing enough to die for his country, "but I'd a heap rather get well & see my mother & my folks again." He hoped so too, Alexander recalled, "but I never knew."[16]

Meanwhile, along the Long Bridge Road to the north, the rest of Cadmus Wilcox's Alabama brigade was in a savage tangle with George Meade's Pennsylvanians. Here too the focus of the fighting was a Federal battery, the six Napoleons of Lieutenant Alanson M. Randol's Battery E, 1st United States regulars. Meade's brigade was severely thinned. It had lost more than a thousand men at Gaines's Mill, including nearly the entire 11th Pennsylvania taken prisoner; for this

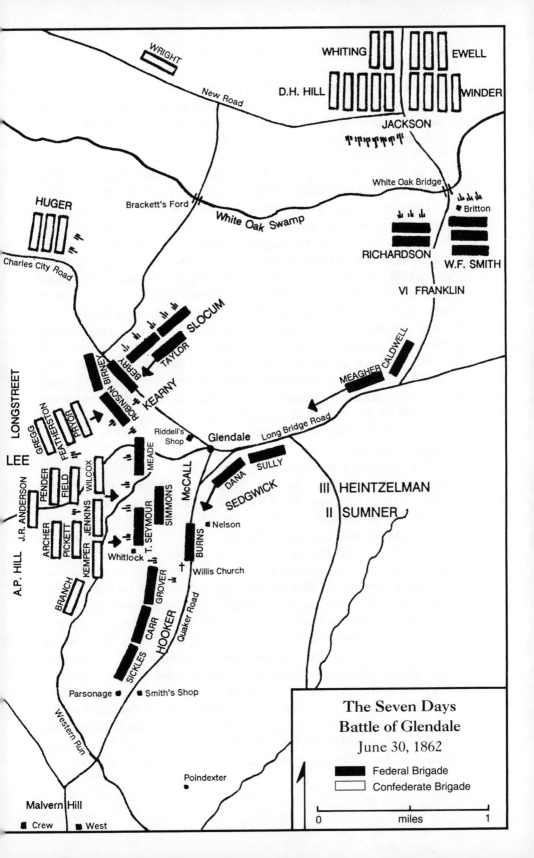

WRIGHT

WHITING

EWELL

D.H. HILL

WINDER

JACKSON

New Road

White Oak Bridge

Brackett's Ford

Britton

HUGER

White Oak Swamp

RICHARDSON

W.F. SMITH

Charles City Road

VI FRANKLIN

SLOCUM

TAYLOR

BERRY

BIRNEY

KEARNY

ROBINSON

CALDWELL

MEAGHER

LONGSTREET

GREGG
FEATHERSTON
PRYOR

Riddell's
Shop

Glendale

Long Bridge Road

LEE

MEADE

McCALL

DANA

SULLY

PENDER
FIELD
WILCOX

SEDGWICK

III HEINTZELMAN

II SUMNER

J.R. ANDERSON

SIMMONS

A.P. HILL

ARCHER
PICKETT
JENKINS
KEMPER

T. SEYMOUR

BURNS

Nelson

Whitlock

Willis Church

BRANCH

GROVER

Quaker Road

CARR

HOOKER

SICKLES

Parsonage

Smith's Shop

Western Run

Poindexter

Malvern Hill

Crew

West

The Seven Days
Battle of Glendale
June 30, 1862

Federal Brigade

Confederate Brigade

0   miles   1

battle the 106 survivors of the 11th would be attached to another regiment, and when the day was over a third of those would be casualties. For a time Meade had fire support from Lieutenant Frank P. Amsden's Battery G of the 1st Pennsylvania Light Artillery, but then Amsden ran low on ammunition and his caissons in the rear could not be found for replenishment, and Battery G had to leave the field. After that Randol's guns and Meade's infantry made the fight alone.

There was some low ground 300 yards in advance of Randol's battery, and the Yankees could see there just the tips of several Rebel battle flags. For a time the flags remained motionless, then they rose and grew larger and behind them men seemed to rise up out of the ground. Witnesses would describe the Battle of Glendale as unique for its hand-to-hand fighting. Porter Alexander said it involved "more actual bayonet, & butt of gun, melee fighting than any other occasion I know of in the whole war." On its first charge the 11th Alabama reached to within 100 yards of Randol's battery before canister and musketry drove it back. It was rallied for a second charge, this time carrying to within 50 yards of the guns before the fire became too much to bear. A watching Yankee soldier wrote of "canister fired by the peck." With that the infantry in immediate support of the battery, the 4th and 7th Pennsylvania, rushed forward with a shout in a spontaneous counterattack.

The two lines came together in front of the guns. The color bearer and every man in the color company of the 7th Pennsylvania went down. A Federal captain shot Lieutenant T. J. Michie in the arm with his pistol and slashed him on the head and face with his sword, whereupon Michie, already several times bayoneted, his wounds mortal, ran the captain through with his sword and killed him. Another Alabamian, Captain Walter Parker, sabered two Yankees and in turn suffered three bayonet slashes and a bullet that broke his leg. With no time to load in the melee, men caught up in a primal fury smashed in each other's heads with rifle butts and grappled with knives and fists.

Now it was the Federals who fell back, and in the heat of the moment they forgot their training and ran straight back toward their own guns, effectively masking them. Randol and his gunners screamed at them to get out of the way and tried to wave them to the flanks, but to no avail. The Rebels came right on the heels of the fleeing men and overran the battery. Color bearer Charley McNeil of the 11th Alabama leaped onto one of the guns and waved his flag and then was shot down. The gunners fought back with handspikes and rammers but were overwhelmed and had to fall back. Among Randol's losses were nearly all his battery horses. In the woods to the rear he rallied the Federals for a second counterattack.

This assault drove the Rebels back — capturing the 11th Alabama's flag and recapturing a Union flag taken in the earlier fighting — but neither side could hold the guns now and both fell back exhausted to sheltering woods to wait for someone else to take up the fight. Between the lines the six Napoleons sat silent, surrounded by heaped dead and helpless wounded. In this fight for Randol's battery the 4th and 7th Pennsylvania lost between them 241 men and the 11th Alabama 181, half its numbers; of the Alabamians' ten company commanders, six were killed and three wounded. General Meade, urging his men on, was hit by two bullets.

Fresh troops were coming on the field now: for the Confederates Longstreet's supporting brigades and some of A. P. Hill's, and on the Federal side William Burns's brigade of Sedgwick's division and, to hold the flanks, Hooker's and Kearny's men from the Third Corps. Sedgwick's other two brigades were coming back from White Oak Bridge at the double-quick, and two other brigades from there were preparing to march.

At the center of the union line George McCall's division was wrecked. Along a half-mile front every one of the twenty-six Federal guns had been taken or withdrawn or abandoned, and those of McCall's troops still on the field were disorganized and leaderless. Of his three brigade commanders, Simmons was dead, Meade badly wounded, and Truman Seymour had disappeared. At about 6:00 P.M. a staff man riding toward Glendale from White Oak Bridge came on General Seymour walking alone along the road, appearing to be in a daze. His horse had been killed and there was a bullet hole in his hat, and he was searching for General Franklin to ask for help. His brigade, he said, "was entirely dispersed."[17]

....

WHEN CONTACT was first made with the enemy that afternoon, Sam Heintzelman had posted himself with his Third Corps division under Phil Kearny to the north, where he anticipated the Confederates would thrust straight down the Charles City Road toward the Glendale crossroads. Nothing happened there, however, except for some sporadic artillery firing — this was Benjamin Huger's feeble bombardment — while off to the south the musketry grew to a roar. "From cheers or yells of the enemy (and they were not to be mistaken)," Heintzelman recalled, he knew there had been a breakthrough in the center.

Quickly he rode that way and saw what he described as "crowds of stragglers" from McCall's division pouring out of the woods and going fast to the rear. He met 150 men of the 1st Pennsylvania, from John Reynolds's old brigade, who assured him that they were all that remained of the regiment. On the Nelson farm he came on Bull Sumner, busily pushing troops toward the battle. To the 15th Massachusetts, just arriving from White Oak Bridge, Sumner called out, "Go in, boys, for the honor of old Massachusetts! I have been hit twice this afternoon, but it is nothing when you get used to it." To Heintzelman he explained that he had indeed been hit twice, on the arm and hand, by spent balls. Just then Heintzelman was burned and badly bruised on the wrist by a grazing shot. Like Sumner, he busied himself putting whatever men and batteries he found into action.

To the west on the Long Bridge Road, marching toward the sound of the guns, came John Caldwell's brigade of Israel Richardson's division. "Here we met a stream of men, cannon, and horses coming to the rear, wounded, disabled, and stragglers," wrote Lieutenant Thomas Livermore of the 5th New Hampshire. "They hurried along, seeming jolly, and spreading reports of the hotness of the battle." At the same time, as if in a mirror image, marching eastward on the Long Bridge Road a mile or so away, came Dorsey Pender's brigade of A. P. Hill's division. "As we advanced we met many stragglers and many wounded men coming out," wrote Lieutenant John Hinsdale. "They told us to go in quickly, that we were whipping the enemy but that our men would need support." Glendale became a battle of reinforcements.[18]

The initial assault by Longstreet's three brigades, striking and breaking open the Federal center, was made on a comparatively narrow front, and to hold his gains Longstreet had quickly to brace both flanks. Two brigades were ordered to the right to relieve Kemper and support Branch. Three went to the left to take over for Wilcox and advance that flank. The brigades of Charles Field and Dorsey Pender were put in to relieve Jenkins in the center, and a single brigade was held back as a reserve. With sunset, eleven of the twelve brigades in Longstreet's and A. P. Hill's divisions were committed to the battle.

At that moment the break in McCall's line was very close to achieving General Lee's design for cutting the Army of the Potomac in half. Should the attack now drive on across the Quaker Road, everything north of that point — better than five divisions — would be isolated from the rest of McClellan's army. To stem this tide there was Bull Sumner's Second Corps: John Sedgwick's division and the two brigades from Israel Richardson's division at White Oak Bridge. Holding the flanks would continue to be the task of Joe Hooker and Phil Kearny of the Third Corps. It was a matter of numbers. With Lee lacking the support of Huger and Magruder, and with Jackson failing to hold Franklin's forces in front of him at White Oak Bridge, those numbers would, if there was time enough, inevitably shift to the Federals' favor.

Joe Hooker managed his part of the battle decisively. Earlier in the day, reconnoitering his position south and east of the Willis Church, he was heard to say, "This would be a good place for a battery; but I guess we won't need it today." His men noticed that the moment the firing intensified on McCall's front a battery was unlimbering on the spot Hooker had indicated. Soon enough Lawrence Branch's North Carolinians emerged from the woods ahead, and Hooker set Cuvier Grover's brigade in their path. The firing intensified as the two battle lines drew closer, and Hooker rode up to Grover's New Hampshire and Massachusetts men and said simply, "Give them hell, boys."

In the still hot air a cloud of battle smoke soon hung low between the lines, but then, as Corporal Asa Smith of the 16th Massachusetts remembered it, the Rebels' gray pants became visible under the slowly rising cloud and the colonel "called for 'three cheers for the old Bay State,' which were given with a will." The battery behind them sent its shells screaming over their heads. "The Johnnies climbed the hill with a rush, causing the line to waver for a moment, then it closed up and gave them a murderous fire." Both sides continued to fire for a time as fresh troops came up, and then "the enemy were rolled back," as Hooker phrased it. The southern flank of the breakthrough was sealed. Branch's men advancing across the open ground had suffered much the worst of the encounter, losing 425 men to Grover's 195.[19]

To the north, on the opposite flank, the scene was tangled and very confusing. Clearings here were fewer and the woods were thick, and the shape of the fighting was hard to discern. "As we filed in among the trees we recognized the battle-field by bullets which splattered into the trees about us," Lieutenant Livermore of the 5th New Hampshire wrote. "We formed line of battle along the edge of the road, lay down, and listened to the roaring around us while we waited our turn. . . . To this day I can recollect one loud-sounding battery, the roar of which would burst out and echo in the forests with an almost gloomy sound followed by the long, horrid shriek of its shell; but such was the confusion of positions to us that we could not tell whether it was a battery of friend or foe. . . ."

The Long Bridge and Charles City roads came together at Glendale at nearly right angles to each other, and Phil Kearny had his division aligned with the Charles City Road, some distance beyond Meade's brigade of McCall's division astride the Long Bridge Road. The brigades of John Robinson and David Birney formed Kearny's front, with Hiram Berry's brigade behind them in reserve. With him Kearny had the six guns of Captain James Thompson's Battery G, 2nd United States, and a two-gun section of Battery E, 1st Rhode Island, Lieutenant Pardon S. Janstram. Confronting Kearny's three brigades were three Confederate brigades: Roger Pryor's and Winfield Featherston's brigades of Longstreet's division in the lead, then Maxcy Gregg's South Carolinians of A. P. Hill's division.

The Rebels' attack, the veteran warrior Kearny reported, came on "in such masses as I had never witnessed." These were Pryor's and Featherston's men, who had been part of the successful charge at Gaines's Mill three days before. At 400 yards Captain Thompson's six Napoleons opened on them with spherical case-shot, fuzed to explode and spray out scores of musket balls. One exploded in the midst of the 14th Louisiana, knocking down half a dozen men and taking off a leg of General Pryor's horse. When the range closed to 150 yards Thompson went to canister, at which, he said, "they appeared to falter."

Yet the Rebels regrouped and charged twice more. To speed the execution, Thompson switched to double charges of canister, fired fast without sponging out the gun barrels between rounds, a highly dangerous expedient that risked a premature explosion while loading. "I never saw such slaughter," Lieutenant Haydon of the 2nd Michigan noted in his diary. "The head of the column seemed to sink into the ground. Beyond a certain point they could not come." The men of the 14th Louisiana would call Glendale "The Slaughter House."

Captain Thompson announced that he was nearly out of ammunition, and the 63rd Pennsylvania, in immediate support of the guns, burst forward in a counterattack. "In a flash, yelling like incarnate fiends, we were upon them," wrote Colonel Alexander Hays. In among some farm buildings ahead of the guns there was another episode of hand-to-hand fighting, and then the two sides fell back exhausted. In this long fight in the smoky dusk individual regiments suffered severe losses. One third of the 63rd Pennsylvania went down making its charge, and a second regiment defending Thompson's battery, the 1st New York, suffered 230 casualties, the highest in any Federal regiment on June 30. In the Confederate ranks, the 19th Mississippi of Featherston's brigade took 130 casualties, and General Featherston went down with a serious wound. In Pryor's brigade the 14th Louisiana lost 122 and the 14th Alabama 245, second only to the Palmetto Sharpshooters in Lee's army that day.[20]

Maxcy Gregg's South Carolinians came up now, and Kearny's reserves, and the fighting spread all along the front. The men of the 20th Indiana had taken the precaution that morning of throwing up a rough breastwork of logs and fence rails, and it saved them from serious loss. Joshua Lewis of the 20th was sure the regiments behind them in reserve suffered more than they did. "We fired so rapidly that our guns were too hot to hold to," he remembered. In the growing darkness it became hard to distinguish friend from foe. At a pause in the firing one of the 20th Indiana's officers went forward to identify troops he thought might be friends, and was politely informed by Colonel Samuel McGowan that he was the prisoner of the 14th South Carolina.

As usual Phil Kearny was leading from up front, and in reconnoitering in the dim woods he somehow got in among Rebel skirmishers. He had just recognized his error when a youthful captain, less observant than he, came to him and asked, "What shall I do next, Sir?" To which Kearny replied (as he later told his wife), " 'Do, damn you, why do what you have always been told to do,' and off I went." (General Kearny's luck would not hold out for long. Two months later, in another such encounter during the Battle of Chantilly, he would be shot dead by the enemy.)

As pressure against his line increased Kearny began receiving help. General Heintzelman, returning to this now threatened flank, saw the need and turned to Slocum's division, just then taking its ease while its guns fended off Huger on the Charles City Road. Slocum offered the New Jersey brigade that Kearny had once commanded. Seemingly the whole brigade heard the request, for it went forward at the double-quick without further orders. Brigade commander George Taylor sent his aide to the front at a gallop, saying to him, "Keep ahead of them and keep them from going too far."

Kearny was also welcoming the 61st New York and Colonel Francis C. Barlow, an uncommonly gifted officer who was looking for a fight to get into. Barlow's regiment, from Israel Richardson's division, was one of those called from White Oak Bridge when the fighting at Glendale began, and in the rush from the bridge it had become separated from the rest of the brigade. Marching toward the sound of the guns,

Colonel Barlow went looking for the first general officer he could find, who happened to be General Robinson of Kearny's division. Robinson put him into action promptly.

Barlow's New Yorkers rushed with a shout at charge bayonets across a field. In the smoke and dim light, Barlow wrote home, "we could not distinctly see the enemy on the open ground but they heard us coming and broke and ran. . . ." He picked up a fallen Confederate battle flag and sent it to the rear. In the woods beyond they ran against the enemy and were challenged, "Throw down your arms or you are all dead men!" Barlow's response was the order to fire. After a "vigorous fire was kept up on both sides for a long time," the 61st New York withdrew to the original line.

Darkness would finally end the fighting here with Kearny's line intact but severely bloodied. The loss in his division came to 1,017 men. The loss in the brigades of Pryor, Featherston, and Gregg totaled 882, but they had not succeeded in widening the breakthrough. "Not a single man of my division fell back," Kearny reported proudly, and he was furious when later he learned that one gun each from Thompson's and Janstram's batteries was left behind on the field that night. For Phil Kearny, losing any of one's guns was the ultimate battlefield sin.[21]

....

As soon as fresh troops came up the fight at the center of the broken Federal line was renewed. The contest for Cooper's and Randol's batteries flared up once more. Yankee troops reached the abandoned pieces first, but they lacked gunners to man them and horses to haul them away, and the twelve guns were still fair game when Charles Field's brigade of A. P. Hill's division came on the field. Passing through Jenkins's and Wilcox's exhausted men, Field's Virginians went in at charge bayonets. Borrowing the tactic of the Texans at Gaines's Mill, the 55th and 60th Virginia rushed ahead without firing, swept right over Cooper's battery, and pursued the defenders into the woods beyond. There were bloody individual clashes among the trees. Private Robert Christian of the 60th Virginia found himself in a duel with four Yankees. Lashing out in every direction, bayoneted several times in turn, he killed three of them. His brother Eli Christian killed the fourth.

To the 47th Virginia, also of Field's brigade, went the honor of capturing Randol's much fought-over battery, this time for good. It so happened that the men of Company K of the 47th had originally enlisted as artillerists, and using that skill they turned one of Randol's Napoleons against the enemy and until dark blazed away with as much ammunition as they found with the gun. At the same time, farther to the south, the 18th Virginia of Longstreet's division overran the two abandoned 20-pounder Parrott rifles of Knieriem's battery and turned them against the Federals as well. That night all fourteen guns in the three batteries would be carried off by the triumphant Virginians.

Among the first of Sedgwick's regiments to arrive back from White Oak Bridge was the 20th Massachusetts, and General Sumner himself sent it into the breach at the center of the line. Through the silent belt of woods west of the Quaker Road it marched, and into the wide field where so much of the earlier fighting had taken place. It passed through the abandoned German battery of Captain Diederichs, surrounded by dead men and horses and wounded crying for help. Then the firing began, both artillery and musketry.

Boston's and Harvard's finest officered the 20th Massachusetts. They ordered the lines dressed for battle, and Captain Oliver Wendell Holmes glanced over at the next company and Captain James Jackson Lowell, of the Boston Lowells. "We caught each other's eye and saluted," Holmes remembered. "When next I looked, he was gone." In Henry Ropes's company, nearly a third of the men were lost in these moments. "One shell dashed Sergeant Holmes' head to pieces and spattered the brains and bits of flesh all about . . . ," Ropes wrote. "Another (or ball) took Corporal Sampson's leg off above the knee knocking it far away. . . . All this was while we steadily advanced over a wide field and before a gun was fired by us."

Then they too were firing and the two battle lines volleyed steadily at each other. Facing them was Dorsey Pender's brigade. Lieutenant Colonel R. H. Gray, commanding the 22nd North Carolina, explained in a letter home that at Glendale he had a brand-new regimental flag, the old one having been shot to ribbons at Mechanicsville and Gaines's Mill. Before long, Gray wrote, "our flag staff was shot in two twice, the Color bearer killed & 6 out of 8 of the color-guard either killed or wounded."

The 7th Michigan, coming up late into this withering fire on the left of the 20th Massachusetts, abruptly collapsed and broke for the rear, with the Massachusetts men jeering them as they ran. That left the 20th out ahead and alone, and soon the word was passed to withdraw. "So we fell back through the woods twice halting, facing to the front and delivering fire," Lieutenant Ropes wrote.[22]

It was after 8:30 P.M. now, and in the gathering darkness it was

increasingly difficult to tell friend from enemy. More of Sumner's men
came onto this part of the field from White Oak Bridge, including
Meagher's Irish Brigade and the rest of John Sedgwick's troops. General Sedgwick, an artillerist in the old army, was personally directing
the fire of a battery. He was nicked twice by bullets and had his horse
killed under him. With their fresh infusion of strength the Federals
were able to retake Diederich's abandoned battery and to stymie the
further advance of Field's and Pender's brigades.

A. P. Hill now committed the last of Lee's reserves, the brigade of
Joseph R. Anderson. He told Anderson to advance along the Long
Bridge Road cheering and making as much noise as possible. "This
seemed to end the contest," Hill wrote, "for in less than five minutes
all firing ceased and the enemy retired." Over on Phil Kearny's front
Lieutenant Haydon saw it somewhat differently. "The enemy cease
firing," he recorded in his diary. "We give tremendous cheers. They
send us a terrible volley which we return. Both parties give three
cheers & the day's work is done." However it ended, the combination
of darkness and the reinforcements from White Oak Bridge sealed off
the break. The Army of the Potomac would not be cut in half on June
30.

Not long before, General McCall had found Phil Kearny and compared notes. "If you can bring on another line in a few minutes I think
we can stop them," Kearny told him, and McCall had gone off to try
to find some of his scattered troops. With three aides he was riding
forward along a wooded byway when he came on a group of men.
"What command is this?" he demanded. "General Field's, sir," came
the reply. "General Field! I don't know him," McCall said, and turned
to ride on. Private S. Brooke Rollins of the 47th Virginia seized his
horse's bridle and said, "Not so fast."

The men of the 47th Virginia would always remember this day,
being credited with capturing one Yankee artillery battery and one
Yankee brigadier general. General McCall was taken back to Longstreet's headquarters. Longstreet had served with McCall in the 4th
Infantry in the old army, and he started to offer his hand, but quickly
saw that his old friend was in no mood for pleasantries. Instead Longstreet sent him off to Richmond with a staff escort.[23]

The thunder of the guns had been plainly heard across the James,
and Edmund Ruffin waited there in suspense for news of the contest.
Every day for nearly a week there had been these same sounds of
battle, sometimes near, sometimes more distant, and Ruffin was opti-

mistic. The news, he wrote in his diary that night, "is now so voluminous that I can merely here state the great results — but so far as heard, all, in the general, is good, & bright for our cause, with the exception of the latest fact, that McClellan has eluded our army, & has gained 12 hours of advance in his retreat toward James River."

Some eight months later, when he came to prepare his report on the Battle of Glendale, General Lee would write, "Could the other commands have co-operated in the action the result would have proved most disastrous to the enemy." Lee politely spared those other commands of criticism, yet even so he stated the case fairly enough. He might claim a narrow tactical victory at Glendale, so far as it went, but it was a victory entirely empty of result. At the time, he did not accept the verdict with equanimity. The morning after the battle, when an officer expressed concern that McClellan might escape, Lee responded with uncharacteristic temper: "Yes, he will get away because I cannot have my orders carried out!"

Casualties on June 30, in both armies, on all fronts, were very nearly equal. The Confederates lost 638 dead, 2,814 wounded, and 221 missing, a total of 3,673. The cost to the Federals came to 297 dead, 1,696 wounded, and 1,804 missing, a total of 3,797. Once again the Confederates in attacking suffered the greater share of the dead and wounded — some 40 percent greater — with Longstreet losing better than a quarter of his division. The defending Federals lost far more in prisoners as well as eighteen pieces of artillery. So far as the Army of the Potomac was concerned, its survival on June 30 was well worth whatever it had cost.[24]

After the last gun had sounded the men of the two armies lay on their arms in the darkness and watched the stretcher bearers' lanterns moving back and forth across the battlefield. The wounded called out their regiments so comrades might find them. "It was the saddest night I ever spent . . . ," a Massachusetts man wrote; "we could hear calls for Mississippi, Georgia and Virginia, mingled with those for Michigan, New York and Massachusetts." They cried out for water, or for someone to put them out of their agony; others groaned and loudly cursed their fate. As the hours passed the cries grew fainter, and a man remembered then hearing the "inexpressible melancholy" of the call of a whippoorwill in the woods. In his diary Lieutenant Haydon wrote, "The enemy sometimes, in looking after their wounded, came within a few feet of our picket line but we did not trouble them."[25]

The Guns of Malvern Hill

···

A T 8:30 THAT Monday evening, in the last light, General McClellan led his escort at a gallop up Malvern Hill from Haxall's Landing on the James, reined in hard before Fitz John Porter's headquarters, and strode inside calling for reports from the battlefield. Back from his excursion aboard the *Galena*, he expressed anxiety for his beloved Army of the Potomac. Before leaving Haxall's he had sent a dispatch boat downriver to Fort Monroe with a telegram for Washington, his first since June 28. "Another day of desperate fighting," he announced. "We are hard pressed by superior numbers. . . . My Army has behaved superbly and have done all that men could do. If none of us escape we shall at least have done honor to the country. I shall do my best to save the Army. Send more Gun Boats."

A report soon came to him from Glendale that the army had already been saved. Bull Sumner was even convinced he had won the battle. When he finally got his corps together, Sumner said, "I then drove the enemy from the field. The fight was a desperate one & continued until some time after dark." At that, General McClellan, as he had claimed he wanted to do after Gaines's Mill, spoke bravely of his willingness to stake "the last chance of battle in that position. . . ." Before he could issue orders for renewing the struggle at Glendale, however, he received word that the army was already falling back from that point. He "could not understand why," he said to the staff, but of course that took the matter out of his hands. In a fresh dispatch he told Washington, "I have taken steps to adopt a new line. . . ."

His lieutenants on the battlefield, having no word and no orders from the general commanding for twelve hours, had once again acted on their own. William Franklin, confronting Stonewall Jackson at White Oak Bridge, was the first to act, slipping away as quietly as possible. At Glendale Sumner and Heintzelman had no choice but to follow. Leaving their dead and wounded behind, the Yankees marched for the James. In his diary Private A. W. Stillwell of Baldy Smith's division wrote disgustedly, "We pulled up stakes again in the night and skedaddled. . . ."

Baldy Smith himself very nearly duplicated John Reynolds's experience at Gaines's Mill, and the Rebels very nearly captured their third brigadier general in as many days. After issuing orders for the retreat, Smith and his staff sought an hour's sleep. Several hours later they woke up and found everyone gone. "We were far behind," Smith recalled, "and in danger of being picked up by the enemy's advance. We did not loiter along the road till we had caught up." Others did not catch up. No one thought to call in the picket line of Slocum's division, and the next morning these Yankees, bewildered and angry, gave themselves up. Through the night men exhausted from combat dragged themselves along the dusty road to Malvern Hill. "What the road was . . . I cannot recall," Lieutenant Thomas Livermore wrote. "I know simply that it was darkness and toil, until we began climbing a hill and were greeted with advancing dawn."[1]

Early on Day Seven — Tuesday, July 1 — General McClellan rode the length of his new line on Malvern Hill. As the troops recognized him his course was marked by cheering. He was greatly heartened by the display. He wrote his wife, "The dear fellows cheer me as of old as they march to certain death & I feel prouder of them than ever." He was himself very tired, he told her: "— no sleep for days — my mind almost worn out — yet I *must* go through it. I still trust that God will give me success. . . ."

McClellan announced to General Dix at Fort Monroe that his army was "in no condition to fight without 24 hours rest — I pray that the enemy may not be in condition to disturb us today." Despite his concern, he then made haste to take himself far from the day's probable battlefield. At 9:15 A.M. he was back at Haxall's Landing and on board the *Galena*, and forty-five minutes later the gunboat cast off. This day his journey was downstream, an hour and a half's steaming time to Harrison's Landing on the north bank of the river. The general went ashore there to inspect what he had determined would be the army's next haven, for the navy told him it could not guarantee control of the river any farther upstream than Harrison's. Once again McClellan made no provision for command of the army in his absence. By being in command at the point of attack, Fitz John Porter would become de facto Union commander at Malvern Hill.[2]

On July 1, for the first time in the Seven Days, the entire Army of the Potomac was united on the same ground. There was scarcely a man in the army who doubted that the fighting would soon resume; these Rebels, it was agreed, were relentless in their attacks. There was also a sense of the last ditch about this place. The river was at their backs and the enemy would soon enough be in front. Veterans looked around them and remarked that at least this Malvern Hill looked like a good place to fight. Andrew A. Humphreys, the army's chief topographical engineer, posted many of the troops that morning, and he wrote his wife, "There was a splendid field of battle on the high plateau where the greater part of the troops, artillery, etc. were placed. It was a magnificent sight. . . ."

For Yankees who had suffered and sweltered for six weeks in the fetid Chickahominy swamps, this place was by comparison a paradise. "It was as beautiful a country as my eyes ever beheld," Lieutenant Haydon wrote in his diary. "The cultivated fields, interspersed with belts & clusters of timber & dotted with delightful residences, extended several miles. The hills were quite high, but the slopes gradual & free from abruptness. Wheat was in the shock, oats were ready for the harvest, & corn was waist high. All were of most luxuriant growth." The day had dawned hot and promised to become hotter, but at least on the higher ground there was the chance of a breeze. Still, numerous men in both armies would fall victim to sunstroke this day.

Malvern Hill was not so much a hill as an elevated, open plateau, about a mile and a quarter north-to-south and three-quarters of a mile wide, just under a mile north of the James and some 130 feet higher than the river. Turkey Island Creek, emptying into the James behind Malvern Hill, had two tributaries, called Turkey Run and Western Run, which framed the sides of the plateau. Malvern Cliffs, the bluff-like face of the plateau on the west, overlooked Turkey Run and the River Road, where General Holmes had been put to flight by the Yankee guns the day before. Western Run, perversely enough, ran along the eastern side of the plateau and then slanted across the northern side, the direction from which the Rebels would be coming. The valley of Western Run was 60 feet below Malvern Hill, but the slope from the run up to the crest of the heights was nearly half a mile long and very gradual.

As Lieutenant Haydon noted, this was good farming country. To the north, along the Quaker Road, the landscape was at about the same elevation as Malvern Hill, only dipping lower into the valley of West-

ern Run and then slanting upward again to the plateau. East of the
Quaker Road and some 1,200 yards north of Malvern Hill was the
Poindexter farm; opposite it, on the west, was the Carter farm. While
these two farms displayed open ground, the course of Western Run,
between them and Malvern Hill, was heavily wooded and swampy,
and Rebel officers were grimly reminded of Boatswain's Swamp on the
Gaines's Mill battlefield.

From the valley of Western Run the ground up to the crest of
Malvern Hill was entirely open. The Crew farm was the largest property in the area, with the Crew house sitting in a pleasant grove on the
western side of the Malvern plateau. A quarter of a mile due east along
the crest was the West house. Between the two houses the Quaker
Road crossed the crest of the hill and ran past the red-brick Malvern
house, sited on the southern edge of the plateau with a panoramic
view of the James. The Malvern house dated from the seventeenth
century, when it had been the seat of Malvern Hills manor, but over
the decades the manor had lost much of its eminence and its plural
form, surviving into the 1860s as simply Malvern Hill.[3]

Reaching Malvern Hill on the morning of June 30, Fitz John Porter
had quickly posted defenses against what seemed the most immediate
threat — from the west, along the River Road. Using Colonel Henry
J. Hunt's artillery reserve, he laid out a daunting line of big guns atop
Malvern Cliffs overlooking the River Road, bracing it with the regulars
of George Sykes's division. As more of his Fifth Corps arrived, Porter
extended the line around to the northern front of the plateau, assigning
George Morell's division to the ground between the Crew and West
houses. Extending the line from there, completing the northern front,
was Darius Couch's division of the Fourth Corps, as yet unbloodied in
the Seven Days' fighting. The other Fourth Corps division and the
corps commander, Erasmus Keyes, remained on the James at Haxall's
Landing, where General McClellan had put him to keep him as far
from any fighting as possible.

By this arrangement, the divisions of Morell and Couch, 17,800
infantrymen, were posted on the north facing the Quaker Road over
which the Rebels were expected to approach from Glendale. As important as the infantry in this line were eight batteries of field artillery,
with thirty-seven guns, thirty-one of which were rifled pieces. Colonel
Hunt had laid out much of this gun line, and he was skilled at such
work. In reserve were additional field artillery and three batteries of
heavy artillery from Hunt's command and from the army's siege train;

this array included five 4.5-inch Rodman and five 20-pounder Parrott rifles and six 32-pounder howitzers. Porter would regard Malvern Hill as the Army of the Potomac's best defensive position of any, with all the open ground and the artillery making it stronger even than Gaines's Mill.

General McClellan's primary concern when he inspected the position was for his right or eastern flank, running back two and a half miles from Couch's division on the north front to the James. This flank was behind the difficult ground of Western Run the whole distance, but having already decided to continue the retreat to Harrison's Landing, McClellan felt the risk of an attack here cutting him off from that point. He had "most cause to feel anxious about the right," he said, and so he posted most of the army there — the two divisions of Heintzelman's Third Corps, and two of Sumner's Second, the two of Franklin's Sixth, and the one of Keyes's Fourth on the James, with George McCall's crippled division in general reserve. The entire line was thus in the shape of a U, the open end on the James and the closed end facing north. "The line I thought too long for our number of troops," Heintzelman noted in his diary, "but we could not well occupy less."

The strength of the Malvern Hill position was at the same time its potential weakness. The northern end of the plateau, guarded by the ranked artillery and the divisions of Morell and Couch, was only some 1,200 yards wide, and only so many guns and men could be pressed into this space. If this relatively narrow front should be stormed by an equal number of men, just as Gaines's Mill was stormed on June 27, it might be overwhelmed and broken before reinforcements could take effect. On Day Seven Malvern Hill looked daunting to the Confederates, and it was daunting, yet there was the example, fresh in everyone's mind, of how one final and finally coordinated assault had won Day Three.[4]

....

GENERAL LEE met early with his generals to plan the pursuit of the enemy. In addition to Longstreet and A. P. Hill, Magruder joined him on the Long Bridge Road for consultation, and then Jackson arrived from White Oak Bridge. The bridge there had been rebuilt, he said, and the Valley army was on the march. As Lee, Jackson, and Magruder rode slowly along together, discussing their plans, they passed a body of troops on the roadside. Like the Yankees on Malvern Hill, these

Rebels recognized their commanding general and raised a cheer. Lee tossed a quick salute and continued his conversation; unlike the Young Napoleon, he expressed no need to feed on their adulation. These meetings of Confederate generals on the Long Bridge Road symbolized something more. As was the case with the Army of the Potomac, Day Seven marked the first time in the Seven Days that the entire Army of Northern Virginia was united on the same field.

Conspicuously absent from these meetings of Lee's lieutenants was Benjamin Huger. The cautious Huger, still worrying the problem of how to get ahead on the Charles City Road to the Glendale crossroads, had finally decided on a flanking movement, and at dawn he directed two of his four brigades, under Lewis Armistead and Rans Wright, to a woods road off to the right. Not until Longstreet sent him notice did Huger realize that the Yankees were gone and his path was clear. That news impelled him to stop and wait for someone to tell him what to do next. At length someone from headquarters arrived and, as Huger put it, "conducted us to the front. . . ."

In the meantime, Armistead and Wright and their brigades reached the Long Bridge Road and reported to Lee. In the absence of their commander, Lee sent them on ahead toward the enemy. General Huger was one to take offense at the thought of anyone else, even the general commanding, issuing orders to his men. He had been treated that way at Seven Pines, he said, and he hoped "this course was accidental." General Huger was thus not in the best of temper for whatever the day might bring.[5]

It was Lee's thought that any fighting on July 1 should be borne by the commands of Jackson, Magruder, and Huger, none of whom had done any fighting the day before. Longstreet and A. P. Hill, who had done all the fighting on June 30, would be held in reserve. Lee apparently expected nothing more of Theophilus Holmes than that he should guard the army's right flank against an unlikely incursion there by the Federals. Holmes himself dismissed any thought of attacking Malvern Hill from the River Road as "out of the question." On July 1, one of Holmes's men wrote, they lay all day in the woods about where they had been the day before, "and could plainly hear the firing of cannon, shell & musketry & cannonades & cheers of the parties engaged."

Lee said to Longstreet that he was feeling fatigued and unwell, and that Longstreet should leave his division in Richard Anderson's care and ride with him that day, to take over if the need arose. The two of them were riding south on the Quaker Road when they encountered D. H. Hill. Hill said that he had been talking to a chaplain in his division who was from the area and who explained that directly ahead of them on the Quaker Road was Malvern Hill, and the chaplain described Malvern Hill as a very imposing position militarily. Harvey Hill, who was not easily impressed by Yankees or their works, was impressed by this. "If General McClellan is there in strength," he said, "we had better let him alone." Longstreet laughed and said, "Don't get scared, now that we have got him whipped."

Old Pete's attitude was more prevalent in the Confederate high command that day than Harvey Hill's; as one of Longstreet's brigadiers put it, "We were on a hot trail." It was obvious that the Yankee army was on the run, and from the evidence left behind, from commissary stores and wagons and arms to stragglers by the hundreds, there was demoralization in that army. One more hard push and it might disintegrate. Robert E. Lee shared that view, and it influenced his decisions on July 1. Each day for five days, starting at Mechanicsville, his designs had been frustrated to one extent or another, from one cause or another. The day before, at Glendale, his frustration had peaked. Now the opportunity to destroy McClellan's army was diminishing with each passing hour, and today might be the last opportunity.[6]

Like the Federals before them, the Confederates on July 1 were greatly hampered by the region's limited number of north-south roads. No Southerner that day discovered the woods road off to the east that Keyes and Baldy Smith had found. Jackson's command of four divisions was to lead the way from Glendale along the Quaker Road, with Magruder following Jackson on the same road. Huger's two brigades under Armistead and Wright had used a lane leading off the Long Bridge Road into the Carter farm, west of the Quaker Road; Huger's other two brigades, when they appeared, would make the best way they could. Finally, the commands of Longstreet and A. P. Hill, in reserve, would move off the Long Bridge Road onto the Carter farm.

Unkind fate continued to lead Prince John Magruder astray. By Major Brent's account, Magruder was shown General Lee's map as they discussed the day's plans, but if he looked at it he did not look closely enough. Back with his command on the Long Bridge Road, Magruder told his guides to take him to the Quaker Road. This they proceeded to do. But, as with the Enroughty/Darby mixup of the day before, their Quaker Road was not *the* Quaker Road, on which just then Stonewall Jackson was marching.

It seemed that at some time past there had been a Quaker meeting-house down along the James River, to which several roads led, and by common usage they came to be known, severally, as the Quaker Road. One of these, the road due south from Glendale to Malvern Hill, was now the site of the Willis Methodist Church, and some of the local people called it the Willis Church Road, but others (including General Lee's mapmaker) still referred to it as the Quaker Road. A second road, turning off the Long Bridge Road at the farm of Nathan En-roughty — who of course was spoken of as Nathan Darby — ran southwesterly to the River Road near Sweeny's tavern, and some of the local people (including General Magruder's guides) called *that* the Quaker Road.

At the moment, Magruder's guides were in the majority, and so Magruder's three divisions proceeded to march obliquely away from the day's battlefield. In common with the misdirection of Stonewall Jackson on the day of Gaines's Mill, no one really was to blame for this; the essential fault lay with the Confederacy's failure to have produced a single good map of the approaches to its own capital.

The farther they marched the more suspicious Magruder became — he "seemed much put out," Major Brent recalled — and he interro-gated his guides, but they insisted this was the only Quaker Road they knew anything about. Longstreet, who had watched in growing amaze-ment as Magruder and his command marched away, finally decided to ride after them and try to persuade Magruder that he had to be on the wrong road. Would he order him to turn back, Magruder asked. He had no authority to do that, Longstreet said, but this surely could not be the right road, whatever its name might be. Magruder had by now come to agree there must be a mistake somewhere, and he ordered the column to reverse course. They returned to the Long Bridge Road, marched east a quarter of a mile, and then turned down the same lane to the Carter farm that Armistead's and Wright's brigades had used earlier. The Quaker Road tangle had consumed three hours and more, and thrown General Lee's plan for deploying his army into a tangle.[7]

....

AS MAGRUDER'S MEN retraced their steps, Major Brent rode on ahead to reconnoiter the ground where they might have to fight. On a knoll facing Malvern Hill he climbed a tree for a better view. The vista that opened out to him was at once beautiful and menacing. The gentle rise up to the crest of Malvern Hill was yellow with ripe wheat, part of which was already harvested and tied in shocks. Along the crest, visible right and left as far as he could see, were the black muzzles of cannon. Through his glasses he could see blue-clad infantry as well. "The Union soldiers were resting in position," Brent recalled, "some sitting or lying down, and others moving at ease or disappearing behind the ridge." He concluded that this part of the field "seemed almost impregnable." When he climbed down out of the tree, a soldier on picket duty nearby remarked that he was surprised to see the major unhurt; Yankee sharpshooters were very active on this front. "I would have preferred his warning before I climbed," Brent wrote, "to his expression of surprise that I had escaped."

Stonewall Jackson's command arrived on the field, and as he had done throughout the campaign, Jackson took the left. Chase Whiting's two brigades turned eastward off the Quaker Road into the Poindexter farm. Behind them, in immediate support or more distant support, came Charles Winder's four brigades and Dick Ewell's three. D. H. Hill, still attached to Jackson's command, positioned his five brigades to Jackson's right, astride the Quaker Road, making up the center of the Confederate position.

Lee had intended Prince John Magruder, marching behind Jackson on the Quaker Road, to take a posting to Hill's right, west of the road. Magruder and his six brigades were nowhere in sight, however, so the place went instead to two brigades already on the scene, Armistead's and Wright's from Benjamin Huger's division. Huger himself and his other two brigades were also among the missing. It was close to noon now, and the problem that had plagued General Lee repeatedly in this week of battle — communication between units, and between Lee and his units — was already once again a problem. It was a problem that would grow worse.

Lee took the blacksmith shop of C. W. Smith, on the Quaker Road opposite the Willis Church parsonage, for his field headquarters. From there he reconnoitered the left himself. He had assigned Longstreet the task of reconnoitering the right, which is what Longstreet was doing when he tried to redirect Magruder's march. On the Carter farm, near Mr. Carter's lane and half a mile west of the Quaker Road, Longstreet discovered a low, open ridgeline that was within artillery range of the crest of Malvern Hill and which, he thought, would hold as many as sixty guns in a kind of "grand battery." On the left, on Jackson's front in Mr. Poindexter's wheat field off the Quaker Road, Lee found similar ground for a second grand battery. Both sites were at an elevation nearly the same as that of Malvern Hill. Moreover, guns posted there would take the guns of Malvern Hill in a crossfire.

Lee and Longstreet compared their findings and quickly agreed on a tactic for the battle. They would establish two grand batteries, left and right, to pound Malvern Hill and its defenders in a converging fire and open the way for the infantry to storm the position. It would be another Gaines's Mill, only this time with the advantage of a preliminary artillery bombardment. Ranks of Federal guns were visible on the hill but could not be precisely counted; in any event it was probable that the fire of two such grand batteries ought to be enough to beat them down. If not, there would be opportunity to develop another tactic. But the guns should be enough. Their crossfire, Longstreet later wrote, ought to "so discomfit them as to warrant an assault by infantry."[8]

Having determined his plan of battle, General Lee announced it to his lieutenants in an order drafted by his chief of staff, Colonel Robert H. Chilton. As he had demonstrated on June 29 in his dispatch on Jackson guarding the Chickahominy line, Chilton lacked skill at drafting orders. This July 1 battle order read: "Batteries have been established to act upon the enemy's line. If it is broken as is probable, Armistead, who can witness effect of the fire, has been ordered to charge with a yell. Do the same. R. H. Chilton, A.A.G."

By this it was left entirely to the discretion of a brigade commander, Lewis Armistead, commanding in his first battle, to judge the effect of an artillery bombardment and then to decide if the army should attack. Furthermore, the only signal for a simultaneous charge by fifteen brigades — the Rebel yell of a single charging brigade — was likely to generate as much confusion as cooperation. To complete his failings, Colonel Chilton marked no time of sending on any copy of his dispatch, which in the case of one recipient would make an already ambiguous order even more ambiguous.

It is highly unlikely that an order so poorly drawn could have been seen and approved by Lee before it was sent; Lee cannot have intended to turn over direction of the Battle of Malvern Hill to a brigade commander. Indeed, why he did not write so important an order himself is puzzling. Perhaps, like Jackson the day before, Lee's extreme fatigue was affecting his judgment. Lafayette McLaws, commanding one of Magruder's divisions, testified that when he sought out Lee to deliver a report that day, he found him sleeping under a tree, with President Davis at hand to see that he was not disturbed.

The general, Davis explained, had been up all night. However that may be, on July 1 General Lee's control over his subordinates was not what it should have been.

The artillery arm of the Army of Northern Virginia had not distinguished itself thus far in the Seven Days' battles. Seldom had it been employed to good effect, and only at White Oak Bridge on June 30 were any number of guns massed against one target. Its employment at Malvern Hill proved to be dismal beyond all previous reckoning. Sharp-tongued D. H. Hill termed the part played by the artillery "most farcical," and after the experiences of the day there were few who would have disagreed with him.

The problems in the left grand battery came down to a matter of numbers. Stonewall Jackson's command was short of artillery to begin with. Most of the guns employed the day before at the bridge were from D. H. Hill's division, and they had shot off all their ammunition. All seven of Hill's batteries were at the rear for replenishment and refitting. This left Jackson ten batteries, but these were divided among three separate commands and were scattered widely along the crowded line of march, and there seemed no way to get them all together at one place, the Poindexter farm, at one time. Jackson's capable artillery chief, Stapleton Crutchfield, might have managed this, but Crutchfield was sick that day and not at the front. Stonewall Jackson, a practiced artilleryman and a one-time instructor in artillery tactics at the Virginia Military Institute, tried to take over Crutchfield's job, but what was needed rather than Old Jack personally placing batteries in the field was someone to bring up the batteries in the first place.

The solution to the problem ought to have been found in Brigadier General William N. Pendleton's artillery reserve, which had been established for just this purpose. General Pendleton had thought deeply about the theory and organization of artillery, but actually directing guns on the battlefield did not seem to be one of his ambitions. If anyone from Lee's headquarters located Pendleton and his guns on July 1, there is no record of it. Pendleton himself said the day "was spent by me in seeking for some time the commanding general, that I might get orders," but he admitted this pursuit was unsuccessful. "To . . . await events and orders, in readiness for whatever service might be called for, was all that I could do." As a consequence, of Pendleton's four battalions of reserve artillery, containing fourteen batteries, just one battery would be employed that day. Colonel J. Thompson Brown, commanding one of the battalions, remarked acidly on "the great superabundance of artillery and the scanty use that was made of it."[9]

Virginian Carter Berkeley, of William Balthis's Staunton Artillery, would never forget his experience that day in the left grand battery in Mr. Poindexter's wheat field. With another Virginia battery, William Poague's Rockbridge Artillery, and James Reilly's Rowan Battery of North Carolina, the Staunton Artillery was standing waiting in the Quaker Road under random fire from the Federal guns. Sergeant Berkley saw Jackson ride by himself far into the Poindexter wheat field, into which the enemy shells were falling with some regularity.

After a time Jackson returned and told Chase Whiting, in command of that part of the field, to order the guns forward. Whiting protested. There were supposed to be fifty guns in this grand battery; these three batteries mounted only sixteen. "They won't live in there five minutes," he said. "Obey your orders, General Whiting, promptly and willingly," Jackson snapped. Whiting snapped back, "I always obey my orders promptly, but not willingly under such circumstances." He told his staff to make witness of his protest, and ordered the battery commanders into the field.

Jackson rode ahead, pointing them to some high ground in the wheat a thousand yards from the Federals on the hill. "Forward, Sir," Old Jack called out. As soon as they unlimbered, Sergeant Berkeley recalled, "all the Yankee batteries on a hill beyond stopped firing into the woods and poured into us the most deadly fire that I ever witnessed during the war." There were no Confederate guns firing yet from the other grand battery, and no crossfire; these sixteen guns, in these moments, constituted the largest concentration of artillery fire Lee's army was able to achieve on July 1.

It was not without effect. "Their shots were not wild," Lieutenant Haydon admitted. "Almost the first shot (12 lbs. solid) struck among the N.Y. 1st as they lay on the ground, killing two & wounding another. One of them was thrown more than 5 ft. in to the air. . . . One struck about 10 ft. short of me in the ground & exploded, nearly burying me in sand & rubble." Matthew Marrin of the 1st Minnesota noted in his diary that the Rebel shelling "tried our pluck to the core. . . ." Bull Sumner ordered his men back out of range and under cover.

The long odds soon told, however — eight batteries against three, thirty-seven guns against sixteen. In the Confederate position gun carriages were shattered and men and horses killed and wounded.

Finally of the three only the Staunton guns were still firing. Captain Balthis, hit seven times by shell fragments, kept urging his men to stand to their guns. Finally they too had to withdraw, out of ammunition. There were barely enough horses left to drag the guns off. Eventually, one at a time, three other batteries would try to establish a presence in the left grand battery, only to be beaten down by the Yankee guns. Losses that day among these gun crews came to 39 men.

This Federal shelling took its toll among others on the Poindexter farm as well. William White of the 18th Georgia in Whiting's division wrote home matter-of-factly that he was wounded by a shell exploding virtually in his face. "The same shell which wounded me wounded four others in my company and killed my bosom friend T. J. Bennett of Marietta." The men of the Stonewall Brigade always remembered the volume of fire from Malvern Hill as enough to shock even the famously profane colonel of the 27th Virginia, Andrew Grigsby, into silence. As Stonewall Jackson rode along with Dick Ewell, wrote Ewell's aide Campbell Brown, a shell "pitched viciously down just at the head of Genl. J.'s horse, which kept on at its shambling gait. Jackson talking earnestly to Genl. Ewell, took no notice, but the latter quickly stooping caught his horse by the bridle & stopped him, a second or two before the shell exploded."

D. H. Hill had a similar narrow escape. He was seated at the base of a tree writing orders when one of the Yankee shells struck close by, tumbling him over in the dirt and ripping his uniform coat. Hill stood up, brushed off the dirt, and then seated himself and resumed writing, this time behind the tree. "I am not going to be killed until my time comes," he observed.[10]

The failure of the right grand battery that afternoon was if anything more dismal. Of Huger's six batteries, only two got to the front and into action. Of sixteen batteries under Magruder's command, just two opened fire. Of the fourteen in General Pendleton's reserve, one was engaged. Seeing the need, A. P. Hill sent his best battery, under Willie Pegram, to join the fight. As they came up and turned into the Carter farm, each battery was thrown into action separately, and each was pounded in its turn by the guns on Malvern Hill. The Federal gunners had now to divide their fire, but this hampered them not at all.

Captain Cary Grimes's Virginia battery had one man killed and three wounded, and three horses hit, even before they could unlimber. Robert Stiles of the Richmond Howitzers complained that several of his guns were set off by shell fragments before the lanyards could be pulled to fire them. Willie Pegram's battery was reduced to a single gun still firing. The only way Greenlee Davidson's Virginia battery could remain in action was to roll the guns down behind a sheltering hill for loading and then push them to the crest for firing.

The six batteries that managed at one time or another to fire from the right grand battery lost among them 59 men. Six other batteries, although close enough to the front to take casualties from the enemy guns, were not put into action. A. S. Cutts, a Georgian commanding the Sumter Artillery battalion in Pendleton's reserve, reported in frustration that his seven guns were "assigned a place near the battle-field of Tuesday, the 1st instant, and, although I am sure that more artillery could have been used with advantage in this engagement, . . . yet I received no orders. . . ." Cutts was speaking for the thirty-five Confederate batteries available for action at Malvern Hill on July 1 which failed to fire a single round.

Of all the Federal guns fired that day, the only ones to prove ineffective were those of the gunboats. From their anchorages in the James the Rebels were out of their direct sight, and they had to fire across Malvern Hill to reach them. A number of their shells fell short, one landing on William Weeden's Rhode Island battery and inflicting seven casualties. General Porter was communicating with the navy by flag, and he signaled, "For God's sake stop your firing, you are killing & wounding our men." They must direct their fire more accurately by compass and flag signal, he told them. Still shells fell short, and finally the gunboats ceased firing. Their big shells, and those of Henry Hunt's heavy batteries on Malvern Hill, tended to land at random well behind the Confederate front lines. When one of them crashed down near an ambulance far to the rear, the driver shook his fist and shouted, "You damn son of a bitch! You haint got no eyes, & would as soon hit a ambulance driver as anybody else."[11]

....

BY THREE O'CLOCK or so that afternoon it was becoming obvious to General Lee that his artillery bombardment was not going to beat down the enemy's guns. If anything, the result was exactly the opposite. Another tactic would have to be tried. He was determined to find a way. Calling Longstreet to his side, Lee rode off to the left, beyond Jackson's front, to see if the Federals' eastern flank might be turned. From their observations it seemed feasible, and it was decided to shift the army's reserve, Longstreet's and A. P. Hill's divisions, to the left to make the effort. Lee had no expectation that McClellan would go any farther in his retreat than Malvern Hill; his position was strong and his gunboats were at hand. Considering the hour and the time that would be required to get the two divisions into their new positions, Lee had now to think of renewing the Battle of Malvern Hill on July 2.

Earlier, Lewis Armistead's brigade, the advance of Huger's division, had taken position opposite the center of the Federal line. While the guns of the right grand battery nearby pressed their uneven contest with the guns on the hill, Yankee skirmishers crept forward to within rifle range of the gun crews, and Armistead felt obliged to drive them off. He gave the task to his 14th, 38th, and 53rd Virginia regiments. They chased the skirmishers back easily enough, but in doing so advanced into a withering fire from the hill. Instead of retreating, they rushed forward "in their ardor" (as Armistead put it) to the cover of a shallow ravine slanting up toward the Crew house. There were too few of them to advance any farther, and to withdraw would mean running the gauntlet a second time, so they stayed where they were, huddled in their precarious lodgement.

Prince John Magruder now arrived in advance of his troops, who were dragging along behind in their second day of misdirected marching. Magruder was very late on the field — it was four o'clock by now — and he knew nothing of Lee's plan or the situation except that he was told to take position on Huger's right — to become, that is, the extreme right of the Confederate line. He made a quick survey of the field and then sent his aide, Captain A. G. Dickinson, to find General Lee and report his arrival and report also Armistead's "success" in advancing three regiments partway up Malvern Hill.

At about the same time, on the other flank, Chase Whiting reported seeing Yankee troops pulling back across Malvern Hill (this was Sumner's men taking cover from the Confederate shells) and the enemy's artillery fire slackening on his front (this was its shift to the new targets on the other flank). General Lee was on his reconnaissance when the two reports reached them. Their exact content is not known, but both must have been assertive and positive, for they impelled him once again to change his plan.

From their evidence — Armistead's successful advance and the Yankee troop withdrawal — it appeared that General McClellan was taking up his retreat again; perhaps he was getting away. Lee gave Captain Dickinson new orders for Magruder. Dickinson made note of them: "General Lee expects you to advance rapidly. He says it is reported the enemy is getting off. Press forward your whole line and follow up Armistead's successes. . . ."

On the face of it, this was a peremptory order to attack immediately. Yet that night Lee would seek out Magruder and demand of him, "General Magruder, why did you attack?" From this, it must be assumed that Lee intended his order carried by Captain Dickinson to be softened with discretion — to be taken by Magruder as an order to attack only if the situation at that time and at that place favored an attack. If this was in fact the case, it argued once again for General Lee to write his own orders instead of relying on staff officers to interpret them for him.

However that may be, Dickinson's return found Prince John in a particular condition of mind. Still suffering from the treatment for his acute indigestion, he was still in a morphine-induced state of agitation and excitement. Just before Captain Dickinson reached him, he had been handed the order written some three hours earlier by Colonel Chilton — and now quite outdated — which to Magruder seemed to outline Lee's plan of attack and which, as it bore no time of writing, he assumed to be a current order. Now came Dickinson's message from Lee, which, on the heels of Chilton's message, had the sound not only of an attack order but of a reiterated attack order. Still smarting from Lee's rebuke of him for lack of aggressiveness at Savage's Station, Magruder had no doubt now of what was expected of him. He must launch a full-blooded attack with the least possible delay.

Thus from an unlikely combination of circumstances — a march down the wrong Quaker Road, misunderstood observations, Armistead's ardent Virginians, a medication laced with morphine, an undeserved rebuke, and General Lee's inability to make his orders understood — would spring the bloody battle for Malvern Hill.[12]

....

PRINCE JOHN MAGRUDER's immediate problems were pulling together enough men for an assault and puzzling out the curious command situation in which he found himself. The only troops immediately at hand were the brigades of Armistead and Rans Wright, both from Huger's command. Those next closest to the front were also Huger's — Little Billy Mahone's brigade and Robert Ransom's. Magruder's three divisions — his own and those of David R. Jones and Lafayette McLaws — were coming up but were not yet ready for deployment. Lee had told Captain Dickinson to have the brigades of Mahone and Ransom at the front, which Magruder took to mean they were his to direct. In any event, it was he who was ordered to make the attack, and he could hardly launch it without employing Huger's troops, who were the first in line.

Benjamin Huger had a different outlook on this. Magruder had some time since sent Major Brent to find out where Huger's lines were so that he might conform his own lines to them. Brent had to ride back through the Carter farm almost to the Long Bridge Road to locate General Huger. The South Carolinian was as courteous and gentlemanly as ever, Brent recalled, yet it was clear that this had become for him a matter of amour-propre. He had not been to the front, Huger said, and he did not know where his brigades were, but he understood that "some of them have been moved without my knowledge by orders independent of me, and I have no further information enabling me to answer your inquiries." This was said, according to Brent, "with great feeling." Clearly General Huger was not marching himself or his men to the sound of the guns.

Magruder, "much perplexed" by Brent's report of the conversation, decided his only chance was to bypass Huger entirely and appeal directly to Huger's brigadiers. Major Brent was hurried to Ransom and Mahone, only to be told that Huger had just sent them strict instructions to ignore any order not issued through him. Ransom said apologetically that therefore he could not go to Magruder's assistance. Little Billy Mahone, who regarded his superior with less reverence, cheerfully volunteered his brigade to Magruder. At 5:30 P.M. Prince John opened the battle as best he could with the brigades of Wright and Mahone and the half of Armistead's already on the field, something over 5,000 men, none of them his own. He thought he ought to have three times that number, but with "the hour growing late" and his orders imperative, he felt he had no choice.[13]

The experience of Rans Wright's brigade — 3rd, 4th, and 22nd Georgia and 1st Louisiana — would prove all too typical of the Confederate brigades that attacked on July 1. Raising the Rebel yell, Wright's men charged out of the woods and into the open and toward the hill. The 22nd Georgia went astray and only a small part of it joined the assault. Then Wright's remaining force got too far out ahead of Mahone's, and Armistead's regiments were pinned down off to the left, and Wright's 1,500 men found themselves quite alone on the slopes of Malvern Hill. David Winn of the 4th Georgia wrote his wife afterward, "It is astonishing that every man did not fall; bullet after bullet too rapid in succession to be counted . . . shell after shell, illuminating the whole atmosphere, burst over our heads, under our feet, and in our faces. . . ." The true measure of a man's courage that day, Winn said, was simply answering the call "for the desperate charge."

The ground north and west of Malvern Hill was planted in wheat, partly harvested and standing in shocks, and behind every shock there seemed to be one of Hiram Berdan's sharpshooters. One of them, Corporal William Kent, watched as "a line of gray coats rush out of the woods towards us. I guess I didn't miss though, for it was only 400 yards, and clear as it could be." The Rebels were perfectly aligned as they emerged from the trees, Kent noticed, but soon enough they broke into groups, "which acted entirely independently of each other, some rushing forward, and others taking cover. . . ." The sharpshooters fell back before the charge to the main line, giving the Yankees there a clear field of fire.

The first line of General Morell's defense on this part of the hill was the variegated brigade of Charles Griffin — 14th New York, 4th Michigan, 9th Massachusetts, and 62nd Pennsylvania — as well as four artillery batteries; Porter had Griffin, a veteran artillerist, commanding the guns as well as the infantry. Wright's charge carried to within 300 yards of this line, losing men at every step, and then it could go no farther. The artillery fire, canister at this range, was deadly. Lieutenant Adelbert Ames's Battery A, 5th U.S. Artillery, would fire the remarkable total of 1,392 rounds on July 1, an average of 232 rounds for each of his six Napoleons. Ames laconically termed the canister "effective." There was a slight depression in the ground here, and Wright's men lay down and took what cover it provided and kept up a fire, but there they remained, waiting for help.[14]

In its turn Little Billy Mahone's brigade made its charge, met the same incessant fire as Wright's, and was driven back. "We hold them," wrote the 4th Michigan's John Bancroft. "Wave our colors. . . ." Just then, off to the left toward the Quaker Road, other Confederate troops could be seen emerging from the woods and advancing on Malvern Hill. D. H. Hill's division was in the fight now.

Harvey Hill had received Colonel Chilton's version of the plan of battle about 2:00 P.M. and called together his brigadiers to prepare for action. When he witnessed the dismal collapse of the artillery barrage, however, Hill, "not knowing how to act under these circumstances," sent to Jackson for further orders. Old Jack's response to Hill, as it had been earlier to Chase Whiting, was to obey orders: when he heard Armistead advance "with a yell" he must advance too. The hours passed and nothing was heard from Armistead's direction, and Hill and his lieutenants began to prepare bivouacs for the night. Abruptly, off to the right where Armistead was supposed to be (but where Rans Wright in fact was) came the unmistakable sound of the Rebel yell, followed by the equally unmistakable sounds of battle. "That must be the general advance!" Hill exclaimed. "Bring up your brigades as soon as possible and join in it."[15]

In his report on the Battle of Malvern Hill, Darius Couch observed that "the enemy continually re-enforced their column of attack. . . ." What General Couch saw as continual reinforcement was in truth stark evidence of the Confederates' failure to coordinate their assaults. D. H. Hill had something over 8,200 men in his five brigades, but rather than one unified sweep forward to overwhelm the Federal line, the reality of the day was five separate attacks. To make the charge his brigades had to flounder through thick woods along the Quaker Road and Western Run, and this played havoc with their organization. For Hill it would be a repetition of the woods march that had so disjointed his attack on Hancock's brigade at Williamsburg two months earlier.

William Calder of the 2nd North Carolina of George B. Anderson's brigade described the charge for his people at home. "Soon the word was passed, 'Up, Second, and at them,' and our Brigade . . . sprang through the woods with a shout," Calder wrote. "We crossed one fence, went through another piece of woods, then over another fence, into an open field on the other side of which was a long line of Yankees. . . ." One regiment lost its way in the woods and later went into action with a neighboring brigade. It seemed to Anderson's men that in this open field they were entirely alone, the object of every Yankee gun on the hill. "Our men charged gallantly at them," Calder wrote. "The enemy mowed us down by fifties." Some of the ground here was planted in oats and some of it was freshly plowed, and all of it was without cover.

In Samuel Garland's brigade, Leonidas Torrence wrote of Malvern Hill, "I think it was as hard a Battle as ever was Fought. The Balls fell around me as thick as hail for 2 or 3 hours." Garland, on the right of the Quaker Road, reported, "I saw no troops of our own in front of me." Colonel John B. Gordon, commanding Rodes's brigade in place of the wounded General Rodes, clawed his way to within 200 yards of the Federal guns before his men wavered under the fire and Gordon ordered them to lie down to carry on the fight. Gordon, the only field officer in his regiment at Seven Pines to escape unhurt, also survived unhurt at Malvern Hill, although he counted the rents of seven bullets in his uniform. His 3rd Alabama lost six color bearers in succession in the charge and saw the regiment's flag literally torn to pieces. The 3rd Alabama would lose 37 dead and 163 wounded on this day, the highest loss in any Confederate regiment on the field and 56 percent of those who went into battle.[16]

The brigades of Alfred Colquitt and Roswell Ripley attacked in their turn and in their turn were hurled back with a loss of 618 men between them. The 10th Massachusetts was in Couch's first line facing Hill's assaults, and in his diary Lieutenant George Hagar wrote that "the rebs poured out of the woods & charged on us. . . . They came within yards of us when they turned & ran, what was left of them." There was a respite and they waited, and then the Southerners came on again: "Pretty soon they poured out in 4 lines & charging our batterys posted on the brow of the hill. . . . We murdered them by the hundreds but they again formed & came up to be slaughtered. . . . I kept firing until I could no longer load my gun & threw it away & took up Hemmenways."

The 61st Pennsylvania, which had broken badly under a surprise attack by D. H. Hill's men at Seven Pines, losing nearly half its men there, this time stood fast against Hill's attack. Making up the extreme right of Couch's position, it fired off its sixty rounds per man without faltering, helping to inflict 264 casualties on Roswell Ripley's Georgians and North Carolinians. "If the Sixty-first Pennsylvania Volunteers ever lost anything previously they more than regained it this time," wrote the Pennsylvanians' brigade commander, John Abercrombie.

General Couch, rallying his three brigades to hold their lines, had his horse killed under him. He warned Porter that if the assaults continued he must have help. Porter sent a call to Bull Sumner for two brigades. Sumner, always expecting an imminent attack on his own lines, responded with John Caldwell's brigade but hesitated to do more. Sam Heintzelman, who was there when Porter's request was received, exclaimed, "By Jove! if Porter asks for help, I know he needs it and I will send it." He dispatched a battery and Dan Sickles's brigade of infantry from the Third Corps. From his Second Corps artillery reserve Sumner sent along a strong eight-gun battery of Parrott rifles.

Colonel Francis Barlow marched his 61st New York, of Caldwell's brigade, to the front to brace Couch's beleaguered line. "The men

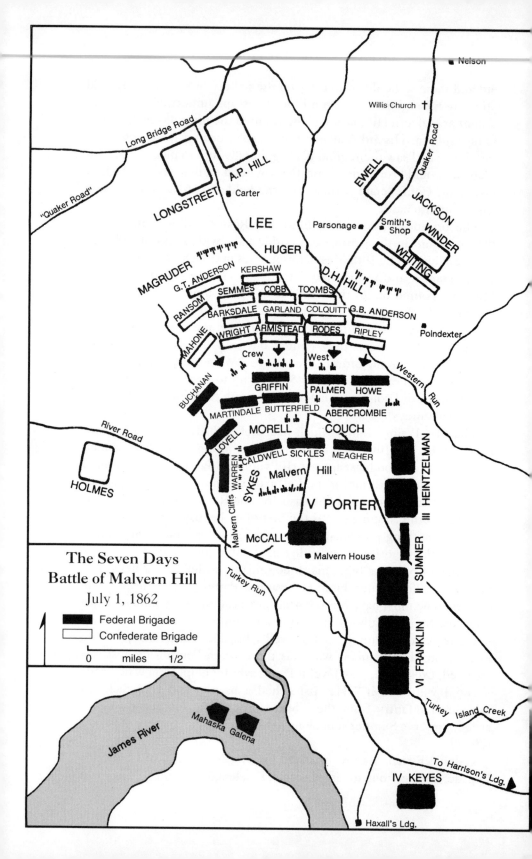

The Seven Days
Battle of Malvern Hill
July 1, 1862

Federal Brigade
Confederate Brigade

0   miles   1/2

fought better than ever before, standing in line with great coolness," Barlow would tell his family. So rapid was their fire that the guns of many of them became fouled with burned powder, making it impossible to ram home the charges. "Then we lay down and prepared to hold the place by the bayonet if the enemy charged out of the woods," Barlow wrote. The Rebels did charge, "with a yell," but the 72nd New York next to them had just enough cartridges left for a last volley, "which broke them and they ran." Barlow remarked that a Federal battery behind them too often fuzed its shells improperly, "and a good many of their shells burst over our heads and even struck behind us which did not add to the pleasure of the occasion."

Another of Caldwell's regiments, the 5th New Hampshire, was ordered to go right to the front to support a battery. This was always dangerous work, but on this occasion the New Hampshire men welcomed it. Confederate artillery fire was sporadic at best in these hours, but at just that moment a battery opened with dead aim on the 5th at its posting near the West house. "Captain," Lieutenant Livermore called out, "we might just as well go across under the fire as to lie here, for we shall get killed here; so let us go!" The captain saw the wisdom of that, and off they went to the front line at the double-quick. "Shells flew all around us," Livermore remembered, "and the wonder was that more were not hurt."

With his assault faltering and increasing numbers of his men streaming to the rear, D. H. Hill called for reinforcements and went in search of them himself. He came first on a part of Robert Toombs's Georgia brigade, from Magruder's command on the right. Political general Toombs was having a bad day and had lost control of his brigade and was somewhere else on the field, and Hill rallied the leaderless Georgians himself and led them forward into the battle. They could not brave the torrent of gunfire from the hill, however, and collapsed to the rear in disorder. The furious Hill would later happen on Toombs in the dusk and rage at him, "For shame! Rally your troops! Where were you when I was riding up and down your line, rallying your troops?" Hill did not restrict his fury to the unfortunate Toombs. Considering how close to the enemy's lines his own division had come on July 1, he asked, "What might have been done had the other nine cooperated with it?" D. H. Hill suffered 1,756 casualties in this series of fruitless charges, more even than he had lost at Gaines's Mill, and this time he had nothing to show for it.[17]

....

AT GAINES'S MILL General Lee won the day by finally getting his
forces assembled and under firm, unified control, and then advancing
in mass and overwhelming the Federal defenders. He would not quite
manage that same tactic at Malvern Hill, yet all the same it was a close-
run thing. "The battle was desperately contested," artillerist Henry
Hunt testified, "and frequently trembled in the balance." At one point
Colonel Hunt positioned several of his reserve batteries far back on
the plateau, to play on the enemy's new line of advance should Porter's
battle line be broken. General Porter, before leading his last reserves
into the fight, would take the precaution of destroying his diary and
dispatch book lest they, and he, fall into the hands of the victorious
Rebels.

In midafternoon the gunboat *Galena* had steamed back from Harrison's Landing with General McClellan aboard, and about 3:30 P.M.
the general once again appeared on Malvern Hill. By now the Federal
gunners had gained the best of the artillery duel and Magruder was yet
to launch his infantry attack, and the battle was in abeyance. After
consulting for a time with Porter at his Malvern house headquarters,
McClellan made a rapid tour of the defensive positions. According to
his aide William Biddle, he was "evidently well satisfied with them."
Then general and staff rode to the extreme right of the line, overlooking the James, and remained there. After a time, Biddle wrote, "we
heard artillery firing away off to the left; we were too far away to hear
the musketry distinctly. . . ." A courier with a message from General
Porter, written at 6:10 P.M., found the general commanding still on this
distant flank. "The enemy has renewed the contest vigorously —
but I look for success again," Porter wrote. "The men cheer most
heartily."

When seeking the presidency in 1864, General McClellan would
suffer the charge, from editorial writers and cartoonists, of dereliction
of duty at Malvern Hill, of taking safe haven aboard the *Galena* while
his army fought for its life. William Brickham of the *Cincinnati Commercial*, for example, wrote that "McClellan on gunboats during the battle
of Malvern Hill was the meanest picture that this bloody rebellion has
painted." The charge was misdirected. Although McClellan boarded
the *Galena* on the morning of July 1 with the all-but-certain knowledge
that his army would be attacked that day and then steamed away ten
miles downriver, at the time the attack finally came he was back on the
field — if as far as possible from the scene of combat.

Yet McClellan was reluctant to correct the record, for in doing so he risked having his excursion aboard the *Galena* during the Glendale battle on June 30 revealed, an excursion that by any definition was a true dereliction of duty. Testifying before a congressional committee, McClellan said he simply could not remember whether or not he was on a gunboat. There remained, however, the verdict rendered by such fighting men as Colonel Francis Barlow of the 61st New York. "I think the whole army feel," Barlow wrote three days after Malvern Hill, "that it was left to take care of itself and was saved only by its own brave fighting."[18]

General Lee was also on the battlefield, but at the very center of it, trying to sort out and salvage a fight that had burst out of his control. Longstreet, who was with the general commanding when the battle erupted, wrote afterward that it opened "in some way unknown to me. . . ." Lee had as little understanding of what had triggered the fighting, but now that it had spread to the commands of Magruder and Huger and D. H. Hill and was beyond stopping, he was determined to make the best of it. He was with Lafayette McLaws's division west of the Quaker Road when a call for help reached him from Magruder. He advanced McLaws himself and sent to Magruder to redirect his assault more toward the right, against the enemy's flank. He also acted on Benjamin Huger, and that general finally released Robert Ransom's big brigade to Magruder's support.

Magruder tried frantically to rush his own three divisions into action in support of Huger's men, but it was a task that frustrated his best efforts. One difficulty was a serious shortage of manpower. On June 30, Day Six, before all his marching and countermarching and misdirection, Magruder had some 12,500 infantry under command. Now, as dusk fell on Day Seven, neither Magruder nor his lieutenants had any real idea of how many of those infantry were still on the scene. Every road and every grove behind Magruder's front was filled with his stragglers.

The two brigades under Lafayette McLaws, commanded by Paul Semmes and Joseph Kershaw, had emerged from the fight at Savage's Station on June 29 with some 3,500 men between them. It is recorded that at Malvern Hill they put into action 1,513 men between them. Semmes laid the blame on "a misconception of orders, the difficulties of the ground, and the lateness of the hour. . . ." If the straggling in these two brigades was excessive, the record of the other four was not much better. All told, Magruder brought hardly 7,100 infantrymen into battle on July 1 — and only two of his sixteen batteries.

Rather than massing these troops for a single, powerful thrust, Magruder impatiently threw them into the fight as they came to the front. He galloped from one end of the battlefield to the other to post them personally, and his staff could never find him to make their reports or obtain fresh orders. "I rode in every direction seeking Magruder in vain," Major Brent remembered. As a consequence, there was no coordination among the forces of his command or with D. H. Hill's forces on the left.[19]

Magruder's own division, the brigades of Howell Cobb and William Barksdale, was first to arrive, and first to go in. Like Hill's brigades then fighting on their left, they attacked piecemeal. Barksdale's Mississippians charged into what their commander called "a terrible fire" of every type of artillery missile imaginable, and lost one-third of their numbers. Cobb's brigade, to the left and separate from Barksdale's, passed through the wreckage of Armistead's Virginians and met the same terrible fire. The 2nd Louisiana lost three color bearers and then the regimental commander. His second-in-command took up the flag and then he too was killed. These Louisianians lost 182 dead and wounded, second only to the 3rd Alabama that day.

Robert Ransom's North Carolina brigade of Huger's division, when it belatedly reached the field, was marched at the double-quick almost half a mile behind the battle line so as to come up on the extreme right of the formation. In the thick woods the 26th North Carolina went astray, encountering "skulkers from all states," as Lieutenant Colonel Henry K. Burgwyn put it. All the skulkers without exception insisted "their regiments had been cut to pieces &c." Burgwyn collared one of these fugitives and at sword's point directed him to lead them toward the battle. The man complied, Burgwyn wrote, "thinking it would be better to risk death from the enemy than to get it from his friends." General Ransom personally led the brigade to within forty yards of a Yankee battery before the wave of charging men broke and fell back down the slope. The charge cost Ransom 499 men, the highest number in any Confederate brigade on July 1.[20]

Virtually every Confederate who stormed Malvern Hill and left a record of his experience spoke in awe of the Federal guns. The ground shook under their cannonade. Brigadier General David R. Jones, commanding one of Magruder's divisions, summed it up for his family by saying, "The fire from the enemy's artillery was truly terrific." D. H. Hill, looking back on Malvern Hill after four years of war, believed more than half the Confederate casualties that day were due to artillery fire, a circumstance he called "unprecedented." The Federals were awestruck as well. A gunner in a battery of big 32-pounders that Hunt unleashed on the attackers admitted to a friend that it made him heartsick to see his shells "cut roads through them some places ten feet wide. . . . They would close up & come ahead. . . ."

General Jones, under conflicting orders first from Longstreet and then from Magruder, suffered his two brigades to enter the battle more than a quarter of a mile apart. Amidst this command confusion some regiments went forward while their neighbors remained behind. The colonel of the 11th Georgia disappeared, and brigade commander Tige Anderson (one of the Georgians wrote) "left his horse and took it afoot rite with us. . . . Some of the companies runn clean off." Anderson had been the 11th Georgia's first colonel, back in 1861, and he "spoak out plain and publicly." If he could not get his old regiment to follow him, he said, he knew at least his old company would: "Boys, stick to your colors." What few there were of the 11th followed their old commander and in a matter of minutes left 72 dead, wounded, and missing on Malvern Hill.

Jones's second brigade, under Robert Toombs, was dispersed even more widely, with part of it going into battle under D. H. Hill's orders and other regiments going in wherever their colonels thought best to take them. Thomas Ware of the 15th Georgia recorded in his diary marching "through a thicket over gullies & swamps" just to reach the battlefield. Then, he wrote, "we marched quick time while our Brigade was exposed to a hot fire of bombs & grape. We commenced ascending a hill in front of the enemy, where we suffered awful. . . . Men could be seen falling in every direction, the grape & bombs falling & bursting just above our heads, taking off a great many heads & cutting some half into." The 15th Georgia charged twice and was thrown back twice, and soon afterward the exhausted Ware dropped down where he was and fell asleep, "while the dead, wounded & dying were lying around me."[21]

Behind the Confederate lines it was chaos. Walking wounded and wrecked batteries and stragglers by the thousands — what Major Brent called "the bashful men" — filled every road and byway and every clearing. Units of the Valley army that Jackson had ordered forward in response to D. H. Hill's appeal for help were held to a virtual standstill by this tide from the battlefield. General Winder and his staff went in among the throngs of stragglers and tried to drive them back to the front, with limited results. Lieutenant McHenry

Howard came on a dozen men lined up behind a single tree, and saw only "a shiver pass up the file when the hindmost was struck with the flat of a sword. . . ." None of Jackson's men would reach the front in time to affect the course of the battle.

It was fast growing dark now, and the battle rushed to its climax. Private Oliver Norton of Morell's divisions watched as "rebels swarmed out of the woods, seemingly without end. . . ." Henry Hunt, pushing fresh batteries to the front to replace those that had exhausted their ammunition, had a second horse killed under him. To Captain Richard Auchmuty of Morrell's staff it seemed as if "much the same scene as at Gaines' Mills was gone through, excepting that the men stood like heroes." Morell's casualty list reflected that stubborn stand. Charles Griffin's brigade in the first line lost 534 men and three of its four regimental commanders killed or mortally wounded. The 62nd Pennsylvania had five color bearers shot down. Morell's two other brigades in support had 566 more casualties between them.

Fitz John Porter called again on Bull Sumner for help, and Sumner sent him Thomas Meagher's Irish Brigade. Porter led the Irishmen to the front himself. As they moved forward, they passed the badly wounded Colonel Thomas Cass of the Irish 9th Massachusetts being carried to the rear. "As they recognized a fellow-countryman," Auchmuty wrote, "they gave a yell that drowned the noise of the guns."

A final desperate charge was made by Lafayette McLaws's two thinned brigades, along with remnants of brigades from earlier attacks, including Lewis Armistead's men and Rans Wright's, who had been clinging to the hill below the Crew house for three hours and more. McLaws called the scene "a slaughter pen." Irishmen of the 69th New York struggled with Irishmen of Semmes's 10th Louisiana. For its full length the crest of Malvern Hill was wreathed in battle smoke, with only angry red flashes to mark the positions of the guns and waving flags to mark the lines of battle.

At almost the center of the line, near the Quaker Road, the spear point of the Rebel thrust reached into the line of guns, forcing Captain John Edwards's battery of Parrott rifles, 3rd U.S. Artillery, to limber up hastily and fall back to avoid being taken. But with that effort the final charge spent its force and slowly receded. Light of day on July 2 would reveal this high-water mark precisely outlined in a line of bodies in gray and butternut. At the farthest point of attack, well inside the line where the guns had been, was the body of a handsome young Louisianian. Major Brent thought the spot deserved a monument to commemorate the hero of Malvern Hill.

In the darkness the Federal guns continued firing, bathing the smoky crest of the hill in a pulsating dull red light, so that it looked like a depiction of the maw of hell. Along the Quaker Road below the hill staunch old Isaac Trimble of Dick Ewell's division doggedly pushed his brigade toward the front. Stonewall Jackson rode up and asked Trimble what he was doing. "I am going to charge those batteries, sir," Trimble said. "I guess you had better not try it," Jackson told him. "General D. H. Hill has just tried it with his whole Division and been repulsed. I guess you had better not try it, sir." Old Jack rode on, and finally the Federal guns stopped their firing, and night closed on Malvern Hill.[22]

This last day of the Seven Days had proved fruitless and expensive for the Army of Northern Virginia. The cost came to 869 dead, 4,241 wounded, and 540 missing (most of whom had to be counted among the dead), a total of 5,650. In the week-long battle only Gaines's Mill had cost more, and at least that could be counted a victory. Malvern Hill could only be counted a defeat. Federal losses were something over half as great: 314 killed, 1,875 wounded, and 818 missing, a total of 3,007. In the harsh verdict of D. H. Hill, the Confederate attacking forces "did not move together, and were beaten in detail. . . . It was not war — it was murder."

Malvern Hill was clearly a battle General Lee did not intend to be fought the way it was fought, and it demonstrated once again his lack of effective control over his lieutenants. When he asked Magruder that night, "Why did you attack?" Magruder replied promptly, "In obedience to your orders, twice repeated." There was nothing Lee could say to that.

It was Prince John's misfortune to arrive on the battlefield three hours late, and then to open the battle on the strength of a misunderstanding. Benjamin Huger's second feeble performance in two days did not actually contribute greatly to the defeat, yet neither would he have contributed anything to another outcome. For all the failings of planning and preparation, however, Malvern Hill was a battle that Lee might well have won, in the same way he won Gaines's Mill, with disastrous consequences to the Army of the Potomac. Better management of their forces by his field commanders — even average management by Magruder and Huger — would have driven the Federals off Malvern Hill in disorder.

However serious the day's results, and in common with Mechanicsville on June 26, General Lee lost the battle but won the larger contest. At 9:30 that night Fitz John Porter signaled McClellan that "against immense odds, we have driven the enemy beyond the battle field and the firing ended at 8:30." He went on to say that if he could be resupplied with food and ammunition, "we will hold our own and advance if you wish." Here was General Porter, the soul of military caution, proposing to follow up the Malvern Hill victory with a counteroffensive. The next morning he said to Baldy Smith that he had spent the night "urging McClellan to move forward on Richmond at daylight."

General McClellan, however, had long since made up his mind. His only thought was safe haven at Harrison's Landing. Without even waiting for Porter's verdict on the day's events, in contradiction to all of Porter's later arguments, he issued the order for the army to continue its retreat.[23]

Richmond Delivered

··

IRST LIGHT ON Wednesday, July 2, revealed Malvern Hill obscured by a ground fog, gray against a threatening gray sky. The sounds of wounded men with enough strength still to cry out echoed eerily through the fog. After a time the fog began to eddy and drift, gradually unveiling a nightmarish scene on the slopes. Colonel William W. Averell of the 3rd Pennsylvania cavalry, commanding the picket line left behind on Malvern Hill, remembered it as an "appalling spectacle." Of the thousands of Rebel soldiers who had fallen the evening before, "enough were alive and moving to give the field a singular crawling effect." Near the crest a row of bodies marked the final failure of the repeated assaults. Emerging from the woods below came men to aid those who might yet be saved.

In the middle of the night Stonewall Jackson's lieutenants had come to him for directions for deploying their forces to meet a Federal attack in the morning. Jackson was awakened with difficulty and then listened patiently to their questions. "McClellan and his army will be gone by daylight," he said, and went back to sleep. His generals thought him mad, Hunter McGuire, Jackson's medical director, remembered, "but the prediction was true." When Old Jack rose that morning, and before it was known that the Yankees had indeed gone, his first order was to remove all the bodies from in front of his lines. If the attack was renewed, he explained, "it won't do to march the troops over their own dead. . . ."[1]

The Federals who had fought the day before at Malvern Hill, or who had watched that fighting, were to a man startled by McClellan's order to take up the retreat once more. It had not always been easy to know who had won or lost in some of the earlier Seven Days' fighting, but there was no doubt who had won on July 1. "The idea of stealing away in the night from such a position, after such a victory, was simply galling," wrote Captain Biddle from the staff. A number of generals in addition to Fitz John Porter spoke out that giving up Malvern Hill was a terrible mistake. Phil Kearny was furious. To his fellow generals in the Third Corps he raged, "I, Philip Kearny, an old soldier, enter my solomn protest against this order for retreat." Instead of retreating they should be launching an immediate counterstroke to capture Richmond. "I say to you all, such an order can only be prompted by cowardice or treason."

General McClellan, back aboard the *Galena* and well out of range of any protest, had his mind fixed only on escape. From Malvern Hill to Harrison's Landing by way of the River Road was eight miles, and by daylight the army was well embarked on the journey. Captain Auchmuty of the Fifth Corps termed it "a regular stampede, each man going off on his own hook, guns in the road at full gallop, teams on one side in the fields, infantry on the other in the woods." Then it began to rain in torrents, and the rain continued for twenty-four hours.

Something about this downpour seemed the last straw, seemed to wash away the bonds that had held the army together during the week of fighting, and what began as a stampede ended as a rout. "The soldiers who had fought so magnificently for the last week, marching by night and fighting by day, were now a mob," wrote General Darius Couch.

The River Road, like every Peninsula road when it rained, quickly became a river of mud. Entire wagon trains bogged down. Quartermaster William Le Duc, trying to sort out one particular snarl, came on an ambulance blocking a narrow passage, its team and driver exhausted and helpless. Passing by on either side were streams of muddy, drenched infantrymen, hurrying along silently in the rain, paying no attention to the teamster's pleas for help. Le Duc himself unloaded the ambulance's medical supplies so that it might be moved on.

Losses of materiel and equipment were enormous. The Potomac army suffered the loss of some 500 wagons and ambulances in the Seven Days, perhaps a third of them in this last retreat. Many men threw away their rifles, and straggling was heavy. The army would officially record 818 men missing as a result of Malvern Hill, and the Confederates captured virtually none of them in battle; they were taken as stragglers. A brigade in the Fourth Corps, for example, posted more than a mile from any fighting on July 1, recorded 121 men missing. The straggling toll would have been considerably higher but for the efforts of a provost guard of hardbitten cavalry regulars, which reported collaring 1,200 stragglers from the rear of the army.

Harrison's Landing, selected personally by General McClellan as his safe haven, was the site of Berkeley Hundred, the historic seat of the Harrisons of Virginia, who had produced a signer of the Declaration of Independence and, in William Henry Harrison, the ninth president of the United States. The Berkeley mansion overlooked the landing wharf; a mile downstream was Westover, the former seat of the Byrds of Virginia. The army's new position, embracing Berkeley and Westover, was bounded on the west by Kimmage's Creek; on the east, and curving around to the north, was the swamp and watercourse of Herring Creek.

Into this area bounded by the creeks, some four miles long and a mile or so deep, crowded the entire Army of the Potomac: 90,000 men, 288 guns, 3,000 wagons and ambulances, 2,500 beef cattle, 27,000 horses and mules. McClellan explained to President Lincoln, "I have not yielded an inch of ground unnecessarily but have retired to prevent the superior force of the Enemy from cutting me off — and to take a different base of operations." Confederate Secretary of the Navy Stephen Mallory took a different view. "The Great McClelland the young Napoleon," Mallory told his wife, "now like a whipped cur lies on the banks of the James River crouched under his Gun Boats. . . ."[2]

That morning, July 2, in the parlor of the Poindexter house east of the Quaker Road, Lee and his generals were pondering the disappearance of the Federals from Malvern Hill. All that was known for certain was that McClellan had marched to the east along the north bank of the James, toward an unknown destination and for an unknown purpose. As he had done following Gaines's Mill, General Lee continued to credit his opponent with a certain degree of military acumen and a fighting spirit; he did not yet understand that some days since, the Young Napoleon had lost his nerve and thrown over his campaign and thought now of nothing but escape. Lee's immediate need was intelligence on the enemy's prospects.

Jeb Stuart, who had come across the Peninsula from White House on the Pamunkey, was sent off to the east with the cavalry to locate the Federals and determine if they were offering battle at some new location. An equally likely prospect, as Lee saw it, was for McClellan to cross the James and advance on Richmond, or on Petersburg, from the south bank of the river. The Federal navy's recent activity on the James and up the Appomattox toward Petersburg seemed to suggest such a plan. To counter this, Theophilus Holmes and his division were ordered back to Drewry's Bluff to defend that key spot. The two commands that had not fought the day before, Longstreet's and Jackson's (less D. H. Hill's division), were to prepare to march in pursuit of the Yankee army.

Longstreet's ride to the Poindexter house had taken him across the battlefield, and Lee invited his observations of the previous day's fight. He had inspected the lines carefully, Longstreet said, and added, "I think you hurt them about as much as they hurt you." That analysis had the sound of faint praise about it, and Lee observed dryly, "Then I am glad we punished them well, at any rate." Jefferson Davis now made his appearance at headquarters, and Lee and the commander-in-chief discussed the situation at some length. The rain was coming down harder than ever now, greatly reducing the chances for effective pursuit over the boggy roads, particularly any road already cut up by the passage of the enemy's army. They agreed they must wait for a day and more information. Jackson said little during these discussions, only observing pointedly, "They have not all got away if we go immediately after them." It was finally the downpour that settled the question.[3]

On July 3, when the rain stopped and they started their pursuit, the Confederates discovered that the direct route, the River Road, had been churned into impassable mud by the retreating Federals, who had also cut down bridges and obstructed the way with felled trees. The columns turned back to a more roundabout route leading off the Quaker Road to the north. Longstreet led the way, followed by Jackson. Jeb Stuart had meanwhile come on the Yankees at Harrison's Landing, chasing their pickets off a ridgeline north of Herring Creek, called Evelington Heights, which commanded the Federal encampment. At about ten o'clock that morning, believing Longstreet to be nearly on the scene, Stuart loosed a few shells at the Yankees from his single piece of horse artillery.

Stuart's bravado had the effect of kicking over a hornet's nest. General McClellan himself galloped to the front to direct personally men and guns to occupy the heights. His was a bravado performance to rival Stuart's. "I at once rode through the troops," he told his wife, "clear in front of them — to let them see there was no danger — they began to cheer as usual, & called out that they were all right & would fall to the last man 'for little Mac'!" Stuart and his outmanned troopers had to beat a hasty retreat.

Jeb Stuart would be criticized for tipping off the Yankees to the importance of Evelington Heights; it was said he should have stayed out of sight until his own army arrived. In fact the position would have been occupied shortly in any event. McClellan had seen the need on his inspection on July 1, and his chief engineer, John Barnard, warned him about it, and the necessary orders had been issued before Stuart opened fire. McClellan expressed anger at the slow response to the orders, and would soon have corrected matters on his inspection tour, which he had delayed that morning so as to see Chief of Staff Marcy off to Washington to plead for reinforcements. "I am ready for an attack now," he told Ellen; "— give me 24 hours even & will defy all Secessia. . . ."

Late in the day Confederate infantry reached the scene, and early the next morning — it was July 4, Independence Day — General Lee came up to measure chances for an attack. He carefully reconnoitered the ground. The Federal troops and guns were in force on every approach. Their flanks were guarded by Herring and Kimmage's creeks, and anchored offshore in the James were the menacing Yankee gunboats, their big guns trained on the Rebel lines. It had the look of another Malvern Hill. This time, and on this ground, Lee decided he would let McClellan alone. "As far as I can see," he told President Davis, "there is no way to attack him to advantage, nor do I wish to expose the men to the destructive missiles of his gunboats." So the battle for Richmond ended, and so Richmond was delivered.[4]

....

JULY 4 was a bright, sunny day, and as the threat of battle receded men stood down from their posts and relaxed. Many on both sides took the occasion of Independence Day to record their impressions. "We have had hard work for several days," Oliver Wendell Holmes wrote his mother, "— marched all night — lain on our arms every morn'g & fought every afternoon — eaten nothing — suffered the most intense anxiety and everything else possible — I'm safe though so far — but you can't conceive the wear & tear. . . ." Georgian William Stillwell wrote his wife, "Molly, it would be folly for me to attempt to describe the hardships and danger that I have come through. . . . God save me from ever seeing the awful sight that I have seen for the last week." Elisha Hunt Rhodes of the 2nd Rhode Island confided to his diary, "Well, the war must end some time, and the Union will be restored. I wonder what our next move will be. I hope it will be more successful than our last."

There was general agreement that it was a special day. Private E. O. Hicks, 1st Massachusetts Sharpshooters, noted in his diary, "Salute was fired & Gen. McClelland was cheered by the troops. We got some pork & that was all the fourth we had." Diarist Charles Haydon of the 2nd Michigan was more effusive. "All our banners were flung to wind," he wrote. "A national salute was fired. The music played most gloriously. Gen. McClellan came around to see us & we all cheered most heartily for country, cause & leader." Over on the Confederate side, Lieutenant Shepherd Pryor of the 12th Georgia told his wife, "I write you a few lines today to let you know that I am yet alive," and he added, "the yanks have a splendid band they have just finished playing Dixy, it cheered me up some to hear it even if it was the yankeys. . . ."

July 4 was also witness to the demise of the Confederacy's aeronautical corps. Attempting to locate McClellan's army, Porter Alexander had again filled his colorful dress-silk balloon at the Richmond gas works, affixed it to the little armed tug *Teaser*, and steamed down the James to Malvern Hill. Alexander made an early morning Independence Day ascension to look for the Yankees, but the wind came up and so the balloon was reeled down, deflated, and stored aboard for future use. Then the *Teaser* ran aground on a mudbank. The tide was ebbing and she stuck fast; only the afternoon flood tide would refloat her. The hours passed with agonizing slowness, and just as the tide was turning a prowling Yankee gunboat, the *Maratanza*, came steaming around the bend from downriver.

The little *Teaser* was heavily outgunned and helpless as a sitting duck, and after firing one round and tying down the boiler's safety valve, captain and crew abandoned ship and waded across the mudbank to shore. The *Maratanza* secured her prize before she blew up and triumphantly carried her off, dress-silk balloon and all. That, Alexander said sadly, "ended my ballooning." As Albert Myer, a Union signal officer and a friend of Alexander's from the old army, told the story, Major Alexander "wept on reaching shore & exclaimed 'What will the ladies say?' "[5]

Lee pulled his army back toward Richmond and set a watch on the Federals, and people began to look on the Seven Days' battles as one great battle, an undoubted turning point in the Peninsula campaign. Hardly a week earlier McClellan's grand army was in sight of Richmond's spires and listening to the city's clock bells chime the hours. Now it was thirty-five miles distant by way of the James and twenty miles away as the crow flies. The Confederacy's capital had truly been delivered.

The Richmond newspapers were filled with praise for the deliverer, General Lee. "No captain that ever lived could have planned or executed a better plan," said the *Dispatch*. The general "has amazed and confounded his detractors" — this was a reference to the "King of Spades" label applied to Lee only a month earlier — "by the brilliancy of his genius, the fertility of his resources, his energy and daring," said the *Whig*. The correspondent of the *Enquirer* remarked the results "achieved in so short a time and with so small cost to the victors. I do not believe the records of modern warfare can produce a parallel. . . ."

The correspondent's judgment of "so small cost to the victors," however, was far off the mark. The cost had been brutally high. In the Seven Days, from Oak Grove on June 25 to Malvern Hill on July 1, the toll for the Army of Northern Virginia came to 3,494 dead, 15,758 wounded, and 952 missing, a total of 20,204. This was 22 percent of the force with which Lee began the Seven Days. Some commands suffered considerably higher percentage losses. A. P. Hill's Light Division, fighting at Mechanicsville, Gaines's Mill, and Glendale, lost 4,191 men, 32 percent of the number it began the week with. At Mechanicsville, Gaines's Mill, and Malvern Hill, D. H. Hill had 3,781 casualties, a 37 percent loss. Longstreet's division, engaged at Gaines's Mill and Glendale, had the highest loss, 4,439, or 40 percent.[6]

Lee was deeply disappointed with an outcome that left McClellan's army, if no longer besieging the capital, still in being and still dangerous. "Our success has not been as great as I could have desired," he told his wife. In his official report on the campaign, prepared some months later, he wrote, "Under ordinary circumstances the Federal Army should have been destroyed." Robert E. Lee was perfectly confident that his strategy ought to have produced that result.

He did not parcel out blame for this failure, but he had no doubt where some of it lay. Of the six major commands with which he opened the Seven Days, he would remove the commanders of three of them, and would do so without undue delay. Benjamin Huger was quietly shifted to a staff position, inspector of artillery, his specialty in the old army. In his time with the Army of Northern Virginia, Huger contributed not a single accomplishment; as with G. W. Smith, exercising a command in the field was beyond him. Much the same had proved true of Theophilus Holmes, and Holmes was sent west to a command in the trans-Mississippi theater.

Prince John Magruder also went to a command in the West. At Savage's Station and afterward he had demonstrated a temperament unsuited to the battlefield, but he had already put his mark on the Peninsula campaign. Probably none other of the army's generals had his peculiar talent for accomplishing what he did in the trench lines at Yorktown and before Richmond. If Prince John contributed little to the outcome of the Seven Days, he contributed greatly to making that outcome possible. This was not widely known or understood at the time, however. "Public opinion is hot against Huger and Magruder for McClellan's escape," noted the Charleston diarist Mary Chesnut.

Of his other lieutenants Lee revealed no similar mistrust of their competence to command in battle. Stonewall Jackson, to be sure, had signally failed to exhibit the initiative expected of him from his record in the Shenandoah Valley, yet Lee would display no lack of confidence in Old Jack because of it. Perhaps he recognized that Jackson, like Lee himself, had taken certain lessons from the experience of the Seven Days. For Lee's part, never again would he attempt such elegant chessboard maneuvers as the converging movements of Mechanics-ville and Glendale; never again would he command with the indirection and deference he showed during this week of battle. Thereafter he would tailor his tactics to better fit his army and hold more tightly to the reins of command. As by an annealing process, Lee — and Jackson — emerged from the fire of the Seven Days stronger generals than before.

In Richmond there was relief at the outcome of the fighting, but no celebration. "There were no noisy jubilations over this succession of victories," Sallie Putnam wrote. "There were no bells rung, no cannon fire, no illuminations. . . ." Instead there was the sight of a seemingly endless procession of ambulances and "dead wagons" in the streets, bringing back the human wreckage from the battlefields. David Winn of the 4th Georgia, in Richmond looking for a wounded comrade, told his wife, "The whole city is a hospital and the very atmosphere is poisoned & loathsome." In addition to nearly 15,800 of its own wounded, Richmond had to care for the sick and wounded the retreating Federals had left behind on every field. All of these were either very sick or severely wounded, or they would not have been left. Lee's medical director Lafayette Guild estimated their number at 4,900. Many Richmonders would remember this hot July of 1862 for one sound. "Day by day," wrote Constance Cary Harrison, "we were called to our windows by the wailing dirge of a military band preceding a soldier's funeral. One could not number those sad pageants. . . ."[7]

....

THE COST OF the Seven Days was also being reckoned by the Federals. The Army of the Potomac lost 1,734 dead, 8,066 wounded, and

6,055 missing, a total of 15,855, or 4,349 fewer than the Confederates. On the defensive in every battle but the first one at Oak Grove, the Federals suffered losses in dead and wounded of just over half those of the Rebels; on the retreat after every battle but that first one, they experienced losses in prisoners more than six times as great. The Federals' materiel loss was enormous, most of it never calculated and beyond calculation. Forty pieces of artillery were taken by the Rebels in the Seven Days, and they also gleaned from the battlefields no fewer than 31,000 small arms. Wagons and ambulances by the hundreds, ordnance stores and ammunition, and equipment of every sort and variety were salvaged by thrifty Confederate quartermasters. The Army of Northern Virginia would re-equip itself at General McClellan's expense. "We had a great swapping around both in infantry & artillery, after the battles," Porter Alexander remembered.

McClellan's practice of haphazard, absentee command produced an imbalanced casualty list in his army. The weight of the fighting — very nearly half the army's total Seven Days' casualties — had fallen most heavily on Fitz John Porter's Fifth Corps, particularly on George Morell's division and George McCall's Pennsylvania Reserves. At Gaines's Mill and Malvern Hill Morell lost 3,136 men, the most in any of the divisions. At Mechanicsville, Gaines's Mill, and Glendale McCall lost just 36 fewer men, and very nearly a third of those he had started the week with. The Fifth Corps as a whole suffered 7,575 casualties, 28 percent of its numbers.

By contrast, Erasmus Keyes's Fourth Corps was called on to fight but once, at Malvern Hill, and with but one of its divisions; the week's loss in the Fourth Corps came to 800 men. Franklin's Sixth Corps also watched much of the time from the sidelines, except for the fierce engagement of Slocum's division at Gaines's Mill. The other Sixth Corps division, under Baldy Smith, lost only 803 men. Some of the army's hardest fighters saw only limited action. Joe Hooker and Phil Kearny were assigned to fight only at Oak Grove on Day One and at Glendale on Day Six; Hooker's loss for the week was 746 men.[8]

One piece of equipment carefully saved on the retreat was General McClellan's portable printing press, and on July 4 the general produced an address to his army. He first explained the events of the Seven Days: "Attacked by vastly superior forces, and without hope of reinforcements, you have succeeded in changing your base of operations by a flank movement, always regarded as the most hazardous of military expedients." He explained further: "You have saved all your material, all your guns, except a few lost in battle. . . . ; and under every disadvantage of numbers, and necessarily of position also, you have in every conflict beaten back your foes with enormous slaughter. Your conduct ranks you among the celebrated armies of history." In his peroration he promised the army would yet "enter the Capital of their so-called Confederacy . . . cost what it may in time, treasure and blood."

This remarkable document was a claim of victory not over the enemy but over adversity — adversity not of the making of the general commanding. Like all General McClellan's commentaries on events of his Civil War career, it rested on his long-standing and well-established foundation of "vastly superior" enemy forces. He would insist to everyone — the authorities in Washington, his political allies at home, newspapers friendly to his cause — that he had been attacked in the Seven Days by a Confederate army of 200,000. Consequently, as he told President Lincoln, his movement to the James "will be acknowledged by all competent judges . . . unparalleled in the annals of war." He had preserved, he said, "above all our honor."[9]

Reaction in the North to the events on the Peninsula was both mixed and predictable. Initially, press reporting on the Seven Days, dependent as it was on McClellan's headquarters, put the best possible face on the retreat. OUR ARMY ON THE JAMES RIVER headed the story in the *New York Tribune* on July 4; MAGRUDER PRISONER, JACKSON KILLED . . . 185,000 REBELS AGAINST 95,000 UNION TROOPS. Reflection on the matter produced more realistic appraisals. Secretary of the Treasury Chase spoke of the "shameful defeat at Richmond, thinly covered from the world's contempt by the pretense of a change of base of operations." His Cabinet colleague Edward Bates, writing on July 8, thought that if the Army of the Potomac "only had a little activity & enterprise, in the governing head, it would not fail to win all desirable success."

Not everyone was that forbearing. General McClellan's radical Republican critics renewed their demands for his dismissal. In the Senate Zachariah Chandler charged him with every military failing imaginable; rather than seeking victory at Richmond the general sought only "another big swamp, and we sat down in the center of it, and went to digging." Republican newspapers lined up against McClellan and Democatic ones lined up behind him. His defenders named Secretary of War Stanton responsible for the failure to take Richmond, by his intrigues against the general and by his refusal to support him, and called for Stanton's dismissal. As had come to be true of anything to do with George McClellan, the debate was loud and heated.[10]

There was growing debate within the army as well. Although probably a majority of the men shared New Yorker Alfred Davenport's view — the general's Fourth of July address to the army, Davenport wrote, "is very eloquent and *about* true" — a considerable number expressed doubts. What they shared was a sense that something had gone very wrong in the "big skedaddle" from the Chickahominy, and that calling it a change of base was not the answer.

"We are at a loss to imagine whether this is strategy or defeat," Sergeant Edgar Newcomb of the 19th Massachusetts said. Lieutenant William Folwell of the engineers wondered why "they deify a General whose greatest feat has been a *masterly* retreat." Felix Brannigan of Joe Hooker's division expressed perhaps the most common view among the men in the ranks — that this had been a serious defeat, no matter how it was sugar-coated, and that there was blame enough to go around. "Who is to blame for all this?" Brannigan asked. "Some say 'the War Department,' others 'the President,' and not a few 'Our General.' "

General McClellan knew precisely where to lay the blame. The authors of his defeat, he told his mentor Samuel Barlow, were the "heartless villains" in Washington who "have done their best to sacrifice as noble an Army as ever marched to battle." From the first, he said, Stanton and his cohorts had wanted him defeated and overthrown, so that disunion would prevail and they might be free to rule unhampered in the North. They recognized him as their paramount enemy who must be destroyed: "They are aware that I have seen through their villainous schemes, & that if I succeed my foot will be on their necks."

The general found solace in his conviction that everything that had happened to him on the Peninsula was God's will, and that consequently nothing was his fault and everything was for the best. The hand of God had dictated the outcome of the Seven Days; his defeat there was actually a blessing in disguise. "I think I begin to see his wise purpose in all this . . . ," McClellan told his wife. "If I had succeeded in taking Richmond now the fanatics of the North might have been too powerful & reunion impossible."[11]

While Harrison's Landing was now guarded by extensive fortifications and by the gunboats and was safe enough, it was a miserable encampment. In these July weeks the James River bottomland was steamy and endlessly hot. On July 15 Lieutenant Haydon recorded in his journal a temperature of 103 degrees in the shade. Everyone and everything were crowded together, the water was bad and the sanitation worse, and plagues of flies drove men and animals to distraction. The list of the sick lengthened, especially those with dysentery, and Chickahominy fever was renamed the James River fever. Private E. O. Hicks noted in his diary on July 19, "A good many of our boys are sick & every where around the hospitals we can see the dead laid out almost every morn." The Potomac army had 42,911 reported cases of illness during July, almost twice that of any other month of the campaign. There were issues of new uniforms and equipment, and the men were kept occupied with drills and work on the fortifications, and reinforcements arrived, yet even so the army grew weaker each day.

On one of these hot July evenings Brigadier Daniel Butterfield of the Fifth Corps called in his brigade bugler, Private Oliver Norton, and, showing him the notes of a melody he had penciled on the back of an envelope, asked Norton to sound them out for him. He had never been happy with the standard lights-out call, Butterfield explained. It was not musical enough, and seemed somehow inappropriate as the last call of the soldier's day. Private Norton dutifully sounded out the melody and Butterfield made a few changes, lengthening some notes and shortening others, until they agreed it was just right. That night at lights-out the haunting strain of "Taps" echoed across the army's encampment for the first time. [12]

....

GENERAL McCLELLAN'S July 4 address to his army was greeted in Richmond with derision. His change of base evasion became a byword among Lee's soldiers. As Captain William Blackwell of the cavalry explained, any time that rain flooded out a campsite, the men would pick up their traps and announce they were changing their base. If two dogs got into a fight in camp and the loser was seen running away, it was remarked sagely that he was merely changing his base. In his military correspondence General D. H. Hill took to calling McClellan "the great Mover of his Base," and Jeb Stuart's cavalry pickets watching Harrison's Landing subjected their opposite numbers to frequent banter on the subject.

The Confederates were recruiting their strength in conditions considerably superior to those of the Yankees at Harrison's Landing. Their encampments were on better ground and had better water, and their closeness to Richmond meant better food. The sick and the recovering wounded were taken into private homes, where recuperation was faster than in the hospitals. While they mourned their many dead, the men accepted it as the price of victory, and morale was high. A popular story ran through the ranks. As William White of the 18th Georgia told it, the reason the Yankees had been defeated before Richmond was that "first, they had to climb two damned steep *Hills*, then came a *Longstreet*, and next a *Stonewall*, which was impregnable." Thomas Verdery's one regret was that the battle for Richmond would likely have to be fought over again, "and it is fearful to contemplate even if we are again successful."

After the casualty lists were published, friends and relatives hurried to Richmond to nurse the injured and grieve for the dead. W. A. Dardan of Jackson's command met the father of a comrade who had been killed in the Seven Days' fighting, and took him to the battlefield where his son was buried. He had come from Georgia to see the spot. "The old man seemed like he was astonished to look at the place where our Regt. fought," Dardan wrote home. "He says that he doesn't see how any of us ever escaped, and it looked much worse than I thought it would, myself. All the small timber on the field is dead and it looks like there had been a big fire."[13]

In these days General Lee occupied himself trying to fathom what the enemy would do next. It was the same situation he had confronted after his victory at Gaines's Mill, when he had held the strategic initiative but could not act until McClellan revealed his hand. Now too Lee would have to grant the enemy the first move, but instead of just one Federal force to watch there were four of them.

The most obvious threat, and the nearest, was McClellan's main army at Harrison's Landing, under observation by Stuart's cavalry. At Newport News, on the tip of the Peninsula, was Ambrose Burnside's command, brought up by transports from the North Carolina coast. To the north, at Fredericksburg and in the Shenandoah Valley, were the two Federal commands that Stonewall Jackson had evaded when he came to the Peninsula in June. It was reported in the Northern papers that they were now incorporated in a new army commanded by General John Pope, from the western theater.

McClellan, commanding the largest of the four, remained the greatest danger to Richmond and claimed the largest share of Lee's attention. Burnside, at Newport News, might be intended as reinforcement for McClellan in a renewed campaign against Richmond; or, supported by McClellan, Burnside might advance on Petersburg and Richmond by way of the south bank of the James. General Pope might revive McDowell's earlier threat by marching on Richmond from the north, from Fredericksburg. Or Pope might attempt to sever the Confederacy's railroad lifeline to the Shenandoah, the Virginia Central, by taking the key junction of Gordonsville. For either of these two purposes Pope might be reinforced by Burnside or even by McClellan. Lee's singular advantage in all this, whatever the Federals might finally do, was his central location, allowing him to move swiftly against any threat as it was discovered.

Lee watched and patiently waited. As soon as Pope was reported moving southward toward the Virginia Central, he sent Jackson with the divisions of Ewell and Winder northward to meet the threat. When Jackson announced that Pope had too much strength to be attacked with profit, Lee sent him the reinforcement of A. P. Hill's Light Division. On the Peninsula, meanwhile, McClellan and Burnside remained quiet. By way of threatening the Young Napoleon, on the last day of July Lee sent a force of artillery down the south bank of the James to a point opposite Harrison's Landing, and that night it opened a surprise bombardment on the Federal encampment. Damage was slight, but General McClellan was given one more thing to think about.

As early as July 19 McClellan's confidant Fitz John Porter observed that the enemy appeared to be "working his way with some parties" northward in the direction of Washington, "but I think he is threatening all around and keeping his forces where he can bring them easily to Richmond. He is feeling everywhere in order to keep reinforcements away from us and Washington." Like Porter, McClellan believed it was only the enemy's vast numbers that allowed him to be "threatening all around," and it was this delusion that gave unwitting credence to General Lee's deadly game.[14]

....

ON JULY 8 Mr. Lincoln had arrived at Harrison's Landing to judge matters for himself. He reviewed the troops and closely questioned General McClellan about their condition. Matters of war strategy were very much on the president's mind. In the wake of the fiasco in the Shenandoah and the conflict over the defense of Washington, Lincoln had gathered together the scattered commands to form the new Army of Virginia and brought John Pope from the western theater to command it. The question now to be addressed was cooperation between the Army of Virginia and the Army of the Potomac. One possibility was withdrawing McClellan's army from the Peninsula to link it with Pope's in a new overland offensive.

Lincoln already knew McClellan's opinion of the matter well enough. The campaign against Richmond should only be renewed from his base at Harrison's Landing, McClellan insisted, and "reinforcements should be sent to me rather much over than much less than 100,000 men." The president posed the question of withdrawal to the army's five corps commanders. Keyes and Franklin said the army should be withdrawn. Porter, Heintzelman, and Sumner said it was secure where it was, and to leave the Peninsula would invite the troops' demoralization. "To withdraw the Army would be the ruin of the country," Heintzelman thought.

General McClellan took advantage of the president's visit to hand him what became famous as the Harrison's Landing letter. It was his broad-ranging outline for conducting the war "upon the highest principles known to Christian Civilization."

McClellan had been formulating these thoughts for some weeks, and now with the war at a critical stage, he told his wife, his conscience dictated that he try to shape war policy in his own image. In the paper he told the president that confiscation of Southerners' property or forced emancipation of Southerners' slaves or any other such "radical views" must not "be contemplated for a moment." Abolitionist sentiment as government policy, he said, "will rapidly disintegrate our present Armies." Lincoln read the letter without comment, leaving General McClellan disappointed. The president, he told Ellen, "really seems quite incapable of rising to the heights of the merits of the question & the magnitude of the crisis."[15]

Concluding he needed better professional military advice than he had been getting, on his return to Washington the president called Henry W. Halleck from the West to become general-in-chief of the Union armies, filling the post vacant since McClellan was relieved of that command on March 11. Upon his arrival Halleck was immediately sent to Harrison's Landing to formulate some strategy to get the war moving again. Halleck even had the president's leave to change the commander of the Army of the Potomac. According to Senator Orville H. Browning, Lincoln said "he was satisfied McClellan would not fight and he had told Halleck so, and that he could keep him in command or not as he pleased." Only a few days before, Lincoln had offered command of the Potomac army to General Burnside, who refused on the grounds that he was not competent for the job. Clearly, however it could be done, Mr. Lincoln would be glad to be rid of General McClellan.

On July 25, under questioning by Halleck at headquarters at Harrison's Landing, McClellan finally revealed a plan for resuming his march on Richmond. At some convenient point, he said, he would cross the James and advance up the south bank and seize Petersburg and entrench himself securely there. This would give him control of all but one of the rail lines entering Richmond from the south. Lee would be forced to abandon Richmond or be starved out, or to attack the Army of the Potomac at Petersburg on ground of McClellan's choosing. At last the Young Napoleon would have his great war-winning, Waterloo-style battle.

General Halleck thought this a highly dangerous idea. On McClellan's word, he said, here was General Lee with 200,000 men (McClellan was sure that by now Lee had made good his Seven Days' losses), and General Lee would surely take advantage of his great numbers and central position to conquer first one and then the other of the two widely separated Union armies. Leaving sufficient force to mask McClellan, Lee might march north to overwhelm John Pope's army, then return and dispose of McClellan; or he might reverse the order. In any event, this separation of armies would be the epitaph of the Union.

McClellan was less impressed with this argument than by a bit of news Halleck imparted to him. It seemed that in the western theater General Don Carlos Buell would not, after all, be able to march on Chattanooga to cut the Confederacy's only direct east-west railroad. This by itself, by McClellan's imaginative reasoning, was enough to doom his Petersburg plan. Now, should he shift his army to Petersburg, he was liable to be trapped between Lee's masses in his front and Rebel masses sent by rail from the West to fall on his rear. In his diary for July 26, General Heintzelman, an advocate of the Petersburg movement, recorded the untimely death of his cherished idea: "There will be no advance on Chattanooga by Buell for some time & in view of this Gen. McClellan opposes taking Petersburg."

Thus Halleck left McClellan with an unpalatable choice: advance on Richmond from Harrison's Landing by way of the north bank of the James, or abandon the Peninsula entirely. In place of the York River Railroad he would have to take the James as his line of supply, overcoming on the way imposing enemy defenses at Malvern Hill and Drewry's Bluff. Still, McClellan had his siege train and the navy's gunboats, and together they might be used to pulverize the Rebel fortifications and the Rebel masses along the river.

This would be his course, he told Halleck — so long as he was reinforced. Halleck said that 20,000 reinforcements were available for him — that part of Burnside's command then at Newport News, and part of David Hunter's command on the South Atlantic coast. Grudgingly McClellan agreed to that number; it would give him, he said, "some chance" of success. Believing this signaled an agreement, Halleck returned to Washington. Thus the Peninsula campaign was saved — for twenty-four hours.[16]

In one of his intuitive leaps of logic that were invariably self-destructive, George McClellan now proceeded once and finally to destroy his grand campaign. Richmond had recently paroled to him a number of Federal sick and wounded, and from their observations McClellan deduced that "reinforcements are pouring into Richmond from the South." Included in this flood he thought he detected troops from his favorite source of Rebel reinforcements, General Beauregard's western army. A new plan must be devised.

Because of this enemy influx, McClellan demanded of Halleck not the agreed-upon 20,000 reinforcements, but more than two and a half times that number. He wanted not just part of Burnside's and Hunter's troops but all of them, to the number of 35,000. He wanted an additional 15,000 or 20,000 men from the West, apparently to counter those westerners of Beauregard's. He was confident, he said, that General Halleck agreed with him that the true defense of Washington "consists in a rapid & heavy blow given by this Army upon Richmond."

Henry Halleck was a pedant and a military bureaucrat, but he was not an easy man to fool, and when he arrived back in Washington to find this dispatch of McClellan's waiting for him, he threw up his hands. Just come from the West himself, he knew very well the whereabouts of the Confederacy's western forces, and McClellan's absurd (and repeated) attempts to put them by the thousands in front of him at Richmond must have amazed him. It was now all too clear to him, Halleck told his wife, that General McClellan "does not understand strategy and should never plan a campaign," and he made up his mind to follow his first instinct and withdraw the Army of the Potomac from the Peninsula. On July 30 he telegraphed to begin evacuating the sick from Harrison's Landing, and on August 3 he made it official: General McClellan was immediately to bring his army north to unite it with Pope's and open a new campaign.[17]

McClellan made bitter and prolonged protest against the decision, but Halleck was adamant. What more than anything else had doomed General McClellan's grand campaign from the first — his hallucinations about the enemy he faced — now came full circle finally to seal its fate. Halleck simply pointed to the numbers: McClellan had 90,000 men, and Pope had 40,000, and squarely between them, by Mc-Clellan's insistent count, Lee had 200,000. Even with their two armies united the Federals would be at risk; individually the two would stand little chance. In explaining his decision Halleck wrote, "There was to my mind no alternative," and against that unblinking logic McClellan's arguments crumbled.

Nevertheless, McClellan would make one final, convulsive effort to turn back the tide of events. On August 5 he assembled an expedition of infantry and cavalry, 17,000 men in all, and sent it under Joe Hooker to retake Malvern Hill. Officially his purpose was to appraise a rumor that the Confederates were giving up Richmond; privately his motivation was to embroil himself in a contest that would forestall Halleck's evacuation order. He would attempt a coup, he told Ellen — lure the Rebels into a misstep, "& follow them up to Richmond. . . ." But when Lee reacted aggressively to the threat, McClellan's resolution evaporated; should he commit to battle and lose, he risked losing even his haven at Harrison's Landing. Hooker was told to abandon the expedition and return, and McClellan said nothing more of a coup.

On the morning of August 7 Lee was surprised to see the Federals for the second time give up Malvern Hill and retreat. In a dispatch to Jackson that day he passed judgment on McClellan: "I have no idea that he will advance on Richmond now." This flight from Malvern Hill served to confirm something Lee already suspected. Several days previously, John Singleton Mosby, Jeb Stuart's scout who had been captured in July by the Yankees, arrived at Fort Monroe as part of a prisoner exchange. From his own spying efforts, and those of a Southern sympathizer there, Mosby learned that Burnside's command at Newport News had been ordered north to the Rappahannock. As soon as he was exchanged, Mosby took this intelligence to Lee.

If Burnside was not to reinforce McClellan or to operate up the James, Lee reasoned, that was certain evidence the enemy was opening a new campaign by land from the north. Furthermore, if Mc-Clellan's army was not being reinforced, the design must be for him too to join that new campaign. McClellan's thrust at Malvern Hill must have been a deception to cover the withdrawal from the Peninsula. General Lee now felt free to turn his attention to the new campaign taking shape in northern Virginia.[18]

So a new campaign began and the Peninsula campaign came to an end. For Robert E. Lee and the Army of Northern Virginia it ended with victory and Richmond delivered. For George B. McClellan and the Army of the Potomac it ended with defeat and ignominious retreat. From the first arrival of the Federals at Fort Monroe on March 20 to their final evacuation on August 26, the campaign lasted 160 days, or five months and one week. In that time some 250,000 men participated in it, on land and at sea (and in the air), more than in any other single campaign of the Civil War. In volume of war materiel too it was unmatched.

In pitched battles and skirmishes, from Yorktown to Malvern Hill, some 25,370 Federals and 30,450 Confederates were killed, wounded, or missing. Of that total of 55,820 for the two armies, at least 8,670 died in battle. Perhaps another 5,000 died of disease in these months, raising the death toll to an estimated 13,670. Even that total is no doubt an undercount, for statistics on disease on the Peninsula were incomplete, and many men reported as missing were surely dead. Better than 24 percent — almost one in four — of the quarter-million men who took part in the Peninsula campaign were counted wounded or missing or dead of battle or disease.

On the Peninsula in these months more even than these men had been lost. General McClellan's grand campaign had always carried within it the dream of ending this civil war while it was still a rebellion and before it became a revolution. He envisioned fighting at Richmond his American Waterloo, so that afterward the contestants might sit down together at the peace table, in the manner of wars of the past. There statesmen would offer certain adjustments and make certain concessions, and the Union would be restored in peace and amity. But the dream died in smoke and fire in the swamps at Gaines's Mill and in the deep woods at Glendale and on Malvern's bloody slopes. No statesmen would meet in the wake of the Seven Days to write an end to "this sad war" and to heal the breach. The war would go on for three more years, and from a rebellion become a revolution.[19]

....

ON THE AFTERNOON of Saturday, August 16, the last units of the Army of the Potomac left Harrison's Landing for the march down the Peninsula to Fort Monroe and embarkation for new fields. The great encampment was empty except for straw-filled dummy sentinels standing guard in the lines and wooden cannon — Yankee Quaker guns — in the embrasures. General McClellan told his wife that he "took a savage satisfaction" in being the last man to leave. He stood on the parapet and figuratively shook his fist at the enemy host he imagined even then was beginning to crowd forward and pursue him and his wrecked campaign. But except for a brigade of Rebel cavalry there was no one there to appreciate his brave gesture. General Lee had left the day before to take command of the new campaign to the north. The war was turning in a new direction, toward the battlefield at Manassas and after that to Antietam Creek in Maryland, far from the gates of Richmond. [20]

APPENDIXES

ACKNOWLEDGMENTS

NOTES

BIBLIOGRAPHY

INDEX

APPENDIXES

....

The following tabulation of forces in the two armies at three points in the Peninsula campaign — May 1 (Appendix I), June 1 (Appendix II), and June 25 (Appendix III), 1862 — is drawn from tables in the *Official Records*, supplemented by additional data from documents and correspondence in those volumes and other primary sources. In the notation of officer casualties, (k) stands for killed, (w) for wounded, (mw) for mortally wounded, and (c) for captured.

APPENDIX I

The Armies at Yorktown

....

Army of the Potomac
Maj. Gen. George B. McClellan

SECOND CORPS: Brig. Gen. Edwin V. Sumner

First Division: Brig. Gen. Israel B. Richardson
  First Brigade: Brig. Gen. Oliver O. Howard

5th New Hampshire	64th New York
61st New York	81st Pennsylvania

  Second Brigade: Brig. Gen. Thomas F. Meagher

63rd New York	88th New York
69th New York	

  Third Brigade: Brig. Gen. William H. French

52nd New York	66th New York
57th New York	53rd Pennsylvania

  Artillery: Capt. George W. Hazzard

1st New York Light, Battery B	2nd Btn. New York Light, Battery A
1st New York Light, Battery G	4th United States, Battery A-C

  Cavalry: 6th New York, Co. D

Second Division: Brig. Gen. John Sedgwick
  First Brigade: Brig. Gen. Willis A. Gorman
    15th Massachusetts (1st Co. Massachusetts Sharpshooters, attached)

1st Minnesota	82nd New York
34th New York	

  Second Brigade: Brig. Gen. William W. Burns

69th Pennsylvania	72nd Pennsylvania
71st Pennsylvania	106th Pennsylvania

  Third Brigade: Brig. Gen. N. J. T. Dana

19th Massachusetts	7th Michigan
20th Massachusetts	42nd New York

Artillery: Col. Charles H. Tompkins
- 1st Rhode Island Light, Battery A
- 1st Rhode Island Light, Battery B
- 1st Rhode Island Light, Battery G
- 1st United States, Battery I

Cavalry: 6th New York, Co. K

Corps Cavalry: John F. Farnsworth
- 8th Illinois

THIRD CORPS: Brig. Gen. Samuel P. Heintzelman

First Division: Brig. Gen. Fitz John Porter
- First Brigade: Brig. Gen. John H. Martindale
  - 2nd Maine
  - 18th Massachusetts
  - 13th New York
  - 25th New York
  - 22nd Massachusetts (2nd Co. Massachusetts Sharpshooters, attached)
- Second Brigade: Brig. Gen. George W. Morell
  - 14th New York
  - 4th Michigan
  - 9th Massachusetts
  - 62nd Pennsylvania
- Third Brigade: Brig. Gen. Daniel Butterfield
  - 16th Michigan (Brady's Co. Michigan Sharpshooters, attached)
  - 12th New York
  - 17th New York
  - 44th New York
  - 83rd Pennsylvania
- Artillery: Capt. Charles Griffin
  - Massachusetts Light, Battery C
  - Massachusetts Light, Battery E
  - 1st Rhode Island Light, Battery C
  - 5th United States, Battery D
- Cavalry: 8th Pennsylvania, Co. A
- Sharpshooters: Col. Hiram Berdan
  - 1st United States Sharpshooters

Second Division: Brig. Gen. Joseph Hooker
- First Brigade: Brig. Gen. Cuvier Grover
  - 2nd New Hampshire
  - 1st Massachusetts
  - 11th Massachusetts
  - 26th Pennsylvania
- Second Brigade: Col. Nelson Taylor
  - 70th New York
  - 71st New York
  - 72nd New York
  - 73rd New York
  - 74th New York
- Third Brigade: Col. Samuel H. Starr
  - 5th New Jersey
  - 6th New Jersey
  - 7th New Jersey
  - 8th New Jersey
- Artillery: Maj. Charles S. Wainwright
  - 1st New York Light, Battery D
  - 1st United States, Battery H
  - 4th New York Independent Light
  - 6th New York Independent Light

Third Division: Brig. Gen. Charles S. Hamilton
  First Brigade: Brig. Gen. Charles D. Jameson

57th Pennsylvania	105th Pennsylvania
63rd Pennsylvania	87th New York

  Second Brigade: Brig. Gen. David B. Birney

38th New York	3rd Maine
40th New York	4th Maine

  Third Brigade: Brig. Gen. Hiram G. Berry

2nd Michigan	5th Michigan
3rd Michigan	37th New York

  Artillery: Capt. James Thompson
    New Jersey Light, Battery B
    1st Rhode Island Light, Battery E
    2nd United States, Battery G
  Corps Cavalry: Col. William W. Averell
    3rd Pennsylvania

FOURTH CORPS: Brig. Gen. Erasmus D. Keyes

First Division: Brig. Gen. Darius N. Couch
  First Brigade: Brig. Gen. John J. Peck

55th New York	98th Pennsylvania
62nd New York	102nd Pennsylvania
93rd Pennsylvania	

  Second Brigade: Brig. Gen. L. P. Graham

65th New York	31st Pennsylvania
67th New York	61st Pennsylvania
23rd Pennsylvania	

  Third Brigade: Col. Henry S. Briggs

7th Massachusetts	2nd Rhode Island
10th Massachusetts	36th New York

  Artillery: Maj. Robert M. West
    1st Pennsylvania Light, Battery C
    1st Pennsylvania Light, Battery D
    1st Pennsylvania Light, Battery E
    1st Pennsylvania Light, Battery H
  Cavalry: 6th New York, Co. F
Second Division: Brig. Gen. William F. Smith
  First Brigade: Brig. Gen. Winfield S. Hancock

5th Wisconsin	43rd New York
6th Maine	49th Pennsylvania

  Second Brigade: Brig. Gen. W. T. H. Brooks

2nd Vermont	5th Vermont
3rd Vermont	6th Vermont
4th Vermont	

Third Brigade: Brig. Gen. John W. Davidson
    7th Maine   49th New York
    33rd New York   77th New York
Artillery: Capt. Romeyn B. Ayres
    1st New York Light, Battery E   5th United States, Battery F
    1st New York Independent Light
    3rd New York Independent Light
Third Division: Brig. Gen. Silas Casey
  First Brigade: Brig. Gen. Henry M. Naglee
    52nd Pennsylvania   100th New York
    104th Pennsylvania   11th Maine
    56th New York
  Second Brigade: Brig. Gen. William H. Keim
    85th Pennsylvania   103rd Pennsylvania
    101st Pennsylvania   96th New York
  Third Brigade: Brig. Gen. Innis N. Palmer
    81st New York   93rd New York
    85th New York   98th New York
    92nd New York
  Artillery: Col. Guilford D. Bailey
    1st New York Light, Battery A   7th New York Independent Light
    1st New York Light, Battery H   8th New York Independent Light
  Cavalry: 6th New York, Co. H

FIRST DIVISION, FIRST CORPS: Brig. Gen. William B. Franklin

First Brigade: Brig. Gen. Philip Kearny
    1st New Jersey   3rd New Jersey
    2nd New Jersey   4th New Jersey
Second Brigade: Brig. Gen. Henry W. Slocum
    16th New York   5th Maine
    27th New York   96th Pennsylvania
Third Brigade: Brig. Gen. John Newton
    18th New York   32nd New York
    31st New York   95th Pennsylvania
Artillery: Capt. Edward R. Platt
    Massachusetts Light, Battery A   New Jersey Light, Battery A
    1st New York Light, Battery F   2nd United States, Battery D
Cavalry: 1st New York

Infantry Reserve, Regular Brigade: Brig. Gen. George Sykes

2nd United States	11th United States
3rd United States	12th United States
4th United States	14th United States
6th United States	17th United States
10th United States	

Artillery Reserve: Col. Henry J. Hunt

1st United States, Battery E	4th United States, Battery K
1st United States, Battery G-K	5th United States, Battery A
2nd United States, Battery A	5th United States, Battery I
2nd United States, Battery B	5th United States, Battery K
2nd United States, Battery E	1st Battalion New York, Battery A
2nd United States, Battery M	1st Battalion New York, Battery B
3rd United States, Battery C-G	1st Battalion New York, Battery C
3rd United States, Battery F-K	1st Battalion New York, Battery D
3rd United States, Battery L-M	9th New York Cavalry
4th United States, Battery G	

Cavalry Reserve: Brig. Gen. Philip St. George Cooke

First Brigade: Brig. Gen. William H. Emory

5th United States	6th Pennsylvania
6th United States	

Second Brigade: Col. George A. H. Blake

1st United States	McClellan Dragoons (Illinois)
8th Pennsylvania	

Engineer Troops

United States Engineer Battalion: Capt. James C. Duane
Companies A, B, C

Volunteer Engineer Brigade: Brig. Gen. Daniel P. Woodbury

15th New York	50th New York

Siege Train: Col. Robert O. Tyler
1st Connecticut Heavy Artillery
5th New York

General Headquarters

2nd United States Cavalry	8th United States Infantry, 2 co.'s
4th United States Cavalry, 2 co.'s	17th United States Infantry, 2 co.'s
Oneida (New York) Cavalry	Sturgis Rifles (Illinois)

Army of Northern Virginia
Gen. Joseph E. Johnston

LEFT WING: Maj. Gen. D. H. Hill

Rodes's Brigade: Brig. Gen. Robert E. Rodes
    5th Alabama   12th Alabama
    6th Alabama   12th Mississippi
       Carter's King William (Virginia) Battery
Featherston's Brigade: Brig. Gen. Winfield S. Featherston
    27th Georgia   4th North Carolina
    28th Georgia   49th Virginia
Early's Brigade: Brig. Gen. Jubal A. Early
    5th North Carolina   24th Virginia
    23rd North Carolina   38th Virginia
       Bondurant's Jeff Davis Alabama Battery
Rains's Brigade: Brig. Gen. Gabriel J. Rains
    13th Alabama   6th Georgia
    26th Alabama   23rd Georgia
       Heavy Artillery: 19 batteries
Ward's Command (attached): Col. George T. Ward
    2nd Florida   2nd Mississippi Battalion
Crump's Command (Gloucester Point): Col. Charles A. Crump
    46th Virginia   Eastern Shore Co.
    9th Virginia Militia   3rd Virginia Cavalry, 1 co.
    21st Virginia Militia   Mathews Light Dragoons
    61st Virginia Militia
       4th Battalion Virginia Heavy Artillery
       Armistead's Mathews (Virginia) Battery

CENTER: Maj. Gen. James Longstreet

A. P. Hill's Brigade: Brig. Gen. A. P. Hill
    1st Virginia   11th Virginia
    7th Virginia   17th Virginia
       Rogers's Loudoun (Virginia) Battery
R. H. Anderson's Brigade: Brig. Gen. Richard H. Anderson
    5th South Carolina   4th South Carolina Battalion
    6th South Carolina   St. Paul's (Louisiana) Foot Rifles
    Palmetto (South Carolina) Sharpshooters
       Stribling's Fauquier (Virginia) Battery
Pickett's Brigade: Brig. Gen. George E. Pickett
    8th Virginia   19th Virginia
    18th Virginia   28th Virginia
       Dearing's Lynchburg (Virginia) Battery

Wilcox's Brigade: Brig. Gen. Cadmus M. Wilcox
- 9th Alabama
- 11th Alabama
- 10th Alabama
- 19th Mississippi
  - Stanard's Richmond Howitzers, 3rd Co.

Colston's Brigade: Brig. Gen. Raleigh E. Colston
- 3rd Virginia
- 14th North Carolina
- 13th North Carolina
  - Maurin's Donaldsonville (Louisiana) Battery

Pryor's Brigade: Brig. Gen. Roger A. Pryor
- 8th Alabama
- 14th Louisiana
- 14th Alabama
  - Macon's Richmond Fayette (Virginia) Battery

RIGHT WING: Maj. Gen. John B. Magruder

McLaws's Division: Brig. Gen. Lafayette McLaws
Semmes's Brigade: Brig. Gen. Paul J. Semmes
- 5th Louisiana
- 15th Virginia
- 10th Louisiana
- Noland's Virginia Battalion
- 10th Georgia
- 1st Louisiana Btn. (Dreux)
  - Garrett's Williamsburg (Virginia) Battery
  - Young's Halifax (Virginia) Battery

Griffith's Brigade: Brig. Gen. Richard Griffith
- 13th Mississippi
- 1st Louisiana Zouave Btn.
- 18th Mississippi
- (Coppens)
- 21st Mississippi
  - McCarthy's Richmond Howitzers, 1st Co.

Kershaw's Brigade: Brig. Gen. Joseph B. Kershaw
- 2nd South Carolina
- 8th South Carolina
- 3rd South Carolina
- Gracie's Alabama Battalion
- 7th South Carolina
  - Kemper's Alexandria (Virginia) Battery

Cobb's Brigade: Brig. Gen. Howell Cobb
- 16th Georgia
- 2nd Louisiana
- 24th Georgia
- 17th Mississippi
- Cobb's Georgia Legion
- 15th North Carolina
  - Page's Morris Louisa (Virginia) Battery

Artillery: Col. H. C. Cabell
- Cosnahan's Peninsula (Virginia) Battery
- Manly's North Carolina Battery
- Read's Pulaski (Georgia) Battery
- Sands's Henrico (Virginia) Battery

D. R. Jones's Division: Brig. Gen. David R. Jones
   Toombs's Brigade: Brig. Gen. Robert Toombs

1st Georgia Regulars	17th Georgia
2nd Georgia	20th Georgia
15th Georgia	

   G. T. Anderson's Brigade: Col. George T. Anderson

7th Georgia	11th Georgia
8th Georgia	1st Kentucky
9th Georgia	

RESERVE: Maj. Gen. Gustavus W. Smith

Hood's Brigade: Brig. Gen. John B. Hood

18th Georgia	4th Texas
1st Texas	5th Texas

Hampton's Brigade: Col. Wade Hampton

14th Georgia	16th North Carolina
19th Georgia	Hampton's South Carolina Legion

   Moody's Madison (Louisiana) Battery

Whiting's Brigade: Brig. Gen. W. H. C. Whiting

4th Alabama	11th Mississippi
2nd Mississippi	6th North Carolina

   Balthis's Staunton (Virginia) Battery
   Reilly's Rowan (North Carolina) Battery

S. R. Anderson's Brigade (attached): Brig. Gen. Samuel R. Anderson

1st Tennessee	14th Tennessee
7th Tennessee	

   Braxton's Fredericksburg (Virginia) Battery

Pettigrew's Brigade (attached): Brig. Gen. James J. Pettigrew

2nd Arkansas Battalion	22nd North Carolina
35th Georgia	47th Virginia

   Andrews's 1st Maryland Battery

Ewell's Command (Williamsburg): Brig. Gen. Benjamin S. Ewell

17th Virginia, 1 co.	68th Virginia Militia
32nd Virginia, 1 co.	115th Virginia Militia
52nd Virginia Militia	

Carter's Command (Jamestown): Col. Hill Carter
   Allen's 10th Battalion Virginia Heavy Artillery
   Rambaut's Independent Company, Virginia Heavy Artillery
   Jordan's Bedford (Virginia) Battery

Cavalry Brigade: Brig. Gen. J. E. B. Stuart

1st Virginia	Jeff Davis Mississippi Legion
3rd Virginia	Wise's Virginia Legion
4th Virginia	

   Stuart Horse Artillery

Artillery Reserve: Brig. Gen. William N. Pendleton
    Pendleton's Corps
        Brown's Richmond Howitzers, 2nd Co.
        Nelson's Hanover (Virginia) Battery
        Southall's Albemarle (Virginia) Battery
        Carleton's Troup (Georgia) Battery
        Richardson's James City (Virginia) Battery
        C. L. Smith's Hampton (Virginia) Battery
        Page's Magruder (Virginia) Battery
    Walton's Corps: Col. James B. Walton
        Washington (Louisiana) Artillery Battalion, 1st, 2nd, 3rd, 4th Co.'s

APPENDIX II

The Armies at Seven Pines

···

Army of the Potomac
Maj. Gen. George B. McClellan

SECOND CORPS: Brig. Gen. Edwin V. Sumner

First Division: Brig. Gen. Israel B. Richardson
  First Brigade: Brig. Gen. Oliver O. Howard (w)
           Col. Thomas J. Parker

5th New Hampshire	64th New York
61st New York	81st Pennsylvania

  Second Brigade: Brig. Gen. Thomas F. Meagher

63rd New York	88th New York
69th New York	

  Third Brigade: Brig. Gen. William H. French

52nd New York	66th New York
57th New York	53rd Pennsylvania

  Artillery: Capt. George W. Hazzard

1st New York Light, Battery B	4th United States, Battery A-C
1st New York Light, Battery G	

  Cavalry: 6th New York, Co. D

Second Division: Brig. Gen. John Sedgwick
  First Brigade: Brig. Gen. Willis A. Gorman
    15th Massachusetts (1st Co. Massachusetts Sharpshooters, attached)
    1st Minnesota (2nd Co. Minnesota Sharpshooters, attached)

34th New York	82nd New York

  Second Brigade: Brig. Gen. William W. Burns

69th Pennsylvania	72nd Pennsylvania
71st Pennsylvania	106th Pennsylvania

  Third Brigade: Brig. Gen. N. J. T. Dana

19th Massachusetts	7th Michigan
20th Massachusetts	42nd New York

Artillery: Col. Charles H. Tompkins
  1st Rhode Island Light, Battery A
  1st Rhode Island Light, Battery B
  1st Rhode Island Light, Battery G
  1st United States, Battery I
Cavalry: 6th New York, Co. K

THIRD CORPS: Brig. Gen. Samuel P. Heintzelman
(jointly commanding Third and Fourth Corps)

Second Division: Brig. Gen. Joseph Hooker
  First Brigade: Brig. Gen. Cuvier Grover

2nd New Hampshire	11th Massachusetts
1st Massachusetts	26th Pennsylvania

  Second Brigade: Brig. Gen. Daniel E. Sickles

70th New York	73rd New York
71st New York	74th New York
72nd New York	

  Third Brigade: Brig. Gen. Francis E. Patterson
          Col. Samuel H. Starr

5th New Jersey	7th New Jersey
6th New Jersey	8th New Jersey

  Artillery: Maj. Charles S. Wainwright

1st New York Light, Battery D	4th New York Independent Light
1st United States, Battery H	6th New York Independent Light

Third Division: Brig. Gen. Philip Kearny
  First Brigade: Brig. Gen. Charles D. Jameson

57th Pennsylvania	105th Pennsylvania
63rd Pennsylvania	87th New York

  Second Brigade: Brig. Gen. David B. Birney
          Col. J. H. Hobart Ward

38th New York	3rd Maine
40th New York	4th Maine

  Third Brigade: Brig. Gen. Hiram G. Berry

2nd Michigan	5th Michigan
3rd Michigan	37th New York

  Artillery: Capt. James Thompson

New Jersey Light, Battery B	2nd United States, Battery G
1st Rhode Island Light, Battery E	

Corps Cavalry: Col. William W. Averell
  3rd Pennsylvania

FOURTH CORPS: Brig. Gen. Erasmus D. Keyes

First Division: Brig. Gen. Darius N. Couch
  First Brigade: Brig. Gen. John J. Peck

55th New York	93rd Pennsylvania
62nd New York	102nd Pennsylvania

  Second Brigade: Brig. Gen. John J. Abercrombie

65th New York	31st Pennsylvania
67th New York	61st Pennsylvania
23rd Pennsylvania	

  Third Brigade: Brig. Gen. Charles Devens (w)
                  Col. Charles H. Innes

7th Massachusetts	36th New York
10th Massachusetts	

  Artillery: Maj. Robert M. West
    1st Pennsylvania Light, Battery C
    1st Pennsylvania Light, Battery D
    1st Pennsylvania Light, Battery E
    1st Pennsylvania Light, Battery H
  Cavalry: 6th New York, Co. F

Second Division: Brig. Gen. Silas Casey
  First Brigade: Brig. Gen. Henry M. Naglee

52nd Pennsylvania	100th New York
104th Pennsylvania	11th Maine
56th New York	

  Second Brigade: Brig. Gen. Henry W. Wessells

85th Pennsylvania	103rd Pennsylvania
101st Pennsylvania	96th New York

  Third Brigade: Brig. Gen. Innis N. Palmer

81st New York	92nd New York
85th New York	98th New York

  Artillery: Col. Guilford D. Bailey (k)
          Maj. D. H. Van Valkenburgh (k)
          Capt. Peter C. Regan

1st New York Light, Battery A	7th New York Independent Light
1st New York Light, Battery H	8th New York Independent Light

  Cavalry: 6th New York, Co. H
Corps Cavalry: Col. David McM. Gregg
  8th Pennsylvania

FIFTH CORPS: Brig. Gen. Fitz John Porter

First Division: Brig. Gen. George W. Morell
  First Brigade: Brig. Gen. John H. Martindale
    2nd Maine   13th New York
    18th Massachusetts   25th New York
    22nd Massachusetts (2nd Co. Massachusetts Sharpshooters, attached)
  Second Brigade: Col. James McQuade
    14th New York   9th Massachusetts
    4th Michigan   62nd Pennsylvania
  Third Brigade: Brig. Gen. Daniel Butterfield
    16th Michigan (Brady's Co. Michigan Sharpshooters, attached)
    12th New York   44th New York
    17th New York   83rd Pennsylvania
  Artillery: Capt. Charles Griffin
    Massachusetts Light, Battery C
    Massachusetts Light, Battery E
    1st Rhode Island Light, Battery C
    5th United States, Battery D
  Sharpshooters: Col. Hiram Berdan
    1st United States Sharpshooters
Second Division: Brig. Gen. George Sykes
  First Brigade: Col. Robert C. Buchanan
    3rd United States   12th United States
    4th United States   14th United States
  Second Brigade: Lt. Col. William Chapman
    2nd United States   11th United States
    6th United States   17th United States
    10th United States
  Third Brigade: Col. Gouverneur K. Warren
    5th New York   1st Connecticut Heavy Art. (inf.)
  Artillery: Capt. Stephen H. Weed
    3rd United States, Battery L-M
    5th United States, Battery I
Artillery Reserve: Col. Henry J. Hunt
  First Brigade: Lt. Col. William Hays
    2nd United States, Battery M   3rd United States, Battery C-G
  Second Brigade: Lt. Col. George W. Getty
    1st United States, Battery E   5th United States, Battery A
    1st United States, Battery G-K   5th United States, Battery K
    4th United States, Battery G

Third Brigade: Maj. Albert Arndt
    1st Btn. New York, Battery A   1st Btn. New York, Battery C
    1st Btn. New York, Battery B   1st Btn. New York, Battery D
Fourth Brigade: Capt. J. Howard Carlisle
    2nd United States, Battery E   4th United States, Battery K
    3rd United States, Battery F-K

SIXTH CORPS: Brig. Gen. William B. Franklin

First Division: Brig. Gen. Henry W. Slocum
  First Brigade: Brig. Gen. George W. Taylor
    1st New Jersey   3rd New Jersey
    2nd New Jersey   4th New Jersey
  Second Brigade: Col. Joseph J. Bartlett
    16th New York   5th Maine
    27th New York   96th Pennsylvania
  Third Brigade: Brig. Gen. John Newton
    18th New York   32nd New York
    31st New York   95th Pennsylvania
  Artillery: Capt. Edward R. Platt
    Massachusetts Light, Battery A   2nd United States, Battery D
    New Jersey Light, Battery A
Second Division: Brig. Gen. William F. Smith
  First Brigade: Brig. Gen. Winfield S. Hancock
    5th Wisconsin   43rd New York
    6th Maine   49th Pennsylvania
  Second Brigade: Brig. Gen. W. T. H. Brooks
    2nd Vermont   5th Vermont
    3rd Vermont   6th Vermont
    4th Vermont
  Third Brigade: Brig. Gen. John W. Davidson
    7th Maine   49th New York
    33rd New York   77th New York
  Artillery: Capt. Romeyn B. Ayres
    1st New York Light, Battery E   5th United States, Battery F
    1st New York Independent Light
    3rd New York Independent Light
  Cavalry: 5th Pennsylvania, 2 co.'s
  Corps Cavalry: 1st New York

RESERVE

Cavalry Reserve: Brig. Gen. Philip St. George Cooke
    First Brigade: Brig. Gen. William H. Emory
        5th United States   6th Pennsylvania
        6th United States
    Second Brigade: Col. George A. H. Blake
        1st United States   8th Pennsylvania
    Advance Guard: Brig. Gen. George Stoneman
        2nd Rhode Island   2nd United States, Battery A
        98th Pennsylvania   2nd United States, Battery B-L
        8th Illinois Cavalry
Engineer Troops
    United States Engineer Battalion: Capt. James C. Duane
        Companies A, B, C
    Volunteer Engineer Brigade: Brig. Gen. Daniel P. Woodbury
        15th New York   50th New York
White House Command: Lt. Col. Rufus Ingalls
        93rd New York, 6 co.'s   1st New York Light, Battery F
        11th Pennsylvania Cavalry, 5 co.'s
General Headquarters
        2nd United States Cavalry   8th United States Infantry, 2 co.'s
        4th United States Cavalry, 2 co.'s   93rd New York, 4 co.'s
        Oneida (New York) Cavalry   Sturgis Rifles (Illinois)
        McClellan Dragoons (Illinois)

Army of Northern Virginia
Gen. Joseph E. Johnston (w)
Maj. Gen. Gustavus W. Smith
Gen. Robert E. Lee

LEFT WING: Maj. Gen. Gustavus W. Smith

Smith's Division: Brig. Gen. W. H. C. Whiting
    Hood's Brigade: Brig. Gen. John B. Hood
        18th Georgia   4th Texas
        1st Texas   5th Texas
    Hampton's Brigade: Brig. Gen. Wade Hampton (w)
        14th Georgia   16th North Carolina
        19th Georgia   Hampton's South Carolina Legion
            Moody's Madison (Louisiana) Battery

Whiting's Brigade: Col. Evander M. Law
    4th Alabama   11th Mississippi
    2nd Mississippi   6th North Carolina
        Balthis's Staunton (Virginia) Battery
        Reilly's Rowan (North Carolina) Battery
Pettigrew's Brigade: Brig. Gen. James J. Pettigrew (w, c)
    2nd Arkansas Battalion   22nd North Carolina
    35th Georgia   47th Virginia
        Andrews's 1st Maryland Battery
Hatton's Brigade: Gen. Robert Hatton (k)
    1st Tennessee   14th Tennessee
    7th Tennessee
        Braxton's Fredericksburg (Virginia) Battery
A. P. Hill's Division: Maj. Gen. A. P. Hill
    Field's Brigade: Brig. Gen. Charles W. Field
        40th Virginia   22nd Virginia Battalion
        55th Virginia
            Pegram's Purcell (Virginia) Battery
    Gregg's Brigade: Brig. Gen. Maxcy Gregg
        1st South Carolina   13th South Carolina
        1st South Carolina Rifles   14th South Carolina
        12th South Carolina
            Davidson's Letcher (Virginia) Battery
    J. R. Anderson's Brigade: Brig. Gen. Joseph R. Anderson
        34th North Carolina   49th Georgia
        38th North Carolina   3rd Louisiana Battalion
        45th Georgia
            McIntosh's Pee Dee (South Carolina) Battery
            Crenshaw's Virginia Battery
    Branch's Brigade: Brig. Gen. Lawrence O'B. Branch
        7th North Carolina   28th North Carolina
        12th North Carolina   33rd North Carolina
        18th North Carolina   37th North Carolina
            Branch's North Carolina Battery
            Johnson's Richmond Battery

            RIGHT WING: Maj. Gen. James Longstreet

Longstreet's Division: Brig. Gen. Richard H. Anderson
    Kemper's Brigade: Col. James L. Kemper
        1st Virginia   11th Virginia
        7th Virginia   17th Virginia
            Roger's Loudoun (Virginia) Battery

R. H. Anderson's Brigade: Col. Micah Jenkins

5th South Carolina	4th South Carolina Battalion
6th South Carolina	

Palmetto (South Carolina) Sharpshooters
1st Louisiana Zouave Btn. (Coppens) & St. Paul's Foot Rifles
    Stribling's Fauquier (Virginia) Battery

Pickett's Brigade: Brig. Gen. George E. Pickett

8th Virginia	19th Virginia
18th Virginia	28th Virginia

    Dearing's Lynchburg (Virginia) Battery

Wilcox's Brigade: Brig. Gen. Cadmus M. Wilcox

9th Alabama	11th Alabama
10th Alabama	19th Mississippi

    Stanard's Richmond Howitzers, 3rd Co.

Colston's Brigade: Brig. Gen. Raleigh E. Colston

3rd Virginia	14th North Carolina
13th North Carolina	

Pryor's Brigade: Brig. Gen. Roger A. Pryor

8th Alabama	14th Louisiana
14th Alabama	32nd Virginia

    Macon's Richmond Fayette (Virginia) Battery

Artillery
    Maurin's Donaldsonville (Louisiana) Battery
    Brown's Richmond Howitzers, 2nd Co.

D. H. Hill's Division: Maj. Gen. D. H. Hill

Rodes's Brigade: Brig. Gen. Robert E. Rodes (w)
               Col. John B. Gordon

5th Alabama	12th Mississippi
6th Alabama	4th Virginia Heavy Art. (inf.)
12th Alabama	

    Carter's King William (Virginia) Battery

Featherston's Brigade: Col. George B. Anderson

27th Georgia	4th North Carolina
28th Georgia	49th Virginia

Garland's Brigade: Brig. Gen. Samuel Garland, Jr.

5th North Carolina	38th Virginia
23rd North Carolina	2nd Florida
24th Virginia	2nd Mississippi Battalion

    Bondurant's Jeff Davis Alabama Battery

Rains's Brigade: Brig. Gen. Gabriel J. Rains

13th Alabama	6th Georgia
26th Alabama	23rd Georgia

    Nelson's Hanover (Virginia) Battery

Wise's Brigade (attached): Brig. Gen. Henry A. Wise
    26th Virginia   47th Virginia
       Armistead's Mathews (Virginia) Battery
       French's Giles (Virginia) Battery
Artillery
       Hardaway's Alabama Battery
       Rhett's Brooks (South Carolina) Battery
Huger's Division: Maj. Gen. Benjamin Huger
    Mahone's Brigade: Brig. Gen. William Mahone
       3rd Alabama   41st Virginia
       12th Virginia
          Grimes's Portsmouth (Virginia) Battery
    Blanchard's Brigade: Brig. Gen. A. G. Blanchard
       3rd Georgia   22nd Georgia
       4th Georgia   1st Louisiana
          Huger's Norfolk (Virginia) Battery
    Armistead's Brigade: Brig. Gen. Lewis A. Armistead
       9th Virginia   53rd Virginia
       14th Virginia   5th Virginia Battalion
          Turner's Virginia Battery

RESERVE: Maj. Gen. John B. Magruder

McLaws's Division: Brig. Gen. Lafayette McLaws
    Semmes's Brigade: Brig. Gen. Paul J. Semmes
       5th Louisiana   15th Virginia
       10th Louisiana   Noland's Virginia Battalion
       10th Georgia
          Garrett's Williamsburg (Virginia) Battery
          Young's Halifax (Virginia) Battery
    Griffith's Brigade: Brig. Gen. Richard Griffith
       13th Mississippi   21st Mississippi
       18th Mississippi
          McCarthy's Richmond Howitzers, 1st Co.
    Kershaw's Brigade: Brig. Gen. Joseph B. Kershaw
       2nd South Carolina   8th South Carolina
       3rd South Carolina   Gracie's Alabama Battalion
       7th South Carolina
          Kemper's Alexandria (Virginia) Battery
    Cobb's Brigade: Brig. Gen. Howell Cobb
       16th Georgia   2nd Louisiana
       24th Georgia   17th Mississippi
       Cobb's Georgia Legion   15th North Carolina
          Page's Morris Louisa (Virginia) Battery

D. R. Jones's Division: Brig. Gen. David R. Jones
   Toombs's Brigade: Brig. Gen. Robert Toombs

1st Georgia Regulars	17th Georgia
2nd Georgia	20th Georgia
15th Georgia	38th Georgia

   G. T. Anderson's Brigade: Col. George T. Anderson

7th Georgia	11th Georgia
8th Georgia	1st Kentucky
9th Georgia	

   Artillery: Col. H. C. Cabell
       Cosnahan's Peninsula (Virginia) Battery
       Manly's North Carolina Battery
       Read's Pulaski (Georgia) Battery
       Sands's Henrico (Virginia) Battery
Cavalry Brigade: Brig. Gen. J. E. B. Stuart

1st Virginia	Jeff Davis Mississippi Legion
3rd Virginia	Hampton's S. C. Legion Cavalry
4th Virginia	Wise's Virginia Legion
9th Virginia	

Cobb's Georgia Legion Cavalry
Stuart Horse Artillary
Artillery Reserve: Brig. Gen. William N. Pendleton
   Pendleton's Corps
       Southall's Albemarle (Virginia) Battery
       Carleton's Troup (Georgia) Battery
       Richardson's James City (Virginia) Battery
       C. L. Smith's Hampton (Virginia) Battery
       Page's Magruder (Virginia) Battery
       Jordan's Bedford (Virginia) Battery
       Clark's Long Island (Virginia) Battery
       Peyton's Orange (Virginia) Battery
       Kirkpatrick's Amherst (Virginia) Battery
   Walton's Corps: Col. James B. Walton
       Washington (Louisiana) Artillery Battalion, 1st, 2nd, 3rd, 4th Co.'s
       Chapman's Dixie (Virginia) Battery

The Armies in the Seven Days

....

Army of the Potomac
Maj. Gen. George B. McClellan

SECOND CORPS: Brig. Gen. Edwin V. Sumner

First Division: Brig. Gen. Israel B. Richardson
First Brigade: Brig. Gen. John C. Caldwell
5th New Hampshire   61st New York
7th New York   81st Pennsylvania
Second Brigade: Brig. Gen. Thomas F. Meagher
               Col. Robert Nugent
63rd New York   88th New York
69th New York   29th Massachusetts
Third Brigade: Brig. Gen. William H. French
52nd New York   66th New York
57th New York   53rd Pennsylvania
64th New York   2nd Delaware
Artillery: Capt. George W. Hazzard (mw)
1st New York Light, Battery B   4th United States, Battery A-C
Cavalry: 6th New York, Co. D
Second Division: Brig. Gen. John Sedgwick
First Brigade: Col. Alfred Sully
15th Massachusetts (1st Co. Massachusetts Sharpshooters, attached)
1st Minnesota (2nd Co. Minnesota Sharpshooters, attached)
34th New York   82nd New York
Second Brigade: Brig. Gen. William W. Burns (w)
69th Pennsylvania   72nd Pennsylvania
71st Pennsylvania   106th Pennsylvania
Third Brigade: Brig. Gen. N. J. T. Dana
19th Massachusetts   7th Michigan
20th Massachusetts   42nd New York

Artillery: Col. Charles H. Tompkins
    1st Rhode Island Light, Battery A
    1st United States, Battery I
Corps Artillery Reserve
    1st New York Light, Battery G   1st Rhode Island Light, Battery G
    1st Rhode Island Light, Battery B

THIRD CORPS: Brig. Gen. Samuel P. Heintzelman

Second Division: Brig. Gen. Joseph Hooker
  First Brigade: Brig. Gen. Cuvier Grover
    2nd New Hampshire   16th Massachusetts
    1st Massachusetts   26th Pennsylvania
    11th Massachusetts
  Second Brigade: Brig. Gen. Daniel E. Sickles
    70th New York   73rd New York
    71st New York   74th New York
    72nd New York
  Third Brigade: Col. Joseph B. Carr
    5th New Jersey   8th New Jersey
    6th New Jersey   2nd New York
    7th New Jersey
  Artillery: Lt. Col. Charles S. Wainwright
    1st New York Light, Battery D   4th New York Independent Light
    1st United States, Battery H
Third Division: Brig. Gen. Philip Kearny
  First Brigade: Brig. Gen. John C. Robinson
    57th Pennsylvania   87th New York
    63rd Pennsylvania   20th Indiana
    105th Pennsylvania
  Second Brigade: Brig. Gen. David B. Birney
    38th New York   3rd Maine
    40th New York   4th Maine
    101st New York
  Third Brigade: Brig. Gen. Hiram G. Berry
    2nd Michigan   1st New York
    3rd Michigan   37th New York
    5th Michigan
  Artillery: Capt. James Thompson
    1st Rhode Island Light, Battery E
    2nd United States, Battery G
  Corps Cavalry: Col. William W. Averell
    3rd Pennsylvania

Corps Artillery Reserve: Capt. Gustavus A. De Russy
New Jersey Light, Battery B   4th United States, Battery K
6th New York Independent Light

FOURTH CORPS: Brig. Gen. Erasmus D. Keyes

First Division: Brig. Gen. Darius N. Couch
First Brigade: Brig. Gen. Albion P. Howe
55th New York   98th Pennsylvania
62nd New York   102nd Pennsylvania
93rd Pennsylvania
Second Brigade: Brig. Gen. John J. Abercrombie
65th New York   31st Pennsylvania
67th New York   61st Pennsylvania
23rd Pennsylvania
Third Brigade: Brig. Gen. Innis N. Palmer
7th Massachusetts   2nd Rhode Island
10th Massachusetts   36th New York
Artillery
1st Pennsylvania Light, Battery C
1st Pennsylvania Light, Battery D
Cavalry: 6th New York, Co. F
Second Division: Brig. Gen. John J. Peck
First Brigade: Brig. Gen. Henry M. Naglee
52nd Pennsylvania   100th New York
104th Pennsylvania   11th Maine
56th New York
Second Brigade: Brig. Gen. Henry W. Wessells
85th Pennsylvania   85th New York
101st Pennsylvania   92nd New York
103rd Pennsylvania   96th New York
81st New York   98th New York
Artillery
1st New York Light, Battery H   7th New York Independent Light
Cavalry: 6th New York, Co. H
Corps Cavalry: Col. David McM. Gregg
8th Pennsylvania
Corps Artillery Reserve: Maj. Robert M. West
1st Pennsylvania Light, Battery E
1st Pennsylvania Light, Battery H
8th New York Independent Light
5th United States, Battery M

FIFTH CORPS: Brig. Gen. Fitz John Porter

First Division: Brig. Gen. George W. Morell
  First Brigade: Brig. Gen. John H. Martindale
      2nd Maine   13th New York
      1st Michigan   25th New York
      22nd Massachusetts (2nd Co. Massachusetts Sharpshooters, attached)
  Second Brigade: Brig. Gen. Charles Griffin
      14th New York   9th Massachusetts
      4th Michigan   62nd Pennsylvania
  Third Brigade: Brig. Gen. Daniel Butterfield
      16th Michigan (Brady's Co. Michigan Sharpshooters, attached)
      12th New York   83rd Pennsylvania
      44th New York
  Artillery: Capt. William B. Weeden
      Massachusetts Light, Battery C
      Massachusetts Light, Battery E
      1st Rhode Island Light, Battery C
      5th United States, Battery D
  Sharpshooters: Col. Hiram Berdan
      1st United States Sharpshooters
Second Division: Brig. Gen. George Sykes
  First Brigade: Col. Robert C. Buchanan
      3rd United States   12th United States
      4th United States   14th United States
  Second Brigade: Lt. Col. William Chapman
               Maj. Charles S. Lovell
      2nd United States   11th United States
      6th United States   17th United States
      10th United States
  Third Brigade: Col. Gouverneur K. Warren
      5th New York   10th New York
  Artillery: Capt. Stephen H. Weed
      3rd United States, Battery L-M
      5th United States, Battery I
Third Division (Pennsylvania Reserves): Brig. Gen. George A. McCall (c)
                           Brig. Gen. Truman Seymour
  First Brigade: Brig. Gen. John F. Reynolds (c)
             Col. Seneca G. Simmons (k)
             Col. R. Biddle Roberts
      1st Pennsylvania Res.   8th Pennsylvania Res.
      2nd Pennsylvania Res.   13th Pennsylvania Res.
      5th Pennsylvania Res.

Second Brigade: Brig. Gen. George G. Meade (w)
    Col. Albert L. Magilton
 3rd Pennsylvania Res.   7th Pennsylvania Res.
 4th Pennsylvania Res.   11th Pennsylvania Res.
Third Brigade: Brig. Gen. Truman Seymour
    Col. C. Feger Jackson
 9th Pennsylvania Res.   12th Pennsylvania Res.
 10th Pennsylvania Res.
Artillery
 1st Pennsylvania Light, Battery A
 1st Pennsylvania Light, Battery B
 1st Pennsylvania Light, Battery G
 5th United States, Battery C
Cavalry: Col. James H. Childs
 4th Pennsylvania, 6 co.'s
Corps Cavalry: Col. John F. Farnsworth
 8th Illinois
Artillery Reserve: Col. Henry J. Hunt
 First Brigade: Lt. Col. William Hays
  2nd United States, Battery A 2nd United States, Battery M
  2nd United States, Battery B-L
 Second Brigade: Lt. Col. George W. Getty
  1st United States, Battery E 5th United States, Battery A
  1st United States, Battery G-K 5th United States, Battery K
  4th United States, Battery G
 Third Brigade: Maj. Albert Arndt
  1st Btn. New York, Battery A 1st Btn. New York, Battery C
  1st Btn. New York, Battery B 1st Btn. New York, Battery D
 Fourth Brigade: Maj. E. R. Petherbridge
  Maryland Light, Battery A Maryland Light, Battery B
 Fifth Brigade: Capt. J. Howard Carlisle
  2nd United States, Battery E 3rd United States, Battery F-K
 Siege Train: Col. Robert O. Tyler
  1st Connecticut Heavy Artillery

SIXTH CORPS: Brig. Gen. William B. Franklin

First Division: Brig. Gen. Henry W. Slocum
 First Brigade: Brig. Gen. George W. Taylor
  1st New Jersey   3rd New Jersey
  2nd New Jersey   4th New Jersey
 Second Brigade: Col. Joseph J. Bartlett
  16th New York   5th Maine
  27th New York   96th Pennsylvania

Third Brigade: Brig. Gen. John Newton

18th New York	32nd New York
31st New York	95th Pennsylvania

Artillery: Capt. Edward R. Platt

Massachusetts Light, Battery A	New Jersey Light, Battery A
2nd United States, Battery D	

Second Division: Brig. Gen. William F. Smith

First Brigade: Brig. Gen. Winfield S. Hancock

5th Wisconsin	43rd New York
6th Maine	49th Pennsylvania

Second Brigade: Brig. Gen. W. T. H. Brooks (w)

2nd Vermont	5th Vermont
3rd Vermont	6th Vermont
4th Vermont	

Third Brigade: Brig. Gen. John W. Davidson

7th Maine	49th New York
20th New York	77th New York
33rd New York	

Artillery: Capt. Romeyn B. Ayres

1st New York Light, Battery E	5th United States, Battery F
1st New York Independent Light	
3rd New York Independent Light	

Cavalry: 5th Pennsylvania, 2 co.'s

Corps Cavalry: 1st New York

Reserve

Cavalry Reserve: Brig. Gen. Philip St. George Cooke

First Brigade: Brig. Gen. William H. Emory

5th United States, 5 co.'s	6th Pennsylvania

Second Brigade: Col. George A. H. Blake

1st United States	4th Pennsylvania, 2 co.'s

Advance Guard: Brig. Gen. George Stoneman

17th New York	6th United States Cavalry
18th Massachusetts	3rd United States, Battery C-G
5th United States Cavalry, 5 co.'s	

Engineer Troops

United States Engineer Battalion: Capt. James C. Duane

Companies A, B, C

Volunteer Engineer Brigade: Brig. Gen. Daniel P. Woodbury

15th New York	50th New York

White House Command: Brig. Gen. Silas Casey

6th Pennsylvania Res.	11th Pennsylvania Cavalry, 5 co.'s
93rd New York, 6 co.'s	1st New York Light, Battery F
4th Pennsylvania Cavalry, 2 co.'s	

General Headquarters

2nd United States Cavalry	8th United States Infantry, 2 co.'s
4th United States Cavalry, 2 co.'s	93rd New York, 4 co.'s
Oneida (New York) Cavalry	Sturgis Rifles (Illinois)
McClellan Dragoons (Illinois)	

Army of Northern Virginia
Gen. Robert E. Lee

JACKSON'S COMMAND: Maj. Gen. Thomas J. Jackson

Cavalry: 2nd Virginia
Jackson's Division: Brig. Gen. Charles S. Winder
  Winder's Brigade: Brig. Gen. Charles S. Winder

2nd Virginia	27th Virginia
4th Virginia	33rd Virginia
5th Virginia	

    Carpenter's Alleghany (Virginia) Battery
    Poague's 1st Rockbridge (Virginia) Battery
  J. R. Jones's Brigade: Brig. Gen. John R. Jones
                    Lt. Col. R. H. Cunningham, Jr.

21st Virginia	48th Virginia
42nd Virginia	1st Virginia Irish Battalion

    Cutshaw's Jackson (Virginia) Battery
    Caskie's Hampden (Virginia) Battery
  Fulkerson's Brigade: Col. S. V. Fulkerson (mw)
               Col. E. T. H. Warren
               Brig. Gen. Wade Hampton

10th Virginia	37th Virginia
23rd Virginia	

    Wooding's Danville (Virginia) Battery
  Lawton's Brigade: Brig. Gen. Alexander R. Lawton

13th Georgia	38th Georgia
26th Georgia	60th Georgia
31st Georgia	61st Georgia

Ewell's Division: Maj. Gen. Richard S. Ewell
  Elzey's Brigade: Brig. Gen. Arnold Elzey (w)
               Col. James A. Walker
               Brig. Gen. Jubal A. Early

12th Georgia	44th Virginia
13th Virginia	52nd Virginia
25th Virginia	58th Virginia
31st Virginia	

Trimble's Brigade: Brig. Gen. Isaac R. Trimble

15th Alabama	21st Georgia
21st North Carolina	16th Mississippi

    1st North Carolina Battalion Sharpshooters
        Courtney's Virginia Battery

Taylor's Brigade: Col. Isaac G. Seymour (k)
              Col. Leroy A. Stafford

6th Louisiana	8th Louisiana
7th Louisiana	9th Louisiana

    1st Louisiana Special Battalion (Wheat)
        Carrington's Charlottesville (Virginia) Battery

Maryland Line: Col. Bradley T. Johnson

1st Maryland	1st Maryland Cavalry, 1 co.

        Brockenborough's Baltimore Battery

Whiting's Division (attached): Brig. Gen. W. H. C. Whiting

  Hood's Brigade: Brig. Gen. John B. Hood

18th Georgia	5th Texas
1st Texas	Hampton's South Carolina Legion
4th Texas	

  Law's Brigade: Col. Evander M. Law

4th Alabama	11th Mississippi
2nd Mississippi	6th North Carolina

  Artillery

        Balthis's Staunton (Virginia) Battery
        Reilly's Rowan (North Carolina) Battery

D. H. Hill's Division (attached): Maj. Gen. D. H. Hill

  Rodes's Brigade: Brig. Gen. Robert E. Rodes
              Col. John B. Gordon

3rd Alabama	12th Alabama
5th Alabama	26th Alabama
6th Alabama	

        Carter's King William (Virginia) Battery

  G. B. Anderson's Brigade: Brig. Gen. George B. Anderson (w)
              Col. C. C. Tew

2nd North Carolina	14th North Carolina
4th North Carolina	30th North Carolina

        Hardaway's Alabama Battery

  Garland's Brigade: Brig. Gen. Samuel Garland, Jr.

5th North Carolina	20th North Carolina
12th North Carolina	23rd North Carolina
13th North Carolina	

        Bondurant's Jeff Davis Alabama Battery

Colquitt's Brigade: Col. Alfred H. Colquitt
    13th Alabama   27th Georgia
    6th Georgia   28th Georgia
    23rd Georgia
       Nelson's Hanover (Virginia) Battery
Ripley's Brigade: Brig. Gen. Roswell S. Ripley
    1st North Carolina   44th Georgia
    3rd North Carolina   48th Georgia
Jones's Artillery Battalion (attached): Maj. Hilary P. Jones
       Rhett's Brooks (South Carolina) Battery
       Clark's Long Island (Virginia) Battery
       Peyton's Orange (Virginia) Battery

HILL'S LIGHT DIVISION: Maj. Gen. A. P. Hill

Field's Brigade: Brig. Gen. Charles W. Field
    40th Virginia   60th Virginia
    47th Virginia   22nd Virginia Battalion
    55th Virginia
Gregg's Brigade: Brig. Gen. Maxcy Gregg
    1st South Carolina   13th South Carolina
    1st South Carolina Rifles   14th South Carolina
    12th South Carolina
J. R. Anderson's Brigade: Brig. Gen. Joseph R. Anderson (w)
                        Col. Edward L. Thomas
    14th Georgia   49th Georgia
    35th Georgia   3rd Louisiana Battalion
    45th Georgia
Branch's Brigade: Brig. Gen. Lawrence O'B. Branch
    7th North Carolina   33rd North Carolina
    18th North Carolina   37th North Carolina
    28th North Carolina
Archer's Brigade: Brig. Gen. James J. Archer
    1st Tennessee   19th Georgia
    7th Tennessee   5th Alabama Battalion
    14th Tennessee
Pender's Brigade: Brig. Gen. William D. Pender
    2nd Arkansas Battalion   34th North Carolina
    16th North Carolina   38th North Carolina
    22nd North Carolina

Artillery: Maj. R. Lindsay Walker
 Pegram's Purcell (Virginia) Battery
 McIntosh's Pee Dee (South Carolina) Battery
 Crenshaw's Virginia Battery
 Johnson's Richmond Battery
 Braxton's Fredericksburg (Virginia) Battery
 Andrews's 1st Maryland Battery
 Bachman's Charleston (South Carolina) German Battery

LONGSTREET'S DIVISION: Maj. Gen. James Longstreet

Kemper's Brigade: Brig. Gen. James L. Kemper

1st Virginia	17th Virginia
7th Virginia	24th Virginia
11th Virginia	

 Rogers's Loudoun (Virginia) Battery

R. H. Anderson's Brigade: Brig. Gen. Richard H. Anderson
         Col. Micah Jenkins

2nd South Carolina Rifles	6th South Carolina
5th South Carolina	4th South Carolina Battalion

 Palmetto (South Carolina) Sharpshooters

Pickett's Brigade: Brig. Gen. George E. Pickett (w)
     Col. Eppa Hunton
     Col. John B. Strange

8th Virginia	28th Virginia
18th Virginia	56th Virginia
19th Virginia	

Wilcox's Brigade: Brig. Gen. Cadmus M. Wilcox

8th Alabama	10th Alabama
9th Alabama	11th Alabama

 Anderson's Thomas (Virginia) Battery

Pryor's Brigade: Brig. Gen. Roger A. Pryor

14th Alabama	14th Louisiana
2nd Florida	3rd Virginia

 1st Louisiana Zouave Btn. (Coppens) & St. Paul's Foot Rifles
 Maurin's Donaldsonville (Louisiana) Battery

Featherston's Brigade: Brig. Gen. Winfield S. Featherston (w)

12th Mississippi	2nd Mississippi Battalion
19th Mississippi	

 Stanard's Richmond Howitzers, 3rd Co.

Artillery: Col. James B. Walton
 Washington (Louisiana) Artillery Battalion, 1st, 2nd, 3rd, 4th Co.'s
 Chapman's Dixie (Virginia) Battery
 Dearing's Lynchburg (Virginia) Battery

MAGRUDER'S COMMAND: Maj. Gen. John B. Magruder

McLaws's Division: Maj. Gen. Lafayette McLaws
  Semmes's Brigade: Brig. Gen. Paul J. Semmes

5th Louisiana	53rd Georgia
10th Louisiana	15th Virginia
10th Georgia	32nd Virginia

    Manly's North Carolina Battery
  Kershaw's Brigade: Brig. Gen. Joseph B. Kershaw

2nd South Carolina	7th South Carolina
3rd South Carolina	8th South Carolina

    Kemper's Alexandria (Virginia) Battery

D. R. Jones's Division: Brig. Gen. David R. Jones
  Toombs's Brigade: Brig. Gen. Robert Toombs

2nd Georgia	17th Georgia
15th Georgia	20th Georgia

  G. T. Anderson's Brigade: Col. George T. Anderson

1st Georgia Regulars	9th Georgia
7th Georgia	11th Georgia
8th Georgia	

  Artillery: Maj. John J. Garnett
    Moody's Madison (Louisiana) Battery
    Brown's Wise (Virginia) Battery
    Hart's Washington (South Carolina) Battery
    Dabney's Virginia Battery
    Lane's Sumter (Georgia) Battalion, Battery E (attached)
    Woolfolk's Ashland (Virginia) Battery (attached)

Magruder's Division: Maj. Gen. John B. Magruder
  Griffith's Brigade: Brig. Gen. Richard Griffith (mw)
            Col. William Barksdale

13th Mississippi	18th Mississippi
17th Mississippi	21st Mississippi

    McCarthy's Richmond Howitzers, 1st Co.
  Cobb's Brigade: Brig. Gen. Howell Cobb

16th Georgia	2nd Louisiana
24th Georgia	15th North Carolina

    Cobb's Georgia Legion
    Carleton's Troup (Georgia) Battery
  Artillery: Col. Stephen D. Lee
    Read's Pulaski (Georgia) Battery
    Sands's Henrico (Virginia) Battery
    Jordan's Bedford (Virginia) Battery
    Richardson's James City (Virginia) Battery
    Page's Magruder (Virginia) Battery
    Kirkpatrick's Amherst (Virginia) Battery (attached)

HUGER'S DIVISION: Maj. Gen. Benjamin Huger

Mahone's Brigade: Brig. Gen. William Mahone
    6th Virginia   41st Virginia
    12th Virginia   49th Virginia
    16th Virginia
       Grimes's Portsmouth (Virginia) Battery
       Moorman's Lynchburg (Virginia) Beauregard Battery
Wright's Brigade: Brig. Gen. Ambrose R. Wright
    3rd Georgia   1st Louisiana
    4th Georgia   44th Alabama
    22nd Georgia
       Huger's Norfolk (Virginia) Battery
       Ross's Sumter (Georgia) Battalion, Battery A (attached)
Armistead's Brigade: Brig. Gen. Lewis A. Armistead
    9th Virginia   53rd Virginia
    14th Virginia   57th Virginia
    38th Virginia   5th Virginia Battalion
       Turner's Virginia Battery
       Stribling's Fauquier (Virginia) Battery
Ransom's Brigade (attached): Brig. Gen. Robert Ransom, Jr.
    24th North Carolina   35th North Carolina
    25th North Carolina   48th North Carolina (June 25–28)
    26th North Carolina   49th North Carolina

HOLMES'S DIVISION: Maj. Gen. Theophilus H. Holmes

Daniel's Brigade: Brig. Gen. Junius Daniel
    43rd North Carolina   50th North Carolina
    45th North Carolina   14th Virginia Cavalry Battalion
Walker's Brigade: Brig. Gen. John G. Walker
               Col. Van H. Manning
    3rd Arkansas   30th Virginia
    27th North Carolina   2nd Georgia Battalion
    46th North Carolina   Petersburg (Virginia) Cavalry
    48th North Carolina (June 29–July 1)
Wise's Brigade (attached): Brig. Gen. Henry A. Wise
    26th Virginia   4th Virginia Heavy Art. (inf.)
    46th Virginia
       Armistead's Mathews (Virginia) Battery
       French's Giles (Virginia) Battery
       Rives's 2nd Nelson (Virginia) Battery
       Andrews's Co. A, Virginia Heavy Artillery

Artillery: Col. James Deshler
    Branch's Petersburg (Virginia) Battery
    Brem's North Carolina Battery
    French's Stafford (Virginia) Battery
    Graham's Petersburg (Virginia) Battery
Cavalry Brigade: Brig. Gen. J. E. B. Stuart

1st Virginia	15th Virginia Battalion
3rd Virginia	1st North Carolina
4th Virginia	Cobb's Georgia Legion Cavalry
5th Virginia	Jeff Davis Mississippi Legion
9th Virginia	Hampton's S.C. Legion Cavalry
10th Virginia	Wise's Virginia Legion

    Stuart's Horse Artillery
Artillery Reserve: Brig. Gen. William N. Pendleton
  1st Virginia Artillery: Col. J. T. Brown
    Southall's Albemarle (Virginia) Battery
    Garrett's Williamsburg (Virginia) Battery
    Young's Halifax (Virginia) Battery
    Brown's Richmond Howitzers, 2nd Co.
    Macon's Richmond Fayette (Virginia) Battery
  Sumter (Georgia) Battalion: Lt. Col. A. S. Cutts
    Price's Battery B
    Blackshear's Battery D
    Hamilton's Georgia Regular Battery
  Richardson's Battalion: Maj. Charles Richardson
    Ancell's 2nd Fluvanna (Virginia) Battery
    Milledge's Georgia Battery
    Masters's Virginia Siege Battery (attached)
    Davidson's Letcher (Virginia) Battery (attached)
  Nelson's Battalion: Maj. William Nelson
    Page's Morris Louisa (Virginia) Battery
    Huckstep's 1st Fluvanna (Virginia) Battery

ACKNOWLEDGMENTS

....

Soldiers' diaries, letters, and memoirs constitute an essential element in this account of the Peninsula campaign, and I am greatly indebted to the curatorial staffs of the manuscript collections in which they were found.

Particular thanks are due Michael P. Musick, the National Archives; Margaret R. Goostray, Boston University Library; Linda McCurdy, William L. Perkins Library, Duke University; Barbara Cain and Kenrick N. Simpson, Division of Archives and History, North Carolina Department of Cultural Resources; John E. White, Southern Historical Collection, University of North Carolina; Barbara A. Filipac, John Hay Library, Brown University; Richard J. Sommers, U.S. Army Military History Institute; Susan Ravdin, Bowdoin College Library; Galen R. Wilson, William L. Clements Library, University of Michigan; Karen M. Mason, Michigan Historical Collections, Bentley Historical Library, University of Michigan; Charlotte Ray, Georgia Department of Archives and History; Ervin L. Jordan, Jr., Alderman Library, University of Virginia; Ann Alley, Tennessee State Library and Archives; Kathy Knox, Robert W. Woodruff Library, Emory University; and Harold B. Simpson, Hill College.

Also, Ellen R. Strong, Earl Gregg Swem Library, College of William and Mary; James M. Mahony, Dinand Library, College of the Holy Cross; Giuseppe Bisaccia, Boston Public Library; Judy Bolton, Hill Memorial Library, Louisiana State University; Rhonda Everson, Minnesota Historical Society; H. T. Holmes, Mississippi Department of Archives and History; Gregory Kendall-Curtis, Maine Historical Society; Debbie Tapley, New Hampshire Historical Society; William F. Hannah, Old Colony Historical Society; Linda A. Ries, Pennsylvania Historical and Museum Commission; Linda J. Long, Stanford University Library; Herbert J. Hartsook, South Caroliniana Library,

University of South Carolina; William H. Richter, Eugene C. Barker Texas History Center, University of Texas; Harold L. Miller, State Historical Society of Wisconsin; Laura H. Katz, Virginia Tech Library; and Corrine P. Hudgins, Museum of the Confederacy.

Edwin C. Fishel of Arlington, Virginia, furnished invaluable guidance in Civil War military intelligence. Mark Grimsley of Columbus, Ohio, kindly granted me access to his translation of the Comte de Paris journal. John Robinson of Chesterland, Ohio, let me see the E. O. Hicks diary, and Gloria Conklin, of Chappaqua, New York, the Brigham Buswell memoir. Generous in sharing information on the campaign were Herbert M. Schiller of Winston-Salem, North Carolina; William Marvel of South Conway, New Hampshire; William F. Howard of Albany, New York; Brian C. Pohanka of Alexandria, Virginia; Edward Maturniak of Allendale, New Jersey; Frederick W. Chesson of Waterbury, Connecticut; Lynne Roffino of Mesquite, Texas; William M. Ferraro of Brown University; Steven Smith of the University of Virginia; and Mary M. Ison, Library of Congress.

Betty L. Krimminger of Chapel Hill, North Carolina, and Paul Bernard of Ann Arbor, Michigan, provided invaluable research assistance.

NOTES

....

Works cited by author and short title in the Notes will be found in full citation in the Bibliography. The following abbreviations are used in the Notes:

CL   William L. Clements Library, University of Michigan
LC   Library of Congress
MHC   Michigan Historical Collections, Bentley Historical Library, University of Michigan
NA   National Archives
NOR   U.S. Naval War Records Office, *Official Records of the Union and Confederate Navies in the War of the Rebellion*, Series 1 unless otherwise noted
OR   U.S. War Department, *The War of the Rebellion: A Compilation of the Official Records of the Union and Confederate Armies*, Series 1 unless otherwise noted
SHC   Southern Historical Collection, University of North Carolina
USAMHI   United States Army Military History Institute

....

Chapter 1. Seven Days to Decision

1. Samuel P. Heintzelman diary, Mar. 8, 1862, Heintzelman Papers, LC; Stephen W. Sears, *George B. McClellan: The Young Napoleon*, pp. 43, 52–53, 116; Richard Smith to Joseph H. Barrett, Feb. 9, Lincoln Collection, University of Chicago Library; Charles Sumner to John A. Andrew, Mar. 2, Andrew Papers, Massachusetts Historical Society; George B. McClellan, *Mc-Clellan's Own Story*, p. 195, and draft, McClellan Papers (D-10:72), LC. McClellan dated his morning meeting with Lincoln and the council of war Mar. 8, but from Heintzelman's diary and Erasmus D. Keyes to Edwin M. Stanton (Mar. 14, Stanton Papers, LC) Mar. 7 is the correct date.

2. Heintzelman diary, Mar. 8, 1862, LC; Henry M. Naglee in *New York World*, Oct. 1, 1864; McClellan to Halleck, Mar. 3, to

Stanton, Feb. 3, 1862, George B. McClellan, *The Civil War Papers of George B. McClellan*, ed. Stephen W. Sears, pp. 195–97, 167–70; Allan Pinkerton to McClellan, Dec. 2, 1861, McClellan Papers (A-32:14), LC; McClellan testimony, *Report of the Joint Committee on the Conduct of the War*, I (1863), p. 425; Irvin McDowell in *New York Herald*, Dec. 4, 1864; Malcolm Ives to James Gordon Bennett, Jan. 15, 1862, Bennett Papers, LC. By the strictest geographical definition, the Peninsula is that area of Virginia, some forty-five miles in length, between the James and York rivers. In defining the Peninsula as a field for military campaigning, however, the confining character of the rivers is extended as far as Richmond by the James and to some twenty miles north of the city by the Pamunkey, the York's chief tributary. For military study, then, the Peninsula is identified as the area bounded by the James and the York-Pamunkey rivers, and extending from Fort Monroe on the east to Richmond on the west.

3. Henry M. Naglee notes, Mar. 7, 1862, Stanton Papers, LC; Barnard to McClellan, Dec. 6, 1861, McClellan Papers (A-32:14), LC; John G. Barnard, *The Peninsular Campaign and Its Antecedents*, p. 94; Heintzelman to Lincoln, Mar. 8, 1862, Lincoln Papers, LC (misidentified as by Salmon P. Chase); Barnard to E. D. Townsend, Oct. 3, 1864, Lincoln Papers, LC; Barnard to Heintzelman, Oct. 23, 1864, Heintzelman Papers, LC; McDowell in *New York Herald*, Dec. 4, 1864;

Heintzelman diary, Mar. 8, 1862, LC.

4. McDowell in *New York Herald*, Dec. 4, 1864; Lincoln to McClellan, c. Dec. 1, 1861, Lincoln, *The Collected Works of Abraham Lincoln*, ed. Roy P. Basler, V, p. 34; Stanton notes, [Mar. 7, 1862], Stanton Papers, LC; John Hay, *Lincoln and the Civil War in the Diaries and Letters of John Hay*, ed. Tyler Dennett, p. 36; Heintzelman diary, Mar. 8, 1862, LC; President's War Orders, Mar. 8, Lincoln, *Works*, V, pp. 149–51; *McClellan's Own Story* draft, McClellan Papers (D-10:72), LC; McClellan corps memorandum, c. Jan. 1862, McClellan Papers (A-50:20), LC. McClellan would have selected Andrew Porter as a corps commander rather than Keyes.

5. McClellan to Stanton, Feb. 3, 1862, to Simon Cameron, Oct. 31, 1861, to Lincoln, Dec. 10, 1861, to Winfield Scott, May 7, 1861, McClellan, *Papers*, pp. 167, 116, 143, 16; Confederate return, Oct. 1861, *OR*, 5, p. 932; Salmon P. Chase memorandum, Sept. 2, 1862, Jacob S. Schuckers, *The Life and Public Services of Salmon Portland Chase*, p. 445; William T. Coggeshall diary, Jan. 31, 1862, Illinois State Historical Library.

6. Stewart Van Vliet to McClellan, Jan. 3, 1862, Virginia topographical study, c. Jan. 1862, McClellan Papers (B-9:47, A-34:14), LC; Louis M. Goldsborough testimony, *Report of Joint Committee*, I (1863), p. 631; Montgomery C. Meigs, "General M. C. Meigs on the Conduct of the Civil War," *American Historical Review*, 26:2

(Jan. 1921), p. 292; "Memorandum of General McDowell" in Henry J. Raymond, *The Life and Public Services of Abraham Lincoln* (New York: Derby and Miller, 1865), pp. 272–77; President's War Order, Jan. 31, 1862, Lincoln, *Works*, V, p. 115; McClellan to Stanton, Feb. 3, to War Dept., c. Mar. 1, McClellan Potomac batteries memorandum, Mar. 1, McClellan, *Papers*, pp. 162–70, 193–95, 195; Charles Sumner to John A. Andrew, Mar. 2, Andrew Papers, Massachusetts Historical Society.

7. Thomas Bragg diary, Feb. 7, 18, 19, 20, 1862, SHC (Bragg quoted Scottish poet Thomas Campbell); Gilbert E. Govan and James W. Livingood, *A Different Valor: The Story of General Joseph E. Johnston, C.S.A.*, p. 20; Confederate return, Feb. 1862, *OR*, 5, p. 1086; Davis to James Phelan, Feb. 18, 1865, *OR*, 47:2, p. 1305; Joseph E. Johnston, *Narrative of Military Operations*, p. 97; Johnston to Davis, Feb. 23, 1862, *OR*, 5, p. 1079.

8. Johnston, *Narrative*, pp. 98–99, 102; Johnston to Whiting, Feb. 28, Mar. 6, 1862, *OR*, 5, pp. 1085, 1091–92; Thomas Bragg diary, Feb. 19, SHC; Johnston to Jubal A. Early, July 6, 1872, Johnston Papers, Perkins Library, Duke University; D. H. Hill to Randolph, Mar. 22, 1862, *OR*, 51:2, p. 512; Mary Alice Wills, *The Confederate Blockade of Washington, D.C., 1861–1862*, p. 156; D. Augustus Dickert, *History of Kershaw's Brigade*, pp. 91–92; W. W. Blackford, *War Years with Jeb Stuart*, p. 60; Sidney J. Richardson to parents, Mar. 27,

Georgia Dept. of Archives and History; Robert A. Moore diary, Mar. 11, Moore, *A Life for the Confederacy* (Jackson, Tenn.: McCowat-Mercer, 1959), p. 108.

9. Wool teleg. to Stanton, Mar. 8–9, 1862, *NOR*, 7, pp. 4–5; Charles D. Brigham teleg., Mar. 9, Lincoln Papers, LC; John G. Nicolay notes, Mar. 9, Helen Nicolay, *Lincoln's Secretary: A Biography of John G. Nicolay*, p. 136; Gideon Welles, *Diary of Gideon Welles*, ed. Howard K. Beale, I, pp. 62–64; McClellan telegs. to Dix, Wool, Mar. 9, McClellan, *Papers*, pp. 198–99; Pinkerton to McClellan, Dec. — , 1861, David D. Porter to McClellan, Nov. 24, 1861, McClellan Papers (A-34:14, A-31:13), LC; Welles in A. K. McClure, ed., *The Annals of the War*, p. 20; John A. Dahlgren to Ulric Dahlgren, Mar. 11, 1862, Dahlgren Papers, LC; McClellan to Stanton, Mar. 9, McClellan, *Papers*, p. 199.

10. Nathaniel P. Banks teleg. to Marcy, Mar. 8, Joseph Hooker teleg. to Seth Williams, Mar. 9, Leavitt Hunt teleg. to Heintzelman, Mar. 9, 1862, McClellan Papers (A-44:18), LC; McClellan teleg. to Lincoln and Stanton, Mar. 9, McClellan, *Papers*, p. 200; Fox telegs. to Welles, McClellan, Mar. 9, *OR*, 9, pp. 21–22, 23–24.

11. Taylor to wife in J. Cutler Andrews, *The North Reports the Civil War*, p. 191; Pinkerton to McClellan, Jan. 27, Marcy telegs. to McClellan, Mar. 11, 12, Dennison to McClellan, Mar. 14, 1862, McClellan Papers (A-38:15, A-45:18, A-46:18), LC; Mar. 11, 13, Edward Bates, *The Diary of*

Edward Bates: 1859–1866, ed. Howard K. Beale, pp. 239–40; President's War Order, Mar. 11, Lincoln, *Works*, V, p. 155; McClellan teleg. to Marcy, Mar. 11, McClellan to wife, Mar. 11, to Lincoln, Mar. 12, McClellan, *Papers*, pp. 201, 202, 207.

12. McClellan teleg. to Stanton, Mar. 11, McClellan to Stanton, c. Apr. 27, Feb. 3, 1862, Mc-Clellan, *Papers*, pp. 201, 247, 168; McClellan in *Battles and Leaders of the Civil War*, eds. Robert U. Johnson and Clarence C. Buel, II, p. 167; George B. McClellan, *Report on the Organization of the Army of the Potomac* (Washington, 1864), pp. 54, 58; McClellan testimony, *Report of Joint Committee*, I (1863), p. 426; Prince de Joinville, *The Army of the Potomac*, p. 27; John C. Ropes in Military and Historical Society of Mass., *The Peninsular Campaign of General McClellan in 1862*, pp. 11–12.

13. Heintzelman diary, Mar. 13, 1862, LC; McDowell testimony, *Report of Joint Committee*, I (1863), p. 270, Barnard testimony, pp. 386, 390; Barnard teleg. to Fox, Mar. 12, *OR*, 9, p. 27; McClellan teleg. to Fox, Mar. 12, Mc-Clellan, *Papers*, p. 206; Wool, Wise, Fox telegs. to McClellan, Mar. 13, McClellan Papers (A-46:18), LC; war council memorandum, Mar. 13, *OR*, 5, pp. 55–56.

14. Heintzelman diary, Mar. 13, 1862, LC; Louis M. Starr, *Bohemian Brigade: Civil War Newsmen in Action*, p. 94; McClellan to Edmund C. Stedman, Mar. 17, McClellan, *Papers*, p. 214; Stanton [Lincoln] teleg. to Mc-

Clellan, Mar. 13, Lincoln, *Works*, V, pp. 157–58.

Chapter 2. Stride of a Giant

1. James H. Wilson, *Under the Old Flag* (New York: Appleton, 1912), I, p. 123; McClellan to Army of the Potomac, Mar. 14, 1862, McClellan, *Papers*, p. 211; copy, Napoleon's address, McClellan Papers (A-107:42), LC; *New York Herald*, Mar. 16; *St. Louis Republican*, Mar. 25.

2. *New York Tribune*, Mar. 15, 1862, Samuel Ward to Barlow, Mar. 16, 18, 22, Stark to Barlow, Mar. 16, 20, Samuel L. M. Barlow Papers, Huntington Library; Mar. 15, E. A. Hitchcock, *Fifty Years in Camp and Field: Diary of Major-General Ethan Allen Hitchcock, U.S.A.* (New York: Putnam's, 1909), p. 439; Apr. 2, Orville H. Browning, *The Diary of Orville Hickman Browning*, eds. Theodore C. Pease and James G. Randall, I, pp. 537–39; McClellan to Barlow, Mar. 16, McClellan, *Papers*, p. 213.

3. Tucker to Stanton, Apr. 5, 1862, *OR*, 5, p. 46; Elisha Hunt Rhodes diary, Mar. 27, Rhodes, *All for the Union: A History of the 2nd Rhode Island Volunteer Infantry*, ed. Robert Hunt Rhodes, p. 61; George A. Townsend, *Rustics in Rebellion: A Yankee Reporter on the Road to Richmond, 1861–1865*, p. 36; George Monteith to mother, Mar. 24, Charles B. Haydon diary, Mar. 18, MCH; Barnard, *Peninsular Campaign*, p. 74. Tucker's manpower figure, from the Mar. 31 return (*OR*, 11:3, p. 53), included Blenker's division, detached on that date.

4. D. H. Hill in *Battles and Leaders,* II, p. 362n; Thomas M. Settles, "The Military Career of John Bankhead Magruder," Ph.D. diss., Texas Christian University, 1972, pp. 37–38, 163–65; Magruder teleg. to Randolph, Mar. 24, 1862, RG 109 (M-618:9), NA; Magruder to Randolph, Mar. 24, *OR,* 11:3, p. 393.

5. Douglas Southall Freeman, *R. E. Lee, A Biography,* II, pp. 8–13; Lee to Magruder, Mar. 26, 29, 1862, Robert E. Lee, *The Wartime Papers of R. E. Lee,* ed. Clifford Dowdey, pp. 136–37, 140; Lafayette McLaws to wife, Apr. 25, McLaws Papers, SHC; Magruder, Cabell reports, *OR,* 11:1, pp. 405–6, 411–12; Magruder to Army of the Peninsula, Mar. 4, *OR,* 9, pp. 53–54. By Mar. 31 Lee had reinforced Magruder with two Alabama regiments and Wilcox's brigade from Johnston (*OR,* 11:3, pp. 404, 412). Artillery in Yorktown-Warwick line: Feb. return, *OR,* 9, p. 49; Magruder to Lee, Apr. 8, *OR,* 11:3, p. 430; C. P. Kingsbury to Marcy, May 5, McClellan Papers (A-56:22), LC.

6. Richard P. Weinert, Jr., and Robert Arthur, *Defender of the Chesapeake: The Story of Fort Monroe,* pp. 32, 38, 72, 87; Settles, "Military Career of Magruder," pp. 22–23; Apr. 1, 1862, Edmund Ruffin, *The Diary of Edmund Ruffin,* ed. William K. Scarborough, II, pp. 269–70; Charles B. Haydon diary, Mar. 19, George Monteith to mother, Mar. 24, MHC; Edward A. Acton to wife, Apr. 8, Acton, " 'Dear Mollie': Letters of Captain Edward A. Acton to His Wife, 1862," *Pennsylvania Magazine of History and Biography,* 89:1 (Jan. 1965), p. 6; Magruder report, Aug. 9, 1861, *OR,* 4, pp. 570–73; Oliver W. Norton to sister, Mar. 26, 1862, Norton, *Army Letters, 1861–1865,* p. 62; Allen A. Kingsbury to parents, Apr. 25, Kingsbury, *The Hero of Medford: Containing the Journals and Letters of Allen Alonzo Kingsbury* (Boston: J. M. Hewes, 1862), p. 74.

7. Pinkerton to McClellan, Nov. 15, Dec. 2, 1861, Feb. 1, 1862, McClellan Papers (A-31:13, A-32:14, A-39:16), LC; *OR Atlas,* plate 18:1; T. J. Cram Peninsula maps, RG 77 (G-77:1, G-77:2), NA; McClellan testimony, *Report of Joint Committee,* I (1863), pp. 428–29; Webb to John C. Ropes, Nov. 16, 1893, Ropes Collection, Boston University Library.

8. Wool teleg. to McClellan, Mar. 12, 1862, *NOR,* 7, p. 100; Woodbury to McClellan, Mar. 19, Porter teleg. to McClellan, Mar. 30, *OR,* 11:3, p. 22, 51:1, p. 564; McClellan teleg. to Stanton, Apr. 3, McClellan, *Papers,* p. 227; Edwin C. Fishel, "Pinkerton and McClellan: Who Deceived Whom?" *Civil War History,* 34:2 (June 1988), pp. 126–27. In reporting the size of his army that met McClellan's advance as 11,000 or 11,500 men (*OR,* 11:1, p. 405, 11:3, p. 436), Magruder failed to include the reinforcement of Wilcox's brigade from Johnston.

9. McClellan teleg. to Stanton, Mar. 18, to Marcy, Mar. 22, to Stanton, Mar. 19, c. Apr. 27, 1862, McClellan, *Papers,* pp. 214, 216–17, 215–16, 247–48; Woodbury to McClellan, Mar. 19, *OR,* 11:3, pp. 22–24.

10. Goldsborough, Fox testimony, *Report of Joint Committee,* I (1863), pp. 632, 630; Barnard to McClellan, Mar. 20, 28, 1862, *McClellan's Own Story* draft, McClellan Papers (A-47:19, A-49:19, D-9:71), LC; Louis M. Goldsborough, "Narrative of Rear Admiral Goldsborough, U.S. Navy," *U.S. Naval Institute Proceedings,* 59 (July 1933), p. 1025; War Board minutes, Mar. 20, Stanton Papers, LC; Goldsborough to Welles, Mar. 23, *NOR,* 7, pp. 165–66; Goldsborough to wife, Apr. 6, Goldsborough Papers, LC; McClellan to Joseph G. Totten, Mar. 28, McClellan, *Papers,* p. 218.

11. McClellan to Banks, Apr. 1, to Lincoln, Mar. 31, 1862, McClellan, *Papers,* pp. 220–21, 219; Lincoln to McClellan, Mar. 31, to Frémont, June 16, Lincoln, *Works,* V, pp. 175–76, 273–74; Frémont to Lincoln, April 21, *OR,* 12:1, p. 7.

12. McClellan to Stanton, Feb. 3, to Banks, Apr. 1, to wife, Apr. 1, 1862, McClellan, *Papers,* pp. 167, 220, 223; Johnston to Lee, Apr. 30, *OR,* 11:3, p. 477; President's War Order, Mar. 8, Stanton [Lincoln] teleg. to McClellan, Mar. 13, Lincoln, *Works,* V, pp. 151, 157. The Confederate high command discussed an offensive north of the Potomac as early as Apr. 14: Gustavus W. Smith, *Confederate War Papers,* pp. 41–42.

13. Stanton to Lincoln, Mar. 30, 1862, Stanton Papers, LC; McClellan to Thomas, Apr. 1, McClellan, *Papers,* pp. 222–23; Wadsworth to Stanton, Thomas and Hitchcock to Stanton, Apr.

2, *OR,* 11:3, pp. 60–62; Federal returns, Mar. 31, Apr. 6, *OR,* 11:3, p. 53, 12:3, pp. 48–51; war council memorandum, Mar. 13, *OR,* 5, pp. 55–56; Stanton to Heman Dyer, May 18, *OR,* 19:2, p. 726; Charles Sumner to John A. Andrew, May 28, Andrew Papers, Massachusetts Historical Society.

14. Goldsborough to G. V. Fox, Apr. 21, 1862, Fox, *Confidential Correspondence of Gustavus Vasa Fox,* eds. Robert M. Thompson and Richard Wainwright, I, pp. 260–61; McClellan to wife, Apr. 2 (teleg.), 3, McClellan, *Papers,* p. 225; Jonathan Stowe diary, Apr. 4, USAMHI; "Instructions for March," Apr. 3, Heintzelman Papers, LC. Army of the Potomac forces: Mar. 31 return, *OR,* 11:3, p. 53; Mar. 31 organization, *OR,* 5, pp. 19–20; Seth Williams to McClellan, Apr. 1, McClellan Papers (A-50:20), LC; Stanton to Lincoln, Mar. 30, Stanton Papers, LC, Heintzelman diary, Apr. 3, LC.

15. McClellan teleg. to Goldsborough, Apr. 4, 1862, *NOR,* 7, p. 200; Heintzelman diary, Mar. 30, LC; McClellan to wife, Apr. 4, McClellan, *Papers,* p. 228; McClellan to Heintzelman, Apr. 4, Heintzelman Papers, LC; Lee teleg. to Johnston, Apr. 4, Magruder teleg. to Lee, Apr. 5, *OR,* 11:3, pp. 420, 422; Magruder teleg. to Randolph, Mar. 25, RG 109 (M-618:9), NA.

16. Virginia topographical study, c. Jan. 1862, Jesse A. Gove to F. J. Porter, Apr. 5, McClellan Papers (A-34:14, A-51:20), LC; Joseph B. Laughton to family, Apr. 14, Laughton Papers, Perkins Li-

brary, Duke University; May 6, Charles S. Wainwright, *A Diary of Battle: The Personal Journals of Colonel Charles S. Wainwright, 1861–1865*, ed. Allan Nevins, p. 58; C. H. Howard to Dellie Gilmore, Apr. 10, C. H. Howard Papers, Bowdoin College Library; Selden Connor to sister, Apr. 9, Connor Papers, John Hay Library, Brown University; Keyes to Marcy, Apr. 5, to McClellan, Apr. 6, *OR,* 11:3, pp. 70, 75; Keyes report, *OR,* 11:1, p. 358. Three soldier-diarists were especially conscientious recorders of weather conditions during the Peninsula campaign: Matthew Marrin, 1st Minnesota, Minnesota Historical Society; William H. Hill, 13th Mississippi, Mississippi Dept. of Archives and History; and Henry C. Wall, 23rd North Carolina, North Carolina State Archives.

17. Apr. 5, 1862, Edmund D. Patterson, *Yankee Rebel: The Civil War Journal of Edmund DeWitt Patterson*, ed. John G. Barrett, p. 17; Robert H. Miller to uncle, Apr. 27, Miller, "Letters of Lieutenant Robert H. Miller to His Family, 1861–1862," ed. Forrest P. Connor, *Virginia Magazine of History and Biography*, 70:1 (Jan. 1962), p. 82; James H. McMath diary, Apr. 5, Alabama Dept. of Archives and History; Mary Chesnut diary, June 29, C. Vann Woodward, ed., *Mary Chesnut's Civil War*, p. 401.

18. McClellan to Lorenzo Thomas, Apr. 5, 1862, McClellan Papers (A-50:20), LC; McClellan to Stanton, Feb. 3, to Goldsborough, Apr. 5, McClellan, *Papers*, pp. 167, 229; Williams to Van

Vliet, Apr. 5, *OR*, 11:3, pp. 71–72.

19. Thomas teleg. to McClellan, Thomas to McClellan, Apr. 4, 1862, *OR*, 11:1, p. 10, 11:3, p. 66; McClellan to wife, Apr. 6, McClellan teleg. to Lincoln, Apr. 5, McClellan, *Papers*, pp. 230, 228; McClellan to Thomas, Apr. 5, McClellan Papers (A-50:20), LC; Barnard, *Peninsular Campaign*, p. 74.

Chapter 3. Siege

1. McClellan, *Report*, p. 77, and *McClellan's Own Story* draft, McClellan Papers (D-7:69, D-9:71), LC; McClellan to Barlow, July 15, 30, Mar. 16, to Stanton, c. Apr. 27, 1862, McClellan, *Papers*, pp. 361, 376–77, 213, 247–48; Marcy to McDowell, Apr. 1, *OR*, 51:1, p. 565; John C. Palfrey in Military and Historical Society of Mass., *Peninsular Campaign*, p. 83.

2. Lowe report, *OR*, Ser. 3, 3, p. 273; Heintzelman diary, Apr. 6, May 6, 1862, LC; Barnard to Fox, May 11, Fox, *Correspondence*, II, p. 296; William F. Smith, *Autobiography of Major General William F. Smith, 1861–1864*, ed. Herbert M. Schiller, pp. 34–35; Hancock report, *OR*, 11:1, pp. 308–9.

3. George H. Bangs interrogation report, [Apr. 7, 1862], McClellan Papers (A-107:42), LC; McClellan teleg. to Stanton, Apr. 7, McClellan to wife, Apr. 8, McClellan, *Papers*, pp. 232, 234; Lincoln to McClellan, Apr. 6 (teleg.), 9, Lincoln, *Works*, V, pp. 182, 185.

4. Magruder teleg. to Lee, Apr. 6,

1862, *OR*, 11:3, p. 425; Magruder report, *OR*, 11:1, p. 404; Lafayette McLaws to wife, Apr. 25, McLaws Papers, SHC; Emory M. Thomas, *The Confederate State of Richmond: A Biography of the Capital*, pp. 81–82, 85; CSA G.O. 16, Mar. 24, *OR*, Ser. 4, 1, p. 1020; Thomas C. DeLeon, *Four Years in Rebel Capitals*, p. 192; *Wilmington* (N.C.) *Journal*, Apr. 14, in Frank Moore, ed., *The Rebellion Record: A Diary of American Events*, IV, Diary, p. 88.

5. Edward M. Burruss to father, Apr. 16, 1862, Burruss Papers, Hill Library, Louisiana State University; DeLeon, *Rebel Capitals*, pp. 191–92; Sallie A. Putnam, *Richmond During the War: Four Years of Personal Observation*, pp. 119–20; G. Moxley Sorrel, *Recollections of a Confederate Staff Officer*, p. 53; *Charleston Mercury*, Apr. 17; Magruder report, *OR*, 11:1, p. 406; Confederate return, c. Apr. 30, *OR*, 11:3, pp. 479–84; Johnston to Lee, Apr. 22, *OR*, 11:3, p. 456. Magruder's Apr. 11 report to Randolph (*OR*, 11:3, p. 436) undercounted his strength by 2,900 men.

6. Apr. 11, 1862, Wainwright, *Diary of Battle*, p. 34; Goldsborough, "Narrative," pp. 1028–29; Tattnall G.O., Apr. 8, *NOR*, 7, pp. 759–60; A. C. Stimers to G. V. Fox, Apr. 14, Fox Papers, New-York Historical Society; Francis W. Dawson, *Reminiscences of Confederate Service, 1861–1865*, pp. 39–41.

7. CSA S.O. 6, Apr. 12, 1862, *OR*, 11:3, p. 438; Davis to Army of Richmond, June 2, *OR*, 51:2, p. 565; Chesnut diary, Dec. 22,

1861, Woodward, *Mary Chesnut's Civil War*, p. 268; Johnston, *Narrative*, pp. 111–13.

8. Johnston, *Narrative*, pp. 114–16; James Longstreet, *From Manassas to Appomattox: Memoirs of the Civil War in America*, p. 66; Smith, *Confederate War Papers*, pp. 41–43; Jefferson Davis, *The Rise and Fall of the Confederate Government*, II, pp. 87–88.

9. Army of the Potomac return, Apr. 30, 1862, *OR*, 11:3, p. 130; Army of Northern Virginia returns, c. Apr. 30, May 21 (despite its date, the May 21 return used late April manpower figures), *OR*, 11:3, pp. 484, 530–31; Magruder proclamation, Apr. 11, *OR*, 11:3, p. 437; Barnard report, *OR*, 11:1, pp. 334–35; McClellan to Wool, Apr. 8, McClellan Papers (C-5:63), LC; McClellan teleg. to wife, Apr. 12, RG 107 (M-504:66), NA; McClellan to wife, Apr. 23, McClellan, *Papers*, p. 245. The order of battle of the two armies, as of May 1, is in Appendix I.

10. Selden Connor to brother, Apr. 24, 1862, Connor Papers, John Hay Library, Brown University; Robert H. Miller to mother, Apr. 9, Miller, "Letters," p. 80; Wilbur Fisk letter, Apr. 24, Fisk, *Anti-Rebel: The Civil War Letters of Wilbur Fisk* (Croton-on-Hudson, N.Y.: Emil Rosenblatt, 1983), p. 19; Oscar J. E. Stuart to aunt, Apr. 29, Mississippi Dept. of Archives and History; E. Augustus Garrison memoir, Schoff Collection, CL; Matthew Marrin diary, Apr. 10, Minnesota Historical Society; A. W. Stillwell diary, Apr. 9, State Historical Society of Wisconsin; Thomas L. Ware

diary, Apr. 19, SHC; Charles B. Haydon diary, Apr. 9, MHC.

11. William F. Bartlett to mother, Apr. 20, 1862, Francis W. Palfrey, *Memoir of William Francis Bartlett* (Boston: Houghton Mifflin, 1878), p. 40; Robert V. Bruce, *Lincoln and the Tools of War*, pp. 109–11; William Y. W. Ripley to wife, Apr. 20, W. Y. Ripley Papers, Perkins Library, Duke University; Nicholas A. Davis, *Chaplain Davis and Hood's Texas Brigade*, ed. Donald E. Everett, p. 56; Robert Stiles, *Four Years Under Marse Robert*, p. 77; E. P. Alexander, *Fighting for the Confederacy: The Personal Recollections of General Edward Porter Alexander*, ed. Gary W. Gallagher, p. 75.

12. Leon Jastremski, "Yorktown and Williamsburg," Louisiana Historical Association Collection, Tulane University; Lee to wife, Mar. 22, 1862, Lee, *Papers*, p. 133; Freeman, *R. E. Lee*, II, pp. 25–29; Nathaniel H. R. Dawson to Elodie Todd, Apr. 4, Dawson Papers, SHC; Jesse W. Reid to wife, Apr. 5, Reid, *History of the Fourth Regiment S.C. Volunteers*, pp. 73–74; John S. Tucker diary, Apr. 27, Tucker, "The Diary of John S. Tucker: Confederate Soldier from Alabama," ed. Gary Wilson, *Alabama Historical Quarterly*, 43:1 (Spring 1981), p. 9.

13. C. H. Howard to Dellie Gilmore, Apr. 10, 1862, C. H. Howard Papers, Bowdoin College Library; Alexander Hays to wife, Apr. 19, Hays, *Life and Letters of Alexander Hays*, ed. George T. Fleming, p. 209; Brigham Buswell memoir, Collection of Gloria Conklin, Chappaqua, N.Y.; Oliver W. Nor-ton to cousin, Apr. 14, Norton, *Army Letters*, p. 68; William H. Beach, *The First New York (Lincoln) Cavalry*, p. 103; Elisha Hunt Rhodes diary, Apr. 15, *All for the Union*, p. 62; Lewis E. Warren memoir, Woodruff Library, Emory University; Charles B. Haydon diary, Apr. 22, MHC; James R. Holmes to aunt, Apr. 15, Holmes, "The Civil War Letters of James Rush Holmes," ed. Ida Bright Adams, *Western Pennsylvania Historical Magazine*, 44:2 (June 1961), p. 116; Moore, *Rebellion Record*, V, Incidents, p. 34.

14. Philip Kearny to wife, Apr. 24, 1862, Kearny, *Letters from the Peninsula: The Civil War Letters of General Philip Kearny*, ed. William B. Styple, pp. 51–52; Heintzelman diary, Apr. 9, 13, LC; Lowe report, *OR*, Ser. 3, 3, p. 274; Townsend, *Rustics in Rebellion*, pp. 92–95; McClellan to wife, Apr. 11, McClellan, *Papers*, p. 235; John R. Bryan in *Confederate Veteran*, 22:4 (Apr. 1914), pp. 161–65; John W. Hinsdale diary, Apr. 27, Perkins Library, Duke University; Bruce, *Tools of War*, pp. 118–19, 198–99; Charles E. Perkins to sister, Apr. 18, Perkins, "Letters Home: Sergeant Charles E. Perkins in Virginia, 1862," eds. Ray Henshaw and Glenn W. LaFantasie, *Rhode Island History*, 39 (Nov. 1980), p. 111; *New York Evening Post*, Apr. 25.

15. McClellan to Smith, Apr. 15, 1862, McClellan Papers (D-9:71), LC; W. F. Smith, Brooks, Hyde, Harrington, Cobb reports, *OR*, 11:1, pp. 364–67, 372–73, 375, 376, 416–18; B. M. Zittler

in *Confederate Veteran*, 8:5 (May 1900), p. 197; Smith, *Autobiography*, p. 35; McClellan to wife, Apr. 18, McClellan, *Papers*, p. 240; George Q. French to "friends," Apr. 18, French, " 'The 3rd Vermont *has won a name*': Corporal Albert C. French's Account of the Battle of Lee's Mill, Virginia," ed. Albert C. Eisenberg, *Vermont History*, 49 (Fall 1981), p. 227; A. W. Stillwell diary, Apr. 16, State Historical Society of Wisconsin; Stephen N. Siciliano, "Major General William Farrar Smith: Critic of Defeat and Engineer of Victory," Ph.D. diss., College of William and Mary, 1984, pp. 91–96; Brooks to father, Apr. 22, W. T. H. Brooks Papers, USAMHI.

16. McClellan to Scott, Apr. 11, to wife, Apr. 19, to Lincoln, Apr. 20, to Stanton, c. Apr. 27, 1862, McClellan, *Papers*, pp. 236, 243–44, 244–45, 248; Stanton teleg. to McClellan, Apr. 11, *OR*, 11:3, p. 90; Associated Press dispatches, Apr. 11, 24, RG 107 (M-473:99), NA; Stanton teleg. to McClellan, Apr. 12, McClellan Papers (A-51:20), LC; McClellan teleg. to Stanton, Apr. 13, *OR*, 11:3, p. 94.

17. Barnard, Doull reports, *OR*, 11:1, pp. 334–35, 354–57; *OR Atlas*, plate 19:2; Thomas B. Leaver diary, May 2, 1862, New Hampshire Historical Society; Matthew Marrin diary, Apr. 9, William W. Folwell diary, Apr. 23, Minnesota Historical Society; Gilbert Thompson diary, May 7, LC; Luther C. Furst diary, Apr. 16, USAMHI.

18. D. H. Hill to Randolph, Apr. 15, 1862, *OR*, 11:3, p. 442; William F. Plane to wife, Apr. 28, Plane, "Letters of William Fisher Plane, C.S.A. to His Wife," ed. S. Joseph Lewis, Jr., *Georgia Historical Quarterly*, 48 (June 1964), p. 221; Hal Bridges, *Lee's Maverick General: Daniel Harvey Hill*, p. 7; Johnston, *Narrative*, pp. 118–19; Mallory to Tattnall, Apr. 18, *NOR*, 7, p. 766; Johnston to Lee, Apr. 27, 29, to Huger, Apr. 27, *OR*, 11:3, pp. 469, 473, 469–70.

19. Johnston to Lee, Apr. 30, to D. H. Hill, May 1, 1862, *OR*, 11:3, pp. 477, 486; Lee to Mallory, Apr. 8, to Johnston, Apr. 30, Lee, *Papers*, pp. 143, 161; Lee to Randolph, Apr. 17, *OR*, 51:2, p. 539; Tattnall to Mallory, Apr. 10, to Johnston, Apr. 30, *NOR*, 7, pp. 764–65, 777; Army of Northern Virginia returns, c. Apr. 30, May 21, *OR*, 11:3, pp. 484, 530–31.

20. Uriah H. Painter testimony, *Report of Joint Committee*, I (1863), pp. 283–84; Porter to McClellan, May 2, McClellan teleg. to W. F. Smith, Apr. 29, 1862, McClellan Papers (A-55:22, C-13:64), LC; Pinkerton to McClellan, May 3, *OR*, 11:1, p. 268; May 3, Wainwright, *Diary of Battle*, p. 44; *McClellan's Own Story*, p. 287; Heintzelman diary, May 3, LC; McClellan teleg. to Goldsborough, May 2, McClellan to Lincoln, Apr. 23, McClellan, *Papers*, pp. 251, 247.

21. George T. Stevens, *Three Years in the Sixth Corps*, p. 47; Heintzelman diary, May 4, 1862, LC; Henry Ropes to father, May 6, Ropes Papers, Boston Public Library; Edgar M. Newcomb to sister, May 6, A. B. Weymouth, ed., *A Memorial Sketch of Lieut.*

Edgar M. Newcomb, of the Nineteenth Mass. Vols., p. 58.

Chapter 4. A Fighting Retreat

1. McClellan telegs. to Stanton, May 4, 1862 (two), McClellan, *Papers*, p. 253; *New York Tribune*, May 4, 5; *New York Journal of Commerce*, May 5; Francis E. Spinner to J. C. Day, May 11, Spinner Papers, Chicago Historical Society; *New York Evening Post*, May 5; Comte de Paris journal, May 12, Fondation Saint-Louis; Robert McAllister to daughters, May 5, McAllister, *The Civil War Letters of General Robert McAllister*, ed. James I. Robertson, Jr., p. 150; Hooker to James Nesmith, May 4, Nesmith Papers, Oregon Historical Society; Doull report, *OR*, 11:1, p. 356; C. P. Kingsbury to Marcy, May 5, McClellan Papers (A-56:22), LC.

2. Milton F. Perry, *Infernal Machines: The Story of Confederate Submarine and Mine Warfare*, pp. 20–27; Rains to Longstreet, Randolph to Longstreet, May 11, 1862, *OR*, 11:3, pp. 510–11; Comte de Paris journal, May 12, Fondation Saint-Louis; McClellan teleg. to Stanton, May 4, McClellan, *Papers*, p. 254; P. A. Hanaford, *The Young Captain: A Memorial of Capt. Richard C. Derby, Fifteenth Reg. Mass. Volunteers, Who Fell at Antietam* (Boston: Degan, Estes, 1865), p. 138.

3. Comte de Paris journal, May 12, 1862, Fondation Saint-Louis; McClellan to Heintzelman, May 4, McClellan Papers (D-9:71), LC; Johnston, *Narrative*, pp. 119–20; Army of the Potomac re-turn, Apr. 30, *OR*, 11:3, p. 130; Franklin to McClellan, Feb. 8, 1884, *McClellan's Own Story*, p. 335.

4. *OR Atlas*, plate 18:2; E. P. Alexander, *Military Memoirs of a Confederate*, p. 66; Alexander, *Fighting for Confederacy*, p. 79; Jennings C. Wise, *The Long Arm of Lee, or The History of the Artillery of the Army of Northern Virginia*, I, pp. 195–96; May 4, 1862, John S. Tucker, "Diary," p. 10; C. C. Cummings in *Confederate Veteran*, 4:3 (Mar. 1896), p. 91; Palmer report, *OR*, 11:1, pp. 426–27; Abram H. Young to sister, May 13, Young, "Civil War Letters of Abram Hayne Young," ed. Mary Wyche Burgess, *South Carolina Historical Magazine*, 78:1 (Jan. 1977), p. 57; Joinville, *Army of the Potomac*, p. 51.

5. Johnston, *Narrative*, p. 120; Magruder to Cooper, Feb. 1, 1862, *OR*, 9, p. 39; May 5, Wainwright, *Diary of Battle*, p. 49. Map: A. A. Humphreys, "Map Showing the Position of Williamsburg," RG 77 (G-447), NA.

6. Hooker, W. F. Smith reports, *OR*, 11:1, pp. 464–65, 526; *McClellan's Own Story* draft, McClellan Papers (D-9:71), LC; Comte de Paris journal, May 12, Fondation Saint-Louis.

7. Hooker to James Nesmith, c. May 10, 1862, Nesmith Papers, Oregon Historical Society; May 5, Wainwright, *Diary of Battle*, pp. 47–52; Longstreet report, *OR*, 11:1, p. 565; Thomas J. Goree to mother, Dec. 14, 1861, Goree, *The Thomas Jewett Goree Letters: The Civil War Correspondence*, p. 111; Wilcox report, *OR*, 51:1, pp. 91–93; Wilcox inter-

view, Dec. 29, 1881, McClellan Papers (D-9:71), LC.

8. Hooker to McKeever, May 5, 1862, *OR*, 11:1, p. 469; W. F. Smith, Keyes reports, *OR*, 11:1, pp. 527, 514–15; Smith, *Autobiography*, pp. 36–37; Heintzelman diary, May 6, LC; John W. De Peyster, *Personal and Military History of Philip Kearny, Major-General United States Volunteers*, p. 282; May 21, Wainwright, *Diary of Battle*, p. 68.

9. David E. Johnston, *The Story of a Confederate Boy in the Civil War* (Portland, Ore.: Glass & Prudhomme, 1914), p. 102; Francis P. Fleming to brother, May 10, 1862, Fleming, "Francis P. Fleming in the War for Southern Independence," ed. Edward C. Williamson, *Florida Historical Quarterly*, 28:1 (July 1949), p. 39; Mather Cleveland, *New Hampshire Fights the Civil War*, pp. 26–27; Warren Lee Goss in *Battles and Leaders*, II, p. 197; Felix Brannigan to sister, May 6, Brannigan Papers, LC.

10. Luther C. Furst diary, May 5, 1862, USAMHI; Wilcox report, *OR*, 51:1, p. 93; May 5, 6, Wainwright, *Diary of Battle*, pp. 54, 58–59; Thomas Newby to mother, May 25, Newby Papers, North Carolina State Archives; James E. Smith, *A Famous Battery and Its Campaigns, 1861–'64*, p. 60; Thomas B. Leaver to brother, May 9, Leaver Papers, New Hampshire Historical Society; Heintzelman diary, May 6, LC; De Peyster, *Kearny*, p. 281; Alfred Bellard, *Gone for a Soldier: The Civil War Memoirs of Private Alfred Bellard*, ed. David Herbert Donald, p. 67; "George" to

"Jim," May 7, Civil War Letters, Alderman Library, University of Virginia.

11. Bruce Catton, *Mr. Lincoln's Army*, p. 32; Smith, *A Famous Battery*, p. 64; Edwin Y. Brown to brother, May 10, 1862, Brown Papers, Swem Library, College of William and Mary; James J. Marks, *The Peninsular Campaign in Virginia, or Incidents and Scenes on the Battle-Fields and in Richmond*, p. 158; Charles B. Haydon diary, May 7, MHC; Joseph B. Laughton to brother, May 11, Laughton Papers, Perkins Library, Duke University; Kearny, *Letters from Peninsula*, p. 60.

12. Hancock, D. H. Hill reports, *OR*, 11:1, pp. 535–40, 602–5; Smith, *Autobiography*, p. 37; William Swinton, *Campaigns of the Army of the Potomac*, p. 115n; Richard L. Maury in *Southern Historical Society Papers*, 8 (1880), p. 287; Jubal A. Early, *Autobiographical Sketch and Narrative of the War Between the States*, p. 69; P. J. Sinclair to "Alexander," May 12, 1862, Sinclair Papers, North Carolina State Archives.

13. Early, D. H. Hill, McRae reports, *OR*, 11:1, pp. 606–8, 603, 610–11; Joinville, *Army of the Potomac*, p. 54; D. H. Hill to Longstreet, Aug. 31, 1885, Longstreet Papers, Perkins Library, Duke University; P. J. Sinclair to "Alexander," May 12, 1862, Sinclair Papers, North Carolina State Archives; Thomas W. Hyde, *Following the Greek Cross or, Memories of the Sixth Army Corps*, p. 51; Selden Connor to mother, May 8, Connor Papers, John Hay Library, Brown University; A. R. Waud drawing,

Prints and Photographs Division, LC.

14. Comte de Paris journal, May 17, 1862, Fondation Saint-Louis; McClellan to wife, May 6, teleg. to Stanton, May 5, McClellan, *Papers*, pp. 257, 255; Francis W. Palfrey in Military Historical Society of Mass., *Peninsular Campaign*, p. 96; McClellan teleg. to wife, May 5, RG 107 (M-504:66), NA; Smith, *Autobiography*, p. 37; McClellan, *Report*, p. 91; *McClellan's Own Story*, pp. 327–28; William Sprague testimony, *Report of Joint Committee*, I (1863), p. 570; Henry J. Hunt to Heintzelman, Aug. 23, 1865, Heintzelman Papers, LC.

15. McClellan telegs. to wife, May 6, to Stanton, May 5, 1862, McClellan, *Papers*, pp. 256–57; Wool teleg. to Stanton, May 6, *OR*, 11:3, p. 143; W. F. Smith to John C. Ropes, Feb. 13, 1898, Ropes Collection, Boston University Library; Heintzelman, Hooker testimony, *Report of Joint Committee*, I (1863), pp. 349, 577. Federal forces and casualties at Williamsburg: *OR*, 11:1, p. 450, 11:3, p. 184; Heintzelman Papers, LC. Confederate forces and casualties: *OR*, 11:1, p. 569; *OR*, 11:3, pp. 479–84, 530–33; *OR*, 51:1, pp. 85–86, 95; P. J. Sinclair Papers, North Carolina State Archives.

16. McClellan telegs. to Stanton, May 5, to wife, May 6, 1862, McClellan, *Papers*, pp. 256–57; McClellan teleg. to Stanton, May 11, *OR*, 11:3, pp. 164–65; Hooker to James Nesmith, May 13, Nesmith Papers, Oregon Historical Society; Hooker to John C. Ten Eyck, May 16, Schoff

Collection, CL; O. O. Howard to wife, May 31, O. O. Howard Papers, Bowdoin College Library; McClellan to wife, May 6, 8, McClellan, *Papers*, pp. 257–58, 260; Thomas B. Leaver to brother, May 9, Leaver Papers, New Hampshire Historical Society; Charles B. Haydon diary, May 6, MHC; Johnston report, *OR*, 11:1, p. 276.

17. Franklin, Alexander, Johnston reports, *OR*, 11:1, pp. 614–17, 137–38, 276; Lewis J. Martin to family, May 8, 1862, Schoff Collection, CL; J.H.L. in *Battles and Leaders*, II, p. 276; Davis, *Hood's Texas Brigade*, p. 134.

18. John B. Hood, *Advance and Retreat: Personal Experience in the United States and Confederate States Armies*, p. 21; G. W. Smith, Hood reports, *OR*, 11:1, pp. 626–28, 630–32; James Brown to family, May 9, 1862, Brown Papers, Maine Historical Society; Robert McAllister to wife, May 8, McAllister, *Civil War Letters*, p. 152; Bartlett Y. Malone diary, May 7, Malone, *Whipt 'em Everytime: The Diary of Bartlett Yancey Malone*, ed. William W. Pierson, Jr., p. 53; casualty return, *OR*, 11:1, p. 618; Franklin to Marcy, May 7, *OR*, 11:1, p. 614; J.H.L. in *Battles and Leaders*, II, p. 276.

Chapter 5. March to the Chickahominy

1. May 3, 7, 1862, Judith White McGuire, *Diary of a Southern Refugee, During the War*, pp. 110, 111–12; Moore, *Rebellion Record*, IV, Diary, p. 95; May 10, 19, John B. Jones, *A Rebel War Clerk's Diary at the Confederate States Cap-*

ital, ed. Howard Swiggett, I, p. 123; Randolph to Cooper, May 10, *OR*, 11:3, p. 504; Putnam, *Richmond During the War*, p. 125; Johnston to Lee, May 7, *OR*, 51:2, pp. 552–53; Alexander, *Fighting for Confederacy*, pp. 82–83.

2. Henry C. Wall diary, May 7, 1862, North Carolina State Archives; May 6, Henry R. Berkeley, *Four Years in the Confederate Artillery: The Diary of Private Henry Robinson Berkeley*, ed. William H. Runge, p. 17; Joel Barnett to wife, May 13, Mills Lane, ed., *"Dear Mother: Don't grieve about me. If I get killed, I'll only be dead.": Letters from Georgia Soldiers in the Civil War*, p. 119; Ruffin Thomson to father, May 24, Thomson Papers, SHC; May 6, John Tucker, "Diary," p. 11; William G. Agnew to parents, May 11, Agnew Papers, Perkins Library, Duke University.

3. Johnston, *Narrative*, p. 127; DeLeon, *Rebel Capitals*, p. 194; Joel Barnett to wife, May 13, 1862, Lane, *Letters from Georgia Soldiers*, p. 119; Johnston to Lee, May 9, *OR*, 11:3, pp. 503–4; Davis to wife, May 13, Dunbar Rowland, ed., *Jefferson Davis, Constitutionalist: His Letters, Papers and Speeches*, V, p. 245; Johnston in *Battles and Leaders*, II, p. 206; Davis, *Rise and Fall*, II, p. 101.

4. Chase to daughter, May 7, 8, 11, 1862, Salmon P. Chase, *Inside Lincoln's Cabinet: The Civil War Diaries of Salmon P. Chase*, ed. David Donald, pp. 75–85; McClellan teleg. to Stanton, May 7, *OR*, 11:3, pp. 148–49; Harry Williams to parents, May 6, Williams-Dameron Papers, North Carolina State Archives; Mansfield teleg. to Wool, Tucker to Mallory, May 8, *NOR*, 7, pp. 330, 786; May 10, Ruffin, *Diary*, II, p. 298; Lincoln to Goldsborough, May 7, Lincoln, *Works*, V, p. 207; E. L. Viele, "A Trip with Lincoln, Chase and Stanton," *Scribner's Monthly*, 16:6 (Oct. 1878), pp. 819–21; Wilson Barstow to sister, May 12, Barstow Papers, LC.

5. Tattnall report and testimony, *NOR*, 7, pp. 335–38, 791–98; John T. Wood in *Battles and Leaders*, I, p. 710; Goldsborough, "Narrative," p. 1029; Davis to wife, May 13, 1862, Rowland, *Jefferson Davis*, V, p. 245; May 12, McGuire, *Diary*, p. 112. A court of inquiry found against Tattnall, but a court martial acquitted him: *NOR*, 7, pp. 789–99.

6. Moore, *Rebellion Record*, V, Documents, pp. 424–25; John H. Reagan, *Memoirs with Special References to Secession and the Civil War* (New York: Neale, 1906), p. 139; *Richmond Whig*, May 16, 1862; Putnam, *Richmond During the War*, pp. 130–31.

7. May 13, 1862, Ruffin, *Diary*, II, p. 303; Rogers, Ferrand, Newman, Van Gieson reports, *NOR*, 7, pp. 357–58, 369–70, 359–62, 358–59; William M. Robinson, Jr., "Drewry's Bluff: Naval Defense of Richmond, 1862," *Civil War History*, 7:2 (June 1961), pp. 167–75; Lee to Johnston, May 10, *OR*, 11:3, p. 505; James R. Soley in *Battles and Leaders*, II, p. 269; Harriet D. Whetten to "Kate," May 8, Whetten, "A Volunteer Nurse in the Civil War: The Letters of Harriet

Douglas Whetten," ed. Paul H. Hass, *Wisconsin Magazine of History*, 48 (Winter 1964–65), p. 133; Goldsborough to Fox, Apr. 24, 28, Fox, *Correspondence*, I, pp. 263–65; Goldsborough, "Narrative," p. 1028; J. Thomas Scharf, *History of the Confederate States Navy* (New York: Rogers & Sherwood, 1887), p. 715. The Federals called the redoubt atop Drewry's Bluff Fort Darling, after a former owner of the property.

8. E. J. Harvie in *Confederate Veteran*, 18:11 (Nov. 1910), p. 521; Johnston in *Battles and Leaders*, II, p. 207; Johnston, *Narrative*, p. 128; Henry C. Wall diary, May 16, 18, 1862, North Carolina State Archives; William Child, *A History of the Fifth Regiment New Hampshire Volunteers*, p. 64; Francis W. Palfrey in Military Historical Society of Mass., *Peninsular Campaign*, p. 116.

9. Johnston to Ewell, May 17, 1862, *OR*, 12:3, pp. 896–97; Johnston, *Narrative*, pp. 108–9, 127; McClellan teleg. to Scott, May 4, McClellan, *Papers*, pp. 253–54. Johnston's forces: c. Apr. 30, May 21 returns, *OR*, 11:3, pp. 484, 530–31, plus Huger's three brigades and Ripley's one, and the brigades of Field, Branch, J. R. Anderson, and Gregg incorporated in A. P. Hill's division, less battle losses. No evidence confirms Thomas N. Conrad's claim that he stole Federal returns from the War Department in Washington: John Bakeless, *Spies of the Confederacy* (Philadelphia: Lippincott, 1970), pp. 74–75.

10. William Allan, *History of the Campaign of Gen. T. J. (Stonewall) Jackson in the Shenandoah Valley of Virginia*, pp. 66, 68; Army of the Valley return, May 3, 1862, *OR*, 12:3, p. 879; Lee to Jackson, Apr. 21, 25, Lee, *Papers*, pp. 151, 156–57; Jackson to Lee, Apr. 28, 29, *OR*, 12:3, pp. 871, 872; Lee teleg. to Jackson, May 6, Lee Headquarters Papers, Virginia Historical Society.

11. McClellan telegs. to Stanton, May 10, Lincoln, May 14, 1862, McClellan to Scott, Aug. 8, 1861, McClellan, *Papers*, pp. 261, 264–65, 79–80; McClellan teleg. to wife, May 10, 1862, McClellan Papers (C-13:64), LC; Adam Gurowski, *Diary* (Boston: Lee & Shephard, 1862), I, p. 99; Fishel, "Pinkerton and McClellan," pp. 125–27.

12. Pinkerton to A. Porter, May 6, 7, 1862, McClellan Papers (A-56:22), LC; McClellan teleg. to Lincoln, May 14, McClellan, *Papers*, p. 264; Lincoln to McClellan, Apr. 9, Lincoln, *Works*, V, pp. 184–85; Army of the Potomac return, May 20, *OR*, 11:3, p. 184; Chase to Murat Halstead, May 24, Schuckers, *Chase*, p. 436; Aug. 31, Welles, *Diary*, I, p. 99; Heintzelman to Henry Wilson, May 21, 1862, to Alfred H. Guernsey, Sept. 30, 1866, Heintzelman Papers, LC.

13. Banks to Stanton, Apr. 30, McDowell teleg. to Lincoln, May 16, Stanton teleg. to McDowell, May 1, Shields to McDowell, May 5, 1862, *OR*, 12:3, pp. 118–19, 195, 121, 134; McDowell testimony, *Report of Joint Committee*, I (1863), p. 268; Stanton teleg. to McDowell, May 17, *OR*, 11:1, p. 28; Lincoln

teleg. to McClellan, May 21, Lincoln, *Works*, V, p. 226.

14. Stanton teleg. to Banks, May 1, Frémont telegs. to Stanton, May 9, 15, Banks teleg. to Stanton, May 12, 1862, *OR*, 12:3, pp. 122, 155, 192, 180; Stanton teleg. to McClellan, May 10, *OR*, 11:3, p. 160; Stanton teleg. to McDowell, May 17, *OR*, 11:1, p. 28.

15. D. H. Hill to wife, May 11, 1862, D. H. Hill Papers, Swem Library, College of William and Mary; McClellan to wife, May 10, McClellan, *Papers*, p. 262; Joel Cook, *The Siege of Richmond*, pp. 169–70, 95–96; Harriet D. Whetten to "Hexie," May 30, Whetten, "Volunteer Nurse," p. 141; Townsend, *Rustics in Rebellion*, p. 53; Van Vliet to Meigs, May 23, *OR*, 11:1, pp. 162–63; Davis to wife, June 11, Rowland, *Jefferson Davis*, V, p. 272. The plantation house at White House replaced the original Martha Custis house, which had burned some years before the war.

16. McClellan, *Report*, pp. 77, 96–97; *McClellan's Own Story*, p. 343; McClellan to Stanton, Feb. 3, May 10 (teleg.), to wife, May 22, to Burnside, May 21, 1862, McClellan, *Papers*, pp. 168, 261, 274, 270; Goldsborough to Fox, May 21, Fox, *Correspondence*, I, p. 271; Goldsborough to Welles, May 23, *NOR*, 7, p. 416; Goldsborough to wife, June 13, Goldsborough Papers, Perkins Library, Duke University; R. O. Tyler to Ingalls, May 17, J. H. Van Alen to C. P. Kingsbury, May 29, McClellan Papers (A-57:22, A-59:23) LC; Alexander S. Webb, *The Peninsula: McClellan's Campaign of 1862*, p. 87.

17. McClellan teleg. to Stanton, May 8, 1862, McClellan, *Papers*, p. 258; *McClellan's Own Story* draft, McClellan Papers (D-9:71), LC; Army of the Potomac G.O. 125, May 18, *OR*, 11:3, p. 181. Heintzelman lost Porter's division to the Fifth Corps, Keyes lost W. F. Smith's division to the Sixth; Sumner had already lost Blenker's division by transfer to Frémont.

18. T. D. Jennings in *Confederate Veteran*, 5:9 (Sept. 1897), p. 477; Charles B. Haydon diary, May 12, 30, 1862, MHC; Newton report, *OR*, 11:1, p. 625; Newton M. Curtis, *From Bull Run to Chancellorsville: The Story of the Sixteenth New York Infantry*, pp. 97–98; Felix Brannigan to sister, June 17, Brannigan Papers, LC; Army of the Potomac circular, May 10, *OR*, 11:3, p. 161; Porter to Manton Marble, May 21, Marble Papers, LC; Urich N. Parmelee to mother, May 8, Parmelee Papers, Perkins Library, Duke University; David E. Cronin, *The Evolution of a Life* (New York: S. W. Greer's Son, 1884), pp. 205–7; Luther C. Furst diary, May 10, 11, USAMHI.

19. J. H. B. Jenkins to Mary A. Benjamin, May 17, 1862, Jenkins Papers, Swem Library, College of William and Mary; Albert Davis to mother, May 16, Charles B. Haydon diary, May 19, MHC; McClellan teleg. to Stanton, May 16, *OR*, 11:3, p. 175; Hyde, *Following the Greek Cross*, pp. 82, 56; May 6, Wainwright, *Diary of Battle*, p. 58; John D. Wilkins to wife, May 14, Schoff Collection, CL; Weymouth, *Memorial Sketch*, pp. 62–63.

20. McClellan to wife, May 22, 1862, McClellan, *Papers*, p. 274; McDowell testimony, *Report of Joint Committee*, I (1863), p. 263; Lincoln telegs. to McClellan, May 24, 25, Lincoln, *Works*, V, pp. 232, 235–36.

Chapter 6. Battle at the Seven Pines

1. McClellan to wife, May 25, 26, McClellan teleg. to Lincoln, May 25, 1862, McClellan, *Papers*, pp. 275, 278, 276; Lincoln telegs. to McClellan, May 21, to McDowell, to Frémont, May 24, Lincoln, *Works*, V, pp. 226, 233, 231.
2. McClellan teleg. to Lincoln, May 26, 1862, McClellan, *Papers*, p. 277; William W. Folwell to wife, May 24, 25, 27, Folwell Papers, Minnesota Historical Society; Woodbury report, *OR*, 11:1, pp. 143–44; Thomas L. Livermore, *Days and Events, 1860–1866*, p. 63; Matthew Marrin diary, May 27, Minnesota Historical Society; Child, *Fifth New Hampshire*, pp. 63–64; Keyes to McClellan, May 26, McClellan Papers (A-58:23), LC.
3. Heintzelman diary, May 27, 1862, LC; Marcy to Cooke, May 25, Grier to Cooke, May 26, *OR*, 11:3, p. 191, 11:1, p. 677; Edwin C. Bennett, *Musket and Sword, or the Camp, March and Firing Line in the Army of the Potomac* (Boston: Coburn, 1900), p. 48; Webb, *The Peninsula*, pp. 94–96.
4. Morell, Martindale, Roberts, Rice, Branch, Lane reports, *OR*, 11:1, pp. 699–700, 705, 709, 731, 741–42, 743–44; William G. Morris to wife, May 30, 1862, Morris Papers, SHC; William

J. H. Bellamy diary, June 2, SHC; Moore, *Rebellion Record*, V, Documents, p. 71; Patrick A. Guiney to wife, May 31, Guiney Papers, Dinand Library, College of the Holy Cross; Porter to McClellan, May 27, McClellan Papers (A-59:23), LC.
5. Walter Clark, ed., *Histories of the Several Regiments and Battalions from North Carolina in the Great War, 1861–'65*, II, p. 654; Porter, Emory reports, *OR*, 11:1, pp. 680, 686–87; Alfred Davenport, *Camp and Field Life of the Fifth New York Volunteer Infantry*, p. 188; McClellan telegs. to wife, May 27, to Stanton, May 28, 1862, McClellan Papers (C-13:64), LC; McClellan teleg. to Stanton, May 30, McClellan, *Papers*, p. 280. Numbers and casualties at Hanover Court House: *OR*, 11:1, p. 685, and reports. Maps: *OR Atlas*, plates 21:2, 21:3, 21:11.
6. Johnston, *Narrative*, pp. 130–32; Gustavus W. Smith, *The Battle of Seven Pines*, pp. 12–14, 21; McDowell to Stanton, May 25, 1862, *OR*, 12:3, p. 232; D. H. Hill report, *OR*, 11:1, p. 943.
7. Cook, *Siege of Richmond*, pp. 104–5; Johnston, *Narrative*, pp. 133–34; Johnston in *Battles and Leaders*, II, pp. 211–12; Smith, *Seven Pines*, pp. 30–31. Maps: *OR Atlas*, plate 92:1; Donald E. Windham, "Seven Days Battles" (1931), maps 7–10, Map Division, LC.
8. Johnston to G. W. Smith, May 29, 30, 1862, Schoff Collection, CL; Johnston to Huger, May 30, 31, *OR*, 11:1, p. 983; Oliver W. Norton to family, May 31, Norton, *Army Letters*, p. 83; A. L. P.

Vairin diary, May 31, July 16, Mississippi Dept. of Archives and History; May 31, Wainwright, *Diary of Battle*, p. 75; Johnston, *Narrative*, p. 133; Smith, *Seven Pines*, p. 147. Confederate forces: May 21 return, *OR*, 11:3, pp. 530–31, plus reinforcements to June 1, less battle losses. Federal forces: May 31, June 20 returns, *OR*, 11:3, pp. 204, 238. The Seven Pines order of battle for both armies is in Appendix II.

9. Smith, *Seven Pines*, pp. 23–26; Alexander, *Military Memoirs*, pp. 77–79; G. W. Smith report (original) in *Seven Pines*, pp. 20–22, and endorsement (June 1865), Schoff Collection, CL; Longstreet, *Manassas to Appomattox*, pp. 88–89. Johnston in fact came to blame Longstreet for Seven Pines, but in his *Narrative of Military Operations* (1874) he refused to add his criticism to that Longstreet was suffering from Southerners for his role in Reconstruction: W. F. Smith, "Memoirs," Vermont Historical Society.

10. D. H. Hill to Longstreet, Aug. 29, 1879, Longstreet Papers, Perkins Library, Duke University; Huger notes, *OR*, 11:1, p. 937; Smith, *Seven Pines*, p. 59; Johnston to Henry Coppee, June 7, 1875, Johnston Papers, Swem Library, College of William and Mary; D. H. Hill, Gordon reports, *OR*, 11:1, pp. 971, 977.

11. McClellan teleg. to Stanton, May 27, 1862, McClellan, *Papers*, p. 278; Robert McAllister to daughter, June 20, McAllister, *Civil War Letters*, p. 179; M. D. McAlester to Barnard, May 29,

Keyes to Marcy, May 30, McClellan Papers (A-59:23), LC; Casey to headquarters, May 28, *OR*, 11:3, pp. 197–98; Marcy to Heintzelman, May 27, 1862, Heintzelman Seven Pines notes, Apr. 1863, Chauncey McKeever to Heintzelman, June 1, 1875, Heintzelman Papers, LC; Keyes, Casey reports, *OR*, 11:1, pp. 873, 914. Maps: Jacob Wells in *Battles and Leaders*, II, p. 240; E. Walter West in George D. Harmon, "General Silas Casey and the Battle of Fair Oaks," *The Historian*, 4:1 (Autumn 1941), opp. p. 96.

12. Lowe's later claim that his balloon rose at noon on May 31 and "I descended at 2 o'clock," and that his observations thus shaped the battle (*OR*, Ser. 3, 3, p. 280), is a falsification — almost surely a deliberate one. The original of this dispatch (McClellan Papers [A-59:23], LC) reads, "I ascended at two o'clock . . ." The journal of the Comte de Paris confirms that because of high winds the balloons had not ascended earlier; Lowe, he wrote, was "too late to boast of his exploits": Fondation Saint-Louis. None of Lowe's later dispatches that afternoon, in the *Official Records* or the McClellan Papers, contains intelligence useful to battlefield commanders.

13. Darius Couch, Civil War record, RG 94 (M-1098:5), NA; Garland report, *OR*, 11:1, p. 961; Thomas Learn memoir, New-York Historical Society; Casey to Heintzelman, June 6, 1862, Heintzelman Papers, LC; Leonidas Torrence to mother, June 8, "The Road to Gettysburg: The

Diary and Letters of Leonidas Torrence of the Gaston Guards," ed. Haskell Monroe, *North Carolina Historical Review*, 36 (Oct. 1959), p. 495; William F. Fox, *Regimental Losses in the American Civil War*, p. 561.

14. Casey to Heintzelman, June 6, 1862, Heintzelman Papers, LC; James Carr letter, June 16, Olde Soldier Books catalogue (June 1990); D. H. Hill report, *OR*, 11:1, p. 943; Bridges, *D. H. Hill*, pp. 42–43; John B. Gordon, *Reminiscences of the Civil War*, pp. 56–57; William E. Dunn, "On the Peninsular Campaign: Civil War Letters from William E. Dunn," *Civil War Times Illustrated*, 14:1 (July 1975), p. 17; Fox, *Regimental Losses*, p. 557; Clark, *North Carolina Regiments*, I, pp. 238–39; Bryan Grimes, *Extracts of Letters of Major-General Bryan Grimes to His Wife*, pp. 14–15; Stephen R. Mallory to wife, June 4, Mallory Papers, SHC.

15. Heintzelman Seven Pines notes, Apr. 1863, Aug. 1865, Heintzelman Papers, LC; Heintzelman telegs. to Marcy, May 31, 1862 (two), McClellan Papers (A-59:23), LC; Richardson, Wilcox reports, *OR*, 11:1, pp. 764, 986; Putnam, *Richmond During the War*, p. 133; Johnston report, *OR*, 11:1, p. 934; Davis, *Rise and Fall*, II, p. 122; John B. De Motte in *Battles and Leaders*, II, p. 365; J. W. Ratchford memoir, North Carolina State Archives; Huger in *Richmond Examiner*, Aug. 25; James H. McMath diary, May 31, Alabama Dept. of Archives and History.

16. Chauncy McKeever to Heintzelman, Mar. 1, 1863, Heintzelman

to wife, May 31, 1862, Heintzelman Papers, LC; Heintzelman teleg. to McClellan, May 31, 1862, *OR*, 51:1, p. 647; Bellard, *Gone for a Soldier*, p. 79; Charles B. Haydon diary, May 31, MHC; George E. Hagar diary, May 31, USAMHI; Keyes, Couch, Civil War records, RG 94 (M-1098:2, 5), NA; Keyes to McClellan, June 3, McClellan Papers (A-60:24), LC; Bridges, *D. H. Hill*, p. 47.

17. Gilbert A. Hays, *Under the Red Patch: Story of the 63rd Regiment, Pennsylvania Volunteers*, p. 97; Gordon, *Reminiscences*, p. 57; George E. Hagar diary, May 31, 1862, USAMHI; Douglas Southall Freeman, *Lee's Lieutenants*, II, p. 237n.

18. Bridges, *D. H. Hill*, p. 58; D. H. Hill, Jenkins reports, *OR*, 11:1, pp. 944, 947–49; Thomas J. Goree to sister, June 17, 1862, *Goree Letters*, pp. 151–52; Fox, *Regimental Losses*, p. 32.

19. May 31, 1862, Ruffin, *Diary*, II, pp. 326–27; Davis, *Rise and Fall*, II, p. 122; Smith, *Seven Pines*, pp. 22, 97; Freeman, *Lee's Lieutenants*, II, p. 237n; Joseph L. Brent, *Memoirs of the War Between the States*, p. 138; Alexander, *Military Memoirs*, p. 92n; Couch report, *OR*, 11:1, p. 880.

20. Oliver Otis Howard, *Autobiography of Oliver Otis Howard, Major General United States Army*, II, p. 237; William D. Sedgwick to cousin, June 5, 1862, John Sedgwick, *Correspondence of John Sedgwick, Major General*, II, p. 58; Henry L. Abbott to father, June 6, Abbott, *Fallen Leaves: The Civil War Letters of Major Henry Livermore Abbott*, p. 128; Ward Osgood

to brother, June 8, Stephen Osgood Papers, Perkins Library, Duke University; Kirby reports, *OR*, 2, p. 407, 11:1, p. 796; Francis W. Palfrey in Military Historical Society of Mass., *Peninsular Campaign*, p. 133; Edward D. Neill in Minnesota MOLLUS, *Glimpses of the Nation's Struggle*, 3rd Ser., p. 460; Cook, *Siege of Richmond*, p. 210.

21. Thomas Herndon memoir, Ben W. Coleman to parents, June 24, 1862, Tennessee State Library and Archives; Brent, *Memoirs*, p. 144; Edgar M. Newcomb to sister, June 5, Weymouth, *Memorial Sketch*, p. 67; O. W. Holmes, Jr., to parents, June 2, Holmes, *Touched with Fire: Letters and Diary of Oliver Wendell Holmes, Jr.*, ed. Mark DeWolfe Howe, p. 51. Casualties at Seven Pines: Federal, *OR*, 11:1, pp. 757-62; Confederate, *OR*, 11:1, pp. 942, 953, 967, 976, 11:2, p. 506.

22. Johnston, *Narrative*, pp. 138-39; Drury L. Armistead in *Southern Historical Society Papers*, 18 (1890), pp. 186-88; Govan and Livingood, *Johnston*, p. 156; Alexander, *Fighting for Confederacy*, p. 88.

23. Alexander, *Fighting for Confederacy*, p. 88; Smith, *Seven Pines*, pp. 103-4; Smith, *Confederate War Papers*, pp. 181-82.

24. Comte de Paris journal, June 13, 1862, Fondation Saint-Louis; May 31, Josiah M. Favill, *The Diary of a Young Officer Serving with the Armies of the United States During the War of the Rebellion*, p. 108; Henry L. Abbott to father, June 6, Abbott, *Fallen Leaves*, p. 129; Livermore, *Days and Events*, pp. 65-66; D. H. Hill to Longstreet, May 14, 1885, Longstreet

Papers, Perkins Library, Duke University; Robert H. Miller to cousin, June 25, 1862, Miller, "Letters," pp. 82-83; Jesse W. Reid to wife, June 2, Reid, *Fourth South Carolina*, p. 92; May 31, John S. Tucker, "Diary," p. 13; D. H. Hill report, *OR*, 11:1, p. 945.

25. Smith, *Seven Pines*, p. 129; Livermore, *Days and Events*, pp. 67, 69; *Cincinnati Commercial*, in Moore, *Rebellion Record*, V, Documents, p. 92; Francis C. Barlow to mother, June 2, 1862, Barlow Papers, Massachusetts Historical Society; Fox, *Regimental Losses*, p. 31; Howard, *Autobiography*, II, p. 251.

26. D. H. Hill to Longstreet, May 14, 1885, Longstreet Papers, Perkins Library, Duke University; Bridges, *D. H. Hill*, p. 49; J. W. Ratchford memoir, North Carolina State Archives; Bellard, *Gone for a Soldier*, pp. 81-82; Hooker report, *OR*, 11:1, p. 819.

27. Francis W. Palfrey in Military Historical Society for Mass., *Peninsular Campaign*, p. 141; Smith, *Seven Pines*, pp. 133, 136-37; Isaac L. Taylor diary, June 1, 1862, Minnesota Historical Society; Bellard, *Gone for a Soldier*, p. 83; McClellan to wife, June 2, McClellan, *Papers*, p. 288; Freeman, *R. E. Lee*, II, p. 77.

Chapter 7. Lee Takes Command

1. Heros Von Borcke, "The Prussian Remembers," *Civil War Times Illustrated*, 19:10 (Feb. 1981), p. 42; Thomas L. Ware diary, June 1, 1862, SHC; Constance Cary Harrison in *Battles and Leaders*, II, pp. 443-45; Putnam, *Richmond During the War*,

pp. 135–36; Alexander Hunter, *Johnny Reb and Billy Yank*, p. 157. Seven Pines casualties: Fox, *Regimental Losses*, p. 549.

2. *McClellan's Own Story* draft, McClellan Papers (D-9:71), LC; George W. Adams, *Doctors in Blue: The Medical History of the Union Army in the Civil War*, p. 71; George W. Barr to wife, June 10, 1862, Schoff Collection, CL; Tripler report, *OR*, 11:1, p. 178; F. L. Olmsted to H. W. Bellows, June 3, Olmsted, *The Papers of Frederick Law Olmsted*, ed. Jane Turner Censer (Baltimore: Johns Hopkins University Press, 1986), IV, p. 363; Katharine P. Wormeley to mother, June 5, Wormeley, *The Other Side of the War; With the Army of the Potomac*, p. 105. Seven Pines casualties: *OR*, 11:1, p. 762.

3. William F. Plane to wife, June 5, 1862, Plane, "Letters of William Fisher Plane, C.S.A. to His Wife," ed. S. Joseph Lewis, Jr., *Georgia Historical Quarterly*, 48 (June 1964), p. 222; Thomas B. Leaver to mother, June 6, Leaver Papers, New Hampshire Historical Society; June 1, Wainwright, *Diary of Battle*, p. 76.

4. McClellan to wife, June 2, to Army of the Potomac, June 2, McClellan telegs. to Stanton, June 2, to Lincoln, June 4, 1862, McClellan, *Papers*, pp. 287, 286–87, 285, 288–89; William W. Folwell to wife, June 3, Folwell Papers, Minnesota Historical Society; Comte de Paris journal, June 13, Fondation Saint-Louis; Comte de Paris to McClellan, Mar. 13, 1875, McClellan Papers (A-95:38), LC.

5. Jesse W. Reid to wife, June 2, 1862, Reid, *Fourth South Caro-*

lina, p. 92; Longstreet report, *OR*, 11:1, p. 940; Longstreet to Johnston, June 7, *OR*, 11:3, p. 580; Huger notes, Sept. 28, *OR*, 11:1, pp. 937–38; [Thomas C. Caffey], *Battle-Fields of the South, from Bull Run to Fredericksburgh*, p. 242; Davis to wife, June 2, Rowland, *Jefferson Davis*, V, p. 265.

6. William Allan conversation with Lee, Dec. 17, 1868, Allan Papers, SHC; Charles Marshall, *An Aide-de-Camp of Lee*, ed. Frederick Maurice, p. 77; Longstreet, *Manassas to Appomattox*, pp. 112–13; Jefferson Davis in *Southern Historical Society Papers*, 17 (1889), p. 369.

7. Boteler teleg. to Randolph, June 1, 1862, RG 109 (M-618:10), NA; Lee to Randolph, to Davis, June 5, Lee, *Papers*, pp. 185, 183–84; Boteler in *Southern Historical Society Papers*, 40 (1915), pp. 164–66; *Richmond Dispatch*, May 29; Jackson to Samuel Cooper, June 9, R. H. Chilton Papers, Museum of the Confederacy.

8. William Allan conversation with Lee, Dec. 17, 1868, Allan Papers, SHC; Brent, *Memoirs*, pp. 154–55; Marshall, *Aide-de-Camp*, p. 84; Pinkerton to McClellan, Apr. 20, Porter to Marcy, June 16, 1862, McClellan Papers (A-52:20, A-64:25), LC; Lee to Randolph, June 11, Lee, *Papers*, p. 191; King to Schriver, June 18, *OR*, 12:3, p. 404; Lincoln teleg. to McClellan, June 19, Lincoln, *Works*, V, p. 277; McClellan teleg. to Lincoln, June 18, McClellan, *Papers*, p. 303.

9. Lee to Davis, June 5, to Stevens, June 3, 1862, Lee, *Papers*, pp. 184, 182–83; Davis to Lee, June

2, *OR*, 11:3, p. 570; Dabney H. Maury, *Recollections of a Virginian in the Mexican, Indian, and Civil Wars* (New York: Scribner's, 1894), p. 161; *Charleston Mercury*, Oct. 14, 1861.

10. Whiting to Lee, June 2, 1862, *OR*, 11:3, pp. 685–86; G. W. Smith to Johnston, July 18, *OR*, 51:2, pp. 593–94.

11. Lee's Seven Days order of battle is in Appendix III. Due to the absence of returns for the Army of Northern Virginia between May 21 (*OR*, 11:3, pp. 530–31, using late April figures) and July 20 (*OR*, 11:3, p. 645), Lee's present-for-duty count of 92,400 entering the Seven Days is derived from these returns supplemented by unit reports, orders and correspondence in the *Official Records*, and from memoirs of participants, with adjustments for battle losses. This count is higher than those in previous accounts, which overlook (at the least) the assignment of new individual regiments to existing brigades.

12. Burnside teleg. to McClellan, June 13, 1862, McClellan Papers (A-63:25), LC; McClellan to wife, June 6, 11, McClellan, *Papers*, pp. 289, 296. McClellan's order of battle for the Seven Days is in Appendix III. The size of his field army — 105,900 present for duty — is determined from the June 20 return (*OR*, 11:3, p. 238) and additional returns in the McClellan and Stanton Papers, LC. (Aggregate present for duty, which included sick and in-arrest, was 117,226.)

13. McClellan teleg. to Stanton, June 10, McClellan to wife, June 22, 1862, McClellan, *Papers*, pp. 295–96, 304–5; Halleck telegs. to Stanton, June 12, 16, *OR*, 16:2, pp. 14, 26–27.

14. Lincoln to Stanton, June 8, 1862, Lincoln, *Works Supplement*, p. 138; Lincoln to McClellan, June 15, 20 (teleg.), to Frémont, June 15, Lincoln, *Works*, V, pp. 272, 277–78, 270–71; William W. Folwell to wife, June 14, Folwell Papers, Minnesota Historical Society.

15. Barnard report, *OR*, 11:1, pp. 114–16; Federal entrenchments map, RG 77 (G-443, 12:1), NA; Cyrus R. Stone to parents, June 15, 1862, Stone Papers, Minnesota Historical Society; Francis C. Barlow to brother, June 18, Barlow Papers, Massachusetts Historical Society; McClellan teleg. to Lincoln, June 20, McClellan to wife, June 15, McClellan, *Papers*, pp. 304, 300–302.

16. Army of the Potomac S.O. 168, June 2, S.O. 189, June 23, 1862, *OR*, 11:3, pp. 210–11, 248; McClellan teleg. to Stanton, June 15, McClellan to wife, June 11, McClellan, *Papers*, pp. 302, 296; *McClellan's Own Story* draft, McClellan Papers (D-9:71), LC.

17. McClellan to wife, June 9, 1862, McClellan, *Papers*, p. 293; James H. Campbell to wife, June 19, Schoff Collection, CL; *St. Louis Republican*, June 16, *New York Tribune*, June 10, *New York Times*, June 24.

18. Key to Stanton, June 16, Stanton to McClellan, June 21, 1862, *OR*, 11:1, pp. 1052–56, 1056; McClellan teleg. to Lincoln, June 20, McClellan, *Papers*, p. 304.

19. J. Ambler Johnston, *Echoes of*

1861–1961, pp. 64–65; W. R. Mason in *Battles and Leaders*, II, p. 277; Robert G. Haile diary, June 10, 1862, Swem Library, College of William and Mary.

20. McClellan to wife, June 22, McClellan telegs. to Stanton, June 25, to Lincoln, June 18, 1862, McClellan, *Papers*, pp. 305, 309–10, 303; Pinkerton to A. Porter, June 15, McClellan to Marcy, June 19, McClellan Papers (A-64:25, A-65:26), LC; Pinkerton to McClellan, June 26, *OR*, 11:1, p. 269; Fishel, "Pinkerton and McClellan," pp. 127–28; Lee to Jackson, June 16, Lee, *Papers*, p. 194; McClellan telegs. to Burnside, June 20, and Rodgers, June 24, McClellan to Barlow, June 23, McClellan, *Papers*, pp. 303, 307, 306.

21. Robert Taggart diary, June 14, 1862, and memoir, Pennsylvania Historical and Museum Commission; *London Times*, July 10; Army of the Potomac return, June 20, *OR*, 11:3, p. 238; Paul E. Steiner, *Disease in the Civil War: Natural Biological Warfare in 1861–1865*, pp. 124, 109–10, 116, 150; A. W. Stillwell diary, June 6, State Historical Society of Wisconsin; Josiah Patterson to family, June 13, Lane, *Letters from Georgia Soldiers*, p. 131; Edward M. Burruss to father, June 25, Burruss Papers, Hill Library, Louisiana State University; Jesse W. Reid to wife, June 7, Reid, *Fourth South Carolina*, pp. 93–94; Jacob Heffelfinger diary, June 17, USAMHI.

22. J. R. C. Ward, *History of the 106th Regiment, Pennsylvania Volunteers* (Philadelphia: McManus, 1906), p. 455; [Caffey], *Battle-Fields of the South*, p. 317; Steiner, *Disease in the Civil War*, p. 134; Charles B. Haydon diary, June 14, 1862, MHC; Giles F. Ward to mother, June 18, Ward Papers, Perkins Library, Duke University; Selden Connor to brother, June 21, Connor Papers, John Hay Library, Brown University; Frank Coker to wife, June 29, Lane, *Letters from Georgia Soldiers*, p. 153; Cyrus R. Stone to parents, June 10, Stone Papers, Minnesota Historical Society.

23. June 17, 1862, Favill, *Diary of a Young Officer*, p. 125; James C. Miller, "Serving Under McClellan on the Peninsula in '62," *Civil War Times Illustrated*, 8:3 (June 1969), p. 25; John A. Fite memoir, Tennessee State Library and Archives; Edgar Allan Jackson to brother, June 23, Jackson Papers, Virginia State Library.

24. James R. Strong to brother, July 21, 1862, Strong Papers, State Historical Society of Wisconsin; Robert Taggart diary, June 21, Pennsylvania Historical and Museum Commission; Matthew Marrin diary, June 20, Minnesota Historical Society; W. F. Smith to Marcy, June 23, McClellan Papers (A-67:27), LC.

25. Robert G. Haile diary, June 6, 1862, Swem Library, College of William and Mary; Jesse W. Reid to wife, June 15, Reid, *Fourth South Carolina*, p. 94; Charles E. Perkins to sister, June 23, Perkins, "Letters Home," pp. 114–15.

26. Stephen M. Weld, *War Diary and Letters of Stephen Minot Weld* (Boston: Massachusetts Historical Society, 2nd ed., 1979), p. 75;

Johnston to Davis, Aug. 10, 1861, *OR*, 5, p. 777; Stuart to Lee, June 4, 1862, J. E. B. Stuart Papers, Huntington Library; Heros Von Borcke, *Memoirs of the Confederate War for Independence*, I, pp. 34–36; John S. Mosby in *Southern Historical Society Papers*, 26 (1898), pp. 246–48; Lee to Stuart, June 11, *OR*, 11:1, pp. 590–91; John S. Mosby, *Mosby's War Reminiscences and Stuart's Cavalry Campaigns*, p. 221; Stuart report, *OR*, 11:1, p. 1038.

27. Von Borcke, *Memoirs*, I, p. 37; Stuart report, *OR*, 11:1, pp. 1036–38; William Campbell, Richard E. Frayser in *Southern Historical Society Papers*, 29 (1911), pp. 86–89, 11 (1883), pp. 506–7; John Esten Cooke, *Wearing of the Gray*, p. 179.

28. Porter telegs. to Marcy, June 13, 1862 (two), McClellan Papers (A-62:25), LC; Cooke, Warren reports, *OR*, 11:1, pp. 1013, 1029–31; Warren to brother, June 16, G. K. Warren Papers, New York State Library.

29. Richard E. Frayser in *Southern Historical Society Papers*, 11 (1883), pp. 507–11; Cooke, *Wearing of the Gray*, pp. 183–87; Ingalls, Reynolds, Warren, Stuart reports, *OR*, 11:1, pp. 1032, 1028–29, 1030, 1039; G. W. Beale, *A Lieutenant of Cavalry in Lee's Army* (Boston: Gorham, 1918), p. 30.

30. *Charleston Mercury*, June 20, 1862; W. T. Robins in *Battles and Leaders*, II, p. 275; Emily J. Salmon, "The Burial of Latané: Symbol of the Lost Cause," *Virginia Cavalcade*, 28 (Winter 1979), pp. 118–29.

31. William Y. Ripley to wife, June 17, 1862, Ripley Papers, Perkins Library, Duke University; Cook, *Siege of Richmond*, pp. 286–87; McClellan teleg. to Stanton, June 14, McClellan, *Papers*, p. 299; McClellan to S. S. Cox, 1884, Charles P. Kingsbury to Marcy, June 17, 1862, McClellan Papers (A-107:42, A-56:26), LC; Clarke, Van Vliet reports, *OR*, 11:1, pp. 169, 159.

32. Marshall, *Aide-de-Camp*, pp. 82–83; Lee to Jackson, June 16, 1862, Lee, *Papers*, p. 194; Jedediah Hotchkiss diary, June 18, Hotchkiss, *Make Me a Map of the Valley: The Civil War Journal of Stonewall Jackson's Topographer*, ed. Archie P. McDonald (Dallas: Southern Methodist University Press, 1973), p. 57; John D. Imboden in *Battles and Leaders*, II, pp. 296–97; Carter S. Anderson, "Train Running for the Confederacy," *Railway and Locomotive Engineering*, 5 (Aug. 1892), pp. 287–89, H. W. Wingfield diary, June 22, Wingfield, "Diary of Capt. H. W. Wingfield," ed. W. W. Scott, *Bulletin of the Virginia State Library*, 16 (July 1927), p. 13; John A. Harmon to brother, June 21, J. William Jones memoir, Hotchkiss Papers (39), LC; Henry Kyd Douglas, *I Rode with Stonewall*, p. 97.

33. D. H. Hill in *Battles and Leaders*, II, pp. 347–48; D. H. Hill to wife, June 24, 1862, Schoff Collection, CL; Lee G. O. 75, June 24, Lee to Davis, June 10, Lee, *Papers*, pp. 198–200, 188; Longstreet, *Manassas to Appomattox*, pp. 121–22; Longstreet to D. H. Hill, Nov. 5, 1877, D. H. Hill Papers, Virginia State

Library; William Allan conversation with Lee, Dec. 17, 1868, Allan Papers, SHC; Marshall, *Aide-de-Camp*, p. 85.

Chapter 8. *"Stonewall Is Behind Them!"*

1. Pinkerton to A. Porter, Farnsworth to Porter, June 24, 1862, *OR*, 51:1, pp. 693–96, 693; Porter in *Lyceum Herald*, 1891 clipping, RG 94 (E-729), NA; McClellan teleg. to Stanton, June 24, McClellan, *Papers*, p. 308; Stanton teleg. to McClellan, June 25, *OR*, 11:1, p. 49; Pinkerton to G. H. Bangs, July 9, Porter to Marcy, June 25, McClellan Papers (C-11:63, A-68:27), LC. Rean's name was spelled variously; Pinkerton supplied McClellan the correct spelling Apr. 18, 1863 (McClellan Papers [A-90:35], LC). By Porter's later account, Rean admitted to being a spy, but he is not so called in McClellan's or Pinkerton's contemporary accounts.
2. McClellan to wife, June 23, 15, 1862, McClellan, *Papers*, pp. 307, 301; McClellan, *Report*, p. 120.
3. Hooker, Grover, Sickles reports, *OR*, 11:2, pp. 108, 120–21, 134; Thomas B. Leaver to mother, June 24, 1862, Leaver Papers, New Hampshire Historical Society; Heintzelman diary, June 25, LC; Francis W. Palfrey in Military Historical Society of Mass., *Peninsular Campaign*, p. 149; Alexander Hays to John B. McFadden, June 26, G. A. Hays, *Under the Red Patch*, pp. 234–35.
4. William Gay to parents, July 20, 1862, Lane, *Letters from Georgia Soldiers*, p. 168; Grover, Ransom, Sickles, Hooker reports, *OR*, 11:2, pp. 121, 791–92, 135, 109; James Reese in *Confederate Veteran*, 4:5 (May 1896), p. 161; Heintzelman teleg. to McClellan, June 25 (9:45 A.M.), N. B. Sweitzer teleg. to Marcy, June 25 (10:30 A.M.), McClellan, *Report* draft, McClellan Papers (A-68:27), LC.
5. Edgar M. Newcomb to brother, June 25, 1862, Weymouth, *Memorial Sketch*, p. 71; Samuel H. Walkup diary, June 25, SHC; Joshua Lewis, Erasmus C. Gilreath memoirs, Indiana State Library; Robinson report, *OR*, 11:2, p. 174.
6. Lee to Davis, June [25], 26, 1862, Lee, *Papers*, pp. 200, 201; Charles B. Haydon diary, June 25, MHC; Comte de Paris journal, Fondation Saint-Louis (the Comte's journal for the Seven Days is in the form of a retrospective entry written in England in May 1863); McClellan teleg. to Stanton, June 25, McClellan, *Papers*, p. 309; Alexander Hays to John B. McFadden, June 26, G. A. Hays, *Under the Red Patch*, p. 235; Elisha Hunt Rhodes diary, June 26, *All for the Union*, p. 71; George E. Hagar diary, June 25, USAMHI. Maps: Donald E. Windham, "Seven Days' Battles" (1931), maps 1, 8, Map Division, LC. Casualties at Oak Grove: Federal, *OR*, 11:2, pp. 37–38; Confederate, *OR*, 11:2, pp. 973–84. Casualty totals for some Confederate brigades in the Seven Days are not broken down by battle; their battle losses are calculated here from

official reports and correspondence, and individuals' letters, diaries, and memoirs.

7. Porter teleg. to Marcy, June 25, Porter to Marcy, June 24, Pinkerton to A. Porter, June 15, 1862, McClellan Papers (A-68:27, A-67:27, A-64:25), LC; Pinkerton to McClellan, June 26, *OR*, 11:1, p. 269; McClellan telegs. to Stanton (two), Burnside, Marcy, Van Vliet, June 25, McClellan, *Papers*, pp. 309–10, 311–12; Rodgers teleg. to McClellan, June 25, *OR*, 11:3, pp. 256–57, Comte de Paris journal, Fondation Saint-Louis.

8. Freeman, *Lee's Lieutenants*, I, pp. 503–4n; B. Y. Malone diary, June 23, 1862, *Whipt 'em Everytime*, p. 57; Anderson, "Train Running" (Oct. 1892), p. 369; A. L. P. Vairin diary, June 23–25, Mississippi Dept. of Archives and History; S. G. Pryor to wife, June 25, Pryor, *A Post of Honor: The Pryor Letters, 1861–63*, ed. Charles R. Adams, Jr. (Fort Valley, Ga.: Garret, 1989), pp. 207–8; Hunter McGuire, "The Seven Days' Fighting Around Richmond," Alderman Library, University of Virginia; Robert L. Dabney, "Jackson's March," Hotchkiss Papers (39), LC; J. W. Melhorn diary, June 23–25, Stanford University Library; J. D. Summers diary, June 24–25, Virginia State Library; Thomas Verdery to Warren Akin, July 22, Lane, *Letters from Georgia Soldiers*, p. 171; Lee G.O. 75, June 24, Lee to Davis, June 26, Lee, *Papers*, pp. 198, 201. Maps: *OR Atlas*, plate 92; Confederate Engineers' Bureau, "Central Virginia, 1863," Gilmer

Collection, Virginia Historical Society.

9. Thomas L. Ware diary, June 25, 1862, SHC; Sara A. R. Pryor, *Reminiscences of Peace and War* (New York: Macmillan, 1904), p. 174; James L. Dinwiddie to wife, June 29, Dinwiddie Papers, Virginia State Library; J. W. Melhorn diary, June 26, Stanford University Library; Marshall, *Aide-de-Camp*, p. 89; Lee to Davis, June 5, Lee, *Papers*, p. 184; Alexander, *Fighting for Confederacy*, p. 77.

10. Lee G.O. 75, June 24, 1862, Lee, *Papers*, pp. 198–200; Davis to wife, June 21, Rowland, *Jefferson Davis*, V, p. 283; W. F. Smith, *Autobiography*, p. 41; E. C. Gordon to William Allan, Nov. 18, 1886, Allan Papers, SHC.

11. Longstreet, A. P. Hill reports, *OR*, 11:2, pp. 756, 834–35; John L. G. Wood to father, June 26, 1862, Wood Papers, Georgia Dept. of Archives and History; Lee to Davis, June 26, Lee, *Papers*, p. 201; McClellan to wife, June 26, McClellan, *Papers*, p. 313; Porter in *Battles and Leaders*, II, pp. 325–27; N. B. Sweitzer to Marcy, June 25, McClellan Papers (A-68:27), LC; Robert McAllister to wife, June 26, McAllister, *Civil War Letters*, p. 184.

12. Jackson to Branch, June 26, 1862 (two), *OR*, 11:3, p. 620; J. W. Melhorn diary, June 26, Stanford University Library; A. L. P. Vairin diary, June 26, Mississippi Dept. of Archives and History; Campbell Brown memoir, Tennessee State Library and Archives; Whiting report, *OR*, 11:2, p. 562; Douglas, *I Rode with*

Stonewall, p. 100; Evander M. Law, "The Fight for Richmond in 1862," *Southern Bivouac*, 2 (1886–87), p. 654; Dabney, "Jackson's March," Hotchkiss Papers (39), LC; council of war memorandum (Jackson copy) in Freeman, *Lee's Lieutenants*, I, pp. 499–500; Lee G.O. 75, June 24, Lee, *Papers*, p. 198. Maps: Confederate Engineers' Bureau, "Hanover County, 1864," Gilmer Collection, Virginia Historical Society; Albert H. Campbell, "Map of the Environs of Richmond, 1862," Museum of the Confederacy.

13. D. R. Clendenin, George Stoneman, Porter, J. F. Reynolds to Marcy, June 26, 1862, McClellan Papers (A-69:27), LC; McClellan teleg. to wife, June 26, McClellan, *Papers*, p. 317.

14. McClellan teleg. to Stanton, June 26, 1862, *OR*, 11:3, p. 257; Brent, *Memoirs*, pp. 160–62; Branch, A. P. Hill reports, *OR*, 11:2, pp. 882, 835.

15. Cook, *Siege of Richmond*, pp. 181, 230; Henry C. Sydnor in *Confederate Veteran*, 20:3 (Mar. 1912), p. 105; Abner Hard, *History of the Eighth Cavalry Regiment, Illinois Volunteers* (Aurora, Ill., 1868), p. 123; John S. Judd diary, June 1, 1862, Kansas State Historical Society; Cordello Collins to parents, July 19, Collins, "A Bucktail Voice: Civil War Correspondence of Pvt. Cordello Collins," ed. Mark Reinsberg, *Western Pennsylvania Historical Magazine*, 48 (July 1965), p. 240; Stone report, *OR*, 11:2, p. 414.

16. Alexander, *Fighting for Confederacy*, p. 95; Dawson, *Reminiscences*, pp. 48–49; William Allan conversation with Lee, Dec. 17, 1868, Allan Papers, SHC; Marshall, *Aide-de-Camp*, p. 94; McClellan teleg. to wife, June 26, 1862, McClellan, *Papers*, p. 315; Marcy telegs. to corps commanders, June 26, McClellan Papers (A-69:27), LC; W. F. Smith, *Autobiography*, p. 41; McClellan teleg. to Stanton, June 26, *OR*, 11:3, p. 257. Maps: Jacob Wells in *Battles and Leaders*, II, p. 328; Donald Windham, "Seven Days' Battles" (1931), map 2, Map Division, LC.

17. McCall, Amsden, A. P. Hill, Field, Thomas reports, *OR*, 11:2, pp. 386, 411, 835, 841, 51:1, p. 117; Josiah R. Sypher, *History of the Pennsylvania Reserve Corps*, p. 211; M. T. Ledbetter in *Confederate Veteran*, 1:8 (Aug. 1893), p. 244.

18. Chesnut diary, July 10, 1862, Woodward, *Mary Chesnut's Civil War*, p. 411; *Richmond Dispatch*, June 26; June 26, Jones, *Rebel War Clerk's Diary*, I, pp. 136–38; Putnam, *Richmond During the War*, p. 146; *Memphis Daily Appeal*, July 5.

19. Pender, D. H. Hill, Estes reports, *OR*, 11:2, pp. 899, 623, 656; John W. Hinsdale diary, June 26, 1862, Perkins Library, Duke University; Robert Taggart diary, June 26, Pennsylvania Historical and Museum Commission; Clark, *North Carolina Regiments*, II, p. 680, I, p. 756; D. H. Hill in *Battles and Leaders*, II, p. 352; Edgar Allan Jackson to mother, July 1, Jackson Papers, Virginia State Library; McClellan telegs. to wife, Stanton, Marcy, June 26, McClellan, *Papers*, p. 317; Selden Connor to

brother, June 26, Connor Papers, John Hay Library, Brown University.

20. Alexander, *Fighting for Confederacy*, p. 96; William Allan conversation with Lee, Dec. 17, 1868, Allan Papers, SHC; Jackson to wife, July 8, 1862, Mary Anna Jackson, *Life and Letters of General Thomas J. Jackson* (New York: Harper, 1892), p. 302. Casualties at Mechanicsvillle: Federal, *OR*, 11:2, pp. 38–39; Confederate, *OR*, 11:2, pp. 973–84 (see Note 6 *supra*).

Chapter 9. Gaines's Mill

1. Porter to John C. Ropes, Feb. 11, William F. Biddle to Ropes, Mar. 27, 1895, Ropes Collection, Boston University Library; G. H. Lyman in Military Historical Society of Mass., *Civil and Mexican Wars* (Boston, 1913), p. 200n; Pinkerton to McClellan, June 27, Van Vliet teleg. to Ingalls, June 27, Marcy teleg. to Franklin, June 27, Marcy to McClellan, June 26, 1862, McClellan Papers (A-70:28), LC; Barnard, *Peninsular Campaign*, p. 41; McClellan, *Report*, p. 124; Comte de Paris journal, Fondation Saint-Louis; Porter, Barnard reports, *OR*, 11:2, p. 223, 11:1, p. 118; McClellan teleg. to Stanton, June 27, McClellan, *Papers*, p. 318.

2. McCall report, *OR*, 11:2, p. 386; Reynolds report, Edward J. Nichols, *Toward Gettysburg: A Biography of General John F. Reynolds* (University Park: Pennsylvania State University Press, 1958), p. 94; William Allan conversation with Lee, Dec. 17, 1868, Allan Papers, SHC; Lee to Huger, June 26, 1862, Lee, *Papers*, pp. 201–2; William Calder to mother, June 29, Calder Papers, SHC; N. J. Brooks to family, July 4, Lane, *Letters from Georgia Soldiers*, p. 160; J. F. J. Caldwell, *The History of [Gregg's] Brigade of South Carolinians*, p. 15.

3. Barnard report, *OR*, 11:1, pp. 117–18; J. D. Richardson to parents, June 8, 1862, Richardson Papers, MHC; Porter, Richard T. Auchmuty in *Battles and Leaders*, II, pp. 333, 340n; Alexander, *Fighting for Confederacy*, p. 95; Alexander, *Military Memoirs*, p. 123; Porter memorandum, c. Apr. 1863, Marcy teleg. to Franklin, June 27, 1862, McClellan Papers (A-89:35, A-70:28), LC; Porter to John C. Ropes, Feb. 11, 1895, Richard Robins memoir, Ropes Collection, Boston University Library; Webb, *Peninsula*, p. 187; Heintzelman diary, June 27, 1862, LC; Porter to Manton Marble, July 22, Marble Papers, LC. Maps: Jacob Wells in *Battles and Leaders*, II, p. 334; Donald E. Windham, "Seven Days' Battles" (1931), map 3, Map Division, LC.

4. Marcy teleg. to Sumner, Sumner teleg. to Marcy, Hooker teleg. to Sumner, Franklin teleg. to Colburn, Marcy teleg. to Van Vliet, Colburn teleg. to Ingalls, June 27, 1862, McClellan Papers (A-70:28), LC; Francis B. Butts in *Personal Narratives of the Events of the War of the Rebellion* (Providence, R.I., 1896), Fifth Series: 6, p. 66; Matthew Marrin diary, June 27, Minnesota Historical Society; Lowe to Humphreys, June 27, *OR*, Ser. 3, 3, p. 290; J.

Duane Squires, "Aeronautics in the Civil War," *American Historical Review*, 42:4 (July 1937), pp. 663–64; E. P. Alexander to father, July 24, Alexander Papers, SHC; June 27, Favill, *Diary of a Young Officer*, p. 131; McClellan teleg. to Stanton, June 27, McClellan to Barlow, July 23, McClellan, *Papers*, pp. 321, 370. Confederate Charles Cevor claimed he also made a balloon ascension on June 27, although no contemporary evidence supports his claim; see Judith Anthis and Richard McMurry, "The Confederate Balloon Corps," *Blue & Gray*, 8:6 (Aug. 1991), pp. 20–24.

5. Lee, Gregg reports, *OR*, 11:2, pp. 492, 853; William Allan conversation with Lee, Dec. 17, 1868, Allan Papers, SHC; [Robert L. Dabney], "What I Saw of the Battle of Chickahominy," *Southern Magazine*, 10 (Jan. 1872), p. 4; Dabney in *Battles and Leaders*, II, p. 353; J. B. Polley, July 12, 1862, Polley, *A Soldier's Letters to Charming Nellie*, p. 53.

6. Lee to Huger, June 27, 1862, Lee, *Papers*, p. 203; [Caffey], *Battle-Fields of the South*, p. 331; Marshall, *Aide-de-Camp*, p. 97; Lee report, *OR*, 11:2, p. 679.

7. D. H. Hill, G. G. H. Kean in *Battles and Leaders*, II, pp. 354, 365; James W. Shinn memoir, Osborne Papers, SHC; Robert McAllister to daughters, May 22, 1862, McAllister, *Civil War Letters*, p. 162 and n; D. H. Hill, Garland, Buchanan, Stuart reports, *OR*, 11:2, pp. 624, 640–41, 359, 515; A. A. Humphreys to wife, July 17, Humphreys Papers, Historical Society of Pennsylvania.

8. Gregg, Griffin, A. P. Hill, Lee, Sykes reports, *OR*, 11:2, pp. 853–54, 313, 836, 492, 348; Caldwell, *Gregg's Brigade*, p. 16; Wise, *Long Arm of Lee*, I, pp. 210–11; Porter teleg. to Marcy, Franklin teleg. to McClellan, June 27, 1862, McClellan Papers (A-70:28), LC.

9. J.B.M. in *Southern Historical Society Papers*, 28 (1900), p. 95; Richard T. Auchmuty to mother, July 5, 1862, Auchmuty, *Letters of Richard Tylden Auchmuty, Fifth Corps, Army of the Potomac*, ed. Ellen S. Auchmuty, p. 69; Gregg report, *OR*, 11:2, pp. 854–55; Brian C. Pohanka, "Like Demons with Bayonets," *Military Images*, 10:6 (May–June 1989), pp. 19–20; Barry G. Benson memoir, SHC.

10. Crenshaw, McIntosh, Haywood, Archer, Pender, J. R. Anderson, Mayo, D. H. Hill reports, *OR*, 11:2, pp. 903, 860, 888, 897, 900, 879, 845, 837; Thomas H. Evans, "There Is No Use Trying to Dodge Shot," *Civil War Times Illustrated*, 6:5 (Aug. 1967), p. 44; Brigham Buswell memoir, Collection of Gloria Conklin, Chappaqua, N.Y.; William C. Kent, "Sharpshooting with Berdan," *Civil War Times Illustrated*, 15:2 (May 1976), p. 8; William H. Powell, *The Fifth Army Corps*, p. 97; William G. Morris to wife, July 21, 1862, Morris Papers, SHC; Norton, *Army Letters*, pp. 315–16.

11. William F. Biddle to John C. Ropes, Mar. 27, 1895, Ropes Collection, Boston University Library; Martindale report, *OR*,

11:2, p. 291; McClellan telegs. to Porter (two) and Franklin, June 27, 1862, McClellan, *Papers*, pp. 319–20; Franklin teleg. to McClellan, Sumner teleg. to Marcy, June 27, McClellan Papers (A-70:28), LC.

12. Robert L. Dabney, *Life and Campaigns of Lieut.-Gen. Thomas J. Jackson*, pp. 443–44; Campbell Brown report, Tennessee State Library and Archives; Ewell report, *OR*, 11:2, p. 605.

13. Ewell, Longstreet, Trimble reports, *OR*, 11:2, pp. 605–6, 757, 614; Campbell Brown report, memoir, Tennessee State Library and Archives; Henry E. Handerson to father, July 13, 1862, Handerson, *Yankee in Gray*, p. 96; Alexander, *Fighting for Confederacy*, p. 120; Terry L. Jones, *Lee's Tigers: The Louisiana Infantry in the Army of Northern Virginia*, p. 104; James C. Nisbit, *Four Years on the Firing Line* (Jackson, Tenn.: McCowat-Mercer, 1963), p. 64; Sidney J. Richardson to parents, July 5, Richardson Papers, Georgia Dept. of Archives and History.

14. Anon. 9th Massachusetts diary, June 27, 1862, *Civil War Times Illustrated*, 29:2 (June 1990), p. 30; Pohanka, "Like Demons with Bayonets," p. 21; James L. Dinwiddie to wife, June 29, Dinwiddie Papers, Virginia State Library; Richard T. Auchmuty to mother, July 5, Auchmuty, *Letters*, p. 146; Cordello Collins to parents, July 19, Collins, "A Bucktail Voice," p. 240; Adam S. Bright to family, July 7, Aida Craig Truxall, ed., *"Respects to All": Letters of Two Pennsylvania Boys in the War of the Rebellion*

(Pittsburgh: University of Pittsburgh Press, 1962), p. 25; Camille Baquet, *History of the First Brigade, New Jersey Volunteers*, p. 315; Brent, *Memoirs*, pp. 171–72.

15. Porter telegs. to McClellan (two), McClellan telegs. to Franklin and Sumner, Franklin and Sumner telegs. to McClellan, Colburn teleg. to Sumner, June 27, 1862, McClellan Papers (A-70:28), LC; McClellan teleg. to Porter, June 27, McClellan, *Papers*, p. 321; A. A. Humphreys to wife, July 17, Humphreys Papers, Historical Society of Pennsylvania.

16. Jackson report, *OR*, 11:2, p. 553; Robert L. Dabney, "Gaines's Mill," Hotchkiss Papers (39), LC; [Dabney], "Battle of Chickahominy," pp. 7–11; Charles Venable, "Personal Reminiscences," McDowell Family Papers, Alderman Library, University of Virginia; John Esten Cooke, *A Life of Gen. Robert E. Lee* (New York: Appleton, 1871), p. 84.

17. [Dabney], "Battle of Chickahominy," p. 12; Dabney, *Life of Jackson*, p. 455; Longstreet to Lee, Mar. 20, 1866, Lee's Headquarters Papers, Virginia Historical Society; James Chesnut to Mary Chesnut, June 29, 1862, Woodward, *Mary Chesnut's Civil War*, p. 403; Stuart, Slocum, D. H. Hill, Seaver reports, *OR*, 11:2, pp. 515, 433, 624–25, 451.

18. Curtis, *Bull Run to Chancellorsville*, p. 120; Cyrus R. Stone to parents, July 11, 1862, and memoir, Stone Papers, Minnesota Historical Society; Grimes, *Extracts of Letters*, p. 17, James W. Shinn memoir, Osborne Papers,

SHC; Sykes report, *OR*, 11:2, p. 349; Evans, "No Use Trying to Dodge Shot," pp. 44–45.

19. Lawton report, *OR*, 11:2, p. 595; I. G. Bradwell in *Confederate Veteran*, 24:1 (Jan. 1916), p. 23, 33:10 (Oct. 1925), pp. 382–83; Richard Robins memoir, Ropes Collection, Boston University Library; McHenry Howard, *Recollections of a Maryland Confederate Soldier and Staff Officer*, p. 140n.

20. Longstreet report, *OR*, 11:2, p. 757; Edmund D. Patterson diary, June 28, 1862, *Yankee Rebel*, p. 32; Robert H. Miller to father, July 23, Miller, "Letters," p. 88; Dabney, *Life of Jackson*, p. 451; Hood, *Advance and Retreat*, p. 25.

21. Law, "Fight for Richmond," pp. 655–56; C. C. Chambers in *Confederate Veteran*, 19:11 (Nov. 1911), p. 511; Clark, *North Carolina Regiments*, I, p. 304; Harold B. Simpson, *Hood's Texas Brigade: Lee's Grenadier Guard*, p. 117n; Davis, *Hood's Texas Brigade*, pp. 83, 87–88; Edmund D. Patterson diary, June 28, 1862, *Yankee Rebel*, p. 33; Comte de Paris journal, Fondation Saint-Louis; Cadmus Wilcox to D. H. Hill, June 17, 1885, D. H. Hill Papers, Virginia State Library.

22. N. J. Brooks to family, July 4, 1862, Lane, *Letters from Georgia Soldiers*, p. 161; John Cheves Haskell, *The Haskell Memoirs*, eds. Gilbert E. Govan and James W. Livingood (New York: Putnam, 1960), pp. 33–34; Val C. Giles, *Rags and Hope: The Recollections of Val C. Giles*, ed. Mary Laswell (New York: Coward-McCann, 1961), p. 111; Charles Venable, "Personal Reminiscences," McDowell Family Papers, Alderman Library, University of Virginia; J. A. Hoyt in *Confederate Veteran*, 7:5 (May 1899), pp. 225–26; Oliver W. Norton to cousin, July 5, Norton, *Army Letters*, pp. 92–93.

23. Comte de Paris journal, Fondation Saint-Louis; O. T. Hanks memoir, Barker Texas History Center, University of Texas; *New York Tribune*, July 4, 1862; C. C. Chambers in *Confederate Veteran*, 19:11 (Nov. 1911), p. 511; Evans, "No Use Trying to Dodge Shot," p. 45; Martin, Weeden, Hyde, Baylor reports, *OR*, 11:2, pp. 284, 282, 285, 580.

24. Porter, Cooke, McArthur reports, *OR*, 11:2, pp. 224–26, 41, 46; W. H. Hitchcock in *Battles and Leaders*, II, p. 346; Simpson, *Hood's Texas Brigade*, pp. 121, 122n; Edmund D. Patterson diary, June 28, 1862, *Yankee Rebel*, p. 33; Law, "Fight for Richmond," p. 656.

25. J. B. Robertson in Moore, *Rebellion Record*, V, Documents, p. 259; Simpson report, *OR*, 11:2, pp. 445–46; Nicholas Pomeroy memoir, Barker Texas History Center, University of Texas; J. B. Polley, July 12, *Letters to Charming Nellie*, p. 59; Baquet, *First New Jersey Brigade*, pp. 316–17.

26. D. R. Jones, Hancock reports, *OR*, 11:2, pp. 689–90, 467; Thomas L. Ware diary, June 27, 1862, SHC; McClellan teleg. to Stanton, June 27, McClellan, *Papers*, p. 321.

27. William H. French, Civil War record, RG 94, (M-1098:1), NA; James C. Miller, "Serving Under McClellan," p. 26; Barry G. Benson memoir, SHC.

Chapter 10. The Flight

1. Alexander, *Fighting for Confederacy*, p. 103. Casualties at Gaines's Mill: Federal, *OR*, 11:2, pp. 39–41; Confederate, *OR*, 11:2, pp. 973–84 (see Chap. 8, Note 6).
2. McClellan telegs. to Heintzelman, Goldsborough, June 27, 1862, McClellan, *Papers*, p. 322; Comte de Paris, *Civil War in America*, II, pp. 105–6; Comte de Paris journal, Fondation Saint-Louis; Townsend, *Rustics in Rebellion*, p. 141; Seth Williams to Keyes, June 27, McClellan Papers (A-70:28), LC; Keyes, Civil War record, RG 94 (M-1098:2), NA; Heintzelman diary, June 27, LC; Heintzelman testimony, *Report of Joint Committee*, I (1863), p. 355.
3. McClellan teleg. to Stanton, June 28, McClellan to wife, July 20, McClellan to Dix, June 29, 1862, McClellan, *Papers*, pp. 322–23, 367, 324–25; David H. Bates, *Lincoln in the Telegraph Office* (New York: Century, 1907), pp. 108–9; Lincoln teleg. to McClellan, June 28, Lincoln, *Works*, V, pp. 289–90; John Nicolay to Therena Bates, June 28, Helen Nicolay, *Lincoln's Secretary*, pp. 146–47; June 28, Ruffin, *Diary*, II, p. 356; John Graeme dispatch, June 28, RG 109 (M-618:10), NA; Frank Coker to wife, June 29, Lane, *Letters from Georgia Soldiers*, p. 151.
4. John M. Bancroft diary, June 27, 1862, MHC; D. H. Hill in *Battles and Leaders*, II, pp. 359–61; J. W. Ratchford memoir, North Carolina State Archives; Oliver W. Norton to sister, June 10, Norton, *Army Letters*, p. 87; Bruce, *Tools of War*, pp. 199–200; Barry G. Benson memoir, SHC; W. A. Kenyon to brother, June 28, M. W. Kenyon Papers, Perkins Library, Duke University; Robert McAllister to wife, June 21, McAllister, *Civil War Letters*, p. 181; Alexander, *Fighting for Confederacy*, p. 113; James L. Dinwiddie to wife, June 29, Dinwiddie Papers, Virginia State Library.
5. A. N. Erskine to wife, June 28, 1862, Erskine Papers, Barker Texas History Center, University of Texas; John W. Hinsdale diary, June 28, Hinsdale Family Papers, Perkins Library, Duke University; William G. Morris to wife, July 21, Morris Papers, SHC; James L. Boulware diary, June 27, Virginia State Library; Spencer G. Welch to wife, June 29, Welch, *A Confederate Surgeon's Letters to His Wife* (New York: Neale, 1911), pp. 16–17; N. J. Brooks to mother, July 4, Lane, *Letters from Georgia Soldiers*, p. 160; Henry R. Berkeley diary, June 27, Berkeley, *Four Years in Confederate Artillery*, p. 19; John S. Judd diary, June 28, Kansas State Historical Society.
6. E. P. Alexander to father, July 24, 1862, Alexander Papers, SHC; Lee report, *OR*, 11:2, pp. 493–94; Barry report, *OR*, 5, p. 69; Tyler, Van Vliet, Clarke reports, *OR*, 11:1, pp. 274, 158, 170; Meigs report, *OR*, Ser. 3, 2, p. 798; McClellan to Army of the Potomac, July 4, McClellan, *Papers*, p. 339. Maps: Jacob Wells in *Battles and Leaders*, II, p. 384; *OR Atlas*, plate 19:1; Donald E. Windham, "Seven Days' Bat-

tles" (1931), map 10, Map Division, LC.

7. Barnard, Keyes reports, *OR*, 11:1, p. 119, 11:2, p. 192; William W. Folwell to wife, July 1, 1862, Folwell Papers, Minnesota Historical Society; Heintzelman diary, June 28, LC; Theodore Reichardt, *Diary of Battery A, First Rhode Island Light Artillery*, p. 49; Charles B. Haydon diary, June 28, MHC; Comte de Paris journal, Fondation Saint-Louis.

8. McClellan teleg. to Lincoln, July 4, 1862, McClellan, *Papers*, p. 338; W. F. Smith to John C. Ropes, Mar. 21, 1895, Ropes Collection, Boston University Library; Lee, Stuart, Lansing reports, *OR*, 11:2, pp. 493, 515–16, 333; Henry M. Naglee to McClellan, June 28, 1862, McClellan Papers (A-71:28), LC; W. W. Blackford, *War Years with Jeb Stuart*, p. 76; John S. Foster to father, July 10, Foster Papers, Hill Library, Louisiana State University.

9. Robert A. Toombs to Alexander S. Stephens, July 14, 1862, Stephens Papers, Woodruff Library, Emory University; D. R. Jones report, *OR*, 11:2, p. 690; Thomas L. Ware diary, June 28, SHC; Bruce, *Tools to War*, p. 200; "Jimmy" to wife, June 29, Lane, *Letters from Georgia Soldiers*, p. 149. Casualties at Garnett's Farm, June 27–28: Federal, *OR*, 11:2, pp. 33–36; Confederate, *OR*, 11:2, p. 977 (see Chap. 8, Note 6). Golding's Farm, a site within the Federal lines, is another name for these engagements.

10. J. F. Mulligan to Randolph, June 28, 1862, *OR*, 11:3, p. 623;

McClellan teleg. to Rodgers, June 24, McClellan, *Papers*, p. 307; Rodgers to Goldsborough, June 29 (two), *NOR*, 7, pp. 523–24, 525.

11. Heintzelman diary, June 28, July 3, 1862, LC; Army of the Potomac circular, June 28, *OR*, 11:3, pp. 272–73; B. S. Alexander testimony, *Report of Joint Committee*, I (1863), p. 592; James F. Rusling, "General McClellan's Baggage-Destroying Order," *Century*, 38 (May 1889), pp. 157–58; Jonathan P. Stowe diary, June 28, USAMHI; Barnard report, *OR*, 11:1, p. 119; Early, *Autobiographical Sketch*, p. 76.

12. Lee to Davis, June 29, 1862, Lee, *Papers*, pp. 205–6; Alexander, *Military Memoirs*, pp. 136–37. Maps: Donald E. Windham, "Seven Days' Battles" (1931), maps 7–10, Map Division, LC.

13. Longstreet, *Manassas to Appomattox*, p. 130; J. W. Jones in *Southern Historical Society Papers*, 9 (1881), pp. 567–68; Magruder report, *OR*, 11:2, pp. 662–63; Brent, *Memoirs*, p. 192.

14. Marks, *Peninsular Campaign*, p. 245; A. W. Stillwell diary, June 29, 1862, State Historical Society of Wisconsin; James C. Miller, "Serving Under McClellan," p. 28; G. B. Adams, *Reminiscences of the Nineteenth Massachusetts Regiment*, p. 33; Asa Smith memoir, *American Heritage*, 22:2 (Feb. 1971), p. 56; June 29, Favill, *Diary of a Young Officer*, p. 136; Livermore, *Days and Events*, p. 79; Heintzelman diary, July 3, LC; Campbell Brown report, memoir, Tennessee State Library and Archives; Handerson, *Yankee in Gray*, p. 48.

15. Marks, *Peninsular Campaign*, pp. 343–44; John S. Judd diary, June 29, 1862, Kansas State Historical Society; Lafayette Guild report, *OR*, Ser. 2, 4, p. 798; Thomas W. Hyde to mother, July 6, Hyde, *Civil War Letters*, p. 33; William G. Le Duc, *Recollections of a Civil War Quartermaster*, p. 82; Comte de Paris journal, Fondation Saint-Louis; Evans, "No Use Trying to Dodge Shot," p. 39; Baker, Averell reports, *OR*, 11:2, pp. 525, 235; Elisha Hunt Rhodes diary, June 29, *All for the Union*, p. 72; Averell in *Battles and Leaders*, II, p. 431.

16. McClellan to wife, June 11, 1862, McClellan, *Papers*, p. 296; Sumner, Barksdale reports, *OR*, 11:2, pp. 50, 750; Matthew Marrin diary, June 29, Minnesota Historical Society; David W. Aiken to wife, July 7, Aiken Papers, South Caroliniana Library, University of South Carolina; Brent, *Memoirs*, p. 180; W. F. Smith, *Autobiography*, pp. 42–43; Franklin to McClellan, June 29, McClellan Papers (A-71:28), LC; Heintzelman diary, July 3, LC; Franklin in *Battles and Leaders*, II, pp. 370–71.

17. Brent, *Memoirs*, pp. 180–82; Lee, Magruder, Huger reports, *OR*, 11:2, pp. 680, 663, 789; Heintzelman diary, June 3, 9, July 3, 1862, LC; Heintzelman in *Battles and Leaders*, II, p. 181n; D. R. Jones to Magruder, June 29, *OR*, 11:3, p. 625.

18. Chilton to Stuart, Jackson to Stuart, June 29, 1862, J. E. B. Stuart Papers, Huntington Library; Lee to Magruder, June 29, Lee, *Papers*, p. 205; Lee report, *OR*, 11:2, p. 680; Dabney, *Life of Jackson*, p. 459; E. P. Alexander to Longstreet, Sept. 29, 1902, Abraham Lincoln Book Shop catalogue (July 1991); Barnard, Trimble reports, *OR*, 11:1, p. 115, 11:2, p. 618; Alexander, *Fighting for Confederacy*, pp. 105–6; Dabney to Jedediah Hotchkiss, Apr. 22, 1896, Hotchkiss Papers (12), LC; McGuire, "Seven Days' Fighting," Alderman Library, University of Virginia. Use of both the Grapevine and Alexander bridges (Trimble reported crossing "at the new bridges"), with confusion over their names, is the only explanation that reconciles contradictions in the Confederate accounts.

19. Lee to Josiah Gorgas, June 5, 1862, Lee, *Papers*, p. 185; George Minor to Lee, June 24, *OR*, 11:3, p. 615; Joel Barnett to wife, July 6, Lane, *Letters from Georgia Soldiers*, p. 164; Franklin in *Battles and Leaders*, II, p. 373; Heintzelman diary, July 3, LC.

20. McLaws report, *OR*, 11:2, p. 716; Lewis E. Warren memoir, Woodruff Library, Emory University; Burns, Franklin in *Battles and Leaders*, II, pp. 374, 373; Matthew Marrin diary, June 29, 1862, Minnesota Historical Society; Brent, *Memoirs*, p. 188; Dickert, *History of Kershaw's Brigade*, p. 129.

21. Semmes, McLaws reports, *OR*, 11:2, pp. 721, 717; John L. G. Wood to father, July 4, 1862, Wood Papers, Georgia Dept. of Archives and History; Lewis E. Warren memoir, Woodruff Library, Emory University; W. F. Smith, *Autobiography*, pp. 43–44; Fox, *Regimental Losses*, p. 150.

22. Lee to Magruder, June 29, 1862, Lee, *Papers*, p. 205. Casualties at Allen's Farm and Savage's Station: Federal, *OR*, 11:2, pp. 24–37, and reports; Confederate, *OR*, 11:2, pp. 973–84 (see Chap. 8, Note 6). Map: Jacob Wells in *Battles and Leaders*, II, p. 374.

23. Charles B. Haydon diary, June 29, 1862, MHC; Elisha Hunt Rhodes diary, June 29, *All for the Union*, p. 72; Jonathan P. Stowe diary, June 29, USAMHI; Stevens, *Three Years in the Sixth Corps*, pp. 105–6; *New York Tribune*, July 4; Le Duc, *Recollections*, pp. 82–84; E. D. Keyes, *Fifty Years' Observation of Men and Events*, pp. 480–81; Sypher, *Pennsylvania Reserve Corps*, p. 254; John M. Bancroft diary, June 29, MHC; L. L. Crounse, "The Army Correspondent," *Harper's Monthly*, 27 (Oct. 1863), p. 632; Joseph K. Newell, *"Ours": Annals of the 10th Regiment, Massachusetts Volunteers, in the Rebellion* (Springfield, Mass.: C. W. Nichols, 1875), p. 195; Beach, *First New York Cavalry*, p. 134.

24. Franklin in *Battles and Leaders*, II, pp. 375–76; Colburn to Delos Sacket, June 29, 1862, Mc-Clellan Papers (A-71:28), LC; W. F. Smith, *Autobiography*, p. 45; Rufus King report, *OR*, 11:2, pp. 57–58.

Chapter 11. Opportunity at Glendale

1. Magruder report, *OR*, 11:2, pp. 665–66; Stiles, *Four Years Under Marse Robert*, pp. 98–99; E. P. Alexander to father, July 24, 1862, Alexander Papers, SHC; Hunter McGuire in G. F. R. Henderson, *Stonewall Jackson and the American Civil War*, p. 382.

2. Holmes report, *OR*, 11:2, p. 906; Comte de Paris journal, Fondation Saint-Louis; Alexander, *Fighting for Confederacy*, p. 110. Map: Donald E. Windham, "Seven Days' Battles" (1931), map 10, Map Division, LC.

3. Colburn to McClellan, Apr. 16, 1863, McClellan Papers (A-90:35), LC; McClellan to Army of the Potomac, June 2, 1862, McClellan, *Papers*, p. 286; Comte de Paris journal, Fondation Saint-Louis; *New York Tribune*, July 4, 1862; log of *Galena*, June 30, 1862, Lincoln Papers, LC, and *NOR*, 7, p. 709; Franklin to John C. Ropes, Mar. 23, 1895, Ropes Collection, Boston University Library; A. A. Humphreys to wife, July 11, 1862, Humphreys Papers, Historical Society of Pennsylvania.

4. Heintzelman testimony, *Report of Joint Committee*, I (1863), p. 350. Glendale order of battle: Donald E. Windham, "Seven Days' Battles" (1931), map 4, Map Division, LC.

5. Asa Smith memoir, *American Heritage*, 22:2 (Feb. 1971), p. 57; Owen report, *OR*, 51:1, p. 104; Comte de Paris journal, Fondation Saint-Louis; Matthew Marrin diary, June 30, 1862, Minnesota Historical Society; Robert Taggart diary, June 30, Pennsylvania Historical and Museum Commission.

6. Frank Coker to wife, June 30, 1862, Lane, *Letters from Georgia Soldiers*, p. 153; Grimes, *Extracts of Letters*, p. 18; John O. Casler, *Four Years in the Stonewall Bri-*

gade, p. 94; Dabney, *Life of Jackson*, pp. 460–61; Jackson report, *OR*, 11:2, p. 556; Isaac L. Taylor diary, June 30, Minnesota Historical Society.

7. Wright, Huger, Mahone, Slocum reports, *OR*, 11:2, pp. 809–10, 789–90, 797, 435; Freeman, *R. E. Lee*, II, pp. 194–95n; [Caffey], *Battle-Fields of the South*, p. 360.

8. Crutchfield, D. H. Hill, Ayres reports, *OR*, 11:2, pp. 561, 627, 465–66; Livermore, *Days and Events*, pp. 86, 87–88; W. F. Smith memoir, Vermont Historical Society; June 30, Favill, *Diary of a Young Officer*, p. 143. Map: Donald E. Windham, "Seven Days' Battles" (1931), map 4, Map Division, LC.

9. Munford to John C. Ropes, Dec. 7, 1897, Ropes Collection, Boston University Library; D. H. Hill in *Battles and Leaders*, II, pp. 387–88; Munford to Hampton, Mar. 23, 1901, Hampton to Alexander, 1902, Alexander, *Military Memoirs*, pp. 148–49, 150–51; Alexander, *Fighting for Confederacy*, pp. 108–9; Hampton to Charles Marshall, June 13, 1871, Marshall, *Aide-de-Camp*, pp. 111–12.

10. D. H. Hill, Longstreet in *Battles and Leaders*, II, pp. 383, 402; Wright, Whiting reports, *OR*, 11:2, pp. 810, 566; Howard, *Recollections*, p. 149; Alexander, *Fighting for Confederacy*, p. 108; Hampton to Charles Marshall, June 13, 1871, Marshall, *Aide-de-Camp*, p. 111; Dabney, *Life of Jackson*, p. 467.

11. Jefferson Davis in *Southern Historical Society Papers*, 14 (1886), pp. 451–52; E. P. Alexander to father, July 24, 1862, Alexander Papers, SHC; Alexander, *Military Memoirs*, pp. 139–40; Longstreet in *Battles and Leaders*, II, pp. 400–401.

12. Rosser, Holmes, Magruder, Porter reports, *OR*, 11:2, pp. 532, 907, 666, 228; Porter in *Battles and Leaders*, II, p. 411n.

13. Clark, *North Carolina Regiments*, III, pp. 163–64; Samuel H. Walkup diary, June 30, 1862, SHC; Daniel, Deshler, Magruder, Cumming reports, *OR*, 11:2, pp. 913–14, 910–11, 666–67, 705; W. D. Carr to mother, July 4, Carr Papers, North Carolina State Archives; D. H. Hill in *Battles and Leaders*, II, p. 390; Brent, *Memoirs*, pp. 193–94; John N. Ware in *American Heritage*, 7:2 (Feb. 1956), p. 120; Magruder report, *OR*, 11:2, p. 684.

14. Longstreet, McCall reports, *OR*, 11:2, pp. 759, 389–91; R. B. Roberts in Freeman Cleaves, *Meade of Gettysburg*, p. 67; Freeman, *R. E. Lee*, II, p. 185n. Other names for the Battle of Glendale include Frayser's Farm, Nelson's Farm, Charles City Crossroads, and Willis Church.

15. Kemper, Arndt, Seymour reports, *OR*, 11:2, pp. 763, 265, 403; A. M. Randol in Cleaves, *Meade of Gettysburg*, p. 67; Hooker report in Walter H. Hebert, *Fighting Joe Hooker*, p. 113.

16. Seymour report, *OR*, 11:2, p. 403; Michael M. Miller to wife, July 11, 1862, Robert K. Murray and Warren W. Hassler, Jr., eds., "Gettysburg Farmer," *Civil War History*, 3:2 (June 1957), p. 185; Robert Taggart diary, June 30, Pennsylvania Historical and Museum Commission; Thomas J.

Goree to mother, July 21, Goree, *Civil War Correspondence*, pp. 161–62; Edmund D. Patterson diary, Aug. 30, *Yankee Rebel*, p. 48; Alexander, *Fighting for Confederacy*, p. 118. Lacking any reports from Jenkins's brigade, Captain Goree's account is followed here. Wilcox credited the capture of Cooper's battery to his 9th and 10th Alabama (*OR*, 11:2, p. 777), but in view of Goree's explicit description and Jenkins's high losses, this must have been its recapture.

17. D. S. Porter report, *OR*, 51:1, p. 114; Powell, *Fifth Army Corps*, pp. 141–42; Alexander, *Fighting for Confederacy*, p. 107; E. W. Warren to father, July 13, 1862, Warren Papers, Perkins Library, Duke University; Amsden, Randol, Seymour, Wilcox reports, *OR*, 11:2, pp. 412, 255–56, 404, 777–78; H. R. Hogan in *Confederate Veteran*, 1:11 (Nov. 1893), p. 333; T. M. Key to Heintzelman, May 26, 1864, Heintzelman Papers, LC.

18. Heintzelman to McCall, Feb. 19, July 9, 1864, Heintzelman Papers, LC; Andrew E. Ford, *The Story of the Fifteenth Regiment Massachusetts Volunteer Infantry* (Clinton, Mass.: W. J. Coulter, 1898), p. 176; Heintzelman diary, July 3, 1862, LC; Livermore, *Days and Events*, p. 91; John W. Hinsdale diary, June 30, Perkins Library, Duke University.

19. Asa Smith memoir, *American Heritage*, 22:2 (Feb. 1971), pp. 57–58; Grover, Hooker reports, *OR*, 11:2, pp. 123, 111–12.

20. Livermore, *Days and Events*, p. 92; Kearny, Thompson, Hays reports, *OR*, 11:2, pp. 162, 171,

178; Hays to J. B. McFadden, July 7, 1862, G. A. Hays, *Under the Red Patch*, p. 241; Jones, *Lee's Tigers*, p. 106; Charles B. Haydon diary, June 30, MHC.

21. Joshua Lewis memoir, Indiana State Library; McGowan, Barlow, Kearny reports, *OR*, 11:2, pp. 870, 65–66, 167–68; Kearny to wife, July 5, 1862, Kearny, *Letters from Peninsula*, p. 118; Heintzelman diary, July 3, LC; Baquet, *First New Jersey Brigade*, p. 327; Francis C. Barlow to mother, July 4, Barlow Papers, Massachusetts Historical Society.

22. Starke, Mayo, Strange reports, *OR*, 11:2, pp. 850–51, 845, 769; Francis W. Palfrey in Military Historical Society of Mass., *Peninsular Campaign*, pp. 185–86; "Memorial Day Address," O. W. Holmes, Jr., *Speeches* (Boston: Little, Brown, 1891), p. 9; Henry Ropes to father, July 5, 1862, Ropes Papers, Boston Public Library; R. H. Gray to father, July 10, Gray Papers, North Carolina State Archives.

23. Leavitt Hunt to Heintzelman, Apr. 24, 1864, Heintzelman Papers, LC; Sedgwick to sister, July 6, 1862, Sedgwick, *Correspondence*, II, pp. 69–70; A. P. Hill, McCall reports, 11:2, pp. 838–39, 391; Charles B. Haydon diary, June 30, MHC; Longstreet, W. Roy Mason in *Battles and Leaders*, II, pp. 401–2, 402n.

24. June 30, 1862, Ruffin, *Diary*, II, pp. 358–59; Lee, Brown reports, *OR*, 11:2, pp. 495, 551; John Goode, *Recollections of a Lifetime* (New York: Neale, 1906), p. 58. Casualties at Glendale: Federal, *OR*, 11:2, pp. 24–37, and re-

ports; Confederate, *OR*, 11:2, pp. 973–84 (see Chap. 8, Note 6). Federal artillery losses: six in Cooper's battery, six in Randol's, two in Knieriem's, one in Thompson's, one in Jastram's, one in Mott's at White Oak Bridge, one 24-pounder from siege train.

25. Adams, *Nineteenth Massachusetts*, pp. 36–37; Livermore, *Days and Events*, p. 93; Charles B. Haydon diary, June 30, 1862, MHC.

Chapter 12. The Guns of Malvern Hill

1. William F. Biddle to John C. Ropes, Mar. 27, 1895, Ropes Collection, Boston University Library; McClellan telegs. to Stanton, June 30, to Thomas, July 1, 1862, McClellan, *Papers*, pp. 326–27; Sumner to McClellan, June 30, 1862, Humphreys to McClellan, Feb. 28, 1864, McClellan Papers (A-71:28, B-14:49), LC; Franklin in *Battles and Leaders*, II, pp. 379–80; A. W. Stillwell diary, July 1, 1862, State Historical Society of Wisconsin; W. F. Smith, *Autobiography*, pp. 46–47; Huger report, *OR*, 11:2, p. 790; Livermore, *Days and Events*, p. 94.

2. Thomas W. Hyde to mother, July 6, 1862, Hyde, *Civil War Letters*, p. 32; McClellan to wife, to Dix, July 1, McClellan, *Papers*, pp. 328–29; log of *Galena*, July 1 (copy), Ropes Collection, Boston University Library.

3. A. A. Humphreys to wife, July 5, 1862, Humphreys Papers, Historical Society of Pennsylvania; Charles B. Haydon diary, July 1,

MHC; Freeman, *R. E. Lee*, II, pp. 582–84; Elizabeth Valentine Huntley, *Peninsula Pilgrimage* (Richmond: Whittet and Shepperson, 1941), pp. 101–2. Maps: Jacob Wells in *Battles and Leaders*, II, p. 412; Donald E. Windham, "Seven Days' Battles" (1931), maps 4, 5, 10, Map Division, LC. Illustrations of Malvern Hill terrain and sites: *Battles and Leaders*, II, pp. 408, 410, 414–16, 418–20, 422.

4. Porter in *Battles and Leaders*, II, p. 409; *McClellan's Own Story*, p. 434; Heintzelman diary, July 3, 1862, LC.

5. Brent, *Memoirs*, pp. 199–202; Huger, Armistead reports, *OR*, 11:2, pp. 790, 818.

6. Holmes report, *OR*, 11:2, p. 908; Samuel H. Walkup diary, July 1, 1862, SHC; Longstreet, *Manassas to Appomattox*, p. 142; D. H. Hill in *Battles and Leaders*, II, pp. 390–91; Cadmus Wilcox to D. H. Hill, June 23, 1885, D. H. Hill Papers, Virginia State Library.

7. Brent, *Memoirs*, pp. 203, 206–8; Magruder report, *OR*, 11:2, pp. 668, 675–77. It is not known what map Lee used on July 1. It cannot have been Albert H. Campbell's "Map of the Environs of Richmond" (Museum of the Confederacy), used for operations north of the Chickahominy, for Campbell showed nothing of the Glendale–Malvern Hill area.

8. Brent, *Memoirs*, pp. 209–11; Lee report, *OR*, 11:2, p. 496; Longstreet, *Manassas to Appomattox*, p. 143; Longstreet in *Battles and Leaders*, II, p. 403.

9. Chilton to Magruder, July 1,

1862, Mass. MOLLUS Collection, Houghton Library, Harvard University; McLaws to "General," Nov. 30, 1885, Longstreet Papers, SHC; D. H. Hill, Pendleton, Brown reports, *OR*, 11:2, pp. 628, 536, 550.

10. Carter Berkeley, William L. Balthis memoirs, Hotchkiss Papers (39), LC; Charles B. Haydon diary, July 1, 1862, MHC; Matthew Marrin diary, July 1, Minnesota Historical Society; Porter in *Battles and Leaders*, II, p. 416; William White to sister, July 20, Lane, *Letters from Georgia Soldiers*, p. 169; Howard, *Recollections*, p. 152n; Campbell Brown memoir, Tennessee State Library and Archives; Gordon, *Reminiscences*, pp. 67–68.

11. Grimes, Wright, Cutts reports, *OR*, 11:2, pp. 802, 813, 547; Stiles, *Four Years Under Marse Robert*, p. 104; Greenlee Davidson report, *Civil War History*, 17:3 (Sept. 1971), p. 202; Reichardt, *Battery A, First Rhode Island Artillery*, p. 51; Porter to John Rodgers, [July 1, 1862], McClellan Papers (A-72:29), LC; Alexander, *Fighting for Confederacy*, p. 118.

12. Longstreet, *Manassas to Appomattox*, p. 144; Thomas J. Goree to mother, July 21, 1862, Goree, *Civil War Correspondence*, p. 163; Armistead, Magruder, Whiting reports, *OR*, 11:2, pp. 819, 668–69, 566; Dickinson to Magruder, July 1, *OR*, 11:2, pp. 677–78; John Lamb in *Southern Historical Society Papers*, 25 (1897), p. 217; Freeman, *R. E. Lee*, II, p. 218n.

13. Dickinson to Magruder, July 1, 1862, *OR*, 11:2, pp. 677–78; Brent, *Memoirs*, pp. 211–12,

215–16; Magruder report, *OR*, 11:2, p. 669.

14. Wright, Griffin, Ames reports, *OR*, 11:2, pp. 814, 314, 260; D. R. E. Winn to wife, July 17, 1862, Winn Papers, Woodruff Library, Emory University; Kent, "Sharpshooting with Berdan," p. 46.

15. John M. Bancroft diary, July 1, 1862, MHC; Wright, D. H. Hill, Garland reports, *OR*, 11:2, pp. 814, 628, 643.

16. Couch, Gordon, Garland, Sands reports, *OR*, 11:2, pp. 204, 634, 643, 637; William Calder to mother, July 4, 1862, Calder Papers, SHC; Leonidas Torrence to parents, July 14, Torrence, "Road to Gettysburg," p. 497; Thomas Caffey in *Confederate Veteran*, 26:3 (Mar. 1918), p. 107.

17. George E. Hagar diary, July 1, 1862, USAMHI; Abercrombie, D. H. Hill reports, *OR*, 11:2, pp. 212, 628; Porter in *Battles and Leaders*, II, pp. 416n, 419; Francis C. Barlow to mother, July 4, Barlow Papers, Massachusetts Historical Society; Livermore, *Days and Events*, pp. 96–97; Pleasant A. Stovall, *Robert Toombs, Statesman, Speaker, Soldier*, Sage (New York: Cassel, 1892), pp. 256–57; D. H. Hill in *Battles and Leaders*, II, p. 394.

18. Hunt, McClellan testimony, *Report of Joint Committee*, I (1863), pp. 574, 436–37; Hunt report *OR*, 11:2, p. 238; Porter in *Battles and Leaders*, II, p. 421; log of *Galena*, July 1, 1862 (copy), William F. Biddle to John C. Ropes, Mar. 27, 1895, Ropes Collection, Boston University Library; Porter to McClellan, July 1, 1862, McClellan Papers (A-72:29), LC;

Sears, *McClellan*, p. 221; Andrews, *North Reports the War*, p. 215; Francis C. Barlow to mother, July 4, Barlow Papers, Massachusetts Historical Society.

19. Longstreet in *Battles and Leaders*, II, p. 403; Lee, Huger, McLaws, Semmes reports, *OR*, 11:2, pp. 680, 790, 719, 723; Brent, *Memoirs*, p. 218.

20. Barksdale, Cobb reports, *OR*, 11:2, pp. 751, 749; Jones, *Lee's Tigers*, pp. 109–10; Henry K. Burgwyn memoir, Burgwyn Family Papers, SHC; John W. Hinsdale diary, July 1, 1862, Perkins Library, Duke University.

21. David R. Jones to sister, July 16, 1862, Schoff Collection, CL; D. H. Hill in *Battles and Leaders*, II, p. 394; George W. Faucett to father, July 18, Faucett Papers, Indiana Historical Society; James T. Thompson to parents, July 15, Thompson, "A Georgia Boy with 'Stonewall' Jackson: Letters of Thomas Thompson," ed. Aurelia Austin, *Virginia Magazine of History and Biography*, 70:3 (July 1962), p. 326; Thomas L. Ware diary, July 1, SHC.

22. Brent, *Memoirs*, pp. 218, 235; Howard, *Recollections*, p. 154; Oliver W. Norton to cousin, July 5, 1862, Norton, *Army Letters*, p. 93; Porter in *Battles and Leaders*, II, p. 419; Richard T. Auchmuty to mother, July 5, Auchmuty, *Letters*, p. 72; Griffin, Edwards reports, *OR*, 11:2, pp. 314, 357; Lafayette McLaws memoir, McLaws Papers, Perkins Library, Duke University; Jones, *Lee's Tigers*, p. 109; George S. Bernard in *Southern Historical Society Papers*, 18 (1890), p. 61; Alexander,

Fighting for Confederacy, pp. 112–13; William C. Oates, *The War Between the Union & the Confederacy* (New York: Neale, 1905), p. 143.

23. D. H. Hill, Porter in *Battles and Leaders*, II, pp. 394, 423n; John Lamb in *Southern Historical Society Papers*, 25 (1897), p. 217; Freeman, *R. E. Lee*, II, p. 218n; Porter to McClellan, July 1, 1862, McClellan Papers (A-72:29), LC; W. F. Smith, *Autobiography*, p. 47. Casualties at Malvern Hill: Federal, *OR*, 11:2, pp. 24–37, and reports; Confederate, *OR*, 11:2, pp. 973–84 (see Chap. 8, Note 6).

Chapter 13. Richmond Delivered

1. Averell in *Battles and Leaders*, II, p. 432; Hunter McGuire in Stiles, *Four Years Under Marse Robert*, p. 105; Blackford, *War Years with Jeb Stuart*, p. 82.

2. William F. Biddle to John C. Ropes, Mar. 27, 1895, Ropes Collection, Boston University Library; E. M. Woodward, *History of the Third Pennsylvania Reserve* (Trenton, N.J.: MacCrellish & Quigley, 1883), pp. 124–25; Richard T. Auchmuty to mother, July 5, 1862, Auchmuty, *Letters*, p. 72; Darius Couch, Civil War record, RG 94 (M-1098:5), NA; Le Duc, *Recollections*, p. 90; Calvin Mehaffey to mother, July 16, Schoff Collection, CL; Meigs report, *OR*, Ser. 3, 2, p. 798; McClellan teleg. to Lincoln, July 2, McClellan, *Papers*, p. 329; Stephen R. Mallory to wife, July 13, Mallory Papers, SHC.

3. Lee to Longstreet, July 2, to Stuart, July 3, 1862, Eldridge

Collection, J. E. B. Stuart Papers, Huntington Library; Lee to Davis, July 2, Lee, *Papers*, pp. 206–7; Robert L. Dabney to Jedediah Hotchkiss, May 7, 1896, Hotchkiss Papers (39), LC; Dabney in Henderson, *Stonewall Jackson*, pp. 391–92; Davis, *Rise and Fall*, II, pp. 149–50.

4. Stuart report, *OR*, 11:2, pp. 519–20; McClellan to wife, July 4, 1862, McClellan, *Papers*, pp. 334–35; Alexander, *Military Memoirs*, pp. 169–70; Barnard to McClellan, July 2, McClellan Papers (A-60:24), LC; Lee to Davis, July 4, Lee, *Papers*, p. 208.

5. O. W. Holmes, Jr., to mother, July 4, 1862, Holmes, *Touched with Fire*, p. 56; William Stillwell to wife, July 4, Lane, *Letters from Georgia Soldiers*, p. 159; Elisha Hunt Rhodes diary, July 4, *All for the Union*, p. 74; E. O. Hicks diary, July 4, Collection of John Robinson, Chesterland, Ohio; Charles B. Haydon diary, July 4, SHC; Shepherd G. Pryor to wife, July 4, Georgia Dept. of Archives and History; E. P. Alexander to father, July 24, Alexander Papers, SHC; Alexander, *Fighting for Confederacy*, p. 117, 572n; T. H. Stevens report, *NOR*, 7, p. 543.

6. *Richmond Dispatch*, July 9, 1862; *Richmond Whig*, July 15; *Richmond Enquirer*, July 1. Confederate casualties in Seven Days: *OR*, 11:2, pp. 973–84, and reports and corrections.

7. Lee to wife, July 9, 1862, Lee, *Papers*, p. 230; Lee report, *OR*, 11:2, p. 497; Chesnut diary, July 10, Woodward, *Mary Chesnut's Civil War*, p. 410; Putnam, *Rich-

mond During the War*, p. 149; D. R. E. Winn to wife, July 9, Winn Papers, Woodruff Library, Emory University; Guild to R. G. Cole, July 3, *OR*, Ser. 2, 4, p. 798; Constance Cary Harrison in *Battles and Leaders*, II, p. 446.

8. F. F. Jones report, *OR*, 11:2, p. 511; Alexander, *Fighting for Confederacy*, p. 122. Federal casualties in Seven Days: *OR*, 11:2, pp. 24–37, and corrections. Lee's claim of fifty-two Federal guns captured (*OR*, 11:2, p. 498) referred probably to the Peninsula campaign as a whole; that actual count was fifty-three.

9. McClellan to Army of the Potomac, July 4, McClellan telegs. to Lincoln, July 4, 11, McClellan to Barlow, July 23, 1862, McClellan, *Papers*, pp. 339, 338, 351–52, 369–70; Halleck to McClellan, Aug. 6, *OR*, 11:1, pp. 82–84.

10. *New York Tribune*, July 4, 1862; Chase to W. C. Bryant, Aug. 4, Chase Papers, Historical Society of Pennsylvania; Bates to Francis Lieber, July 8, Lieber Collection, Huntington Library; Sears, *McClellan*, pp. 229–32.

11. Alfred Davenport to mother, July 8, 1862, Lydia M. Post, *Soldiers' Letters from Camp, Battle-field and Prison* (New York: Bunce & Huntington, 1865), p. 147; Edgar M. Newcomb to wife, July 4, Weymouth, *Memorial Sketch*, p. 75; William W. Folwell to wife, July 17, Folwell Papers, Minnesota Historical Society; Felix Brannigan to sister, July 16, Brannigan Papers, LC; McClellan to Barlow, July 15, 30, to wife, July 10, McClellan, *Papers*, pp. 361, 376–77, 349.

12. Charles B. Haydon diary, July 15, 1862, MHC; Aug. 10, Wainwright, *Diary of Battle*, p. 83; E. O. Hicks diary, July 19, Collection of John Robinson, Chesterland, Ohio; Steiner, *Disease in the Civil War*, p. 124; Norton, *Army Letters*, pp. 327–29.

13. Blackwell, *War Years with Jeb Stuart*, pp. 76–77; D. H. Hill to G. W. Smith, Aug. 17, 1862, Schoff Collection, CL; William White to sister, July 20, Thomas Verdery to Warren Akin, July 22, Lane, *Letters from Georgia Soldiers*, pp. 171, 173; W. A. Dardan to sister, Aug. 5, Hightower Papers, Georgia Dept. of Archives and History.

14. Lee to Jackson, July 23, 25, 27, to Randolph, July 28, 1862, Lee, *Papers*, pp. 235, 236, 239–40, 240–41; S. G. French report, *OR*, 11:2, pp. 940–42; Porter to G. H. Heap, July 19, Schoff Collection, CL.

15. McClellan to Stanton, July 3, to Lincoln, July 7, to wife, July 9, 17, 1862, McClellan, *Papers*, pp. 333, 344–45, 348, 362–63; Lincoln memorandum, July 8–9, Lincoln, *Works*, V, pp. 309–12; Heintzelman diary, July 9, LC.

16. July 25, 1862, Browning, *Diary*, I, p. 563; Burnside testimony, *Report of Joint Committee*, I (1863),

p. 650; Halleck to Stanton, July 27, to McClellan, Aug. 6, *OR*, 11:3, pp. 337–38, 11:1, p. 83; Heintzelman diary, July 26, LC.

17. McClellan to Halleck, July 26, 1862, McClellan, *Papers*, p. 372; Halleck to wife, July 28, James Grant Wilson, "General Halleck — A Memoir," *Journal of the Military Service Institution of the United States*, 36 (May–June 1905), p. 557; Halleck telegs. to McClellan, July 30, Aug. 3, *OR*, 11:1, pp. 76–77, 80–81.

18. McClellan teleg. to Halleck, Aug. 4, McClellan to Marcy, Aug. 5, to wife, Aug. 8, to Hooker, Aug. 6, 1862, McClellan, *Papers*, pp. 383–84, 386, 388, 386–87; Halleck to McClellan, Aug. 6, *OR*, 11:1, pp. 82–84; Lee to Jackson, Aug. 7, to Randolph, Aug. 14, to Davis, Aug. 14, Lee, *Papers*, pp. 247–48, 252, 253–54; Mosby, *War Reminiscences*, pp. 243–44.

19. Between-battles skirmishing casualties are extrapolated from *OR*, 11:2, p. 117, deaths from disease from data in Steiner, *Disease in the Civil War, passim*.

20. *McClellan's Own Story*, p. 505; A. R. Waud drawing, Prints and Photographs Division, LC; McClellan to wife, Aug. 17, 1862, McClellan, *Papers*, p. 395.

BIBLIOGRAPHY

....

Manuscript Sources

Alabama Department of Archives and History, Montgomery
    James H. McMath diary
Boston Public Library
    Henry Ropes letters
Boston University Library
    John C. Ropes Collection: Papers of the Military Historical Society of
        Massachusetts
Bowdoin College Library, Brunswick, Maine
    Charles Henry Howard letters
    Oliver Otis Howard letters
John Hay Library, Brown University, Providence, R.I.
    Selden Connor letters
William L. Perkins Library, Duke University, Durham, N.C.
    William G. Agnew letters
    John W. Hinsdale diary
    Joseph E. Johnston Papers
    W. A. Kenyon letters
    Joseph B. Laughton letters
    James Longstreet Papers
    Lafayette McLaws Papers
    Ward Osgood letters
    Urich N. Parmelee letters
    William Y. Ripley letters
    Giles F. Ward letters
    E. W. Warren letters
Robert W. Woodruff Library, Emory University, Atlanta
    Robert A. Toombs letters: Alexander S. Stephens Papers
    Lewis E. Warren memoir
    D. R. E. Winn letters

Fondation Saint-Louis, Amboise, France
    Comte de Paris journal
Georgia Department of Archives and History, Atlanta
    Shepherd G. Pryor letters
    Sidney J. Richardson letters
    John L. G. Wood letters
Dinand Library, College of the Holy Cross, Worcester, Mass.
    Patrick A. Guiney letters
Huntington Library, San Marino, Calif.
    Samuel L. M. Barlow Papers
    J. E. B. Stuart Papers
Indiana State Library, Indianapolis
    Joshua Lewis memoir
Kansas State Historical Society, Topeka
    John S. Judd diary
Manuscript Division, Library of Congress, Washington
    Felix Brannigan letters
    Bruce Catton research notes, Doubleday & Co.
    Samuel P. Heintzelman Papers and diary
    Jedediah Hotchkiss Papers
    Abraham Lincoln Papers
    George B. McClellan Papers
    Manton Marble Papers
    Edwin M. Stanton Papers
    Gilbert Thompson diary
Map Division, Library of Congress
    Donald E. Windham, "The Seven Days' Battles" (1931), maps
    1–10
Hill Memorial Library, Louisiana State University, Baton Rouge
    Edward M. Burruss letters
    John S. Foster letters
Maine Historical Society, Portland
    James Brown letters
Massachusetts Historical Society, Boston
    John A. Andrew Papers
    Francis C. Barlow letters
William L. Clements Library, University of Michigan, Ann Arbor
    James S. Schoff Civil War Collection
Michigan Historical Collections, Bentley Historical Library, University of
Michigan, Ann Arbor
    John M. Bancroft diary
    Albert Davis letters
    Charles B. Haydon diary

George Monteith letters
J. D. Richardson letters
Minnesota Historical Society, St. Paul
William W. Folwell diary
Matthew Marrin diary
Isaac L. Taylor diary
Mississippi Department of Archives and History, Jackson
William H. Hill diary
Oscar J. E. Stuart letters
A. L. P. Vairin diary
National Archives, Washington
Record Group 77: Records of the Office of the Chief of Engineers: Civil
War maps
Record Group 94: U.S. Generals' Reports
Record Group 107: Records of the Office of the Secretary of War
Record Group 109: Confederate Records
New Hampshire Historical Society, Concord
Thomas B. Leaver diary
New York State Library, Albany
G. K. Warren letters
Southern Historical Collection, University of North Carolina, Chapel Hill
Edward Porter Alexander letters
William Allan Papers
William J. H. Bellamy diary
Barry G. Benson memoir
Thomas Bragg diary
Henry K. Burgwyn memoir
William Calder letters
Nathaniel H. R. Dawson letters
James Longstreet Papers
Lafayette McLaws Papers
Stephen R. Mallory letters
William G. Morris letters
James W. Shinn memoir: Augustus Osborne Papers
Ruffin Thomson letters
Samuel H. Walkup diary
Thomas L. Ware diary
North Carolina State Archives, Raleigh
R. H. Gray letters
Thomas Newby letters
J. W. Ratchford memoir
P. J. Sinclair letters
Henry C. Wall diary

Oregon Historical Society, Portland
    Joseph Hooker letters: James Nesmith Papers
Pennsylvania Historical and Museum Commission, Harrisburg
    Robert Taggart Papers and diary
Historical Society of Pennsylvania, Philadelphia
    Andrew A. Humphreys letters
South Caroliniana Library, University of South Carolina, Columbia
    David W. Aikin letters
Stanford University Library, Stanford, Calif.
    J. W. Melhorn diary
Tennessee State Library and Archives, Nashville
    Campbell Brown Papers
    Ben W. Coleman letters
    John A. Fite memoir
    Thomas Herndon memoir
Eugene C. Barker Texas History Center, University of Texas, Austin
    O. T. Hanks memoir
    Nicholas Pomeroy memoir
U.S. Army Military History Institute, Carlisle Barracks, Pa.
    W. T. H. Brooks letters
    Luther C. Furst diary
    George E. Hagar diary
    Jacob Heffelfinger diary
    Jonathan Stowe diary
Vermont Historical Society, Montpelier
    William F. Smith memoir
Virginia Historical Society, Richmond
    Lee's Headquarters Papers
    Confederate Engineers' Maps: Jeremy Francis Gilmer Collection
Virginia State Library, Richmond
    James L. Boulware diary
    James L. Dinwiddie letters
    D. H. Hill Papers
    Edgar Allan Jackson letters
    J. D. Summers diary
Alderman Library, University of Virginia, Charlottesville
    Civil War Letters
    Hunter McGuire Papers
    Charles Venable memoir: McDowell Family Papers
Earl Gregg Swem Library, College of William and Mary, Williamsburg, Va.
    Edwin Y. Brown letters
    Robert G. Haile diary
    D. H. Hill Papers

J. H. B. Jenkins letters
Joseph E. Johnston Papers
State Historical Society of Wisconsin, Madison
A. W. Stillwell diary
James R. Strong letters

Books and Articles

Abbott, Henry L. *Fallen Leaves: The Civil War Letters of Major Henry Livermore Abbott.* Ed. Robert Garth Scott. Kent, Ohio: Kent State University Press, 1991.

Acton, Edward A. " 'Dear Mollie': Letters of Captain Edward A. Acton to His Wife, 1862." *Pennsylvania Magazine of History and Biography,* 89:1 (January 1965), pp. 4–51.

Adams, G. B. *Reminiscences of the Nineteenth Massachusetts Regiment.* Boston: Wright & Potter, 1899.

Adams, George W. *Doctors in Blue: The Medical History of the Union Army in the Civil War.* New York: Schuman, 1952.

Alexander, Edward Porter. *Fighting for the Confederacy: The Personal Recollections of General Edward Porter Alexander.* Ed. Gary W. Gallagher. Chapel Hill: University of North Carolina Press, 1989.

Alexander, Edward Porter. *Military Memoirs of a Confederate.* New York: Scribner's, 1907.

Allan, William. *The Army of Northern Virginia in 1862.* Boston: Houghton Mifflin, 1892.

Allan, William. *History of the Campaign of Gen. T. J. (Stonewall) Jackson in the Shenandoah Valley of Virginia.* Philadelphia: Lippincott, 1880.

Anderson, Carter S. "Train Running for the Confederacy." *Railway and Locomotive Engineering,* 5 (August 1892), pp. 287–89; 5 (October 1892), pp. 369–71.

Andrews, J. Cutler. *The North Reports the Civil War.* Pittsburgh: University of Pittsburgh Press, 1955.

Andrews, J. Cutler. *The South Reports the Civil War.* Princeton: Princeton University Press, 1970.

Auchmuty, Richard T. *Letters of Richard Tylden Auchmuty, Fifth Corps, Army of the Potomac.* Ed. Ellen S. Auchmuty. Privately printed, 1895.

Baquet, Camille. *History of the First Brigade, New Jersey Volunteers, from 1861 to 1865.* Trenton, N.J.: MacCrellish & Quigley, 1910.

Barnard, John G. *The Peninsular Campaign and Its Antecedents.* New York: Van Nostrand, 1864.

Bates, Edward. *The Diary of Edward Bates, 1859–1866.* Ed. Howard K. Beale. Washington: Government Printing Office, 1933.

Battles and Leaders of the Civil War. Eds. Robert U. Johnson and Clarence C. Buel. 4 vols. New York: Century, 1887–88.

Beach, William H. *The First New York (Lincoln) Cavalry from April 19, 1861 to July 7, 1865.* Milwaukee: Burdick & Allen, 1902.

Bellard, Alfred. *Gone for a Soldier: The Civil War Memoirs of Private Alfred Bellard.* Ed. David Herbert Donald. Boston: Little, Brown, 1975.

Berkeley, Henry R. *Four Years in the Confederate Artillery: The Diary of Private Henry Robinson Berkeley.* Ed. William H. Runge. Chapel Hill: University of North Carolina Press, 1961.

Bill, Alfred Hoyt. *The Beleaguered City: Richmond, 1861–1865.* New York: Knopf, 1946.

Blackford, W. W. *War Years with Jeb Stuart.* New York: Scribner's, 1945.

Brent, Joseph L. *Memoirs of the War Between the States.* New Orleans: Fontana, 1940.

Bridges, Hal. *Lee's Maverick General: Daniel Harvey Hill.* New York: McGraw-Hill, 1961.

Browning, Orville H. *The Diary of Orville Hickman Browning.* Eds. Theodore C. Pease and James G. Randall. 2 vols. Springfield: Illinois State Historical Library, 1925, 1933.

Bruce, Robert V. *Lincoln and the Tools of War.* Indianapolis: Bobbs-Merrill, 1956.

[Caffey, Thomas C.] *Battle-fields of the South, from Bull Run to Fredericksburgh.* By an English Combatant. New York: Bradburn, 1864.

Caldwell, J. F. J. *The History of [Gregg's] Brigade of South Carolinians.* Philadelphia: King & Baird, 1866.

Casler, John O. *Four Years in the Stonewall Brigade.* Guthrie, Okla.: State Capital Printing, 1893.

Catton, Bruce. *Mr. Lincoln's Army.* New York: Doubleday, 1951.

Chambers, Lenoir. *Stonewall Jackson.* 2 vols. New York: Morrow, 1959.

Chase, Salmon P. *Inside Lincoln's Cabinet: The Civil War Diaries of Salmon P. Chase.* Ed. David Donald. New York: Longmans, Green, 1954.

Child, William. *A History of the Fifth Regiment New Hampshire Volunteers, in the American Civil War, 1861–1865.* Bristol, N.H.: R. W. Musgrove, 1893.

Clark, Walter, ed. *Histories of the Several Regiments and Battalions from North Carolina in the Great War, 1861–'65.* 5 vols. Raleigh: State of North Carolina, 1901.

Cleaves, Freeman. *Meade of Gettysburg.* Norman: University of Oklahoma Press, 1960.

Cleveland, Mather. *New Hampshire Fights the Civil War.* New London, N.H.: privately printed, 1969.

Collins, Cordello. "A Bucktail Voice: Civil War Correspondence of Pvt. Cordello Collins." Ed. Mark Reinsberg. *Western Pennsylvania Historical Magazine,* 48 (July 1965), pp. 235–48.

Confederate Veteran. Nashville, Tenn.: 1–40 (1893–1932).

Cook, Joel. *The Siege of Richmond: A Narrative of the Military Operations of Major-General George B. McClellan During the Months of May and June, 1862.* Philadelphia: George W. Childs, 1862.

Cooke, John Esten. *Wearing of the Gray; Being Personal Portraits, Scenes, and Adventures of the War.* New York: E. B. Treat, 1867.

Cullen, Joseph P. *The Peninsula Campaign 1862: McClellan & Lee Struggle for Richmond.* Harrisburg, Pa.: Stackpole, 1973.

Curtis, Newton M. *From Bull Run to Chancellorsville: The Story of the Sixteenth New York Infantry.* New York: Putnam's, 1906.

Dabney, Robert L. *Life and Campaigns of Lieut.-Gen. Thomas Jackson.* New York: Blelock, 1866.

[Dabney, Robert L.] "What I Saw of the Battle of Chickahominy." *Southern Magazine,* 10 (January 1872), pp. 1–15.

Davenport, Alfred. *Camp and Field Life of the Fifth New York Volunteer Infantry (Duryee Zouaves).* New York: Dick and Fitzgerald, 1879.

Davis, Jefferson. *The Rise and Fall of the Confederate Government.* 2 vols. New York: D. Appleton, 1881.

Davis, Nicholas A. *Chaplain Davis and Hood's Texas Brigade.* Ed. Donald E. Everett. San Antonio, Tex.: Principia Press of Trinity University, 1962.

Dawson, Francis W. *Reminiscences of Confederate Service, 1861–1865.* Ed. Bell I. Wiley. Baton Rouge: Louisiana State University Press, 1980.

DeLeon, Thomas C. *Four Years in Rebel Capitals: An Inside View of Life in the Southern Confederacy, from Birth to Death.* Mobile, Ala.: Gossip Printing, 1892.

De Peyster, John W. *Personal and Military History of Philip Kearny, Major-General United States Volunteers.* New York: Rice and Gage, 1869.

Dickert, D. Augustus. *History of Kershaw's Brigade.* Newberry, S.C.: E. A. Aull, 1899.

Douglas, Henry Kyd. *I Rode With Stonewall.* Chapel Hill: University of North Carolina Press, 1940.

Dowdey, Clifford. *The Seven Days: The Emergence of Lee.* Boston: Little, Brown, 1964.

Dunn, William E. "On the Peninsular Campaign: Civil War Letters from William E. Dunn." *Civil War Times Illustrated,* 14:1 (July 1975), pp. 14–19.

Early, Jubal A. *Autobiographical Sketch and Narrative of the War Between the States.* Philadelphia: Lippincott, 1912.

Evans, Thomas H. "There Is No Use Trying to Dodge Shot." *Civil War Times Illustrated,* 6:5 (August 1967), pp. 40–45.

Favill, Josiah M. *The Diary of a Young Officer Serving in the Armies of the United States During the War of the Rebellion.* Chicago: Donnelley, 1909.

Fishel, Edwin C. "Pinkerton and McClellan: Who Deceived Whom?" *Civil War History,* 34:2 (June 1988), pp. 115–42.

Fleming, Francis P. "Francis P. Fleming in the War for Southern Independence: Soldiering with the 2nd Florida Regiment." Ed. Edward C. Williamson. *Florida Historical Quarterly*, 28:1 (July 1949), pp. 38–52.

Fox, Gustavus V. *Confidential Correspondence of Gustavus Vasa Fox, Assistant Secretary of the Navy, 1861–1865*. Eds. Robert M. Thompson and Richard Wainwright. 2 vols. New York: Naval History Society, 1920.

Fox, William F. *Regimental Losses in the American Civil War, 1861–1865*. Albany: Albany Publishing, 1889.

Freeman, Douglas Southall. *Lee's Lieutenants: A Study in Command*. 3 vols. New York: Scribner's, 1942–44.

Freeman, Douglas Southall. *R. E. Lee, A Biography*. 4 vols. New York: Scribner's, 1934–35.

Goldsborough, Louis M. "Narrative of Rear Admiral Goldsborough, U.S. Navy." *U.S. Naval Institute Proceedings*, 59 (July 1933), pp. 1023–31.

Gordon, John B. *Reminiscences of the Civil War*. New York: Scribner's, 1903.

Goree, Thomas J. *The Thomas Jewett Goree Letters: The Civil War Correspondence*. Ed. Langston James Goree. Bryan, Tex.: Family History Foundation, 1981.

Govan, Gilbert E., and James W. Livingood. *A Different Valor: The Story of General Joseph E. Johnston, C.S.A*. Indianapolis: Bobbs-Merrill, 1956.

Grimes, Bryan. *Extracts of Letters of Major-General Bryan Grimes to His Wife*. Raleigh, N.C.: Edwards, Broughton, 1883.

Handerson, Henry E. *Yankee in Gray: The Civil War Memoirs of Henry E. Handerson*. Cleveland: Press of Western Reserve University, 1962.

Harman, George D. "General Silas Casey and the Battle of Fair Oaks." *The Historian*, 4:1 (Autumn 1941), pp. 84–101.

Hay, John. *Lincoln and the Civil War in the Diaries and Letters of John Hay*. Ed. Tyler Dennett. New York: Dodd, Mead, 1939.

Hays, Alexander. *Life and Letters of Alexander Hays*. Ed. George T. Fleming. Pittsburgh: privately printed, 1919.

Hays, Gilbert A. *Under the Red Patch: Story of the Sixty-third Regiment, Pennsylvania Volunteers*. Pittsburgh: Press of Market Review, 1908.

Hebert, Walter H. *Fighting Joe Hooker*. Indianapolis: Bobbs-Merrill, 1944.

Henderson, G. F. R. *Stonewall Jackson and the American Civil War*. New York: Longmans, Green, 1936.

Holmes, James R. "The Civil War Letters of James Rush Holmes." Ed. Ida Bright Adams. *Western Pennsylvania Historical Magazine*, 44:2 (June 1961), pp. 105–27.

Holmes, Oliver Wendell, Jr. *Touched with Fire: Letters and Diary of Oliver Wendell Holmes, Jr*. Ed. Mark DeWolf Howe. Cambridge: Harvard University Press, 1946.

Hood, J. B. *Advance and Retreat: Personal Experiences in the United States and Confederate States Armies*. New Orleans: privately printed, 1880.

Howard, McHenry. *Recollections of a Maryland Confederate Soldier and Staff*

Officer Under Johnston, Jackson, and Lee. Baltimore: Williams & Wilkins, 1914.

Howard, Oliver Otis. *Autobiography of Oliver Otis Howard, Major General United States Army.* 2 vols. New York: Baker & Taylor, 1907.

Hunter, Alexander. *Johnny Reb and Billy Yank.* New York: Neale, 1905.

Hyde, Thomas W. *Civil War Letters by General Thomas W. Hyde.* Privately printed, 1933.

Hyde, Thomas W. *Following the Greek Cross or, Memories of the Sixth Army Corps.* Boston: Houghton Mifflin, 1895.

Johnston, J. Ambler. *Echoes of 1861–1961.* Richmond: privately printed, 1970.

Johnston, Joseph E. *Narrative of Military Operations.* New York: D. Appleton, 1874.

Joinville, Prince de. *The Army of the Potomac: Its Organization, Its Commander, and Its Campaign.* New York: Anson D. F. Randolph, 1862.

Jones, John B. *A Rebel War Clerk's Diary at the Confederate States Capital.* Ed. Howard Swiggett. 2 vols. New York: Old Hickory Bookshop, 1935.

Jones, Terry L. *Lee's Tigers: The Louisiana Infantry in the Army of Northern Virginia.* Baton Rouge: Louisiana State University Press, 1987.

Kearny, Philip. *Letters from the Peninsula: The Civil War Letters of General Philip Kearny.* Ed. William B. Styple. Kearny, N.J.: Belle Grove Publishing, 1988.

Kent, William C. "Sharpshooting with Berdan: William C. Kent's Eyewitness Account of the Seven Days' Battles." *Civil War Times Illustrated,* 15:2 (May 1976), pp. 4–9, 42–48.

Keyes, E. D. *Fifty Years' Observation of Men and Events, Civil and Military.* New York: Scribner's, 1885.

Lane, Mills, ed. *"Dear Mother: Don't grieve about me. If I get killed, I'll only be dead.": Letters from Georgia Soldiers in the Civil War.* Savannah, Ga.: Beehive Press, 1977.

Law, Evander M. "The Fight for Richmond in 1862." *Southern Bivouac,* 2 (1886–87), pp. 649–60, 713–23.

Le Duc, William G. *Recollections of a Civil War Quartermaster: The Autobiography of William G. Le Duc.* St. Paul, Minn.: North Central Publishing, 1963.

Lee, Robert E. *The Wartime Papers of R. E. Lee.* Ed. Clifford Dowdey. New York: Bramhall House, 1961.

Lincoln, Abraham. *The Collected Works of Abraham Lincoln.* Ed. Roy P. Basler. 9 vols. New Brunswick, N.J.: Rutgers University Press, 1953–55.

Livermore, Thomas L. *Days and Events, 1860–1866.* Boston: Houghton Mifflin, 1920.

Longstreet, James. *From Manassas to Appomattox: Memoirs of the Civil War in America.* Philadelphia: Lippincott, 1896.

McAllister, Robert. *The Civil War Letters of General Robert McAllister.* Ed. James I. Robertson, Jr. New Brunswick, N.J.: Rutgers University Press, 1965.

McClellan, George B. *The Civil War Papers of George B. McClellan: Selected Correspondence, 1860–1865.* Ed. Stephen W. Sears. New York: Ticknor & Fields, 1989.

McClellan, George B. *McClellan's Own Story.* New York: Charles L. Webster, 1887.

McClellan, George B. *Report on the Organization of the Army of the Potomac, and of Its Campaigns in Virginia and Maryland.* Washington: Government Printing Office, 1864.

McClure, A. K., ed. *The Annals of the War, Written by Leading Participants, North and South.* Philadelphia: Times Publishing, 1879.

McGuire, Judith White. *Diary of a Southern Refugee, During the War.* New York: E. J. Hale, 1867.

Malone, Bartlett Y. *Whipt 'em Everytime: The Diary of Bartlett Yancey Malone.* Ed. William S. Pierson, Jr. Jackson, Tenn.: McCowat-Mercer, 1960.

Manarin, Louis H. *Richmond at War: The Minutes of the City Council, 1861–1865.* Chapel Hill: University of North Carolina Press, 1966.

Marks, James J. *The Peninsular Campaign in Virginia, or Incidents and Scenes on the Battle-fields and in Richmond.* Philadelphia: Lippincott, 1864.

Marshall, Charles. *An Aide-de-Camp of Lee: Being the Papers of Colonel Charles Marshall.* Ed. Frederick Maurice. Boston: Little, Brown, 1927.

Meigs, Montgomery C. "General M. C. Meigs on the Conduct of the Civil War." *American Historical Review,* 26:2 (January 1921), pp. 285–303.

Military and Historical Society of Massachusetts. *The Peninsular Campaign of General McClellan in 1862.* Boston: James R. Osgood, 1881.

Miller, James C. "Serving Under McClellan on the Peninsula in '62." *Civil War Times Illustrated,* 8:3 (June 1969), pp. 24–30.

Miller, Robert H. "Letters of Lieutenant Robert H. Miller to His Family, 1861–1862." Ed. Forrest P. Connor. *Virginia Magazine of History and Biography,* 70:1 (January 1962), pp. 62–91.

Moore, Frank, ed. *The Rebellion Record: A Diary of American Events.* 11 vols. and supplement. New York: Putnam's, 1861–63; Van Nostrand, 1864–68.

Mosby, John S. *Mosby's War Reminiscences and Stuart's Cavalry Campaigns.* New York: Dodd, Mead, 1887.

Neill, Edward D. "Incidents of the Battles of Fair Oaks and Malvern Hill." *Glimpses of the Nation's Struggle.* Minnesota Commandery, Military Order of the Loyal Legion of the U.S., 3rd Series, 1893, pp. 454–79.

Nicolay, Helen. *Lincoln's Secretary: A Biography of John G. Nicolay.* New York: Longmans, Green, 1949.

Norton, Oliver W. *Army Letters, 1861–1865.* Chicago: privately printed, 1903.

Paris, Comte de. *History of the Civil War in America.* 4 vols. Philadelphia: Porter & Coates, 1875–88.

Paris, Comte de. "We Prepare to Receive the Enemy Where We Stand." Ed.

Mark Grimsley. *Civil War Times Illustrated*, 24:3 (May 1985), pp. 18–26.

Patterson, Edmund D. *Yankee Rebel: The Civil War Journal of Edmund DeWitt Patterson*. Ed. John G. Barrett. Chapel Hill: University of North Carolina Press, 1966.

Perkins, Charles E. "Letters Home: Sergeant Charles E. Perkins in Virginia, 1862." Eds. Ray Henshaw and Glenn W. LaFantasie. *Rhode Island History*, 39 (November 1980), pp. 107–31.

Perry, Milton F. *Infernal Machines: The Story of Confederate Submarine and Mine Warfare*. Baton Rouge: Louisiana State University Press, 1965.

Plane, William F. "Letters of William Fisher Plane, C.S.A. to His Wife." Ed. S. Joseph Lewis, Jr. *Georgia Historical Quarterly*, 48 (June 1964), pp. 215–28.

Pohanka, Brian C. "Like Demons with Bayonets." *Military Images*, 10:6 (May–June 1989), pp. 12–22.

Polley, J. B. *A Soldier's Letters to Charming Nellie*. New York: Neale, 1908.

Powell, William H. *The Fifth Army Corps (Army of the Potomac)*. New York: Putnam's, 1896.

Putnam, Sallie A. *Richmond During the War: Four Years of Personal Observation*. New York: G. W. Carleton, 1867.

Reed, Rowena. *Combined Operations in the Civil War*. Annapolis: Naval Institute Press, 1978.

Reichardt, Theodore. *Diary of Battery A, First Rhode Island Light Artillery*. Providence: N.B. Williams, 1865.

Reid, Jesse W. *History of the Fourth Regiment S.C. Volunteers*. Greenville, S.C.: Shannon, 1892.

Report of the Joint Committee on the Conduct of the War. 3 vols. Washington: Government Printing Office, 1863.

Rhoades, Jeffrey L. *Scapegoat General: The Story of Major General Benjamin Huger, C.S.A.* Hamden, Conn.: Archon Books, 1985.

Rhodes, Elisha Hunt. *All for the Union: A History of the 2nd Rhode Island Infantry in the War of the Great Rebellion As Told by the Diary and Letters of Elisha Hunt Rhodes*. Ed. Robert Hunt Rhodes. Lincoln, R.I.: Andrew Mowbray, 1985.

Robertson, James I., Jr. *General A. P. Hill: The Story of a Confederate Warrior*. New York: Random House, 1987.

Robinson, William M., Jr. "Drewry's Bluff: Naval Defense of Richmond, 1862." *Civil War History*, 7:2 (June 1961), pp. 167–75.

Ropes, John C. *The Story of the Civil War*. 2 vols. New York: Putnam's, 1895–98.

Rowland, Dunbar, ed. *Jefferson Davis, Constitutionalist: His Letters, Papers and Speeches*. 10 vols. Jackson: Mississippi Department of Archives and History, 1923.

Ruffin, Edmund. *The Diary of Edmund Ruffin, II: The Years of Hope, April,*

1861–June, 1863. Ed. William Kauffman Scarborough. Baton Rouge: Louisiana State University Press, 1976.

Schuckers, Jacob S. *The Life and Public Services of Salmon Portland Chase*. New York: D. Appleton, 1874.

Sears, Stephen W. *George B. McClellan: The Young Napoleon*. New York: Ticknor & Fields, 1988.

Sedgwick, John. *Correspondence of John Sedgwick, Major General*. 2 vols. New York: privately printed, 1903.

Settles, Thomas Michael. "The Military Career of John Bankhead Magruder." Ph.D. diss., Texas Christian University, 1972.

Siciliano, Stephen N. "Major General William Farrar Smith: Critic of Defeat and Engineer of Victory." Ph.D. diss., College of William and Mary, 1984.

Simpson, Harold B. *Hood's Texas Brigade: Lee's Grenadier Guard*. Dallas: Alcor Publishing, 1983.

Smith, Asa. "Asa Smith Leaves the War." *American Heritage*, 22:2 (February 1971), pp. 54–59, 103–5.

Smith, Gustavus W. *The Battle of Seven Pines*. New York: C. G. Crawford, 1891.

Smith, Gustavus W. *Confederate War Papers*. New York: Atlantic Publishing, 1884.

Smith, James E. *A Famous Battery and Its Campaigns, 1861–'64*. Washington: W. H. Lowdermilk, 1892.

Smith, William F. *Autobiography of Major General William F. Smith, 1861–1864*. Ed. Herbert M. Schiller. Dayton, Ohio: Morningside, 1990.

Sorrel, G. Moxley. *Recollections of a Confederate Staff Officer*. New York: Neale, 1905.

Southern Historical Society Papers. Richmond: 1–52 (1876–1959).

Squires, J. Duane. "Aeronautics in the Civil War." *American Historical Review*, 42:4 (July 1937), pp. 652–69.

Starr, Louis M. *Bohemian Brigade: Civil War Newsmen in Action*. New York: Knopf, 1954.

Starr, Stephen Z. *The Union Cavalry in the Civil War*. 3 vols. Baton Rouge: Louisiana State University Press, 1979–85.

Steiner, Paul E. *Disease in the Civil War: Natural Biological Warfare in 1861–1865*. Springfield, Ill.: C. C. Thomas, 1968.

Stevens, George T. *Three Years in the Sixth Corps*. New York: Van Nostrand, 1870.

Stiles, Robert. *Four Years Under Marse Robert*. New York: Neale, 1903.

Swinton, William. *Campaigns of the Army of the Potomac*. New York: Charles B. Richardson, 1866.

Sypher, Josiah R. *History of the Pennsylvania Reserve Corps*. Lancaster, Pa.: Elias Barr, 1865.

Taylor, Walter H. *Four Years with General Lee*. New York: D. Appleton, 1878.

Thomas, Emory M. *Bold Dragoon: The Life of J. E. B. Stuart.* New York: Harper & Row, 1986.

Thomas, Emory M. *The Confederate State of Richmond: A Biography of the Capital.* Austin: University of Texas Press, 1971.

Thompson, James T. "A Georgia Boy with 'Stonewall' Jackson: The Letters of James Thomas Thompson." Ed. Aurelia Austin. *Virginia Magazine of History and Biography,* 70:3 (July 1962), pp. 314–31.

Torrence, Leonidas. "The Road to Gettysburg: The Diary and Letters of Leonidas Torrence of the Gaston Guards." Ed. Haskell Monroe. *North Carolina Historical Review,* 36 (October 1959), pp. 476–517.

Townsend, George Alfred. *Rustics in Rebellion: A Yankee Reporter on the Road to Richmond, 1861–1865.* Chapel Hill: University of North Carolina Press, 1950.

Tucker, John S. "The Diary of John S. Tucker: Confederate Soldier from Alabama." Ed. Gary Wilson. *Alabama Historical Quarterly,* 43:1 (Spring 1981), pp. 5–33.

U.S. Naval War Records Office. *Official Records of the Union and Confederate Navies in the War of the Rebellion.* 30 vols. Washington: Government Printing Office, 1894–1922.

U.S. War Department. *The War of the Rebellion: A Compilation of the Official Records of the Union and the Confederate Armies.* 128 parts in 70 vols. and atlas. Washington: Government Printing Office, 1880–1901.

Vandiver, Frank E. *Mighty Stonewall.* New York: McGraw-Hill, 1957.

Veile, Egbert L. "A Trip with Lincoln, Chase, and Stanton." *Scribner's Monthly,* 16 (October 1878), pp. 813–22.

Von Borcke, Heros. *Memoirs of the Confederate War for Independence.* 2 vols. New York: Peter Smith, 1938.

Wainwright, Charles S. *A Diary of Battle: The Personal Journals of Colonel Charles S. Wainwright, 1861–1865.* Ed. Allan Nevins. New York: Harcourt, Brace & World, 1962.

Webb, Alexander S. *The Peninsula: McClellan's Campaign of 1862.* New York: Scribner's, 1881.

Weinert, Richard P., Jr., and Robert Arthur. *Defender of the Chesapeake: The Story of Fort Monroe.* 3rd edition. Shippensburg, Pa.: White Mane Publishing, 1989.

Welles, Gideon. *Diary of Gideon Welles.* Ed. Howard K. Beale. 3 vols. New York: Norton, 1960.

Weymouth, A. B., ed. *A Memorial Sketch of Lieut. Edgar M. Newcomb, of the Nineteenth Mass. Vols.* Malden, Mass.: Alvin G. Brown, 1883.

Whetten, Harriet D. "A Volunteer Nurse in the Civil War." Ed. Paul H. Hass. *Wisconsin Magazine of History,* 48 (Winter 1964–65), pp. 131–51; 48 (Spring 1965), pp. 205–21.

Wills, Mary Alice. *The Confederate Blockade of Washington, D.C., 1861–62.* Parsons, W.Va.: McClain, 1975.

Wise, Jennings C. *The Long Arm of Lee, or the History of the Artillery Arm of the Army of Northern Virginia*. 2 vols. Lynchburg, Va.: J. P. Bell, 1915.

Woodward, C. Vann, ed. *Mary Chesnut's Civil War*. New Haven: Yale University Press, 1981.

Wormeley, Katharine P. *The Other Side of the War; With the Army of the Potomac: Letters from the Headquarters of the U.S. Sanitary Commission During the Peninsular Campaign*. Boston: Ticknor & Co., 1888.

Young, Abram H. "Civil War Letters of Abram Hayne Young." Ed. Mary Wyche Burgess. *South Carolina Historical Magazine*, 78:1 (January 1977), pp. 56–70.

INDEX

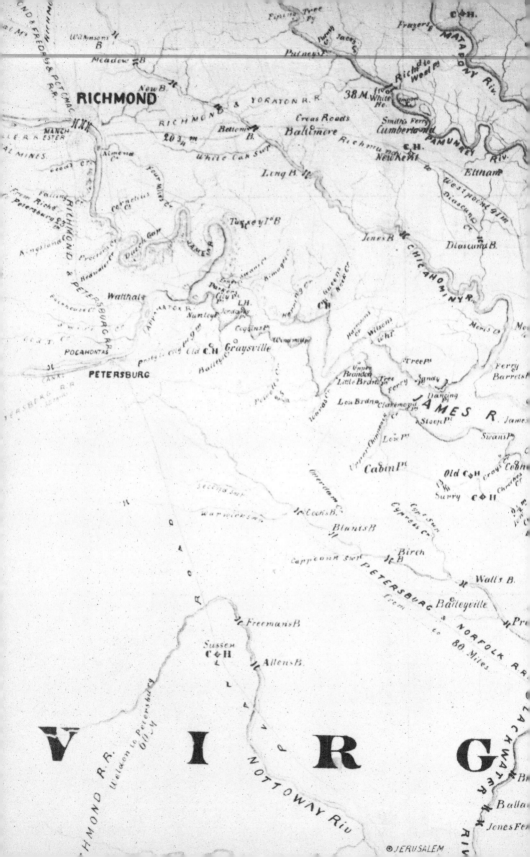